just JAVA™ 2

FIFTH EDITION

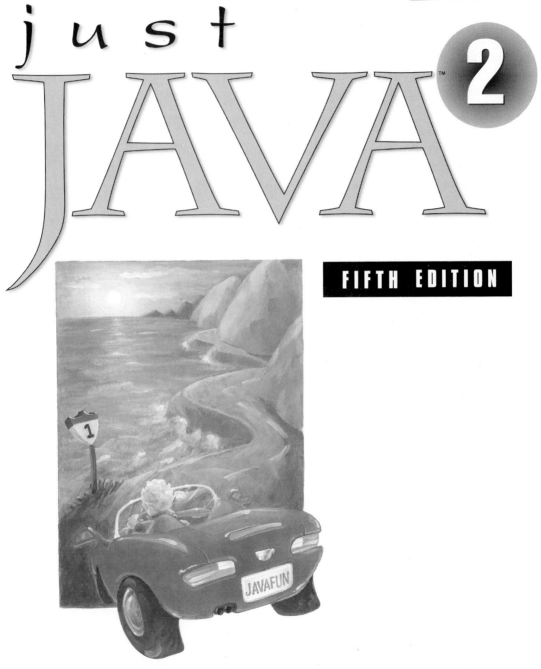

SUN MICROSYSTEMS PRESS
A Prentice Hall Title

PETER van der LINDEN

The publisher offers discounts on this book when ordered in bulk quantities.
For more information, contact Corporate Sales Department, Prentice Hall PTR,
One Lake Street, Upper Saddle River, NJ 07458. Phone: 800-382-3419; FAX: 201-236-7141.
E-mail: corpsales@prenhall.com.

Editorial/production supervision: *Patti Guerrieri*
Cover design director: *Jerry Votta*
Cover designer: *Nina Scuderi*
Cover illustration: *Karen Strelecki*
Manufacturing manager: *Alexis R. Heydt-Long*
Marketing Manager: *Debby vanDijk*
Acquisitions editor: *Gregory G. Doench*
Sun Microsystems Press publisher: *Michael Alread*

10 9 8 7 6 5 4 3 2

ISBN 0-13-032072-2

Sun Microsystems Press
A Prentice Hall Title

I would like to dedicate this book
to my wife; to my family; and to
hard-working programmers everywhere;
to you.

Contents

XV

Part Four Client Java

XXV

Acknowledgments

I would like to express my thanks to Bob Lynch and Peter Jones who read all the new chapters for this edition and kept me on the straight and narrow. Other chapters were improved by suggestions from Chris Riesbeck and Jon Skeet.

I take responsibility for remaining errors, except the ones to do with quotation marks or source listing layout—blame FrameMaker for those. If you notice an error that isn't in the errata sheet at *www.afu.com*, please let me know by email (my address is at the end of the errata sheet).

I am grateful to all the programmers who were willing to let me showcase their excellent work, and in many cases add it to the CD: William Brogden, Toby Downer, Wilson Fletcher, Carl Ginnow, Marcus Green, Karl Hörnell, Dean Jones, Karsten Lentzsch, the Limewire team,Walter Pullen, Burkhard Ratheiser, Kerry Shetline, Robin Southgate.

The layout and design of this book was improved by Patti Guerrieri and previous editors who have earned my warmest appreciation. Thanks go to the copy editor, Barbara, who blue-pencilled out my anachronisms like "whence," "especial," and "hitherto." Barbara also got the 'ell out of "marvellous."

Thanks to the hardworking people at Sun Microsystems Press and Prentice Hall: Greg Doench, Rachel Borden, Michael Alread, Eileen Clark, Debbie Van Dijk, and Brandt Kenna.

I would also like to thank the following people who provided significant help, code for the CD, moral support, beer recipes, programming assistance, etc.:

Josh Bloch,

Matthew Burtch,

John F. Dumas,

Jane Erskine,

Roedy Green,

Steve Griffiths,

Roger Lindsjö,

Nicholas J. Morrell (what a taste he has for expensive Scotch),

Alec Muffet,

Jef Poskanzer,

Kathy Stark,

Al Sutton,

Greg Turner,

Tom van der Linden (who instilled in me his love for reading, writing, and consolidated statements of stockholder equity),

Wendy van der Linden (who pointed out that Citrus was a subclass of Fruit, and conceived the "Wendy Wand" pointing device),

Sean Willard.

We're doing something right.

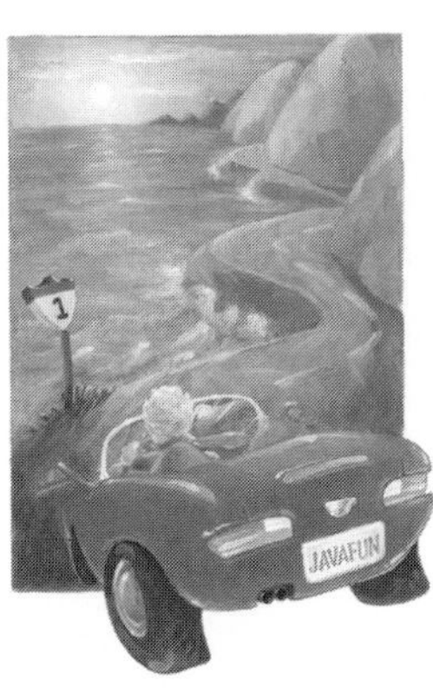

Using the Just Java CD-ROM

About the CD-ROM

Welcome to the *Just Java* CD-ROM—a disk packed with Java tools and source code discussed in the book and lots more.

This CD is for any reasonably modern system that can read a CD with a UDF file system. That includes Unix, Windows, and MacOS but may exclude some vintage PCs.

There is a huge amount of useful, entertaining, or educational material on this CD. Some of the content (and there is a *lot* more) is:

- **Useful** — Java Programmer's FAQ and Glossary. Decompilers and obfuscators.
- **Educational** — Translators for Perl, TCL, Eiffel, C, C++, Python, etc. CIA World Fact Book—your tax dollars at work. Java Digital Simulator.
- **Entertaining** — Java program to solve crossword puzzles. The Jargon File The Sherlock Holmes books. Java Bible Code software. Look for hidden messages.

Explore the CD-ROM using a browser. Put the CD in your computer and point your browser at the index.html file in the root directory with a URL like "file:/e:/index.html" (substitute the right letter for the CD drive if it is not 'e').

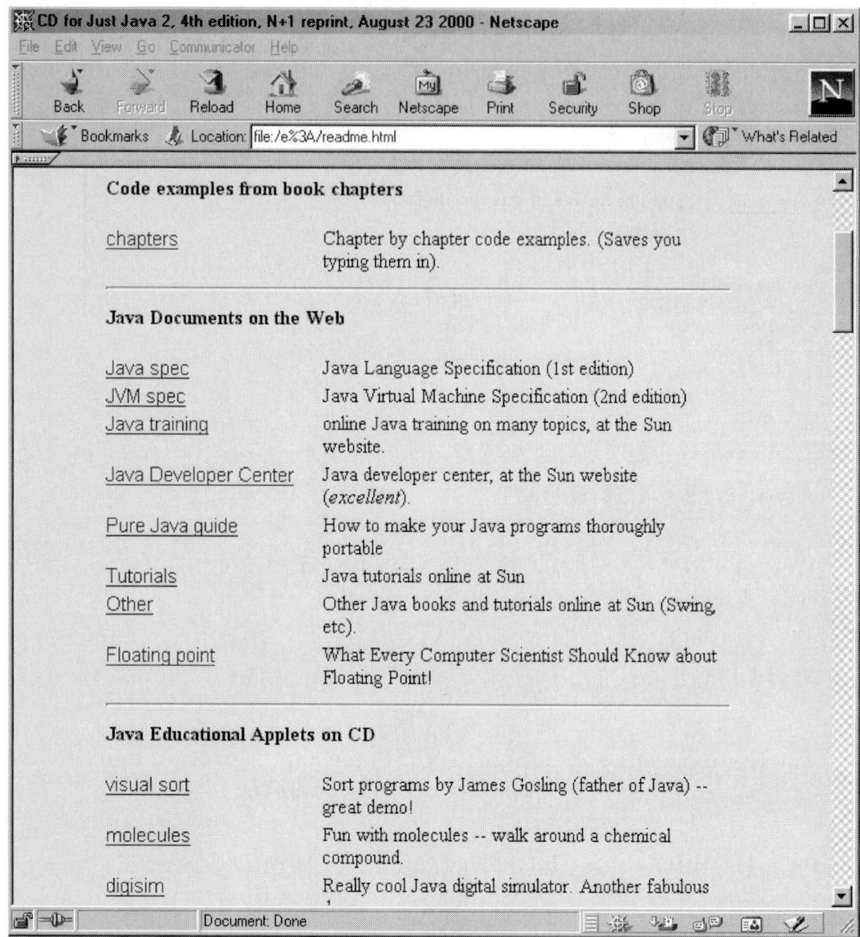

Figure P–1 Browsing the CD.

You'll see a display like that shown in Figure P-1.

If you click on, for example, the "digisim" link at the bottom of the page, the browser will take you to that directory, and the display will now look like Figure P-2.

Some of the content on the CD is in applet form, and you can run the programs as you browse them. The program shown in Figure P-2 is a digital simulator applet, allowing you to drag and drop icons representing electronic components to make circuits. It comes with a demo LED circuit (shown).

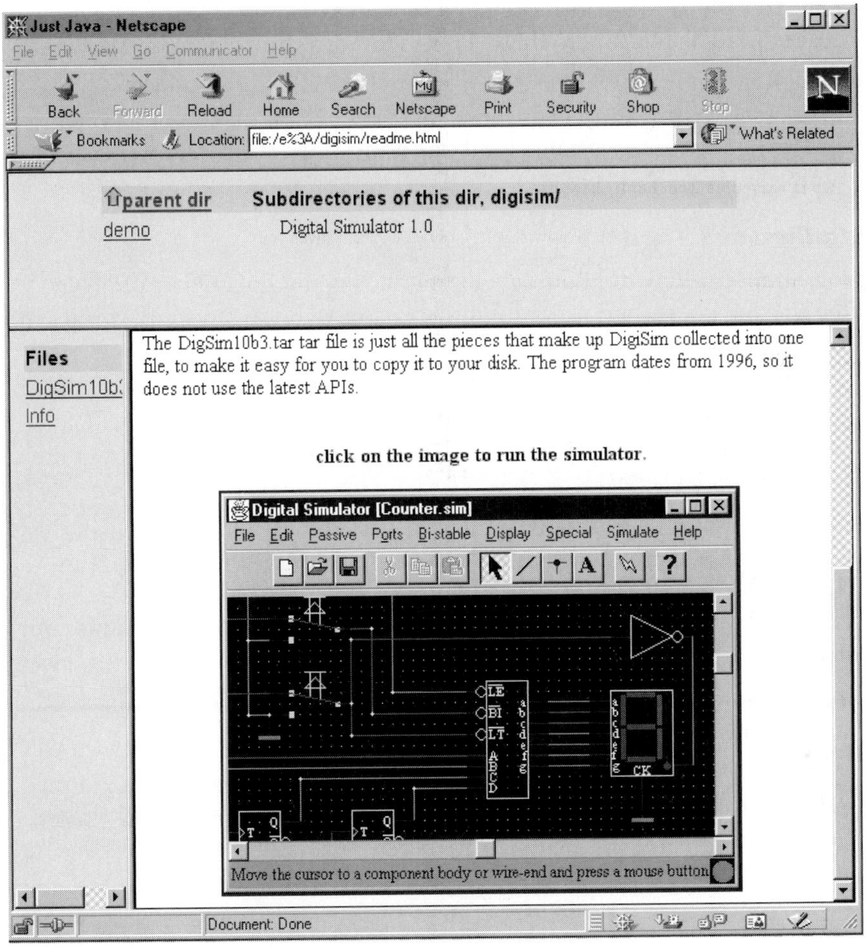

Figure P–2 Java Digital Simulator.

You can carry on exploring the CD, and also use the "back" and "forward" buttons in the browser. There are hundreds of megabytes of data of interest to a professional programmer on this CD, including many freeware or shareware compilers for other programming languages.

Your next step should be to download and install a Java Development Kit. That used to be called a "JDK," but recently Sun has started calling it the "Java 2 Standard Edition SDK." The JDK software is not on the CD, but there are links to the download sites on the CD. Choose the latest (highest version number) JDK for your system. You should also download and install the HTML documentation for the release. You will be refering to that a lot as you read through these chapters.

The J2 SDK is about a 40 Mbyte download, which will take about two hours to download on a 56 Kb dial-up connection. The Java 2 SDK documentation is about a 30 Mbyte download, taking about one and a half hours to download.

Follow the instructions at the download site to install these downloads.

Running the Java Tools

Many programmers today do their development using an IDE. Other programmers, often those who learned programming on non-Windows systems, prefer to use command line tools.

There are many excellent IDEs available that support Java—some free and even some open source. Sun allows free download of the "Forte for Java" IDE. It runs on Solaris, Linux, and Windows, and can be found at *www.sun.com/forte/ffj/buy.html*.

My recommendation is that you write your first few Java programs using only an editor and the command line tools from an MS DOS window (on Windows). The Windows Notepad editor (under Start-> Programs -> Accessories) works fine. That way, you can focus on just Java, and you don't have to figure out an IDE at the same time

---

Editing Command Lines in Windows 9x

There is a very useful, but easily-overlooked, utility in Windows 9x that remembers the last few dozen commands you typed and lets you recall and edit them. The command is known as "doskey," and you get its benefits by putting a line like this in your \autoexec.bat file:

```
doskey /insert /keysize:64
```

Once you have added that line and rebooted, the up and down cursor keys will move you backwards and forwards through the list of commands you previously entered. The left and right cursor keys will move you along the line. The insert key will let you add characters by typing, and delete or backspace will remove them.

This lets you easily modify and re-issue long command lines. You can type "doskey /?" at the command line to see some of the additional options that the program supports.

Pathnames Used Throughout This Book. The source code for the Java runtime library is supplied as part of the JDK. It's in a file called src.jar that you need to unpack using winzip or other utility. Jar files have the exact same format as zip files.

From time to time, I will refer you to particular files in the runtime library. The first part of the pathname will depend on where you installed JDK, and I'll represent this by "$JAVAHOME."

The separators in a pathname are different on Unix than on Windows. For example, I may recommend you look at a file located here:

$JAVAHOME/src/java/awt/Window.java

If you installed Java on your PC at C:\jdk1.4, then the file to review is here:

C:\jdk1.4\src\java\awt\Window.java.

Enough of the administrative details! Let's go on to look at our first Java program.

Part 1

Language

Chapter 1

What Is Java?

- ▼ Compiling and Executing a Sample Program
- ▼ The Biggest Java Benefit: Future-Proofing
- ▼ Java Virtual Machine
- ▼ The "Java Platform"
- ▼ The Java Language
- ▼ Java Libraries
- ▼ Three Execution Environments
- ▼ Some Light Relief—A Java Desktop Application

Java is a programming language from Sun Microsystems, but Java is more than just a programming language. Java works well for server-based applications with great features like easy database access, object-oriented programming, professional-looking GUI support, network libraries, and built-in security.

One of the biggest assets of Java is its ability to run on all computers. You can compile a Java program on a Linux system, take the binary over to your Windows PC, IBM mainframe, or Macintosh system, and just run it. Java achieves this by layering a common runtime library on top of each operating system and having one common executable format that runs on all computers. Java is really a complete computing platform, just as the Macintosh, Windows XP, and OS/390 are platforms.

The computer industry has flocked to Java for solid practical reasons. A study by Evans Data Corp in 2001 found that more than half of North American programmers already use Java. By 2002 more developers will be using Java than

C/C++/C# or Visual Basic. Java usage is even stronger outside North America, with around 60% of developers doing some part of their work in Java.

Java provides a robust way for organizations to streamline and integrate incompatible computer systems. And yet Java is not complicated. Programmers seem to enjoy working in Java because they can accomplish more, more quickly. You hear many stories about C++ programmers who try Java and never switch back. You can be more productive in Java than in other similar languages for two reasons:

- Java has a large (almost overwhelming) set of rich libraries. These libraries are "building blocks" for your systems. The libraries are identical on all Java implementations on all computers. There are libraries for data structures, for speech processing, for image manipulation, for database access, for cryptography, and many more.
- The language was designed so that some common bugs either can't happen, or are caught as soon as they occur. For example, array indexes are always checked to be within bounds; the language is strongly typed; type conversions are checked for validity as a program runs; and memory address arithmetic, a frequent source of bugs in C, is not allowed.

Java was released to the public in the summer of 1995, and its popularity has grown faster than anyone imagined. In a 1996 meeting of the Mountain View, California, Java Users Group, I asked the designer of Java, James Gosling, how long it would be before we could throw away our C++ books in favor of Java. He started to giggle because the question seemed so audacious at that time. By summer 2001, developers downloaded the compiler more than 5.5 million times from Sun's website alone.

Since Java runs anywhere, the total potential market for all these developers is the 350+ million computer systems in the world. Java is well positioned to replace Windows as the high-volume platform of the computer industry. With only one exception (guess who doesn't want to see Windows replaced by something better), Java has united all the players in the software industry behind it.

No programming language in the past has ever gathered so many developers in such a short space of time. Due to the attention it has received, programmers (especially students) frequently ask, "Should I learn Java or Perl, C++, C?" The answer is, "Yes." You should learn several programming languages and be familiar with several more.

Java is easy to learn. The language is covered in the first few chapters of this book, and the rest of the book introduces the Java libraries, which are extensive.

Compiling and Executing a Sample Program

For those who want to get off to a quick start, this section walks through the compilation and execution of a Java program. Just follow these numbered steps:

1. Download and install the Java Software Development Kit (SDK) as described in the previous section, "Using the Just Java CD-ROM."

2. Follow these rules *very carefully* when you write and compile your own programs:

    - The name of your Java class or module must match the name of the file that it is in. This means an *exact* match, including letter case and spelling! If you call your Java class `TrYmE`, then it *must* be in a source file called "`TrYmE.java`". Letter case matters throughout Java such that, for example, the word "System" is different from the word "system," and you cannot use one in place of the other.

    - Avoid development environments at first—they just add another thing to learn at this stage. Use an editor that saves in an ASCII text format, not a word processor format, and make sure it doesn't change the file name. On a PC, EDIT works. Notepad works if you put quotes around the file name when you save it, as in "myframe.java".

3. Type the program on the next page into a file called `myframe.java,` or you can simply copy the file off the CD. Put the file in a separate little directory called, say, c:\work. Don't put the file anywhere in the directories belonging to the Java compiler you just installed. Stay out of those directories.

    Note: It is tempting fate to print these lines in a book and ask readers to copy them exactly. Such examples are notoriously prone to proofreading and printing errors. Just copy this file off the top directory of the CD if you have trouble. This program is explained in detail in Chapter 3, "Explanation of a Sample Program."

    Ensure that you follow that rule about the file name matching the class name, even to the letter case! The file name must have the suffix of `.java,` too.

Sample Java Program

```
// 40 line Java demo, Peter van der Linden
// rolls colored text across the screen
import java.awt.*;
class myframe extends Frame {
    static int x=0,y=120; // x,y position to display message
    static int i=0;
    static int horizScroll=1;     // 1->we are moving msg L-to-R

    Font fb = new Font("TimesRoman", Font.BOLD, 36);
    String msg[]={"Java", "Portable", "Secure", "Easy"};
    Color color[]={Color.blue, Color.yellow, Color.green, Color.red};

    public void paint(Graphics g) { // gets called by runtime library
        g.setFont( fb );
        g.setColor( color[i] );
        g.drawString(msg[i],x,y);
    }

    static public void main(String s[]) throws Exception {
        myframe mf = new myframe();
        mf.setSize(200,200);
        int pixelsPerLine=200, totalLines=4;
        mf.setVisible(true);
        for (int j=0;j<pixelsPerLine*totalLines; j++) {
            Thread.sleep(25);
            mf.repaint();
            if (horizScroll==1) { // increase x to scroll horizontally
                if ( (x+=3) < 200) continue;
                i = ++i % 4;          // move index to next msg/color
                x=50; y=0; horizScroll=0;  // scroll vertically next time
            } else { // increase y to scroll vertically
                if ( (y+=3) < 200) continue;
                i = ++i % 4;          // move index to next msg/color
                x=0; y=120; horizScroll=1; // horiz scroll next time
            }
        }
        System.exit(0);
    }
}
```

4. Open a command line window to get a DOS prompt on Windows or a command shell on Unix (see Figure 1-1). Compile the program by typing:

```
javac myframe.java
```

There should be no error messages from this compilation. If there are, you probably typed something wrong in the file or the command. Correct it and try again.

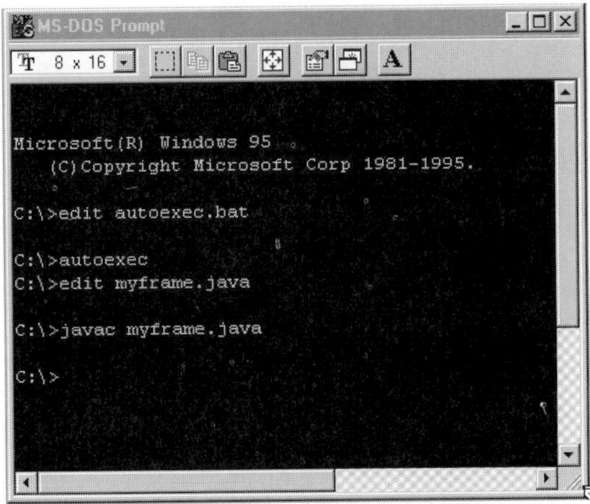

Figure 1–1 The process of compilation.

5. A successful compilation will create file `myframe.class`. Execute the Java class file like this:

```
java myframe
```

If you have entered everything correctly, your results will look like Figure 1-2, which shows a screen capture of the program running on Windows 95.

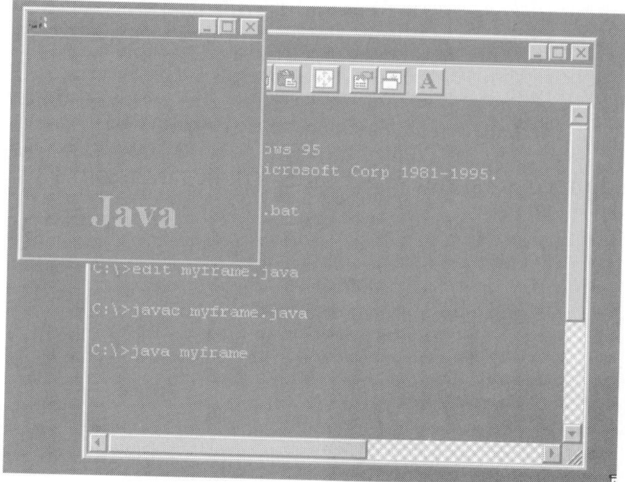

Figure 1–2 Running the program on Windows 95.

The program goes through a few iterations and then exits. For simplicity, there isn't any code to let you terminate the program prematurely. We explain this code in full in Chapter 3.

It's exciting that such a program can be written in less than a page of code. Copy the `myframe.class` file onto a floppy disk and walk it over to a different system. Run it on the Java system you install there and marvel at the possibilities of universally portable software.

Book Website/Author Email

In spite of strenuous efforts, all technical books contain at least one error. If you find an error in this text, please let me know by email.

There is an errata sheet for this book at *www.afu.com*. That site also hosts the Java Programmers FAQ. My email address is given at the end of the errata sheet at the website.

The Biggest Java Benefit: Future-Proofing

Java executables run on all computer systems, as shown in Figure 1-3. You compile a Java program once on any system and run it anywhere—on a Macintosh, on Windows 98, NT, 2K, XP, on Solaris, Linux, BSD or any of the varieties of Unix, on IBM's mainframe operating systems, and even on cell phones, Personal Digital Assistants (PDAs), embedded processors, and smart cards (credit cards with a microprocessor and memory).

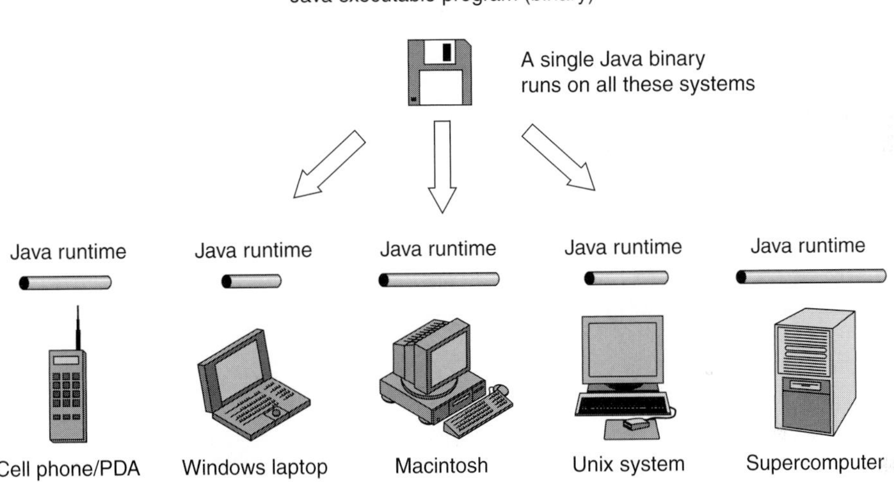

Figure 1–3 Future-proof software: Your Java application runs on every system that supports Java. No more "123 for DOS, 123 for Windows 3.1, 123 for Windows 95"; just "123 for Java," and you're done.

Why Software Portability Matters

You may be thinking that portability does not affect you: Your software runs on your PC and that's all you ever use. That's true, right up until the time you want to buy a new system. Then you are faced with the "choice" of walking away from your investment in existing software, or buying a system that has some compatibility with your previous system. You've been locked in.

For businesses, the problem is worse and far more expensive. Even if your whole organization has standardized on, say, Microsoft Windows, there have been very many releases over just the last decade: MS-DOS, Win 3.1, Win3.11, Win95A, Win95B, Win98, ME, NT 3.1, NT3.5, NT3.51, NT4, 2K, numerous service packs, and now XP. These platforms have subtle and different incompatibilities between them. Even applications running on a single platform have limited interoperability. Office 95, for example, cannot read files produced by default from Office 97, even when the files don't use any of the new Office 97 features.

Software Portability for Office Applications

There is an alternative to incompatible and frequent MS Office updates. You can download the StarOffice software and use it instead of MS Office. MS Office 2002 costs $339 for the word processor alone—for one computer. StarOffice has a word processor, spreadsheet, drawing program, image editor, and presentation manager, as well as other modules. StarOffice is free.

StarOffice can read and write files in MS Office formats. Its appearance is quite similar to MS Office, so it doesn't take long to become familiar with it. You can even get the source code. Over six million users have downloaded it, and you can get your copy at:

www.sun.com/star/staroffice/get.html

There are versions available for Linux, Windows, and Solaris, in eleven different national languages. Sun is adding a library that lets Java code interact with StarOffice applications.

Microsoft will eventually switch to a 64-bit operating system to match the Intel Merced/Itanium/McKinley 64-bit processor line. It will break a lot of existing C/C++/C# code, just as moving from Win 3.1 to Windows 95 obsoleted most of our software. To use the new 64-bit architecture, the majority of C-based programs will have to be ported or rewritten.

Many of us remember past transitions. Few DOS applications survived under Windows 3.1, and none prospered. Few 16-bit applications survived Windows 95. They looked clumsy or had problems running, where in Windows 3.1 they looked great and worked fine. In five years' time, it's unlikely you'll be using the OS you use today. But if you code your programs in Java today and avoid OS dependencies, your software will keep running regardless of the operating system and hardware changes. Java's cross-platform design already runs unchanged in 64-bit mode on Solaris, and protects users from system evolution.

Software portability is about "future-proofing" your software. Rewrite it in Java, and that's the last port you'll ever need to do. Portability is the Holy Grail of the software industry. It has long been sought, but never before attained. Java brings the industry closer to true software portability than any previous system has.

Software Portability Case Study

Java portability was a very ambitious goal, and at first, platform differences showed through in some libraries. Today the issue has been overcome. The most troublesome area was GUI code portability. That has now been solved by a new library written in Java. Here is the Java portability experience of one developer.

Gene McKenna works for a software company in San Francisco producing e-commerce applications. He recently took a complex distributed database Java application with a web front end, and ported it from NT to Solaris with no recompilation at all. This is a real enterprise system from the database to the web interface and everything in between; the port involved simply reinstalling the software and fixing up a batch script. Bugs are occasionally fixed on the deployed system, and the code is transferred back. The portability of source and binaries works both ways.

This system was developed and tested on an NT box, but deployed on Solaris and Linux. "Anyone new to programming may think nothing of this," Gene commented, "but before Java, it was time-consuming and expensive to port a system. With Java, our applications now run on all platforms."

Java portability poses a real threat to Microsoft. Software that can run on any operating system has a larger market than software that is Windows-only. Over time ISVs will move their products away from Windows-only to Java—unless Java can somehow be spoiled or broken.

It is unfortunate for you, me, and all computer users that Microsoft's Java strategy is to try and undermine the language. At first, Microsoft introduced deliberate incompatibilities into the Java product it licensed from Sun. Microsoft paid $20M to Sun to settle the resulting court case. The current Microsoft plan is to push the C# language, which is barely different enough from Java to avoid another lawsuit. There's a lot of window-dressing about getting some hapless standards body to rubber stamp C# the way they did with Activex, but the key libraries will be only be available on Windows, and Redmond will control them. You might want to bear this in mind as you think how to future-proof your software investment.

J2EE, J2ME, J2SE Editions

It's not easy to support software that runs on everything from a cell phone to a supercomputer. Sun has achieved it by defining three different "editions." The language is the same everywhere; the bundled libraries are subsets in smaller editions.

Enterprise Edition (the "large" platform). This development product is intended for those building enterprise-class server-based applications. It contains everything in the standard edition, and additional libraries for enterprise directories, transaction management, and enterprise messaging.

The Enterprise Edition is also known as Java 2 Enterprise Edition or "J2EE" for short.

Micro Edition (the "small" platform). The Micro Edition is a very low-footprint Java runtime environment, intended for embedding in consumer products like cell phones and other wireless devices, palmtops, or car navigation systems. You will develop your code using J2SE, and then deploy onto the various small devices.

The Micro Edition is also known as Java 2 Micro Edition or "J2ME" for short.

The J2ME environment is further subdivided into "profiles." There is a profile that defines the libraries available to PDAs. Another profile fits wireless devices. The smallest profile, which runs in just 128 Kbytes of memory, is intended for smart cards.

The J2ME environment is enjoying enormous success and shipped in more than 4.5M cell phones by 2001. The year 2002 marks the point at which the number of handheld computing devices sold exceeded the number of PCs sold, so Java's success in this challenging sector is a real landmark.

Standard Edition (the "medium" platform). Most people will use this development product. It is the standard development kit, including a compiler and a runtime system. Using it, you can write, deploy, and run Java applications and applets for desktops and low-end servers.

The Standard Edition is also known as Java 2 Standard Edition or "J2SE" for short. This text covers J2SE. There have been more than 5.5 million downloads of J2SE, and it is the right place to start learning Java. The different releases of the Java Development Kit over the years, and the most important content each introduced, are outlined in Table 1-1.

You should install and run the most up-to-date version of the JDK available to you, but don't use a beta release for a production system. Check Sun's Java website for the latest download.

The intention is to ship new releases on a regular 12-18 month cycle, with each update including a combination of quality and performance improvements and a small amount of new features. That's the intention, but some releases (like 1.4) have a *lot* of new features.

Table 1–1 Java Development Kit Releases

JDK Version	Date	Content
JDK 1.0.2	Jan. 1996	Standard libraries for I/O, networking, applets, file I/O, basic windowing.
JDK 1.1	Feb. 1997	Inner classes, new event handling model, RMI, java beans, JDBC, serialization, internationalization, the Calendar class, performance.
JDK 1.2	Dec. 1998	Floating point changes, "Swing" GUI library, collections, Java 2D graphics, and accessibility (GUI support for people with visual impairments), reference objects, performance. *This release and later ones were rebranded to "Java 2."*
JDK 1.3	May 2000	Performance improvements, CORBA compatibility, Java sound, Java naming and directory interface.
JDK 1.4	Dec. 2001	Assertion statement, 64-bit address space on Solaris, new I/O, pattern matching, mouse wheel support, IPv6, some XML, Webstart support, performance improvements. Code named "Merlin."
JDK 1.5	July 2003	Generics (code templates), possibly some operator overloading. Code named "Tiger.

Java Virtual Machine

So how do you get the amazing portability that allows a single executable to run on systems with different instruction sets? Java source code is compiled to produce object code, known as *bytecode*. So far, this is just like any other language. The critical difference is that bytecode is not the binary code of any existing computer. It is an architecture-neutral machine code that can quickly be interpreted to run on any specific computer. You execute a Java program by running another program called the Java Virtual Machine, or JVM. The JVM is typically invoked by running the program called `java`. The JVM reads the bytecode program and interprets or translates it into the native instruction set.

This feature is highly significant! Running bytecode on a JVM is the reason that Java software is "Write Once, Run Everywhere." A Java executable is a binary file that runs on every processor. A Java program is compiled on any computer, and run on any computer.

Application Binary Interface (ABI)

This is the environment that a program sees at runtime. It is the format of an executable file; the OS-specific process address space, and hardware details including the number, sizes, and reserved uses of registers.

Only a compiler-writer has to know the details of an ABI. Binary standards, such as the SPARC Compliance Definition, specify an ABI. Every processor architecture, such as Intel x86, Apple/Motorola Power PC, and Sun SPARC, has its own native ABI.

Java uses the same ABI on all computers. A Java Runtime Environment (JRE) including a Java Virtual Machine (JVM) bridges the gap between the Java ABI and the native hardware/OS ABI.

The Java Virtual Machine—a fancy name for an interpreter—needs to be implemented once for each computer system; then all bytecode will run on that system. There are several alternative JVMs available for the PC, the Macintosh, and Linux, and they differ in speed, cost, and quality.

Program portability through use of an interpreter for common bytecodes is not a new idea. The UCSD Pascal system ran the same way. Smalltalk, popularized a while back at Xerox PARC and more recently by IBM, uses the same approach.

Bytecode is not just for Java. If you modify a compiler for some other language, such as Ada, COBOL, or Visual Basic, so that it outputs bytecode, you can

run it equally well on the JVM on any computer. One developer drew up a list[1] of 160 languages that had been retargeted to run on the JVM. The list included Perl, Forth, Pascal, C, COBOL, many varieties of BASIC, C++, Lisp, some functional programming languages, Scheme, Prolog, many research languages, Ada, Python, Modula-2, and more.

Today, every Solaris system ships with Java. Both Compaq and Dell preinstall Java on their Windows XP systems. These companies are the top two vendors of PCs worldwide. Apple ships Java 2 as part of Mac OS X, and many of its system tools are written in Java. Sharp's latest palmtop PDA runs Java. Sony ships Java as part of the Playstation 2. Java is everywhere.

The "Java Platform"

The Java platform has several pieces:

- Java programming language
- Java Virtual Machine (interpreter/compiler)
- Software libraries accompanying the system
- Runtime environments

While mentioning the pieces that make up Java, note there is some software that includes the Java name but is only marginally related to Java. JavaScript is used in the Netscape browser to prompt the user for input and then to read it, open and close additional windows, and so on. JavaScript supports an elementary browser programming capability, but is not a general-purpose applications language as Java is. You don't need to learn JavaScript to be a Java programmer. If you already know JavaScript, it neither helps nor hurts.

As you read through the following sections describing the features of Java, you may recognize various good ideas that were pioneered by earlier systems. Java does not introduce many things that are wholly new; the innovation is in the blending of so many established good ideas from several sources.

1. See *grunge.cs.tu-berlin.de/~tolk/vmlanguages.html*, or do a web search.

The Java Language

Java is an object-oriented programming language in the same family as C++, Pascal, or Algol 60. It adopts ideas from non-mainstream languages like Smalltalk and Lisp, too. Java is a strongly typed language, has data declarations, and has statements that operate on the data. The statements are grouped into what other languages call functions, procedures, or subroutines. Since Java is an object-oriented language, we call the functions *methods*. Methods can call other methods and can be recursive (call themselves). Program execution begins in a method with the special name `main()`.

If you are already familiar with object-oriented programming, great! If not, Chapter 2, "The Story of O: Object-Oriented Programming," explains the terminology, the ideas behind it, and how the ideas are expressed in Java.

Java is immediately recognizable to many programmers. The statements and expressions are similar to those in other languages and, in most cases, identical to those of C or C++.

Although Java adds some new things, it is equally notable for what is left out. The designer of C++ once wrote, "Within C++, there is a much smaller and cleaner language struggling to get out," (Bjarne Stroustrup, *The Design and Evolution of* C++, Addison-Wesley, 1994: 207). Of the people who agree with that prophetic statement, many think that the name of that smaller and cleaner language is Java.

The size of the basic datatypes, such as integers, characters, and floating-point numbers, is laid down in the language and is the same on all platforms. If a computer system doesn't support, say, 64-bit long integers, it must simulate them in software for Java. In this way, you get the same numeric results no matter what computer runs your program. The Java specification was adjusted recently to provide a better fit for the Intel x86 platform that does some floating-point calculations in 80 bits, even though it only has 64-bit registers to store the results.

We'll also be covering the following Java language features in later chapters:

- **Threads.** Threads let a program do more than one thing at once, just as time-sharing lets a computer system do more than one thing at once.
- **Exceptions.** Exceptions let a programmer deal with error conditions when most convenient, instead of cluttering up the main flow of control with lots of error-checking and code-handling.
- **Garbage collection.** With garbage collection, the runtime library, not the programmer, manages the use of dynamic storage and reclaims (frees) memory no longer in use in a program.

For those who like to study language reference manuals, the Java specification is online at *java.sun.com/docs/books/jls/html/index.html*. It is also published in book form as *The Java Language Specification*.

Note that there are no royalties due for the use of Sun's Java compilers, runtimes, or the software you build with them. Sun has written a perpetual, irrevocable, free, and royalty-free license for the Java specification. Sun realizes that Java has the best chance of succeeding if everyone in the computer industry can share in the benefits. In other words, use of Java does not exchange one monopoly for another. Instead, Java enables open competition on a level playing field, with participation by all.

Java Libraries

Much of the real value of Java is in the set of cross-platform APIs (described in the following box) that come with the system. Java has possibly the easiest-to-use networking and windowing (GUI) of any language, and that has helped its widespread adoption. For example, there is a library function to read a JPEG file and display it on the screen. There is another library function to make a method call to a Java program running on another computer, making distributed systems easy to build.

Application Programmer Interface (API)

This is the set of libraries the programmer sees and uses when writing source code. An API consists of the names of the routines in a library and the number and types of arguments they take. For example, the POSIX 1003.1 standard says that every system complying with the standard will have a function with the following prototype that returns nonzero if ch is in the range of the 7-bit ASCII codes:

```
int isascii(int ch);
```

A program that uses only the routines specified in an API is compatible at the source code level with any OS that implements the API. Standard APIs make life easier for software vendors. Java supports a common API on all computers.

The Java libraries can be divided into two categories:

- **Core libraries bundled with the Java Development Kit (JDK):** These are the class libraries that every JDK must support.
- **Optional standard additions to the JDK:** These are the class libraries that are optional. If the feature is supported, however, it must be supported with this API.

There are so many additional libraries and packages announced for Java at this point, they alone would make a topic for a pretty thick book. The following Tables 1-2 and 1-3 provide an overview of the Java libraries; in the second half of the book, we'll cover the use of the mainstream class libraries.

These libraries will give you some idea of the richness of the Java platform. I suggest you glance over them at this time. Later, when you have mastered the basics of the language and are looking to try different application areas, you can return and take a longer look.

The following API families were public when JDK 1.4 was released. Sun occasionally adds a library or uses a different grouping. You can always find the most up-to-date information on Sun's Java web page *java.sun.com*.

Table 1–2 Core APIs and Their Purposes

Core API	Purpose
Java runtimes	Standard runtime libraries for I/O, networking, applets, basic windowing, data structures, internationalization, math operations, and more.
Java Foundation Classes	"Swing" GUI library, Java 2D graphics, and accessibility (GUI support for people with visual and other impairments).
Security	Support for digital signatures, X.509 certificates, and message digests. Exportable worldwide.
Java IDL	(Java Interface Definition Language) Used to talk to CORBA middleware.
JDBC	(Java Database Connectivity) Library for database access.
JavaBeans	Software component library.
Java RMI	(Java Remote Method Invocation) For communicating with other Java processes, possibly on other systems.

Table 1-3 shows some of the Optional Package APIs—some additional libraries that can be downloaded and added to one of the editions. When installed, optional packages are treated exactly like other parts of the runtime library, giving them some extra privileges over user code.

Optional packages are the new name for what used to be known as "standard extensions." Standard Extension was a very poor choice of name: if something is standard, how can it be an extension? Thank heavens Sun finally fixed this.

Table 1–3 Some Optional Packages and Their Purposes

Optional Package	Purpose
Java Communications	Support for reading and writing the RS232 serial and IEEE 1284 parallel ports on a computer. Enables faxing, voice mail, and smart cards.
Infobus	A library contributed to Java by Lotus. Used to send data between communicating components and applets.
JavaHelp	Platform-independent framework for online help. Can be embedded in a program or used stand-alone in a browser for online documentation. Content can be client-side (fast) or server-side (shared).
JavaMail	Protocol-independent framework for building Java-based mail and messaging applications. Supports IMAP (client/server mail) and SMTP (Internet mail transfer).
Java Media	Large API set containing individual packages for 3D imaging, MIDI sound, remote collaboration, each processing, telephony, and video and audio streaming.
JNDI	(Java Naming and Directory Interface) A library to get information from LDAP, NIS, or other enterprise directory service. This became a standard part of J2SE in release 1.3.

The Java Media libraries are optional packages because they make heavy demands on the hardware (like video streaming) or require special peripherals (like the telephony library). If your low-end laptop can't do this, there is no value in burdening it with the libraries.

The optional packages are typically separate downloads from the JDK. Each API family generally contains several related APIs, and each API (termed a *package* in Java) may be composed of several classes. This hierarchy is shown in Figure 1-4.

How New Libraries are Developed

From quite early on several companies besides Sun Microsystems played a role in Java development. The Calendar class introduced in JDK 1.1 was developed by IBM and contributed by them to the release. Sun quickly saw the value of industry help with shaping the content and future of Java. A formal collaboration policy, known as the Java Community Process, was established in 1998.

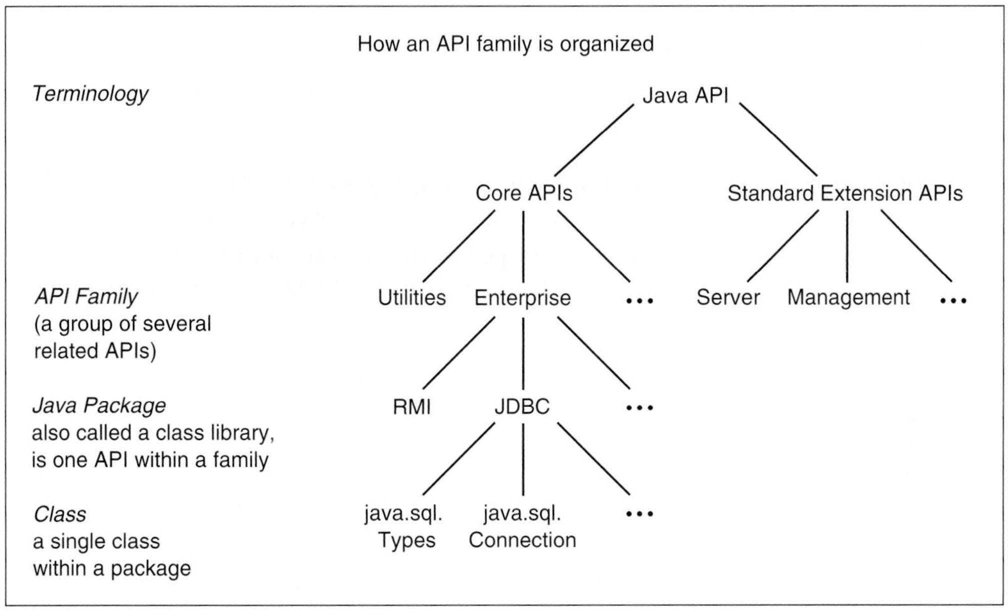

Figure 1–4 The hierarchy of an API family.

The Java Community Process (JCP) is the way the Java platform evolves. It's an open forum of about 300 companies and developers from around the world. The charter is to develop and revise Java technology specifications and their reference implementations.

The JCP has developed from the informal process that Sun used beginning in 1995, to a formalized process overseen by representatives from many organizations across the Java community. Anyone can join the JCP and have a part in its process, and you don't even have to join to contribute as a public participant.

Various subgroups of experts within the JCP create proposals for the development of a new library or a significant revision to an existing library. The proposal is written in the form of a Java Specification Request (JSR), which is published on the web. There are currently around 90 Java technology specifications in development, and you can see them at *www.jcp.org/jsr/all/index.jsp*.

The JDK 1.4 release was developed as JSR59. The new I/O API was developed as JSR51. There is a computer game profile for J2ME under development as JSR134! The JDK 1.5 release is being specified with a JSR, but has not yet been given a number. When it does get one, you'll be able to review the contents of the release months before it is available.

A Java Specification Request (JSR) moves through four stages to become a final specification and potentially become part of the Java platform. The steps are Initiation Draft, Community Draft, Public Draft, and Maintenance. They involve wider and wider review and comment.

The JCP is driven by the computer industry participants, not by Sun. As an example of that, fewer than half of all Java Specification Requests (JSRs) under review were submitted by Sun. Two of Sun's own submissions, JSR 76 and JSR 78, were even voted down by the JCP.

Finally, all Java source code is available under the Sun Community Source License (SCSL). Community Source creates a community of widely available software source code just as the Open Source model does, but with two significant differences:

- compatibility among deployed versions of the software is required and enforced through testing.
- proprietary modifications and extensions including performance improvements are allowed, as long as compatibility is retained.

Most people don't need the Java source code, but if you want it, it is available at *www.sun.com/communitysource/*. You don't need a separate download for the runtime library source code. That comes with J2SE. Most of the library is written in Java, and it is sometimes very handy to be able to look at the source.

There is a very active and rich developer community at the portal *developer.java.sun.com*. You need to register at the site, but it is free and quick, and the content is very worthwhile.

Three Execution Environments

There are three execution environments for Java programs:

- Stand-alone programs, known as *applications*.
- Programs that run in web browsers, known as *applets*. An applet is simply an application program that runs inside a browser.
- Programs that run in a web server, known as *servlets*. A servlet is simply an application program that is run on demand by a web server.

Applets

There are very few differences between programming an applet versus programming an application. In fact, a single binary can even be both. Everything you learn about Java application programming carries over to applet programming, and vice versa.

You can put a web page on a server, and browser clients can download the page on demand to see the formatted text. Applets work in the same way. You write and compile a Java applet program, then place a URL or HTML reference to it in the web page. When a client browses that page, the Java applet binary is downloaded to the client along with the text and graphics files. The browser contains a JVM, and it executes the applet on the client computer.

Before Java, the World Wide Web (WWW) was a read-only interface. You browsed URLs, it served you pages. Now that web pages can cause programs to run, the browser is on the way to becoming the universal computer interface. Originally, an applet was considered a little application, but in fact there is no size restriction on applets. Because the model is useful, applets of all sizes exist. Java applets fit very neatly into the client/server model of computing. A later chapter is devoted to applets.

Applets in general are more popular for in-house enterprise systems than for high-profile ISV software. Applets have been hampered by less-than-stellar support in browsers, and were a casualty of the Microsoft-Netscape browser wars. Applets have been overshadowed in recent years by server-side Java. However, there are some excellent example applets on the CD accompanying this book.

Server-Side Java

Java is hugely popular on servers, where it is being used to replace CGI scripts. This kind of program is called a *servlet*. A servlet is a Java program that is executed when a user browses the URL corresponding to the servlet. Its input comes from a server and its output goes to the server, usually for onward transmission to the client. Other than that, a servlet is virtually no different from a regular Java program. Think of a servlet as an application that, like an applet, requires a web server software environment in which to run.

On the CD, there is a web server that supports servlets, including source code, and the subject has a chapter of its own in this book. One of the benefits of servlets is that you can now use one language consistently on the client, on the server, in your middleware, and for accessing the corporate database. It replaces a muddle of different languages and scripts, and the "Write Once, Run Anywhere" feature is a bonus that makes Java servlets irresistible.

Some Light Relief—A Java Desktop Application

Do you have trouble keeping track of your disk usage? Do you sometimes need to free up space, but have no idea what to start deleting? Have a look at jDiskReport, which is a Java application written by expert programmer Karsten Lentzsch of Kiel in Germany.

jDiskReport is a free cross-platform graphical disk report utility. It lets you understand how much space the files and directories consume on your hard disks. Figure 1-5 shows jDiskReport but really doesn't do justice to the program.

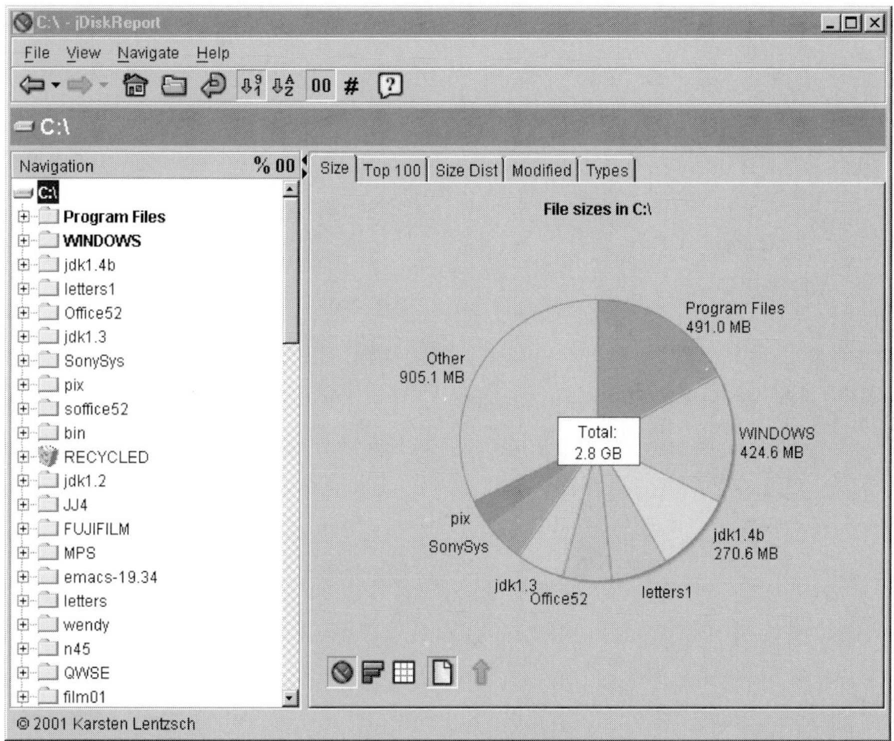

Figure 1–5 The jDiskReport: keeping track of hard disk space.

The jDiskReport software is freely distributable, and there is a copy on the CD that comes with this book. Use a browser to view the CD contents, and you will see a link to jDiskReport. Click on the link, and the browser will let you save the zip file to disk. Do so and then unzip the file. There is a readme.txt and a jar file. Go to the directory containing those files, and start the program with the command line

```
java -jar jdiskreport.jar
```

The application will summarize the disk usage on your system and display it in a large variety of formats: oldest, largest, by type of file, pie chart, bar graph, text, tree display. This software was written once, and it runs on Linux, the Mac, Solaris, the DEC Alpha, and so on. It is a very user friendly program, fast, and a superb advert for the Java GUI library known as "Swing." Karsten has a website at *www.jgoodies.com* with additional software. If someone tells you that Java is only good for server software, show them this desktop application. Try it yourself; you'll probably find it very useful.

Chapter 2

The Story of O: Object-Oriented Programming

- ABSTRACTION
- ENCAPSULATION
- COMPARING PRIMITIVE TYPES TO CLASS TYPES
- THE ONE-MINUTE OBJECT MANAGER
- CREATING NEW OBJECTS: CONSTRUCTORS
- PER-INSTANCE AND PER-CLASS MEMBERS
- THE "FINAL" MODIFIER
- ACCESS MODIFIERS
- EXERCISES
- SOME LIGHT RELIEF—IT'S NOT YOUR FATHER'S IBM

It's a surprising observation, but software development trends seem to be running in the opposite direction from the universe in general. The universe has entropy—it is gradually "winding down," or proceeding to a less and less coherent state. In contrast, software development methodologies over the past 30 years have become more disciplined and more organized. We're making fast progress because it is still a young field of research. The prime example of this is object-oriented programming (OOP), an idea enjoying a powerful revival.

Java is an object-oriented language, and to understand Java you have to understand OOP concepts. Fortunately, the big, well-kept secret of object-oriented programming works in our favor here: OOP is based on simple ideas. If you already know OOP, you can breeze through this chapter to pick up the Java way of doing things. If you haven't done any OOP before, this chapter will explain it from first principles.

Object-oriented programming is based on a small number of common-sense fundamentals. Unfortunately, OOP has some special terminology, and it suffers from the "surfeit of Zen" problem: to fully understand any one part, you need to understand most of the other parts. Most programmers can understand OOP instinctively when it is explained clearly.

The Great Big Well-Kept Secret of Object-Oriented Programming

Although there are zillions of language-specific details, object-oriented programming is based on a few simple ideas.

It is not usually explained clearly, however. Look at the kind of turbo-babble you can find in many books on C++, for example:

> Object-Oriented Programming is characterized by inheritance and dynamic binding. C++ supports inheritance through class derivation. Dynamic binding is provided by virtual class functions. Virtual functions provide a method of encapsulating the implementation details of an inheritance hierarchy.

True but incomprehensible gibberish to someone encountering the topic for the first time. Here we describe OOP in simple English, and relate it to familiar programming language features.

Teach Yourself OOP the Hard Way

Alan Kay, an OO expert who is now an Apple distinguished Fellow, began studying the topic in the early 1970s. He was leafing through an 80-page Simula-67 listing. Simula was the first OO language, but Alan hadn't seen it before and didn't know that. He thought it was Algol or an Algol-variant.

He literally taught himself the principles of OOP from reading 80 pages of code in the first object-oriented language. Not everyone will want to duplicate that achievement, so this chapter provides the missing background.

Object-oriented programming is not a new idea; Simula-67 pioneered it around 30 years ago. Most experts agree that OOP is based on four key principles: abstraction, encapsulation, inheritance, and polymorphism (see Figure 2-1).

We'll deal with the first two in this chapter, and the other two in a later chapter. We'll describe the concepts in terms of real-world examples and programming abstractions. At the end of this chapter, you'll have enough knowledge to read and write basic object-oriented programs. You'll need to read the second OOP chapter to finish learning all the OOP features, though.

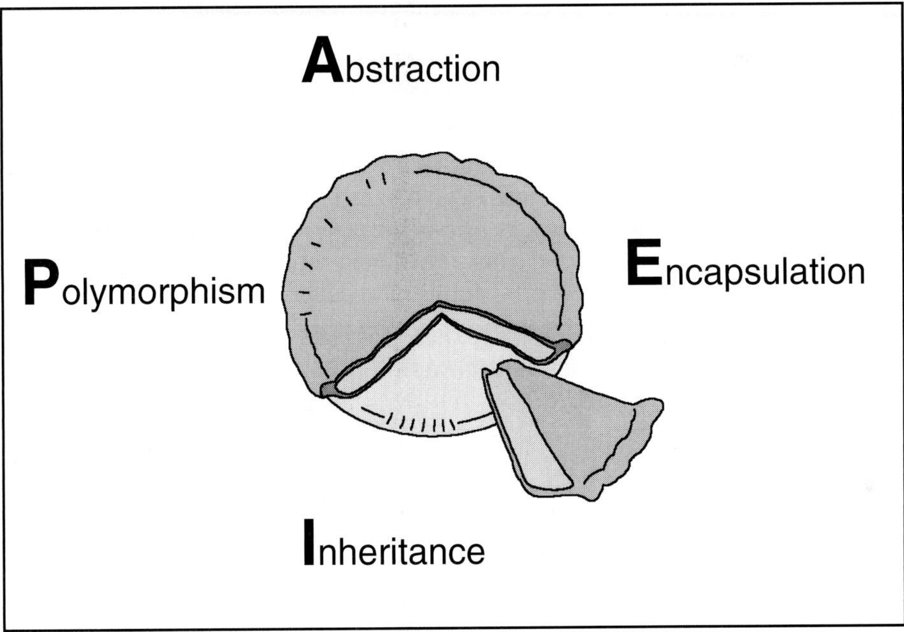

Figure 2–1 OOP has four key concepts which you can remember by thinking of A PIE: Abstraction, Polymorphism, Inheritance, and Encapsulation.

Abstraction

To process something from the real world on a computer, we have to extract the essential characteristics. The data representing these characteristics are how we will process that thing in a system.

The characteristics that we choose will depend on what we are trying to do. Take a car, for example. A registration authority will record some details like the Vehicle Identification Number (the unique code assigned by the manufacturer), the license plate, the current owner, the tax due, and so on. When the car checks into a garage for a service, the garage will represent it in their computer system by other details such as make and model, work description, billing information, and owner. In the owner's home budgeting system, the abstraction may be the car description, service history, gas mileage records, and so on.

These are all examples of data abstractions. Data abstraction is the process of refining away the unimportant details of an object, so that only the appropriate characteristics that describe it remain. These, together with the operations on the data, form an abstract data type. We just mentioned three different data abstractions for a car (see Figure 2-2). Abstraction is where program design starts.

All mainstream programming languages provide a way to store pieces of related data together. It is usually called something like a structure or record. OOP adds a disciplined way to bundle it together with the operations on that data.

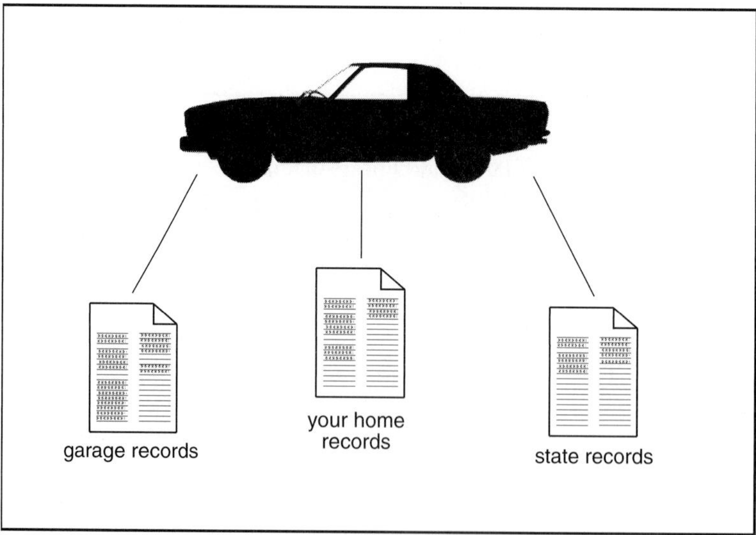

Figure 2–2 Three abstractions of "a car."

Encapsulation

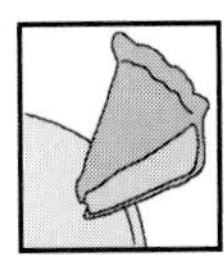

One step beyond abstraction is the recognition that, equally as important as data, are the operations that are performed on it. Encapsulation simply says that there should be a way to associate the two closely together and treat them as a single unit of organization. In language terms, data and related functions should be bundled together somehow, so you can say, "This is how we represent a blurf object, and these are the *only* operations that can be done on blurfs."

Non-OOP languages (like C, Fortran, or Perl) support encapsulation well for built-in types, but not at all for user-defined types. For example, take strings. In most languages, the kinds of things you can do with strings are copy, search, extract, or join them. If you try to divide by a floating-point number, the compiler knows that this is not a valid operation for a string type, as shown below:

```
float f = 2.0;
String s = "hello";

s = s / f;
      ^ invalid operator for type
```

The valid operations for a string are *encapsulated*, or bundled together with other information about the type, and arithmetic division isn't one of them. The compiler enforces the rule that each type (int, float, string, char, etc.) has a certain number of operations that are compatible with the type. Only those operations can be done to values of the type.

Some languages support "header files" that group together variables, definitions of user types, and function declarations, but this is not true encapsulation. Header files do not enforce the integrity of a type (i.e., prevent invalid operations, like assigning a float to an int that represents month_number), nor do they provide any information hiding. Any program that includes a header file can access individual fields as desired and can create new functions that operate on the internals of the structures. So this is not true encapsulation.

OOP languages support encapsulation—bundling together types and the functions that operate on those types and restricting access to the internal representation—on user-defined types, not just on built-in types. The operations on built-in types tend to be arithmetic operations like +, -, *, and /. The operations on user-defined types tend to be expressed as functions, also known as procedures, and known as methods in the OOP world.

There is considerable debate in the Java world at present over whether Java should be changed to make it possible to use arithmetic operators, not just functions, to express operations on user-defined types. This feature is known as "operator overloading," and it is not in Java 1.4, but it may come in the future. It was left out of Java because the feature is easy to misuse and can result in confusing, hard-to-maintain programs. You may know what you are doing when you write the code, but operator overloading makes it more difficult for the maintenance programmer who follows you.

Comparing Primitive Types to Class Types

OOP is all about special support for class types and the operations on them. We will explain OOP by comparing it to the support for built-in types that you are already familiar with in other languages. Java has eight built-in types: byte, short, int, long, float, double, char, and boolean. The names suggest what they represent, and we will look at them in detail in Chapter 4.

These eight types are known in Java as "primitive types," because they do not contain any other types, in contrast to class types or array types. We will point out how some rules for class types are very similar to some rules for primitive types, and also how there are some different rules.

Defining a Type

Defining a Primitive Type. The OOP term for "datatype and operations bundled together with special restrictions on how they can be used" is a *class*. A class is another word for a user-defined type. Here is how you define a primitive type:

```
int
```

You just mention its name. That means that what follows is a 32-bit binary integer. No further definition of the type is needed. All the operations on it are already known to the language. That is what makes int a built-in type.

Defining a Class Type. Here is how you define a class:

```
class SomeName { membersOfTheClass }
```

I use italics here to represent the kind of thing that you can put there. The non-italic characters are taken literally. A class is defined by starting with the keyword class, then giving it a name, then an opening brace, followed by any number of members (the data fields and functions), and finishing up with a closing brace. The data fields and the functions in your class are what give it meaning and behavior. If you were using a class to represent a car, you'd have fields matching one of the abstractions we mentioned earlier. You'd have functions that could update those fields, change ownership, and calculate costs. The fields and functions together are the *members* of a class.

We'll build our examples around a class that we'll call "Fruit." By convention, class names all begin with a capital letter. That helps us to tell classes and other things apart. Fruit will be our user-defined data type to store information abstracted from the qualities of fruit. Defining a class doesn't bring any of its objects into existence. For that, we'll declare variables like plum, apple, and banana that refer to individual objects of the Fruit type. Objects of a class are also known as *instances*.

Fruit isn't usually something that is data processed, but this example keeps everything focused on the new abstraction, rather than the bits and bytes.

Assume we are primarily concerned with the nutritional value of fruit. Here's an example definition of a class:

```
class Fruit {
    int grams;

    int totalCalories() {
         return grams*10;
    }
}
```

The example class is called Fruit. It has two members:

- a field called "grams" which is an int.
- a method called "totalCalories" that returns an int value and has no arguments.

Try typing that example in and compiling it. Don't forget that the file name for a class must be the same as the class name, and add the extension ".java" for an overall file name of Fruit.java. If you get any compiler error messages, you probably mistyped a character, so just correct it. The command to compile this example is "javac Fruit.java".

Declaring Variables

Declaring a Primitive Variable. Here is how you declare some variables of a primitive type:

```
int count, total, i;
```

Those declarations mean that count, total, and i have the type "int," and can be used in all the operations and places where an int is expected.

The declaration of a primitive variable...

creates a place in memory that holds a value.

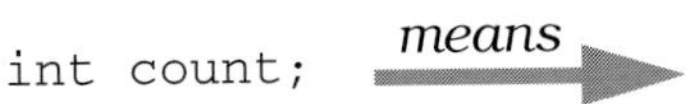

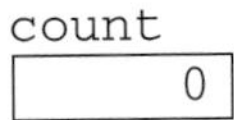

count

0

Declaring an Object Variable. Variables of a class type are called *objects*. Just as with built-in types, to declare some variables you first write the type name, then follow it by a comma-separated list of all the names that refer to a thing of that type. Here is how you declare some variables of a class type:

```
Fruit lemon, apple, f;
```

Java has one primitive type called int, but a program can contain zero or zillions of variables of type int. So it is with objects. There is exactly one of any given user-defined type, such as Fruit. But there is an arbitrary number of objects of that type in your program.

Perhaps surprisingly, an object is *not* created for you when you declare a variable of class type. Read on for the full story!

Newsflash: Object vs. Reference to an Object!

Those declarations above mean that lemon, apple, and f have the type "reference to a Fruit object." Those variables can be used anywhere a Fruit or reference to a Fruit is expected.

"Object" vs. "Reference-to-Object"

You only ever have a reference-to-an-object in Java. What looks like the declaration of an object variable:

```
Fruit lemon;
```

is actually the declaration of a variable that is a *reference to* an object. There is no way in Java to declare a variable that directly contains an object. Variables of a class type always hold the address of some object, not the object itself. This is a big difference from built-in types and from other OOP languages.

When declared, the reference variable contains a null pointer. It does not point to any object. You cannot start accessing anything until you make the variable point to some object.

The compiler keeps track of when you are using the variable directly, and when you are using it indirectly to access a member of an object. It generates the right code for you in each case.

There's a *big* semantic difference here between variables of a primitive type and variables of a class type. Variables of some class type are called "reference variables." They do not directly hold an object; they only hold the address of an object (i.e., they reference it, hence the name reference variable).

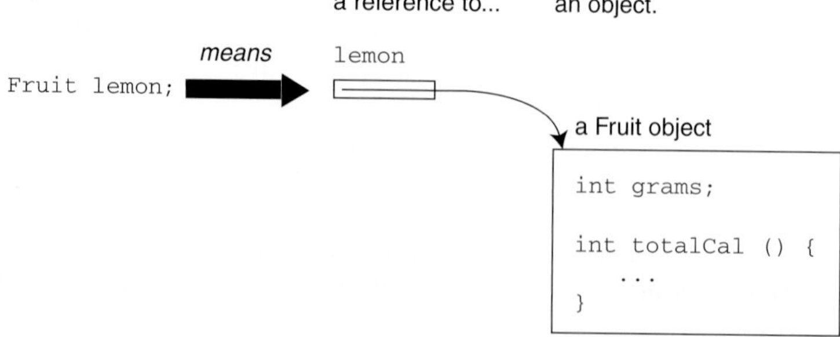

When you declare a variable of primitive type, it allocates the memory, and you can start assigning into the variable right away. When you declare a variable of class type, it is initialized with a null value (points to nothing), and you can't start assigning into object data fields until you make the variable point to an object.

It may not sound like a big deal, but this aspect of Java is unlike most other OOP languages, and results in some simplifications. An entire class of C bugs (forgetting to dereference a pointer) goes away.

In everyday use, most Java programmers usually say "object" when they mean "reference to an object," and it's perfectly understandable. We'll follow that practice here, and only make a distinction in places where it makes a difference. But it's important to understand the difference.

Operations on Primitive Types/Methods on Objects

Here is how you express some operation on a variable of a built-in type:

```
j + 5;
```

This statement takes the operand j and does the *add* operation to it, with 5 as the other operand.

You do operations on objects in a similar way. As we already mentioned, operations on an object are expressed with method calls rather than operators. You need to specify which object you intend, and then which method call you want.

The methods and fields in an object are called its *members* (they belong to the object). An individual data item (as opposed to a method) in an object is a *field*. To get to any member of an object you say what reference variable you are using, follow that by a "dot," and then say what member you want. This "dot selection" is a common notation in several languages. Here's an example:

```
lemon.grams
```

This says "go to the object that lemon is pointing to and get its "grams" field. Now that we know how to select a member, it should be clear how we express some operation on a variable of a class type. It looks like this:

```
lemon.totalCalories();
```

This statement takes lemon and invokes the totalCalories method on the object that it references. The whole point here is that the compiler restricts you to calling the methods defined inside the class. So if you want to "frobnicate" an object, you better make sure that its class contains a "frobnicate" method to do that.

If lemon is not currently pointing at an object, a runtime error occurs so silly mistakes are caught. Reference variables are always pointing at a valid object, or they contain the value null. They can never get random junk as their contents.

This particular totalCalories() method has no arguments—that's what the empty parentheses mean. Inside the body of the totalCalories method, the statements will operate on some of the data fields that were defined in the class. Every object has its own copy of those data fields. Which of the zillions of Fruit objects gets its data modified? The object that you invoked the method on! That is the object pointed to by the lemon variable, in this case. Accessing the right data is implemented by passing an extra, hidden argument to all methods. It is called the "this" pointer, and it is just a copy of the reference variable used to invoke the method. All data fields in an object are referenced indirectly through the "this" pointer.

The notation

```
object_reference.memberName
```

is very common in Java. You see it everywhere. It dereferences the object variable for you, and then selects that member in it. Classes can be nested inside packages or inside classes so you can have multilevel references, like `a.b.c.d()`.

Here are a couple of complete statements showing how to call the methods after you have created the objects. Note that "//" makes the rest of the line a comment in Java. We'll often annotate code examples using that.

```
// call totalCalories() on the plum object
int i = plum.totalCalories();

// call totalCalories() of several different objects
int j = plum.totalCalories() +
            apple.totalCalories() +
                pear.totalCalories();
```

We refer to the functions that are in the class as "methods" because they are the method for processing some data of that type. There aren't any global functions or data. Everything is in some class in Java.

The One-Minute Object Manager

You have already covered two of the four cornerstones of object-oriented programming: abstraction and encapsulation. This section summarizes what we've seen.

Objects and methods belong together in a strong way. The methods in a class can only be invoked on objects that belong to that class. If you don't have an object, you cannot invoke one of the object methods. You cannot write a method in class A that is invoked on an object of some unrelated class B. There is no way to get that past the compiler in Java.

The rest is just details (although there are a lot of them). That should have taken about one minute to read, although it may take a little longer to re-read and sink in.

There are plenty of keywords—public, private, and protected—to control whether other classes can access a class or the members of a class. We'll cover those later. Let's summarize the distinctions between a class type, an object variable, and a primitive type and variable, as shown in Table 2-1.

There are no structures or records in Java. The most important way to group related things together is to put them in a class. You can also put classes together into a package. Packages are usually implemented as directories in the filesystem, though they don't have to be. You can have several levels of package.

The preceding sections described the philosophy of OOP. Now we'll dive into the details of Java and look at how to create objects.

Table 2–1 Summary of a Class, an Object, a Primitive Type, and a Primitive Variable

Name	Description	Example Java Code

Class	A user-defined type describing the field and methods that we group together to represent something.
	The only way to update the fields should be by invoking the methods. A class is also known as a *non-primitive type.*
		`class Fruit {`
		`    int grams;`
		
		`    int totalCalories() {`
		`        return grams *10;`
		`    }`
		`}`

Object	An object belongs to some class type. An object holds values in its fields, and can have its methods called.
	There are typically many objects for any given class. We say an object is an *instance* of a class. You get to an object through a reference variable, like those to the right. You have to allocate an object before you can use a reference variable.
		`Fruit apple;`
		
		`Fruit orange, lemon, plum;`

Primitive Type	A primitive type is one of the eight basic data types in Java, such as int, char, boolean, and more.
	A primitive type is not composed of any other types, and it contrasts with the non-primitive, or class types.
		`byte`
		`short`
		`int`
		`long`
		`char`
		`float`
		`double`
		`boolean`

Primitive Variable	You get a primitive variable by declaring it as one of the eight basic data types in Java. That directly allocates the memory for the data.	`char c = 'X';`
		
		`double pi = 3.142;`

Creating New Objects: Constructors

Whenever you declare an object variable, you must make it point to an object instance before you can actually do anything with it. You can assign an existing object reference into it, or you can create a new object using a constructor—a process known as *instantiation*. It looks like this:

```
myBasket = new Fruit();
```

The keyword "new" says that we are calling a constructor. A constructor is a special kind of method that you write as part of a class. An expression with the "new" keyword is the *only* way to get a new object created (sole exception: cloning, described in Chapter 8). Even if it looks like you got an object some other way (like a string literal, or a factory class) a constructor was called for you behind the scenes. It is common to combine the declaration and instantiation into one like this:

```
Fruit myBasket = new Fruit();
```

The general form of a call to a constructor is:

```
objectOfSomeClass = new SomeClass();
```

A constructor is like a special kind of method that can be used only to create and initialize a new object. The longer name "MemoryAllocatorAndInitializer" would be more accurate, but the OOP world has already settled on constructor. One reason a constructor (or at least an ordinary method) is needed is because no one outside the class is able to access data whose scope is limited to the class (known as "private data"—there is a keyword to label data in this way).

Therefore, you need a privileged function inside the class to fill in the initial data values of a newly minted object. This is a bit of a leap from other languages, where you just initialize a variable with an assignment in its definition, or even leave it uninitialized.

Constructor functions always have the same name as the class, and have this general form:

```
optionalAccessModifier ClassName ( parameterlist ) optionalThrows {
     statements
}
```

We can ignore the optional parts for now. Note that there is no explicit return type, nor the keyword "void." In some sense, the constructor name (the same as the classname) *is* the return type.

Here is the Fruit class with some constructors added:

```
class Fruit {
     int grams;
     int calsPerGram;

     Fruit() {                    // constructor
          grams=55;               // no-arg constructor - has no arguments
          calsPerGram=0;
     }


     Fruit(int g, int c) {    //another constructor
          grams=g;
          calsPerGram=c;
     }
}
```

Here are some examples of objects being constructed:

```
...
// invoking a constructor in a declaration
Fruit melon=new Fruit(4,5);

Fruit banana = new Fruit();

// invoking a constructor in a statement
melon=new Fruit(60,3);
// melon now points to a different newly created object
```

In the first line, a Fruit object referenced by `melon` is created with grams = 4 and calsPerGram = 5. Similarly, a Fruit object, referenced by `banana`, is created with grams = 55 and calsPerGram = 0. We get that because those are the defaults that the no-arg (no arguments) constructor uses.

Most classes have at least one explicit constructor. You can define several different constructors and tell them apart by their parameter types. Sometimes you may want one constructor to call another. You may have a series of constructors that accept several different types of arguments and call a single constructor with the arguments in a standardized form to do the rest of the processing in one place, which is quite common. You may use `this()` to call a different constructor in the same class. Normally, `this` in a method means "the object I was invoked on." Here it is reused to mean "one of my other constructors; pick the one with the matching signature."

When one constructor explicitly invokes another, that invocation must be the very first statement in the constructor. This is required for a couple of reasons. First, you can't call a constructor on something that has already had its memory allocated, and second, memory has already been allocated by the time the system starts executing your statements in a constructor.

Here is an example of one constructor invoking another with `this()`:

```
class Fruit {
        // data fields
    int grams;
    int calsPerGram;

    Fruit() {            // constructor
        this(55, 10);
    }

    Fruit(int g, int c) {    //another constructor
        grams=g;
        calsPerGram=c;
    }

         // ... other methods ....

}
```

Calls the sibling constructor whose arguments match.

A constructor cannot be invoked explicitly by the programmer other than in object creation, although this might otherwise be quite a useful operation to, say, reset an object to a known initial state. This is because a constructor is deemed to allocate storage for an object, as well as to set values in its fields. The language specification says that constructors are not counted as members of a class other than that they are like methods and contain ordinary statements.

Since almost everything in Java is an object, almost everything is created by a call to a constructor. Constructors have the same name as the class, so it is very common to see something declared and initialized with calls like this:

```
Bicycle schwinn = new Bicycle();
Cheese cheddar = new Cheese(matured);
Beer ESB = new Beer(London, bitter, 1068);
```

The repeated classname in the code above looks quite odd to some programmers at first.

A First Glimpse at Inheritance

You may also see an object initialized like this:

```
Fruit lime = new Citrus();
```

That doesn't repeat the class name. One class can be based on another class, and this is an example of how their types are then compatible.

It's a neat thing: A class can be related to another class in a parent/child relationship. You are saying "this class *extends* that class over there, with these additional members or changes."

```
class Fruit { ... }
class Citrus extends Fruit { ...}

... Fruit lime = new Citrus();
```

In these lines of code, there is obviously a class called Fruit and a class called Citrus that extends Fruit. That means Citrus will have all the behavior that Fruit does, plus its own special operations that apply only to citrus fruit. Citrus is a child class of Fruit. It is also termed a subclass or subtype. Subclass objects can always be assigned to parent objects, but not the other way round. All Citrus are Fruit. But not all Fruit are Citrus (it might be AppleVariety or FruitContainingA-Nut).

The technique of basing one class on another is called "inheritance." Inheritance is what you get from your parent, and a child class has all the fields and methods that are in the parent. We'll discuss inheritance in detail in an upcoming OOP chapter. It is the third of the four cornerstones of OOP.

Even if you don't explicitly give it one, all classes that you write have a parent class. If you do not specify a parent, your class extends the root system class known as *Object*. A class is a type, and a child class is just a subtype. All objects in the system are subtypes of `java.lang.Object`, and have all the members of that root class.

How Constructors Are Invoked

When you do not provide any explicit constructors for your class (you are allowed to do this), then the default no-arg constructor is assumed for you. The *default no-arg* (meaning "no arguments") constructor for a class takes no arguments and does nothing, but it does ensure that every class always has at least one constructor.

Some classes shouldn't have a no-arg constructor. So when you provide any constructor at all, you do not get the default no-arg constructor. In this case, if you also want a no-arg constructor, you must provide one explicitly.

When an object is instantiated, this is the order in which things happen:

1. The memory for the object is allocated.
2. That memory is cleared, causing data fields to be filled in with the default values zero, 0.0, null, and so on. Thus, all objects start with a known state.

3. The constructor is called and might explicitly call another constructor in the same class. For example, a no-arg constructor might call one of the other constructors with some preset values for arguments, like this:

```
Fruit() {                 // constructor
     this(55,10); // explicitly calls the Fruit(int, int)
}                        // the constructor
```

4. A constructor in the object's parent class is *always* called, either explicitly with `super(someArguments)`, or implicitly. This is recursive, meaning that it then calls a constructor in its parent and so on all the way back to the Object class. Object is the direct or indirect parent of all other classes in the system. Constructing a new object can take several method calls and be expensive.

```
Fruit(int g, int c) {    //another constructor
     // parent constructor implicitly called here
     // as though you had written super();
     grams=g;
     calsPerGram=c;
}
```

5. Any data fields with explicit initializers have those initial assignments executed. Any *Instance Initializers* are executed. These are a hack introduced with JDK1.1 so that anonymous classes (which cannot have constructors because—with no name—there is no way to call them) can be initialized. An instance initializer is simply a block of code in a class outside the body of any method. There's an example in a later section. The initializations take place in the order in which they appear in the source code.

6. The rest of the statements in the object's constructor are executed.

People sometimes doubt that a constructor calls a constructor in the parent class, even if you didn't explicitly code it that way. Take a look at this example. There are three classes (Grandparent, Parent, and Child) in a superclass, class, subclass relationship. The "class A extends B" phrase makes class A a child of class B.

```
class Grandparent {
        Grandparent() {
          System.out.println("Grandparent");
     }
}



class Parent extends Grandparent {
     Parent() {
          System.out.println("Parent");
     }
}



public class Child extends Parent {
     // has a default no-arg constructor

     public static void main(String[] args) {
          Child c = new Child();
     }
}
```

The class called "Child" has a default no-arg constructor. However, when you instantiate a child object, you will see that the parent and grandparent constructors are called, even though there is no explicit statement doing that. You should compile and run the program, and check that you see this output:

```
Grandparent
Parent
```

Grandparent is printed first because its constructor is called before the first statement in the Parent constructor is executed.

No Destructors

Java has automatic storage management, including automatic reclamation of objects no longer in use. The runtime system does not therefore need to be told when an object has reached the end of its lifetime. Accordingly, there are no destructor methods to reclaim an object. Just delete, overwrite, or null out the last reference to an object, and it becomes available for destruction so the memory can be reused. We'll cover more about this when we discuss garbage collection further on.

Methods

Methods are the OOP name for functions. A method is always declared inside a class; methods can't exist outside a class. A method has this general form:

This part is known as the "method signature"

```
optAccess returnType methodName ( optArgumentList ) optionalThrowsClause {
      ... statements...
}
```

The parts marked *"opt"* in the example above are optional. So an example method may look like this:

```
void someMethod() {
      i = this.totalCalories();
}
```

Or, it could look like this, and this is how the main routine looks where execution starts.

The "method signature"

```
public static void main ( String[] args ) {
      ... statements...
}
```

You invoke a method by its name. You can have several methods with the same name in a class. The same-named methods are said to *overload* the name.

```
void someMethod(int i) {
      ... // some statements
}

void someMethod(double d, char c) { // overloaded
      ... // some statements
}
```

The two methods above are overloaded. As long as they have different arguments, the compiler will be able to tell which one you intend to call. The ten-dollar way of saying this is, "The method signature is used to disambiguate overloaded method calls."

Methods with the same name should do the same thing. Don't have a method called `validate()` that validates a customer record, and another one in the same class called `validate(int i)` that calculates the square root of its argument.

Unlike primitive instance variables, primitive variables declared inside a method have an undefined initial value. For those familiar with compiler internals, it's too big a performance hit to keep clearing stack frames, so it's not done. Primitive local variables get an initial value of whatever old junk was left on the stack. So it's really important to initialize them before use.

You can call other methods in the same class without explicitly saying what object you are invoking the method on. It assumes the "this" object.

```
class Fruit {
     int totalCalories() {
      ...
     }

     void someMethod() {
        int i = totalCalories();
         // it assumes i = this.totalCalories()
          ...
     }
```

You can write the "this" reference explicitly, with the exact same meaning, but most people don't.

```
class Fruit {
     int totalCalories() {
      ...
     }

     void someMethod() {
        int i = this.totalCalories();
          ...
     }
```

You can also prefix "`this.`" onto a data member name. One reason for writing it that way is if you gave a parameter the same name as a data member, the parameter name hides the simple data member name. So you qualify it by saying it is the so-and-so field of this object:

```
class Fruit {
     int i;                        // the field "i"

     void someMethod(int i) {  // "i" is the parameter
          this.i = i;          // "this.i" is the field
     }
```

The following boxes summarize how to call a method in the same class versus another class:

Calling a Method in the Same Class	Calling a Method in Another Class

`class Fruit {`
 	
`    int totalCalories() { ... }`
 	
`    void someMethod() {`
`        int i = totalCalories();`
`        // it knows you mean this.`
`}`
	`class Cooking{`
	
	`    Fruit lime = ...`
	
	`    void otherMethod() {`
	`        int i = lime.totalCalories();`
	`        // tell it which object`
	
	`}`

OOP stresses the importance of objects rather than procedural statements. Consider it analogous to the expression "-5", indicating "take the object known as '5' and do the '-' operation on it." Here we have "take the object called 'plum' and do the 'totalCalories()' method on it."

Now it is time to review the object versus object reference paradigm.

You Always Get to an Object with a "Reference Variable"

All objects in Java are always and only accessed through a memory reference to them. This is termed *indirect addressing*. You never deal with an object directly; you always deal with a variable that holds the address of an object.

References, Pointers, Addresses—The Same Thing

Some people say that Java doesn't have pointers, it has references. They mean that references are a refinement of pointers with restricted semantics.

That is splitting hairs: a reference is another name for a pointer, which is another name for a memory address. If Java doesn't have pointers, it is very suspicious that a common error condition in Java is called a "Null**Pointer**Exception."

Java doesn't have arbitrary arithmetic on pointers (the source of so many bugs in C++), and Java automatically dereferences pointers as needed, making it easy to use.

When you declare a variable, what you get depends on the type. If you declare a primitive type (simple built-in types like int, char, boolean, and float), you actually get the variable, and you can immediately read, write, and process it. An example follows:

```
int i;
i =0;  i++; i=myNumber; // all fine.
```

If, however, you declare a variable of any class type, since you do *not* immediately get an object of that class, you cannot immediately read, write, or call its methods! What you get is a *reference variable*—a location that can hold a reference to the desired object *when you fill it in.* A reference to something is just its address in memory. In practice, objects may be doubly-indirect because that is more convenient for garbage collection. You can't tell and never need know. A reference variable is all you need to get to an object.

```
Fruit i;     // "i" is a Fruit reference, we must still create it

i.grams =0; // Not fine. The "i" Fruit does not exist yet
            // executing the statement will cause a runtime error
```

Note that this is a big difference from most other languages, where declaring an object variable reserves space for the object then and there. The Java way allows useful implementation simplifications—object sizes never have to be known on compilation, because they are *all* simply dealt with as a reference to the actual object. So you can compile code that uses a class the compiler hasn't seen yet.

The point you should take away is that objects of non-primitive types—objects and arrays—need to be created before use, and are always and exclusively referenced indirectly. *Dereferencing*, or going first to the reference variable to get the memory address and then going to that address to get the fields, is done automatically for you. When the compiler needs an address, it uses the address; when the compiler needs a member of an object, it dereferences the address in the variable to get to it.

If you have had to grapple with C or C++ pointers, this is an incredible boon, and is one reason that people are so productive in Java. The concept that variables are really references to objects is so strong in Java that "reference type" is used synonymously for "class" in the language specification.

This declaration gets you a variable myName that can reference an object of String:

```
String myName;
```

This is after you have filled in the reference so it points to such an object. Create a String object for myName, or you can make it point to an existing String object.

If you compare two reference variables, you are actually comparing whether the address in one matches the address in the other; meaning: do these two variables point to the same one object?

```
String yourName = "Anne";
if (yourName == myName) ... // compares String addresses
```

Frequently you are more interested in comparing two different objects for equal content in the data fields. That kind of comparison is done using a method call. The standard Java String class defines a method `equals()`, and you might use it like this:

```
if ( yourName.equals(myName) ) // compares String contents
```

If you have two variables, the assignment shown does not *copy* the apple object:

```
Fruit apple = new Fruit();
Fruit myfruit;

myfruit = apple;
```

it simply takes the memory address that is in apple and also writes it into myfruit. The variables myfruit and apple now reference the same one object. Changes made through myfruit will be seen by apple!

```
myfruit.grams = 37;
```

The field `apple.grams` (that is, the field `grams` in the object that `apple` references) is now 37, too.

The "null" Reference

References can be assigned a special value that says, "I don't refer to anything." In Java, this is called the *null* value. When you declare a reference type, it is initialized with the value "null," usually represented as zero in the underlying system. You can explicitly assign null or check for it using the literal value "null" like this:

```
Window MyWindow;  // MyWindow has the value null
MyWindow = new Window(); // MyWindow points to a Window object

if (MyWindow==null) . . .
```

There is a similar keyword for the return type of methods to say "this method doesn't return any value." That keyword is `void`.

Summary: Object Variables Hold References to Objects, Not Objects

This summarizes the implications of Java's philosophy that non-primitive variables hold references to objects, meaning that they hold the address of an object.

- Declaring an object variable does not create a corresponding object.
- Comparing two object variables with the "==" operator really compares the pointers held in the variables, not the contents of the objects pointed to. So you usually want to define an `equals()` method for comparisons.
- An object is passed as a parameter by pushing a copy of the reference to it on the stack. The fields in the original object may therefore be changed or updated by the method, and you cannot make the original version of the reference point to a different object.
- It's easy to declare a class that has an instance of itself as a field. For example, a linked list contains a linked list, and a binary tree contains two binary trees. If you declare the field "Foo," it will be a "reference to Foo."
- Since a reference variable is dereferenced automatically to get the contents of fields in the object, it's easy for you to overlook that assignments and comparisons are of pointers, not objects.

Conceptually, each object has its own copy of the methods in the class. In practice, methods don't change (unlike the values in data fields), so we don't need to keep multiple copies of them. We do need to make sure that when a method references a field, it refers to that field in that object. The compiler takes care of it for you.

Reference Variables and Passing Parameters to Methods

The difference between variables of primitive types and objects (reference types) has implications for parameter passing to methods. Variables of primitive types are passed by value; objects are passed by reference.

"Passing by value" means that the argument's value is copied and is passed to the method. Inside the method this copy can be modified at will, and doesn't affect the original argument.

"Passing by reference" means that a reference to (i.e., the address of) the argument is passed to the method. Using the reference, the method is actually directly accessing the argument, not a copy of it. Any changes the method makes to the parameter are made to the actual object used as the argument. After you return from the method, that object will retain any new values set in the method.

What's really going on here is that a *copy* of the value that references an object argument is passed to the method. This is why some Java books say (misleadingly) "everything is passed by value"—the copy of the *object reference* is passed by *value* which effectively passes the *object itself* by *reference*.

The one difference is that with "references passed by value" (as in Java), there is nothing you can do to an argument to change where the original parameter points. With true "pass by reference," assigning to the argument will make the original parameter change too. In Java, a method can change the contents of an object parameter, but not which object it is.

Dynamic Data Structures

The first question that most programmers ask when they hear that Java does not feature pointers is, "How do you create dynamic data structures?" How, for instance, do you create a binary tree class in which objects of the class can point to each other?

The answer is that reference variables can do this. Here are the data members for a Tree class in Java:

```
class Tree {
    private Object data;
    private Tree left;
    private Tree right;
        ...
```

Java scores in allowing memory references, but disallowing the unsafe behavior frequently associated with them. By allowing arithmetic on pointers, unchecked deallocation, dangling pointers, pointers into the stack, and other evils, C/C++ gives the programmer too much rope. Sooner or later, most of us end up tying ourselves in knots with it.

Per-Instance and Per-Class Members

We have seen how a class defines the fields and methods that are in an object, and how each object stores its own data for these members. That is usually what you want.

Sometimes, however, you have some fields of which you want only one copy, no matter how many instances of the class exist. A classic example of this is a field that represents a total. The objects contain the individual amounts, and it would be handy to have a single field that represents the total over all the objects for the class. There is an obvious place to put this kind of "one-per-class" field too—in the object that represents the class.

This is the purpose of the keyword "static"—it makes something exist per-class, not per-instance, and it moves it into the runtime object representing the class. There are four varieties of static thing (once-only) in Java:

- **Data.** This is one set of data that belongs to the class, not individual objects.
- **Methods.** These are methods that belong to the class.
- **Blocks.** These are blocks that are executed only once.
- **Classes.** These are classes that are nested in another class. Static classes were introduced with JDK 1.1.

Static Is a Crummy Name

Of all the many poorly chosen names in Java, "static" is the very worst. It comes from the confusing and confused static keyword in C. Static never made much sense as a keyword in C either. The term originated with data that was allocated statically in the data segment at compile time, but the term was re-used with other meanings, too. Whenever you see "static" in Java, think "once-only" or "per-class."

When you apply the keyword `static` to some data, it causes the data to be stored in the object that represents that class. All objects share that one copy of the static data.

Static Data

Static data belongs to the class, not an individual object of the class. There is exactly one instance of static data, regardless of how many instances of the class there are. To make a field "per-class," apply the keyword "static," as shown here.

```
class Employee {
     String name;                    // per-object field
     long     salary;                // per-object field
     short    employee_id;           // per-object field

     static int total_employees; // per-class field (one only)

           ...
}
```

The purpose of the Employee class is to store and process data on an individual employee. However, we also use the class to hold the total number of employees that we have on the payroll. The variable `total_employees` is a quantity associated with employees in general, so this class might be a good home for it. It's wasteful and error-prone, however, to duplicate this value in every employee object. While `total_employees` is a value associated with the class as a whole, it is not associated with each object of it. Applying the storage modifier "static" to a data field makes that happen.

Inside the class, static data is accessed by giving its name. Outside the class, static data can be accessed by prefixing it with the name of an object *or* the name of the class. Either works, as the following example shows:

```
Employee newhire = new Employee();
newhire.total_employees = 1;        // reference through an instance

Employee.total_employees = 1; // reference through the class
```

The second form, referencing static variables through the class name, is preferred because it provides a cue that this is not instance data. Static variables are also called class variables.

Static Methods

Just as there can be static data that belongs to the class as a whole, there can also be static methods, also called *class methods,* that do some class-wide operations and do not apply to an individual object. Again, these are highlighted by using the "static" modifier before the method name. Again, you can call a static method by prefixing it with the name of an object or the name of the class.

It is always better to call a static method using the name of the class so that people don't confuse it with per-instance methods. Here is an example:

```
class Employee {
     String name;
     long      salary;
     short     employee_number;

     static int total_employees;

     static void clear() {
          total_employees = 0;
     }
}
     ...

     newhire.clear();  // reference through an instance

     Employee.clear();  // better: reference through the class
```

Static Method Pitfalls

A common pitfall is to reference *per-object* data from a *static* method. This "does not compute," since a static method doesn't have the implicit "this" pointer to the individual object data. The compiler won't know which object you want and will emit an error message if you try to access an instance variable from a static method. The error message will say something like:

"Can't make static reference to non-static variable."

```
public static void main(String[] args) {

    salary = 50000;      // BZZT!  does not work

    Employee e = new Employee("Fred", 50000);

    e.salary = 50000;    // WORKS fine.
```

One way to reference instance (per-object) data and methods from a static method is to declare and instantiate an object in the static method. You can then access the data and methods of that instance.

We've already let the cat out of the bag about not really keeping "per-instance" copies of instance methods. So what is a static method used for? You declare a method static when it does something relating to the class as a whole, rather than specific to one instance. The class `java.lang.String` has several `valueOf()` methods that take a primitive type (boolean, int, etc.) argument and return its value as a String. These methods are static, so you can invoke them without needing a string instance, as in:

```
String s=String.valueOf(123.45); // OK
```

The `java.lang.Math` package is all static methods: abs(), sin(), cos(), exp(), and so on. Use them like this: double d = Math.abs(-12.0);

Finally, the main() method where execution starts is static. If it weren't, some magic would be needed to create an instance before calling it, as is done for applets and servlets.

Static Blocks

The third kind of static thing is a static block. A block of code is a series of statements contained in a pair of curly braces. It can occur anywhere in a class that a member declaration can occur. A static block is a block prefixed by the keyword `static`. A static block must be inside a class and outside all methods. A static block belongs to the class and is most commonly used for initialization.

Each static block is executed once only, when the class is first loaded into the JVM. *Loading a class* means reading in and converting a stream of bits from a .class file or URL into a known class inside the JVM. A class is loaded on demand when another class references it.

The keyword "static" precedes the curly braces that delimit the static block, as shown here:

```
public class Employee {
     String name;
     long      salary;
     short     employee_number;

     static int totalPayroll;

     static {
          System.out.println("Calculating money for payroll");
          if ( IncludingTempsAndContractors ) // some condit'n
               totalPayroll =  ... // some value
          else totalPayroll = ... // some other value
     }
```

Reloading Classes and Re-Executing Static Blocks

There was a subtle bug in pre-JDK 1.2 compilers. If a class dropped out of use, meaning that there were no instances of it left, it could be completely removed from the VM to save memory. If you later created an instance of the class, it would be loaded again, and the static initializers would execute again.

This was potentially disastrous if you were relying on the "once only" semantics. The bug was fixed in JDK1.2, and the language specification was clarified: Classes are guaranteed not to be unloaded unless the class that loaded them is also unloaded. Essentially, classes stay in memory unless you are starting over from scratch.

Once again, static blocks can only access static data. There can be multiple static blocks in a class, and they are executed in the order in which they occur in the source. They are most useful for initializing data or guaranteed one-time only initialization. You can do more in a block of code than you can in an initializer expression that is attached to a variable declaration.

Static Classes

The final kind of static thing is a nested static class. A nested static class is just the declaration of an entire class—constructors, methods, fields, and all—as a static member of another class.

Making a nested class static means that it is nested purely for reasons of convenience, and not because of any special need to access member data of the containing class. A nested static class can be accessed independently from outside the containing class. We go into the details of nested classes, including nested static classes, in Chapter 9.

The "final" Modifier

The last part of this chapter deals with some keywords that can be used to modify declarations. The next section looks at several keywords which make a class or the members of a class more visible or less visible to other classes, and this section looks at `final`, which makes something constant. Why was the word "const" or "constant" not chosen? Because "final" can also be applied to code, as well as data, and the term "final" makes better sense for both.

A class or a class member (that is, a data field or a method) can be declared final, meaning that this is the immediate value to use, and it won't change. We will look at what it means for a class or a method not to change in the advanced OOP chapter. A couple of final data declarations are:

```
final static int myTotal = 100000;
final Fruit banana = new Fruit(200, 35);
```

When a reference variable is declared final, it means that you cannot make that variable point at some other object. You can, however, access the variable and change its fields through that final reference variable. The reference is final, not the referenced object.

JDK 1.1 introduced the ability to mark method arguments and variables local to a method as final, such as:

```
void someMethod(final MyClass c, final int a[]) {
     c.field = 7;        // allowed
     a[0] = 7;           // allowed
     c = new MyClass(); // final means this line is NOT allowed
     a = new int[13];    // final means this line is NOT allowed
}
```

Marking a declaration as final is a clue to the compiler that certain optimizations can be made. In the case of final primitive data, the compiler can substitute the value in each place the name is used. This optimization is known as constant propagation. That in turn may lead to other optimizations becoming possible.

The "Blank Final Variable"

JDK 1.1 also introduced something called a *blank final variable,* which is simply a final variable (of any kind) that doesn't have an initializer. A blank final variable must be assigned an initial value, and that can be assigned only once. If you give a value to a blank final in a constructor, every constructor must give it a value. This is because you don't know which constructor will be called, and it must end up with an initialization.

```
class Fruit {

     final String consumer;// blank final variable - has no initializer

     Fruit (String s) {     // constructor
          consumer = s;     // the blank final is initialized
     }

     ... // more stuff
}
```

You could also initialize a blank final in an instance initializer, as follows:

```
class Fruit {

     final String packedOn;// blank final variable


    {// this instance initializer is
      // executed for every instantiation
     packedOn = (new java.util.Date()) . toString();
    }


    public static void main(String[] args) {
        Fruit f = new Fruit();
        System.out.println("packed on: "+ f.packedOn);
    }

}
```

Notice how Java lets you chain expressions together so that we can invoke the "toString()" method on the Date returned by the constructor without needing a temporary variable. Compile and run this sample code, and you will see output like this:

```
javac Fruit.java
java Fruit
packed on: Sun Sep 23 12:15:58 PDT 2001
```

Use a blank final when you have a value that is too complicated to calculate in a declaration, or that might cause an exception condition (more on that later), or where the final value depends on an argument to a constructor.

Access Modifiers

There are several keywords that control the visibility of a class and the members of a class. Table 2-2 explains these modifiers (private, no keyword, protected, and public). You do have to know this material, but you can skim this section on the first reading.

There are plenty of other keywords (static, final, abstract, native, and so on) that affect other things about a member or class. We have already seen static. Some of the keywords can occur together, such as "static final."

You can have only one access modifier though, and if you leave it off you get the default, which is "the field can be accessed by anything in the same package." We'll talk more about packages later, but a package is just a group of related classes that you want to bundle together. Think "package = directory."

Table 2-2 is just a summary to look over. We'll be seeing it in action when we start some programming. Do notice how the modifiers form a logical increasing progression from no access to maximum access. Each is a true superset of the previous modifier. That will help you remember them.

In general, you should give fields the most restricted visibility that still makes it possible for them to work. Don't make any fields public without good reason. Doing so destroys encapsulation.

Here is an OOP code idiom allowing read-only access to a field:

```
public class Employee {
     private long salary;      // is NOT visible to other classes

     public long getSalary() { // is visible to other classes
          return salary;
     }
}

class SomeOtherClassEntirely {

     public void main() {
          Employee e = ...

          long pay = e.getSalary();// gets the salary field of e
```

In the example above the salary field is private and cannot be accessed outside the `Employee` class. However, the `Employee` class can define an accessor function which is not private and that reads the value and returns it. Accessor functions frequently occur in pairs, with the name `getSomething()` to read it, and `setSomething(x newValue)` to set it.

Table 2–2 Keywords and Their Effects

Keyword	Effect	Example of Use

`private`	Members are not accessible outside this class.
	Making a constructor private prevents the class from being instantiated by other classes.
	Making a method private means that it can only be called from some other method in the class.
		`class Fruit {`
		`    private static int tot_grams;`
		`    private int grams;`
		`    private int calsPerGram;`
		
		`    private Fruit() { // constructor`
		`        grams=55;`
		`        calsPerGram=0;`
		`    }`
		`}`

(none) often called "package access"	Members are accessible from classes in the same package (loosely, directory) only.
	A class can be given package access or public access.
		`class Employee { // package access`
		`    String name;`
		`    long    salary;`
		`    static int total_employees;`
		
		`    static void clear() {`
		`        total_employees = 0;`
		`    }`
		`...`

`protected`	Members are accessible in the package and in subclasses of this class.
	Note that protected is *less* protected than the default of package access.
		`class Employee {`
		`    protected String name;`
		`    protected long    salary;`
		
		`    protected void`
		`     giveRaise(int amount) {`
		`    salary = salary+amount;`
		`    }`
		`...`

`public`	Members are accessible anywhere the class is accessible.
	A class can be given package access or public access.
		`public class Employee {//public access`
		
		`    public static void main() {`
		`    }`
		`...`
		`}`

Exercises

1. Distinguish between class and object, member and field, primitive type and class type.

2. Write a sample program that demonstrates the compiler will not let you change a final value, but that you can change the fields of an object variable that is final. (Compile the first part, compile and run the second part.)

3. Write a class with a static block, some constructors, and instance initializers that print out the order in which these are executed.

Some Light Relief—It's Not Your Father's IBM

Probably the biggest single supporter of Java is IBM. The largest computer company on the planet demonstrates its support with products, with research, with free downloadable code, and with open participation in the user community. IBM's Java initiative mirrors its Linux initiative, and the company supports these two technologies for the same reasons: software compatibility across product lines, freedom from proprietary operating systems that IBM doesn't own, and recognition that these technologies have become a major force in IT. IBM is also very interested in promoting Linux to fill the embedded processor niche that Microsoft CE has noticeably failed to win.

IBM announced in late 2000 that it would invest $1 billion in Linux over the next year. This isn't "the standard is whatever we sell" IBM of a generation ago! The company is showing a new face that is lively, cooperative, and engaging. For example, to show how the Linux operating system is viable across all platforms—from large enterprise servers to the smallest embedded devices—IBM demonstrated a wristwatch-sized Linux device at a San Jose conference in August 2000 (see Figure 2-3). The wristwatch had wireless capability, and could be used to read email. It ran Linux 2.2 and the X/11 window system!

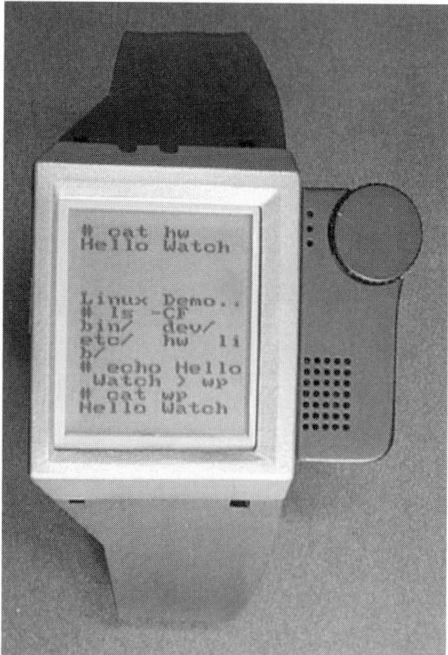

Figure 2–3
The IBM Linux wristwatch.

On the Java side, IBM has released a large amount of useful software through its Alphaworks early release research program. One Java package that you can download from Alphaworks is the Robocode software.

Robocode is an intriguing "learn Java while having fun with a game" system. Recreational software is one of the last things I would have expected to come out of IBM! The game part is shown in the screenshot in Figure 2-4. There is a troop of robot battle tanks that roll all over the window, chasing and shooting one another. The Java part is that each tank is programmed in Java. There is a library of tank-actions to change speed or direction and fire the gun. Other tanks are detected and reported asynchronously. It's wonderfully easy to get started with this software. You can have tanks clanking around blasting each other within minutes of the download, and read the documentation later!

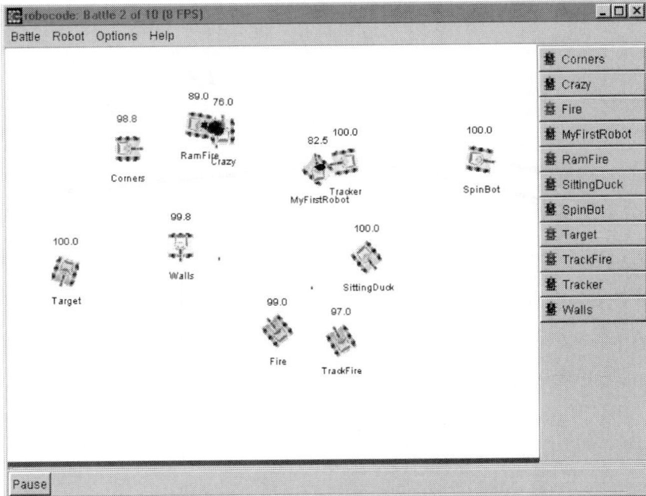

Figure 2–4
Java's Robocode.

There is a simple editing and compiling environment built in so you can very quickly start programming and deploying your own robot tanks (see Figure 2-5).

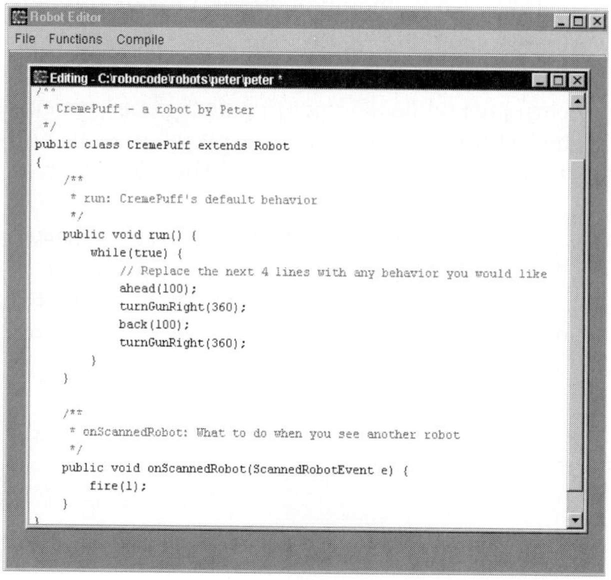

Robot Editor

File Functions Compile

Editing - C:\robocode\robots\peter\peter *

```
/**
 * CremePuff - a robot by Peter
 */
public class CremePuff extends Robot
{
    /**
     * run: CremePuff's default behavior
     */
    public void run() {
        while(true) {
            // Replace the next 4 lines with any behavior you would like
            ahead(100);
            turnGunRight(360);
            back(100);
            turnGunRight(360);
        }
    }

    /**
     * onScannedRobot: What to do when you see another robot
     */
    public void onScannedRobot(ScannedRobotEvent e) {
        fire(1);
    }
}
```

Figure 2–5
Robocode software.

It is very similar to the old "Turtle Graphics" educational software, but instead of guiding a toothless old turtle that can draw a line, you control a radar-guided tank that chases down and explodes other tanks. That's *much* more educational. You can download IBM's Java Robocode software from *robocode.alphaworks.ibm.com/home/home.html.*

Robocode is all the work of one talented guy: IBM researcher Mat Nelson. The Alphaworks site has a community bulletin board, regular software updates, and robot competitions. What are you waiting for, General Patton? Roll those tanks!

Chapter 3

Explanation of a Sample Program

- EXPLANATION OF THE EXAMPLE PROGRAM
- WHERE AN APPLICATION STARTS
- RUNTIME INTERNALS: STACK AND HEAP
- THE CLASS "OBJECT"
- READING THE JAVA API
- SOME LIGHT RELIEF—NAPSTER AND LIMEWIRE

Ever since *The C Programming Language* (Brian Kernighan and Dennis Ritchie, Prentice Hall) was published in 1978, writers of programming textbooks have been using the "Hello World" program as an introductory example. Programmers deserve a bit of innovation. Java is the first popular language to support graphics, networking, multimedia, multithreaded code, and software portability. Surely we can do a bit better than a first example that spits up a bit of text on the screen?

Chapter 1, "What Is Java?," introduced an example program that did some GUI work to display a window and to roll some text across it in several directions and colors. In this chapter we'll look at that code in more detail and explain how it works. Then we'll round off the chapter with a discussion of the stack and the heap and what they do.

If you haven't yet installed the JDK and tried running the `myframe` example from Chapter 1, now would be an excellent time to do that. As the great Arnold Schwarzenegger once said, "You can't get muscles by watching me lift weights."

The source listing appears on the following page with the annotations appearing on the page after that.

```
// 40 line Java demo, Peter van der Linden
// rolls colored text across the screen
1 import java.awt.*;

2 3 class myframe extends Frame {
    static int x=0,y=120; // x,y position to display message
  4 static int i=0;
    static int horizScroll=1;     // 1->horiz, 0->vertical

    Font fb = new Font("TimesRoman", Font.BOLD, 36);
  5 String msg[]={"Java", "Portable", "Secure", "Easy"};
    Color color[]={Color.blue, Color.yellow, Color.green, Color.red};

6   public void paint(Graphics g) { // gets called by runtime library
        g.setFont( fb );
        g.setColor( color[i] );
        g.drawString(msg[i],x,y);
    }

    static public void main(String s[]) throws Exception {
7     8 myframe mf = new myframe();
        mf.setSize(200,200);
        int pixelsPerLine=200, totalLines=4;
        mf.setVisible(true);
        for (int j=0;j<pixelsPerLine*totalLines; j++) {
            Thread.sleep(25);
          9 mf.repaint();
            if (horizScroll==1) {
                if ( (x+=3) < 200) continue;
                i = ++i % 4;          // move index to next msg/color
                x=50; y=0; horizScroll=0;  // move msg up next time
            } else {
                if ( (y+=3) < 200) continue;
             10 i = ++i % 4;          // move index to next msg/color
                x=0; y=120; horizScroll=1; // move msg L-to-R next
            }
        }
        System.exit(0);
    }
}
```

Explanation of the Example Program

1. The `import` keyword saves the programmer from having to write out the full package names of all the library classes that will be used in this source file. Here we are importing `java.awt.*` which means all the classes in the java.awt package, just as * means all the files in a directory. Doing this import means we can write `Frame` or `Font` instead of `java.awt.Frame` or `java.awt.Font`. The `java.awt` package contains basic windowing support.

2. This box encloses the class we have written. The class is called `myframe`, and it has some field members (boxes 4 and 5) and two method members (boxes 6 and 7).

3. To say that we want this class to be a subclass of the Frame class, use `extends Frame`. Frame is a class in the AWT package that displays a basic window on the screen. By saying we extend Frame, we get all the things that Frame can do, plus we can add our own specializations or variations.

4. These four fields (`x, y, i, horizScroll`) are declared static so that we can reference them without an instance of the class existing. The field horizScroll controls whether the text is scrolled horizontally or vertically across the screen. The program alternates every few words between the two directions.

5. These three fields represent the text that we are going to move across the screen and its color and font. `Font` and `Color` are two classes from the java.awt package. We declare a Font variable called `fb` and create an instance of it using a constructor from the Font class. The variables `msg` and `color` are both four-element arrays which we initialize here.

6. The `paint()` method is a standard part of many classes in the awt package. The convention is that the Java runtime calls it when the window system needs to update what is on the screen. Since we *extended* the Frame class, our version of `paint()` here *replaces* the basic one in Frame. (This is a piece of OOP that we haven't yet covered.)

   When you call `setVisible(true)` on a `Frame`, the window system knows it has to display it. It does that by calling our `paint` method at the right times to put it up on the screen. It will call `paint` when execution starts and any time after that when we request it. The statements inside `paint` set the default font and color, and then write some text from `msg[i]` onto the graphics context argument at location `x,y`. The window system translates that into pixels on the screen.

7. The `main()` method has a special *signature*, or method name and arguments, that is recognized as the place where a program starts executing when you run the class that it is in. More about this in the next section.

8. The first variable we declare inside the main routine is a `myframe`. That gives us an instance variable on which we can invoke the ordinary (non-static) methods of `myframe` and its parent `Frame`. The first statement is a method call, `mf.setSize(200,200)`, to set `mf`'s size to 200 pixels wide and 200 pixels high. Again, this is a method we inherit by virtue of extending `java.awt.Frame`.

9. This is in the body of a loop that is executed a few hundred times. Our first action is to go to sleep and delay the program for 25 milliseconds. Since the method `sleep()` is a static method of the standard Java runtime class `Thread`, we can just invoke it with the classname. Animation looks better if you match the speed of display changes to the persistence quality of the human eye. About 40 changes per second is plenty.

After the loop delay, we ask for the `mf` instance of `myframe` to be scheduled for repainting on the screen. What we are going to do here is change the location where we display the text a little bit each time through the loop. The overall effect will be to make the text appear to glide across the screen.

10. This is the "else" part of an "if...then...else" statement that is in the body of the big loop. Just for fun, the program alternates between rolling the text across the screen horizontally and vertically. This "if" statement is where the choice is made. If the horizScroll variable has the value 1, we execute the "then" part. Otherwise, we execute the "else" part that drops the text vertically.

First, we increase y by three and check that the result is less than 200, that being the height of the screen. The variable y, of course, is used in paint as one of the coordinates for locating the text message. By changing its value, we change where the text is drawn. If y is less than 200, then `continue`. That means branch immediately to the head of the loop. If y is greater than 200, then we are at the end of scrolling the text down, and we want to select another message and color, and scroll the other way. We increment `i`, ensuring it stays in the range 0–3, we reset `x,y` and we change `horizScroll` so that the "then" part of the "if" statement before 10 will be chosen. That clause is similar to the "else" clause, but increments the x variable, instead of y, to move text horizontally.

Applications vs. Applets vs. Servlets

A Java program can be written to run in these three different ways:

- As a stand-alone program that can be invoked from the command line, termed an *application*. The sample program we were reviewing is an application.
- As a program embedded in a web page, to be downloaded to the client and run in the browser when the page is browsed, termed an *applet*. Just as a booklet is a little book, an applet is a little application.
- As a program invoked from a web server, to be run on the server when a particular URL is browsed, termed a *servlet*.

The execution vehicles differ in the default execution privileges they have and the way in which they indicate where to start execution. Almost all the code and examples are the same whether you are writing an application, an applet, or a servlet. Only a few trivial startup details differ. We will deal with applications in this chapter. Applets appear in a later chapter.

How and why to set up a servlet is dealt with at length towards the end of the book. The Tomcat add-on to the Apache web server is included on the CD, so you can actually turn your system into an servlet server. Apache is the most widely used web server in the world, according to statistics at *www.netcraft.com/Survey/Reports/200108/platform.html.*

Netcraft also keeps statistics on how long different servers have been running, and it publishes them at *uptime.netcraft.com/up/today/top.avg.html.*

The top end is completely dominated by Unix servers running Apache. Other systems and servers do not even rate a mention in the top fifty available and reliable web sites.

Where an Application Starts

Looking at the signature[1] of main(), which is the method in which every application starts execution, we see the following:

```
public static void main(String args[]) {
```

The keywords say that the function is:

- **public**—visible everywhere.
- **static**—a class method that can be called using the classname without needing an object of the class. Static methods are often used where you would use a global function in C or C++. That is, you are not doing something to some specific object, you are just doing something that generally needs doing.
- **void**—the method does not return a value.

That last point is a difference between Java and C/C++. In C, main() is defined to return an int. In Java, main() is defined to return a void, that is "no value." Java has a better way to indicate program failure, namely, throwing an exception.

A Common Pitfall

A very common and frustrating pitfall is trying to access an object member from the static method called main(), as we mentioned in Chapter 2, "The Story of O: Object-Oriented Programming."

There are two ways to get past this. The simplest way is to make a referenced field static, too. If the field has to be non-static because each object needs its own copy, then instantiate an object whose purpose is to be an instance variable allowing you to reference the member or invoke a call on it.

```
class myframe { ...
    public static void main(String args[]) {
         // we want to invoke the instance method setSize()
         myframe mf = new myframe(); // so declare an instance
         mf.setSize(200,200); // then use it for the call
```

It looks weirdly recursive the first time you see it. Think of it this way: The class definition is a datatype. All you are doing is instantiating an object of that type at a point when you need one, which happens to be inside the original datatype definition.

1. Strictly speaking, the signature doesn't include the access modifiers or return type.

The `main()` routine where execution starts is a static method. That means it can be invoked before any individual instance objects have been created.

Passing over the modifiers, the actual function is as follows:

```
void main(String args[]) {
```

It declares a function called "main" that has no return value, and takes just one argument here called "args" (the parameter name doesn't matter, just its data type) which is an array of Strings. The empty array bracket pair is a reminder that the function is not restricted to any one size of array. The strings are the command-line arguments with which the program was invoked. "String" is a class in Java with more to it than just the nul-terminated character array that it is in C.

You don't need a separate count of the number of arguments, because all arrays have a length field holding the size of the array. Simply use `args.length`, which gets the number of strings in the `args` array.

The zeroth argument in the args array is the first command-line argument, *not* the program name as in C and C++. The program name is already known inside the program: It is the name of the class that contains the "main()" function. The name of this class will match the name of the file it is in. This framework is all that is needed to indicate the entry point program where execution will start.

We're working from the middle out here. Having seen our first reasonable Java program, we'll look at the small building blocks of individual tokens that the compiler sees in the next chapter.

For the rest of this chapter we'll cover the stack and the heap—which are a couple of popular runtime data structures common to many programming languages—we'll review how to read the Java API, then we'll finish up with some light relief.

Runtime Internals: Stack and Heap

The *stack* is a runtime data structure for keeping track of memory to support functions and recursive function invocation. All modern block-structured languages use a stack. Many processors have some hardware support for them.

When you call a method, some housekeeping data, known as an *activation record* or *stack frame*, is pushed onto the stack. The activation record contains the return address, the arguments passed to the function, the space for local variables, and so on. When you return from a function, the record is popped from the stack. The next function call will push another record into the same space (see Figure 3-1).

If you have any pointers back into the old activation record on the stack, memory can be corrupted, as the pointer references an area that the next function call will reuse for a different purpose. This is a common problem in C/C++, and can be hard to debug. In other words, the lifetime of stack-based storage is tied to the scope in which it was allocated, and although some languages let you get this wrong, Java doesn't!

The *heap* is another runtime data structure used to support your program. It is a large storage area that is managed dynamically. All objects in Java are allocated on the heap; no objects are ever allocated on the stack.

Many programming languages support heap-based memory allocation. Different pieces of storage can be allocated from and returned to the heap in no particular order. Whenever something is allocated on the heap, its lifetime is independent of the scope in which it was allocated.

```
Fruit saveIt;
void foo() {
     Fruit f = new Fruit();
     saveIt = f;
}

... foo();
saveIt.grams = 23;  // is it valid? f was allocated in foo
                    // and foo is no longer live
```

In the code above, a Fruit object is allocated in a method and a reference to that Fruit is stashed away for later use. Later, after the method has returned, the reference is used to access the Fruit. This is valid for heap-based storage. It is not valid in stack-based storage and is the source of a large number of high-profile bugs and failings in C/C++ code. The Internet Worm of 1988 used this flaw to subvert a system. Ten years later, the Hotmail bug of 1998 fell vulnerable to the same flaw! Since Java uses only heap-based storage for variables accessed

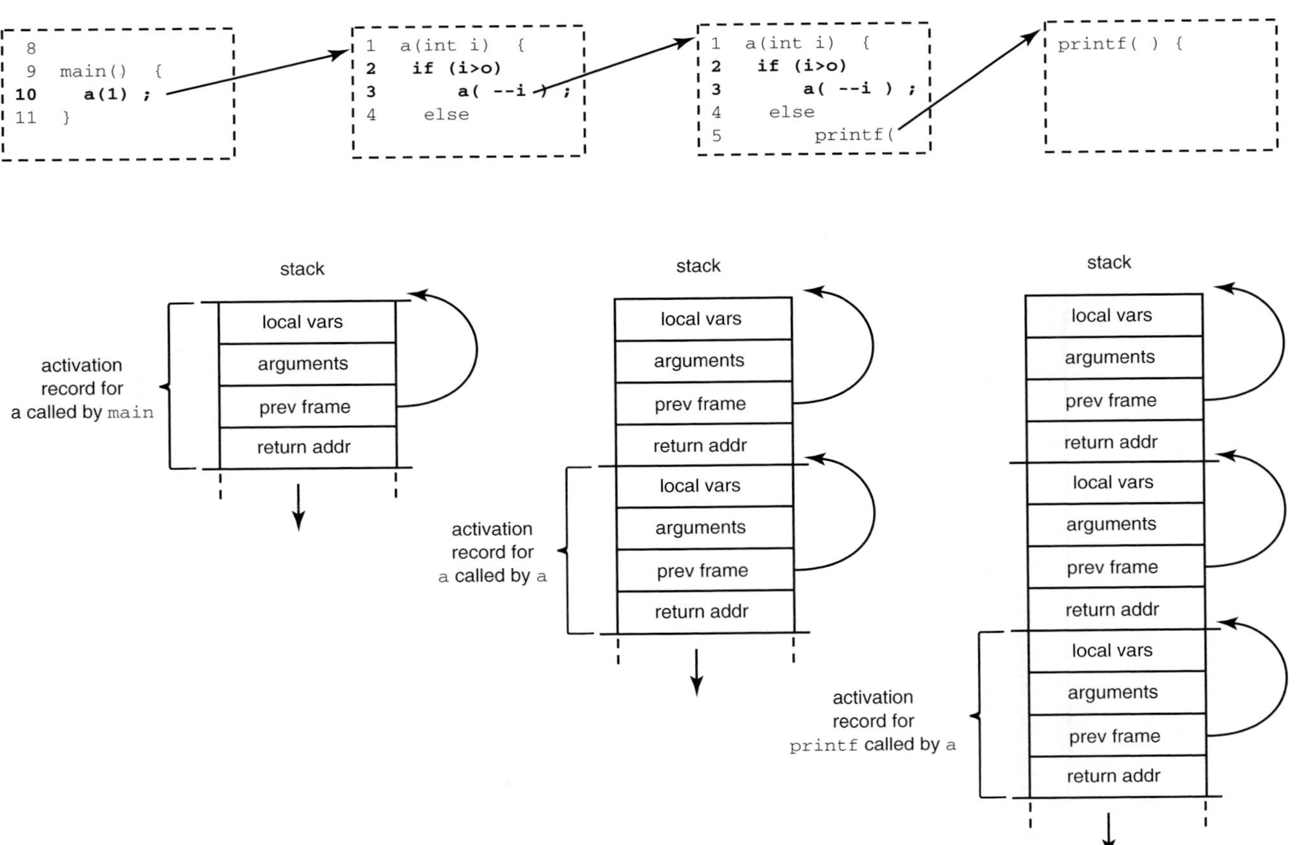

Figure 3–1 Stacks in Java.

through references, objects can and do happily live on after the scope in which they were created.

Since the heap and the stack both grow dynamically on demand, they are usually put at opposite ends of the address space and grow into the hole between them.

Looking for an Argument?

Here is a little bit of compiler terminology common to most languages.

A parameter is a variable declared in a method declaration. It provides a name for referring to the different arguments with which the method will later be called. In the following code, the variables param1 and param2 are parameters:

```
void foo(int param1, char param2) {
    param1 = ... ;
    ... = param2;
}
```

Some people call a parameter a formal parameter.

Notice how the string array parameter to the main routine is usually called "arg" even though it is a parameter, not an argument. This is a carryover from the same mistaken convention in C.

An argument is a value used in a particular call to a method. In the following code the values 23 and c are arguments:

```
plum.foo( 23, c );
```

Some people call an argument an actual parameter.

More Terminology. These characters are called parentheses: ( ). They go around expressions and parameter lists.

These characters are called square brackets: [ ]. They go around array indexes.

These characters are called braces or curly braces: { }. They indicate the start and end of a new block of code, or an array literal.

The Class "Object"

Most of the following chapters will present a brief listing of one of the standard built-in classes. You should just scan the list, look at the typical methods, and then go on. Later when you want to refer to the class in detail, you can look back at the appropriate chapter.

Related Java classes are grouped into packages. Packages are software libraries, and they correspond to file directories in most implementations. They are hierarchical, just like directories. All the classes in one directory are in the same package.

You write a line at the top of a source file to give the name of the package a class it belongs to. You can refer to packages by name in your Java code to reference some other class. The name of a package is the same as the name of the directory it is in. Java comes with a very large standard library stored in a package called "java." Part of the java package is a subpackage called "lang." The lang (language) package contains 20 or 30 standard classes that are imported automatically into every compilation. One such class is `java.lang.Object`.

We've mentioned a couple of times that there is a class called "Object" that is the ultimate superclass (parent class) of all other classes in the system. The members that exist in Object are thus inherited by every class in the system. Whatever class you have, an instance of it can call any of these methods. Here is what Object has:

```
public class Object {
     public java.lang.Object();
     public java.lang.String toString();

     protected native java.lang.Object clone() throws
                                 CloneNotSupportedException;

     public boolean equals(java.lang.Object);
     public native int hashCode();

     public final native java.lang.Class getClass();

     // methods relating to thread synchronization
     public final native void notify();
     public final native void notifyAll();
     public final void wait() throws InterruptedException;
     public final native void wait(long) throws
                                        InterruptedException;
     public final void wait(long, int) throws
                                        InterruptedException;
}
```

The "throws SomeException" clause is an announcement of the kind of unexpected error return that the method might give you.

There are several variations on the standard OS synchronization primitives `wait()` and `notify()`. These are described in Chapter 11. The remaining methods in Object, and thus in every class, are further highlighted below.

In each case, the method offers some useful, though often elementary, functionality. Programmers are supposed to provide their own version of any of these methods to replace the basic one if necessary. When an object (any object) calls a method, its own version of that method is preferred over an identically named method in a parent class, as we'll see in the second chapter on OOP.

`String toString();` This is a very handy method! You can call it explicitly, and it will return a string that "textually represents" this object. Use it while doing low-level debugging to see if your objects really are what you thought they were. Here's what I get for Fruit:

```
public class Fruit {
     int grams;
     int cals_per_gram;

     public static void main (String args[]) {
          Fruit f = new Fruit();
          System.out.println( " f = " + f.toString() );
     }
}
```

When you run the program, the output is as follows:

```
f = Fruit@a04c8d82
```

It is also invoked implicitly when any object and a String object are joined in a "+" operation. That operation is defined as *String concatenation.* To turn the other object into a String, its `toString()` method is called. It constitutes a piece of "magic" extra operator support for type String. The "+" operator is the only operator that can be applied to an object, at least until operator overloading is brought into Java, possibly with JDK 1.5.

`Object clone() throws CloneNotSupportedException.` The "native" keyword says that the body of this method is not written in Java, but will be provided in a native library linked in with the program.

Java supports the notion of cloning, meaning to get a complete bit-for-bit copy of an object. Java does a shallow clone, meaning that when an object has

data fields that are other objects, it simply copies the reference. The alternative is to recursively clone all referenced classes, too, known as a *deep clone.*

As a programmer, you can choose the exact cloning behavior you want. If a class wants to support deep cloning on its objects, it can provide its own version of `clone()`. When you provide your own version of clone, you can also change the access modifier to `public` (so other classes can call it and hence clone this object) rather than the default `protected` (outside this package, only subclasses can clone).

Note that `clone()` returns an Object. The object returned by `clone()` is usually immediately cast to the correct type. "Cast" is the Java term for type conversion, and it is written as the new type in parentheses immediately before the thing that is being converted, as in this example:

```
Vector v = new Vector();
Vector v2;

Object o = v.clone(); // clone the Vector
v2 = (Vector) o;      // cast it back to Vector type
```

Casting is "type safe," meaning that the validity of the type conversion is checked at runtime, and it will cause an error if you try to cast an object to a type that it does not have.

Not every class should support the ability to clone. If I have a class that represents unique objects, such as employees in a company, the operation of cloning doesn't make sense. Since methods in Object are inherited by all classes, the system places a further requirement on classes that want to be cloneable—they need to implement the cloneable interface to indicate that cloning is valid for them. Implementing an interface is described later.

`boolean equals(Object obj).` The method does a comparison of reference types, such as:

```
if (obj1.equals(obj2) ) ...
```

This is equivalent to the following:

```
if (obj1 == obj2 ) ...
```

The method is provided so that you can supply your own version of `equals()` to give it whatever semantics make sense for your class. This has already been done for String, because two Strings are usually considered equal if they contain the exact same sequence of characters, even if they are different objects. When you override `equals()`, you should also override `hashCode()` to make certain equal Objects get the same hashcode. If you fail to do this, your objects will fail to work in certain data structures, which are described later.

`native int hashCode ().` Ideally, a hashcode is a value that uniquely identifies an individual object. For example, you could use the memory address of an object as its hashcode if you wanted. It's used as a key in the standard `java.util.Hashtable` class. We'll say more about hashtables later.

`final native Class getClass().` All class types have an object that represents them at runtime. This runtime representation is known as *Run Time Type Identification* or RTTI. The method getClass( ) gets that RTTI information, returning it in an object of type `java.lang.Class`.

The class whose name is `Class` has several methods to tell you more about the class to which an arbitrary object belongs. You invoke the `getClass` method in the usual way:

```
Class whatAmI = myobject.getClass();
```

Reading the Java API

This is a very important section! You should do the download and try the steps shown. We will use java.lang.Object as an example to demonstrate how to use Java's documentation. The Java Application Programmer Interface (API) is a vast collection of libraries. Luckily, it is well documented, and the documentation is easily accessed in a browser.

The API documentation is a separate download from the JDK. You can also browse it online. I find it most convenient to download the API documentation, which you can do by following these steps:

1. Go to *java.sun.com* and follow the links to "Products and APIs" then to "Java 2 Platform, Standard Edition." Or just search for "J2SE documentation."

   That will take you to a J2SE page which offers you three downloads for each of the various releases:

   - J2SE software development kit (also known as the JDK)
   - J2SE runtime library for running programs only (aka JRE)
   - J2SE API documentation

2. For the downloadable documentation, click on the *first* of these, not the API documentation link (I know, it's perverse). You can choose any release, but I recommend the most recent that is available there. The API documentation link takes you to a page full of documentation links to online documentation. Browse that, too, according to time and interest.

3. The Java 2 SDK link takes you to a page with a prominent link marked "Download documentation." Finally! If you have not yet downloaded the JDK, you can and should do it from this page first.

   Click on the "download documentation" link, and then on the "continue" button. Then "accept" the click-through license. Finally, finally, click on "FTP download."

4. That lets you save a file called something like j2sdk-1_4_0-doc.zip onto your system. It's about 30 MBytes, so that's a couple of hours of download using a 56Kbps modem. 56Kbps is about 5 Kbytes per second.

5. Once the zip file is on your system, you want to unpack it into the same directory where you installed the JDK. Let's say that was C:\jdk1.4. Enter the directory with the command "cd c:\jdk1.4". Move the zip file here, too.

6. You can use any unzip utility to unpack the documentation. I like to use the "jar" utility that is part of the JDK. Once you are in the correct directory, the command is: "`jar -xf j2sdk-1_4_0-doc.zip`". That creates a docs subdirectory of the directory you are in and puts the files there.

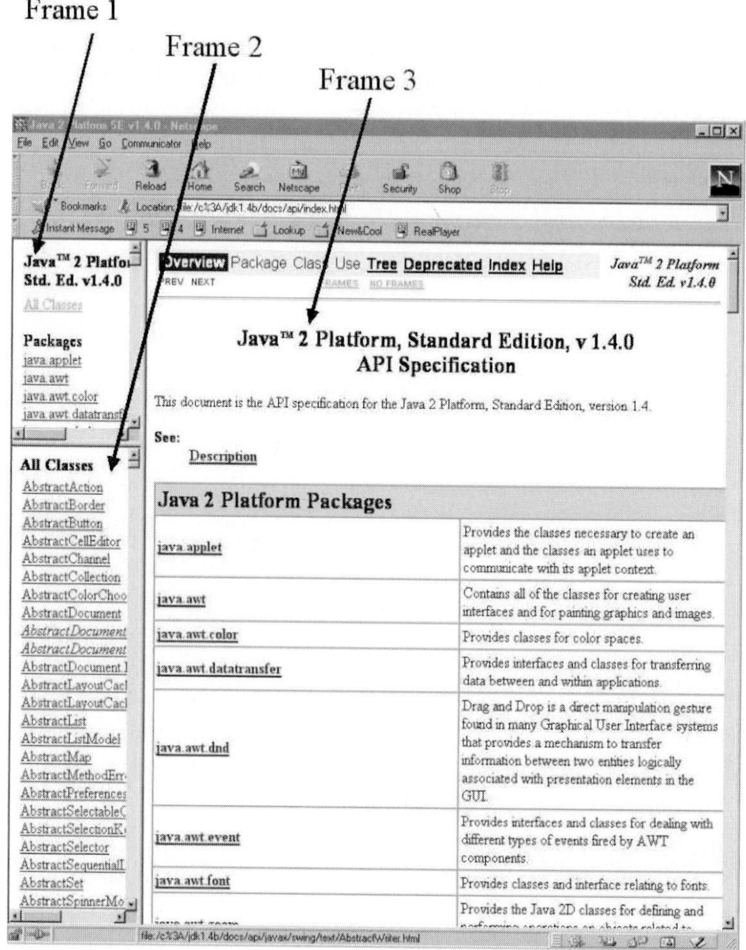

Figure 3–2 The API documentation.

7. At last you are in a position to look at the API documentation. Start up your favorite browser and browse the URL file:/c:/jdk1.4/docs/api/index.html. When the page comes up, set a bookmark for it. Your browser should be displaying something like Figure 3-2.

This is the standard form of the Java API documentation. There is a tool called "javadoc" that reads Java source code and generates this HTML documentation. All the Java library code is heavily annotated with comments, which javadoc processes and displays to you (see Figure 3-3).

There are three frames in the window. Frame 1 has a scrolling list of all package names in the release. Frame 2 has an alphabetical list of all classes. Frame 3 starts off by displaying more detail on each package.

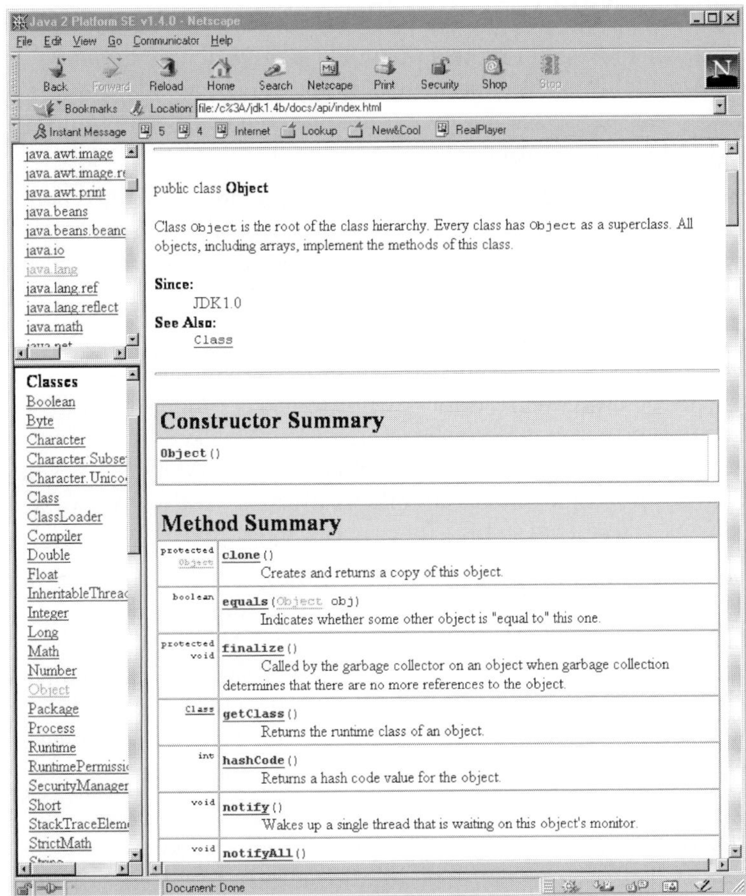

Figure 3–3 Detailed and general information in Frame 2.

To look at a particular class, you can either click on its name in Frame 2, or if you know the package it is in, you can click on that package in Frame 1. That causes Frame 2 to display all the classes in that package. Try it now, with package java.lang. Then click on class "Object" in Frame 2.

That brings up all the information about class java.lang.Object in Frame 3. You will see documentation on all the methods of the class, the constructors, the error conditions it can hit, and often some more general information too.

You should get into the habit of using the javadoc documentation heavily. You should not use any library class without first reading through its API in your browser. You should supplement the library classes presented in this book by reading the HTML from javadoc.

Some Light Relief—Napster and LimeWire

Everyone knows the story of Napster by this point. College student Shawn Fanning (baby nickname: "the napster" because of his sleeping habits) threw together some rickety old Windows software to broadcast the titles of any music tracks you had on your PC to a central database.

Other users could search that database looking for titles they wanted. When they found a match, the Napster software would set up a peer-to-peer connection and allow direct transfer of the music bits from your PC to the unknown fan elsewhere. Your incentive to share was that you in turn would be able to get files from other people similarly sharing their titles.

That was the concept at least. In practice, the record companies and some bands took exception to freelance distribution. By this time, Fanning had parlayed his idea and some prototype software into a start-up venture backed by premier venture capitalist company Kleiner Perkins Caulfield and Byers. At its peak, Napster claimed it had 70 million users, and even if they only exaggerated by the industry standard factor of five, that's still a lot of users.

Napster's demise took a couple of years to wind through the legal system, but the central point never seemed that subtle to me: you cannot legally broker the wholesale transfer of other people's intellectual property. Naturally, the record companies conducted themselves with their usual rapacious shortsightedness. Instead of licensing the Napster software and charging a membership fee, they tried to sue Napster out of existence. It's a reprise of 1992 when they killed DAT (Digital Audio Tape) by encumbering it with anticopying hardware backed by law.

Which brings us to the current situation. Napster is just about completely dead. Shawn Fanning will resume his college education if he has any sense. And a number of open source, distributed peer-to-peer music-sharing databases have replaced Napster's centralized model. All the file sharing goes on as before, but in a decentralized way, so the record companies have no deep-pockets adversary to sue. Ironic, isn't it? By killing Napster, they also killed their best chance to make money on the net.

When I first tried the Napster software in its heyday, all the way back in the last millennium, my first thought was, "why on earth didn't they write this in Java?" It was a simple network database lookup with peer file transfer capability front-ended by a simple GUI. Tailor-made for Java! Fanning was not familiar with Java, so he churned out his Windows-only software. Though Napster has now passed on to that great big recording studio in the sky, others still carry the conductor's baton.

Bearshare, Gnutella, and LimeWire are currently the most popular applications for sharing files (including .mp3 music files) across the net. They use the Gnutella client protocol, which is a search engine and file serving system in one. It

is wholly distributed. Anyone can implement it to share their content (any files) with others. The great thing about LimeWire is that it is written in Java.

You can download the application from *www.limewire.com* and see for yourself. The main screen is shown in Figure 3-4.

Since LimeWire is written in Java, the program runs on Windows, Macintosh, Linux, Solaris, IBM mainframes, and other computing platforms. The application has a solid, professional feel to it, and is fully functional. It has more than 3 million users, and is estimated to be present on 1.5% of all PCs.

LimeWire is now being sued by the record industry. Win or lose, they will probably be able to drive LimeWire out of business. LimeWire has responded by going open source, so download a copy of the application while you can, and see how the experts write Java GUIs.

When someone asks me about Java client applications, LimeWire is one of the programs I like to show them.

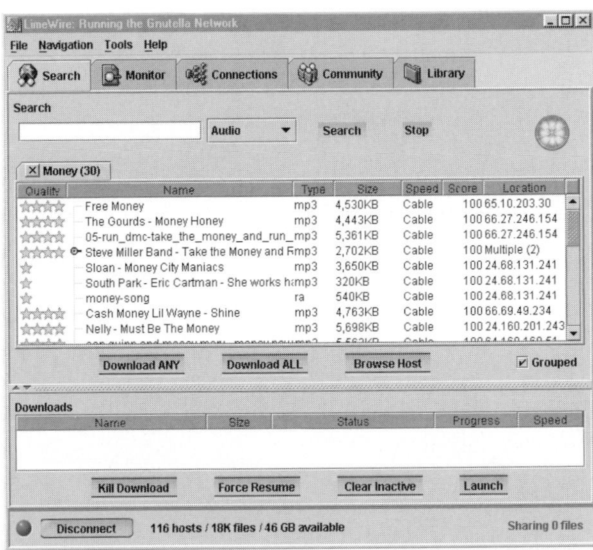

Figure 3–4 LimeWire: Napster's successor.

Chapter 4

Identifiers, Keywords, and Types

The great majority of operating systems in use today employ the ASCII codeset to represent characters. ASCII, the American Standard Code for Information Interchange, started out as a 7-bit code that represented uppercase and lowercase letters, the digits 0–9, and a dozen or so control characters like NUL and EOT. As computing technology became pervasive in Western Europe, users demanded the ability to represent all characters in their national alphabets. ASCII was extended to 8 bits, with the additional 128 characters being used to represent various accented and diacritical characters not present in English. The extended 8-bit code is known as the ISO 8859-1 Latin-1 codeset. It is reproduced for reference as an appendix at the end of this book.

Java and Unicode

An even more general solution was needed for Java that included support for Asian languages with their many thousands of ideograms. The solution that was chosen is Unicode. It is an ISO[1] standard 16-bit character set supporting 65,536 different characters. About 21,000 of these are devoted to Han, the ideograms seen in Chinese, Japanese, and Korean. The ISO Latin-1 code set forms most of the first 256 values, effectively making ISO Latin-1 a subset of Unicode, just as ASCII is a subset of Latin-1.

Java takes 2 bytes to represent each character internally, and uses the Unicode encoding. If you're only working with ASCII or Latin-1, then the encoding is the same, but you're carrying an extra byte for each character.

On Unix, Windows, and Macintosh, the default character sets are all 8-bit based. When Java gets a character on these systems, the operating system gives it 8 bits, but Java squirrels it away in a 16-bit datatype and always processes it as 16 bits. This does away with some hideous multibyte char complications in C and the special wide versions of the string-handling routines.

JDK 1.4 introduces some new classes that manage the conversion from external character representation to internal, and back again. These are covered in the second of the two chapters on I/O, later in the book. The one-sentence summary is: "the right conversions happen by default when you read in or write out 16-bit Unicode characters into an ASCII world, and if you want something different, there's a way to ask for it." This chapter explains how chars and strings are processed once you have got them into your program.

You can read more about the Unicode standard at *www.unicode.org*. Be warned: For something that is conceptually so simple, the Unicode standard sets some kind of world record in obscurity and all-around lack of clarity. An example can be seen at *www.unicode.org/unicode/standard/utf16.html*, reproduced in the following box.

1. ISO is the International Organization for Standardization, a federation of national standards bodies.

Extended UCS-2 Encoding Form (UTF-16)

The basic Unicode character repertoire and UCS-2 encoding form is based on the Basic Multilingual Plane (BMP) of ISO/IEC 10646. This plane comprises the first 65,536 code positions of ISO/IEC 10646's canonical code space (UCS-4, a 32-bit code space). Because of a decision by the Unicode Consortium to maintain synchronization between Unicode and ISO/IEC 10646, the Unicode Character Set may some day require access to other planes of 10646 outside the BMP. In order to accommodate this eventuality, the Unicode Consortium proposed an extension technique for encoding non-BMP characters in a UCS-2 Unicode string. This proposal was entitled UCS-2E, for extended UCS-2. This technique is now referred to as UTF-16 (for UCS Transformation Format 16 Bit Form).

Another way of saying all that is, "Unicode characters are 16 bits, and UCS-4 characters are 32 bits. Right now, Unicode forms the least significant 16 bits of the 32-bit code, but that might get jumbled up in the future in a new coding system called UTF-16." It's ironic—some programmers would say "predictable"—that a standard whose purpose is to foster communication is so poorly written that it actually hinders the ready transmission of meaning.

Scanning

When a Java compiler reads in program source, the very first thing that it does, even before forming tokens out of the characters, is to look for any six-character sequences of the form `\uxxxx`, where `xxxx` is exactly four hexadecimal digits, as in `\u3b9F`. These six-character sequences are translated into the corresponding one Unicode character whose value is xxxx, which is pushed back into the input stream for rescanning.

Because this early scanning takes place before tokens are assembled, the six-character sequence `\uxxxx` will be replaced even if it appears in a quoted string or character literal! It is done so that Java programs with arbitrary Unicode characters in them can be translated to and from ASCII and processed by ASCII tools with no loss of information. Relax, though: You never see this in practice.

Identifiers

Identifiers, which are names provided by the programmer, can be any length in Java. They must start with a letter, underscore, or dollar sign, and in subsequent positions can also contain digits.

A letter that can be used for a Java identifier doesn't just mean uppercase and lowercase A–Z. It means any of the tens of thousands of Unicode letters from any of the major languages in the world including Bengali letters, Cyrillic letters, or Bopomofo symbols. Every Unicode character above hex 00C0 is legal in an identifier. Table 4-1 shows some example valid Java identifiers.

Table 4–1 Legal Java Identifiers

`calories`	`Häagen_Dazs`	`déconnage`
`_99`	`Puñetas`	`fottío`
`i`	`$__`	`p`

The more accented characters you use in your variable names, the harder it is for others to edit them and maintain the code. So you should try to stick to ASCII characters.

Comments

Java has comment conventions that are similar to C++. Comments starting with "//" go to the end of the line, as follows:

```
i = 0;  // the "to end-of-line" comment
```

Comments starting with "/*" end at the next "*/", as follows:

```
/* the "regular multiline" comment
*/
```

There's a third variety of comment starting with "/**". This indicates text that will be picked up by javadoc, an automatic documentation generator. This is the tool that generates the HTML files for the Java API, reviewed in the previous chapter. You can also use javadoc on your own code and generate some HTML documentation for it. Many professional packages, including LimeWire, are documented using javadoc.

Javadoc is an implementation of the *literate programming* system invented by Donald Knuth. The javadoc tool (part of the JDK) parses source code with these special comments and extracts them into a set of HTML pages describing the API.

```
/** the API comment for HTML documentation
    @version 1.12
    @author A.P.L. Byteswap
    @see SomeOtherClassName
    HTML tags can also be put in here.
  */
```

The javadoc comments must be outside a method. Take a look at the source of the Java runtime library (distributed with the JDK) to see examples. There is a whole set of comments preceding each class, and each individual method in the class.

Try javadoc. You can easily annotate your own code with comments javadoc recognizes. Javadoc works on .java files, not .class files, because the .java files contain the comments. Add some of the javadoc tags to the myframe example and run javadoc like this:

```
javadoc myframe.java
```

This will create several HTML files and a style sheet, listing their names as it generates them. A style sheet is an update to HTML that lets you customize the appearance of other tags. You can change colors, fonts, and sizes throughout a document by using a style sheet that overrides the default appearance.

The javadoc output can be viewed in your web browser. It shows the chain of class inheritance and all the public fields in the class, along with your comments.

Commenting Out Code

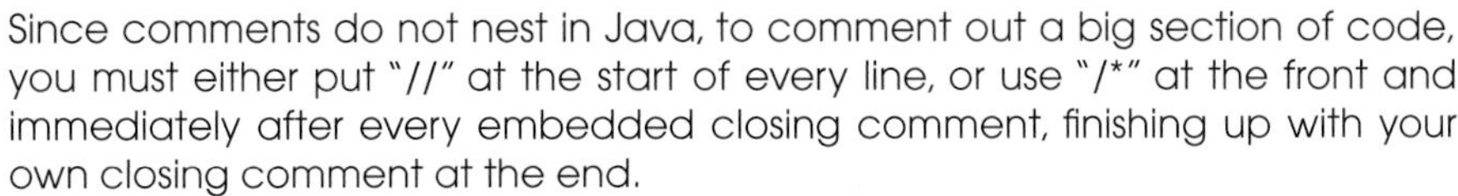

Since comments do not nest in Java, to comment out a big section of code, you must either put "//" at the start of every line, or use "/*" at the front and immediately after every embedded closing comment, finishing up with your own closing comment at the end.

You can also use the following around the section you want to temporarily delete:

```
if ( false ) {
     ...


 }
```

Each of these approaches has drawbacks. My preference is to use a smart editor that knows how to add or delete "//" from the beginning of each line. That way it is absolutely clear what is commented out.

Whether or not you agree with the idea of using web pages to store program documentation, it offers some compelling advantages. Documentation automatically generated from the program source is much more likely to be available, accurate (what could be more accurate than the documentation and the source being two views of the same thing?), and complete (the documentation is written at the same time as the code and by the same person).

Keywords

Keywords are reserved words, and they cannot be used as identifiers. ANSI C has only 32 keywords. Java has almost 50 keywords, including some reserved for future use in case the language designers add to the language. The keywords can be divided into several categories as follows according to their main use:

Used for built-in types:

```
boolean
char
byte   short    int      long
float  double   strictfp
void
```

Used for objects:

```
new        this        super
```

Used in statements:

selection statements	`if else` `switch case break default`
iteration statements	`for continue` `do while`
transfer of control statements	`return` `throw`
exception statements	`try catch finally` `assert`
thread statements	`synchronized`

Used to modify declarations (visibility, sharing, etc.):

```
static
abstract   final
private    protected  public
```

Used for other method or class-related purposes:

```
class        instanceof    throws    native
transient    volatile
```

Used for larger-than-a-single-class building blocks:

```
extends
interface    implements
package      import
```

Reserved for possible future use:

```
const    goto
```

The Primitive Types

Java has eight built-in, non-object types, also known as primitive types. They are:

- `boolean` (for truth values)
- `int, long, byte, short` (for arithmetic on integers)
- `double, float` (for arithmetic on the real numbers)
- `char` (for character data, ultimately to be input or printed)

All class types are ultimately represented in terms of primitive types. Primitive types are simpler than class types, and are directly supported in hardware on most computers. That is, most of the operations on primitive types are a single machine instruction, like ADD, whereas the operations on class types are specified as statements in a method.

Most high-level languages don't specify the sizes of primitive data types. That allows compiler writers the freedom to select the best sizes on each architecture for performance. The freedom turns out to be a false economy, since it greatly impedes program portability, and programmer time is a lot more expensive than processor time.

Java does away with all the uncertainty by rigorously specifying the sizes of the primitive types and making clear that these sizes are identical on all platforms. Let us examine the properties of each of these in turn.

`boolean`

This is the data type used for true/false conditions. To optimize memory access time, more than one bit is used to store a boolean value. In the Sun JVM, all integer types smaller than 32 bits are promoted to 32 bits when pushed on the stack during execution. An array of booleans is treated as an array of bytes.

range of values: false, true

literals: A "literal" is a value provided at compile-time. Just write down the value that you mean, and that's the literal. Literals have types just like variables have types. For boolean, the literals are false, true. In the code below, the assignment will always occur.

```
if (true) x = 33;
```

You cannot cast (convert) a boolean value to any other type. However, you can always get the same effect by using an expression, for example,

```
if (bool) i=1; else i=0; // set int according to bool value.
bool = (i==0? false:true); // set bool according to int value.
```

In Java, the boolean type is not based on integers. In particular, the programmer cannot increment, decrement, or add boolean values. Inside a JVM, there are no instructions dedicated to booleans, and integer operations are used.

int

The type int is a 32-bit, signed, two's-complement number, as used in virtually every modern cpu. It will be the type that you should choose by default whenever you are going to carry out integer arithmetic.

range of values: –2,147,483,648 to 2,147,483,647

literals: Int literals come in any of three varieties:

- A decimal literal, e.g., 10 or –256
- With a leading zero, meaning an octal literal, e.g., 077777
- With a leading 0x, meaning a hexadecimal literal, e.g., 0xA5 or 0Xa5

Uppercase or lowercase has no significance with any of the letters that can appear in integer literals. If you use octal or hexadecimal, and you provide a literal that sets the leftmost bit in the receiving number, then it represents a negative number. (Brush up on two's-complement format if you're not sure why.)

A numeric literal is a 32-bit quantity, even if its value could fit into a smaller type. But provided its actual value is within range for a smaller type, an int literal can be assigned directly to something with fewer bits, such as byte, short, or char. If you try to assign an int literal that is too large into a smaller type, the compiler will insist that you write an explicit conversion, termed a "cast."

Integer literals can be assigned to floating-point variables without casting. When you cast from a bigger type of integer to a smaller type, the high-order bits are just dropped.

A Word About Casts (Type Conversion)

All variables have a type in Java, and the type is checked so that you can't assign two things that are incompatible. You cannot directly assign a floating point variable to an integer variable.

It is reasonable, however, to convert between closely related types. That is what a cast does. Although casting can be used between two objects of related classes and between two primitives, you cannot cast an object to a primitive value or vice versa.

You cast an expression into another type by writing the desired new type name in parentheses before the expression, as follows:

```
float f = 3.142;
int i = (int) f; // a cast
```

Some numeric conversions don't need a cast. You are allowed to directly assign from a smaller-range numeric type into a larger range—as in byte to int, or int to long, or long to float—without a cast.

long

The type long is a 64-bit, signed, two's-complement quantity. It should be used when calculations on whole numbers may exceed the range of int. Using longs, the range of values is -2^{63} to $(2^{63}-1)$. Numbers up in this range will be increasingly prevalent in computing, and 2^{64} in particular is a number that really needs a name of its own. In 1993, I coined the term "Bubbabyte" to describe 2^{64} bytes. Just as 2^{10} bytes is a Kilobyte, and 2^{20} is a Megabyte, so 2^{64} bytes is a Bubbabyte. Using a long, you can count up to half a Bubbabyte less one.

range of values: –9,223,372,036,854,775,808 to 9,223,372,036,854,775,807

literals: The general form of long literals is the same as int literals, but with an "L" or "l" on the end to indicate "long." However, never use the lowercase letter "l" to indicate a "long" literal as it is too similar to the digit "1." Always use the uppercase letter "L" instead. The three kinds of long literals are:

- A decimal literal, e.g., 2047L or –10L
- An octal literal, e.g., 0777777L
- A hexadecimal literal, e.g., 0xA5L or OxABADCAFEDEADBE30L

All long literals are 64-bit quantities. A long literal must be cast to assign it to something with fewer bits, such as byte, short, int, or char.

byte

The byte type is an 8-bit, signed, two's-complement quantity. The reasons for using byte are to hold a generic 8-bit value, to match a value in existing data files, or to economize on storage space where you have a large number of such values. Despite popular belief, there is no speed advantage to bytes, shorts, or chars—modern CPUs take the same amount of time to load or multiply 8 bits as they take for 32 bits.

range of values: –128 to 127

literals: There are no byte literals. You can use, without a cast, int literals provided their values fit in 8 bits. You can use char, long, and floating-point literals if you cast them.

You always have to cast a (non-literal) value of a larger type if you want to put it into a variable of a smaller type. Since arithmetic is always performed at least at 32-bit precision, this means that assignments to a byte variable must always be cast into the result if they involve any arithmetic, like this:

```
byte b1=1, b2=2;
byte b3 = b2 + b1; // NO! NO! NO! compilation error
byte b3 = (byte) (b2 + b1); // correct, uses a cast
```

People often find this surprising. If I have an expression involving only bytes, why should I need to cast it into a byte result? The right way to think about it is that most modern computers do all integral arithmetic at 32-bit or 64-bit precision (there is no "8-bit add" on modern CPUs). Java follows this model of the underlying hardware. An arithmetic operation on two bytes potentially yields a bigger result than can be stored in one byte. The philosophy for numeric casts is that they are required whenever you assign from a more capacious type to a less capacious type.

short

This type is a 16-bit, signed, two's-complement integer. The main reasons for using short are to match external values already present in a file or to economize on storage space where you have a large number of such values.

range of values: –32,768 to 32,767

literals: There are no short literals. You can use, without a cast, int literals provided their values will fit in 16 bits. You can use char, long, and floating-point literals if you cast them.

As with byte, assignments to short must always be cast into the result if the right-hand side of the assignment involves any arithmetic.

The next two types, double and float, are the floating-point arithmetic types.

double

The type double refers to floating-point numbers stored in 64 bits, as described in the IEEE[2] standard reference 754. The type double will be the default type you use when you want to do some calculations that might involve decimal places (i.e., not integral values).

range of values: These provide numbers that can range between about –1.7E308 to +1.7E308 with about 14 to 15 significant figures of accuracy. The exact accuracy depends on the number being represented. Double precision floating-point numbers have the range shown in Figure 4-1.

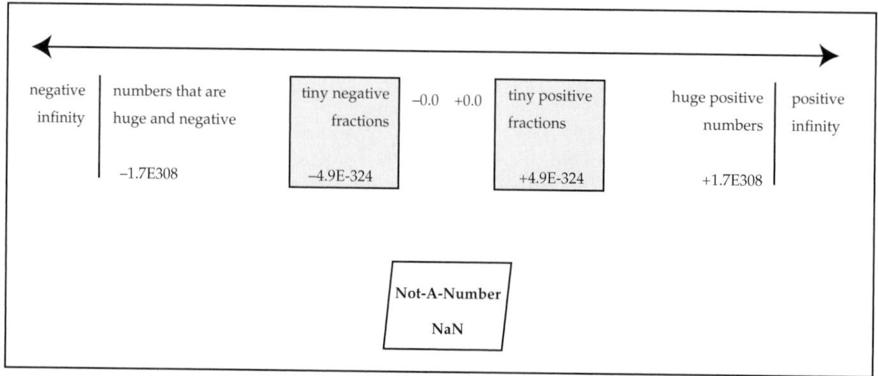

Figure 4–1 Type double should be used when calculations involve decimal places.

IEEE 754 arithmetic has come into virtually universal acceptance over the last decade, and it would certainly raise a few eyebrows if a computer manufacturer proposed an incompatible system of floating-point numbers now. IEEE 754 is the standard for floating-point arithmetic, but there are several places where chip designers can choose from different alternatives within the standard, such as rounding modes and extended precision. Java originally insisted on consistency on all hardware by specifying the alternatives that must be used. That is now being loosened somewhat.

2. IEEE is the Institute of Electrical and Electronic Engineers, a U.S. professional body.

IEEE 754 has an ingenious way of dealing with the problem of representing, on limited hardware, the unlimited amount of infinite precision real-world numbers. The problem is resolved by reserving a special value that says, "Help! I've fallen off the end of what's representable and I can't get up." You're probably familiar with infinity, but the "Not-a-Number" might be new if you haven't done much numerical programming. Not-a-Number, or NaN, is a value that a floating point can take to indicate that the result of some operation is not mathematically well-defined, like dividing zero by zero.

If you get a NaN as an expression being evaluated, it will contaminate the whole expression, producing an overall result of NaN—*which is exactly what you want!* The worst way to handle a numeric error is to ignore it and pretend it didn't happen.

You may never see a NaN if your algorithms are numerically stable, and you never push the limits of your datasets. Still, it's nice to know that NaN is there, ready to tell you your results are garbage, if they head that way.

literals: It is easiest to show by example the valid formats for double literals:

```
1e1    2.    .3     3.14     6.02e+23d
```

The format is very easy-going; just give the compiler a decimal point or an exponent, and it will recognize that a floating-point literal is intended. A suffix of "D", "d", or no suffix, means a double literal. In practice, most people omit the suffix.

It is also permissible to assign any of the integer literals or character literals to floats or doubles. The assignment doesn't need a cast, as you are going from a less capacious type to a more capacious type. So a line like this, while perverse, is valid:

```
double cherry = '\n';
```

It takes the integer value of the literal (0x0a in this case), floats it to get 10.0d, and assigns that to "cherry." Don't ever do this.

Make Mine a Double: How Large Is 1.7E308?

The largest double precision number is a little bit bigger than a 17 followed by 307 zeroes.

How large is that? Well, the volume of the observable universe is about (4pi/3)(15 billion light-years)^3 = 10^{85} cm^3. The density of protons is about 10^{-7} cm^{-3}. This value seems so sparse because it is an average for all space—on a planet the value is much, much denser, of course. The number of protons in the observable Universe is about 10^{78}, or "only" 1 followed by 78 zeros, give or take two-fifty.

The largest double precision number is even bigger than a googol. A googol is the number description suggested by 9 yr. old Milton Sirotta in 1938 at the request of his uncle, mathematician Edward Krasner. A googol is 10^{100}, meaning that it is only a 1 followed by 100 zeroes. Is the largest double precision number bigger than Madonna's capacity for self-promotion? No, we have to admit, it probably isn't that big.

It's possible to come up with problems where you want accuracy to 14 significant figures, such as figuring the national debt, but it is most unusual to need to tabulate numbers that are in orders of magnitude greater than the number of protons in the universe.

float

The type float refers to floating-point numbers stored in 32 bits, as described in the IEEE standard reference 754.

The justification for using single precision variables used to be that arithmetic operations were twice as fast as on double precision variables. With modern extensively pipelined processors and wide data buses between the cache and CPUs, the speed differences are inconsequential. The reasons for using floats are to minimize storage requirements when you have a very large quantity of them or to retain compatibility with external data files.

range of values: The type float provides numbers that can range between about –3.4E38 to 3.4E38 (i.e., 340,000,000,000,000,000,000,000,000,000,000,000,000) with about 6–7 significant figures of accuracy. The exact accuracy depends on the number being represented.

literals: The simplest way to understand what is allowed is to look at examples of valid float literals, as follows:

```
1e1f   2.f   .3f   3.14f   6.02e+23f
```

A suffix of "F" or "f" is always required on a float literal. A common mistake is to leave the suffix off the float literal, as follows:

```
float cabbage = 6.5;
 Error: explicit cast needed to convert double to float.
```

The code must be changed to the following:

```
float cabbage = 6.5f;
```

Also, a double literal cannot be assigned to a float variable without a cast, even if it is within the range of the float type. This is because some precision in decimal places may potentially be lost. The next section explains more about this interesting, and sometimes subtle, topic.

char

This type is a 16-bit unsigned quantity that is used to represent printable characters. Since it is an integer-based type, all the arithmetic operators are available on it. Unlike all the other arithmetic types, char is unsigned—it never takes a negative value. You should only use char to hold character data or bit values. If you want a 16-bit quantity for general calculations, don't use `char`, use `short`. This will avoid the possible surprise of converting between signed and unsigned types. Otherwise, a cast of a negative value into char will magically become positive without the bits changing.

Java provides the framework that is capable of handling characters from just about any locale in the world. The cost is that we store and move 16 bits for each character instead of just 8 bits.

range of values: a value in the Unicode code set 0 to 65,535

You have to cast a 32- or 64-bit result if you want to put it into a smaller result. This means that assignments to char must always be cast into the result if they involve any arithmetic. An example would be:

```
char c = (char) (i + 42); // cast
```

literals: Character literals appear between single quotes or in Strings. They can be expressed in four ways, and can be used for all of the types: char, byte, short, int, and long.

- A single character, `'A'`
- A character escape sequence. The allowable values are:

`'\n'` (linefeed)	`'\r'` (carriage return)	`'\f'` formfeed
`'\b'` (backspace)	`'\t'` (tab)	`'\\'` (backslash)
`'\"'` (double quote)	`'\''` (single quote)	

- An octal escape sequence. This has the form `'\nnn'` where `nnn` is one-to-three octal digits in the range 0 to 377. Note the odd fact that you can only set the least significant 8 bits of a 16-bit char when using an octal escape sequence. Some examples are `'\0'` or `'\12'` or `'\277'` or `'\377'`.

- A Unicode escape sequence. This has the form `'\uxxxx'` where xxxx is exactly four hexadecimal digits. An example is:

```
'\u0041' is the character A
```

Choosing Unicode for the char type was a bold and forward-looking design choice. Although a few people complained about the cost and waste of using 16 bits per character, these are the same pikers who a few years ago didn't want to shift from two-digit years to four-digit years, and who still hold onto their abacuses while they evaluate the "cutting edge" slide rules.

Switching to Unicode

OS vendors missed a big opportunity to move from ASCII to Unicode as the native character set of various operating systems. It could all have been done as part of the transition to 64-bit system software. Since that didn't happen, we'll all have two big "flag-days" in our future: one to make our applications 64-bit compatible, and one to make our applications globally compatible by converting all ASCII text to Unicode.

The extra storage requirements of Unicode are a no-brainer. Rotating magnetic media just keeps getting cheaper and cheaper. Even if my 1GB of data doubled in size—which it won't because I have a lot of non-text files—that is only about another $2-$3 worth of disk.

When the operating system vendors catch up, Java is already there.

Designers of forward-looking systems like Java have a responsibility to include proper support for more than just Western alphabets. Apart from anything else, customers are more likely to buy your software if it supports their native language. Until all systems have adopted Unicode, however, handling it on an ASCII system is clumsy, so avoid sprinkling Unicode literals through your code.

String

To round out this chapter, here is the standard Java class String. As a class type, it contrasts with the primitive types described up to this point in the chapter.

As the name suggests, String objects hold a series of adjacent characters like an array. It takes a method call, however (not an array reference), to pull an individual character out. You will use String instances a lot—whenever you want to store zero or more characters in a sequence or do character I/O. Arrays of char do some of these things, too, but String is a lot more convenient for comparing several characters and using literal values.

literals: A string literal is zero or more characters enclosed in double quotes, like this:

```
"" // empty string
"That'll cost you two-fifty \n"
```

Because Strings are used so frequently, Java has some special built-in support. Everywhere else in Java, you use a constructor to create an object of a class, such as:

```
String filmStar = new String( "Arnold Alois Schwarzenegger" );
```

String literals count as a shortcut for the constructor. So this is equivalent:

```
String filmStar = "Arnold Alois Schwarzenegger";
```

Each string literal behaves as if it is a reference to an instance of class String, meaning that you can invoke methods on it, copy a reference to it, and so on. For the sake of performance, the compiler can implement it another way, but it must be indistinguishable to the programmer.

Like all literals, string literals cannot be modified after they have been created. Variables of class String have the same quality—once you have created a String, you cannot change a character in the middle to something else. Some people refer to this by saying, "Strings are immutable." You can always discard any String and make the same reference variable refer to a different one in its place. You can even construct a new String out of pieces from another, so being unable to change a given String after it has been created isn't a handicap in practice.

String Concatenation

The other String feature with special built-in support is concatenation. Whenever a String is one operand of the "+" operator, the system does not do addition. Instead, the other operand (whatever it is, object or primitive thing) will be converted to a String by calling its `toString()` method, and the result is the two Strings joined together. You will use this feature in many places. Here are a few examples:

- To print out a variable and some text saying what it is:

```
System.out.println( "x has value " + x
                   + " and y has value " + y );
```

- to break a long String literal down into smaller strings and continue it across several lines:

```
  "Thomas the Tank Engine and the naughty "
+ "Engine-driver who tied down Thomas's Boiler Safety Valve"
+ "and How They Found Pieces of Thomas in Three Counties."
```

- To convert the value to a String (concatenating an empty String with a value of a primitive type is a Java idiom):

```
int i = 256;
    ...
... "" + i // yields a String containing the value of i.
```

That's much shorter than the alternative of using the conversion method of the String class `String.valueOf( i )`.

String Comparison and intern()

Just a reminder about String comparisons. Compare two Strings like this:

```
if ( s1.equals(s2)) ....
```

not this:

```
if (s1 == s2) ....
```

The first compares string contents, the second, string addresses. Failing to use "equals()" to compare two strings is probably the most common single mistake made by Java novices.

There is one exception to this string comparison rule. The exception has been put in place as a performance optimization. String has a method called intern(). You can call intern on one of your strings, and it will go into a private program-wide pool that the string class maintains. It gives you back a pointer to that string in the pool. Each string is only in that pool once. If you later call intern on a string that is already in the pool, you get the shared version back to use. This works because string contents never change after creation.

All string literals and String-valued constant expressions are interned for you automatically. That ensures that you don't have two copies of a string literal with the same contents. You can call intern() on your own strings in addition, if you wish. There is some cost to interning a string, so only do it when the number of string comparisons in your program is a lot more than the number of string creations.

The key reason to use intern() is that all strings returned from intern() can be compared for equality by using s == t instead of s.equals(t)! (Exercise: why?) The reference comparison is obviously quicker than invoking the equals method. A second benefit is that since all references to Strings of the same value use only a single object, you may save memory.

String uses another built-in class called StringBuffer to help it operate. StringBuffer differs from String in that you can change characters in the middle of a StringBuffer after it has been instantiated. StringBuffer doesn't have any support for searching for individual characters or substrings though. StringBuffer is widely used by the compiler to implement support for concatenating two Strings into a longer String. You'll use the class String a lot more than StringBuffer.

The following code shows the important methods of the String class. You can look at the entire source in file $JAVAHOME/java/src/lang/String.java. Also look at the HTML API, by choosing package java.lang.

```
public final class String implements CharSequence, Comparable, Serializable {
        // constructors with various arguments
    public String();
    public String(java.lang.String);
    public String(java.lang.StringBuffer);
    public String(byte[]);
    public String(byte[],int);
    public String(byte[],int,int);
    public String(byte[],int,int,int);
    public String(byte[],int,int,java.lang.String)
                                throws UnsupportedEncodingException;
    public String(byte[],java.lang.String) throws UnsupportedEncodingException;
    public String(char[]);
    public String(char[],int,int);
        // comparisons
    public char charAt(int);
    public int compareTo(java.lang.Object);
    public int compareTo(java.lang.String);
    public int compareToIgnoreCase(java.lang.String);
    public boolean endsWith(java.lang.String);
    public boolean equals(java.lang.Object);
    public boolean equalsIgnoreCase(java.lang.String);
    public boolean regionMatches(int, java.lang.String, int, int);
    public boolean regionMatches(boolean, int, java.lang.String, int, int);
    public boolean startsWith(java.lang.String);
    public boolean startsWith(java.lang.String, int);
        // search, extract and other routines
    public String concat(java.lang.String);
    public static String copyValueOf(char[]);
    public static String copyValueOf(char[], int, int);
    public byte [] getBytes();
    public void getBytes(int, int, byte[], int);
    public byte [] getBytes(java.lang.String)throws UnsupportedEncodingException;
    public void getChars(int, int, char[], int);
    public int hashCode();
    public int indexOf(int);
    public int indexOf(int, int);
    public int indexOf(java.lang.String);
    public int indexOf(java.lang.String, int);
    public native java.lang.String intern();
    public int lastIndexOf(int);
    public int lastIndexOf(int, int);
    public int lastIndexOf(java.lang.String);
    public int lastIndexOf(java.lang.String, int);
```

```
    public int length(); // gets the length of the string
    public String replace(char, char);
    //new in JDK 1.4, splits the string according to the pattern
    public String[] split (String pattern);
    public String[] split (String pattern, int limit);

    public String substring(int);
    public String substring(int, int);
    public char toCharArray()[]; public java.lang.String toLowerCase();
    public String toLowerCase(java.util.Locale);
    public String toString();
    public String toUpperCase();
    public String toUpperCase(java.util.Locale);
    public String trim(); // chops off leading & trailing spaces
        // conversion to String
    public static String valueOf(char);
    public static String valueOf(double);
    public static String valueOf(float);
    public static String valueOf(int);
    public static String valueOf(long);
    public static String valueOf(java.lang.Object);
    public static String valueOf(boolean);
    public static String valueOf(char[]);
    public static String valueOf(char[], int, int);
}
```

Some Light Relief—Hatless Atlas

Here's a cheery song that was written by top programmer David H. Zobel and circulated on the Internet for more than a while. It's sung to the tune of *Twinkle, Twinkle, Little Star*, but to sing it you have to know how some programmers pronounce the shifted and control characters on a keyboard. The "^" character above the "6" is often pronounced "hat" because it looks like a little hat. Some people give the name "huh" to "?", and "wow" to "!". Both of those are a lot shorter than more conventional names.

The song is called *Hatless Atlas* and it goes like this:

```
^ < @ < . @ *          Hat less at less point at star,
} " _ #   |            backbrace double base pound space bar.
- @ $ & / _ %          Dash at cash and slash base rate,
!(    @ | = >          wow open tab at bar is great.
; ' + $ ? ^?           Semi backquote plus cash huh DEL,
, # " ~ | ) ^G         comma pound double tilde bar close BEL.
```

This song can be enjoyed on more than one level. While the theme is not totally transparent, key elements are revealed. The bare-headed strong man relishes nature ("point at star"), and then enjoys the full hospitality of a tavern ("Wow, open tab at bar is great"). Soon he finds that the question of payment does arise, after all; hence, the veiled reference to Alan Greenspan ("slash base rate") and the finality overshadowing that closing lament "bar close BEL"!

I like to think that in the years to come wherever programmers gather in the evening, after the pizza is all eaten and a sufficient quantity of beer has been drunk, a piano may start to play softly in the corner. Quietly, one member of the group will sing, and then more and more of the programming staff will join in. Any systems analysts who haven't yet quaffed themselves unconscious might sway unsteadily with the beat. Soon several choruses of *Hatless Atlas* will roll lustily around the corners of the room. Old-timers will talk of the great bugs they have overcome and the days of punching clocks, cards, and DOS.

Or maybe we'll all stay home and watch reruns of *Star Trek: Kirk Violates the Prime Directive with Xena, Warrior Princess* instead, who knows?

Chapter 5

Names, Arrays, Operators, and Accuracy

This chapter covers more of the language basics: names, arrays, how operators work, and the accuracy you can expect in arithmetic. The chapter finishes up by presenting the standard class java.lang.Math.

Names

What is the difference between an *identifier* and a *name?* As we saw in Chapter 4, "Identifiers, Keywords, and Types," an identifier is just a sequence of letters and digits that don't match a keyword or the literals "true," "false," or "null." A name, on the other hand, can be prefixed with any number of further identifiers to pinpoint the namespace from which it comes. An identifier is thus the simplest form of name. The general case of name looks like the following:

```
package1.Package2.PackageN.Class1.Class2.ClassM.memberN
```

Since packages can be nested in packages, and classes nested in classes, there can be an arbitrary number of identifiers separated by periods, as in:

```
java.lang.System.out.println( "goober" );
```

That name refers to the `java.lang` package. There are several packages in the `java` hierarchy, and `java.lang` is the one that contains basic language support. One of the classes in the `java.lang` package is `System`. The class `System` contains a field that is an object of the `PrintStream` class, called `out`. `PrintStream` supports several methods, including one called `println()` that takes a `String` as an argument. It's the way to get text sent to the standard output of a program.

By looking at a lengthy name in isolation, you can't tell where the package identifiers stop and the class and member identifiers start. You have to do the same kind of evaluation that the compiler does. Since the namespaces are hierarchical, if you have two identifiers that are the same, you can say which you mean by providing another level of name. This is called *qualifying the name.* For example, if you define your own class called `BitSet`, and you also want to reference the class of the same name that is in the `java.util` package, you can distinguish them like this:

```
          BitSet myBS = new BitSet();
java.util.BitSet theirBS = new java.util.BitSet();
```

A *namespace* isn't a term that occurs in the Java Language Specification. Instead, it's a compiler term meaning "place where a group of names are organized as a whole." By this definition, all the members in a class form a namespace. All the variables in a method form a namespace. A package forms a namespace. Even a local block inside a method forms a namespace.

A compiler will look for an identifier in the namespace that most closely encloses it. If not found, it will look in successively wider namespaces until it finds the first occurrence of the correct identifier. Java also uses the context to resolve names. You won't confuse Java if you give the same name to a method, to a data field, and to a label. It puts them in different namespaces. When the compiler is looking for a method name, it doesn't bother looking in the field namespace.

When Can an Identifier Be Forward-Referenced?

A forward reference is the use of a name before that name has been defined, as in the following:

```
class Fruit {
     void foo() { grams = 22; } // grams not yet declared

     int grams;
}
```

A primitive field needs to appear before it is used only when the use is in the initialization of a field, like this:

```
int i = grams;
```

In the first example above, the use is in a method, so this is a valid forward reference to the field `grams`. The declaration of a class never needs to appear before the use of that class, as long as the compiler finds it at some point during that compilation.

Expressions

There's a lengthy chapter in the Java Language Specification on expressions covering many cases that would be interesting only to language lawyers. What it boils down to is that an expression is any of the alternatives shown in Table 5-1.

Table 5–1 Expressions in Java

Expression	Example of Expression
a literal	`245`
this object reference	`this`
a field access	`plum.grams`
a method call	`plum.total_calories()`
an object creation	`new Fruit( 3.5 )`
an array creation	`new int[27]`
an array access	`myArray[i][j]`
any expression connected by operators	`plum.grams * 1000`
any expression in parens	`( plum.grams * 1000 )`

You *evaluate* an expression to get a result that will be a variable (as in evaluating `this` gives you an object you can store into), a value, or nothing (a void expression). You get the last by calling a method with a return value of void.

An expression can appear on either side of an assignment. If it is on the left-hand side of an assignment, the result designates where the evaluated right-hand side should be stored.

The type of an expression is known either at compile time or checked at run-time to be compatible with whatever you are doing with the expression. There is no escape from strong typing in Java.

Arrays

In this section we introduce arrays and describe how to use them.

In Java, arrays are objects. That means array types are reference types, and your array variable is really a reference to an array.

Java arrays are allocated dynamically and keep track of their length. It's the same drill that we saw with classes. What looks like the declaration of an array:

```
int day[];
```

is actually a variable that will point to an array-of-ints. When we finally fill in the pointer, it's good for any size of int array, and in the course of execution it can point to different arrays of different sizes.

For example, when you write an array as the parameter to a method, you write it like this:

```
void main(String[] args) { ...
```

That allows arrays of arbitrary bounds as parameters, because String[] matches any size array of strings.

Array Subscripts Start at Zero

Array subscripts always start at zero. People coming to Java from another language often have trouble with that concept. After all, when you're counting anything, you always start "one, two, three"—so why would array elements be any different?

This is one of the things carried over from C. C was designed by and for systems programmers. In a compiler, a subscript is translated to "offset from array base address." You can save an instruction in subscript-to-address translation if you disallow subscripts with an arbitrary starting point. Instead, require the first offset to be zero, and use offset-from-base-address directly.

Watch out! It means that when you declare the following, valid subscripts for "day" are in the range 0 to 364:

```
int day[] = new int[365];
```

A reference to "day(365)" is invalid. If this causes distress in terms of program readability (perhaps you want days numbered from 1 to 365 to match the calendar), you can declare the array one larger than it needs to be, and don't use element zero.

Array indexes are all checked at runtime. If a subscript attempts to access an element outside the bounds of its array, it causes an exception and the program will cease execution rather than overwrite some other part of memory. Exceptions are described in a later chapter.

Here are some ways in which arrays *are* like objects:

- They *are* objects because the language specification says so (section 4.3.1).
- Array types are reference types, just like object types.
- Arrays are allocated with the "new" operator, similar to constructors.
- Arrays are always allocated on the heap, never on the stack.
- The parent class of all arrays is `Object`, and you can call any of the methods of `Object`, such as `toString()`, on an array.

On the other hand, here are some ways arrays *are not* like objects:

- You can't make an array be the child of some class other than Object.
- Arrays have a different syntax from other object classes.
- You can't define your own methods for arrays.

Regard arrays as funny kinds of objects that share some key characteristics with regular objects. Operations that are common to all objects can be done on arrays. Operations that require an Object as an operand can be passed an array. The length of an array (the number of elements in it) is a data field in the array class. For example, you can get the size of an array by referencing the following:

```
myArray.length        // yes
```

People always want to treat that as a method call, and write the following:

```
myArray.length()      // NO! NO! NO!
```

To remember this, remind yourself that arrays only have the method calls defined in java.lang.Object, and length() isn't one of them. So length must be a field for arrays. java.lang.String, on the other hand, is a regular class in all respects, and it has a length() method.

The Length of an Entire Array Versus a String in an Array

Think back to the String argument array and the main() routine. You may be wondering how to get the length of the array (the total number of Strings) versus the length of a given String in the array. Here is some code that demonstrates the two scenarios:

```
public static void main(String args[]) {
     int i=0;
     System.out.println( "number of String args:" + args.length );
     System.out.println( "length of i'th String:" +args[i].length() );
}
```

Contrast how "length" is a data field for arrays and is a method for the class String. This is a frequent point of confusion for beginners.

Creating an Array

When you declare an array, as in the following example, that declaration says the "carrot can hold a reference to any size array of int."

```
int carrot [];
```

You have to make the reference point to an array before you can use it, just as with class types. You might make it point to an existing array, or you might create the array with a `new` expression, just as with objects.

```
carrot = new int[100];
```

Once an array has been created, it cannot change in size. You can make the reference variable point to a bigger array into which you copy the same contents.

Array Size

You can never specify the size of an array in a C-style declaration like this:

```
int sprout [256];                    // NO! NO! NO!
```

The array's size is set when you assign something to it, either in an initializer or a regular assignment statement.

```
int carrot [] = new int[256];
```

Once an array object has been created with a given size, it cannot change for that array, although you can replace it by assigning a differently-sized array object to it.

When you create an object, the fields that are primitive types are created and initialized to zero. The fields that are reference types are initialized to null (don't point to anything yet). It is exactly the same with arrays.

If the array element type is a primitive type, the values are created when the array is new'd.

```
carrot = new int [256]; // creates 256 ints
carrot[7] = 32;          // ok, accesses 1 element.
```

If the array elements are a reference type, you get 256 references to objects *and you must fill them in before use!*

```
Fruit carrot [] = new Fruit[256]; // creates 256 references
carrot[7].grams = 32; // NO! NO! NO!
```

You need to make each individual reference element point to an object before you can access the object. You need to do something like this:

```
Fruit carrot [] = new Fruit[256];
     for (int i=0; i<carrot.length; i++) {
          carrot[i] = new Fruit();
     }
```

Failing to create the objects in an array of reference types is the most common novice mistake with arrays, and it causes a `NullPointerException` error.

Initializing an Array

You can initialize an array in its declaration with an *array initializer* like this:

```
byte b[] = { 0, 1, 1, 2, 3 };
String wkdays[] = { "Mon", "Tue", "Wed", "Thu", "Fri", };
```

A superfluous trailing comma is allowed in an initialization list—an unnecessary carryover from C. The permissible extra trailing comma is claimed to be of use when a list of initial values is being generated automatically.

A new array object is implicitly created when an array initializer expression is evaluated. You can't use an array initializer anywhere outside a declaration, like in an assignment statement. So this is not valid:

```
wkdays = { "Mon", "Tues" }; // NO! NO! NO!
```

But it is really useful to be able to allocate and initialize an array in a statement, so *array creation expressions* were brought to the rescue. It provides the explicit extra information about the type of the thing in braces. This is valid:

```
wkdays = new String[] { "Mon", "Tues" };
```

That `new type[] {values... }` is an array creation expression, and it was introduced in JDK 1.1. You *can* use an array creation expression in a declaration or anywhere a reference to an array is expected. Here is one in a declaration.

```
Fruit orchard[] = new Fruit [] {new Fruit(),
                                new Fruit(4,3),
                                null };
```

There is a method called `arraycopy()` in class `java.lang.System` that will copy part or all of an array, like this:

```
String midweek[] = new String[3];
System.arraycopy ( wkdays /*src*/, 1 /*offset*/,
                   midweek /*dest*/, 0 /*offset*/, 3 /*len*/ );
```

You can clone an array, like this:

```
int p[] = new int[10];
int p2[] = (int[]) p.clone(); // makes a copy of p
```

Whereas cloning creates the new array, arraycopy just copies elements into an existing array. As with the clone of anything, you get back an Object which must be cast to the correct type. That's what `( int[] )` is doing.

Arrays of Arrays of ...

The language specification says there are no *multidimensional* arrays in Java, meaning the language doesn't use the convention of Pascal or Ada to put several indexes into one set of subscript brackets. Ada allows multidimensional arrays like this:

```
year : array(1..12, 1..31) of real;
```

Ada code for multidimensional array.

```
year(i,j) = 924.4;
```

Ada also allows arrays of arrays, like this:

```
type month is array(1..31) of real;
```

Ada code for array of arrays.

```
year : array(1..12) of month;
year(i)(j) = 924.4;
```

What "Multidimensional" Means in Different Languages

The Ada standard explicitly says arrays of arrays and multidimensional arrays are different. The language has both.

The Pascal standard says arrays of arrays and multidimensional arrays are the same thing.

The ANSI C standard says C has what other languages call arrays of arrays, but it also calls these multidimensional.

The Java language only has arrays of arrays, and it only calls these arrays of arrays.

Java arrays of arrays are declared like this:

```
Fruit plums [] [] ;
```

Array "plums" is composed of an array that is composed of an array whose elements are Fruit objects. You can allocate and assign to any arrays individually.

```
plums = new Fruit [23] [9]; // an array[23] of array[9]
plums [i] = new Fruit [17]; // an array[17]
plums [i][j] = new Fruit(); // an individual Fruit
```

Because object declarations do not create objects (I am nagging about this repeatedly—it's an important point), you will need to fill out or *instantiate* the elements in an array before using it. If you have an array of arrays, like the one below, you will need to instantiate both the top-level array and at least one bottom-level array before you can start storing ints:

```
int cabbage[][];
```

The bottom-level arrays do not have to all be a single uniform size. Here are several alternative and equivalent ways you could create and fill a triangular array of arrays:

- Use several array creation expressions, like this:

```
int myTable[][] = new int[][] {
                              new int[] {0},
                              new int[] {0,1},
                              new int[] {0,1,2},
                              new int[] {0,1,2,3},
                  };
```

- Lump all the initializers together in a big array initializer, like this:

```
int myTable[][] = new int[][] {
                    {0},
                    {0,1},
                    {0,1,2},
                    {0,1,2,3}, };
```

- Initialize individual arrays with array creation expressions, like this:

```
int myTable[][] = new int[4][];
// then in statements
myTable[0] = new int[] {0};
myTable[1] = new int[] {0, 1};
myTable[2] = new int[] {0, 1, 2};
myTable[3] = new int[] {0, 1, 2, 3};
```

- Use a loop, like this:

```
int myTable[][] = new int[4][];
... // later in statements
for( int i=0; i<myTable.length; i++) {
     myTable[i] = new int [i+1];
     for (int j=0; j<=i; j++)
          myTable[i][j]=j;
}
```

This could be done in a static block (if myTable is static) or in a constructor.

If you don't instantiate all the dimensions at one time, you must instantiate the most significant dimensions first. For example:

```
int cabbage[][] = new int[5][];   // ok
int cabbage[][] = new int[5][3];  // ok
```

but:

```
int cabbage[][] = new int[][3];   // NO! NO! NO!
```

Arrays with the same element type, and the same number of dimensions (in the C sense, Java doesn't have multidimensional arrays) can be assigned to each other. The arrays do not need to have the same number of elements because (as you would expect) the assignment just copies one reference variable into another. For example:

```
int eggs[] = {1,2,3,4};
int ham[] = new int[2] {77, 96};
ham = eggs;
ham[3] = 0;     // OK, because ham now has 4 elements.
```

This doesn't make a new copy of eggs; it makes ham and eggs reference the same array object.

Watch the size of those arrays of arrays. The following declaration allocates an array of 4 * 250 * 1000 * 1000 = 1GB.

```
int bubba[][][] = new int[250][1000][1000];
```

Do you have that much memory on your system? In 1998, that was a joke. In 2001, 1GB was about $120 worth of synchronous 133MHz DRAM, with free shipping from the Yahoo store, and you could buy a Solaris UltraSPARC 64bit workstation running a 64 bit operating system, with a 64 bit version of Java preinstalled for $995. This is the power of Moore's Law.

Have Array Brackets, Will Travel

There is a quirk of syntax in that the array declaration bracket pairs can "float" to be next to the element type, to be next to the data name, or to be in a mixture of the two. The following are all valid array declarations:

```
int a [] ;
int [] b = { a.length, 2, 3 } ;

char c [][] = new char[12][31];
char[] d [] = { {1,1,1,1}, {2,2,2,2} }; // creates d[2][4]
char[][] e;

byte f [][][] = new byte [3][3][7];
byte [][] g[] = new byte [3][3][7];

short [] h, i[], j, k[][];
```

If array brackets appear next to the type, they are part of the type, and apply to *every* variable in that declaration. In the code above, "j" is an array of short, and "i" is an array of arrays of short.

This is mostly so declarations of functions returning arrays can be read more normally. Here is an example of how returning an array value from a function would look following C rules (you can't return an array in C, but this is how C syntax would express it if you could):

```
int funarray()[] { ... }                Pseudo-C CODE
```

Here are the alternatives for expressing it in Java (and it is permissible in Java), first following the C paradigm:

```
int ginger ()[]   { return new int[20]; }
```

Java CODE

A better way is to express it like this:

```
return type
|
int []   ginger ()   { return new int[20]; }
         method
```

Java CODE

The latter allows the programmer to see all the tokens that comprise the return type grouped together.

Arrays are never allocated on the stack in Java, so you cannot get into trouble returning an array stack variable. If you declare an array as a local variable (perhaps in a method), that actually creates a reference to the array. You need a little more code to create the array itself and that will allocate the array safely on the heap. In C, it is too easy to return a pointer to an array on the stack that will be overwritten by something else pushed on the stack after returning from the method.

Indexing Arrays and 64-Bit Java

Arrays are indexed by "int" values. Values of types "byte," "short," and "char" are promoted to "ints" when they are used as an index, just as they are in other expression contexts.

Arrays may not be indexed by "long" values. That means arrays are implicitly limited to no more than the highest 32-bit int value, namely, 2,147,483,647. That's OK for the next year or so—but the lack of 64-bit addressing will eventually make itself felt in Java arrays, and the rule will need to be relaxed.

So what is meant by a 64-bit version of Java, available for the Solaris 64-bit operating system? It means that the JVM on that platform does not incur the emulation penalty of a 32-bit application on 64-bit hardware.

Instead, the JVM has been compiled as a 64-bit program, and supports 64-bit operation on 64-bit Sparc-v9 platforms when using the Java HotSpot Server VM. With a 64-bit address space, more than four gigabytes of heap memory is available.

Two implementations of the Java virtual machine are available for J2SE 1.3 on Solaris: the client, and the server versions of the JVM. The client JVM has been optimized for quicker startup and reduced memory use, and only runs as a 32-bit application. The Server VM has been optimized for peak operating speed in large, long running applications, and has 64-bit support.

The Java HotSpot Server VM includes support for both 32-bit and 64-bit operations, and users can select either 32-bit or 64-bit operation by using command-line flags -d32 or -d64, respectively. Users of the Java Native Interface will need to recompile their code to be able to run it on the 64-bit VM, but pure Java makes the transition to 64 bits and the extended heap space without recompiling.

Operators

Most of the operators in Java will be readily familiar to any programmer. One novel aspect is that the order of operand evaluation in Java is well-defined. For many older languages, the order of evaluation has been deliberately left unspecified. In other words, in C and C++ the following operands can be evaluated and added together in any order:

```
i + myArray[i] + functionCall();
```

The function may be called before, during (on adventurous multiprocessing hardware), or after the array reference is evaluated, and the additions may be executed in any order. If the functionCall() adjusts the value of i, the overall result depends on the order of evaluation. The trade-off is that some programs give different results depending on the order of evaluation. A professional programmer would consider such programs to be badly written, but they exist nonetheless.

The order of evaluation was left unspecified in earlier languages so that compiler-writers could reorder operations to optimize register use. Java makes the trade-off in a different place. It recognizes that getting consistent results on all computer systems is much more important than getting varying results a trifle faster on one system. In practice, the opportunities for speeding up expression evaluation through reordering operands seem to be quite limited in many programs. As processor speed and cost improve, it is appropriate that modern languages optimize for programmer sanity instead of performance.

Java specifies not just left-to-right operand evaluation, but the order of everything else, too, such as:

- The left operand is evaluated before the right operand of a binary operator. This is true even for the assignment operator, which must evaluate the left operand (where the result will be stored) fully before starting on the right operand (what the result is).
- In an array reference, the expression before the square brackets "[]" is fully evaluated before any part of the index is evaluated.
- A method call for an object has this general form:

  ```
  objectInstance.methodName(arguments);
  ```

- The objectInstance is fully evaluated before the methodName and arguments. This can make a difference if the objectInstance is given to you by a method that has side effects. Any arguments are evaluated one by one from left to right.
- In an allocation expression for an array of several dimensions, the dimension expressions are evaluated one by one from left to right.

The Java Language Specification (James Gosling, Bill Joy, and Guy L. Steele, Addison-Wesley, 1996) uses the phrase, "Java guarantees that the operands to operators *appear to be* evaluated from left-to-right." This is an escape clause that allows clever compiler-writers to do brilliant optimizations, as long as the appearance of left-to-right evaluation is maintained.

For example, compiler-writers can rely on the associativity of integer addition and multiplication. This means that a+b+c will produce the same result as (a+b)+c or a+(b+c). This is true in Java even in the presence of overflow, because what happens on overflow is well-defined. We have a section on overflow later in this chapter.

If one of the subexpressions occurs again in the same basic block, a clever compiler-writer might be able to arrange for its reuse. In general, because of complications involving infinity and not-a-number (NaN) results, floating-point operands cannot be trivially reordered.

Note that the usual operator precedence still applies. In an expression like the one below, the multiplication is always done before the addition.

```
b + c * d
```

What the Java order of evaluation says is that for all binary (two argument) operators the left operand is always fully evaluated before the right operand. Therefore, the operand "b" above must be evaluated before the multiplication is done (because the multiplied result is the right operand to the addition).

Left-to-right evaluation means in practice that all operands in an expression (if they are evaluated at all) are evaluated in the left-to-right order in which they are written down on a page. Sometimes an evaluated result must be stored while a higher precedence operation is performed. Although *The Java Language Specification* only talks about the apparent order of evaluation of operands to individual operators, this is a necessary consequence of the rules.

Java Operators

The Java operators and their precedence are shown in Table 5-2. The arithmetic operators are undoubtedly familiar to the reader. We'll outline some of the other operators in the next section.

Table 5–2 Java Operators and Their Precedence

Symbol	Note	Precedence (highest number= highest precedence)	COFFEEPOT Property (see next section)
`++ --`	pre-increment, decrement	16	right
`++ --`	post-increment, decrement	15	left
`~`	flip the bits of an integer	14	right
`!`	logical not (reverse a boolean)	14	right
`- +`	arithmetic negation, plus	14	right
`( typename )`	type conversion (cast)	13	right
`* / %`	multiplicative operators	12	left
`- +`	additive operators	11	left
`<< >> >>>`	left and right bitwise shift	10	left
`instanceof <` `<= > >=`	relational operators	9	left
`== !=`	equality operators	8	left
`&`	bitwise and	7	left
`^`	bitwise exclusive or	6	left
`|`	bitwise inclusive or	5	left
`&&`	conditional and	4	left
`||`	conditional or	3	left
`? :`	conditional operator	2	right

`= *= /= %=`
`+= -=`
`<<= >>= >>>=`
`&= ^= |=`
	assignment operators	1	right

Char is considered to be an arithmetic type, acting as a 16-bit unsigned integer.

The ++ and -- Operators

The pre- and post-increment and decrement operators are shorthand for the common operation of adding or subtracting one from an arithmetic type. You write the operator next to the operand, and the variable is adjusted by one.

```
++i;        // pre-increment
      j++; // post-increment
```

It makes a difference if you bury the operator in the middle of a larger expression, like this:

```
int result = myArray[++i]; // pre-increment
```

This will increment i *before* using it as the index. The post-increment version will use the current value of i, and after it has been used, add one to it. It makes a very compact notation. Pre- and post-decrement operators (`--x`) work in a similar way.

The % and / Operators

The division operator "/" is regular division on integer types and floating point types. Integer division just cuts off any decimal part, so -9/2 is -4.5 which is cut to -4. This is also (less meaningfully) termed "rounding towards zero."

The remainder operator "%" means "what is left over after dividing by the right operand a whole number of times." Thus, -7%2 is -1. This is because -7 divided by 2 is -3, with -1 left over.

Some people call "%" the modulus operator, so "-7 % 2" can be read as "-7 modulo 2". If you have trouble remembering what modulo does, it may help to recall that all integer arithmetic in Java is modular, meaning that the answer is modulo the range. If working with 32 bits, the answer is the part of the mathematically correct answer that fits in a 32-bit range. If working with 64 bits, the answer is the part of the answer that fits in 64 bits. If doing "-8 modulo 3", the answer is that remainder part of the division answer that fits in 3, i.e., -2.

The equality shown below is true for division and remainder on integer types:

```
(x / y) * y + x%y == x
```

If you need to work out what sign some remainder will have, just plug the values into that formula.

The << >> and >>> Operators

In Java the ">>" operator does an arithmetic or signed shift right, meaning that the sign bit is propagated. In C, it has always been implementation-defined whether this was a logical shift (fill with 0 bits) or an arithmetic shift (fill with copies of the sign bit). This occasionally caused grief, as programmers discovered the implementation dependency when debugging or porting a system. Here's how you use the operator in Java:

```
int eighth = x >> 3; // shift right 3 times same as div by 8
```

One new Java operator is ">>>" which means "shift right and zero fill" or "unsigned shift" (do not propagate the sign bit). The ">>>" operator is not very useful in practice. It works as expected on numbers of canonical size, ints, and longs.

It is broken, however, for short and byte, because negative operands of these types are promoted to int with sign propagation before the shift takes place, leaving bits 7-or-15 to 31 as ones. The zero fill thus starts at bit 31! Not at all what you probably intended!

If you want to do unsigned shift on a short or a byte, mask the bits you want and use >>.

```
byte b = -1;
b = (byte)((b & 0xff) >> 4);
```

That way programs won't mysteriously stop working when someone changes a type from `int` to `short`.

The `instanceof` Operator

The other new operator is `instanceof`. We've said a couple of times that a class can be set up as a subclass of another class. The `instanceof` operator is used with superclasses to tell if you have a particular subclass object. For example, we may see the following:

```
class vehicle { ...
class car extends vehicle { ...
class convertible extends car { ...

vehicle v; ...
if (v instanceof convertible) ...
```

The `instanceof` operator is often followed by a statement that casts the object from the base type to the subclass, if it turns out that the one is an instance of the other. Before attempting the cast, `instanceof` lets us check that it is valid. There is more about this in the next chapter.

The & | and ^ Operators

The "&" operator takes two boolean operands, or two integer operands. It always evaluates both operands. For booleans, it ANDs the operands, producing a boolean result. For integer types, it bitwise ANDs the operands, producing a result that is the promoted type of the operands (as in long or int).

```
int flags = ... ;
int bitResult = (flags & 0x0F );
```

You can get the two nibbles out of a byte with this code:

```
byte byteMe = 0xC5;
byte loNibble = (byte) (byteMe & 0x0F);
byte hiNibble = (byte) ((byteMe >> 4) & 0x0F);
```

If that looks like a lot of casting, the section coming up called "Widening and Narrowing Conversions" explains what is happening.

"|" is the corresponding bitwise OR operation.

"^" is the corresponding bitwise XOR operation.

The && and || Operators

The "&&" is a conditional AND that takes only boolean operands. It avoids evaluating its second operand if possible. If a is evaluated to false, the AND result must be false and the b operand is not evaluated. This is sometimes called *short-circuited evaluation.* "||" is the corresponding short-circuited OR operation. There is no short-circuited XOR operation.

You often use a short-circuited operation to check if a variable refers to something before calling a method on it.

```
if ((anObject != null) && (anObject instanceof String)) { ...
```

In the example above, if the variable anObject is null, then the second half of the expression is skipped. Possible mnemonic: The longer operators "&&" or "||" try to shorten themselves by not evaluating the second operator if they can.

The ? ... : Operator

The "? ... :" operator is unusual in that it is a ternary or three-operand operator. It is best understood by comparing it to an equivalent `if` statement:

```
if (someCondition)      truePart      else falsePart
someCondition ? trueExpression       :    falseExpression
```

The conditional operator can appear in the middle of an expression, whereas an `if` statement cannot. The value of the expression is either the true expression or the false expression. Only one of the two expressions is evaluated. If you do use this operator, don't nest one inside another, as it quickly becomes hard to follow. This example of ? is from the Java runtime library:

```
int maxValue = (a >= b) ? a : b;
```

The parentheses are not required, but they make the code more legible.

The Assignment Operators

Assignment operators are another notational shortcut. They are a combination of an assignment and an operation where the same variable is the left operand and the place to store the result. For example, these two lines are equivalent:

```
i += 4;          // i gets increased by 4.
i = i + 4;       // same thing.
```

There are assignment operator versions of all the arithmetic, shifting, and bit-twiddling operators where the same variable is the left operand and the place to store the result. Here's another example:

```
ypoints[i] += deltaY;
```

Assignment operators are carried over from C into Java, where they were originally intended to help the compiler-writer generate efficient code by leaving off a repetition of one operand. That way it was trivial to identify and reuse quantities that were already in a register.

The Comma Operator Is Gone

Finally, note that Java cut back on the use of the obscure comma operator. Even if you're quite an experienced C programmer, you might never have seen the comma operator, as it was rarely used. The only place it occurs in Java is in "for" loops. The comma allows you to put several expressions (separated by commas) into each clause of a "for" loop.

```
for (i=0, j=0; i<10; i++, j++)
```

It's not actually counted as an operator in Java, so it doesn't appear in Table 5-2. It's treated as an aspect of the `for` statement.

Associativity

Associativity is one of those subjects that is poorly explained in many programming texts, especially the ones that come from authors who are technical writers, not programmers. In fact, a good way to judge a programming text is to look for its explanation of associativity. Silence is not golden.

There are three factors that influence the ultimate value of an expression in any algorithmic language, and they work in this order: precedence, associativity, and order of evaluation.

Precedence says that some operations bind more tightly than others. Precedence tells us that the multiplication in a + b * c will be done before the addition, i.e., we have a + (b * c) rather than (a + b) * c. Precedence tells us how to bind operands in an expression that contains different operators.

Associativity is the tie breaker for deciding the binding when we have several operators of equal precedence strung together. If we have `3 * 5 % 3,` should we evaluate it as `(3 * 5) % 3`, that is `15 % 3`, which is `0`? Or should we evaluate it as `3 * (5 % 3)`, that is `3 * 2`, which is `6`? Multiplication and the "%" remainder operation have the same precedence, so precedence does not give the answer. But they are left-associative, meaning when you have a bunch of them strung together you start associating operators with operands from the left. Push the result back as a new operand, and continue until the expression is evaluated. In this case, `(3 * 5) % 3` is the correct grouping.

Associativity is a terrible name for the process of deciding which operands belong with which operators of equal precedence. A more meaningful description would be, "***C****ode* ***O****rder* ***F****or* ***F****inding/****E****valuating* ***E****qual* ***P****recedence* ***O****perator* ***T****ext-strings.*" This is the "COFFEEPOT property" mentioned in Table 5-2.

Note that associativity deals solely with deciding which operands go with which of a sequence of adjacent operators of equal precedence. It doesn't say anything about the order in which those operands are evaluated.

Order of evaluation, if it is specified in a language, tells us the sequence for each operator in which the operands are evaluated. In a strict left-to-right language like Java, the order of evaluation tells us that in `(i=2) * i++`, the left operand to the multiplication will be evaluated before the right operand, then the multiplication will be done, yielding a result of 4, with i set to 3. Why isn't the auto-increment done before the multiplication? It has a higher precedence after all. The reason is because it is a *post* increment, and so by definition the operation is not done until the operand has been used. In C and C++, this expression is undefined because it modifies the same i-value more than once. It is legal in Java because the order of evaluation is well defined.

How Accurate Are Calculations?

The accuracy when evaluating a result is referred to as the *precision* of an expression. The precision may be expressed either as number of bits (64 bits), or as the data type of the result (double precision, meaning 64-bit floating-point format). In Java, the precision of evaluating each operator depends on the types of the operands. Java looks at the types of the operands around an operator and picks the biggest of what it sees: double, float, and long, in that order of preference. Both operands are then promoted to this type, and that is the type of the result. If there are no doubles, floats, or longs in the expression, both operands are promoted to int, and that is the type of the result. This continues from left to right through the entire expression.

A Java compiler follows this algorithm to compile each operation:

- If either operand is a double, do the operation in double precision.
- Otherwise, if either operand is a float, do the operation in single precision.
- Otherwise, if either operand is a long, do the operation at long precision.
- Otherwise, do the operation at 32-bit int precision.

In summary, Java expressions end up with the type of the biggest, floatiest type (double, float, long) in the expression. They are otherwise 32-bit integers.

Most programmers already understand that floating-point numbers are approximations to real numbers. They may inherently contain tiny inaccuracies that can mount up as you iterate through an expression. (Actually, most programmers learn this the hard way.) Do not expect ten iterations of adding 0.1 to a float variable to cause it to exactly equal 1.0F! If this comes as a surprise to you, try this test program immediately, and thank your good fortune at having the chance to learn about it before you stumble over it as a difficult debugging problem.

```
public class inexact1 {
     public static void main(String s[]) {
          float pear = 0.0F;
          for (int i=0; i<10; i++) pear = pear + 0.1F;

          if (pear==1.0F) System.out.println("pear is 1.0F");
          if (pear!=1.0F) System.out.println("pear is NOT 1.0F");
     }
}
```

You will see this results in the following:

```
pear is NOT 1.0F
```

Since 0.1 is not a fraction that can be represented exactly with powers of two, summing ten of them does not exactly sum to one. This is why you should never use a floating-point variable as a loop counter. A longer explanation of this thorny topic is in "What Every Computer Scientist Should Know about Floating Point" by David Goldberg, in the March 1991 issue of *Computing Surveys* (volume 23, number 1). You can find that paper from a link on the CD, or with a web search at the site *docs.sun.com*. Note that this is a characteristic of floating-point numbers in all programming languages, and not a quality unique to Java.

Accuracy is not just the range of values of a type, but also (for real types) the number of decimal places that can be stored. Since the type float can store about six to seven digits accurately, when a long (which can hold at least 18 places of integer values) is implicitly or explicitly converted to a float, some precision may be lost.

```
public class inexact2 {
     public static void main(String s[]) {
          long  orig = 9000000000000000000L;
          float castMe = orig; // assign the long into a float

          orig = (long) castMe; //cast the float back into a long
          System.out.println(
               "orig (started as 9e18, assigned to float) is: \n"
               +orig);
     }
}
```

The output is as follows:

```
orig (started as 9e18, assigned to float) is:
9000000202358128640
```

As you can see, after being assigned to and retrieved back from the float variable, the long has lost all accuracy after six or seven significant figures. The truth is that if a float has the value shown, it could stand for any real value in the interval between the nearest representable floating-point number on each side. The library is entitled, within the bounds of good taste and consistency, to print it out as any value within that interval. If all this makes you fidget uncomfortably in your seat, maybe you better take a look at that Goldberg article.

The limitations of floating point arithmetic apply to all programming languages. But people notice them a lot more in Java because Java doesn't round floating point numbers to six decimal places when it prints them. The C and C++ languages do round by default, hiding the floating point limitations from the unwary. The chapter on I/O has some examples of formatting numbers using class java.text.DecimalFormat to get the desired number of decimal places displayed.

Floating-Point Extension

A new keyword was added to JDK 1.2: `strictfp`. Without this keyword, a method or class is free to use IEEE 754 extended precision (80-bit) when calculating intermediate results.

This matches what the hardware does by default on an Intel x86 processor or an IBM PowerPC. The keyword `strictfp` disallows this time optimization and requires the use of standard precision. The two alternatives can produce slightly different results.

There are more details at *java.sun.com/docs/books/jls/strictfp-changes.pdf.*

Here's the wording for telling a method not to use extended precision:

```
strictfp void doCalc (float x, float y) {
     // some calculations not to be done in extended precision...
}
```

The `strictfp` keyword is used when you need strictly portable floating point arithmetic on all your different platforms, and this is more important than slightly more accurate results on some platforms. If the `strictfp` keyword is not present, extended accuracy can be used, allowing slightly different arithmetic results.

Widening and Narrowing Conversions

This section provides more details on when a cast is needed, and also introduces the terminology of type conversions. This is explained in terms of an assignment between one variable and another, and exactly the same rules apply in the transfer of values from actual parameters to formal parameters.

When you assign an expression to a variable, a *conversion* must be done. Conversions among the primitive types are either identity, widening, or narrowing conversions.

- **Identity conversions** are an assignment between two identical types, like an int to int assignment. The conversion is trivial: just copy the bits unchanged.
- **Widening conversions** occur when you assign from a less capacious type (such as a short) to a more capacious one (such as a long). You may lose some digits of precision when you convert either way between an integer type and a floating point type. An example of this appeared in the previous section with a long-to-float assignment. Widening conversions preserve the approximate magnitude of the result, even if it cannot be represented exactly in the new type.
- **Narrowing conversions** are the remaining conversions. These are assignments from one type to a different type with a smaller range. They may lose the magnitude information. Magnitude means the largeness of a number, as in the phrase "order of magnitude." So a conversion from a long to a byte will lose information about the millions and billions, but will preserve the least significant digits.

Widening conversions are inserted automatically by the compiler. Narrowing conversions always require an explicit cast.

The previous section explained how expressions are evaluated in one of the canonical types (int, long, float or double). That means if your expression is assigned to a non-canonical type (byte, short, or char), an identity or a narrowing conversion is going to be required. If a narrowing conversion is required, you must write a cast. The cast tells the compiler, "OK, I am aware that the most significant digits are being lost here. Just go ahead and do it."

Now it should be clear why we have to use a cast in:

```
byte loNibble = (byte) (byteMe & 0x0F);
```

Each operand in the expression "`byteMe & 0xOF`" is promoted to int, then the "and" operation is done yielding a 32-bit int result. The variable receiving the expression is an 8-bit byte, so a narrowing conversion is required. Hence, the cast "`(byte)`" is applied to the entire right hand side result to mollify the compiler.

Casts and Assignment Operators

As a reminder, assignment operators are expressions like:

```
b += 7;
```

If b is a byte and you had written that as the equivalent

```
b = b + 7; // NO! NO! NO!
```

you will find that the first statement compiles fine, but the second produces an error message about loss of precision. You have to use an explicit cast in the second statement, like this:

```
b = (byte) (b + 7);
```

Why is a cast required in one case, but not in an apparently equivalent one? For an answer, we have to travel to *The Java Language Specification*, which is online at *java.sun.com/docs/books/jls/second_edition/html/*.

Section 15.26.2 "Compound Assignment Operators" says:

> A compound assignment expression of the form E1 op= E2 is
>
> equivalent to E1 = (T)((E1) op (E2))
>
> where T is the type of E1, except that E1 is evaluated only once. Note that the implied cast to type T may be either an identity conversion (§5.1.1) or a narrowing primitive conversion (§5.1.3).

That last sentence is the key one. It says that you get the cast for free ("implied cast ... to a narrowing primitive conversion"). This was done for pragmatic reasons: the assignment operators would be totally lame if they didn't work on non-canonical types. And a cast is needed when they do. Ergo, it is provided automagically.

Not all questions are answered so easily in the JLS, but it is always worth checking. I have it bookmarked in my browser.

What Happens on Overflow?

When a result is too big for the type intended to hold it because of a cast, an implicit type conversion, or the evaluation of an expression, something has to give! What happens depends on whether the result type is integer or floating-point.

Integer Overflow

When an integer-valued expression is too big for its type, only the low end (least significant) bits get stored. Because of the way two's-complement numbers are stored, adding one to the highest positive integer value gives a result of the highest negative integer value. Watch out for this (it's true for all languages that use standard arithmetic, not just Java).

There is one case in which integer calculation ceases and overflow is reported to the programmer: division by zero (using / or %) will throw an exception. To "throw an exception" is covered in a later chapter.

There is a class called `Integer` that is part of the standard Java libraries. It contains some useful constants relating to the primitive type `int`.

```
public static final int   MIN_VALUE = 0x80000000; // class Integer
public static final int   MAX_VALUE = 0x7fffffff; // class Integer
```

There are similar values in the related class `Long`. Notice how these constants (`final`) are also `static`. If something is constant, you surely don't need a copy of it in every object. You can use just one copy for the whole class, so make it static.

One possible use for these constants would be to evaluate an expression at long precision, and then compare the result to these int endpoints. If it is between them, then you know the result can be cast into an int without losing bits, unless it overflowed long, of course.

Floating Point Overflow

When a floating-point expression (double or float) overflows, the result becomes infinity. When it underflows (reaches a value that is too small to represent), the result goes to zero. When you do something undefined like divide zero by zero, you get a NaN. Under no circumstances is an exception ever raised from a floating-point expression.

The class `Float,` which is part of the standard Java libraries, contains some useful constants relating to the primitive type `float`.

```
public static final float POSITIVE_INFINITY;
public static final float NEGATIVE_INFINITY;
public static final float NaN;
public static final float MAX_VALUE = 3.40282346638528860e+38f;
public static final float MIN_VALUE = 1.40129846432481707e-45f;
```

One pitfall is that it doesn't help to compare a value to NaN, for NaN compares false to everything (including itself)! Instead, test the NaNiness of a value like this:

```
if (Float.isNaN( myfloat ) ) ... // It's a NaN
```

There are similar values in the class Double.

Overflow Summary

- Integer arithmetic:

  Division by zero (using / or %) will throw an exception.
  Out of range values drop the high order bits from the result.
- Floating point arithmetic:

  Never throws an exception.
  Out of range values are indicated by a NaN result.

Arithmetic That Cannot Overflow

There is a class called `java.math.BigInteger` that supports arithmetic on unbounded integers, and a class called `java.math.BigDecimal` that does the same thing for real numbers. We'll give some examples of these classes later. They simulate arbitrary precision arithmetic in software. They are not as fast as arithmetic on the primitive types, but they offer arbitrary precision operands and results.

The Math Package

Let's introduce another of the standard classes. This one is called `java.lang.Math` and it has a couple of dozen useful mathematical functions and constants, including trig routines (watch out—these expect an argument in radians, not degrees), pseudorandom numbers, square root, rounding, and the constants pi and e.

There are two methods in Math to convert between degrees and radians:

```
public static double toDegrees(double); // new in JDK 1.2
public static double toRadians(double); // new in JDK 1.2
```

You'll need these when you call the trig functions if your measurements are in degrees.

You can review the source of the Math package at $JAVA-HOME/src/java/lang/Math.java and in the browser looking at the Java API.

How to Invoke a Math.method

All the routines in the Math package are static, so you typically invoke them using the name of the class, like this:

```
double cabbage = java.lang.Math.random(); // value 0.0..1.0
```

There is a way to shorten the method call to name just the class and method using the `import` statement (to be explained later).

```
double cabbage = Math.random();
```

The Math.log() function returns a natural (base e) logarithm. Convert natural logarithms to base 10 logarithms with code like this:

```
double nat_log = ...

double base10log = nat_log / Math.log(10.0);
```

The list of members in the java.lang.Math class is:

```
public final class Math {
     public static final double E = 2.7182818284590452354;
     public static final double PI = 3.14159265358979323846;
     public static native double IEEEremainder(double, double);
     public static double abs(double);
     public static float abs(float);
     public static int abs(int);
     public static long abs(long);

// trig functions
     public static double toDegrees(double);
     public static double toRadians(double);
     public static native double sin(double);
     public static native double cos(double);
     public static native double tan(double);
     public static native double asin(double);
     public static native double acos(double);
     public static native double atan(double);
     public static native double atan2(double, double);
     public static native double exp(double);
     public static native double pow(double, double);
     public static native double log(double);
     public static native double sqrt(double);

// rounding and comparing
     public static native double ceil(double);
     public static native double floor(double);
     public static double max(double, double);
     public static float max(float, float);
     public static int max(int, int);
     public static long max(long, long);
     public static double min(double, double);
     public static float min(float, float);
     public static int min(int, int);
     public static long min(long, long);
     public static long round(double);
     public static int round(float);

// returns a random number between 0.0 and 1.0
     public static synchronized double random();

// rounds the argument to an integer, stored as a double
     public static native double rint(double);
}
```

All the Math methods are "strictfp".

Further Reading

"What Every Computer Scientist Should Know About Floating-Point Arithmetic" by David Goldberg, *Computing Surveys*, March 1991, published by the Association for Computing Machinery.

> It explains why all floating-point arithmetic is approximate and how errors can creep in. There is a hyperlink to an online copy of this paper in the Java Programmers FAQ which is on the CD.

ANSI/IEEE Standard 754-1985 for Binary Floating-Point Arithmetic

> Institute of Electrical and Electronic Engineers, New York, published 1985. Reprinted in SIGPLAN 22(2) pages 9–25.

Some Light Relief—Too Much Bread

Dough. Spondulicks. Moolah. Cabbage. Oof. Bread.

It's what we get for writing programs that other people want, instead of spending all our time writing programs that interest us. Since we program for money, we might as well try to maximize the flow that comes our way. There are various ways to do that, all involving trade-offs. One way, not unusual in Silicon Valley where I work, is to put the perfection of the programming craft above all other life-style considerations. That can get a bit dire in the long run, though. This story concerns a programmer who tried to maximize his income with unexpected results. We'll call him "Archie" here, because that's his name.

Archie made a vast pile of loot by contract programming. Archie wasn't all that good at programming and often had to skip to a new contract every few months. He was very good at selling himself, though, and giving the appearance of competence, which is how he survived as a contract programmer for so long. He fiddled his taxes by fixing things so that he appeared to be an employee of a shell company in an offshore tax haven. Actually, he was a *partner* in that shell company, paid himself a pittance in the taxable country, and stashed a tax-free fortune offshore. He did this for a number of years.

So, Archie lived a jet-set life and never missed a chance to rub it in the faces of us wage slaves. Archie had everything: badly-written code, oodles of cash, regular ski trips, and many girlfriends (whom he gleefully two-timed). In short, he was a bit of a reptile who thought he'd figured out a way to beat the system.

Eventually, Archie had so much stashed away in his offshore bank account that he decided to put the money to use. Since he couldn't easily spend the money domestically, he bought a sandwich shop franchise in Barcelona. The sandwich shop was doing fine under its current owner and was almost certain to continue to prosper. Archie hired a local manager to replace the old owner, and everything ran well for about a month.

Then Archie received an urgent call from the bank in Spain saying that the venture wasn't generating enough cash to meet its payroll. Archie transferred the funds and put it down to start-up costs. The same thing happened the next month. At great cost, Archie hired a local auditor who eventually determined the local manager was skimming from the profits! Archie flew to Barcelona, fired the manager, and stayed in a hotel for three weeks until he was able to hire a new manager. This investment was already proving expensive.

The new manager wasn't any more honest than the last one, and Archie had to fly out and hire another one. That manager lasted only a couple of weeks, and Archie realized that he had a serious problem on his hands. So far, all the flights, hotels, payroll, auditing, and advertising had cost him about as much again as his original investment. He needed to put more cash in every month to keep the venture solvent. He didn't have a new manager, and worst of all, since it now had a

track record of six months of losses, he could no longer sell the business as a going concern.

Archie quickly figured out that he'd have to take charge personally to solve these problems. This is why you could find Archie—jet-setter and lavishly paid contract programmer—waiting tables in a sandwich shop in Barcelona throughout 1998. While he's serving sandwiches and trying to build up a record of profitability for the business so he can unload it, Archie has no time to work as a contract programmer. Thus, his losses also include what he'd make in a year of contract programming. It couldn't happen to a nicer guy.

The last time I passed through Barcelona on business, I felt like having a snack, so I called in at the sandwich store. Archie was neatly dressed in a green apron and a hair net, and he was standing behind a counter slicing a towering pile of loaves. "Hi Archie. How's things?" I called out. Archie glanced up and gestured at the loaves all around him. "Too much bread," he muttered. I could only nod my silent agreement with his pronouncement. Yes, way too much bread.

Chapter 6

More OOP—Extending Classes

- INHERITANCE
- POLYMORPHISM
- THE CLASS WHOSE NAME IS CLASS
- EXERCISES
- SOME LIGHT RELIEF—THE NERD DETECTION SYSTEM

We now come to the second part of object-oriented programming where we cover another two parts of "A PIE:" inheritance and polymorphism. You need a solid understanding of these to successfully use the Java library routines. Despite the unusual names, they describe some clean concepts.

Inheritance means basing a new class on a class that is already defined to extend it in some way. Inheritance is what you acquire from past generations. Just as inheritance in real life is "what you get from a parent," inheritance in OOP is "what you get from a parent class." Every class has one immediate parent class. This is either a parent that you name explicitly or the parent that you get implicitly. For example, the implicit parent if you don't name one is java.lang.Object.

```
class A { ... }
```

actually means:

```
class A extends java.lang.Object { ... }
```

The class `java.lang.Object` is the root of all classes. The keyword `extends` followed by the name of some other class is how you indicate that the other class is the parent class of this class, also known as a *superclass*. All the non-private members of the superclass are available in a subclass just as though they were declared directly in the subclass. Some terminology:

class	A data type.
extend	To make a new class that inherits the contents of an existing class.
superclass	A parent or "base" class. Superclass wrongly suggests that the parent class has more than the subclass. It means "super" in the sense of "above." The superclass is above its children in the inheritance tree.
subclass	A child class that inherits, or extends, a superclass. It is called a subclass because it only represents a subpart of the universe of things that make up the superclass. It usually has more fields to represent its specialization, however.

Inheritance

To see what inheritance means in practice, consider a real-world example of the Linnaean taxonomy of the animal kingdom, as shown in Figure 6-1.

In biology, animals are classified by whether they have a spinal cord or not. All mammals have a spinal cord. They inherit it as a characteristic because they are a subclass of the chordata phylum (fancy words for "the group with spines"). Mammals, like humans, also have specialized characteristics: they feed their young milk, they have hair, they have two generations of teeth, and so on. Primates inherit all the characteristics of mammals, including the quality of having a spinal cord, which mammals inherited from their parent type. The primate subclass is specialized with forward facing eyes, a large braincase, and so on to increasingly specialized subtypes.

We can also show how inheritance applies in theory to the Java primitive types, but that model only goes so far. Although byte is a subset or subtype of short, and short is a subtype of int, that makes them assignment-compatible and that's about it. An important part of OOP is figuring out and advantageously using the hierarchies of the abstract data types in your application. That doesn't

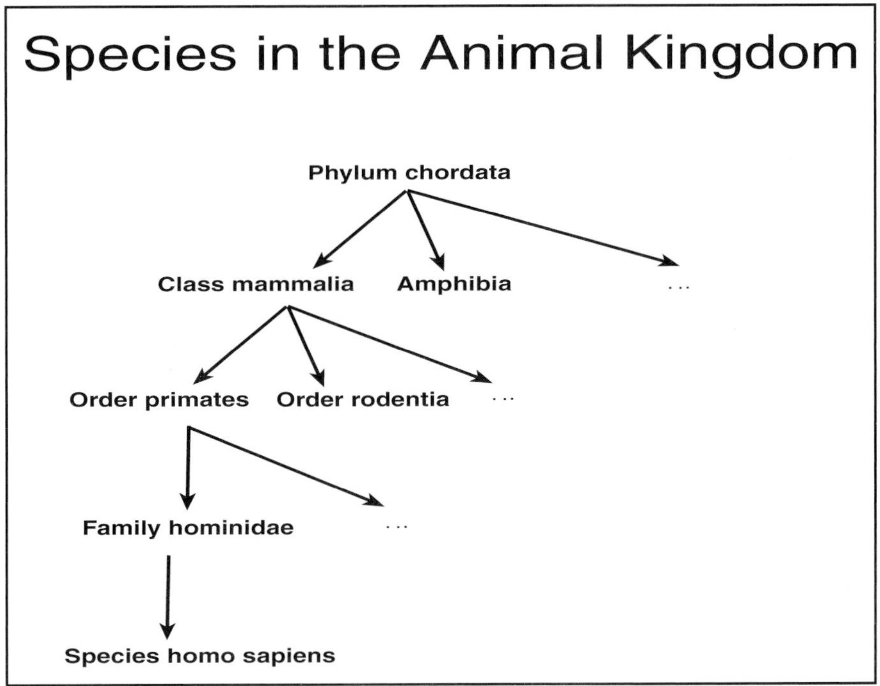

Figure 6–1 A real-world example of an inheritance hierarchy.

really work on the primitives in Java, so we have to leave them behind in our examples at this point.

To summarize, inheritance occurs when a class adopts or adapts the data structures and methods of a base or *parent class*. That creates a hierarchy, similar to a scientific taxonomy. Each level is a specialization of the one above. Inheritance is one of the concepts people mean when they say object-oriented programming requires a special way of thinking. Get ready to spring forward with that "conceptual leap."

A Java Example of Inheritance

There is a GUI library class in Java called Window that implements the simplest kind of window. The class Window doesn't even have borders or a menubar, so you can't move it or close it using a mouse. The source for the Java runtime library is part of the JDK, and you can look at *Window.java at $JAVAHOME/src/java/awt/Window.java*. If you look at the Window source file, you'll see the following code:

```
package java.awt;

import several-packages;
public class Window ... {
... // about 900 lines of code of methods and fields

    public Window(Frame owner) { // a constructor
        ...

}
```

Read the code carefully on this and the following pages, as we're going to stick with this example for much of the chapter.

A Window object can be moved or written on by your code and can hold other GUI objects. Here's a program to instantiate a Window object and display it on the screen:

```
import java.awt.*;
public class example {
    public static void main(String args[]) {
        Frame f = new Frame();// Window must belong to a Frame
        Window w = new Window(f);
        w.setSize(200,100);
        w.setVisible(true);
        w.setLocation(50,50);
    }
}
```

Looking at the Source Code for the Java Runtime Library!

The JDK ships with all the source code for the runtime library. You don't have to sign or download anything further.

You should always figure out how to use a class by looking at the Javadoc API in your favorite browser, but for learning value or those occasions when you really need to know what is going on, you can review the actual code.

When you install the JDK, you typically want to set an environment variable like this: set JAVAHOME=C:\jdk1.4

The $JAVAHOME environment variable represents where you installed the release. It will have a value like C:\jdk1.4 if you installed it in the standard place. You should unzip the file $JAVAHOME\src.jar to create a directory tree with the source for the runtime library.

The directory name hierarchy follows the package name hierarchy, so we will find the source for class java.awt.Window in file $JAVAHOME/src/java/awt/Window.java.

The constructor for Window requires a more fully-featured GUI object, namely, a Frame, so we create one here just to give it to the constructor. We don't do anything else with the Frame. We don't even bother making it visible. Similarly, our window has no title bar or border, so you can't grab it with the mouse. If you compile and run the code, you will get the window shown in Figure 6-2.

For the sake of this inheritance example, let's assume that your program needs a slightly different kind of window: a WarningWindow. The only change from Window is that you want WarningWindows to be colored red to highlight their importance. Everything else should work exactly like Window and should have all the same methods and fields.

There are at least three possible ways to implement WarningWindow:

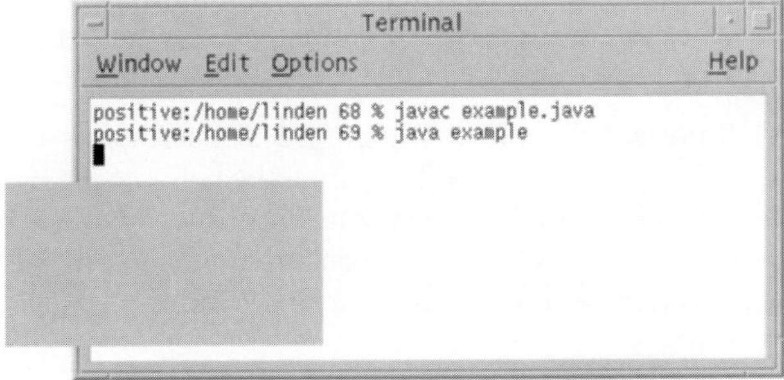

Figure 6–2 Window and Frame.

1. Change the Window class and add a constructor for a special Window that is colored red. This is a bad approach because you never, ever want to change the standard runtime library, even if you get the source for it.
2. Copy all the code in Window.java into file WarningWindow.java, making the change you need. This is a bad approach because it is impossible to keep duplicated code in synchronization. Whenever the code for class Window changes in future releases, class WarningWindow will be out of sync and may well stop working.
3. Make WarningWindow a *subclass* of Window, so it *inherits* all the functionality from Window. *Add* a small amount of code for the different behavior you want.

The preferred OOP approach is the third one: make WarningWindow *extend* the class Window so that WarningWindow inherits all the data and methods of Window.

```
class WarningWindow extends java.awt.Window {
     ... // put any additional members in here
}
```

This is exactly how the OOP process is supposed to work: Find a class that does most of what you want, and then subclass it to provide the exact functionality. There's nothing special about the libraries that come with Java. You are supposed to subclass system classes and your own classes as needed.

There are two points to watch here. First (unlike real life), the child class chooses its parent class. The parent has some say in the matter in that it can control its visibility with access modifiers, and it can make itself `final` to say "no class is permitted to extend me." Second, you have to know what a class does and how it is implemented in order to extend it successfully. Despite the goals of encapsulation, you cannot treat a superclass like a black box and completely ignore its inner workings. This is because a subclass is essentially a statement that says, "I belong to the same black box as the superclass."

I happen to know that the Window class, like many graphical classes, has a method called `setBackground()` that can be used to change the color of its background.[1] All we have to do is make sure that every WarningWindow calls that method when it is being instantiated. A good way to ensure that is to put the call in a constructor. The code should go in a file called WarningWindow.java, as follows:

1. Actually, `setBackground()` and many of the other "Window" routines truly come from a parent of Window; in this case, the class called `Component`.

```
class WarningWindow extends java.awt.Window {

    WarningWindow(java.awt.Frame anyFrame) { //a constructor
        super(anyFrame);
        setBackground(java.awt.Color.red);
    }
}
```

We have to add a constructor anyway because Windows take a Frame argument in their constructor, so we can't rely on the default no-arg constructor. We write a WarningWindow constructor with the Frame argument, have it call the constructor of its superclass (that's the "super(anyFrame)" statement), and then call setBackground() to set the window color to red.

Here's an example program that instantiates a regular window and a WarningWindow. As you can see, all the non-private members of the superclass are available in the subclass just as if they were declared directly in the subclass.

```
import java.awt.*;
public class example { // example use of 2 kinds of Window

    public static void main(String args[]) {
        Frame f = new Frame();

        Window w = new Window(f); // standard Window
        w.setSize(200,100);
        w.setVisible(true);
        w.setLocation(300,300);

// The new red-hued WarningWindow we created
        WarningWindow ww = new WarningWindow(f);
        ww.setSize(200,100); // setSize is in a superclass
        ww.setVisible(true);
        ww.setLocation(370,370);
    }
}
```

We can call the three setSomething() methods, even though we didn't declare them in WarningWindow. We inherited them from Window.

Try running the program and you will see the result shown in Figure 6-3. Since the red window won't show up red in a printed book, you're going to have to try it to prove that I'm not kidding you.

That's your first example of inheritance. We have reused the functionality of 900 lines of code in a new six-line class that is in a separate file and only contains the differences and specializations from its superclass. How is this any different from a library? What we have here is a powerful way to take an existing library and *modify* some of its behavior without modifying the library itself.

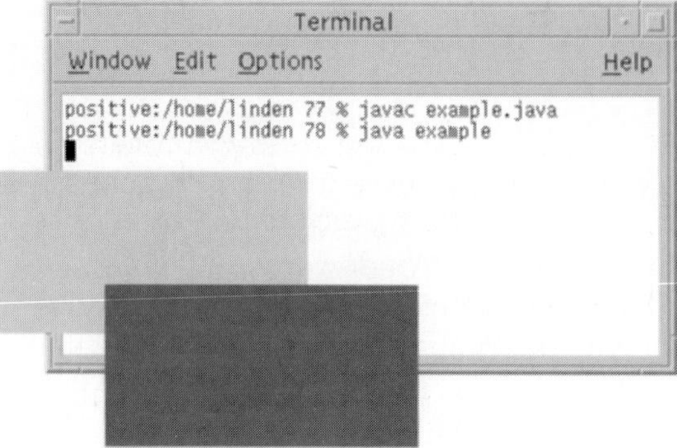

Figure 6–3 Program results: A regular window and a WarningWindow.

You might ask how this is any different from instantiating an ordinary Window and always remembering to color it red. The answer is that inheritance lets the compiler and runtime do the hard work of keeping track of what an object is, and whether it has the library behavior or the modified behavior. Inheritance lets you *superimpose* some new behavior on a class to create essentially a new library, but without copying everything. I use this all the time when debugging or prototyping some code. "What if I did it this way?" I ask myself, and I write a subclass that extends the original class and contains my experimental changes. If the idea is bad, I just throw away the new class, and I haven't changed one line of source code in the underlying class.

Take another look at the constructor in the WarningWindow class. That line of code that reads `super(anyFrame)` is a common idiom when one class extends another. The code `super( )` is the way you express "call the constructor of my superclass." That's exactly what we want here: a regular Window is constructed, and its color is changed to red.

"Is a" vs. "Has a"

Don't confuse inheritance with nesting (having a member that refers to another object).

Declaring an object as a data field inside a class just sets up a reference variable to the object with no special privileges or relationship. In contrast, inheritance says the subclass is a variation of the superclass that extends its semantics in some way.

The way to distinguish between these two cases is to ask yourself the "is a" versus "has a" question. Let's assume you have a "car" class and an "engine" class, and you want to decide whether to use inheritance or nesting to associate the two. Would you say "a car has an engine" or "a car is an engine?" If the answer is "has a," use nesting. If the answer is "is a," use inheritance. Similarly, if we have a "mammal" class and a "dog" class, we know that a "dog is a mammal." We would use inheritance to add the canine specializations to the mammal class resulting in the dog class.

The rule of thumb is that inheritance is for specialization of a type or changing its behavior. Container classes are for data structure reuse.

As we saw in Chapter 2, a superclass constructor is *always* invoked when you create a subclass object. If you don't explicitly call a superclass constructor, then the no-arg constructor of the superclass is called for you. If the superclass doesn't have a no-arg constructor (either an implicit one because you didn't provide any constructors or an explicit no-arg constructor that you did provide), then you will get a compilation error along the lines of "no constructor found in superclass."

The most common use of `super` is the call `super()` which invokes a constructor in the superclass. The keyword is also used to access fields of any superclass (not just the immediate superclass) that are hidden by an identically-named feature in the subclass.

Java Does Not Use Multiple Inheritance

You may have heard about "multiple inheritance." That means having more than one immediate parent class. The resulting subclass thus has characteristics from all its immediate parent types.

Multiple inheritance is much less common than single inheritance. Where it has appeared in languages (like C++), it has been the subject of considerable debate on whether it should be in the language at all. Multiple inheritance poses additional problems in both implementation and use. Say there is a class A with some data members, and classes B and C inherit from A. Now have a class D that multiply-inherits from B and C. Does D have one copy of A's data members, or two identical copies? When you access something else in A, do you get B's or C's version of it? All this can be worked out, if you don't mind having a language reference manual the size of the Gutenberg Bible.

Some people say that no convincing examples have been produced where there was no alternative design avoiding multiple inheritance. Java bypasses any difficulties by not permitting multiple inheritance. The interface feature described in a later chapter fills in the gap left by multiple inheritance.

There is no way to "chain" several supers together, however, and reach back higher into the parent class hierarchy. Do not think that because `super.x` means "the x of a superclass" therefore "`super.super.x`" means "the x of grandparent." This is a very common mistake. There is no `super.super.x`.

Inheritance usually provides increasing specialization as you go from a general superclass class (e.g., vehicle) to a more specific subclass (e.g., passenger car, fire truck, or delivery van). It can equally well restrict or extend the available operations, though.

Summary of Key Idea: Inheritance

The purpose of inheritance in an OOP language is twofold:

1. To model a hierarchy in the domain that you are programming.

2. To provide code reuse while allowing customizations.

Inheritance means being able to declare a type which builds on the fields (data and methods) of a previously declared type. As well as inheriting all the operations and data, you get the chance to declare your own versions and new versions of the methods to refine, specialize, replace, or extend the ones in the parent class.

What Happens When Names Collide?

If a field in the subclass has the same name as a field in the superclass, then it supersedes, or *hides*, the superclass field. The visible subclass field is said to *shadow* (put in the shade) the superclass field. The superclass field is still available by using the "super" keyword. It is also available if you assign the subclass to the superclass type. Be careful here. Don't hide names as a general practice.

```
class Fruit {        // example of variable name hiding
     boolean zestySkin= false;
}

public class Citrus extends Fruit {
     boolean zestySkin= true;    // same name hides the Fruit one

     public static void main (String args[]) {
          Citrus c = new Citrus();
          Fruit f = c; // f and c now refer to the same object
          System.out.println( " f.zesty = " + f.zestySkin );
          System.out.println( " c.zesty = " + c.zestySkin );
          System.out.println( " cast = " + ((Fruit) c).zestySkin );
     }
}
```

When you run the above code, you get this output:

```
f.zesty = false
c.zesty = true
cast = false // surprise!
```

Be sure to note that a cast of something to its superclass makes it see the superclass variables where there is name hiding. The reason Java allows name duplication is to permit new fields to be added later to superclasses without breaking existing subclasses that might already use that name. The subclasses will continue to use their own copies of those fields, except when you tell them to behave like superclass objects.

A variable may have the same name as a method in its own class or superclass without either hiding the other.

```
class Example {
     public int total = 22;// overloading field and method is dumb,
     public int total () {    // but it works OK
          ...
```

Name duplication should be rare, because the Java Language Specification says that method names should be based on verbs, while field names should be based on nouns (JLS, sect. 6.8).

In the case of a method with the same name in both a superclass and the subclass, the runtime system figures out exactly what class this object really is and calls the method that is a member of that particular class. This is dealt with in the section on overriding later in this chapter.

It turns out that all objects carry around a little bit of extra information about their type and the characteristics of that type. The runtime system needs to keep track of the type of an object reference to check casts to invoke the right version of overloaded methods. The information is known as Run Time Type Information (RTTI), and it is kept in an object of its own. You get to the RTTI object through the `getClass()` method that is in class `Object` and thus inherited by every class. The type of an RTTI object is a reference type whose name is `Class`. That class called `Class` is featured at the end of this chapter.

Compatibility of Superclass and Subclass

One of the nice things about inheritance is that it lets you treat a specialized object as a more general one. In other words, my `WarningWindow`, by virtue of being a subclass of `Window`, counts as a `Window` and can be used anywhere in code where a `Window` is used. If you have a method that expects a `Window` as an argument, you can pass it a `WarningWindow`, and it will work fine.

If you have a `Window` variable, you can assign a `WarningWindow` into it, like this:

```
WarningWindow ww = new WarningWindow( new Frame() );
Window w = ww; // the Window obj now refers to a WarningWindow
```

Here's the really magical thing: that `Window` object will continue to behave as a `WarningWindow`! It will display with a red background whenever someone invokes a `Window` operation on it that causes it to be updated on the screen.

This is a *key point* of OOP. When you have a variable of SomeClass, it might actually be referring to a much more specialized subclass. If a method takes some particular superclass type as a parameter, you can actually call it with any of its subclasses and it will do the right thing. Add some lines of code to the example class a few pages back to try this. You can even assign a `WarningWindow` object to an `Object`, then later cast it back to a `WarningWindow`, and it won't have lost its type information.

Casting

Let's look a little more closely into compatibility between subclass and superclass. We'll use the following code for examples:

```
public class Mammal { ... }
public class Dog extends mammal { ... }
public class Cat extends mammal { ... }
Mammal m;
Dog fido = new Dog();
Cat kitty = new Cat();
     ... m = fido;
```

Notice the assignment of `fido` (a `Dog` object) into `m` (a `Mammal` variable). You can always make a more general object hold a more specialized one, but the reverse is not true without an explicit type conversion. All dogs are mammals, but not all mammals are dogs. Cats, horses, pigs, and people are also mammals. You can assign `m=fido`, but not (directly) `fido=m`, because `m` could be referring to a `Cat` object. Just as you can cast (convert) an integer into a double, you can cast a superclass into one of its more specialized subclasses. You can't directly assign the following:

```
fido = m;    // causes compilation error
```

You can, however, cast it. To cast any type, write the typename in parentheses immediately before the object being cast. In this case:

```
fido = (Dog) m;     // The cast allows the compilation to work
                    // and the conversion is checked at runtime
```

Type hierarchies are often drawn as tree diagrams with `Object` (the ultimate superclass) at the top, and all subclasses beneath their superclass as Figure 6-4 exemplifies. In a drawing of this kind, you can only cast "downward" from a superclass to some subclass (or subclass of a subclass, and so on). You can never cast "sideways" to force an object to become something it is not.

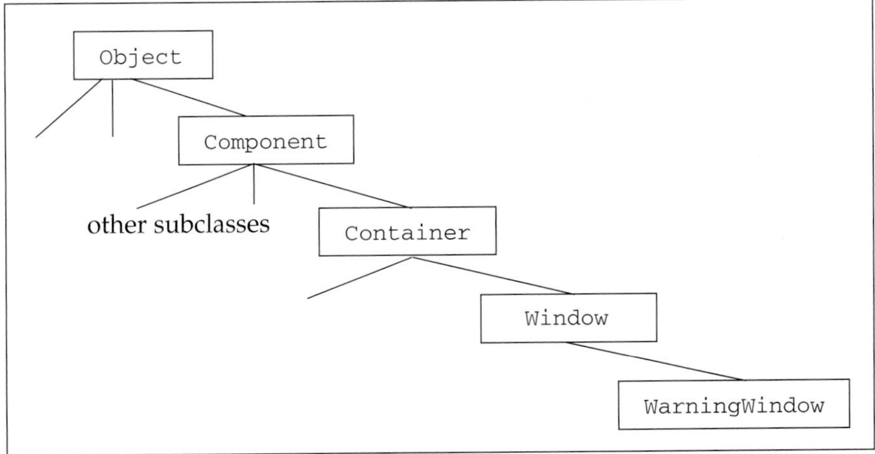

Figure 6–4 An inheritance hierarchy may be many levels deep.

The general rules for casting classes are:

- You can always assign parent = child; a cast is not needed because a specific child class also belongs to its general parent class. You can assign several levels up the hierarchy; that is, the parent may be a more remote ancestor. `Chordata c = new Dog()` is valid.
- You can cast child = (child) parent, and it will be checked at runtime. If the parent is referring to the correct child type, the assignment will occur. If the parent refers to some unrelated subclass, an exception `ClassCastException` will be raised. Exceptions are a recoverable interruption to the normal flow of control. They are described later.
- You cannot assign or cast at all between arbitrary unrelated classes, as in `fido=kitty;`.

Because every class is a subclass of the built-in system class `Object`, every object can be assigned to something of type `Object`, and later cast back to the type that it really is. In this way, the type `Object` can be used as a general reference to anything.

Some Java utility classes store and manipulate `Object`. You can use them for any object, later casting to get back the same type that you put in. You can be certain that, if a cast succeeds, you really have an object of the type you cast to. This is another illustration that there is no evading strong typing in Java.

You can probably guess how the `instanceof` operator is used. We met `instanceof` in the last chapter. It allows you to compare a reference variable with a type, and it returns a value at runtime based on what type of object the variable is truly pointing to at that moment.

```
Mammal m;
if (Math.random() < 0.5) m = new Dog(); else m = new Mammal();
if (m instanceof Dog) // Check the type before attempting cast
     fido = (Dog) m; // the cast will always succeed.
```

Summary: Superclass/Subclass Compatibility

They must really love this topic on the Java Certification exam, because they ask it in several different questions. Make sure you have it down before taking that test. Here are possible assignments and a note about their compatibility:

```
superclass = subclass // always valid
subclass = (subclass) superclass //valid at compile time, checked at runtime
subclass = superclass // not valid as written, requires a cast to compile
someClass = someUnrelatedClass // won't even compile
someClass = (someClass) someUnrelatedClass // won't even compile
```

Polymorphism

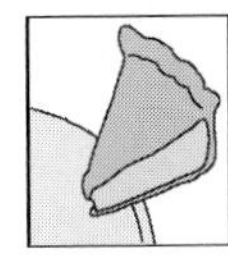

Polymorphism is a complicated name for a straightfoward concept. It is Greek for "many shapes," and it merely means using the same one name to refer to different methods. "Name reuse" would be a better term. There are two types of polymorphism in Java: the really easy kind (overloading) and the interesting kind (overriding).

Overloading

The really easy kind of polymorphism is called *overloading* in Java and other languages, and it means that in any class you can use the same name for several different (but hopefully related) methods. The methods must have different signatures, however, so that the compiler can tell which of the synonyms is intended. Here are two overloaded methods:

```
public static int parseInt(String s) throws NumberFormatException
public static int parseInt(String s, int radix)
                                        throws NumberFormatException
```

These methods come from the class `java.lang.Integer`, which is a class wrapper[2] for the primitive type `int` and has some helper functions like these. The first method tries to interpret the String as an int. The second method does the same thing, but uses an arbitrary base. You could parse a hexadecimal String by supplying 16 as the radix argument.

The return type and the exceptions that a method can throw are not looked at when resolving same-named functions in Java.

The I/O facilities of a language are one typical place where overloading is used. You don't want to have an I/O class that requires a different method name depending on whether you are trying to print a short, an int, a long, and so on. You just want to be able to say "print(thing)." Note that C fails to meet this requirement. Although it's the same routine, "printf," it also needs a format specifier (which is a statement in a particularly ugly programming language in its own right) to tell printf what argument types to expect and to output. If you change the type of the C value you are outputting, you usually need to change the format specifier, too.

Overriding

The second, more complicated kind of polymorphism, true polymorphism, is resolved dynamically at runtime. It occurs when a subclass class has a method with the same signature (number, type, and order of parameters) as a method in

2. A *class wrapper* is a class wrapped around a primitive type so you can treat that primitive value as an object and send it to data structures and methods that process only objects.

the superclass. When this happens, the method in the derived class overrides the method in the superclass. Methods cannot be overridden to be more private only to be more public.

An example should make this clear. Let's go back to our base class `Window`, and our subclass `WarningWindow`. I happen to know that one of the operations you can do with a `Window` is `setSize()` on it. That's even in our example program. We will give `WarningWindow` its own version of `setSize()` to reflect the fact that `WarningWindows` are more important and should be bigger than regular `Windows`. We add a `setSize()` method to our subclass:

```
class WarningWindow extends java.awt.Window {

     WarningWindow(java.awt.Frame apple) { // constructor
          super(apple);
          setBackground(java.awt.Color.red);
     }

     public void setSize(int x, int y) { // overriding method
          int bigx = (int) (x*1.5);
          int bigy = (int) (y*1.5);
          super.setSize(bigx, bigy);
     }
}
```

The method setSize() in WarningWindow replaces or overrides the superclass's version of setSize() when the method is invoked on a WarningWindow object. C++ programmers will note that you do not need to specifically point out to the compiler (with the C++ "virtual" keyword) that overriding will take place. Here's some example code:

```
public static void main(String args[]) {
        Frame f = new Frame();
        { Window w = new Window(f);
          w.setSize(200,100);
          w.setVisible(true);
          w.setLocation(300,300);
        }
        { Window w = new WarningWindow(f); // the only change
          w.setSize(200,100);
          w.setVisible(true);
          w.setLocation(370,370);
        }
}
```

I have simply duplicated some code and put it in separate blocks (separate scopes) so that the duplication of the variable `w` doesn't cause a compiler error. In the first block, I assign a regular window to `w`; in the second, I assign a WarningWindow. Even though `w` remains a Window object, different methods are called on it.

When you try running this, you will note that when we apply the setSize() method to a Window, we get the base class version, meaning it comes out the regular size. When we apply the setSize method to a WarningWindow, we get the WarningWindow specialized version which it displays 50% bigger in each direction as shown in Figure 6-5. Wow!

When we invoke the method on something that started out as a general Window, but may have been assigned a WarningWindow at runtime, the correct method is chosen at runtime based on what the object actually is. And *that* is polymorphism. It is a powerful tool for letting a class implement an operation in a way that is unique to itself.

It would clearly be bad design to override a method in a way that fundamentally changes what it does. You probably wouldn't *really* want to make `setSize()` use different values from its arguments. It makes a great demonstration for teaching purposes, though, because the difference is so visible.

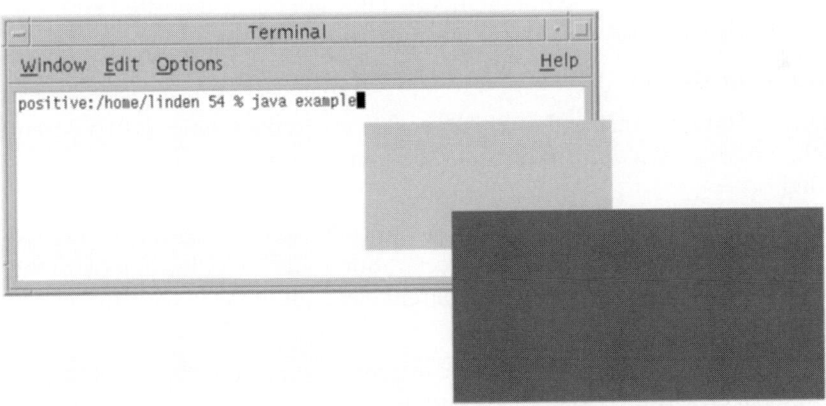

Figure 6–5 WarningWindow invokes setSize() but ends up bigger!

The Difference Between Overloading and Overriding

Overloading, the shallow kind of polymorphism, is resolved by the compiler at compile time. Overloading allows several methods to have the same one name, and the compiler will choose the one you mean by matching on argument types.

Overriding, the deep kind of polymorphism, is resolved at runtime. It occurs when one class extends another, and the subclass has a method with the same signature (exact match of number and argument types) as a method in the superclass.

Question: Which of them gets invoked?

Answer: If it's an object of the subclass, the subclass one; if it's an object of the superclass, the superclass one. The reason this is "fancy" is that sometimes you cannot tell until runtime, so the compiler must plant code to work out which method is appropriate for whatever this object turns out to be, then call that at runtime.

The technical term for "choosing the correct method for whatever object this is at runtime" is *late binding* or *delayed binding*. Polymorphism is the language feature that allows two methods to have the same name, such that late binding may be applied.

Constructor declarations are not members. They are never inherited and therefore are not subject to hiding or overriding.

Inheriting from Object

So the meaning of inheritance is that a class has access to the members of a parent class. If a class has its own version of a method in a parent class, its own version will be called.

This has implications for program maintenance. When you see a class accessing some member, if you cannot find the declaration in the class itself, look in the parent class, and then in the parent of the parent class, all the way back to the ultimate base class `Object`, if necessary.

Inheritance is the reason why you can call `toString()` on any object. If you look back at the listing of `Object` at the end of Chapter 3, you'll see it has a number of methods that are inherited by every class. The method `toString()` is one of these.

When to Override Object. toString()

The method `toString()` has some magic language support. The language rule is that when the compiler sees a String and any other object whatsoever as the two operands to a "+" operator, the system will call a method with the name `toString` to create a String representation of that object and then concatenate the two Strings. You thus have two choices for the `toString` method for any class:

- You can let the inheritance hierarchy pick up the `toString` method from superclass Object. This will return a String containing the classname and something that looks like the address of the instance.
- You can provide in your class your own version of a method with this signature:

  ```
  public String  toString()
  ```

  You will write the method to print out the value of key fields, nicely formatted. It will override the Object version of `toString`.

It's better to take the second alternative and provide more meaningful output. The method `toString()` will be invoked on any object that is concatenated with a String.

```
Fruit lemon = new Fruit();
String s = "Your object is " + lemon;
// the + invokes method lemon.toString()
```

Defining `toString` for your classes and printing an object this way is a useful debugging technique.

Forcing Overriding off: Final

There are two further adjustments to fine-tune inheritance: abstract and final. You will be able to use this to great advantage when you become more expert. Let's go back to the class java.lang.Math that we met at the end of Chapter 5. One feature of the class is that all trig operations are done in radians, not degrees. Would it be possible to *extend* java.lang.Math and *override* just the trig functions so that they worked with degrees instead? You could leave all the other rounding and comparing Math functions alone, and you would have specialized the subclass for your needs.

Your code might look like this:

```
public class DegreeMath extends java.lang.Math { // won't work
     public double sin(double d) {
          double rads = super.toRadians(d);
          double result = super.sin(rads);
          return super.toDegrees(result);
     }
...
}
```

That is a great idea in theory, but it cannot be done this way for the `Math` class in practice for two reasons. One, the Math class is labeled as `final`, so cannot be extended. Two, all the Math methods are `static`.

```
public final class Math { ...
     public static native double sin(double a);
```

Static methods do not participate in overriding. Overriding is used when an object might be one type or might be a more specialized subtype. Class methods don't belong to an object and never have this possible ambiguity. Acting as a reminder that a method will not be overridden is another reason why you should always invoke class methods using the name of the class, not an instance of it.

When the keyword `final` appears at the start of a class declaration, it means "no one can extend this class." Similarly, an individual method can be made `final`, preventing it from being overridden when its class is inherited. It is final in the sense that it is a leaf of an inheritance tree. Typically, you might wish to prevent further inheritance to avoid further specialization or for security reasons: you don't want to permit this type to be further adjusted. A "final" method is also a clue to the compiler to inline the code. Inlining the code means optimizing out the overhead of a method call by taking the statements in the body of the method and duplicating them inline instead of making the call. This is a classic space versus time trade-off.

The class `java.lang.Math` is labeled as `final` for reasons of performance. Overriding can be "turned off" on a method or class by using the keyword `final` on a method or class. A method call can be made much more quickly if the compiler can compile it in, rather than having the runtime system figure out which is the right overriding method at execution time. (This performance cost is the reason overriding is off by default in C++.)

The class `java.lang.String` is labeled as `final` for reasons of security and performance. As well as being a final class, String objects are read-only. If you could override String, you could write a subclass that was not read-only, but could be used in all the places that String is used. Specifically, you could change the String pathname to a file after it had been checked for access permission, but before the open operation had been done.

Forcing Overriding: Abstract

Just as `final` tells the compiler "this thing is complete and must not be changed or extended or overridden," there is a keyword to force overriding to take place. The keyword `abstract` tells the compiler "this thing is incomplete and must be extended to be used." You can think of `final` and `abstract` as opposites of each other, as they cannot occur together for a method or class. The keyword `final` or `abstract` can be applied to an individual method or an entire class. We have already seen `final` applied to data.

When the keyword `abstract` appears at the start of a class declaration, it means that zero or more of its methods are abstract. An abstract method has no body; its purpose is to *force* some subclass to override it and provide a concrete implementation of it. Labeling a method `abstract` requires you to label the class `abstract`.

You make a class `abstract` when three conditions are fulfilled:

- There will be several subclasses.
- You want to handle all the different subclasses as an instance of the superclass.
- The superclass alone does not make sense as an object.

That set of conditions for deciding when to use an abstract class probably made no sense at all, so I'll try to show what it means in terms of an example. Think back to the GUI class Window. We showed a few pages back how Window is a subclass of Component (not directly, but two levels down). It turns out that Component is the window toolkit superclass for many Java library objects that you can display on the screen. In particular, many screen widgets (Unix terminology) or controls (Microsoft terminology) are Components. Scrollbars, panels, dialogs, tabbed panes, cursors, labels, textfields, and so on are all subclasses of Component. Thus, it meets the first condition of abstract classes: there is more than one subclass.

There are many operations that we can do on a control without precisely knowing or caring which control it is. One common operation is to add it to a container for display. A container is a GUI backdrop or pinboard whose purpose is to arrange and display the group of components it is given. We don't want to have umpteen individual methods—one for adding each individual type of control to a panel—we just want to be able to say the following:

```
myContainer.add(Component c);
```

We have the second condition: for convenience, you want to handle all the different subclasses as an instance of the superclass. The most frequently seen case is where the superclass is a parameter to a method, as it is here.

Finally, all the subclasses of Component are real, concrete objects. You can actually display them on the screen. Component itself is not a concrete object. You cannot sensibly display the Component superclass on the screen (what would be drawn?). Only the subclasses have the actual semantics of shape, behavior, and look. An instance of Component itself doesn't really make sense. You need an instance of a concrete subclass of Component. In this way, the third condition has been met: an instance of the superclass does not make sense as an object. Hence, `java.awt.Component` is an abstract class.

Although making a class `abstract` forces a programmer to extend it and fill in some more details in the subclass before it can be instantiated, it allows the class to stand in for any of the concrete subclasses. Saying a class is abstract imposes the requirements "you must implement the abstract method(s) in a subclass" and "you cannot instantiate an object of the abstract class, it is incomplete in some way." Abstract has no connection with data abstraction we saw in Chapter 2.

Here's the general form that Component has in source code:

```
public abstract class Component {
     public void setBackground(java.awt.Color){...}
     public void setVisible(boolean) { ...}
     public void setLocation(int, int){ ...}
     ... // 3800 lines of code omitted
     public abstract void DrawMeOnScreen();
}


// some concrete subclasses of Component
public class Button extends Component {
     public void DrawMeOnScreen(){ ...}
}

public class Scrollbar extends Component { ...
     public void DrawMeOnScreen(){...}
}



// Some other class entirely that wants to operate
// on any of the above subclasses
public class Container {
     public void remove(Component comp) { ...}
     public Component add(Component comp){ comp.DrawMeOnScreen(); }
     void setFocusOwner(Component c) { .. }
}
```

I have fudged a bit on the name and use of `DrawMeOnScreen()` to make the example simpler. That's what the method does, but it is called something less intuitive—`paint()`, if you must know. We'll meet it in a later chapter.

The use of `extends` is at least twenty times more common than the use of `abstract` to fine-tune class hierarchies in the Java runtime library.

The Class Whose Name Is `Class`

Here's where the terminology admittedly can get a little confusing. We saw a few pages back that every object has some Run Time Type Information associated with it. The RTTI for any object is stored in an object whose class is called "Class." Class could certainly use a better, less self-referential name.

A big use of `Class` is to help with loading new classes during program execution. A lot of other languages load an entire program before they start execution. Java encourages dynamic loading. Classes only need to be loaded on demand when they are first referenced.

When you compile the class `Fruit`, it creates the bytecode file Fruit.class. Fruit.class contains the bytecode for `Fruit`. When the first reference to a Fruit type or object is encountered at runtime, the JVM asks the java.lang.ClassLoader class to find and load that class file. Typically, the ClassLoader transforms the fully qualified name into a file name and looks for that in certain places locally and across the net. Class objects are created automatically by the JVM as part of loading the class. `Class` provides the information for checking casts at runtime, and it lets a program look at all the members of a class—the data fields and the methods. These are systems programming activities, unlikely to occur in your programs, but providing `Class` makes it easy to program them without stepping outside the Java system. You can safely skim over the rest of this section and return when you have a specific need to look at RTTI.

To access the runtime type information for a class, you need an object of type Class. You can get one in three ways. Here's some code showing the alternatives:

```
Fruit lemon = new Fruit();

Class which = lemon.getClass(); // getClass is a method in Object
```

or

```
Class which = Class.forName("Fruit"); // forName is a static method
```

or

```
Class which = Fruit.class; // class literal
```

The last alternative is called a *class literal*. You can jam the characters `.class` onto the end of any type at all, even a primitive type like `int`, and it gets you the Class RTTI associated with the type. You'll choose which of the alternatives to use depending on whether you have an object, the classname in a String, or the class.

Once you have the class object you can invoke its methods. The strict left-to-right evaluation of Java allows method calls to be chained together in one statement. You can do this with any methods where the result of one method is the reference used in the next:

```
String name = myobject.getClass().getName();
```

The class whose name is Class looks like this:

```
public final class java.lang.Class  {
     public java.io.InputStream getResourceAsStream(java.lang.String);
     public java.net.URL getResource(java.lang.String);

     public native String getName();
     public static native java.lang.Class forName(java.lang.String);
     public native java.lang.Object newInstance();

     static native Class getPrimitiveClass(java.lang.String);

     public native boolean isInstance(java.lang.Object);
     public native boolean isAssignableFrom(java.lang.Class);
     public native boolean isInterface();
     public native boolean isArray();
     public native boolean isPrimitive();

// security related
     public native ClassLoader getClassLoader();
     public native Object getSigners()[];
     native void setSigners(java.lang.Object[]);

// introspection on the class, its ancestors, members and constructors
     public native Class getSuperclass();
     public native Class getInterfaces()[];
     public native Class getComponentType();
     public native int getModifiers();
     public Class getDeclaringClass();
     public Class getDeclaredClasses()[];
     public Class getClasses()[];
     public reflect.Constructor getConstructors()[];
     public reflect.Constructor getConstructor(java.lang.Class[]);
     public reflect.Constructor getDeclaredConstructors()[];
     public reflect.Constructor getDeclaredConstructor(java.lang.Class[]);

     public reflect.Field getFields()[];
     public reflect.Field getField(java.lang.String);
     public reflect.Field getDeclaredFields()[];
     public reflect.Field getDeclaredField(java.lang.String);

     public reflect.Method getMethods()[];
     public reflect.Method getMethod(java.lang.String, java.lang.Class[]);
     public reflect.Method getDeclaredMethods()[];
     public reflect.Method getDeclaredMethod(
                                java.lang.String, java.lang.Class[]);

     public java.lang.String toString();
}
```

It can be useful to print out the names of classes while debugging code that deals with arbitrary objects. A description of this and other popular methods of Class follow. The first returns the name of the Class.

```
public native String getName();
```

The next method takes a String that should be the name of a class and retrieves the Class (RTTI) object for that class. It's an alternative to getClass(), used when you have the name of the class in a String, rather than having any objects of it.

```
public static native Class forName(String className)
                           throws ClassNotFoundException
```

This next example is a surprising method—it allows you to create an object of the class for which this is the RTTI. Coupled with the forName() method, this lets you create an object of any class whose name you have in a String. Highly dynamic! The no-arg constructor of the appropriate class is called, so it better have one.

```
public native Object newInstance()
throws InstantiationException, IllegalAccessException
```

In the following example, if you have an instance of a class, and you cast it to the class that you know it is, you can call its methods!

```
String s = "Fruit";
    ...
Object f = Class.forName(s).newInstance();
```

Use the classloader that loaded this next class to get a resource (e.g., a file) from the same place. That place might be a zip or Jar file, a local filesystem, or a network connection.

```
public InputStream getResourceAsStream(String name)
```

Similar to the previous method, this one returns a URL that can access the resource rather than a Stream with its contents.

```
public java.net.URL getResource(String name) {
        name = resolveName(name);
```

This checks if the Class it is invoked on is the same as, or a superclass of, the `obj`. This is the dynamic equivalent of the `instanceof` operator. If true, it means you could assign the `obj`, possibly with a cast, into the object for whom this is the RTTI.

```
public native boolean isInstance(Object obj);
```

Exercises

1. What are the four attributes that distinguish object-oriented programming? What are some advantages and disadvantages of OOP?

2. Give three examples of primitive types and three examples of predefined Java classes (i.e., object types).

3. What is the default constructor, and when is it called? What is a no-arg constructor?

4. Describe overriding, and write some code to show an example.

5. Consider the following three related classes:

```
class Mammal {}
class Dog extends Mammal { }
class Cat extends Mammal { }
```

There are these variables of each class:

```
Mammal m;
Dog d = new Dog( );
Cat c = new Cat( );
```

Which of these statements will cause an error at compile time and why? Which of these statements may cause an error at runtime and why?

```
m = d; // 1.
d = m; // 2.
d = (Dog) m; // 3.
d = c; // 4.
d = (Dog) c; // 5.
```

6. Create a class that provides all the same methods as java.lang.Math, but which operate on degrees not radians. Do this by creating a wrapper for each method in Math, in your class.

Some Light Relief—The Nerd Detection System

Most people are familiar with the little security decals that electronic and other high-value stores use to deter shoplifters. The sticker contains a metallic strip. Unless deactivated by a store cashier, the sticker sets off an alarm when carried past a detector at the store doors.

These security stickers are actually a form of antenna. The sticker detector sends out a weak RF signal between two posts through which shoppers will pass. It looks for a return signal at a specific frequency, which indicates that one of the stickers has entered the field between the posts.

All this theory was obvious to a couple of California Institute of Technology students Dwight Berg and Tom Capellari, who decided to test the system in practice. Naturally, they selected a freshman to (unknowingly) participate in the trials. At preregistration, after the unlucky frosh's picture was taken but before it was laminated onto his I.D. card, Dwight and Tom fixed a couple of active security decals from local stores onto the back of the photo.

The gimmicked card was then laminated together, hiding the McGuffin, and the two conspirators awaited further developments. A couple of months later they caught up with their victim as he was entering one of the stores. He was carrying his wallet above his head. In response to a comment that this was an unusual posture, the frosh replied that something in his wallet, probably his bank card, seemed to set off store alarms. He had been conditioned to carry his wallet above his head after several weeks of setting off the alarms while entering and leaving many of the local stores.

The frosh seemed unimpressed with Dwight and Tom's suggestion that perhaps the local merchants had installed some new type of nerd detection system. Apparently, the comment got the frosh thinking, because on the next occasion when he met Dwight he put him in a headlock until he confessed to his misdeed. **Moral:** Never annoy a computer programmer.

Chapter 7

Java Statements

Statements are the way we get things done in a program. Statements live in methods and in blocks. Any statement may be prefixed by a label, as shown here:

```
months: for(int m = 1; m <= 12; m++) { ...
```

The general syntax for a statement is this:

```
optIdentifier: statement
```

Java doesn't have a `goto` statement. If a label appears, it is either just empty documentation (rare—use a comment instead), or it is used to break out of certain enclosing statements in a clean way.

Statements in Java can be conveniently divided into several groups:

- "Organizing" statements
- Expression statements

- Selection, Iteration, and Transfer statements
- Guarding statements

First we will describe all but the guarding statements. We will then introduce the topic of exceptions, which provides the context in which to talk about guarding statements.

An entirely new kind of statement was introduced with JDK 1.4: the assert statement. We will describe the assert statement after the material on exceptions. Exceptions and asserts are two ways of dealing with unexpected and unwanted error situations. Exceptions give you a chance to recover from the error and continue program execution. Assert statements provide a way to stop a program dead when it hits some kind of error. You can configure at runtime whether you want this "stop on error" behavior or not.

Most of Java's statements are pretty much identical to their counterparts in other languages and will be readily recognizable to any programmer. Accordingly, we can limit our discussion to showing the general form of each statement and noting any special rules or "gotchas" that apply.

"Organizing" Statements

There are two statements whose purpose is primarily to organize your code. It is convenient to group them in with the other statements because the Java Language Specification says they are regular statements. The two *organizing* statements (my term) are the block statement and the empty statement.

A block statement is a pair of curly braces, "`{ ... }`", that contains zero or more statements and local variable declarations in any order. Wherever you can legally put one statement, you can put a block statement. We've seen block statements many times. Use them to put a whole group of statements in an "if" branch or to declare a variable that will be used just within the block. A block statement looks like this:

```
{
     Window w = new WarningWindow(f);
     w.setSize(200,100);
     w.setVisible(true);
}
```

An empty statement is simply a semicolon by itself. The empty statement does nothing. Wherever you can legally put a statement, you can put an empty statement. In the example below, we are saying "if the condition is true, do nothing; otherwise, invoke the method."

```
boolean noRecordsLeft = ...
if (noRecordsLeft)
     ; // empty statement
else {
          alertTheMedia(); ...
```

The code is written this way for a reason: rewriting it so the "else" part becomes the "then" part causes the condition to become a double negative ("not no records left"). It's usual to comment the empty statement and put it on a line by itself.

Expression Statements

Certain kinds of expression are counted as statements. You write the expression, put a semicolon after it, and voila, it's an expression statement. In particular, an assignment, method invocation, the instantiation of a class, and pre-increment, post-increment, and decrement are all expressions that can be statements.

```
new WarningWindow(f); // instance creation
w.setSize(200,100);   // method invocation
i++;                  // post increment
a = b;                // assignment
```

An expression statement is executed by evaluating the expression. Any ultimate result after an assignment has taken place is discarded. You usually save a reference to something that you create an instance of. For example, you have:

```
foo = new WarningWindow(f); // instance creation
```

not:

```
new WarningWindow(f); // instance, but no ref saved
```

However, there are certain classes that you can instantiate for which you don't necessarily need to save a reference, like Threads and inner classes. So, you might see this either way.

Selection Statements

---

if

The general form of the "if" statement looks like this:

```
if ( Expression ) Statement  [ else  Statement ]
```

Statement Notes

- ✔ The `Expression` must have boolean type. This has the delightful side-effect of banishing the old "`if (a=b)`" problem, where the programmer does an assignment instead of a comparison, `(a==b)`. If that typo is written, the compiler will give an error message that a boolean is needed in that context—unless a and b are booleans. At least you're protected for all the other types.
- ✔ The Statement can be any statement, in particular a block statement, `{ ... },` is normal.

---

switch

The general form of the "switch" statement is impossible to show in any meaningful form in a syntax diagram with less than about two dozen production rules. That tells you something about how badly designed the statement is right there. If you look at Kernighan and Ritchie's C book, *The C Programming Language*, you'll note that even they were not up to the task of showing the syntax in any better way than this:

```
switch (Expression) Statement
```

Neither has any other C book since. Ignoring syntax diagrams, the switch statement is a poor man's "case" statement. It causes control to be transferred to one of several statements depending on the value of the Expression, which must be of type `char, byte, short,` or `int`. It generally looks like this:

```
switch (Expression) {
   case constant_1 : Statement; break;
   case constant_5 :
   case constant_3 : Statement; break;
        ...
   case constant_n : Statement; break;
        default : Statement; break;
  }
```

Statement Notes

- ✔ If you omit a "break" at the end of a branch, control falls through to execute any remaining branches after that branch is executed, up to the next break! This is almost *never* what you want.
- ✔ There can be only one "default" branch, and it doesn't have to be last. The "default" branch can be omitted. If it is present, it is executed when none of the "case" values match the Expression.
- ✔ A Statement can be labeled with several cases. (This is actually a trivial case of fall-through.)
- ✔ If none of the cases match, and there is no default case, the statement does nothing.
- ✔ Implicit fall-through (in the absence of "break") is a bug-prone misfeature.

Switch Is Badly Designed

Looking through about 100,000 lines of the Java Development system source, there are about 320 switch statements. Based on a random sample of files, implicit fall-through is used in less than 1% . A statement in which you must take explicit action 99% of the time to avoid something is a disaster. Death to the switch statement!

JDK 1.4 has a compiler option to check for and warn about switch fall-through. Use this command line:

```
javac -Xswitchcheck filename.java
```

Iteration Statements

The "for" statement looks like this:

`for (` *Initial; Test; Increment* `)` *Statement*

for

Statement Notes

✔ Initial, Test, and Increment are all Expressions that control the loop. Any or all of them is optional. A typical loop will look like this:

```
for( i=0; i<100; i++ ) { ...
```

A typical infinite loop will look like:

```
for (;;)
```

✔ It is possible to declare the loop variable in the "for" statement, like this:

```
for( int i=0; i<100; i++ ) { ...
```

This is a nice feature created for the convenience of the programmer.

✔ The comma separator "," is allowed in the Initial and Increment sections of loops. This is so you can string together several initializations or increments, like this:

```
for(i=0,j=0; i<100; i++, j+=2 ) { ...
```

The "while" statement looks like this:

`while (` *Expression* `)` *Statement*

while

Statement Notes

- ✔ While the boolean-typed expression remains true, the Statement is executed.
- ✔ This form of loop is for iterations that take place zero or more times. If the Expression is false on the first evaluation, the Statement will not execute.

The "do while" statement looks like this:

do *Statement* while (*Expression*) ;

Statement Notes

- ✔ The Statement is executed, and then the boolean-typed expression is evaluated. If it is false, execution drops through to the next statement. If it is true, you loop through the Statement again.
- ✔ This form of loop is for iterations that take place at least one time. If the Expression is false on the first evaluation, the Statement will already have executed once.

There may be "continue" statements in a loop. These look like:

continue;
continue *Identifier*;

Continue statements occur only in loops. When a continue statement is executed, it causes the flow of control to pass to the next iteration of the loop. It's as though you say, "Well, that's it for iteration N; increment the loop variable (if this is a "for" loop), do the test, and continue with iteration N+1."

The "continue *Identifier*" form is used when you have nested loops, and you want to break out of an inner one altogether and start with the next iteration of the outer loop.

The loop which you want to continue is labeled at its "for" statement with the matching identifier, and it does the same trick. Namely, that's it for iteration N of the labeled loop; increment the loop variable (if this is a "for" loop), do the test, and continue with iteration N+1. You continue with the *next iteration*, even though

the label is (confusingly) at the beginning, rather than labeling, say, the end of the loop. Here is an example "continue" statement:

```
months: for (int m=1; m<=12; m++) {

            // do something
            // nested loop
            for (int d=1; d<=31; d++) {
                  // some daily thing
                  if (m==2 && d==28) continue months;
                  // otherwise something else
            }
            // more guff
}
```

There may be "break" statements in a loop or switch. These look like this:

```
break;
```

Or they look like this:

```
break identifier;
```

Break is a more dramatic version of continue. Break with no identifier causes control to pass to just after the end of the enclosing "for, do, while," or "switch" statement. The loop or switch statement is "broken out of." Break with no identifier can appear only in a statement by virtue of the whole thing being nested in an iteration or switch statement. You will break to the end of the iteration or switch, *not* the statement it's immediately nested in.

```
for (int i=1; i<=12; i++){
     if (LeapYear()) {
          if (i==2) break;
     }
     getTotalforMonth(i);
}
// break to here. Is that what you want?
```

If an identifier is included, it must be an identifier matching the label on some enclosing statement. The enclosing statement can be *any* kind of statement, not just an iterative or switch statement. In other words, it's OK to break out of any kind of enclosing block as long as you explicitly indicate it with a label. In practice, it's almost always a loop or switch that you break out of, not an if or block. Again, there is the slightly confusing feature that statements are labeled at their *beginning*, but "break" causes you to jump to their *end*. Here is an example:

```
months: for (int m=1; m<=12; m++) {

            // do something
            // nested loop
            for (int d=1; d<=31; d++) {
                  // some daily thing
                  if (cost > budget)  break months;
            }
}
cost=0;
```

Transfer of Control Statements

A "return" statement looks like this:

return

```
    return;
return  Expression;
```

Statement Notes

- ✔ "Return" gets you back to where you were called from.
- ✔ A "return *Expression*" can be used only with something that actually does return a value, meaning never with a "void" method. There is another statement that causes transfer of control: the "throw" statement that raises an exception. We will cover this in the chapter that deals with exceptions.

There is a reserved word "goto" in Java, but there is no goto statement. The designers grabbed the keyword to ensure that no one uses it as a variable name in case it later turns out to be convenient to support (perhaps for automatically generated code).

How to Look at Bytecode Instructions for a Statement

You can look at the Java code output by the compiler by using the javap command, like this:

```
javap -c  class
```

The javap command is an abbreviation for "java print." It can be instructive and fun to look at the bytecode output for various Java statements. You can find answers to questions about the code something is compiled into.

Javap will also tell you the sourcefile from which the class came, which is sometimes a useful check that you are executing the code you want. Here's the result of running javap on the WarningWindow class we compiled in the last chapter:

```
javap -c WarningWindow
Compiled from example.java // first it lists the class API
class WarningWindow extends java.awt.Window {
    WarningWindow(java.awt.Frame);
    public void setSize(int, int);
}

Method WarningWindow(java.awt.Frame) // really a constructor
   0 aload_0
   1 aload_1
   2 invokespecial #6 <Method java.awt.Window(java.awt.Frame)>
   5 aload_0
   6 getstatic #7 <Field java.awt.Color red>
   9 invokevirtual #8 <Method void setBackground(java.awt.Color)>
  12 return

Method void setSize(int, int)
   0 iload_1
   1 i2d
   2 ldc2_w #10 <Double 1.5>
   5 dmul
   6 d2i
   7 istore_3
   8 iload_2
   9 i2d
  10 ldc2_w #10 <Double 1.5>
  11 ... etc
```

You can decode the bytecode instructions by looking at the JVM specification at *java.sun.com/docs/books/vmspec/2nd-edition/html/VMSpecTOC.doc.html*.

Exceptions

At several points in the preceding text I mentioned exceptions, only to defer discussion. This is where I deliver on the promise of describing the purpose and use of exceptions following this order:

1. The purpose of exceptions.
2. How to cause an exception (implicitly and explicitly).
3. How to handle ("catch") an exception within the method where it was thrown.
4. Handling groups of related exceptions.
5. How the exception propagates if not handled in the method where it was thrown.
6. How and why methods declare the exceptions that can propagate out of them.
7. Fancy exception stuff.

The Purpose of Exceptions

Exceptions are for changing the flow of control when some important or unexpected event, usually an error, has occurred. They divert processing to a part of the program that can try to cope with the error, or at least die gracefully. The error can be any condition at all, ranging from "unable to open a file" to "array subscript out of range" to "no memory left to allocate" to "division by zero." Java exceptions are adapted from C++, which itself borrowed them from the research language ML. Like C and C++, ML (Meta Language) was developed at Bell Labs. Java exception terminology is presented in Table 7-1.

Table 7–1 Exception Terminology of Java

Note	Java	Some Other Languages
An error condition that happens at runtime	Exception	Exception
Causing an exception to occur	Throwing	Raising
Capturing an exception that has just occurred and executing statements to resolve it in some way	Catching	Handling
The block that does this	Catch clause	Handler
The sequence of method calls that brought control to the point where the exception happened	Stack trace	Call chain

An exception can be set in motion explicitly with the "throw" statement, or implicitly by carrying out some illegal or invalid action. The exception then diverts the normal flow of control (like a goto statement).

If the programmer has made provision, control will transfer to a section of the program that can recover from the error. That section can be in the same method, in the method that called the one where the exception occurred, or in the one that called that method. If no catch clause is found there, the thrown object continues up the stack of calls that were made at runtime. You might want to refresh your memory on how the stack is used to keep track of method invocations by looking at the diagram that was presented back in Chapter 3.

If the thrown object gets to the top where your program execution started, and no handler for the exception has yet been found, then program execution will cease with an explanatory message.

Therefore, the places that you can jump to are strictly limited. You must even explicitly stipulate, "In this block, I will listen for and deal with this type of exception."

How to Cause an Exception (Implicitly and Explicitly)

Exceptions are caused in one of two ways: the program does something illegal (common case), or the program explicitly generates an exception by executing the throw statement (less common case). The throw statement has this general form:

```
throw   ExceptionObject;
```

The *ExceptionObject* is an object of a class that extends the class java.lang.Exception.

Triggering an Exception

Here is a simple program that causes a "division by zero" exception:

```
class melon {
   public static void main(String[] a) {
      int i=1, j=0, k;

      k = i/j;    // Causes division-by-zero exception
   }
}
```

Compiling and running this program gives this result:

```
> javac melon.java
> java melon
     java.lang.ArithmeticException: / by zero
           at melon.main(melon.java:5)
```

There are a certain number of predefined exceptions, like ArithmeticException, known as the runtime exceptions. Actually, since *all* exceptions are runtime events, a better name would be the "irrecoverable" exceptions. They mean "runtime" in the sense of "thrown by the runtime library code, not your code."

Runtime exceptions contrast with the user-defined exceptions which are generally held to be less severe, and in some instances can be recovered from. If a filename cannot be opened, prompt the user to enter a new name. If a data structure is found to be full, overwrite some element that is no longer needed. You don't have to make provisions for catching runtime exceptions. You do have to make provisions for catching other exception types

Some Predefined Exceptions and How They Extend More Basic Classes

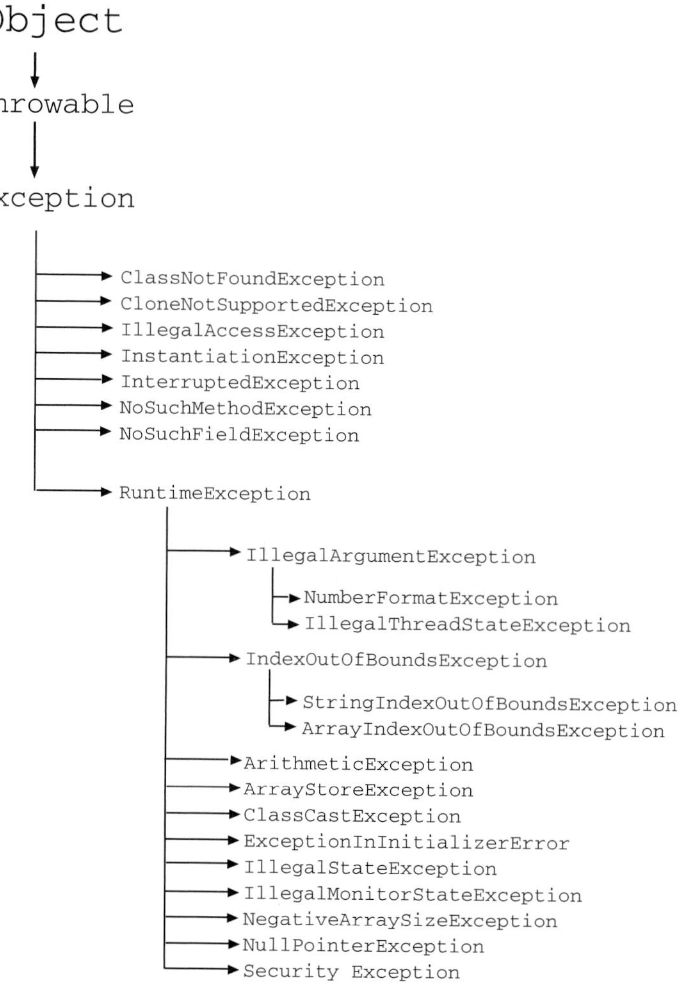

The names are intended to suggest the condition each represents. The source files for these can be found in $JAVAHOME/src/java/lang.

Why is there a class "Throwable?" Why doesn't Exception extend Object directly? The reason is that there is a second class called "Error," which also extends Throwable. In other words, both Exceptions and Errors can be thrown, but Errors are not meant to be caught. They usually indicate some catastrophic failure. Typical Errors are: LinkageError, OutOfMemoryError, VerifyError, and IllegalAccessError. Throwable is the common superclass for all.

User-Defined Exceptions. Here is an example of how to create your own exception class by extending System.exception:

```
class OutofGas extends Exception {}

class banana {
        :

      if (fuel < 0.1) throw   new OutofGas();
}
```

Any method that throws a user-defined exception must also either catch it or declare it as part of the method interface. What, you may ask, is the point of throwing an exception if you are going to catch it in the same method? The answer is that exceptions don't *reduce* the amount of work you have to do to handle errors. Their advantage is they let you collect it all in well-localized places in your program so you don't obscure the main flow of control with zillions of checks of return values.

How to Handle ("Catch") an Exception Within the Method Where It Was Thrown

Of the types of statements we defined at this chapter's opening, here is where *guarding statements* fit in.

Here is the general form of how to catch an exception:

```
try            block
[ catch (arg)   block   ]
[ finally       block   ]
```

There must be at least one (or both) of the two choices below.

[catch (arg) block] ← There can be zero or many of these.

[finally block] ← There can be zero or one of these.

A "block" is a group of statements in curly braces.

The "try" statement says, "Try these statements and see if you get an exception." The "try" statement must be followed by at least one "catch" clause or the "finally" clause.

Each catch says, "I will handle any exception that matches my argument." Matching an argument means that the thrown exception could legally be assigned to the argument exception. There can be several successive catches, each looking for a different exception. Don't try to catch *all* exceptions with one clause, like this:

```
catch (Exception e) { ...
```

That is way too general to be of use and you might catch more than you expected. You are better off letting the exception propagate to the top and give you a reasonable error message.

The "finally" block, if present, is a "last chance to clean up" block. It is *always* executed—even if something in one of the other blocks did a "return!" The "finally" block is executed whether an exception occurred or not and whether it was caught or not. It is executed after the catch block, if present, and, regardless of the path taken, through the try block and the catch block.

The "finally" block can be useful in the complete absence of any exceptions. It is a piece of code that is executed irrespective of what happens in the "try" block. There may be numerous paths through a large and complicated "try" block. The "finally" block can contain the housekeeping tasks that must always be done (counts updated, locks released, and so on) when finishing this piece of code.

Here is an example of an exception guarding statement in full adapted from the window toolkit code:

```
public void printComponents(Graphics g) {
     // ... some code omitted ...
     Graphics cg = g.create();
     try {
          cg.clipRect(i.left, i.top, vs.width, vs.height);
          cg.translate(p.x, p.y);
          c.printAll(cg);
     } finally {
          cg.dispose();
     }
}
```

The method prints components in a scrolling window. It puts a pixel representation of the components onto `g`, the Graphics context. Graphics contexts are an operating system concept, not a Java concept.The finally clause was designed for recycling (releasing) resources like this.

Cleaning Up with finally

Most resources in a program are simply memory, but there are a few resources known to the operating system outside the program. Graphics contexts are one example. They are used to keep track of something on the screen and carry around a lot of information about font, resolution, size, color, and pixel data. There are usually a limited number of graphics contexts available at any one time.

Sockets, file descriptors, database connections, and window handles are other common examples. Many of these have a dispose() method to hand the resource back to the operating system. If you just null out the last pointer to the resource, it will eventually be garbage collected, but that doesn't do anything about recycling the native resource.

By putting a call to dispose in the finally clause, we can be certain that the scarce resource will always be given back to the operating system, regardless of any exceptions raised or avoided.

After the whole *try ... catch ... finally* series of blocks are executed, if nothing else was done to divert it, execution continues after the last catch or finally (whichever is present). The kinds of things that could make execution divert to elsewhere are the regular things: a continue, break, return, or the raising of a different exception. If a "finally" clause also has a transfer of control statement, then that is the one that is obeyed.

Handling Groups of Related Exceptions

We mentioned before that "matching an argument" means that the thrown exception can be assigned legally to the argument exception. This permits a subtle refinement. It allows a handler to catch any of several related exception objects with common parentage. Look at this example:

```
class Grumpy extends Exception {}
class TooHot   extends Grumpy {}
class TooTired extends Grumpy {}
class TooCross extends Grumpy {}
class TooCold  extends Grumpy {}

    .
    :

      try {
        if ( temp > 40 ) throw (new TooHot() );
        if ( sleep < 8 ) throw (new TooTired() );
      }
      catch (Grumpy g) {
           if (g instanceof TooHot)
              {System.out.println("caught too hot!"); return;}
           if (g instanceof TooTired)
              {System.out.println("caught too tired!"); return;}
      }
      finally {System.out.println("in the finally clause.");}
   }
```

The catch clauses are checked in the order in which they appear in the program. If there is a match, then the block is executed. The instanceof operator can be used to learn the exact identity of the exception.

How the Exception Propagates If Not Handled in the Method Where It Was Thrown

If none of the catch clauses match the exception that has been thrown, then the finally clause is executed (if there is one). At this point (no handler for this exception), what happens is the same as if the statement that threw the exception was not nested in a try statement at all. The flow of control abruptly leaves this method, and a premature return is done to the method that called this one. If that call was in the scope of a try statement, then we look for a matching exception again, and so on.

Figure 7-1 shows what happens when an exception is not dealt within the routine where it occurs. The runtime system looks for a "try . . . catch" block further up the call chain, enclosing the method call that brought us here. If the exception propagates all the way to the top of the call stack without finding a matching exception handler, then execution ceases with a message. You can think of this as

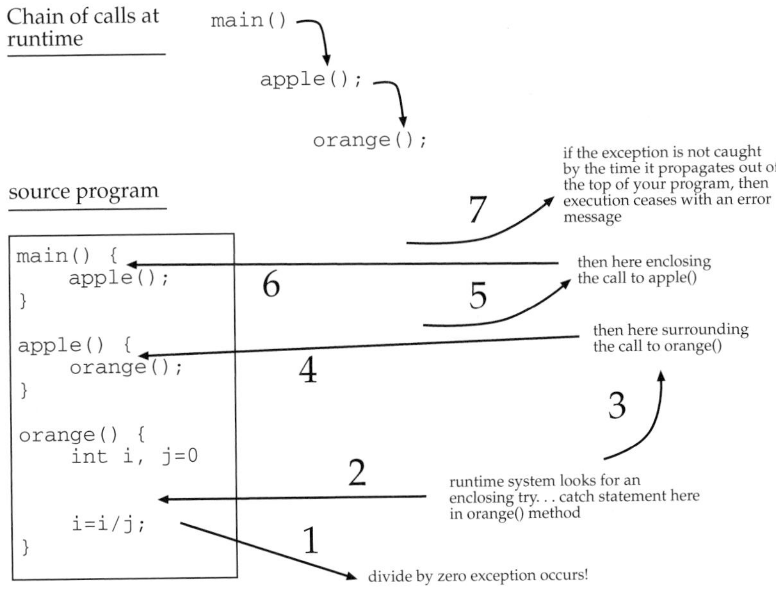

Figure 7–1 The result of an exception not dealt within the occurring routine.

Java setting up a default catch block for you around the program entry point that just prints an error message and quits.

There is no overhead to putting some statements in a "try" statement. The only overhead comes when an exception occurs.

How and Why Methods Declare the Exceptions That Can Propagate Out of Them

Earlier we mentioned that a method must either catch the exceptions that it throws or declare it along with its signature,[1] meaning it must announce the exception to the outside world. This is so that anyone who writes a call to that method is alerted to the fact that an exception might come back instead of a normal return.

This allows the programmer calling that method to make the choice between handling the exception or allowing it to propagate further up the call stack. Here is the general form of how a method declares the exceptions that might be propagated out of it:

```
modifiers_and_returntype name (params)  throws e1, e2, e3  { }
```

1. The exceptions a method throws are not part of the signature, though.

The names e1 through e3 must be exception or error names (that is, any type that is assignable to the predefined type Throwable). Note that just as a method declaration specifies the return *type*, it specifies the exception *type* that can be thrown, rather than an exception object.

An example, taken from the Java I/O system, follows:

```
 byte readByte() throws IOException;
short readShort() throws IOException;
 char readChar() throws IOException;
```

The interesting thing to note here is that the routine to read a char can return a char—not the int that is required in C. C requires an int to be returned so that it can pass back any of the possible values for a char, plus an extra value (traditionally –1) to signify that the end of file (EOF) was reached. Some of the Java routines just throw an exception when the EOF is hit. Out-of-band-signaling can be effective in keeping your code well organized. The EOF exception is a subclass of the IOException, so the technique suggested above for handling groups of related exceptions can be applied.

The rules for how much and what must match when one method that throws an exception overrides another work in the obvious way. Namely, if you never do this, you will never obviously be bothered by it. Well, OK, another way to think about it is to consider the exception as an extra parameter that must be assignment-compatible with the exception in the class being overridden.

Fancy Exception Stuff

When you create a new exception by subclassing an existing exception class, you have the chance to associate a message string with it. The message string can be retrieved by a method. Usually, the message string will be some kind of message that helps resolve the problem or suggests an alternative action.

```
class OutofGas extends Exception {
     OutofGas(String s) {super(s);}  // constructor
}

    ...
// in use, it may look like this
try {
        if (j<1) throw  new OutofGas("try the reserve tank");
      }
catch ( OutofGas o) {
         System.out.println( o.getMessage() );
      }
   ...

//At runtime, this message will appear:
  try the reserve tank
```

Another method that is inherited from the superclass Throwable is "print-StackTrace()." Invoking this method on an exception will cause the call chain at the point where the exception was thrown (not where it is being handled) to be printed out. For example:

```
// catching an exception in a calling method

class test {
   static int myArray[] = {0,1,2,3,4};

   public static void main(String[] a) {
      try {
          bob();
      } catch (Exception e) {
          System.out.println("caught exception in main()");
          e.printStackTrace();
      }
   }

   static void bob() {

      try {
        myArray[-1] = 4; //obvious out of bounds exception
      }
      catch (NullPointerException e) {
         System.out.println("caught a different exception");
      }

   }
}
```

At runtime it will look like this:

```
caught exception in main()
java.lang.ArrayIndexOutOfBoundsException: -1
     at test.bob(test5p.java:19)
     at test.main(test5p.java:9)
```

Summary of Exceptions

- Their purpose is to allow safer programming by providing a distinct path to deal with errors.
- Use them. They are a useful tool for organized error-handling.
- The main use of exceptions is getting a decent error message explaining what failed, where, and why. It's a bit much to expect recovery. Graceful degradation is often the most you can obtain.

We will next review the assert statement, then conclude this chapter with a look at our featured class, Integer.

The Assert Statement

Introduced with Java 1.4, the assert statement helps to debug code and also troubleshoot applications after they have been deployed. You write an assert statement stating some very important condition that you believe will always be true at this point in your program. If the condition is not true, the assertion throws an Error (an exception that is not intended to be caught). You can do that already in Java. The part that is new is that assertion statements let you choose at runtime whether the assertion checking is done or not. There are two key pieces to using asserts.

First, you sprinkle assert statements at a few critical places in your program. For example, after calculating a checksum, you could assert that the calculated value equals the stored checksum. You only use assert statements for fatal errors—something has gone so wrong that the only thing to do is stop before more data disappears or whatever.

The second half of assert statements is that you control whether the assert statements are in effect, or not, at runtime. There is a command line option to the JVM that enables or disables whether the assertions are executed, and this can be applied to individual packages and even classes.

The usual scenario is that you keep the assert statements on during debugging and testing. After testing, when you are confident that the application works correctly, you no longer need to do all that checking. So you disable the assert statements, but leave them compiled in the source code. If the application later hits a problem, you can enable asserts and rerun the failure case to see if any assertions are untrue. This can be done in the field or over telephone support.

An "assert" statement looks like either of these alternatives:

```
assert booleanExpression;
assert booleanExpression : Expression2;
```

If the boolean is not true, a java.lang.AssertionError is thrown. The second form of the statement allows you to write an expression that will be passed to the constructor of the AssertionError. The expression is supposed to resolve to a message about what went wrong. You should just pass a String. An expression of other types (such as int) is allowed to accommodate any nimrods who want to number their error messages or label them with a character instead of using self-identifying strings.

Here's a complete example of the use, compilation, and run of a program with assert.

```
public class asst {
    public static void main(String[] args) {

        int a = Integer.parseInt(args[0]);
        System.out.println("a = "+a);

        assert a>0 : "argument too negative";

        // if a OK, go on with program
    }
}
```

That assert statement is equivalent to this line of code:

```
if (a<=0) throw new java.lang.AssertionError("argument too negative");
```

except that you have the additional ability to configure whether such statements should be executed or not.

For backwards compatibility, the compiler will only accept code containing assertions when you use the "-source 1.4" command line option. So people who have tried to create their own version of assertions in the past and used the identifier "assert" will not have their code broken. Compile as follows:

```
javac -source 1.4 asst.java
```

By default, assertions are disabled. Here is a regular program execution where no error occurs, even though we provided a command line argument that triggers the problem.

```
java asst -3
```

To turn on the assertion checking for a particular run, use the "-ea" (enable assertions) option:

```
java -ea asst -3
Exception in thread "main" java.lang.AssertionError: argument too negative
at asst.main(asst.java:1)
```

There is also a syntax for enabling just one package tree or a class, but you might as well do everything. A separate switch is provided to enable asserts in the system classes (i.e., to set the assertion status for java.* packages to true).

```
java  -esa  MyProgram
```

If you ever get a runtime error in the JVM, such as a core dump, try running with the "-esa" option and including the output in your bug report to Sun. You can search and file bug reports on the JDK at the Java Developer Connection site *developer.java.sun.com*.

There are a couple of caveats with assertion statements. First, you must test your code both ways, with assertions enabled and disabled. Second, you must avoid side effects in the assertion expression. Otherwise, program behavior would be different depending on whether you run with assertions on or off. A "side effect" is a change to the value of some variable, as part of evaluating the expression, e.g.,

```
boolean noMoreData = true;
boolean checkingMethod() {
    noMoreData = false;
    return noMoreData;
}
assert checkingMethod();
```

Now, variable noMoreData has a different value from this point in the program, depending on whether assertions are on or off! Avoid this.

Finally, assertions are supposed to be unrecoverable errors, so do not try to repair the problem and continue. That is what exceptions are for. Assert statements provide the ability to check for significant errors and to make the checking configurable at runtime.

The Class Integer. In the previous chapter we referred to the class `java.lang.Integer` as a class wrapper for the primitive type `int`. There is a similar class wrapper for all the primitive types boolean, char, int, long, etc., as shown in Table 7-2.

Table 7–2 Primitive Types and Their Corresponding Classes

Primitive Type	Corresponding Class (in src/java/lang)
`boolean`	`Boolean`
`char`	`Character`
`byte`	`Byte`
`short`	`Short`
`int`	`Integer`
`long`	`Long`
`float`	`Float`
`double`	`Double`
`void`	`Void`

There are three purposes for having a class version of each basic type:

- To provide an object wrapper for data values. A wrapper is useful because most of Java's utility classes require the use of Objects. Since variables of the primitive types are not objects in Java, it's convenient to provide a simple way to "promote" them when needed.
- To support some useful constants and methods associated with the type, like range boundaries and conversion to and from String.
- To give primitive types the same kind of introspection as non-primitive types. "Introspection" is a Java term for looking at the characteristics of a Java object. It allows you to write component software, debuggers, class inspectors, and other systems programs in Java.

Void (no return value from a method) isn't a type, but it was included for completeness. Here is an example of moving an int to an Integer object and back again, using methods from the Integer class:

```
// changes int to Integer and back
Integer myIntObj;
int i=42;

myIntObj = new Integer(i);  // int to an Integer object
i = myIntObj.intValue();    // Integer object to an int
```

As with Strings, once one of these objects has been created with a given value, that value cannot be changed. You can throw away that object and create a new one, but the object itself doesn't change its identity once assigned. If you need a class that can hold an int that changes, it is trivial to declare. Here it is:

```
public class AnyInt { public int i; }
```

Here is the declaration of class java.lang.Integer:

```
public final class java.lang.Integer extends java.lang.Number
                            implements java.lang.Comparable {
    public static final int MIN_VALUE = 0x80000000; // -2147483648
    public static final int MAX_VALUE = 0x7fffffff; // +2147483647
    public static final java.lang.Class TYPE; // synonym for Integer.class
// constructors
    public java.lang.Integer(int);
    public java.lang.Integer(java.lang.String) throws
                        java.lang.NumberFormatException;
// integer/string conversion
    public static int parseInt(java.lang.String) throws
                                NumberFormatException;
    public static int parseInt(java.lang.String, int) throws
                                NumberFormatException;
    public static java.lang.String toBinaryString(int);
    public static java.lang.String toHexString(int);
    public static java.lang.String toOctalString(int);
    public java.lang.String toString();
    public static java.lang.String toString(int);
    public static java.lang.String toString(int, int);
    public static java.lang.Integer valueOf(java.lang.String)
                        throws java.lang.NumberFormatException;
    public static java.lang.Integer valueOf(java.lang.String, int)
                        throws java.lang.NumberFormatException;
    // converts between Integer values & system properties
    public static java.lang.Integer getInteger(java.lang.String);
    public static java.lang.Integer getInteger(java.lang.String, int);
    public static java.lang.Integer getInteger(java.lang.String, Integer);
    public static java.lang.Integer decode(java.lang.String) throws
                        java.lang.NumberFormatException;
    public int compareTo(java.lang.Integer);
    public int compareTo(java.lang.Object);
    public byte byteValue();
    public short shortValue();
    public int intValue();
    public long longValue();
    public float floatValue();
    public double doubleValue();

    public boolean equals(java.lang.Object);
    public int hashCode();
}
```

You might be wondering about that "`implements Comparable`" clause at the start of the class. That says, "This class has the methods demanded by the interface whose name is `Comparable`." It is the subject of the very next chapter.

Further Reading

There is more information on the assert statement, including a couple of clever idioms, at the Sun site *java.sun.com/j2se/1.4/docs/guide/lang/assert.html*. One of the idioms is code to prevent a program from running if assertions are turned off.

Exercises

1. Write the "if" statements that call different methods do0_9(), do10_99(), and do100_999() based on the value of i being in the range 0-9, 10-99, or 100-999. Don't forget to allow for other values of i, including negative values.

2. Write a switch statement that corresponds to the if statement in question 1. Which is more compact? Which is easier to read?

3. Dump out the byte code for the statements in questions 1 and 2. Use "javap -c" to do this. Review the online JVM specification, and write a description of which byte codes each statement is translated to.

4. Write a method that uses ands, ors, and shifts to reverse the order of bytes in an int. Instead of b1 b2 b3 b4, your routine should rearrange in byte-swapped order to b4 b3 b2 b1.

5. Write a method that counts the number of "1" bits in an int value. Write another method that counts the number of "1" bits in a long value. Is there any way to share code between the two? (Hint: a long is two ints wide.) Would you do so in practice? Explain why or why not. Then reimplement it using java.math.BigInteger.bitCount().

Some Light Relief—MiniScribe: The Hard Luck Hard Disk

Most readers will know the term "hard disk," which contrasts with "floppy disk," but how many people know about MiniScribe's pioneering efforts in the fields of *very* hard disks, inventory control, and accounting techniques?

MiniScribe was a successful start-up company based in Longmont, Colorado, that manufactured disk drives. In the late 1980s, Miniscribe ran into problems when IBM unexpectedly cancelled some very big purchasing contracts. The venture capitalists behind MiniScribe, Hambrecht & Quist, brought in turnaround expert Q.T. Wiles to get the company back on track.

Wiles mercilessly drove company executives to meet revenue targets, even as sales fell still further. In desperation, the beleaguered executives turned to outright record falsification. It must have seemed so easy. Over the space of a couple of years they came up with an impressive range of fraudulent techniques for making a failing company have the appearance of prospering.

The Miniscribe executives started off with the easy paper-based deceit, like:

- Counting raw inventory as finished goods (with a higher value).
- Anticipating shipments before they were made to customers.
- Counting imaginary shipments on non-existent ships.

When they were not found out, they graduated to more brazen activities like parading inventory past the accountants twice, so it would be counted twice, and shipping obsolete product to a fake customer called "BW." "BW" stood for "Big Warehouse" and was a MiniScribe storage building. And so it went, with smaller crimes leading to bigger crimes, just the way your kindergarten teacher warned it would.

Miniscribe employed more than 9,000 people worldwide at the height of its fortunes, so this was no fly-by-night, two-guys-in-a-garage undertaking. This was a fly-by-night, 9,000-guys-in-a-Big-Warehouse undertaking. The companies that supplied Miniscribe were doing less and less business with them and were finding it hard to get paid. One analyst surveyed the entire computer industry and found only one large MiniScribe customer. At the same time, MiniScribe was issuing press releases talking about "record sales."

The most breathtaking coup, though, was the brick scam. Desperate to show shipments on the books, executives brought in their assistants, spouses, and even children for a crazy weekend of filling disk shipping boxes with house bricks. They also created a special computer program called "Cook book" (these guys were well aware of what they were doing) that facilitated shipping the bricks to good old "BW" and recognizing the "revenue" from that customer. These bricks were surely the ultimate hard drive.

Of course, it all came unglued in the end. On January 1, 1990, MiniScribe announced massive layoffs and filed for bankruptcy. Chief Financial Officer

Owen Taranto, the genius who devised the brick shipment plan, was granted immunity for his testimony. The stock went into a precipitous decline, but not before the aptly-named Wiles had unloaded a parcel of it at premium prices. So the people who lost their jobs and the stockholders bore the brunt of all this dishonesty.

There was plenty of blame to go around. After a trial, Cooper & Lybrand, Hambrecht & Quist, and 16 MiniScribe executives were ordered to pay $568 million in restitution to defrauded stockholders. Wiles was sentenced to three years in the Big House. The remains of MiniScribe were bought out by rival Maxtor. The later Maxtor model 8541s looked just like Miniscribe 8541s, so they were still being made, but any resemblance to a brick was long since gone.

You want to know the thing that really kills me about this case, though? It's just not that unusual an event. I taught a programming class at beautiful Foothill College, in Los Altos Hills, California, recently. As well as filling the students' heads with knowledge about stacks, interrupts, kernels, device drivers, heaps, and such, I took pains to talk about the computer industry as a whole. As part of that, I wanted to give a brief lecture on ethics in the computer industry.

I figured I'd dredge up a few shocking tales about benchmark shenanigans, mention whatever was the most recent deceit from Microsoft corporate executives, and remind the class to avoid dealing from the bottom of the deck. I started collecting news stories and reports of ethical lapses within the computer industry to provide material for the lecture.

To my horror, I found that lack of integrity at high levels within a company was not as rare as I had supposed. My files swelled up with material and case studies to the point where I stopped collecting it. So if the MiniScribe story tells us anything, it is this: you will likely be confronted with something ethically wrong at some point in your programming career. When that happens, you'll have a choice between going along with it, or refusing to. If you have thought about it beforehand, it will be easier to do the right thing. That's all.

Chapter 8

Interfaces

Interfaces are an important concept in Java. In this chapter we'll explain how you use interfaces and how they work. We'll start by describing the problem that they solve.

What Problem Does an Interface Solve?

We've seen in previous chapters how classes can be related in a hierarchy, with the common behavior higher up the tree. An example is given in Figure 8-1.

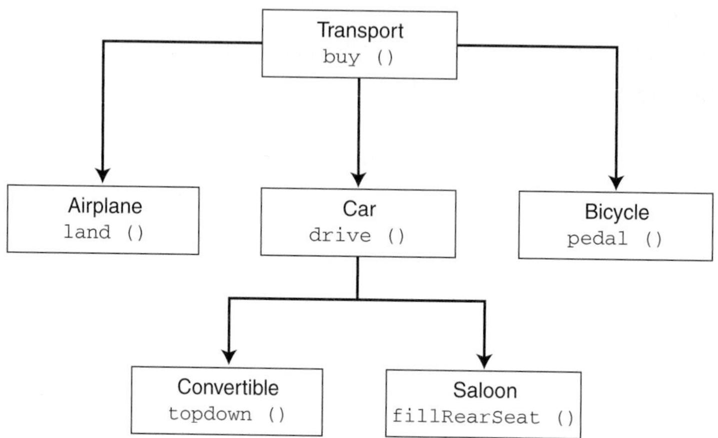

Figure 8–1 Where should the `refuel()` method go?

The figure shows some classes relating to means of transport. Each box is a class, labeled with the class name, and with an example method that belongs in that class. The parent class is called "Transport" and has a method called "buy()". Whatever kind of vehicle you have, you have to buy it before it becomes yours. Putting the method in the parent class means that all subclasses inherit it.

Transport has three child classes. The class called "Car" has a method called "drive()," and this is inherited by its two subclasses, Convertible and Saloon. Whatever kind of car it is, the way you move it is to drive(). It belongs in Car, not Transport, because you don't drive a bicycle or an airplane.

Now let's imagine we want to keep refuelling information in this class hierarchy. We want to add a method called "refuel( )" that fills the fuel tank of each vehicle. The class that keeps track of our supply depot will call the refuel method on vehicle objects. Where is the right place to add refuel() in the tree of classes?

We cannot add a refuel() method in the transport class, because Bicycle would inherit it, and bicycles are not refuelled. We can add the method individually to Airplane and Car and any other unrelated Classes, like Generator, that represent something that can be refuelled.

That's good, but it causes problems for our supply depot class. The supply depot class will call an object's refuel() method. What should be the type of the things we pass to it for refuelling? We cannot pass a Transport, because not all

transport objects have a refuel method(), and some non-Transport things (like Generator) need refuelling

We could overload service() with one version for each type that has a refuel method. But that's not very convenient. Even worse, if we come along with some new thing that is capable of being refuelled, like a JetSki, we now have to modify the SupplyDepot class to add a `service (JetSki thingToSupply)` method. Well-designed systems don't cause changes to ripple across classes this way.

We are looking for a way to say "I represent any type that has a refuel() method" (see Figure 8-2). Then we just make the argument to service() be that type. Some OOP languages allow classes to have more than one parent, a feature known as "multiple inheritance." Multiple inheritance would solve this problem by having a class called "CapableOfBeingRefuelled" with a single method called "refuel()." Everything that can be refuelled will be where it is now in the class hierarchy, but it will also have CapableOfBeingRefuelled as a second parent.

When a language has multiple inheritance, it often proves to be a controversial feature because it seems to need a great many confusing and unintuitive language rules. Java does not have a multiple inheritance feature, but it has something that fills a similar role in a simpler way. Step forward, interfaces!

Interfaces are in the Java language to allow a class to say it has some particular behavior and to act as a placeholder for real classes in any place where that behavior is expected.

We already saw something similar with inheritance, but you can inherit only from one class. A class can implement any number of interfaces. Interfaces say, "I offer this kind of behavior, and you can later use any object from a class that implements me in any place you are using me." Interfaces provide the functionality of multiple inheritance, without the difficulties.

Remember some of the sample Java classes, like java.lang.String and java.lang.Integer we have presented, saying "here is the API" and showing a list

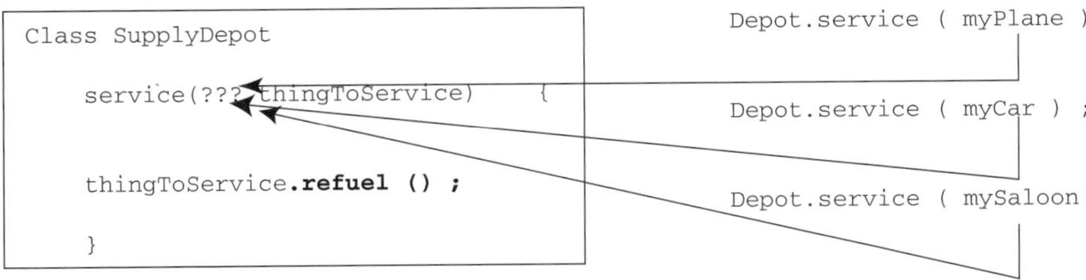

Figure 8–2 What type should `thingToService` be to represent everything that has a `refuel( )` method?

of the method names? The "I" in API even stands for "Interface" (Application Programmer Interface). That is exactly what a Java interface is: a class-like thing that just has a list of method names, not the method bodies. For this reason, some people say that "Java has multiple inheritance of interface, but not multiple inheritance of implementation."

An interface is a skeleton of a class showing the methods the class will have when someone implements it. An interface looks like this:

```
public interface CapableOfBeingRefuelled {
     public int refuel();
}
```

An interface looks a bit like a class (actually, more like an abstract class), is counted as a reference type, and can generally be used in most of the same places as a class. It doesn't have any behavior, though—it's just a description of promised behavior. The declarations in an interface—the fields and methods—are always public, even if you don't label them. The fields in an interface are final, even if you don't label them so. The methods in an interface are abstract, even if you don't label them so.

Any class that has a refuel method should say that it implements the CapableOfBeingRefuelled interface, like this:

```
public class Airplane implements CapableOfBeingRefuelled {
     public int refuel() {
          purgeWingTanks();
          leftTank += this.capacity;
     }
     ... // more methods, omitted
}
```

Now here comes the clever part. The SupplyDepot's service method will take an argument that is type CapableOfBeingRefuelled! Class Airplane, Generator, JetSki, Car and so on all have that type by virtue of implementing that interface. Therefore, they can all be passed to the service method. SupplyDepot will look like this.

```
public class SupplyDepot {
     public void service(CapableOfBeingRefuelled thingToService) {
          thing.refuel();
     }
     ... // more methods, omitted
}
```

And when we come along with something additional that needs to be refuelled, like a snowmobile, no further change is needed in the SupplyDepot class. The snowmobile will be declared as follows, and it is therefore already compatible with the argument to SupplyDepot's service() method:

```
public class Snowmobile implements CapableOfBeingRefuelled {
     public int refuel() {
               ...
     }

     ... // more methods, omitted
}
```

The fundamental reason for interfaces is to decouple or *separate some behavior* that you know some classes have from the classes that *use that behavior.* In summary:

- Use the interface type as a parameter for a method. *Inside the method you can invoke any of the methods promised by the interface parameter.* When you actually call the method, you will have to provide an object that implements the interface and thus has all the methods promised by the interface.
- Interfaces let you compile your code now. But you need to provide an object with actual code for the thing to work at runtime.
- The interface specifies the exact signatures of the methods that must be provided by the implementing classes.

With interfaces, you can write code that makes calls on classes that haven't even been written yet. A class can come along later and be used in the places where you have used the interface— as long as it says it implements the interface.

Comparable

Interfaces are used frequently in the Java runtime library. Here is a complete example of interface Comparable in the java.lang package:

```
public interface Comparable {
     public int compareTo(Object o);
}
/**
 * Compares this object with the specified Object o for order.
 *
 * Returns a negative integer, zero, or a positive integer
 * if this object is less than, equal to, or greater than the
 * specified object.<p>
 */
```

An interface name often includes the suffix "-able." That happens naturally because interfaces describe some capability. The package java.lang has four interfaces, three of which are "-able":

- `java.lang.Cloneable`—this interface is an example of the "marker" design pattern. It has no members, but signals to the compiler that some behavior is permitted. There is a full description of Cloneable later in the chapter.
- `java.lang.Comparable`—this interface promises a method that allows two objects of the same class to be placed in order with respect to one another, i.e., they can be compared. We'll show a complete example of using the Comparable interface.
- `java.lang.Runnable`—this interface promises a run() method which allows an object to execute as a separate thread of control. A couple of later chapters deal with threads of control.

A class that fulfills the interface will use the keyword "implements" like this:

```
public class Double implements Comparable { ...
```

If you want to peek ahead, this class is the standard `java.lang.Double` class featured at the end of this chapter. Double is an object wrapper for double precision floating-point numbers, meaning that it provides a thin object layer over the primitive type. It thus allows you to send along a double primitive type argument to all the classes that require an object as an argument.

When we see the line of code above, we know at once that Double has a method with the `compareTo` signature because that's what the `Comparable` interface promises. Objects of class Double can be used anywhere you have used the `Comparable` interface.

A class can extend only one superclass, but it can implement any number of interfaces. Two interfaces can make the same demand for a method of a given

name in a class without problems (one of the situations that causes *tic douloureux* among the multiple inheritance crowd). Different classes can implement the same interface each in their own special way.

Here's some more code from the Double class. The class Double implements the Comparable interface by providing a body for the compareTo method. This is the actual source code from the runtime library. The runtime library source code is distributed as part of the JDK, and it is instructive to read it.

```
public class Double implements Comparable { ...

     public int compareTo(Object o) {
          anotherDouble = (Double) o;
          double anotherVal = anotherDouble.value;
          double thisVal = value;

          if (thisVal < anotherVal)
               return -1; // Neither val is NaN, thisVal is smaller

          if (thisVal > anotherVal)
               return 1; // Neither val is NaN, thisVal is larger

          // tricky code dealing with NaN's, omitted
          return 0;
     }

// other methods in the class omitted ...
}
```

Look at the source in $JAVAHOME/src/java/lang/Double.java if you are curious about the NaN trickiness which I have left out of this example.

The code here says that if I see anything that takes a Comparable as an argument, I can actually call it with a Double object. The reason is that Double has all the behavior promised by Comparable. Here's an example showing it being used as an argument type:

```
void howBigIsIt(Comparable c) {
     ...
}
 ...
Double myDouble = new Double(22.0);
howBigIsIt( myDouble ); // can call method using a Double
```

Getting more detailed, I can write a data structure that sorts an array. Instead of making it an array of some fixed type like, say, Integer, I can make it process an array of Comparables. Then anything that implements the interface can use my sort class! Here's how some of the code might look:

```
// first, a reminder of the interface
public interface Comparable {
     public int compareTo(Object o);
}

// next, my sortingClass to sort anything that can be
// compared, making use of the Comparable interface

public class sortingClass {
     // holds the data
     static java.lang.Comparable [] d;

     // a constructor, to fill up the d array
     sortingClass(java.lang.Comparable data[]) { d=data; }

     int findLargest() {
          java.lang.Comparable largestSoFar = d[0];
          int where = 0;
          for (int i=1; i<d.length; i++) {
               if ( largestSoFar.compareTo(d[i]) == -1) {
                    largestSoFar = d[i]; // new element is bigger
                    where = i;           // so record where it is
               }
          }
          return where;
     }

     ... // more methods, omitted
```

In the body of the `findLargest()` method, we look at successive elements of the array called d, and compare them *using the compareTo method*. This is a neat trick. We have promised only that method so far and not actually supplied a body for it. It's enough to allow compilation to take place. We can't actually run the code until we supply a class that implements the interface.

To keep the example small, I haven't filled up the page with code showing the rest of a sort algorithm. You'll have to believe me when I say that by finding the largest thing left in a pile of objects, you can sort the objects. That is how the bubblesort algorithm works, though everyone knows that the only virtue of bubblesort is that it is easy to understand. It is too slow to use when you actually want to sort, instead of teach.

Here's how some code to fulfill the interface might hook up with the sortingClass. Double implements Comparable, so we can pass a Double array to the sortingClass constructor that expects a Comparable array:

```
public static void main(String[] args) {
     Double dubs [] = { new Double(4.0), new Double(10),
                        new Double(-9.2), new Double(0.6),
                        new Double(1),    new Double(99),
                        new Double(6.00)
                  };

     sortingClass s = new sortingClass( dubs );
     int i = s.findLargest();
     String val = s.d[i].toString();
     System.out.println("Largest is "+ val + " at element "+i);
}
```

Sure enough, when we run that code, it will print out the following message:

```
% java Try
Largest is 99.0 at element 5
```

This demonstrates that the correct substitution of Double's version of compareTo() was made in the sortingClass. Better yet, the very same sortingClass works if we instantiate it with Integer objects.

```
Integer ints [] = { new Integer(4),new Integer(10),
                    new Integer(9), new Integer(6),
                    new Integer(1), new Integer(99),
                    new Integer(600) };

sortingClass s = new sortingClass( ints );
int i = s.findLargest();
String val = s.d[i].toString();
System.out.println("Largest is "+ val + " at element "+i);
```

This results in the following:

```
% java Try
Largest is 600 at element 6
```

Don't be misled into thinking that interfaces are a replacement for C++ templates (i.e., writing a single method body and then having some compiler magic so it can operate on several types that are not related to each other). Templates or generic types form a different feature that is planned for JDK 1.5.

The point is that the interface allows the class that uses it to be freed from any one specific datatype as an argument. The interface lets you use sortingClass with any type that implements the Comparable interface, even a type that hadn't been thought of when sortingClass was written. If the class implements Comparable, you can use the sortingClass on it.

Think of interfaces as being like a library of stub bodies against which you can compile, but you have to supply a real library at runtime before you actually make the calls.

Interfaces vs. Abstract Classes

While an interface is used to specify the form that something *must* have, it does not actually provide the implementation for it. In this sense, an interface is a little like an abstract class that must be extended in exactly the manner that its abstract methods specify.

An interface differs from an abstract class in the following ways:

- An abstract class is an incomplete class that requires further specialization. An interface is just a specification or prescription for behavior.
- An interface doesn't have any overtones of specialization that are present with inheritance. It merely says, "We need something that does 'foo' and here are the ways that users should be able to call it."
- A class can implement several interfaces at once, whereas a class can extend only one parent class.
- Interfaces can be used to support callbacks (inheritance doesn't help with this). This is a significant coding idiom. It essentially provides a pointer to a function, but in a type-safe way. The next section explains callbacks.

Here's the bottom line: You'll probably use interfaces more often than abstract classes. Use an abstract class when you want to initiate a hierarchy of more specialized classes and provide a partial implementation with fine control over what is private, public, protected, etc. Use an interface when you need multiple inheritance of design to say, "this class has behavior (methods) A, B, and C."

An interface can be extended, but only by another interface. It is legal for a class to implement an interface but only have some of the methods promised in the interface. You must then make it an abstract class that must be further extended (inherited) before it can be instantiated.

Granting Permission Through an Interface—Cloneable

When we looked at the Object class in Chapter 3, we saw that it has this method:

```
protected native Object clone() throws CloneNotSupportedException;
```

Java supports the notion of *cloning*, meaning to get a complete bit-for-bit duplicate of an object.

Not every class should support the ability to clone. If I have a class that represents a set of objects that are unique in the real world, such as the ships in a company fleet, the operation of cloning doesn't make sense, as it doesn't represent anything in the real world. However, methods (including the clone() method) in the class java.lang.Object are inherited by all classes.

So Java places a further requirement on classes that want to be cloneable: they must implement the cloneable interface to indicate that cloning is valid for them. The cloneable interface is this:

```
public interface Cloneable { } // completely empty
```

The empty interface as a marker is not the most common use of interfaces, but you do see it in the system libraries. To have a class that can be cloned, you must state that the class implements the `Cloneable` interface.

```
public class ICanBeCopied implements Cloneable { ...
```

Why wasn't the method `clone()` of `Object` made part of the `Cloneable` interface? That seems like the obvious place to put it, instead of in Object. The reason is that we have two conflicting aims. We want to provide a default implementation of clone so that any cloneable class can automatically inherit it, and that implementation cannot be put in an interface. We also want individual classes to take an extra step to permit cloning on their object.

The end result is that we require, at minimum, an extra step of having cloneable classes implement the Cloneable interface. The class Object does *not* implement Cloneable itself, otherwise all its descendants (which is every object in existence) would too. We provide a default implementation by putting the method clone, with a body, into the root superclass Object. That implementation could not be placed in an interface, since interfaces only hold method signatures and final data.

Shallow vs. Deep Clone

There is some subtlety to a class that has data fields that are other classes. Do you simply copy the reference and share the referenced object (a *shallow clone*), or do you recursively clone all referenced classes too (a *deep clone*)? While Object.clone() does a shallow clone, supplying the method in class Object and making it overridable allows you to choose the behavior you want. You can disallow any kind of clone. You can override clone as public rather than the default protected (outside this package, only subclasses can clone). You can even implement a deep clone, if you wish.

Note that `clone()` returns an `Object`. The object returned by `clone()` is usually cast immediately to the correct type, as in this example:

```
Vector v = new Vector();
Vector v2;

v2 = (Vector) v.clone();
```

Since Arrays are considered to implement Cloneable, they can be copied by System.arrayCopy or by clone().

What Protected Really Means

A Common Pitfall with Clone

There is a very commonly-encountered pitfall with cloning. When you try to clone an object in the most obvious way, you get a compilation error:

```
class b implements Cloneable {
    int bi = 22;
}

public class c {
    public static void main(String [] args) {
        b thing = new b();
        b duplicate = (b) thing.clone();
    }
  }
```

```
ERROR: clone has protected access in java.lang.Object
```

It's true, too. The relevant signature in java.lang.Object is:

```
protected native Object clone() throws CloneNotSupportedException;
```

Read on for the details!

Object.clone() is protected because subclasses might want to restrict access to cloning, and if Object.clone() were declared public, subclasses could never make it more restrictive. Subclasses can make access to their overriding methods less restrictive, but never more restrictive.

This means that a method can clone its own objects, but a method cannot clone objects of another class unless or until you open up access like this:

```
class b implements Cloneable {
     public Object clone()
             throws CloneNotSupportedException {
            return super.clone();
     }

     int b = 22;
}
```

i.e., override clone() to make it public, and call the superclass clone().

Cloning, perhaps surprisingly, does not invoke any constructor.

This is a good place to clarify what the "protected" access modifier does. The JLS (Java Language Specification, which is online at *java.sun.com/docs/books/jls/second_edition/html/jTOC.doc.html*) says in section 6.6.2:

> Let C be the class in which a `protected` member m is declared. Access is permitted only within the body of a subclass *S* of C. In addition, if *id* denotes an instance field or instance method, then if the access is by a qualified name *Q.id*, where *Q* is an *ExpressionName*, then the access is permitted if and only if the type of the expression *Q* is *S* or a subclass of *S*.

Loosely rephrasing that in English, protected access means that other classes in the same package can access the member, and subclasses in other packages can access the member. To understand exactly what that means, consider these two classes, which we will put in different packages to be sure we are testing the subclasses part of the rule:

```
package somePackage;
class Parent {
     protected int x;
}
```

and

```
class Child extends Parent { ..... }
```

The class Child can only access "x" on objects that are of type Child or that are a subtype of Child. If an equal() method is added to Child, then the following two uses of "x" are both legal:

```
boolean equal(Child other) {
     return x == other.x;
}
```

They are legal because the left-most "x" is implicitly "this.x", and both "this" and "other" are of type Child. However, adding this method to Child will cause a compilation error:

```
int getIt(Parent p) {
     return p.x; /// BAD! BAD! BAD!
}
```

The problem is that the class Child can only access "x" on objects that are of type Child or that are a subtype of Child. The type p is not Child or a subtype, it is the Parent type. You don't have access to protected members of your superclass, only to protected members of your own class that you inherited because they are accessible members of your superclass.

"static" protected variables and methods are accessible from any child class since there is no "object" through which to access them. "`super.protectedMethod(...)`" is always legal.

People learning about this subtlety often wonder if they have wandered into a C++ book by mistake. Don't worry! There are hardly any other pitfalls like that in Java. Well, at least compared with some other languages, I mean. For historians and language theologians, this meaning of protected was a change made to Java between JDK 1.0 Beta 1 and Beta 2 in December 1995.

Interfaces in the Java Runtimes

Interfaces are used in many places in the Java runtimes. The utility class java.util.Vector implements three interfaces, as shown below:

```
public class Vector extends AbstractList
     implements List, Cloneable, java.io.Serializable { ...
```

The Cloneable class is described above. By implementing a List, the class is announcing that it can be used wherever a List is used. It can also do all the things a List can do, meaning it can have elements added or removed, can be checked for being empty, can tell you its size, and so on.

By implementing Serializable, the class Vector is saying that it and all of its subtypes have the ability to be serialized. Being serialized is the conversion into a stream of bytes that can be written out to disk and later reconstituted into an object. This is the same permission-granting use of an interface that we saw with Cloneable.

Call Backs

The examples of interfaces thus far have solved compile time issues. There is an additional way that an interface can be used to obtain more dynamic behavior, which forms the basis of GUI programming in Java. We have already seen this; the explanation here has a different nuance.

Once we have defined an interface, we can use it as the type of some parameter to a method. Inside the method we can use that parameter to invoke the operations that the interface promises. Whenever we make a call to that method, we can pass it a class that implements the interface, and it will call the appropriate method of that class. The following four steps should make this a little clearer.

1. Define an interface that promises a method called *run* like this:

```
interface Runnable {
     public void run();
}
```

2. Now sprinkle calls to "run" throughout our code, even though we don't yet have anything that fulfills the interface.

```
void vitalSystemThing(Runnable r) {
     r.run();
}
```

This code can be compiled, and may even be part of the Java runtime library.

3. At a later time and in another file, provide a class (or several classes) that implements the following interface:

```
class myCode implements Runnable {
     public void run() {
          System.out.println("You called myCode.run()");
     }
     // other code ...
}
```

4. Pass myCode object to the vitalSystemThing:

```
myCode myobj = new myCode()
vitalSystemThing( myobj );
```

`vitalSystemThing` can even save a reference to `myobj` and later call its methods as needed. This is how event handling works in the GUI.

Whenever the vitalSystemThing is invoked, it results in `myCode.run()` being called back. This is therefore known as a *callback*. It's a drawn-out way of doing what you do with a function pointer in C or C++, and this has led some people to call for the addition of function pointers to Java. That won't happen since Java callbacks are type-safe, but function pointers might not be.

The main reason for writing your code this way is that it decouples the calling routine from the called-back routine. You could have several different classes that implement the Runnable interface. Callbacks allow any of them to be sent to the vitalSystemThing and hence to be called back. The correct class is called back, based on the type at runtime.

There actually *is* a built-in Java interface, called *Runnable*, that is used in this way for threads. It is described in Chapter 10. The use of an interface allows the runtime system to schedule and control threads that you implement and compile later. Here is another example of an interface used as a callback:

```
interface runnable {
    public void run();
}

public class VeryDynamic {
   public static void main(String args[]) {
        runnable r;
        try {
           Class unknown = Class.forName(args[0]);
           r = (runnable) unknown.newInstance();
           r.run();
        } catch (Exception e){ e.printStackTrace();}

   }
}

class Coffee implements runnable {
   public void run() { System.out.println("Coffee.run called"); }
}

class Tea implements runnable {
   public void run() { System.out.println("Tea.run called"); }
}
```

The try and catch statements are required to accommodate the exceptions that the enclosed statements might cause. If you compile this program, you can run it like this:

```
java VeryDynamic Tea
```

Try executing it with an argument of "Coffee" and an argument of "Bogus." The three lines in bold simply get the runtime type information for the class

whose name you give as an argument. They then create an instance of that class that is cast to runnable, and call the run() method of that class.

The example demonstrates how a callback can work for an object of a class that isn't even known until runtime. It doesn't get any more dynamic than that! The technique is used extensively in the Java GUI library to tell your code about events happening on screen.

Using Interfaces for Named Constants

There's another unorthodox way to use an interface that forms a useful programming idiom. If you have a group of related constants, perhaps of the kind you would put in an enumerated type (if the language has enumerated types), you might gather them in a class like this:

```
public class FightingWeight {
   public static final int         flyweight = 100;
   public static final int      bantamweight = 113;
   public static final int     featherweight = 118;
   public static final int       lightweight = 127;
   public static final int      welterweight = 136;
   public static final int      middleweight = 148;
   public static final int lightheavyweight = 161;
   public static final int       heavyweight = 176;
}
```

Then, to use the constants in another class, you would have to do something like this:

```
static int title = FightingWeight.heavyweight;
```

Let's say you make FightingWeight an *interface*, like this:

```
public interface FightingWeight {
   public static final int         FLYWEIGHT = 100;
   public static final int      BANTAMWEIGHT = 113;
   public static final int     FEATHERWEIGHT = 118;
   public static final int       LIGHTWEIGHT = 127;
   public static final int      WELTERWEIGHT = 136;
   public static final int      MIDDLEWEIGHT = 148;
   public static final int LIGHTHEAVYWEIGHT = 161;
   public static final int       HEAVYWEIGHT = 176;
}
```

You can then reference the names directly. Wow!

```
class gooseberry implements FightingWeight {
   ...
     int title = HEAVYWEIGHT;
```

Final variables are usually written in all capitals (a holdover from C). The interface `javax.swing.WindowConstants` uses this technique. Name inheritance works for classes, too, but it's considered poor style to extend a class just for better name visibility.

The Class Double

Here is the declaration of class java.lang.Double:

```
public final class java.lang.Double extends java.lang.Number
                                    implements java.lang.Comparable {
     // constructors
     public java.lang.Double(double);
     public java.lang.Double(java.lang.String)
                         throws java.lang.NumberFormatException;
     public static final double POSITIVE_INFINITY = 1.0 / 0.0;
     public static final double NEGATIVE_INFINITY = -1.0 / 0.0;
     public static final double NaN = 0.0d / 0.0;
     public static final double MAX_VALUE = 1.79769313486231570e+308;
     public static final double MIN_VALUE = longBitsToDouble(1L);
     public static final java.lang.Class TYPE=
                                    Class.getPrimitiveClass("double");

     public byte byteValue();
     public short shortValue();
     public int intValue();
     public long longValue();
     public float floatValue();
     public double doubleValue();

     public int compareTo(java.lang.Double);
     public int compareTo(java.lang.Object);
     public boolean isInfinite();
     public static boolean isInfinite(double);
     public boolean isNaN();
     public static boolean isNaN(double);
     public boolean equals(java.lang.Object);
     public int hashCode();
     public static native long doubleToLongBits(double);
     public static native double longBitsToDouble(long);

     public static double parseDouble(java.lang.String) throws
                                    java.lang.NumberFormatException;
     public java.lang.String toString();
     public static java.lang.String toString(double);
     public static java.lang.Double valueOf(java.lang.String) throws
                                    java.lang.NumberFormatException;
}
```

Exercises

1. Describe, without excessive handwaving, two common uses for interfaces.
2. Use the sorting class shown in this chapter to find the "largest" of a set of Strings you provide. The class java.lang.String implements the Comparable interface.
3. Take any class that you have written and make it cloneable by making it implement the Cloneable interface. The Cloneable source code is at $JAVA-HOME/src/java/lang/Cloneable.java.
4. Override Object.clone() to do a shallow copy for your class, and also keep count of the number of objects of your class that have been created. Don't forget to count those created via a constructor, too.
5. Write some code to clone an object of your class. Change your version of clone() to do a deep copy for your class. Run the clone program again, and make it print out enough details that you can tell the difference between a shallow clone and a deep clone.

Some Light Relief—The Odyssey of Naming Hal

To close out the chapter, let's peek at another example of naming and the confusion that can arise. There's a pervasive industry legend that the antihero computer HAL in the film *2001: A Space Odyssey* was so-named to indicate that he was one step ahead of IBM. Alphabetically, "H," "A," and "L" precede "I," "B," and "M" by one letter.

Similarly, people say that Windows NT (WNT) is one step away from VMS. Dave Cutler designed VMS when he was at Digital and then joined Microsoft to become the chief architect of Windows NT. I believe that the name was chosen with this in mind. It's a moot point, now that the product has been renamed Windows 2000, to make it look like a continuation of the Windows line. In a sense it *is* now, since the Windows XP release drops the Windows 3.1, 95, 98, ME line of products, and tries to migrate all consumers to the NT source base under the XP name.

Arthur C. Clarke, the author of *2001: A Space Odyssey,* emphatically denies the HAL legend in his book *Lost Worlds of 2001,* claiming that HAL is an acronym for "Heuristically-programmed Algorithmic Computer." Clarke even wrote to the computer magazine *Byte* to place his denial on record. Methinks he doth protest too much.

Certainly, the claims of an involved party are one piece of evidence, but there is no particular reason why they should be accepted uncritically as complete truth. Consider them rather in the context of all pieces of evidence, as happens in courts of law every day. For one thing, "Heuristically-programmed Algorithmic Computer" is a contrived name that does not properly form the desired acronym. For another, all the working drafts of the 2001 story had HAL named "Athena," and it would have remained so had not Clarke deliberately rechristened it. The odds of him accidentally latching onto the one name that mimics one of the world's largest computer companies are a few thousand to one.

Why would Clarke deny it if it were true? IBM logos appear in several places in the movie, and the filmmakers clearly cut a deal with IBM for product placement. It may be that Clarke decided to assert some artistic independence by deciding on a name change as a subtle dig at IBM: HAL is a homicidal maniac who goes berserk. Perhaps he was just suggesting that his creation was one step ahead of IBM. Later, when the story got out, Clarke realized he would look foolish, or at the very least ungracious, by lampooning them. So he tried to bluff his way out.

An interesting concern is why the name was changed at all. If Clarke provided an explanation of *that* along with his denials, the denials would have more credibility.

Chapter 9

Packages and Visibility

In this chapter, we'll look at the "how" and "why" of packages. Java uses the term *package* to mean a collection of related .class files in a directory. Speaking very strictly, packages and classes do not *have* to be directories and files. The Java Language Specification is written to allow implementations that store source code in a database or any other kind of repository, and some IDEs do that. However, "package equals directory" and "class equals file" is the simplest implementation, and the easiest way to understand the topic. It is how we'll describe it here.

Thus, a package is both a directory and a library. How do you tell the compiler that a class belongs to some package? It's simplicity itself—just write the first non-comment line in the file like this:

```
package identifier.identifier.identifier... ;
```

You can have one or more identifiers. They denote a deeper and deeper depth in the package and filesystem hierarchy. A package clause might be this:

```
package java.lang;
```

That says that the classes in the file belong to the java.lang package. It also says that the class file will be in directory `java\lang\` (on Windows) or `java/lang/` (on Unix). Java can use the computer's filesystem to organize and locate packages.

We already know that the name of a public class must match the name of the file containing the source code. Java also requires a *package name* to match the last part of the *directory name* where it is kept. Since it's most convenient to keep source and bytecode together, the source will usually be in the same directory.

The requirement means that if you know the name of a class, you also know where to find it. Classes that are part of the same package will be in the same directory. It simplifies things for the compiler-writer, and gives the programmer less to remember.

What Are Packages For?

Packages (as the name suggests) are for parcelling up several class files and having a convenient way to give that group a name of its own. When you're just writing a few programs for your personal use, you can put them in any old directory and use any old names. When you have a team of twenty programmers working on five different software products that interact, you need a better way to organize your files than "putting them in any old directory."

Packages solve the problem of name conflicts. Unlike many other language or compiler systems, Java doesn't link all your code into one big, freestanding program. Instead, it leaves everything in separate classfiles.

The Cost of Loading Code

When you say "java myclass" to run a program, the JVM follows a set of rules to locate the file myclass.class, and then loads that class into the execution environment. As execution proceeds, the JVM dynamically looks for and loads the classes that myclass references as it needs them, and then it loads all the classes that *those* classes reference, and so on throughout program execution.

Java linking is done at runtime. This has the advantage that programs can be very small, flexible, and dynamic. It has the disadvantage that you have to pay the cost of runtime linking every time you execute a program, just as you do with a dynamically-linked C program.

The cost is greater in Java because you're doing it all twice: first, the OS has to map in and load the JVM program, then the JVM has to map in and load the Java Runtime Library (JRE) and your class. It accounts for the brief pause after you invoke an executable and before anything starts happening. It makes Java more suited to longer-running applications than small, frequently-invoked utilities such as directory listers. There are some things an OS manufacturer could do to alleviate this burden, like keep a JVM already loaded and ready for use. We'll see.

If a class was identified purely by its classname and nothing else, we'd have to demand that classnames be unique. Otherwise, if I wrote a class called `ReadData` that was part of my program installed on a customer's system, and you wrote a class called `ReadData` that was part of your program installed on the same customer's system, the JVM wouldn't know which of the two classes to load when it hit a reference to `ReadData`.

Packages give the programmer a way to qualify a class name. The system can then use more than just the identifier that comes after "`public class ...`" to locate and name a class.

```
package java.util.zip;
public class ZipFile ... {
```

In the code above, you are actually specifying that the full name of this class is the following:

```
java.util.zip.ZipFile
```

That is what the JVM will look for at runtime, and that is how you distinguish the class from any other `ZipFile` class that someone else may have written. There is an algorithm for choosing package names that ensures we all end up with different, fully-qualified class names. Part of the algorithm is that names starting with "java" are reserved for the Java system itself, and you may not write any packages that start with that name.

An additional function of packages is to provide namespaces to the programmer, and we review how that works a little later in the chapter.

How to Choose a Package Name

Package names are hierarchical, just like mailing addresses. If you want to send a letter, you can't just write "Mr. James Brown" on the envelope. There are thousands of people with that name. It's not even good enough to just include the street name. You don't know where to start looking unless you know the country and town. We make the address unique by giving enough further qualifiers. Two different addresses for two different people might have some components that match, like this:

Mr. James Brown,	*Mr. James Brown,*
27, Main Street,	*27 Main Street,*
Cricklewood,	*Hollywood,*
London,	*California*
England	

As long as there is some identifier that is different, they are different addresses. A mailing address can satisfactorily identify which recipient is meant, and these different addresses can be different lengths. Reading from the bottom up, the address goes from most general to most specific. Package names are formed the same way.

The Java Language Specification tells us that package names should be formed from Internet domain names. If an organization that is writing software for sale doesn't have an Internet domain name at this point, they should go into some other, slower-paced line of work. Domain names are guaranteed to be unique and the JLS tells us to reverse them so they are sorted from most general to least general. That means that all java class libraries coming out of IBM should be in packages whose names start with `com.ibm`.

IBM will probably want to impose further levels of package names so that its different divisions don't conflict with each other. How, and how far, they subdivide it further is totally up to them. They'll probably want to add, at minimum, "division" and "product within division." Another example package name, representing the online real-time arbitrage system that I am coding for the multinational software giant AFU, Inc., is `com.afu.applications.arby`.

That distinguishes my arby package from all the other Java code on which AFU is working, namely, com.afu.applications.gambling.horses, com.afu.applications.office2010, and com.afu.OSkernel.

In this way, the most significant part of your package name has already been chosen for you, and the least significant part you can subdivide as you wish. Those parts of a package name are called the *members*. Just as classes have members, packages have members. The members of a class or interface are the fields (data) and methods (code). The members of a package are the subpackages and classes or interfaces.

By following this protocol, you can also easily create package names that are unique across the entire Internet since domain names have this quality. It allows different vendors to provide class libraries with no danger of namespace collisions.

How the JVM Finds Classes

We just saw that the full name of a class includes the package name and might be something like `com.afu.applications.arby.ReadData`.

We also saw that the JVM will expect the class file to be in `com\afu\applications\arby\ReadData.class` (on Windows) or `com/afu/applications/arby/ReadData.class` (on Unix). Clearly, that's the final part of a complete pathname. Where does the JVM start looking for the first part?

Rooting about for Packages

Java has seen a bit of evolution in the area of where to look for the roots of your packages. The support in JDK 1.0 was downright horrid. In JDK 1.1, it was only mildly ugly. From JDK 1.2, things are OK. To avoid confusion, I'll describe only the vastly improved JDK 1.2 support here. If you want to get things working under one of the earlier releases, read and follow the directions in the readme file that comes with that version of the JDK.

You no longer have to tell the JVM where to find the runtime library. For your own classes, you either have to tell the JVM the directories where it might find the roots of your packages, or you have to put your packages in a place where it automatically looks.

The first point to note is that you can gather all your class files into a *jar file*, so you don't really need umpteen levels of directory on the customer's system. A jar file (Java Archive) works exactly like a zip file and can be used to store a whole directory tree in a single file. You can put other files that the application needs, such as image files, sound files, and translations for Strings in the jar, too. In the case of my world-beating arbitrage program, I jar'ed everything into a file called all.jar. We now have to put the jar file (or the complete directory tree) where Java can find it, or tell Java the possible places to look for it.

Putting the Jar File Where Java Will Find It

Java looks in the directory $JAVAHOME/jre/lib/ext for jar files. You can install your programs just by placing the jar file containing them in this directory. They will be found automatically without further action on the user's part. Strictly speaking, this directory is reserved for use by the Java system, and it is intended for optional system libraries that don't come with the JDK. However, it is super-convenient to put your jar files there while you are learning about Java. Just don't do it for any deployed applications.

Java also looks in the directory $JAVAHOME/jre/classes for a directory hierarchy containing class files that corresponds to your package hierarchy. You may have to create the classes subdirectory the first time. If your program doesn't use

packages, you can just dump the .class files directly in this directory, although that gets messy for more than a few files.

Telling Java Where to Look for the Jar File or Package Roots

Java will look at the CLASSPATH environment variable, typically set in the autoexec.bat file (on Windows 95, 98, ME), or in the system section of the control panel (NT or XP), or in a shell initialization file (on Unix). CLASSPATH tells the class loader all the possible places (roots) to begin looking for Java packages to import in a compilation or to load at runtime.

The CLASSPATH will be set to a list of one or more pathnames separated by ";" (Windows) or ":" (Unix). It may look like this, for instance, on Windows:

```
SET CLASSPATH = c:\all.jar;c:\project\test;.
```

It may look like this on a Unix system using C shell:

```
setenv CLASSPATH /all.jar:/project/test/:.
```

That tells Java to look, in order, for the arby code in the following:

```
/all.jar
/project/test/com/afu/applications/arby/*.class
./com/afu/applications/arby/*.class
```

One of these had better be a match or the compilation, or run, will fail with the error, "Class not found." The first match found is the class for which it is looking. Java tools that expect classes can cope with package names. Thus, the following works to run a program:

```
java com.afu.applications.arby.go
```

Zip Files and Jar Files

Zip files were introduced in December 1995 for classes. A zip file is a collection of .class files grouped together in one physical file, as can be done on Windows with the standard Windows zip software.

Jar files replaced zip files in the JDK 1.1 release. Jar files are in zip format and can contain an extra "manifest" file listing all the files in the jar. The standard Java runtime library is kept in a 10MB jar file called *jre/lib/rt.jar.* Jar files can also contain any other file resources the program needs, such as image files or property files. You can bundle an entire program up into a Jar file.

Jar files are convenient for a browser opening a connection to a remote URL applet. The browser need open only one connection for a package, not one for each class. Since opening the TCP/IP connection often takes more time than transmitting the data, this is a win. Jar files offer improvement in both performance and convenience.

Packages and Access Modifiers

We mentioned above that another role packages play is to provide namespaces to the programmer. That is, the package has implications for the visibility of classes and fields. This is simply the access modifiers that we met at the end of Chapter 2. In order of most accessible to least accessible, they are:

1. **`public`**, world access. Everyone can see this member.
2. **`protected`**, accessible in *this* package/directory and also in subclasses in *other* packages/directories.
3. Default, package access (access by any class in the package/directory).
4. **`private`**, accessible only in this class. No other class can see this member.

The interaction between classes and subclasses, along with things in the same package and things in other packages, can be downright confusing. Figures 9-1 through 9-3 illustrate the interaction of public, protected, default (package), and private.

What About C++ "Friend"?

The keyword "friend" in C++ is a hack to allow a piece of code to access the protected or private member declarations of another class.

Java does not permit access to private members from outside the class. If another class needs to see those members, you would do this by labeling not the friend, but the private members. Instead of making them private, give them either protected, package (no keyword), or public access.

Java has no exact equivalent of the C++ protected modifier that says, "This field can only be accessed by this class and its subclasses." The Java protected modifier has a slightly different meaning that says, "This field can be accessed only by this class and its subclasses, *plus anything else in the same package.*"

They just love asking questions about this on the Java Certification exam to try to catch all the C++ programmers.

When you start to build bigger systems you will use a package statement at the top of each source file to say to which package the class belongs. The package names must match the directory names. The package name is concatenated with the class name and stored as the full name of the class.

Access Between Two Classes in the **Same** *Package*

```
package A;

public class Foo {
   int x;

   void bar() {
     Example e = new Example();
     x = e.i;
     x = e.j;
     x = e.k;
     x = e.l;
   }
}
```

```
package A;

public class Example {
      public int i;

          int j; //package

   protected int k;

   private int l;

}
```

Notes:

1. The arrow reaching a member indicates that the access is valid.

2. The access does not change if Foo is a subclass of Example, and they remain in the same package. The reason is that the only modifier that is affected by being/not being a subclass is protected. "Protected" grants access to subclasses, or classes in the same package. Since Foo and Example are in the same package, they can access one another'sprotected members anyway, regardless of a parent/child relationship.

Figure 9–1 Access between two classes in the *same* package.

Access Between Two Unrelated Classes in Different Packages

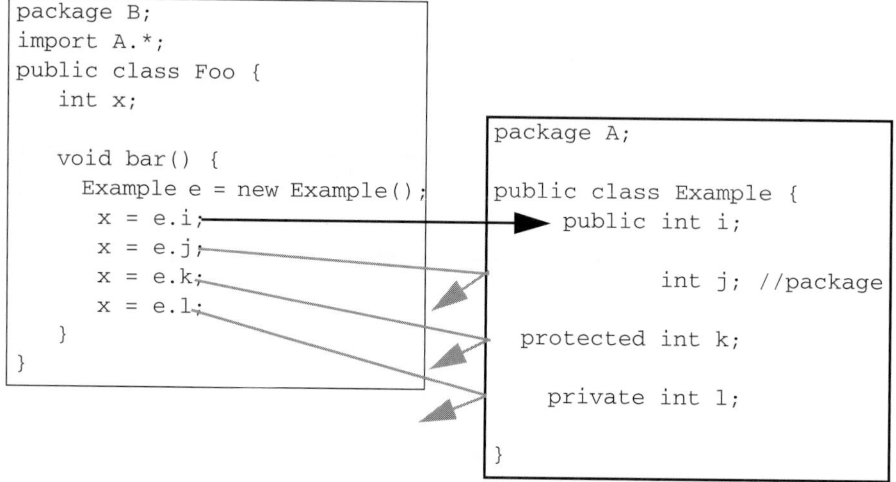

You should compile and run these examples as follows:

1. Choose a main directory for the example; call it "main."
2. Create a subdirectory main\A and put file Example.java there.
3. Create a subdirectory main\B and put file Foo.java there.
4. Stay in the main directory, and compile Example with:

   ```
   javac A\Example.java
   ```

   There should be no compiler error messages.
5. Stay in the main directory, and compile Foo with:

   ```
   javac B\Foo.java
   ```

   There will be compiler error messages pointing out the invalid accesses.

Figure 9–2 Access between two unrelated classes in *different* packages.

Access Between a Parent and Child Class in Different Packages

```
package B;
import A.Example;
public class Foo
extends A.Example {
  int x;

  void bar() {
    Example e = new Example();
     x = e.i;
     x = e.j;
     x = e.k;
     x = e.l;

     x = this.k; //OK!
  }
}
```

```
package A;

public class Example {
        public int i;

                int j; //package

     protected int k;

       private int l;

}
```

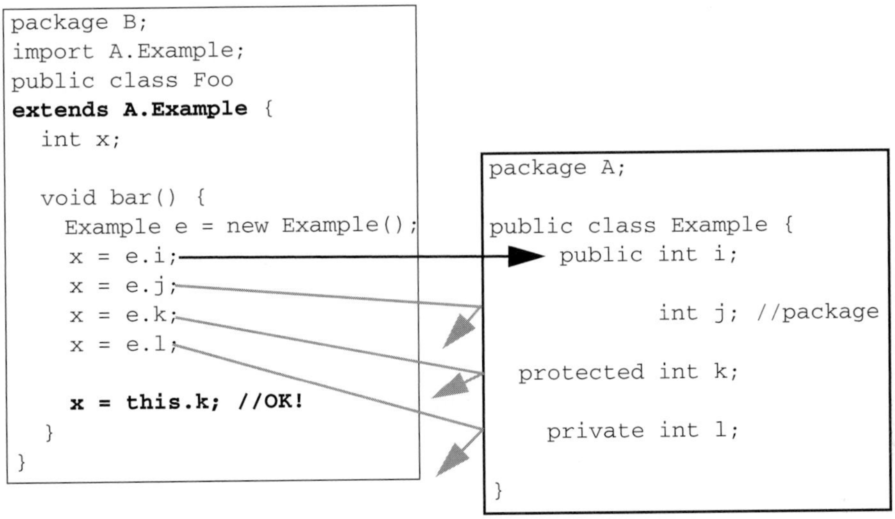

Notes
1. If subclass Foo is in the same package as Example, you have the access shown in Figure 9-1.
2. You can reference your own protected field that you *inherited* from your parent, but you cannot reference a *parent object's* protected field! See the notes under Cloneable in the previous chapter for an explanation of this.

Figure 9–3 Access between a parent and child class in *different* packages.

Here are some examples from the java.* hierarchy of each kind of access:

- `public`: most methods in the Java API are public. These are the methods you call to do your work.
- *package*: class java.awt.Button has a field that holds the button label:

  ```
  String label;
  ```

  The lack of any other access modifier gives this field package access, allowing other classes that are internal to the GUI library to read and update the label directly. There are also get and set accessor methods with public access, allowing controlled access from outside the class.

- `protected`: class java.awt.Button has a method intended for debugging:

  ```
  protected String paramString()
  ```

  It returns a string giving the current state of the button, armed or disarmed. The method is protected because only subclasses should have the right to access the internal state of the Button class.

- `private`: class java.util.Random has a field like this

  ```
  private long seed;
  ```

  That field contains a seed value that starts the generation of a sequence of random numbers. You don't want any other class being able to adjust that value in the middle of calculations, and so the field is private. Even subclasses of Random should not be able to get their hands on it. Otherwise, the guaranteed properties of Random may not hold true any more.

How Many Packages in a Directory?

The requirement that a package name match the source file directory name also means that any given directory can contain files of, at most, one named package. If you don't put your classes into a package, they are compiled by default into an anonymous package in the current directory. When you are building a big system across several directories, you will want to make sure everything goes into a named package.

Using the host filesystem to structure a Java program, and particularly to help organize the program namespace, is a very good idea. It avoids unnecessary generality and provides a clear model for understanding (see Figure 9-4).

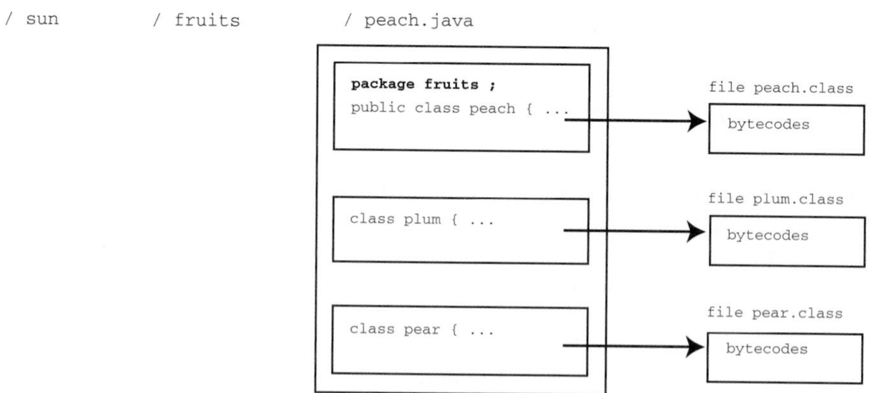

Figure 9–4 How package names relate to directory names.

Compilation Units

Since a source file is what you present to a Java compiler, the contents of a complete source file are known as a "Compilation Unit." Think of it as the unit of compilation, just as the gram is a unit of mass.

Java tries hard not to let you build a system using some components that are out-of-date. When you invoke the compiler on a source file, the compiler does not just translate that in isolation. It looks to see what classes it references, and tries to determine if they are up-to-date. If the compiler decides another class needs compiling, it adds it in, and recursively applies the same procedure to it.

In other words, Java has a "make"-like utility built into it. Say the class you are compiling makes reference to a class in another file. That utility is capable of noticing when the second .class file does not exist but the corresponding .java does, and of noticing when the .java file has been modified without a recompilation taking place. In both these cases, it will add the second .java file to the set of files it is recompiling.

Here is an example. This is the contents of file plum.java:

```
public class plum {
     grape g;
}
```

This is the contents of file grape.java:

```
public class grape { }
```

If we now compile plum.java, the compiler will look for grape.class, check that it is up-to-date with respect to its source file, and if not, it will recompile grape.java for you!

Here is the output from such a compilation:

```
javac -verbose plum.java
[parsed plum.java in 1312 ms]
[loaded /home/linden/jdk1.4/jre/lib/rt.jar(java/lang/Object.class) in 71
ms]
[checking class plum]
[parsed ./grape.java in 2 ms]
[wrote plum.class]
[checking class grape]
[wrote ./grape.class]
[done in 2718 ms]
```

As you can see, grape.java got compiled as well, creating grape.class.

What we're explaining here is how the rules work when you use the default case of source and object files in the same directory. If you use the "-d" option to javac to make your class files be written in a different directory to the source, then the rules below are modified accordingly.

A compilation unit (source file) has several rules:

1. It can start with a package statement, identifying the package (a library) to which the class will belong.

   A package statement looks like this:

   ```
   package mydir;
   ```

   When starting out, it's simplest not to use packages. Your class files will belong to a default anonymous package and be visible to other classes in the same directory.

2. Next can come zero or more import statements, each identifying a package or a class from a package that will be available in this compilation unit.

   An import statement looks like this:

   ```
   import java.io.*;
   ```

3. The rest of the compilation unit consists of class declarations and interface declarations.

4. At most, one of the classes in the file can be public. This class must have a name that corresponds to the file it is in, as shown in Figure 9-5.

   ```
   public class plum    // must be in file plum.java.
   ```

The underlying host system should allow filenames with the same form as Java classnames: unbounded length, contain "$" or "_" as well as Unicode alphabetics, and be case-sensitive. The more restrictions there are on filenames on your host system, the more restrictions there are on the classnames you can use. This will form a practical impediment to the total portability of the software. Avoid using characters in classnames that are problematic for any host file systems.

Each of the classes in a .java file will create an individual .class file to hold the generated bytecodes. If you have three classes in a source file, the compiler will create three . class files.

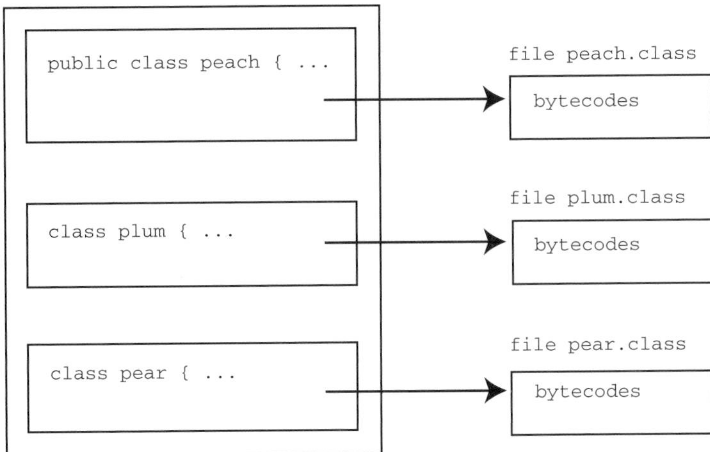

Figure 9–5 Classes and corresponding file names.

Simplicity is a major advantage of Java. Programmers can devote all their brain power to solving the problem rather than trying to learn and remember the ten thousand complicated rules and the five thousand special cases of language or system. One of Silicon Valley's top programmers (and I mean really *top* programmers) confided to me, "Thank heavens for Java. It means I won't have to learn C++."

A lot of programmers share that sense of relief at finally getting a simpler programming language with rich, well-designed libraries.

Import

Packages put classes into a group. Imports let you use a more convenient form for referring to a package or its members in your code. You never have to use the import clause. When you do use it, its effect is to allow you to use a class name directly, instead of fully qualifying it with the package name.

An import statement always has at least two components. The final component is either a class name or a "*" (meaning all classes in that package), like this:

```
import package.classname;    or    import package.*;
```

You cannot import a subpackage and expect to supply the rest of the name in your code. So you can do this:

```
import java.util.Date;                      // no import used
class Pie {                     or          class Pie {
     Date whenMade;                           java.util.Date whenMade;
```

but not

```
import java.*;
class Pie {
     util.Date whenMade // does not work!
```

There is no good reason for this restriction.

Some people say, "Just use the 'import all classes' form." Others recommend that you import only the minimum number of packages and libraries you require, to provide a clear sign of what the actual dependencies are. Whatever you import, only the code that is needed is written to the .class file. Superfluous imports are discarded. You should be able to conclude this from what you already know about how Java loads a program dynamically. There is no compilation or runtime performance difference to the two forms.

All compilations import the standard Java package `java.lang.*` without specifically naming it. That package contains interactive I/O classes, objects representing some of the built-in types, predefined exceptions, and mathematical operations, among other useful items.

Now that we've looked at how you can group classes into packages and subpackages, we will look at how you can group classes within classes, namely *nested classes* (see Figure 9-6).

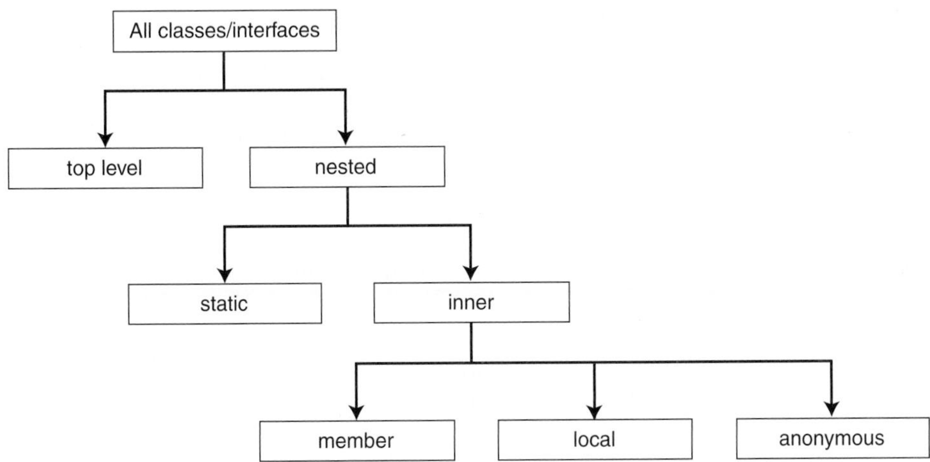

Figure 9–6 All classes are either top level or nested. All nested classes are either static or inner classes.

Nested Classes

One of the criticisms that people sometimes (rightly) make of OOP is that everything has to be a class. In particular, even if you just want a single function for some utilitarian purpose, you still have to create a class and instantiate an object of that class and invoke a method on that instance. The code for that class might have to be pages and pages away from the place in the source file where you use it. It's a bit heavyweight if your utility function is just a few lines of code. Inner classes are intended to improve the situation.

In JDK 1.0, Java had only *top-level classes* that had to be members of packages. In JDK 1.1, Java gained *nested classes*, which are classes that are defined within the body of another class. See Table 9-1 for further explanation.

Table 9–1 Nested Classes in Java

Java Term	Description	Example Code

Nested Static Class	A nested class that *is* declared "static."
	This is not an inner class, but acts like a top-level class.
		`class Top {`
		`static class MyNested {...}`
		`}`

Member Class	This is an inner class.
	It is a nested class that *is not* declared "static." It is declared as a member of a class.
		`class Top {`
		`class MyMember {...}`
		`}`

Local Class	This is an inner class.
	It is declared within a block, typically within a method.
		`void foo() {`
		`class MyLocal { ... }`
		`}`

Anonymous Class	This is an inner class.
	It is a variation on a local class.
	The class is declared and instantiated within a single expression.
		`void foo () {`
		`JFrame jf = new JFrame();`
		`jf.addKeyListener(`
		`new KeyAdapter() {`
		`public void`
		`keyPressed(KeyEvent k)`
		`{...}`
		`}`
		`);`
		`}`

Table 9-1 summarizes the different kinds of classes (and interfaces) that Java has in addition to top-level classes. The ellipsis ("...") in the example code column is not part of the syntax, but represents anything that can be declared in any class. We will look at the special features of each of these kinds of classes and how to use them in the pages ahead.

Nested classes will make a lot more sense when we have covered event-handlers (Chapter 19), so you want to just glance over Table 9-1. For now, you can note that there are ways you can nest classes inside each other like Russian dolls, and postpone an in-depth reading until you need it.

Nested Static Classes

A nested class is any class whose declaration occurs within the body of another class or interface. Up to now, we have been dealing exclusively with top-level classes. A top-level class is any class that is not nested.

A nested class may be a static member of its enclosing class or interface. We saw nested static classes at the end of Chapter 2, as one of the four "static" (once-only) things that a class can contain. We can say, loosely, that the static keyword always marks a construct (variable, method, or class) that belongs to the class as a whole, not to any one instance of the class.

We mention nested static classes again here to contrast them with inner classes. A nested static class works exactly like any top-level class, the only distinction being that its name includes the name of the class in which it is nested. For example, you might see code like this:

```
class Top {
     int i,j;

     static class SomeClass {
          int k;
          void foo() { ... }
     }

     void bar () {
          SomeClass sc = new SomeClass();
     }
}

class someOther {
     Top.SomeClass mySc = new Top.SomeClass();
}
```

Since it is static and therefore does not have a "this" pointer to an instance of the enclosing class, a nested class has no access to the instance data of objects for its enclosing class. In the code example, Top is the enclosing class.

You would typically use a nested top-level class when you have a significant data structure that strongly relates to the enclosing class, but contains enough substance to warrant a class of its own. You can see two examples of a nested static class used this way in the class `java.lang.Character` which is featured at the end of this chapter.

Another example of a nested static class occurs in java.lang.String:

```
public class String  {
        private static class CaseInsensitiveComparator
                    implements Comparator, java.io.Serializable { ... }
```

This class is private to String, and is used to do case-insensitive comparisons. The comparator interface is part of package java.util. By nesting this class inside String, we tie it strongly to String. Since it is private, it is not even part of the API. We can implement and debug the two classes largely independently. Code maintenance is simpler than if everything were written in one larger class.

Nested classes can be declared final, private, protected, or public, just like other members. Access protection protects against classes outside the enclosing class. It never affects the enclosing class or other classes inside it. They have full visibility.

Member Classes

Java supports one class being declared within another class, just as a method or data field is declared within a class. It is called an inner class, and the class is associated with each instance of the class in which it is nested. The three varieties of inner class are *member class, local class,* and *anonymous class,* each one being a refinement of the one before it.

A member class looks exactly like the nested static class—with the keyword `static` removed. That says, "The class appears in every instance." Just as any member in a class can see all the other members, the scope of the inner class is the entire parent in which it is directly nested. That is, the inner class can reference any members in its parent. The parent must declare an instance of an inner class before it can invoke the inner class methods, assign to data fields (including private ones), and so on.

```
class top {
     int i=33;

     class myNested {     // member inner class
          int k=i;
          void foo() {}
     }

     void bar () {
          myNested mn1 = new myNested(); //instantiate member class
          myNested mn2 = new myNested(); // get another one too
          mn1.k = 564 * mn2.k;
     }

}
```

A good way to think of an inner class object is that, because it is associated with an instance of its enclosing class, it really has two "this" pointers: one to itself and one to its enclosing object.

Unlike nested static classes, inner classes are not directly part of a package and are not visible outside the class in which they are nested. One of the main uses of inner classes is for GUI event handlers, and we'll see plenty of real examples of them in Chapter 19. They allow you to put the event handling class and method right next to the place where you declare the GUI objects.

The class java.awt.ScrollPane has a member class, like this:

```
public class ScrollPane extends Container implements Accessible {
   // lots of code, omitted

   class PeerFixer implements AdjustmentListener, java.io.Serializable {
       // methods, omitted
   }
}
```

The member class PeerFixer is used to keep the native window system Scrolling window aligned with the Java scrolling window object when the user makes adjustments.

Local Classes

A local class is an inner class. It is a class that is declared within a block of code, so it is not a member of the enclosing class. Typically, a local class is declared within a method.

Figure 9-7 shows a local inner class. The class is declared inside the method `init()`. This inner class is the event handler for a button. You will find the code on the CD in the directory `book\ch09\` and you can try compiling and running it.

You could easily convert this local class to a member class by moving it outside the method. The distinction between member classes and local classes is a fine one. The most important limitation is that local classes can access only `final` variables or parameters. The reason for this apparently strange restriction is given later in the chapter. It has to do with the way it is implemented.

```
//<applet code=f.class height=100 width=200> </applet>
   import java.applet.*;
   import java.awt.*;
   import java.awt.event.*;

   public class f extends Applet {

      Button apple = new Button ("press me");
      public void init() {

      class MyinnerBHClass implements java.awt.event.ActionListener {
              int i=1;
              public void actionPerformed (ActionEvent e) {
              // this gets called when button pressed . . .
              System.out.println ("button pressed" + i++ +" times");
              }
      }

           add (apple);
           apple.addActionListener (new MyinnerBHClass () );

    }

  }
```

Inner Class

The inner class can be placed wherever any declaration can go, including inside the init ( ) method.

Figure 9–7 A local inner class.

Anonymous Classes

It's possible to go one step further from a local inner class to something called an *anonymous class.* An anonymous class is a refinement of inner classes, allowing you to combine the *definition* of the class with the *instance allocation.*

Instead of just nesting the class like any other declaration, you go to the "`new SomeClass ()`" statement where an object is instantiated and put the entire class there in brackets, as shown in Figure 9-8.

```
//<applet code=f.class height=100 width=200> </applet>
import java.applet.*;
import java.awt.*;
import java.awt.event.*;

public class f extends Applet {

      Button apple = new Button("press me");

      public void init() {
              add(apple);
              apple.addActionListener(
                     new ActionListener ()
          {
                  public void actionPerformed(ActionEvent e) {
                      System.out.println ( e.paramString () +" pressed");
                  }
          } // end anon class

          ); // end method call
    }
}
```


Figure 9–8 An anonymous class.

Try compiling and running this example. Your `f.java` file will generate class files called `f.class` and `f$1.class`. The second of these represents the anonymous `ActionListener` inner class.

Be sure you are clear on what is going on here, even if the code won't make sense until we reach Chapter 19. This is saying that there is an Interface (or class—we can't tell from looking at the code here) called ActionListener. We are declaring an object of an anonymous class type that either implements the interface or extends the class. If it extends the class, then any methods we define will override the corresponding methods of the base class.

You should only use inner classes and anonymous classes where the event handler is just a few lines long. If the event handler is more than a screenful of text, it should be in a named top-level class. We have to admit, however, that the notational convenience for smaller cases is considerable. Just don't get carried away with it.

How Inner Classes Are Compiled

You might be interested to learn that inner classes are completely defined in terms of a source transformation into corresponding freestanding classes, and that this is how the Sun compiler implements them. An inner class "pips" is defined to be transformed into JDK 1.0 compatible code.

```
public class orange {
     int i=0;
     void foo() {  }

     class pips {
          int seeds=2;
          void bar() { }
     }
}
```

First, separate out the inner class and prefix the containing class to its name.

```
public class orange {
     int i=0;
     void foo() {  }
}

class orange$pips {
     int seeds=2;
     void bar() { }
}
```

Then, give the inner class a private field that keeps a reference to the object in which it appears. Also, ensure all the constructors initialize this extra field.

```
class orange$pips { // the transformed inner class
     private orange this$0;   // the saved copy of orange.this

     orange$pips(orange o) {  // constructor
          this$0 = o; // initialize the ref to enclosing obj
     }
     int seeds=2;
     void bar() { }
}
```

The manufactured field `this$0` allows the inner class to access any fields of its containing class, even private fields which could not otherwise be accessed. If you try compiling this example, you will note that the compiler produces class files with names like `orange$pips.class`.

That embedded dollar sign in the name of nested classes is part of the definition. Having a consistent explicit policy for naming inner classes allows everyone's tools (debugger, linker, and so on) to work the same way.

One restriction on local and anonymous inner classes is that they can't access variables of the method in which they are embedded. The reason is clear if you think it through. The source transformation shown above lets an inner class get back to its outer class, but the scoping rules don't give it any way to see the local variables of a method in that class. If you break this rule, as in the following code, the compiler will give an error message like the one shown:

```
public void init() {
     int i = 20; // local variable i
          ... // lines omitted
     s.addAdjustmentListener(
          new AdjustmentListener() {
               public void adjustmentValueChanged(
                              AdjustmentEvent ae) {
                    something.setSize( i, ae.getValue()  );

^  Attempt to use a non-final variable i from a different method. From
enclosing blocks, only final local variables are available.
```

The simplest fix is to make the variable final if possible. A constant (final) variable can be used because the compiler will pass a copy of it to the inner class constructor as an extra argument. Since it is final, that value won't later change to something else.

Some people feel that inner classes take more away from the simplicity and purity of model than they provide. Don't make the problem worse by using them for large classes. We now finish the chapter by featuring the class Character.

The Class Character

Here is the declaration of class `java.lang.Character`. Notice the two examples of a nested top-level class in the following listing:

```
public final class java.lang.Character
        implements java.io.Serializable, java.lang.Comparable {
    public java.lang.Character(char); // constructor

    public static final int MIN_RADIX = 2;
    public static final int MAX_RADIX = 36;
    public static final char MIN_VALUE = '˘0000';
    public static final char MAX_VALUE = '˘ffff';
    public static final java.lang.Class TYPE = Class.getPrimitiveClass("char");
    public static final byte UNASSIGNED;//about 20 other Unicode types
    public static final byte UPPERCASE_LETTER;
    public static int getType(char); // returns the Unicode type

    public char charValue();
    public int compareTo(java.lang.Character);
    public int compareTo(java.lang.Object);
    public static int digit(char, int);
    public boolean equals(java.lang.Object);
    public static char forDigit(int, int);
    public static int getNumericValue(char);
    public int hashCode();

    public static boolean isDefined(char);
    public static boolean isDigit(char);
    public static boolean isISOControl(char);
    public static boolean isIdentifierIgnorable(char);
    public static boolean isJavaIdentifierPart(char);
    public static boolean isJavaIdentifierStart(char);
    public static boolean isJavaLetter(char); // deprecated
    public static boolean isJavaLetterOrDigit(char); // deprecated
    public static boolean isLetter(char);
    public static boolean isLetterOrDigit(char);
    public static boolean isLowerCase(char);
    public static boolean isSpace(char);
    public static boolean isSpaceChar(char);
    public static boolean isTitleCase(char);
    public static boolean isUnicodeIdentifierPart(char);
    public static boolean isUnicodeIdentifierStart(char);
    public static boolean isUpperCase(char);
    public static boolean isWhitespace(char);
    public static char toLowerCase(char);
    public java.lang.String toString();
    public static char toTitleCase(char);
    public static char toUpperCase(char);

    // class Character is continued on the next page ...
    // class Character continued ...
```

```
    // Character contains two top-level nested classes

    public static class java.lang.Character.Subset {
// represents a particular subset of the Unicode characters
        protected java.lang.Character.Subset(java.lang.String);
        public final boolean equals(java.lang.Object);
        public final int hashCode();
        public final java.lang.String toString();
    } // end of Subset

    public static final class java.lang.Character.UnicodeBlock
                            extends java.lang.Character.Subset {
// Names for Unicode Blocks. Any given character is contained by
// at most one Unicode block.
          public static final UnicodeBlock BASIC_LATIN;
          public static final UnicodeBlock LATIN_1_SUPPLEMENT;
          public static final UnicodeBlock LATIN_EXTENDED_A;
          public static final UnicodeBlock LATIN_EXTENDED_B;
          public static final UnicodeBlock IPA_EXTENSIONS;
          public static final UnicodeBlock SPACING_MODIFIER_LETTERS;
          public static final UnicodeBlock COMBINING_DIACRITICAL_MARKS;
          public static final UnicodeBlock GREEK;
          public static final UnicodeBlock CYRILLIC;
          public static final UnicodeBlock ARMENIAN;
          public static final UnicodeBlock HEBREW;
          public static final UnicodeBlock ARABIC;
          public static final UnicodeBlock DEVANAGARI;
              ... there are about 65 of these in all ...
          public static final UnicodeBlock COMBINING_MARKS_FOR_SYMBOLS;
          public static final UnicodeBlock LETTERLIKE_SYMBOLS;
          public static final UnicodeBlock NUMBER_FORMS;
          public static UnicodeBlock of(char);
    } // end of UnicodeBlock class

} // end of Character class
```

Java Coding Style

This seems like a good point in the text to tell you about the recommended coding style for Java. These recommendations are actually in section 6.8, "Naming Conventions," in the Java Language Specification.

- Package names are guaranteed unique by using the Internet domain name in reverse order, as in `com.afu.applications.arby`.The `com` (or `edu`, `gov`, etc.) part used to be in uppercase, but now lowercase is the recommendation.
- Class and interface names should be descriptive nouns with the first letter of each word capitalized, as in `PolarCoords`. Interfaces are often (not always) called *`something`*`-able`, e.g., `Runnable`, or `Sortable`. There is a caution here: `java.util.Observable` is not an interface, though `java.util.Observer` is. These two are not well designed.

- Object and field names are nouns or noun phrases with the first letter lowercase and the first letter of subsequent words capitalized, as in `currentLimit`.
- Method names are verbs or verb phrases with the first letter lowercase and the first letter of subsequent words capitalized, as in `calculateCurrentLimit`.
- Constant (final) names are in caps, as in `UPPER_LIMIT`

If you keep to these simple conventions, you'll be giving useful stylistic hints to those who must maintain your code. Maybe they will do the same for you. There aren't any recommendations in the JLS on brace style, but all the Java runtime code I've ever seen uses this style:

```
compoundStatement {
     statement;
     statement;
}
```

```
void someMethod() {
          statement;
          statement;
}
```

It's a slight variant of "K&R style" (it comes from Kernighan and Ritchie who developed C), known as "The Original One True Brace Style" (TOOTBS).[1] With this style, the else part of an if-else statement and the while part of a do-while statement appear on the same line as the close brace. With most other styles, the braces are always alone on a line. When maintaining someone else's code, *always* use the style used in that code.

The One True Brace Style has methods formatted like this:

```
void someMethod()
{
          statement;
          statement;
}
```

The *Original* One True Brace Style, and Java, has them like this:

```
void someMethod() {
          statement;
          statement;
}
```

The Java way is more consistent, but makes it a little harder to find functions and review their signatures. You'll be enchanted to hear that there are many further styles and variations that different programmers champion. Stick with TOOTBS.

1. I'm not making another one of my acronym wisecracks here—this is all true.

Exercises

1. Use a browser to review the javadoc documentation for the classes java.lang.Comparable and java.util.Comparator. What are the two different interfaces used for?
2. Describe the three different kinds of inner class. Find an example of one kind of inner class in the Java runtime library source code. Describe it.
3. What is a static nested class? Give an example of where you might use one.
4. Find an example of a local inner class in the Java runtime library, and explain why it is used there.
5. What is the CLASSPATH environment variable used for?

Some Light Relief—The Domestic Obfuscated Java Code Non-Competition

Readers of my book *Expert C Programming* will be aware of the International Obfuscated C Code Competition (IOCCC). It's an annual contest run over Usenet since 1984 to find the most horrible and unreadable C programs of the year. Not horrible in that it is badly written, but in the much subtler concept of being horrible to figure out what it does and how it works.

The IOCCC accepts entries in the winter, which are judged over the spring, and the winners are announced at the summer Usenix conference. It is a great honor to be one of the dozen or so category winners at the IOCCC, as many very good programmers turn their talents to the dark side of the force for this event. If you know C pretty well, you might be interested in figuring out what this IOCCC past winner does:

```
main() {printf(&unix["\021%six\012\0"],(unix)["have"]+"fun"-0x60);}
```

Hint: It doesn't print "have fun."

Here, in the spirit of the IOCCC, are two Java programs that I wrote for April Fool's Day. You should be pretty good at reading Java code at this point, so I won't spoil your fun. This program is on the CD in directory book/ch09/h.java. It looks like one big comment, so it should compile without problems. When you run it, it greets you! But how?

```
/*   Just Java
     Peter van der Linden
     April 1, 1996.

\u0050\u0076\u0064\u004c\u0020\u0031\u0020\u0041\u0070\u0072\u0039\u0036
 \u002a\u002f\u0020\u0063\u006c\u0061\u0073\u0073\u0020\u0068\u0020\u007b
  \u0020\u0020\u0070\u0075\u0062\u006c\u0069\u0063\u0020\u0020\u0020\u0020

\u0073\u0074\u0061\u0074\u0069\u0063\u0020\u0020\u0076\u006f\u0069\u0064

\u006d\u0061\u0069\u006e\u0028\u0020\u0053\u0074\u0072\u0069\u006e\u0067

\u005b\u005d\u0061\u0029\u0020\u007b\u0053\u0079\u0073\u0074\u0065\u006d

\u002e\u006f\u0075\u0074\u002e\u0070\u0072\u0069\u006e\u0074\u006c\u006e

\u0028\u0022\u0048\u0069\u0021\u0022\u0029\u003b\u007d\u007d\u002f\u002a

 */
```

The second program is my attempt to greatly improve program portability. This one source file can be compiled by an ANSI C compiler and executed. The same code can also be compiled by a Java compiler and executed—and by a C++ compiler! Am I having a great day, or what? True source portability! Every program should do as well. This program is on the CD.

```
/*  Peter van der Linden,    "Just Java"
    April 1, 1996
    Real portability: a Java program, C program and C++ program.

    Compile and run this Java program with:  javac b.java     java b
    Compile and run this C program with:     cc    b.c          a.out
    Compile and run this C++ program with:   CC    b.c          a.out
    \u002a\u002f\u002f*/

#define String char*
#define t struct
#include <stdio.h>
t{t{int(*print)(const char*,...);}out;}
System={{printf}};/*\u002a\u002f

public class b {
                               public static void
/* The main routine                          */     main (
/* The number of arguments \u002a\u002f\u002f*/          int    argc,
/* The array of argument strings             */          String argv[] )
                       {
                             System.out.print("Hi!\n");
                       }

/*\u002a\u002f}/**/
```

How does this trilingual program work?

Please don't suggest an International Obfuscated Java Code Competition! It works for C because there are so many opportunities to abuse the preprocessor, the expression semantics, the library calls, and so on. Computer consultant Mike Morton suggested to me that these *should* be an Obfuscated Java competition, just so we could name it the "OJ trial."

Java doesn't offer half as many opportunities to unscrew the unscrutable, so let's keep things that way, OK?

Chapter 10

Doing Several Things at Once: Threads

- What Are Threads?
- Two Ways to Obtain a New Thread
- The Lifecycle of a Thread
- Thread Groups
- Four Kinds of Threads Programming
- Some Light Relief—The Motion Sensor Solution

Multithreading is not a new concept in software, but it is new to come into the limelight. People have been kicking around experimental implementations for 20 years or more, but it is only in the last few years that desktop hardware (especially desktop multiprocessors) became powerful enough to make multithreading popular.

There is a POSIX[1] document P1003.4a (ratified June 1995) that describes a threads API standard. The threads described by the POSIX model and the threads available in Java do not exactly coincide. The Java designers didn't use POSIX threads because the POSIX model was still under development when they implemented Java. Java threads are simpler, take care of their own memory management, and do not have the full generality (or overhead) of POSIX threads.

1. POSIX is an operating system standard heavily weighted to a common subset of Unix.

What Are Threads?

Everyone is familiar with time-sharing: A computer system can give the impression of doing several things simultaneously by running each process for a few milliseconds, then saving its state and switching to the next process, and so on. Threads simply extend that concept from switching between several different programs to switching between several different functions executing simultaneously within a single program, as shown in Figure 10-1. A thread isn't restricted just to one function. Any thread in a multithreaded program can call any series of methods that could be called in a single-threaded program. You might have one thread that waits for input from a GUI and another thread that processes the input when it arrives.

When the operating system switches from running one process to running another for its time slice, there is quite a costly overhead of saving the program state (virtual memory contents and map, file descriptors, interrupt settings, etc.). When the JVM switches from running one of your threads to running another of your threads, a low-overhead context switch (saving just a few registers, a stack pointer, the program counter, etc.) within the same address space is done. Threads can actually achieve the counterintuitive result of making a program run faster, even on uniprocessor hardware. This occurs when there are calculation steps that no longer have to wait for earlier output to complete, but can run while the I/O is taking place.

Threads (an abbreviation of "threads of control," meaning control flow) are the way we get several things to happen at once in a program. Why is this a good idea? In an unthreaded program (what you have been using to date in Java, and what you have always used in Fortran, Pascal, C, Basic, C++, COBOL, and so on), only one thing happens at a time. Threads allow a program to do more than one thing at a time. There are three reasons why you would do this:

- You will have interactive programs that never "go dead" on the user. You might have one thread controlling and responding to a GUI, while another thread carries out the tasks or computations requested, while a third thread does file I/O, all for the same program. This means that when one part of the program is blocked waiting on some resource, the other threads can still run and are not blocked.

- Some programs are easier to write if you split them into threads. The classic example is the server part of a client/server. When each request comes in from a client, it is very convenient if the server can spawn a new thread to process that one request. The alternative is to have one larger server program algorithmically try to keep track of the state of each individual request.

- Some programs are amenable to parallel processing. Writing them as threads allows the code to express this. Examples include some sorting and merging algorithms, some matrix operations, and many recursive algorithms.

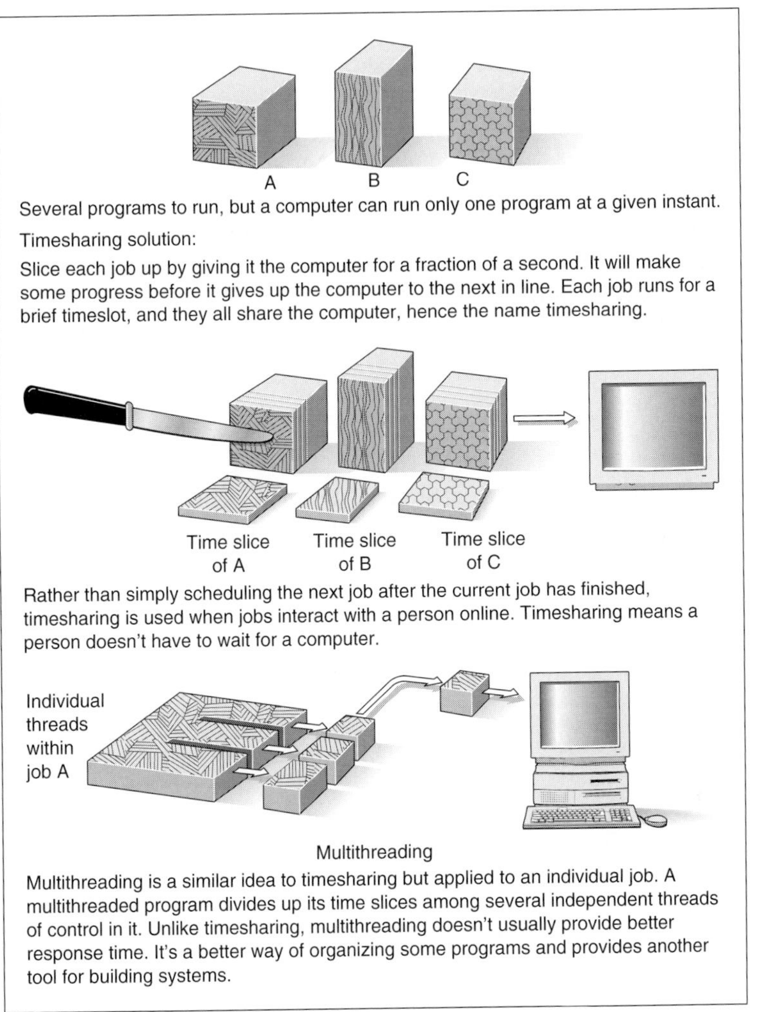

A
B
C
Several programs to run, but a computer can run only one program at a given instant.
Timesharing solution:
Slice each job up by giving it the computer for a fraction of a second. It will make some progress before it gives up the computer to the next in line. Each job runs for a brief timeslot, and they all share the computer, hence the name timesharing.
Time slice of A
Time slice of B
Time slice of C
Rather than simply scheduling the next job after the current job has finished, timesharing is used when jobs interact with a person online. Timesharing means a person doesn't have to wait for a computer.
Individual threads within job A
Multithreading
Multithreading is a similar idea to timesharing but applied to an individual job. A multithreaded program divides up its time slices among several independent threads of control in it. Unlike timesharing, multithreading doesn't usually provide better response time. It's a better way of organizing some programs and provides another tool for building systems.

Figure 10–1 An explanation of timesharing and multithreading.

Two Ways to Obtain a New Thread

There are two ways to obtain a new thread of control in Java. Either extend the Thread class, or write a class to implement the java.lang.Runnable interface and use it in the Thread constructor. The first way can be used only if your class doesn't extend any other class (as Java disallows multiple inheritance).

1. Extend class "java.lang.Thread" and override "run()":

```
class mango extends Thread {
     public void run() { ... }
}
mango m= new mango();
m.start();
```

or

2. Implement the "Runnable" interface (the class "Thread" itself is an implementation of "Runnable"), and use that class in the Thread constructor:

```
class Pineapple implements Runnable {
     public void run() { ... }
}


Pineapple pine = new Pineapple();

Thread t1 = new Thread( pine );
t1.start();
```

Your applets extend class Applet by definition, so threads in applets must always use the second way. If the thread doesn't have to run in the Applet object, it can use the first approach.

Figure 10-2 shows how a subclass of Thread is created by extending Thread.

Creating a thread by extending class Thread looks confusing, because you have to start the thread running by calling a method that you do not have, namely `P.start()` in Figure 10-2. You extended Thread with a subclass, so your class will inherit `Thread.start()` and all will be well.

Then, continuing to refer to Figure 10-2, declaring an object of class Plum gives you a new thread of control whose execution will start in the method "`run()`". That isn't an OOP mechanism, it's just a name convention you have to know. Declaring two Plums (or more likely one Plum and one object of some

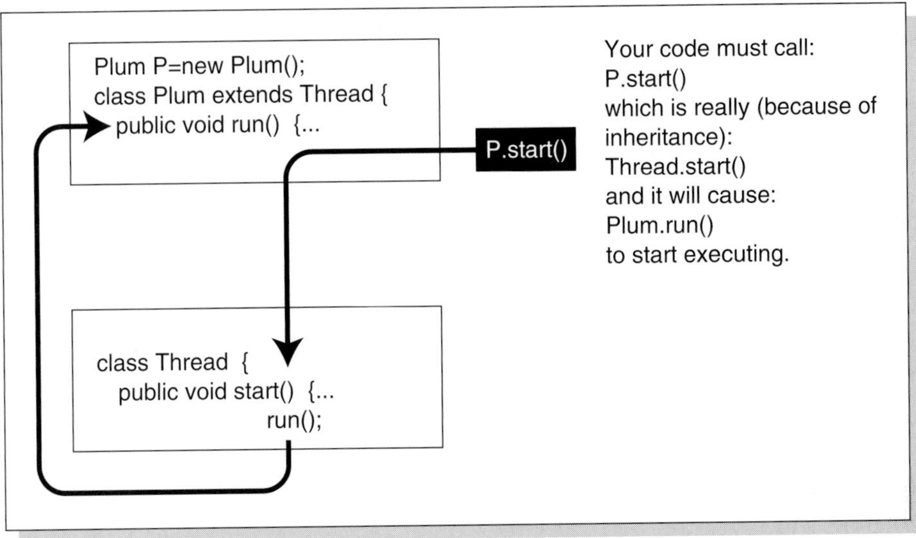

Figure 10–2 Subclass of Thread created by extending Thread.

other thread subclass) will give you two independently executing threads of control, and declaring and filling an array of Plums will give you an entire array.length of threads of control.

New threads do not start executing on creation. For some applications, programmers (or maybe the runtime system—we'll talk about this in the chapter on applets) want to create threads in advance, then explicitly start them when needed, so this has been made the way it works. Create a thread like so:

```
Plum p = new Plum();
```

You start it running by calling the "start()" method, like so:

```
p.start();
```

Or you can create and start it in one step, like this:

```
new Plum().start();
```

Execution will then begin in the "run()" method, from where you can call other methods in this and other classes as usual. Remember: "run()" is the place where it starts, and "start()" will get it running. Arrrgh! Perhaps another way to think of this is that "run()" is the equivalent of "main()" for a thread. You do not call it directly, but it is called on your behalf.

A Few Words on Runnable

The Runnable interface just looks like this:

```
public interface Runnable {
     public void run();
}
```

All it does is promise that an implementing class will have a method called run.

To get a Runnable object running, you pass it as an argument to a Thread constructor, like this:

```
class Pear implements Runnable {
     public void run() { ... }
}
   ...

Thread t1 = new Thread(new Pear());
```

You can then invoke all the Thread methods on t1, such as:

```
t1.start();
t1.stop();
```

You have to call `start()` to get the Runnable implementation executing (just as with a thread). It's common to instantiate and start in one statement like this:

```
new Thread (new Pear()).start();
```

However, you cannot have statements *within the Runnable interface implementation* of "run()" that invoke the Thread methods, like "sleep()" or "getName()" or "setPriority()." This is because there is no Thread "this" in Runnable, whereas there is in Thread. This perhaps makes an implementation of Runnable slightly less convenient than a subclass of Thread. There is a simple workaround shown after this code example.

```
// Show the two ways to obtain a new thread
//    1.  extend class java.lang.Thread and override run()
//    2.  implement the Runnable interface,

class example {
   public static void main(String[] a) {

      // alternative 1
       ExtnOfThread t1 = new ExtnOfThread();
       t1.start();

      // alternative 2
       Thread t2 = new Thread (new ImplOfRunnable());
       t2.start();
   }
}

class ExtnOfThread extends Thread {
   public void run() {
          System.out.println("Extension of Thread running");
          try {sleep(1000);}
          catch (InterruptedException ie) {return;}
   }
}

class ImplOfRunnable implements Runnable {
   public void run() {
          System.out.println("Implementation of Runnable running");

// next two lines will not compile
//           try {sleep(1000);}
//           catch (InterruptedException ie) {return;}
   }
}
```

The class Thread has many other methods shown later in the chapter. You can only call these Thread methods if you have a Thread object to invoke them on. You don't get that automatically in a class that implements Runnable.

To get a Thread object, you call the static method `Thread.currentThread()`. Its return value is simply the currently running thread. Once you have that, you can easily apply any thread methods to it, as shown in the next example.

```
class ImplOfRunnable implements Runnable {
   public void run() {
         System.out.println("Implementation of Runnable running");
         Thread t = Thread.currentThread();
         try { t.sleep(1000); }
         catch  (InterruptedException ie) { return; }
   }
}
```

A call to `currentThread()` can appear in any Java code, including your main program. Once you have that thread object, you can invoke the thread methods on it.

The official word from the Java team is that the Runnable interface should be used if the "run()" method is the only one you are planning to override. The thinking is that, to maintain the purity of the model, classes should not be subclassed unless the programmer intends to modify or enhance the fundamental behavior of the class.

As with exceptions, you can provide a string argument when you create a thread subclass. If you want to do this, you must provide a constructor to take that string and pass it back to the constructor of the base class. The string becomes the name of the object of the Thread subclass and can later be used to identify it.

```
     class Grape extends Thread {
           Grape(String s){ super(s); } // constructor

           public void run() { ... }
}
    ...
     static public void main(String s[]) {
          new Grape("merlot").start();
          new Grape("pinot").start();
          new Grape("cabernet").start();
    ...
```

You cannot pass any parameters into the "run()" method because its signature would differ from the version it is overriding in Thread. A thread can, however, get the string with which it was started, by invoking the "getName()" method. This string could encode arguments or be an index into a static array of arguments as needed.

You have already seen enough to write an elementary Java program that uses threads. So do it. Write two classes that extend Thread. In one, the run() method should print "I like tea" in a loop, while the other prints "I like coffee." Create a third class with a main() routine that instantiates and starts the other two threads. Compile and run your program.

The Lifecycle of a Thread

We have already covered how a thread is created, and how the "start()" method inherited from Thread causes execution to start in its run() method. An individual thread dies when execution falls off the end of "run()" or otherwise leaves the run method (through an exception or return statement). If an exception is thrown from the run method, the runtime system prints a message saying so, the thread terminates, but the exception does not propagate back into the code that created or started the thread. What this means is that once you start up a separate thread, it doesn't come back to interfere with the code that spawned it.

Priorities

Threads have priorities that can be set and changed. A higher priority thread executes ahead of a lower priority thread if they are both ready to run.

Java threads are preemptible, meaning that a running thread will be pushed off the processor by a higher priority thread before it is ready to give it up of its own accord. Java threads might or might not also be time-sliced, meaning that a running thread might or might not share the processor with threads of equal priority.

A Slice of Time

Not guaranteeing time-slicing may seem a somewhat surprising design decision as it violates the "Principle of Least Astonishment"—it leads to program behavior that programmers find surprising (namely threads suffer from CPU starvation). There is some precedent in that time-slicing can also be missing in a POSIX-conforming thread implementation. POSIX specifies a number of different scheduling algorithms, one of which (round robin) does do time-slicing. Another scheduling possibility allows a local implementation. In the Solaris case of POSIX threads only the local implementation is used, and this does not do any time-slicing.

Many people think that the failure to require time-slicing is a mistake that will surely be fixed in a future release.

Since a programmer cannot assume that time-slicing will take place, the careful programmer assures portability by writing threaded code that does not depend on time-slicing. The code must cope with the fact that once a thread starts running, all other threads with the same priority might become blocked. One way to cope with this would be to adjust thread priorities on the fly. That is *not* recommended because the code will cost you a fortune in software maintenance.

A better way is to yield control to other threads frequently. CPU-intensive threads should call the "`yield()`" method at regular intervals to ensure they don't hog the processor. This won't be needed if time-slicing is made a standard part of Java. Yield allows the scheduler to choose another runnable thread for execution.

Up to and including the 1.4 version of Java, priorities run from 1 (lowest) to 10 (highest). Threads start off with the same priority as their parent thread (the thread that created them), and the priority can be adjusted like this:

```
t1.setPriority ( t1.getPriority() +1 );
```

On operating systems that have priorities, most users cannot adjust their processes to a higher priority (because they may gain an unfair advantage over other users of the system).[2] There is no such inhibition for threads, because they all operate within one process. The user is competing only with himself or herself for resources.

2. Hence, the infamous message from the system operator, "I've upped my priority, now up yours."

Thread Groups

A Thread group is (big surprise!) a group of Threads. A Thread group can contain a set of Threads as well as a set of other Thread groups. It's a way of lumping several related threads together and doing certain housekeeping things to all of them, like starting them with a single method invocation.

There are methods to create a Thread group and add a Thread to it. Applets are not allowed to manipulate Threads outside the applet's own Thread group. You may want to save a reference to that group for later use:

```
public class myApplet extends Applet{
   private ThreadGroup mygroup;
   public void init(){
      mygroup=Thread.currentThread().getThreadGroup();
```

Thread groups exist because it turned out to be a useful concept in the runtime library. There was no reason not to just pass it through to application programmers, too.

How Many Threads? Sometimes programmers ask, "How many threads should I have in my program?" Ron Winacott of Sun Canada has done a lot of thread programming, and he compares this question to asking, "How many people can I take in my transport?"

The problem is that so much is left unspecified. What kind of transport is it? Is it a motorbike or a jumbo jet? Are the people children or 250-pound wrestlers like Ric Flair? How many are needed to help get to where you want to go (e.g., driver, radio operator, navigator, fuel purchaser)? In other words, what kind of program is it, what's the workload, and what hardware are you running it on?

The bottom line is this: Each thread has a default stack size of 400K in the JDK current release. It will also use about 0.5K to hold its internal state, but the stack size is the limiting factor. A 32-bit Unix process (Unix is the most capable of all the systems that Java has been ported to) effectively has a 2GB user address space, so in theory you could have around 5,000 threads. In practice, you would be limited by CPU availability, swap space, and disk bandwidth before you got up there. In one experiment, I was able to create almost 2,000 threads before my desktop system ground to a halt. That was just to create them; I'm not making any claims about them doing any useful work.

Now, back to the real question. Overall, there is no unique correct answer. How many is "reasonable"? There is only one person who can accurately answer this question, and that is the programmer writing the threaded application. The runtime library used to have a comment mentioning 26 threads as being the maximum concurrency that one might reasonably expect. That's just a rule of thumb.

The best estimate is "the number of threads needed to perform the task." If this number is too high for the address space or the CPU power, then you must redesign the tasks (and the number of threads) to use what is available. Use threads to achieve concurrency or to gain overlapping I/O. Do not try to create a new thread for every single method, class, or object in your program.

The CD contains a program that I wrote to solve crossword puzzles. The program reads in a big dictionary of words at the start of execution, and I put that file processing into a separate thread. The rest of the program can thus proceed with constructing the user interface while the I/O is taking place in the background. Everything would otherwise just stall until the data had been read. It works well and is a good example of where to use threads effectively.

Inner Class Thread

One Java expert on the HotJava team pointed out that you can write the following to create and start a background thread close to the place where it's relevant:

```
(new Thread() {
     public void run() {
          // 2 or 3 lines to do in the background
     }
} ).start();
```

That's true, but for goodness sake, don't make your programs impossible to maintain by putting more than two or three lines in an inner class. In theory, you can nest an inner class in an inner class, but don't let me catch you doing it.

Four Kinds of Threads Programming

Coordination between different threads is known as *synchronization*. Programs that use threads can be divided into the following four levels of difficulty, depending on the kind of synchronization needed between the different threads.

1. Unrelated Threads
2. Related but Unsynchronized Threads
3. Mutually-Exclusive Threads
4. Communicating Mutually-Exclusive Threads

We will deal with the first two here and the second two in the next chapter. Figure 10-3 is the key for all illustrations dealing with this topic.

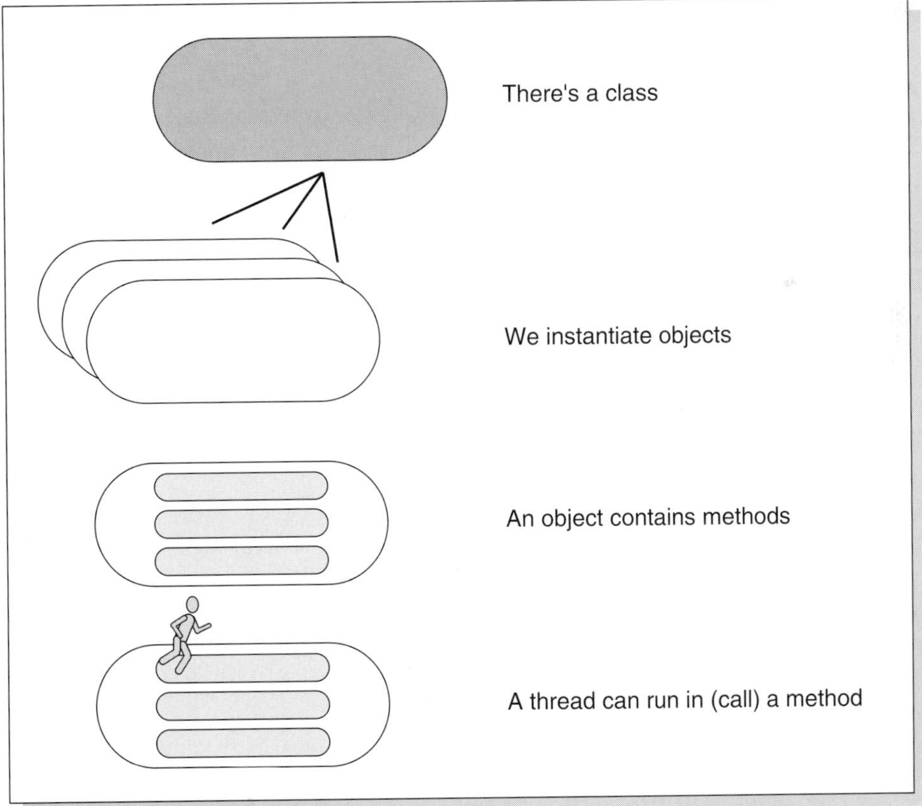
There's a class
We instantiate objects
An object contains methods
A thread can run in (call) a method

Figure 10–3 Key to threads diagrams.

Unrelated Threads

The simplest threads program involves threads of control that do different things and don't interact with each other.

A good example of unrelated threads is the answer to the programming challenge set a few pages back.

The code follows:

```
public class drinks {
   public static void main(String[] a) {
      Coffee t1 = new Coffee();
      t1.start();
      new Tea().start();  // an anonymous thread
   }
}

class Coffee extends Thread {
   public void run() {
         while(true) {
              System.out.println("I like coffee");
              yield();  // did you forget this?
         }
   }
}

class Tea extends Thread {
   public void run() {
         while(true) {
              System.out.println("I like tea");
              yield();
         }
   }
}
```

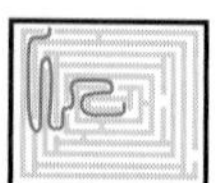

When you run this program, you will see the output:

I like coffee
I like tea
I like coffee
I like tea
I like coffee
I like tea

It is repeated over and over again until you press control-C or otherwise interrupt program execution. This type of threads programming is easy to get working, and it corresponds to Figure 10-4.

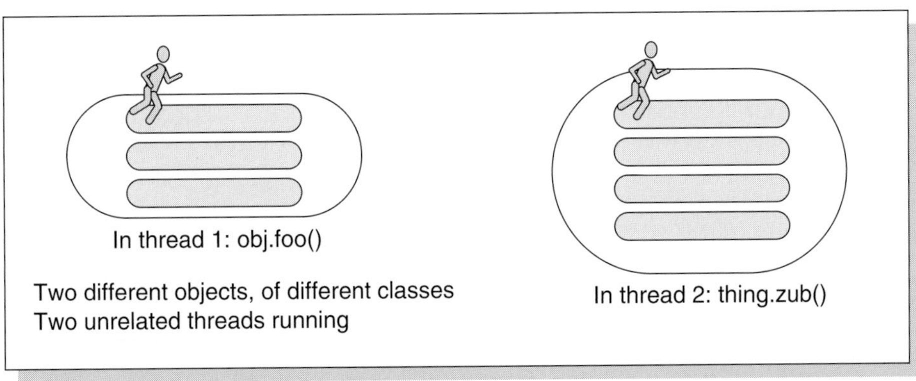

Figure 10–4 Unrelated threads.

Related but Unsynchronized Threads

This level of complexity uses threaded code to partition a problem, solving it by having multiple threads work on different pieces of the same data structure. The threads don't interact with each other. Here, threads of control do work that is sent to them, but they don't work on shared data, so they don't need to access it in a synchronized way.

An example of this would be spawning a new thread for each socket connection that comes in. A Thread that just does "work to order" like that is a good example of a demon thread—its only purpose is to serve a higher master. See Figure 10-5 for a graphical representation of how this kind of thread interacts with objects.

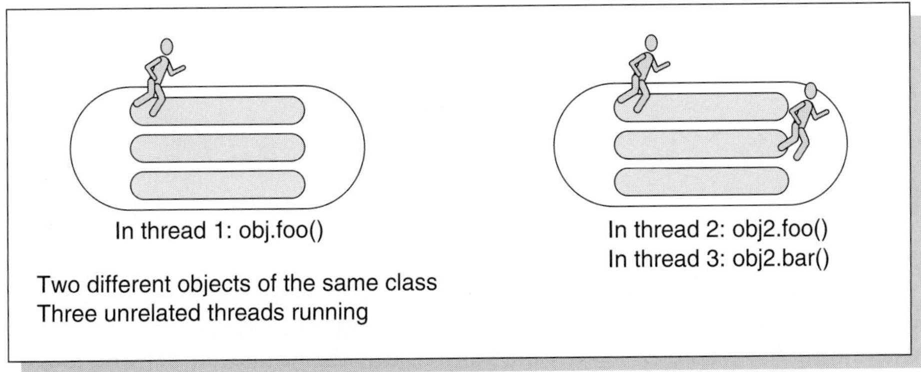

Figure 10–5 Related but unsynchronized threads.

Demon Threads

A thread can also be marked as a demon or daemon (the spelling varies) thread. Demon threads are those that exist only to carry out work on behalf of others. The following will mark a thread as a demon:

```
myThread.setDemon(true);
```

If a Java program finds that only demon threads are running, it has nothing further to do and so terminates. A thread that maintains a queue for a printer is an example of a system demon thread.

A less common but still interesting example of related but unsynchronized threads involves partitioning a data set and instantiating multiple copies of the same thread to work on different pieces of the same problem. Be careful not to duplicate work, or even worse, to let two different threads operate on the same data at once.

Here is an example program that tests whether a given number is a prime number. That involves a lot of calculations that don't affect each other so it's a good candidate for parcelling the work out among a number of threads. Tell each thread the range of numbers it is to test-divide into the possible prime. Then let them all loose in parallel.

The driver code is:

```
// demonstrates the use of threads to test a number for primality

public class testPrime {

   public static void main(String s[]) {
        long possPrime = Long.parseLong(s[0]);
        int centuries = (int)(possPrime/100) +1;

        for(int i=0;i<centuries;i++) {
             new testRange(i*100, possPrime).start();
        }

   }
}
```

This main program gets its argument, which is the value to test for primality, and then calculates how many 100s there are in the number. A new thread will be created to test for factors in every range of 100. So if the number is 2048, there are twenty 100s. Twenty one threads will be created. The first will check whether any of the numbers 2 to 99 divide into 2048. The second will check the range 100 to

199. The third will check 200 to 299, and so on, with the 21st thread checking the numbers 2000 to 2100.

The line "`new testRange(i*100, possPrime).start();`" instantiates an object of class testRange, using the constructor that takes two arguments. That object belongs to a subclass of Thread, so the ".start()" jammed on the end starts it running. This is the Java idiom of invoking a method on the object returned by a constructor or method invocation. The listing of class testRange follows:

```
class testRange extends Thread {

   static long possPrime;
   long from, to;

   // constructor
   //   record the number we are to test, and
   //   the range of factors we are to try.
   testRange(int argFrom,long argpossPrime) {
       possPrime=argpossPrime;
       if (argFrom==0) from=2; else from=argFrom;
       to=argFrom+99;
   }

   public void run() {
      for (long i=from; i<=to && i<possPrime; i++) {
         if (possPrime%i == 0) {  // i divides possPrime exactly
             System.out.println(
                    "factor "+i+" found by thread "+getName());
             break;  // get out of for loop
         }
         yield();
      }
   }

}
```

The constructor just saves a copy of the number we are to test for primality, and it saves the start of the range of potential factors for this thread instance to test. The end of the range is the start plus 99.

All the run() method does is count through this range, trying each divisor. If one divides the number exactly, then print it out and stop this thread. We have the answer that the number is not prime. There are many possible improvements to the algorithm (for instance, we need only test for factors up to the square root of the possible prime). These improvements have been omitted so as not to clutter up the code example.

A sample run of this program might look like this:

```
% java testPrime 2048
 factor 2 found by thread Thread-4
 factor 512 found by thread Thread-9
 factor 1024 found by thread Thread-14
 factor 128 found by thread Thread-5
 factor 256 found by thread Thread-6
```

So, 2048 is not a prime number and five of the 21 threads found factors. The default name for the first thread you create is Thread-4 (not Thread-1) because there are already several threads running in your program, including the garbage collector and your main program.

Deprecated Thread Methods and Interrupting I/O

When a method or class in the Java API is replaced, the old one is said to be "deprecated." It is left in the library so that old programs don't fail, but you should use the newer version.

Three methods in the thread class have been deprecated:

```
Thread.suspend();
Thread.resume();
Thread.stop();
```

Suspend and resume were always just a bad idea. They were methods in the runtime code that someone thought would be helpful to make available as part of the API. Most applications shouldn't be doing thread scheduling.

Most uses of stop should be replaced by code that just modifies some variable to tell the target thread it should stop running. The target thread should poll this synchronized variable regularly, and return from its run method when some other thread sets it.

If you wanted to stop a thread because it is hung in I/O, send it an exception instead, by calling probablyBlockedThread.interrupt(); If it is blocked in I/O that will send it one of two exceptions. We will see them in Chapter 17.

There is more information about all of these in the Java HTML documentation.

The following code shows the non-private members of the class `java.lang.Thread`. You can look at the full source at $JAVA-HOME\src\java\lang\Thread.java.

```
public class java.lang.Thread implements java.lang.Runnable {
     java.lang.InheritableThreadLocal$Entry values;
     public static final int MIN_PRIORITY;
     public static final int NORM_PRIORITY;
     public static final int MAX_PRIORITY;
// constructors
     public java.lang.Thread();
     public java.lang.Thread(java.lang.Runnable);
     public java.lang.Thread(java.lang.Runnable,java.lang.String);
     public java.lang.Thread(java.lang.String);
     public java.lang.Thread(ThreadGroup,java.lang.Runnable);
     public Thread(ThreadGroup, Runnable, String);
     public java.lang.Thread(ThreadGroup,String);

     public static int activeCount();
     public final void checkAccess();
     public static native java.lang.Thread currentThread();
     public void destroy();
     public static void dumpStack();
     public static int enumerate(java.lang.Thread[]);
     public java.lang.ClassLoader getContextClassLoader();
     public final java.lang.String getName();
     public final int getPriority();
     public final java.lang.ThreadGroup getThreadGroup();
     public void interrupt();
     public static boolean interrupted();
     public final native boolean isAlive();
     public final boolean isDaemon();
     public boolean isInterrupted();
     public final void join() throws java.lang.InterruptedException;
     public final synchronized void join(long) throws
                                         InterruptedException;
    public final synchronized void join(long, int) throws
                                    InterruptedException;
     public void run();
     public void setContextClassLoader(java.lang.ClassLoader);
     public final void setDaemon(boolean);
     public final void setName(java.lang.String);
     public final void setPriority(int);
     public static native void sleep(long) throws
                                    java.lang.InterruptedException;
public static void sleep(long, int) throws java.lang.InterruptedException;
     public java.lang.String toString();
     public static native void yield();
     public native synchronized void start();

// deprecated methods: do not use.
     public native int countStackFrames();            // deprecated
     public final void stop();                        // deprecated
     public final synchronized void stop(java.lang.Throwable);
//deprecated
     public final void suspend();                     // deprecated
     public final void resume();                      // deprecated
}
```

Some Light Relief—The Motion Sensor Solution

A while back I moved into a new office building. This was good in that it gave me an excuse to discard all the flotsam and jetsam I had not yet unpacked from the previous such move. You should move your office every three years for that reason alone. Not me, you. But my move was bad in that there were a few things about the new office that didn't suit me.

Number one on the list was the motion sensor connected to the lights. All modern U.S. office buildings have power-saving features in the lighting, heating, and ventilation. These building services are usually installed in a false floor at the top of a building, but that's another storey. Improving the energy efficiency of buildings is part of the U.S. government's Energy Star program. Energy Star is the reason that the photocopier is always off when you go to use it. There are Energy Star power management guidelines that apply to desktop computers, too. At that time, I was responsible for Sun's desktop power management software, so I know how essential it is to allow users to retain control over power-saving features. Apparently, our building designers did not appreciate this.

The light in my new office was wired up to a motion sensor, and it would automatically switch itself off if you didn't move around enough. This was something of a nuisance as there are long periods in the day when the only thing moving in my office are my fingertips flying over the keyboard. Periodically, my office would be plunged into darkness, a sharp transition which spoils my concentration. And concentration is very important to programmers.

After that unpleasant business with the glitter booby trap[3] I installed in the VP's office, it would have been futile to ask the facilities guys to replace the motion sensor with a regular switch. So I considered other alternatives. A gerbil on an exercise wheel? They're too high-maintenance, noisy, smelly, and they keep erratic hours. One of my colleagues suggested installing folks from the marketing department in my office and having them flap their arms intermittently, thus getting some productive use out of them. I did consider it, but they have some of the same disadvantages as the gerbil, and may not be so easy to train.

The final answer was one of those kitschy dippy bird things. I position it next to the sensor and dip the beak in the glass of water in the morning. It continues to rock backwards and forwards for a good long time, and everyone is happy. I plan to camouflage the dippy bird with a water lily in a dish, which motivates the housekeeping staff to keep the water level topped up. That makes it zero mainte-

3. Booby-trapped ceiling tile, hinged like a trapdoor and piled with confetti on top. The trap is triggered by a thread attached to the back of a desk drawer. It pulls out the safety latch when the drawer is opened. Treat your boss to one today.

nance from my perspective and the closest we'll get to perpetual motion, but at least the lights no longer go out on me.

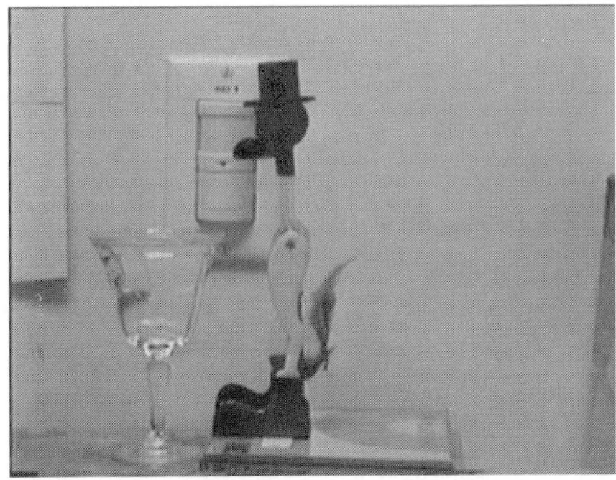

Figure 10–6
Perceptual motion: The dippy bird.

How Do Dippy Birds Work?

Dippy birds work on the same general principle as the steam engine, but with less splendor.

The bird is essentially two balanced globes connected by a small tube, with the lower globe full of a very volatile (easy to evaporate) liquid. You start it going by tipping the upper globe forward into a glass of water, and releasing it back upright.

Water evaporation from the surface of the upper globe soon cools it, cooling the air inside too, thus dropping its pressure. The lowered air pressure in the upper globe sucks some of the fluid up the tube from the lower globe. That change in delicate weight distribution causes the bird to tip forward, and dunk its beak in the water.

Now that the bird is tipped forward, the bottom of the tube comes out of the volatile liquid. A bubble of normal pressure air will travel up the tube, thus releasing the column of fluid to the bottom of the bird. That weight change in turn makes the bird bob upright again. Why does the liquid have to be volatile? So it doesn't inhibit the tiny cooling effect of water evaporation from a surface.

As the water droplets left on its beak start to evaporate, the pressure in the higher globe drops again, and the cycle repeats until the water source is used up.

You can get a dippy bird of your own (see Figure 10-6) from Edmunds Scientific at *www.edsci.com*. Don't forget about the glitter trap, either.

Chapter 11

Advanced Thread Topics

- More Thread Programming
- Piped I/O for Threads
- Garbage Collection
- Design Patterns
- Further Reading
- Exercises
- Some Light Relief—Are You Certifiable?

In this chapter we will cover the advanced thread topics. Specifically, we will explain how threads synchronize with each other when they have data that they must pass to each other. That is, they cannot solve the problem merely by staying out of each other's way and ignoring each other.

More Thread Programming

In the last chapter, we saw the easy parts of thread programming as items 1 and 2. This chapter covers items 3 and 4 from the same list and are the hard parts of thread programming. We are about to plunge into level 3: when threads need to exclude each other from running during certain times.

Mutually-Exclusive Threads

Here's where threads start to interact with each other, and that makes life a little more complicated. In particular, we use threads which need to work on the same pieces of the same data structure.

These threads need to take steps to stay out of each other's way so they don't each simultaneously modify the same piece of data, leaving an uncertain result. Staying out of each other's way is known as *mutual exclusion*. You may not believe mutual exclusion is necessary if I just say so, so we will motivate the discussion with some code, which you should type in and run.

This code simulates a steam boiler. It defines some values (the current reading of and the safe limit for a pressure gauge), and then instantiates ten copies of a thread called "pressure," storing them in an array. Each pressure object looks to see if we are within safe boiler limits, and if so, increases the pressure. The main routine concludes by waiting for each thread to finish (this is the "join()" statement) and then prints the current value of the pressure gauge. Here is the main routine:

```
public class p {
     static int pressureGauge=0;
     static final int safetyLimit = 20;

     public static void main(String[]args) {
          pressure []p1 = new pressure[10];
          for (int i=0; i<10; i++)  {
               p1[i] = new pressure();
               p1[i].start();
          }
          try{
               for (int i=0;i<10;i++)
                         p1[i].join();
          } catch(Exception e){ }

          System.out.println(
               "gauge reads "+pressureGauge+", safe limit is 20");
     }

}
```

Now let's look at the pressure thread. This code simply checks if the current pressure reading is within safety limits, and if it is, it waits briefly, then increases the pressure. Here is the thread:

```
class pressure extends Thread {

     void RaisePressure() {
          if (p.pressureGauge < p.safetyLimit-15) {
               // wait briefly to simulate some calculations
               try{sleep(100);} catch (Exception e){}
               p.pressureGauge += 15;
          }  else ; // pressure too high -- don't add to it.
     }

     public void run() {
          RaisePressure();
     }
}
```

If you haven't seen this kind of thing before, it should look pretty safe. After all, before we increase the pressure reading we always check that our addition won't push it over the safety limit. Stop reading at this point, type in the two dozen lines of code, and run them. Here's what you may see:

```
% java p
gauge reads 150, safe limit is 20
```

Although we always checked the gauge before increasing the pressure, it is over the safety limit by a huge margin! Better evacuate the area! So what is happening here?

This is a classic example of what is called a *data race* or a *race condition*. A race condition occurs when two or more threads update the same value simultaneously. What you want to happen is:

- Thread 1 reads pressure gauge
- Thread 1 updates pressure gauge
- Thread 2 reads pressure gauge
- Thread 2 updates pressure gauge

But it may happen that thread 2 starts to read before thread 1 has updated, so the accesses take place in this order:

- Thread 1 reads pressure gauge
- Thread 2 reads pressure gauge
- Thread 1 updates pressure gauge
- Thread 2 updates pressure gauge

In this case, thread 2 will read an erroneous value for the gauge, effectively missing the fact that thread 1 is in the middle of updating the value based on what it read. For this example we helped the data race to happen by introducing a tenth-of-a-second delay between reading and updating. But whenever you have different threads updating the same data, a data race can occur even in statements that follow each other consecutively. It can even occur in the middle of expression evaluation!

In this example we have highlighted what is happening and rigged the code to exaggerate the effect, but in general data races are among the hardest problems to debug. They typically do not reproduce consistently and they leave no visible clues as to how data got into an inconsistent state.

To avoid data races, follow this simple rule: Whenever two threads access the same data, they must use mutual exclusion. You can optimize slightly, by allowing multiple readers at one instant. A reader and a writer must never be accessing the same data at the same time. Two writers must never be running at the same time. As the name suggests, mutual exclusion is a protocol for making sure that if one thread is touching some particular data, another is not. The threads mutually exclude each other in time.

In Java, thread mutual exclusion is built on data Objects. Every Object in the system has its own semaphore[1] (strictly speaking, this will only be allocated if it is used), so any Object in the system can be used as the "turnstile" or "thread serializer" for threads. You use the `synchronized` keyword and explicitly or implicitly provide an Object, any Object, to synchronize on. The runtime system will take over and apply the code to ensure that, at most, one thread has locked that specific object at any given instant, as shown in Figure 11-1.

The `synchronized` keyword can be applied to a class methods, to a method, or to a block of code. In each case, the mutex (mutual exclusion) lock of some named object is acquired, then the code is executed, then the lock is released. If the lock is already held by another thread, then the thread that wants to acquire the lock is suspended until the lock is released.

The Java programmer never deals with the low-level and error-prone details of creating, acquiring, and releasing locks, but only specifies the region of code and the object that must be exclusively held in that region. You want to make your regions of synchronized code as small as possible, because mutual exclusion really chokes performance. Here are examples of each of these alternatives of synchronizing over a class, a method, or a block, with comments on how the exclusion works.

Mutual Exclusion Over an Entire Class. This is achieved by applying the keyword `synchronized` to a class method (a method with the keyword `static`). Making a class method synchronized tells the compiler, "Add this method to the

1. A semaphore is the basic operating system primitive that supports mutual exclusion. It's a hardware lock plus a couple of operations on it to maintain a queue of threads and let them through one at a time.

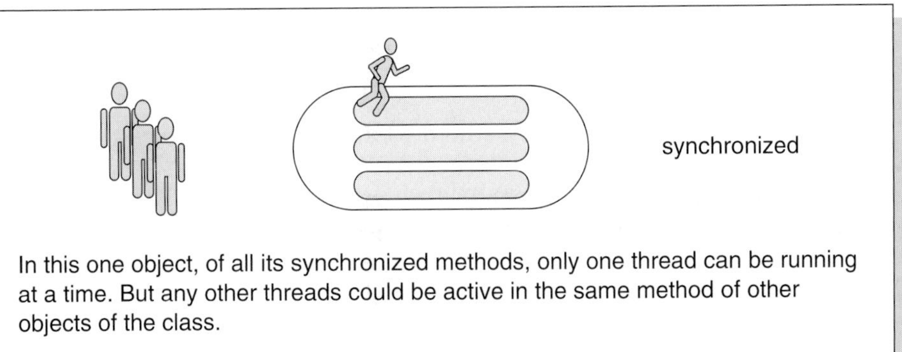

synchronized
In this one object, of all its synchronized methods, only one thread can be running at a time. But any other threads could be active in the same method of other objects of the class.

Figure 11–1 Mutually-exclusive threads.

set of class methods that must run with mutual exclusion," as shown in Figure 11-2. Only one `static synchronized` method for a particular class can be running at any given time, regardless of how many objects there are. The threads are implicitly synchronized using the class object.

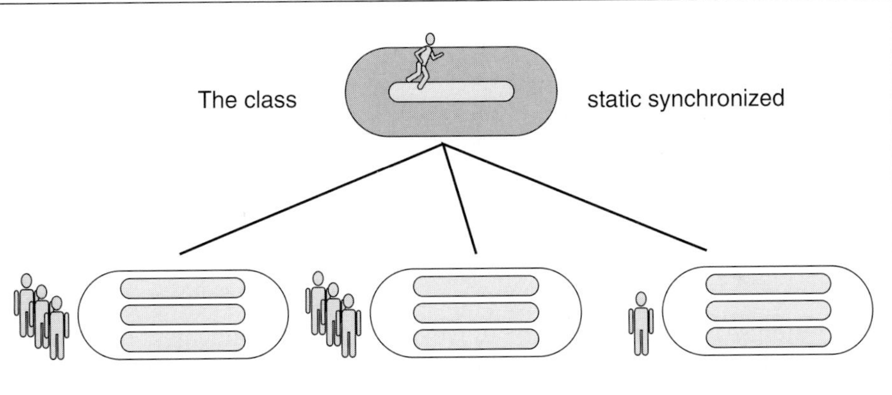

Figure 11–2 Mutual exclusion over the static methods of a class.

In the preceding pressure example, we can make RaisePressure a static synchronized method by changing its declaration to this:

```
static synchronized void RaisePressure() {
```

Since there is only one of these methods for the entire class, no matter how many thread objects are created, we have effectively serialized the code that accesses and updates the pressure gauge. Recompiling with this change and rerunning the code will give this result (and you should try it):

```
% java p
gauge reads 15, safe limit is 20
```

Mutual Exclusion Over a Block of Statements. This is achieved by attaching the keyword "`synchronized`" before a block of code. You also have to explicitly mention in parentheses the object whose lock must be acquired before the region can be entered. Reverting to our original pressure example, we could make the following change inside the method RaisePressure to achieve the necessary mutual exclusion:

```
void RaisePressure() {
    synchronized(O) {
      if (p.pressureGauge < p.safetyLimit-15) {
            try{sleep(100);} catch (Exception e){} // delay
            p.pressureGauge += 15;
      }  else ; // pressure too high -- don't add to it.
    }
}
```

We will also need to provide the object O that we are using for synchronization. This declaration will do fine:

```
static Object O = new Object();
```

We could use an existing object, but we do not have a convenient one at hand in this example. The fields "pressureGauge" and "safetyLimit" are ints, not Objects, otherwise either of those would be a suitable choice. It is always preferable to use the object that is being updated as the synchronization lock wherever possible. Recompiling with the change and rerunning the code will give the desired exclusion:

```
% java p
 gauge reads 15, safe limit is 20
```

Mutual Exclusion Over a Method . This is achieved by applying the keyword "synchronized" to an ordinary (non-static) method. Note that in this case the

object whose lock will provide the mutual exclusion is implicit. It is the "this" object on which the method is invoked.

```
synchronized void foo() { ...  }
```

This is equivalent to:

```
void foo() {
  sychronized (this) {
      ...
  }
}
```

Note that making the obvious change to our pressure example will not give the desired result!

```
// this example shows what will NOT work
synchronized void RaisePressure() {
      if (p.pressureGauge < p.safetyLimit-15) {
            try{sleep(100);} catch (Exception e){} // delay
            p.pressureGauge += 15;
      }  else ; // pressure too high -- don't add to it.
}
```

The reason is clear: The "this" object is one of the ten different threads that are created. Each thread will successfully grab its own lock, and there will be no exclusion between the different threads at all. Synchronization excludes threads working on the *same* one object; it doesn't synchronize the same method on different objects.

Be sure you are clear on this critical point: Synchronized methods are useful when you have several threads that might invoke methods simultaneously *on the same one object*. It ensures that, at most, one of all the methods designated as synchronized will be invoked *on that one object* at any given instant.

In this case we have the reverse. We have one thread for each of several different objects calling the same method simultaneously. Some system redesign is called for here.

Note that synchronized methods all exclude each other, but they do not exclude a non-synchronized method, nor a (synchronized or non-synchronized) static (class) method from running.

Communicating Mutually-Exclusive Threads

Warning: Specialized Threads Topics Ahead

Here's where things become downright complicated until you get familiar with the protocol. This is a complicated section, and you don't need to understand it unless you are tackling advanced concurrent programming. You can safely jump over this material to the end of the chapter, returning to study it in depth when you see the words wait/notify in a program.

The hardest kind of programming with threads is when the threads need to pass data back and forth. Imagine that we are in the same situation as the previous section. We have threads that process the same data, so we need to run synchronized. In our new case, however, imagine that it's not enough just to say, "Don't run while I am running." We need the threads to be able to say, "OK, I have some data ready for you," and to suspend themselves if there isn't data ready. There is a convenient parallel programming idiom known as *wait/notify* that does exactly this. Figure 11-3 shows this in four stages.

Wait/notify is a tricky language-independent protocol that has been developed by ingenious minds. Wait/notify wasn't invented by Java, and it's not Java-specific. If you've ever taken a college-level course in operating system concurrency, you have probably seen it. Otherwise, you just need to appreciate it as the accepted solution to this problem. Wait/notify is used when synchronized methods in the same class need to communicate with each other. The most common occurrence of this is a producer/consumer situation—one thread is producing data irregularly and another thread is consuming (processing) it.

Methods in the threads are only ever called from within synchronized code, which means they are only ever called when a mutex lock is held. However, simple synchronization is not enough. The consumer might grab the lock and then find that there is nothing in the buffer to consume. The producer might grab the lock and find that there isn't yet room in the buffer to put something. You could make either of these spin in a busy loop continually grabbing the lock, testing whether they can move some data, releasing the lock if not. But busy loops are never used in production code. They burn CPU cycles without any productive result.[2] The correct approach lies in the two method calls wait() and notify().

2. Well, OK, one of my colleagues pointed out a research paper that showed a brief busy loop followed by a wait/notify was superior to either used alone. Let's leave research papers out of this for now.

1.

wait()

the blocked list

blocked for monitor

the wait list

The executing thread may notice that some data isn't ready for it yet, and wait() for it.

It executes wait() and goes to the wait list.

2.

the blocked list

the wait list

It releases the monitor, allowing one thread to proceed from the blocked list. Threads on the blocked list are blocked until they can get the synchronization object, but are otherwise ready to run.

3.

the blocked list

notify()

the wait list

Eventually that thread will produce some data, then it will call notify(), waking something on the wait list, moving it to the blocked list.

4.

the blocked list

the wait list

When the thread that just called notify() leaves the method, it gives something else the chance to run.

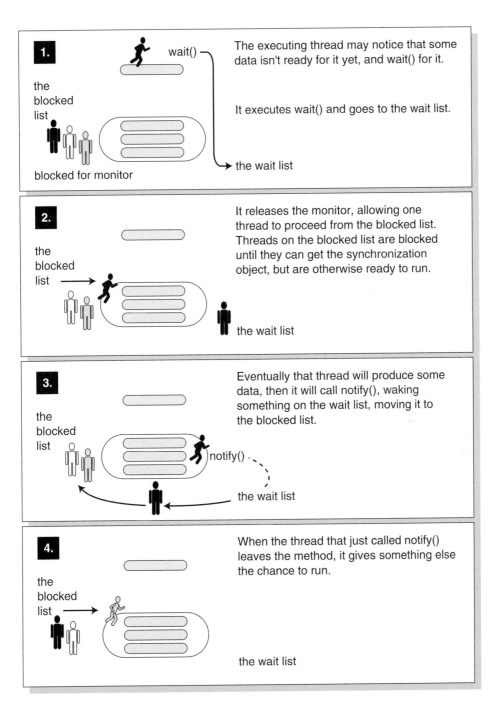

Figure 11–3 Communicating mutually-exclusive threads.

- Wait() says, "Oops, even though I have the lock I can't go any further until you have some data for me, so I will release the lock and suspend myself here. One of you notifiers carry on!"
- Notify() says, "Hey, I just produced some data, so I will release the lock and suspend myself here. One of you waiters carry on!"

  The pseudo-code for the way the producer works is:

```
// producer thread
enter synchronized code (i.e. grab mutex lock)
produce_data()
notify()
leave synchronized code (i.e. release lock)
```

  The pseudo-code for the consumer is:

```
// consumer thread
enter synchronized code
while( no_data )
     wait()
consume_the_data()
leave synchronized code
```

The consumer waits in a loop, testing whether there is yet data, because a different consumer may have grabbed the data, in which case it needs to wait again. As we have already seen, entering and leaving synchronized code is trivially achieved by applying the keyword "synchronized" to a method, so the templates become like this:

```
// producer thread
produce_data()
notify()

// consumer thread
while( no_data )
     wait()
consume_the_data()
```

Usually, the producer is storing the produced data into some kind of bounded buffer, which means the producer may fill it up and will need to wait() until there is room. The consumer will need to notify() the producer when something is removed from the buffer.

The pseudo-code is:

```
// producer thread—produces one datum
while( buffer_full )
     wait()
produce_data()
notify()

// consumer thread—consumes one datum
while( no_data )
     wait()
consume_the_data()
notify()
```

The reason we walked through this step-by-step is that it makes the following program a lot easier to understand. If you didn't follow the pseudo-code above, go back over the previous section again. This code directly implements the pseudo-code, and demonstrates the use of wait/notify in communicating mutually-exclusive threads.

There are three classes that follow. The first is a class that contains a main driver program. It simply instantiates a producer thread and a consumer thread and lets them go at it.

```
public class plum {
  public static void main(String args[]) {
     Producer p = new Producer();

     Consumer c = new Consumer(p);
     p.start();
     c.start();
  }
}
```

The second class is the Producer class. It implements the pseudo-code above and demonstrates the use of wait/notify. It has two key methods: one that produces data (actually, it just reads the number of millisecs the program has been running) and stores it into an array. The other method, called consume(), will try to return successive values from this array. The value of this setup is that produce() and consume() can be called from separate threads: they won't overrun the array; they won't get something before it has been produced; they won't step on each other; and neither ever gets in a busy wait.

```
class Producer extends Thread {
    private String [] buffer = new String [8];
    private int pi = 0;  // produce index
    private int gi = 0;  // get index

    public void run() {
       // just keep producing
       for(;;) produce();
    }

    private final long start = System.currentTimeMillis();
    private final String banana() {
        return "" + (int) (System.currentTimeMillis() - start);
    }

    synchronized void produce() {
       // while there isn't room in the buffer
       while ( pi-gi+1 > buffer.length ) {
           try {wait();} catch(Exception e) {}
       }
       buffer[pi&0x7] = banana();
       System.out.println("produced["+(pi&7)+"] " + buffer[pi&7]);
       pi++;
       notifyAll();
    }

    synchronized String consume(){
       // while there's nothing left to take from the buffer
       while (pi==gi) {
           try {wait();} catch(Exception e) {}
       }
       notifyAll();
       return buffer[ gi++&0x7 ];
    }
}
```

Produce () puts a datum in the buffer, and consume () can be called by a Consumer topull something out to give it to the consumer.

Those expressions like “`pi&0x7`” are a programming idiom to mask off the bits of the subscript we want. In this case, it is a cheap way to let the subscript be incremented without limit, but always get the value modulo 8. It requires the buffer size to be a power of two, which is a hidden dependency that makes the program fragile. If this coding idiom makes you uneasy (it does me), change the program to use subscripts that are incremented modulo the buffer size. I don’t recommend code that does modulus by and’ing, but you will see it in the work of others.

Finally, the third class is another thread that will be the consumer in this example. It starts off with a common Java idiom: another class is passed into the constructor, and all the constructor does is save a copy of this object for later use. This is the way that the consumer can call the consume() method of the producer.

```
class Consumer extends Thread {
   Producer whoIamTalkingTo;
   // java idiom for a constructor
   Consumer(Producer who) { whoIamTalkingTo = who; }

   public void run() {
      java.util.Random r = new java.util.Random();
      for(;;) {
          String result = whoIamTalkingTo.consume();
          System.out.println("consumed: "+result);
          // next line is just to make it run a bit slower.
          int randomtime = Math.abs(r.nextInt() % 250);
          try{sleep(randomtime);} catch(Exception e){}
      }
   }
}
```

The technique of passing an object into a constructor that saves the reference to it, for later communicating something back, is a common idiom known as a "callback." You should make a special note of it. Make sure you understand the previous example, to see how this is written and used.

The run method of this consumer simply repeats over and over again a get, printing what it got, followed by a sleep for a random period. The sleep is just to give the producer some work to do in adapting to an asynchronous consumer.

When you compile these three classes together and try running them, you will see output like this:

```
% java plum     produced[0] 12
    produced[1] 18
    produced[2] 20
    produced[3] 22
    produced[4] 24
    produced[5] 26
    produced[6] 29
    produced[7] 31
    consumed: 12
    produced[0] 47
    consumed: 18
    produced[1] 213
    consumed: 20
    produced[2] 217
```

And so on. Notice that the producer filled up the buffer before the consumer ran at all. Then each time the slow consumer removed something from the buffer, the producer reused that now empty slot. And always the consumer got exactly what was stored there with no data race corruption. If this explanation of wait/notify seems complicated, your impression is correct. Programming threaded code is hard in the general case and these methods supply a specialized feature that makes one aspect of it a little easier. The good news is that, for simple producer/consumer code, you don't have to bother with any of this! Two classes, PipedInputStream and PipedOutputStream, in the I/O library can be used in your code to support simple asynchronous communication between threads. We will look at this later.

Wait and notify are methods in the basic class Object, so they are shared by all objects in the system. There are several variants:

```
public final native void notify();
public final native void notifyAll();

public final void wait() throws InterruptedException;
public final void wait(long time, int nanos) throws InterruptedException;
public final native void wait(long timeout) throws InterruptedException;
```

The difference between notify() and notifyAll() is that notifyAll() wakes up all threads that are in the wait list of this object. That might be appropriate if they are all readers or they are all waiting for the same answer, or can all carry on once the data has been written. In the example there is only one other thread, so notify() or notifyAll() will have the same effect. There are three forms of wait, including two that allow a wait to timeout after the specified period of milliseconds or milliseconds and nanoseconds(!) have elapsed. Why have a separate wait list or wait set for each object, instead of just blocking waiting for the lock? Because the whole point of wait/notifying is to take the objects out of contention for systems resources until they are truly able to run! A notify notifies an arbitrary thread in the wait list. You can't rely on FIFO order.

A Thread Bug in the Collections Library

Thread programs are notoriously difficult to get right. Up to and including JDK 1.3, there was a thread bug in the library class java.util.Vector. The code involved two versions of the lastIndexOf() method, one of which invokes the other. The code is:

```
public int lastIndexOf(Object elem) {
    return lastIndexOf(elem, elementCount-1);
}
public synchronized int lastIndexOf(Object elem, int index) {
    if (elem == null) {
    for (int i = index; i >= 0; i--)
    if (elementData[i]==null)
    return i;
    // ...
}
```

Vectors do offer the feature of being properly synchronized in the presence of threads. Now, imagine if one thread calls the first method and evaluates the argument involving elementCount. What happens if another thread comes along at the same time (because that first method is not synchronized) and changes the size of the Vector? Then the elementCount given to the second method when it is called from the first method could refer to a value that is not even in the Vector any more. This code was fixed in JDK 1.4.

Interrupting a Thread

Now we have all that theory behind us, let's explain the minor point of why statements like this have an exception handler:

```
try {sleep(randomtime);} catch(Exception e){}
try {wait();} catch(Exception e) {}
```

It's quite easy. One thread can interrupt another sleeping thread by calling its `interrupt()` method. This will make the interrupted thread wake up and take the exception branch. The thread has to be able to tell the difference between waking up because it has been "notified" and waking up because it has been "interrupted." So the second case is detected by raising the exception `InterruptedException` in the thread. Statements like sleep(), join(), and wait() that are potentially prone to being interrupted in the middle need to catch this exception, or declare that their method can throw it.

The interrupt() method of Thread sets the interrupt state (a boolean flag) of a thread to "true." A thread can query and clear its own interrupt state using the Thread.interrupted() method. (You call it twice to clear it!) You can query the interrupted state of any thread using isInterrupted(). The method interrupt() will not wake a thread that is waiting to acquire a synchronization lock.

Two further points: In this text, I generally use the parent type Exception, instead of the correct subtype, InterruptedException. This is to minimize the size of the lines in the example. Always catch the narrowest type of exception you can or you may catch more than you bargained for. And do something sensible with it, like print an error message. Finally, note that the interrupt() method was not implemented in the first major release of the JDK.

Synchronized code isn't a perfect solution, because a system can still get into deadlock. Deadlock or *deadly embrace* is the situation where there is a circular dependency among several threads between resources held and resources required. In its simplest form, Thread "A" holds lock "X" and needs lock "Y," while Thread "B" holds lock "Y" and is waiting for lock "X" to become free. Result: that part of the system grinds to a halt. This can happen all too easily when one synchronized method calls another. The "volatile" keyword may also be applied to data. This informs the compiler that several threads may be accessing this simultaneously. The data therefore needs to be completely refreshed from memory (rather than a value that was read into a register three cycles ago) and completely stored back on each access.

Volatile is also intended for accessing objects like real time clocks that sit on the memory bus. It is convenient to glue them on there, because they can be read and written with the usual "load" and "store" memory access instructions, instead of requiring a dedicated I/O port. They can return the current time via a single cycle read, but the value will change unpredictably due to actions outside the program. Volatile isn't really intended for general use on arbitrary objects in applications. The keyword isn't used anywhere in the current version of the runtime library.

Generalized thread programming is a discipline in its own right and one that will become increasingly significant now that Java makes it so easy. The Solaris operating system kernel is a multithreaded implementation, and multithreaded is definitely the future trend. Consult the threads books listed at the end of this chapter for a thorough grounding in the topic of threads programming.

Piped I/O for Threads

A pipe is very easy way to move data between two threads. One thread writes into the pipe, and the other reads from it. This forms a producer/consumer buffer, ready-programmed for you! There are two stream classes that we always use together in a matched consumer/producer pair:

- `PipedInputStream`—Gets bytes from a pipe (think "hosepipe"; it's just a data structure that squirts bytes at you).
- `PipedOutputStream`—Puts bytes into a pipe (think "drainpipe"; it's just a data structure that drinks down bytes that you pour into it).

An object of one of these classes is connected to an object of the other class, providing a safe way (without data race conditions) for one thread to send a stream of data to another thread.

Pipe Pitfall

Most operating systems support a pipe feature to communicate between threads or processes. All of these have one very common pitfall! The pipe between the threads is implemented by a buffer in shared memory, and this buffer has a limited capacity.

If your input and output happens at different rates, the availability of data will become a bottleneck. The faster thread will block until the slower thread has either added something to the empty buffer (the output thread is slower), or made some room in an otherwise full buffer by reading something from the buffer (the input thread is slower).

If your system design relies on the two threads taking turns, your program may deadlock and not run satisfactorily. This pipe problem is common to all languages. You can extend these two streams to give the buffer a different size, but that may merely postpone but not solve the pipe problem.

As an example of the use of piped streams, the program below reimplements the Producer/Consumer problem, but uses piped streams instead of `wait/notify`. If you compare, you'll see that this is considerably simpler. There is no visible shared buffer—the pipe stream between the two threads encapsulates it.

The next example shows one thread sending primitive types to another. You can also send Strings using the classes `PipedWriter` and `PipedReader`. These four Piped classes are part of the java.io package. Their use should be clear from the examples here, and it is fully explained in the two chapters on I/O.

```
import java.io.*;
public class expipes {

  public static void main(String args[]) {
     Producer p = new Producer();

     Consumer c = new Consumer(p);
     c.start();
     p.start();
  }
}
```

```
///// This class writes into the pipe until it is full, at which
///// point it is blocked until the consumer takes something out.

class Producer extends Thread {
    protected PipedOutputStream po = new PipedOutputStream();
    private DataOutputStream dos = new DataOutputStream(po);

    public void run() {
       // just keep producing numbers that represent the
       // amount of millisecs program has been running.
       for(;;) produce();
    }

    private final long start = System.currentTimeMillis();
    private final long banana() {
        return (System.currentTimeMillis() - start);
    }

    void produce() {
       long t = banana();
       System.out.println("produced " + t);
       try {dos.writeLong( t );}
       catch (IOException ie) { System.out.println(ie); }
    }

}
```

```
///// This class consumes everything sent over the pipe.
///// The pipe does the synchronization.  When the pipe is full,
///// this thread's read from the pipe is blocked.
```

```
class Consumer extends Thread {
   private PipedInputStream pip;
   private DataInputStream d;

   // java constructor idiom, save argument.
   Consumer(Producer who) {
      try {
          pip = new PipedInputStream(who.po);
          d = new DataInputStream( pip );
      } catch (IOException ie) {
          System.out.println(ie);
      }
   }

    long get(){
       long i=0;
       try {   i= d.readLong();  // read from pipe.
       } catch (IOException ie) {System.out.println(ie);}
       return i;
    }

   public void run() {
      java.util.Random r = new java.util.Random();
      for(;;) {
          long result = get();
          System.out.println("consumed: "+result);
          // next lines are just to make things asynchronous
          int randomtime = r.nextInt() % 1250;
          try{sleep(randomtime);} catch(Exception e){}
      }
   }
}
```

The output of this program is a list of numbers that represent the number of milliseconds the program has been running. The numbers are passed in a buffer in a thread-safe way from the producer thread to the consumer thread. The piped streams allow for real simplification in interthread communication.

Thread Local Storage

Thread local storage is a term for data which is accessible to anything that can access the thread, but which can hold a value that is unique in each thread. A common use for thread local storage is giving a different value to each of several newly-constructed threads that lets them identify themselves (as in, "if I am thread 5,...").

Thread local storage was introduced with JDK 1.2 and allows each thread to have its own *independently initialized* copy of a variable. It's easy enough to give threads their own variables. The bit that's tricky is in getting them initialized with a value that's different in each thread in a thread-safe way. It's tough for the thread to do it because each copy of the same thread is (naturally) executing the same code. ThreadLocal objects are typically private static variables used to associate some state with a thread (e.g., a user id, session id, or transaction id).

You typically extend the ThreadLocal class and override variables as needed. Here's how you give your threads an int id. First, the subclass of ThreadLocal is:

```
class MyThreadLocal extends ThreadLocal {
     private static int id = 0;

     protected synchronized Object initialValue() {
          return new Integer(id++);
     }
}
```

If you look at the source code for java.lang.ThreadLocal, you'll see that this just overrides the initialValue() method to make it an Integer. The underlying int is incremented each time the method is called (so everyone gets a different initial value). You should override it to set up whatever value you want the thread local storage to be. Now you have the following program that creates a few threads:

```
public class t3 {
     private static MyThreadLocal tls = new MyThreadLocal();

public static void main(String args[]) {
     /* Start the threads */
     for(int i=0; i<5; i++) {
          Thread t = new Thread() {
          public void run() {
          System.out.println("I'm thread " + tls.get());
          System.out.println("That's thread " + tls.get());
          } };

          t.start();
     }
     }
}
```

The lines in italic are a thread anonymous inner class. The real point here is our `tls` thread local storage object. When you try running the program you'll see each different thread has its own value for the integer that MyThreadLocal maintains.

Here is some sample output:

```
java t3
     I'm thread 0
     That's thread 0
     I'm thread 1
     That's thread 1
     I'm thread 2
     That's thread 2
     I'm thread 3
     That's thread 3
     I'm thread 4
     That's thread 4
```

We make it print out the number twice to prove that the `tls` value is not simply being incremented in the get() routine. You can call the get() routine multiple times from the same thread and get the same value. How can that be?

What's happening behind the scenes is that the class ThreadLocal is maintaining a table of threads versus values. Any thread can get its local value from the table and any thread can set a new value for itself into the table. The access is through tls.get(0) and tls.set(). The ThreadLocal class translates that into table lookup, indexed by thread id. How does it know thread id? It's just the value returned by Thread.currentThread!

Wait—I hear you ask, "How does the initial value get set?" It doesn't! At least, it doesn't until you call ThreadLocal's get() for the first time. When you do, it calls initialValue() as its first action to put a value in the table for you to get.

You could have achieved the same effect without using ThreadLocal by extending Thread, but this doesn't scale. Suppose you have one package that wants to associate a numerical ID with a thread, and a second that wants to associate a userId. If both demand that you use a particular subclass of Thread, you're out of luck. You can't use both at the same time. This is exactly the problem that ThreadLocal solves.

Thread local storage is another thread idiom, and you won't use it in many (perhaps any) of your Java threaded programs. But when you want it, it is there. It's designed and implemented in a particularly clever way that makes it easy for the programmer to use, but also makes the maximum use of Java features to do all the work. The Thread API didn't change at all for the addition of thread local storage. It gets "two thumbs up" from this reviewer. We'll finish the chapter by reviewing memory management, a system feature that relies on threads.

Garbage Collection

Now that you've seen how a Java program can have more than one thing going on at once, we'll look at a practical place where that is used in the runtime library, namely, automatic memory reclamation. Languages with dynamic data structures (structures that can grow and shrink in size at runtime) must have some way of telling the underlying operating system when they need more memory. C does this with the malloc() library call. Java does this with the "new" operator.

Conversely, you also need some way to indicate memory that is no longer in use (e.g., threads that have terminated, objects that are no longer referenced by anything, variables that have gone out of scope, etc.) and hand it back to the runtime system for reuse. C does this with the free() library call, C++ uses delete, but Java takes a different approach to reclaiming memory.

C and C++ require explicit deallocation of memory. The programmer has to say what memory (objects) to give back to the runtime system, and when. In practice, this has turned out to be an error-prone task. It's all too easy to create a "memory leak" by not freeing memory before overwriting the last pointer to it. It can then neither be referenced nor freed, and is lost to further use for as long as the program runs.

Compiler writers for algorithmic languages have the concept of a "heap" and a "stack." Pushing and popping on the stack takes care of dynamic memory requirements related to procedure call and return. The heap is responsible for all other dynamic memory. In Java, that's a lot because object allocation is always from the heap. The only variables allocated on the stack are the local variables of a method.[3]

To avoid the problems of explicit memory management, Java takes the burden off the shoulders of the programmer and puts it on the runtime storage manager. One subsystem of the storage manager will be a "garbage collector." The automatic reclaiming of memory that is no longer in use is known as "garbage collection" in computer science. Java has a thread that runs in the background whose task is to do garbage collection. It looks at memory, and when it finds objects that are no longer referenced, it reclaims them by telling the heap that memory is available to be reallocated.

Why Do We Need Garbage Collection?

Taking away the task of memory management from the programmer gives him or her one less thing to worry about, and makes the resulting software more reliable in use. It may take a little longer to run compared with a language like C++ with

3. Java actually has multiple stacks: it starts out with one for Java code and another stack for C native methods. Additional stacks are allocated for every thread created. This aspect of Java requires a virtual memory mapping system to operate efficiently.

explicit memory management, because the garbage collector has to go out and look for reclaimable memory rather than simply being told where to find it. On the other hand, it's *much* quicker to debug and get the program running in the first place. Most people would agree that in the presence of ever-improving hardware performance, a small performance overhead is an acceptable price to pay for more reliable software.

What is the cost of making garbage collection an implicit operation of the runtime system rather than a responsibility of the programmer? It means that at unpredictable times, a potentially large amount of behind-the-scenes processing will suddenly start up when some low water mark is hit and more memory is called for. This has been a problem with past systems, but Java addresses it somewhat with threads. In a multithreaded system, the garbage collector can run in parallel with user code and has a much less intrusive effect on the system.

We should mention at this point that there is almost no direct interaction between the programmer and garbage collection. It is one of the runtime services that you can take for granted, like keeping track of return addresses, or identifying the correct handler for an exception. The discussion here is to provide a little more insight into what takes place behind the scenes.

If you want to tell the system that you are done with a data structure and it can be reclaimed, all you do is remove all your references to it, as in:

```
myBigDataStructure = null;
```

If there are other references to the data structure, it won't be garbage-collected. But as soon as nothing points to it, it is a candidate for sweeping away.

You might be wondering, "What about my threads?" What if you start a thread and then overwrite the reference to it, as was shown in the thread local storage example a few pages back. Will that be reclaimed? The answer is no. You may not have a reference to the thread, but the runtime system still does, and the thread will not be reclaimed until it falls off the end of its run method. This is also the reason your GUI programs don't terminate when they come to the end of your main() method: there are still some window system threads running.

Garbage Collection Algorithms

A number of alternative garbage collection algorithms have been proposed and tried over the years. Three popular ones are "reference counting," "mark and sweep," and "stop and copy."

Reference counting keeps a counter for each chunk of memory allocated. The counter records how many pointers directly point at the chunk or something inside it. The counter needs to be kept up to date as assignments are made. If the reference count ever drops to zero, nothing can ever access the memory and so it can immediately be returned to the pool of free storage. The big advantage of reference counting is that it imposes a steady constant overhead, rather than needing periodic bursts of the cpu. The big disadvantage of reference counting is that in its simplest incarnation it is fooled by circular references. If A points to B, and B points to A, but nothing else points to A and B they will not be freed even though they could be. It's also a little expensive in multithreaded environments because reference counts must be locked for mutual exclusion before reference counts are updated.

Adjusting Garbage Collection

Up to JDK 1.1, you were able to turn off garbage collection by starting Java with this option:

```
java -noasyncgc  ...
```

One reason for doing this might be to experiment and see how much of a difference in performance it makes, if any. The command line option is no longer supported from JDK 1.2. You should not turn off garbage collection in a program that may run for an extended period. If you do, it is almost guaranteed to fail with memory exhaustion sooner or later.

You can call the following method to request to run the garbage collector at any point you choose.

```
System.gc();
```

The current Java implementation from Sun uses the "mark and sweep" garbage collection algorithm. The marker starts at the root pointers. These are things like the stack and static (global) variables. You can imagine marking with a red pen every object that can be accessed from the roots. Then the marker recursively marks all the objects that are directly or indirectly referenced from the objects reachable from the roots. The process continues until no more red marks can be placed. The entire virtual process may need to be swapped in and looked at, which is expensive in disk traffic and time. A smart garbage collector knows it doesn't have to bring in objects that can't contain references like large graphics images and the like. Then the "sweep" phase starts, and everything without a red mark is swept back onto the free list for reuse. Memory compaction also takes place at this point. Memory compaction means jiggling down into one place all the memory that is in use, so that all the free store comes together and can be merged into one large pool. Compaction helps when you have a number of large objects to allocate.

Another garbage collection algorithm is "stop and copy." As the name suggests, it stops all other threads completely and goes into a garbage collection phase, which is simplicity itself. The heap is split into two parts: the currently active part and the new part. Each of these is known as a "semi-space." It copies all the non-garbage stuff over into the new semi-space and makes that the cur-

rently-active semi-space. The old currently-active semi-space is just discarded completely. Non-garbage is identified by tracing active pointers, just as in mark and sweep.

The advantage of "stop and copy" is that it avoids heap fragmentation, so periodic memory compaction is not needed. Stop and copy is a fast garbage collection algorithm, but it requires twice the memory area. It also can't be used in real-time systems, as it makes your computer appear to just freeze from time to time.

Finalizers

A "finalizer" is a Java term related to but not the same as a C++ destructor. When there are no further references to an object, its storage can be reclaimed by the garbage collector.

A finalizer is a method from class Object that any class may override. If a class has a finalizer method, it will be called on dead instances of that class before the memory occupied by that object is reused. You only need to use finalizers if you have some special reason for wanting to get hold of objects as they are garbage collected. You have no such reason 99.9% of the time, and you can ignore finalizers.

Interpose a finalizer by providing a body for the method finalize() in your class to override the Object version. It will look like this:

```
class Fruit {

        protected void finalize() throws Throwable {
     // do finalization ...
};
```

It must have the signature shown (protected, void, and no arguments).

The Java Language Specification says:

> The purpose of finalizers is to provide a chance to free up resources (such as file descriptors or operating system graphics contexts) that are owned by objects but cannot be accessed directly and cannot be freed automatically by the automatic storage management. Simply reclaiming an object's memory by garbage collection would not guarantee that these resources would be reclaimed.

Finalization was carried over from the Oak language and justified on the grounds that it would help provide good resource management for long-running servers.

If present, a class's finalizer is called by the garbage collector at some point after the object is first recognized as garbage and before the memory is reclaimed, such that the object is garbage at the time of the call. A finalizer can also be called explicitly. In JDK 1.0 there is no guarantee that an object will be garbage collected, and hence there is no guarantee that an object's finalizer will be called. A program may terminate normally without garbage collection taking place. So you could not rely on a finalizer method being called, and you cannot use it to carry out some essential final housekeeping (release a lock, write usage statistics, or whatever). If the method `System.runFinalizersOnExit()` is called (and accepted by the SecurityManager) before exit, Java 1.1 will guarantee that finalizers are run.

Finally (uh...), don't confuse "final" (a constant) or "finally" (a block that is always executed after a "try{}") with "finalize"—the three concepts are unrelated.

Weak References

JDK 1.2 brought in the notion of *weak references.* Weak references allow a program to have a reference to an object that does not prevent the object from being considered for reclamation by the garbage collector. This is an advanced technique that won't appear in your programs very often. I've been writing Java programs for a few years, and only needed something like this once or twice.

They also allow a program to be notified when the collector has determined that an object has become eligible for reclamation. Weak references are useful for building caches that are flushed only when memory is low, and for scheduling post-mortem cleanup actions in a more flexible way than is possible with the Java finalization mechanism.

If you studied the section on thread local storage a few pages back, you'll already have seen one place where weak references are used. The thread local storage used a table that connected threads with corresponding data items. Each thread has a regular reference to the thing that it uses for a key in the table, and to the entry. The table is a data structure that ties these together, allowing quick retrieval of an entry corresponding to a key. The thread has regular references, but the table just has weak references to all its keys/entries. A key and entry stay around as long as the strong references from the thread do. But when the thread ends, and is garbage collected, there are only now weak references to that key/entry in the table. Voila, key and entry are suddenly and automatically also candidates for garbage collection.

Design Patterns

There's an area of OOP technology that seems to be increasing in importance known as *design patterns.* A design pattern is a set of steps for doing something, like a recipe is a set of steps for cooking something.

There is a key book on the topic called *Design Patterns—Elements of Reusable Object-Oriented Software* by Erich Gamma, Richard Helm, Ralph Johnson, and John Vlissides (Addison Wesley, 1994: ISBN 0-201-63361-2). As the authors explain, design patterns describe simple, repeatable solutions to specific problems in object-oriented software design. They capture solutions that have been improved over time; hence, they aren't typically the first code that comes to mind unless you know about them. They are code idioms writ large. They are not unusual or amazing, or tied to any one language. Giving the common idioms names and describing them, helps reuse. Some common idioms/design patterns are shown in Table 11-1.

Table 11–1 Common Idioms and Design Patterns

Design Pattern	Purpose and Use
Factory Method	Supplies an interface to create any of several related objects without specifying their concrete classes. The Factory figures out the precise class that is needed and constructs one of those for you.
Adapter	Converts the interface of a class into another interface that the client can use directly. Adapter lets classes work together that couldn't otherwise. Think "hose to sprinkler interface adapter."
Observer	Defines a many-to-one dependency between objects, so that when the observed object changes state, all the Observers are notified and can act accordingly. Think "monitoring the progress of something coming in over the network."
Strategy	Defines a family of algorithms and makes them interchangeable. Strategy lets the algorithm vary independently from the clients that use it. Think "let the client specify if speed or space is the preferred optimization."

The recommended book describes a couple of dozen design patterns, and is worth further study.

Further Reading

There are several great websites giving additional information on the SCJP tests described in the Light Relief section. Marcus Green has one at *www.jchq.net/*, and Bill Brogden's is at *www.lanw.com/java/javacert/*. These sites have examples of the kinds of questions you'll face, FAQs, advice, and suggestions on books that prepare you for the tests. Heather MacKenzie has an excellent set of review points at *www.software.u-net.com/javaexam/JavaTips.htm*. The web is quite a resource.

Exercises

1. Give three examples of when threads might be used to an advantage in a program. Describe a circumstance when it would not be advantageous to use threads.
2. What are the two ways of creating a new thread in Java?
3. Take your favorite sorting algorithm and make it multithreaded. ***Hint***: A recursive partitioning algorithm like quicksort is the best candidate for this. Quicksort simply divides the array to be sorted into two pieces, then moves numbers about until all the numbers in one piece are smaller (or at least no larger) than all the numbers in the other piece. Repeat the algorithm on each of the pieces. When the pieces consist of just one element, the array is sorted.
4. What resources are consumed by each individual thread?
5. Refer back to the text giving the information about the synchronization bug in the thread library. What code would you recommend to fix that bug and why? Look at the source code for Vector in the Java runtime library for JDK1.4. Did they follow your recommendation?

Some Light Relief—Are You Certifiable?

These Light Relief sections are pieces of "infotainment" about Java and the computer industry. This one is heavy on the info, and light on the 'tainment.

Sun Microsystems, the company that originated Java, started offering a Java test and pass certificate to programmers back in 1996. People take these tests for different reasons. Some companies send their employees on Java training courses and buy them this test at the end so they will have a qualification they can take away with them. Other people (like me) took the test at the invitation of the folks at Sun running the program to help them calibrate the results. Some people just like an extra qualification to put on their resume.

The Four Java Technology Certifications

Java 2 Standard Edition:

- Sun Certified Programmer for Java 2 Platform
- Sun Certified Developer for Java 2 Platform

Java 2 Enterprise Edition:

- Sun Certified Web Component Developer for the J2EE Platform
- Sun Certified Enterprise Architect for J2EE Technology

The four certifications roughly correspond to (in order) programming in Java, designing applications in Java, servlet/JSP programming, and designing Enterprise applications in Java.

I've never seen a job advert that mentioned Java certification as a prerequisite for the position, but I think it's safe to assume that if you were a hiring manager trying to choose between two otherwise equal candidates, one of whom had demonstrated commitment and interest by obtaining a Java technology certification, you'd probably choose that applicant first. It's a rough, tough world out there in software development, and any steps you can take to boost your own career are worth considering.

As the computer industry started to invest heavily in Java, a multivendor partnership was created in 1999 to sponsor common standards for Java skills certification. The initiative included leading IT companies like BEA Systems, Hewlett-Packard, IBM, Oracle, Sybase, and, of course, Sun. You can visit their JCert website at *www.jcert.org*. These vendors have developed additional qualifications, but the starting point remains the "Sun Certified Java Programmer" test.

Sun Certified Java Programmer

After you have learned Java from this book, the way to become a "Sun Certified Java Programmer"(SCJP) is straightforward, but it takes an investment of time. The steps are:

1. **Learn the SCJP curriculum.**

   What are they testing for? The test objectives can be found online at *suned.sun.com/US/images/certification_progj2se_07_01.pdf* (just search for "certification" at java.sun.com if they move it about). Testing covers only four packages: java.lang, java.io, java.util, and java.awt (GUI). So you're wasting your time boning up on other packages, until the test is updated. There are plenty of questions on things you use only infrequently, like wait() and notify() in threads.

2. **Learn the SCJP test rubric.**

   The exam lasts two hours and has 59 questions with no optional parts. You should attempt every question, and spend no more than two minutes on each. There are three kinds of question:

   Multiple-choice questions with *a single* correct answer.

   Multiple-choice questions with *multiple* correct answers.

   Fill-in-the-blank questions requiring your typed response.

3. **Practice on the sample tests.**

   Sample tests and sample questions can be found at the websites listed in "Further Reading" and at this URL:
   suned.sun.com/US/certification/java/index.html
   Some of these resources are free, and some of them are for sale.

4. **Take the SCJP test.**

   You sign up with Sun Education Services for $150 (in the U.S.). The tests are locally administered in centers run by a company called Prometric, who also run the Novell and Microsoft certifications. You have to make an appointment for the test with Prometric, then on the due day go along to their local branch. The test is computer-administered and marked, so you get your result immediately after completing it. Sun sends you official confirmation a week or two later in the form of a nice letter that includes a Java lapel pin (if you passed).

You might think you can skip some of the preparatory steps, but that would be a big mistake. You should maintain a healthy respect for the SCJP examination. It is not easy to pass, and many inadequately-prepared candidates fail on their first try.

Some of the questions on the test have the form "if you were to run this really stupid piece of code that no one would ever write in practice, what would the output be?" People don't like those kind of questions, but you may encounter that code when you are helping maintain someone else's code.

Other questions are downright tricky, and focus on a difference between Java and other OOP languages. But they are not phrased that way! You just have to know how Java does something, and a familiarity with C++ could hurt you.

A sticking point for me was the multiple choice questions that expected multiple answers. Such a question may say something like this:

What can cause a thread to stop executing?

1) The program exits via a call to System.exit(0);

2) Another thread is given a higher priority.

3) A call to the thread's stop method.

4) A call to the halt method of the Thread class.

You may read this list and choose an answer like "1." The correct answer is "1," "2," and "3." If you miss one of these, you still got two-thirds right, but your score is zero. If you get too many questions like this, you risk failing even though you know quite a bit of the material.

The bottom line on all this is that Java certification can't hurt, and as long as you know what you're getting into you'll succeed. Plus, you get the cool lapel pin (Figure 11-4).

Figure 11–4
A pin to prove it.

Chapter 12

Practical Example Explained

- Case Study Java Program: Fritter Engine Shunt
- Exercises
- Some Light Relief—Apple Armchair Advice

This chapter contains a nontrivial Java program annotated with a running commentary. The program source appears on the CD accompanying this book, so you can look at it without the annotation, and you can try compiling and running it without typing it in.

The program generates anagrams (letter rearrangements). You give it a word or phrase, and it comes back with all the substring combinations that it can find in the dictionary. It uses a wordlist as a dictionary (there's one of those on the CD, too), and you can also specify the minimum length of words in the anagrams that it generates.

For any phrases more than a few letters long, there are a lot more anagrams than you would ever think possible.

Case Study Java Program: Fritter Engine Shunt

Here is an example of running the program on the infamous "surfing the Internet" phrase, specifying words of length four or longer. It finds dozens and dozens of them, starting like this:

```
java anagram "surfing the internet" 4
reading word list...
main dictionary has 25144 entries.
least common letter is 'f'

fritter engine shunt
fritter hung intense
surfeit Ghent intern
surfeit ninth regent
furnish greet intent
furnish egret intent
furnish tent integer
further stint engine
further singe intent
further tinge tennis
further gin sentient
freight nurse intent
freight runt intense
freight turn intense
freight run sentient
freight nun interest
freight sen nutrient
freeing Hurst intent
   ...
```

If you specify a length argument, it will try to use words with at least that many characters, but the final word it finds to complete the anagram may be shorter.

Here is the annotated program source:

```
/*
 * Usage: anagram string-to-anagram [[min-len] wordfile]
 * Java Anagram program, Peter van der Linden .
 */

import java.io.*;
```

Note: The "using an interface to hold useful constants" idiom was explained in Chapter 8.

```
interface UsefulConstants {
    public static final int MAXWORDS = 50000;
    public static final int MAXWORDLEN = 30;
    public static final int EOF = -1;
```

Note the way a reference variable can be used to provide a shorter name for another object.

We can now say "o.println()" instead of "System.out.println()".

```
    // shorter alias for I/O streams
    public static final PrintStream o = System.out;
    public static final PrintStream e = System.err;
}

class Word {
    int mask;
    byte count[]= new byte[26];
    int total;
    String aword;
```

This is an important data structure for representing one word. We keep it as a string, and we note the total number of letters in the word, the count of each letter, and a bitmask of the alphabet. A zero at bit N means the letter that comes Nth in the alphabet is in the word. A one means that letter is not in the word. This allows for some fast comparisons later on how much overlap there is between these two strings.

```
    Word(String s)  // construct an entry from a string
    {
        int ch;
        aword = s;
        mask = ~0;
        total = 0;
        s = s.toLowerCase();
        for (int i = 'a'; i <= 'z'; i++) count[i-'a'] = 0;

        for (int i = s.length()-1; i >= 0; i--) {
            ch = s.charAt(i) - 'a';
            if (ch >= 0 && ch < 26) {
                total++;
                count[ch]++;
                mask &= ~(1 << ch);
            }
        }
    }
}
```

The program has the following steps:

1. Read in a list of real words, and convert each word into a form that makes it easy to compare on the quantity and value of letters.
2. Get the word or phrase we are anagramming, and convert it into the same form.
3. Go through the list of words, using our helpful comparison, to make a second list of those which can be part of a possible anagram. Words that can be part of a possible anagram are those which only have the same letters as appear in the anagram, and do not have more of any one letter than appears in the anagram.
4. Go through our extracted list of candidate words. Choose the most difficult letter (the one that appears least often) to start with. Take words with it in, and call the anagram finder recursively to fill out the rest of the letters from the candidate dictionary.

The class "Word" above is the class that deals with one word from the word list and puts it in the special "easy to compare" form.

In several places in this program, characters are used as the basis for an index into an array. The line here, from the Word() constructor, is an example of this.

```
for (int i='a'; i <= 'z'; i++) count[i-'a'] = 0;
```

In C, this is the classic example of something that would work on a system with an ASCII codeset, but fail on an EBCDIC machine since the alphabetic letters are not contiguous in EBCDIC. Java's use of Unicode ensures that this idiom works on all systems. On, say, a Sun Ultra workstation, the following code gives the expected "i = 97":

```
int i='a';
System.out.println("i = " + i);
```

This is because that is the decimal value that represents lowercase A in both ASCII and Unicode. However, you would even get the same result on an IBM System/390 where an EBCDIC 'a' is decimal 121, as Java guarantees and requires the internal representation of a character to be 16-bit Unicode. The runtime system will do the translation from/to EBCDIC on input/output.

The class "WordList" below is the one that reads in a word list and builds up an entire dictionary of all words in the special format:

```
class WordList implements UsefulConstants {
    static Word[] Dictionary= new Word[MAXWORDS];
    static int totWords=0;

    static void ReadDict(String f)
    {
```

The half dozen lines that follow are a very common idiom for opening a file. This can throw an exception, so we either deal with it here or declare it in the method. It is usually easiest to deal with exceptions closest to the point where they are raised, if you are going to catch them at all.

Here we catch the exception, print out a diagnostic, then rethrow a Runtime-Exception to cause the program to stop with a backtrace. We could exit the program at this point, but rethrowing the exception ensures that it will be recognized that an error has occurred. We throw RuntimeException rather than our original exception because RuntimeException *does not have to be handled or declared.* Now that we have printed a diagnostic at the point of error, it is acceptable to take this shortcut:

```
FileInputStream fis;
try {fis = new FileInputStream(f);}
catch (FileNotFoundException fnfe) {
    e.println ("Cannot open file of words '" + f + "'");
    throw new RuntimeException();
}
e.println("reading dictionary...");
```

It is better not to have any arbitrary fixed size arrays in your code. This one is done for convenience. Removing the limitation is one of the programming challenges at the end of this example. The buffer holds the characters of a word as we read them in from the word list and assemble them.

```
char buffer[] = new char[MAXWORDLEN];
String s;
int r =0;
while (r!=EOF) {
    int i=0;
    try {
        // read a word in from the word file
        while ( (r=fis.read()) != EOF ) {
            if ( r == '\n' ) break;
            buffer[i++] = (char) r;
        }
    } catch (IOException ioe) {
        e.println ("Cannot read the file of words ");
        throw new RuntimeException();
    }
```

This simple looking constructor to create a new Word object actually does the complicated conversion of a string into the form convenient for further processing (the dozen or so lines of code in class Word).

```
            s=new String(buffer,0,i);
            Dictionary[totWords] = new Word(s);
            totWords++;
        }

        e.println("main dictionary has " + totWords + " entries.");
    }

}
```

An example of a class that is both a subclass and an implementation follows. It extends and implements:

```
class anagram extends WordList implements UsefulConstants {

    static Word[] Candidate = new Word[MAXWORDS];
    static int totCandidates=0,
               MinimumLength = 3;
```

We just made it implement UsefulConstants to show that a class can implement and extend at the same time. In practice, since anagram's parent class implements UsefulConstants, that namespace is already present in the subclass.

This is the main routine where execution starts:

```
public static void main(String[] argv)
{
    if ( argv.length < 1 || argv.length > 3) {
       e.println("Usage: anagram  string-to-anagram "
                 + "[min-len [word file]]");
       return;
    }
    if (argv.length >= 2)
     MinimumLength = Integer.parseInt(argv[1]);
```

If the name of a word list isn't explicitly provided as an argument, the program expects to find a file called "words.txt" in the current directory. This will simply be an ASCII file with a few hundred or thousand words, one word per line, no definitions or other information.

```
  // word filename is optional 3rd argument
    ReadDict( argv.length==3? argv[2] : "words.txt" );
    DoAnagrams(argv[0]);
}

static void DoAnagrams(String anag)
{
    Word myAnagram = new Word(anag);

    myAnagram.mask = ~myAnagram.mask;
```

The next couple of lines go through the list of words that we read in, and extract the ones that could be part of the phrase to anagram. These words are extracted into a second word list or dictionary called "Candidates." The dictionary of Candidate words is sorted.

```
getCandidates(myAnagram);

int RootIndexEnd = sortCandidates(myAnagram);
```

The call below says "Find an anagram of the string 'myAnagram,' using this working storage, you're at level 0 (first attempt), and considering candidate words zero through RootIndexEnd."

```
    FindAnagram(myAnagram, new String[50], 0,0, RootIndexEnd);

    o.println("----" + anag + "----");
}
```

This is how a word becomes a candidate:

1. The candidate must have only letters that appear in the anagram (this is the fast overlap test that a bit mask representation provides).
2. It must also be no shorter than the minimum length we specified.
3. It must not be too long.
4. It must not have more of any one letter than the anagram has.

If the word meets all these conditions, add it to the candidates dictionary.

```
static void getCandidates(Word d)
{
    for (int i = totCandidates = 0; i < totWords; i++)
        if (    (   (Dictionary[i].mask | d.mask) == (int)~0)
            && (    Dictionary[i].total >= MinimumLength    )
            && ( Dictionary[i].total + MinimumLength <= d.total
                || Dictionary[i].total == d.total)
            && ( fewerOfEachLetter(d.count,
                Dictionary[i].count) )   )

            Candidate[totCandidates++]=Dictionary[i];

    e.println(
      "Dictionary of words-that-are-substring-anagrams has "
              + totCandidates + " entries.");
//    PrintCandidate();
}



static boolean fewerOfEachLetter(byte anagCount[], byte entryCount[])
{
    for (int i = 25; i >= 0; i--)
        if (entryCount[i] > anagCount[i]) return false;
    return true;
}

static void PrintCandidate()
{
    for (int i = 0; i < totCandidates; i++)
        o.print( Candidate[i].aword + ", "
                + ((i%4 == 3)?"\n":" " ) );
    o.println("");
}
```

Here's where we start trying to assemble anagrams out of the words in the candidates dictionary.

```
static void FindAnagram(Word d,
                        String WordArray[],
                        int Level, int StartAt, int EndAt)
{
    int i, j;
    boolean enoughCommonLetters;
    Word WordToPass = new Word("");

    for (i = StartAt; i < EndAt; i++) {
      if ( (d.mask | Candidate[i].mask) == (int)~0) {
          enoughCommonLetters = true;
          for (j = 25; j >=0 && enoughCommonLetters; j--)
              if (d.count[j] < Candidate[i].count[j])
                  enoughCommonLetters = false;

          if (enoughCommonLetters) {
            WordArray[Level] = Candidate[i].aword;
            WordToPass.mask = 0;
            WordToPass.total = 0;
            for (j = 25; j >= 0; j--) {
```

What is going on with the data structures here is a little involved. The source code on the CD has more annotation and comments, if you want to fully understand it. The cast to (byte) is needed whenever a byte receives the value of an arithmetic expression. It assures the compiler that the programer realizes the expression was evaluated in at least 32 bits and the result will be truncated before storing in the byte.

```
    WordToPass.count[j] =
        (byte) (d.count[j] - Candidate[i].count[j] );
    if ( WordToPass.count[j] != 0 ) {
        WordToPass.total +=
           (int)WordToPass.count[j];
        WordToPass.mask |= 1 << j;
    }
}
if (WordToPass.total == 0) {
    /* Found a series of words! */
    for (j = 0; j <= Level; j++)
        o.print(WordArray[j] + " ");
    o.println();
} else if (WordToPass.total < MinimumLength) {
      ; /* Don't call again */
} else {
```

Finally, we see the recursive call to find anagrams for the remaining letters in the phrase.

```
                    FindAnagram(WordToPass, WordArray, Level+1,
                        i, totCandidates);
                }
            }
        }
    }
}


static int SortMask;

static int sortCandidates(Word d)
{
    int [] MasterCount=new int[26];
    int LeastCommonIndex=0, LeastCommonCount;
    int i, j;

    for (j = 25; j >= 0; j--) MasterCount[j] = 0;
    for (i = totCandidates-1; i >= 0; i--)
        for (j = 25; j >= 0; j--)
            MasterCount[j] += Candidate[i].count[j];

    LeastCommonCount = MAXWORDS * 5;
    for (j = 25; j >= 0; j--)
        if (    MasterCount[j] != 0
             && MasterCount[j] < LeastCommonCount
             && (d.mask & (1 << j) ) != 0   ) {
            LeastCommonCount = MasterCount[j];
            LeastCommonIndex = j;
        }

    SortMask = (1 << LeastCommonIndex);

    quickSort(0, totCandidates-1 );

    for (i = 0; i < totCandidates; i++)
        if ((SortMask & ~Candidate[i].mask) == 0)
            break;
```

The root breadth is the first word in the sorted candidate dictionary that doesn't contain the least common letter. Since the least common letter will be hard to match, we plan to start out by using all the words with it in as the roots of our search. The breadth part is that it represents the number of alternatives to start with.

```
    e.println("least common letter is '"
        + (char)(LeastCommonIndex+'a') + "'" );
    e.println("words with least common letter: " + i + " words");
    return i;
}
```

Sort the dictionary of Candidate words using the standard quicksort algorithm from any Algorithm book. This one was adapted from page 87 of K&R Edition 2. Again, it shows that recursion is fine in Java.[1]

```
    static void quickSort(int left, int right)
    {
        // standard quicksort from any algorithm book
        int i, last;
        if (left >= right) return;
        swap(left, (left+right)/2);
        last = left;
        for (i=left+1; i<=right; i++)   /* partition */
            if (MultiFieldCompare( Candidate[i],
                                   Candidate[left] ) == -1 )
                swap( ++last, i);

        swap(last, left);
        quickSort(left, last-1);
        quickSort(last+1,right);
    }

    static int MultiFieldCompare(Word s, Word t)
    {
        if ( (s.mask & SortMask) != (t.mask & SortMask) )
            return ( (s.mask & SortMask)>(t.mask & SortMask)? 1:-1);

        if ( t.total != s.total )
            return (t.total - s.total);

        return (s.aword).compareTo(t.aword);
    }

    static void swap(int d1, int d2) {
        Word tmp = Candidate[d1];
        Candidate[d1] = Candidate[d2];
        Candidate[d2] = tmp;
    }
}
```

1. This anagram program was based on a C program that my colleague Brian Scearce wrote in his copious free time.

When I wrote the above Java code, my first version had a bug in it. In the following code, I had omitted to subtract 1 from the String length (also I did not check that the character was alphabetic before putting it in the data structure). Instead of looking like this:

GOOD CODE

```
for (int i = s.length()-1; i >= 0; i--) {
          ...s.charAt(i)...
```

I had it like this:

BAD CODE

```
for (int i = s.length(); i >= 0; i--) {
          ...s.charAt(i)...
```

In a C program, this would cause no anagrams to be found, but the program would run to completion. There would not be any indication that an error had occurred, or where. A naive tester would report that the program worked fine. Works fine? Ship it!

In my Java program, this was the output from my first test run:

```
java.lang.StringIndexOutOfBoundsException: String index out of range: 4
        at java.lang.String.charAt(String.java)
        at Word.<init>(anagram.java:35)
        at WordList.ReadDict(anagram.java:77)
        at anagram.main(anagram.java:104)
```

It told me an error had occurred, what the error was, why it was an error, where it happened, and how execution reached that point. Some other languages have this kind of comprehensive runtime checking (Ada comes to mind), but Java is the only one that is also both object-oriented and has a C flavor. At that moment, as they say, I became enlightened.

Exercises

1. (Complexity: Easy) After it has completed one anagram, make the program go back and prompt for more. Don't make it reload the word list!

2. (Complexity: Easy) Modify the program so it doesn't use arrays of fixed size, but uses the Vector class from package "java.util" to grow arrays as needed at runtime. Don't forget to add this line to the start of the program:

```
import java.util.Vector;
```

3. (Complexity: Medium) Create a version of the program that has the word list compiled into it. You'll probably want to first write a java program that reads a word list and prints out the array initialization literals for you to edit into your source program. What difference does this make to program start-up time? Runtime? Size?

4. (Complexity: Medium) Create a version of the program that uses several threads to sort the candidate words. Use a heuristic like "if the partition is larger than 4 elements, spawn a thread to sort it using quicksort, otherwise sort it directly by decision tree comparison." Decision tree comparison means this:

```
if ( a>b )
     if ( a>c )
          if (a>d)   // a is largest
          else       // d is largest, then a
               if (b>c) // order is d,a,b,c
               else     // order is d,a,c,b
// and so on
```

5. (Complexity: Easy) Identify a part of the anagram program to reimplement as an inner class, and do that.

Some Light Relief—Apple Armchair Advice

Apple Computer is the darling of the "Why the heck don't they...?" armchair strategy crowd. Since the Mac introduction back in January 1984, people have second-guessed Apple executives, critiqued their initiatives, and suggested different plans to them. To be honest, Apple has invited this behavior over the years with more than its fair share of executives who didn't seem quite up to the task. Apple's no/yes/no policy towards clones is thought to have cost Motorola about $1B. Steve Jobs cancelled the Newton message pad in February 1998, probably because he anticipated that Windows CE would corner the market. It didn't. Apple was left without a PDA just as the PDA market took off. Apple completely missed the significance of mp3 music files, and for a long time had no cdrw product. It has now put that right, and is one of the first to offer a DVD burner. There used to be a joke in Silicon Valley asking, "what's the difference between a scout troop and Apple?" The answer was that the scout troop has adult supervision.

People are always asking why doesn't Apple build Intel x86-based systems, or port their OS to the PC? It's technically feasible—Mac OS X is just a variant of Unix with a cool GUI, and many Unix ports run on x86 hardware. Linux is the best known of these. Apple computers cost 10-20% more than similarly equipped x86 systems. By developing PC-based products, Apple would get access to cheap hardware, or to new customers using their existing PC hardware.

Here are the things Apple would lose by porting to the PC: compatibility with their entire installed base of 25M users; the guarantee that all device drivers work with all hardware; the extra costs of two development environments for themselves and ISVs; most importantly, by making itself a rival on Microsoft's x86 home turf, Apple would lose the cooperation of Microsoft. MS Office for Mac would be dropped or sidelined.

To stand any chance of success, Apple would have to cut deals with PC manufacturers to preload Mac OS. These OEMs will treat Mac OS the same way they treat Linux, and bump up the price of Mac OS PCs since they are not the dominant product. Apple would thus have to manufacture its own hardware in order to benefit from the "cheaper hardware."

That would leave Apple with, uh, 10-20% higher prices than comparable PCs, a raft of new problems, and still facing all the problems they have now: insufficient marketing and sales resources, lack of a visible Windows coexistence strategy, and consumer fear of stepping outside the mainstream.

In 1997 Microsoft invested $150M in Apple to boost user confidence and to keep them in business, to get Internet Explorer installed as the Mac's default browser, and to order Apple not to enthusiastically promote Java. Microsoft would turn on Apple the minute Apple stepped out of its "nature reserve" onto Windows turf. It would have been embarrassing for Microsoft if their market share of desktop operating systems went from 95% to 100% right before their "we deny everything" monopoly trial.

Since an x86-based product is out, what can Apple do to grow its 5%-and-shrinking share of the shrinking desktop market? A big part of the answer is getting the word out. How many people realize that every model of every Apple computer sold today comes with video-editing software, with mp3 music software, with first class digital photo support, and with Java bundled?

For anyone used to fussing with buggy and complicated CD-burning software and PCI cards on Windows, the seamless Mac system is a dream come true. Every Mac laptop, iMac, desktop, and server has an easy-to-use video playing and editing application (Figure 12-1). High-end Mac models come with a DVD burner, so you can create videos to mail to your family and friends. These Apple applications are good to look at, and you can learn them by using them. You recoup that 15% price premium the first time you don't waste hours trying to coax something incompatible to work.

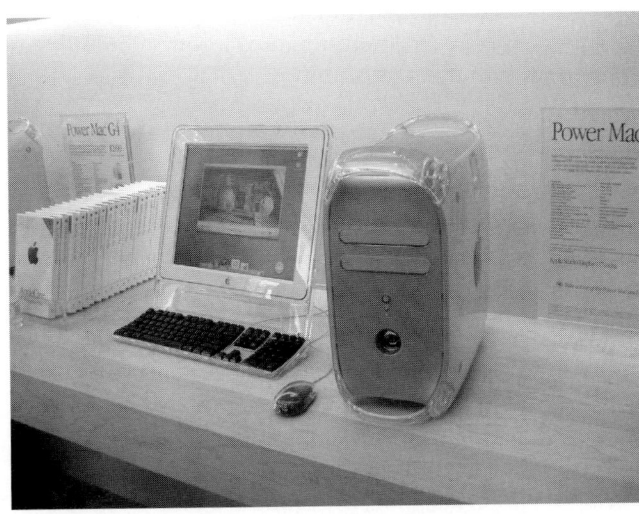

Figure 12–1 All Apple computers now come with video editing software.

Figure 12–2 Lining up for Apples.

To help get the word out about its products, Apple is opening 35 stores in premium locations. Figure 12-2 shows people lining up outside the Palo Alto store on opening day October 6, 2001. This is Apple's first venture into storefront retailing, and no one can yet predict whether it will meet its ambitious goals.

Apple is already making a substantial though silent investment in Java, and has included several Java-based applications in Mac OS X. Java enhances Apple's products in two ways: all Java applications run on the Mac, boosting the pool of available software, and Java's portability makes the Mac acceptable to developers for any platform who want to enjoy the Mac's superior GUI environment.

Another part of gaining market share is to show potential customers that Apple is a safe choice in a Windows-dominated world. Apple already has mindshare among Macolytes. It needs to reach beyond them to risk-averse Windows users. The company should create simple documents and Java tools for transferring data files to and from Windows. Apple should also bundle or subsidize one of the Windows-on-Mac emulators. If the Connectix Virtual PC for MacOS product was a "check this box" $50 option at order time, everyone would buy it. Let customers see how a Mac is a safe choice, with an easy way to run legacy Windows programs.

Apple should put some buzz back in their name by engaging and empowering the open source community. Become super-compatible with Linux. Establish a "hacker support" organization just like the ISV support organization. Send Linus Torvalds flowers and a G4 Power Mac—whatever it takes to get the support of the

open source opinion leaders. Then encourage businesses to run reliable Linux servers with productive/preconfigured Mac clients. The next thing Apple has to do is get out from under Microsoft, and their ongoing threat to drop Office for the Mac if Apple displeases them in any way.

Apple should port StarOffice to the Mac, and bundle it free with every system. After all, Sun has made the StarOffice sources available under its Community Source License initiative, and StarOffice for the Mac would serve Sun's goals too. I'm estimating the biggest part of the port could be done by 5 or 10 good Mac programmers within a year. So it would only cost $2-3M. A reimplementation of key components in Java along the way would be awesome too.

You will never see this because, undoubtedly, Apple's 1997 agreement with Microsoft required them not to compete in certain areas. This is one of the ways an unregulated monopoly harms consumers: certain products never appear on the market.

Part

2

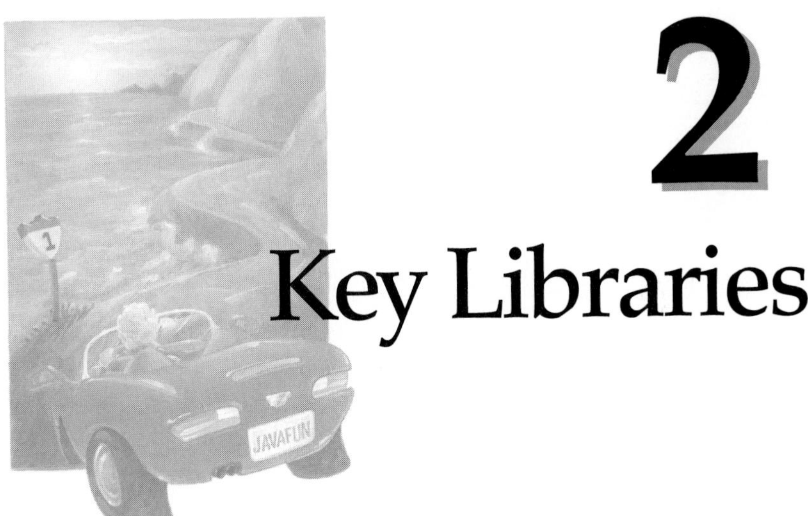

Key Libraries

Chapter 13

Simple Input Output

- Design Philosophy
- File and FileDescriptor Classes
- Output
- Outputting Double-byte Characters
- Other Writer Wrappers
- Outputting ASCII Characters and Binary Values
- Input
- Reader Wrappers
- Inputting ASCII Characters and Binary Values
- Input Stream Wrappers
- Further Reading
- Exercises
- Some Light Relief—The Illegal Prime Number!

SCSI-wuzzy was a bus.
SCSI-wuzzy caused no fuss.
SCSI-wuzzy wasn't very SCSI, was he?

Designing input/output (henceforth "I/O") libraries is a lot harder than it might appear. There have been some spectacular blunders in the past. One language, Algol 60, gave up on I/O altogether, leaving it out of the language specification and making it an implementation defined detail! Pascal has the deficiency that you can't test for end-of-file until you have read from the file, distorting all while loops that control input. The C library `gets()` call to read a string from a stream is probably the biggest single security hole in Unix history. It was responsible for the November 1988 Morris Worm that permeated all the then 50,000 (!) hosts on the Internet.[1] Classic Fortran I/O is so ugly because John Backus's team

1. See The Cornell Commission on Morris and the worm; T. Eisenberg, D. Gries, J. Hartmanis, D. Holcomb, M. S. Lynn and T. Santoro; Commun. ACM vol. 32, 6 (June 1989), pp. 706–709).

decided to reuse an existing IBM 704 assembler library instead of designing their own language support.

So what are the problems with Java I/O? There are several. First, it is a very large library, with 75 classes and interfaces. Size alone doesn't make an interface poor, but there are too many low-value classes (like SequenceInputStream) and not enough high-value classes (like proper support for interactive I/O). Sun got the API wrong the first time and had to add many more classes in the JDK 1.1 release to properly cope with internationalization. Interactive I/O (text input-output to keyboard/screen) is particularly poorly supported. The Java I/O package is not intuitive to use, and there are a number of peculiar design choices often reflecting the use of the underlying standard C I/O library. That's the same mistake the Fortran team committed 40 years earlier. Finally, because this library makes heavy use of wrapper classes, you need to use two or three classes to do simple file I/O.

Enough of the criticism. Let's describe the philosophy of the java.io package. Obviously, its purpose is to conduct I/O on data and on objects. You will use this package to write your data into disk files, into sockets, into URLs, and to the system console, and to read it back again. There is some support for formatting character data, and for processing zip and jar files. Several other packages are involved in this, and the key ones are listed in Table 13-1. The point of presenting this table is to indicate the vast range of Java I/O features.

In this chapter we will cover the I/O basics. By the end of this chapter and the next, you will be versed in the use of the first five packages listed in Table 13-1. The "further reading" section at the end of each chapter will point out resources for more information on some of the other packages.

Table 13–1 Java Packages Involved with I/O

Package Name	Purpose
`java.io`	contains the 75 or so classes and interfaces for I/O.
`java.nio`	(new in JDK 1.4) an API for memory-mapped I/O, non-blocking I/O, and file locking.
`java.text`	for formatting text, dates, numbers, and messages according to national preferences and conventions.
`java.util.regex`	(new in JDK 1.4) for matching a string against a pattern or regular expression.
`java.util.zip`	used to read and write zip files.
`java.util.logging`	(new in JDK 1.4) a framework for recording and processing system or application messages to help with later problem diagnosis and resolution.
`java.util.jar`	used to read and write Jar files.
`javax.xml.parsers`	(new in JDK1.4) an API to read in and parse XML trees. Covered in Chapter 28.
`javax.imageio`	(new in JDK 1.4) an API for image file I/O (jpegs, gifs, etc.) together with common operations for handling them, such as thumbnail processing, conversions between formats, and color model adjustment.
`javax.print`	(new in JDK 1.4) the third attempt at providing a decent, enterprise-ready printing service.
`javax.comm`	support for accessing serial (RS-232) and parallel (IEEE-1284) port devices. Not part of the basic JDK.
`javax.sound.midi`	(new in JDK 1.3) provides interfaces and classes for I/O, sequencing, and synthesis of MIDI (Musical Instrument Digital Interface) data.
`javax.speech`	Speech recognition and output API under development. Third-party implementations are available now. This library will have the biggest impact in Java 2 Micro Edition on telephony applications.

Design Philosophy

The design philosophy for Java I/O is based on these principles:

- **I/O is based on streams.** A stream has a physical "device" at one end (like a file or a location in memory). That physical device is managed by some class, and you wrap (layer) additional logical classes on top of that for specific kinds of I/O.
- **Programs that do I/O should be portable**, even though I/O has some non-portable aspects. Platform differences in file names and line terminators must be handled in a way that ensures the code runs everywhere.
- **There are lots of small classes that do one thing**, instead of a few big classes that do many things. There is one class that interprets data in binary format, and another class that reads data from a file. If you want to read binary data from a file, you use both of these classes. The constructors make it convenient to use the classes together.

We'll see examples of these principles throughout the chapter. This is a long chapter, but a worthy one. To help you get the best out of it, Figure 13-1 represents the topics that will be covered, and how they are grouped together. As you can see, many of the I/O topics are freestanding and only relate to each other in a general way. If you feel lost at some point in this chapter, refer back to this diagram.

The first three boxes are covered in this chapter, and the next two in the following chapter on advanced I/O topics. Before looking at actual input/output classes, we'll first cover the File and FileDescriptor classes that provide a convenient way to represent a filename in Java.

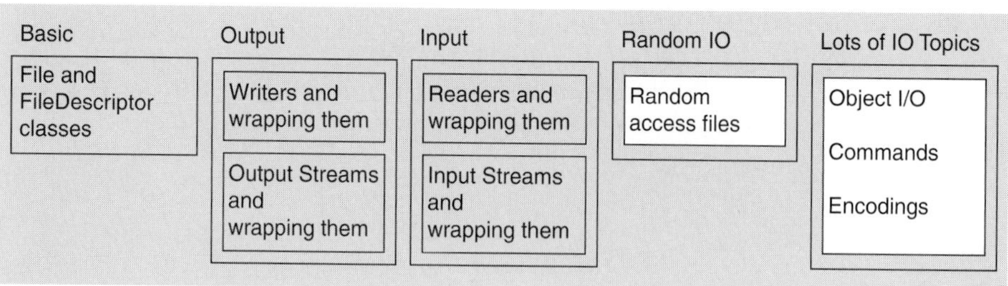

Figure 13–1 Topics in I/O.

File and FileDescriptor Classes

These two classes can't actually do any I/O! The class "java.io.File" should really be called "Filename" since most of its methods are concerned with querying and adjusting filename, and pathname information, not the contents of a file. Directory, filename and pathname information is often called "metadata," meaning "data about data." Methods of java.io.File allow you to access metadata to:

- return a File object from a String containing a pathname
- test whether a file exists, is readable/writable, or is a directory
- say how many bytes are in the file and when it was last modified
- delete the file, or create directory paths
- get various forms of the file pathname.

Here are all the public members of java.io.file. Method names are in bold for visibility.

Public members of java.io.File

```
public class File implements Serializable, Comparable {
    public static final char separatorChar;
    public static final String separator;
    public static final char pathSeparatorChar;
    public static final String pathSeparator;

// constructors:
    public File(String path);
    public File(String directory,String file);
    public File(File directory,String file);

// about the file:
    public String getName();
    public String getParent();
    public File getParentFile();
    public String getPath();
    public String getAbsolutePath();
    public File getAbsoluteFile();
    public String getCanonicalPath() throws IOException;
    public File getCanonicalFile() throws IOException;

    public boolean canRead();
    public boolean canWrite();
    public boolean exists();
    public boolean isAbsolute();
    public boolean isDirectory();
    public boolean isFile();
    public boolean isHidden();
    public long lastModified();
    public long length();

// about the directory
    public String[]  list();
    public String[] list(FilenameFilter);
    public File[] listFiles();
    public File[] listFiles(FilenameFilter);
    public File[] listFiles(FileFilter);
    public static File[] listRoots();
    public boolean mkdir();
    public boolean mkdirs();
```

```
// using temporary files
   public boolean createNewFile() throws IOException;
   public boolean delete();
   public void deleteOnExit();
   public static File createTempFile(String, String) throws IOException;
   public static File createTempFile(String, String, File) throws IOException;

// miscellaneous:
   public boolean renameTo(File);
   public boolean setLastModified(long);
   public boolean setReadOnly();
   public int compareTo(File);
   public int compareTo(Object);
   public boolean equals(Object);
   public int hashCode();
   public String toString();
   public URL toURL() throws java.net.MalformedURLException;
}
```

You create a File object by giving strings for the directory and filename. The file doesn't actually have to exist when you instantiate the File object, and you can go on to create it using createNewFile(). You only bother to instantiate a File object if one of the operations listed above is of interest to you. If you just want to do some I/O, then keep reading—that information is coming soon. Most of the method names in File give a clear indication of what they do. Here are the details on some of the less obvious ones.

public int **compareTo**(File);

This method compares the pathnames of two files for equality or otherwise. Filename comparisons are platform-dependent, as Microsoft Windows does not distinguish letter case in filenames. A straight alphabetic comparison would give the wrong result on Windows, but the compareTo method ensures the correct ordering for the platform.

public static File **createTempFile**(String prefix, String suffix) throws IOException;

This routine creates a temporary file in the default temporary directory. A unique filename will be generated for you, and it will have the prefix and suffix that you provide. This lets you give all temporary files created by, e.g., your mail program—a name that starts with "mail" and ends with ".tmp." There is another form of this method that takes a third parameter, a File object, to specify the directory.

```
public boolean createNewFile() throws IOException;
public void deleteOnExit();
```

These two routines could be used together to provide a simple file-locking protocol, giving exclusive access to some other file or resource. The createNewFile method would either atomically create a new file, or return "false" if the file already existed. "Atomically create" means that the check for the existence of the file, and the creation of the file if it does not exist, form a single operation. If there are several copies of your program running and making the same call at the same time, only one of them will succeed in creating the file. JDK 1.4 introduces the java.nio package which provides more direct support for file locking. See Chapter 14 for details.

```
public boolean mkdir();
public boolean mkdirs();
```

The first method creates just that directory. The second creates that directory plus any non-existent parent directory as needed.

```
public String[]  list();
public File[] listFiles();
```

The first method returns an array of strings representing the files and directories in the directory the method is invoked on. The second method returns the same information, but as File objects, not strings.

```
public static File[] listRoots();
```

This method lists all the available filesystems on this system. On Windows systems, the array will hold File objects for "A:\", "C:\", "D:\", and so on, allowing the programmer to learn what active drives there are. On Unix, the root drive is just "/" the root filesystem. On Windows, File objects for the root directories of the local and mapped network drives will be returned. Windows UNC pathnames (Universal Naming Convention pathnames that start with "//") indicate a non-local file and are not returned by this method.

FileDescriptor

The basic operating system object used to manipulate files is called a file descriptor, but you're not expected to create them or work with them much in Java.

For interest, we will mention what descriptors are, and then move on to some tips on portable I/O. A file descriptor is a non-negative integer, 0,1,2,3... etc., that is used by the native I/O system calls to index a control structure containing data about each open file or socket. Each process has its own table of file descriptors, with each entry pointing to an entry in a system-wide file descriptor table. The size of the process descriptor table places a limit on the number of files or sockets that a process can have open simultaneously. A typical size is 128 or 256 file descriptors.

Java applications should not create their own file descriptors. The FileInputStream and FileOutputStream classes have methods that get the file descriptor for a file that you have open, and that open the file for a descriptor that you have. The class java.io.FileDescriptor is used when the operating system needs a file descriptor, perhaps for a JNI call, or as part of the runtime library.

Portability of I/O

The basic portability approach of the Java runtime library is to have the same method do slightly different things appropriate to each platform. The standard end of line sequence on Windows is "carriage return, linefeed," while on Unix it is just "linefeed." Any library method that writes an end of line sequence, such as `System.out.println()`, will output a "carriage return, linefeed" pair on Windows, a linefeed on Unix, and a carriage return when run on the Mac. In contrast, any string data where you wrote a literal `'\n'` (line feed) or `'\r'` (carriage return) in a string will be output on every platform exactly as you wrote it.

There is a field in the class java.io.File that contains the filename separator, which is a backslash on Windows and a forward slash on Unix. Instead of writing a pathname as "`a/b/c.txt`," you can write it using the separator character, ensuring that it will be correct on all platforms. If you insist on reducing portability by using literal strings for pathnames, remember that backslash is also the string escape character. Therefore, you have to write it twice (to escape itself) when writing literal file names for the PC. Here is an example:

```
String myFile = "a\\b\\c.txt";
```

You can actually use "/" to separate components in a Windows pathname in a program. The Windows file system calls all use it internally. The Windows interactive shell, COMMAND.COM, is the only part of the system that can't handle it. This is an interesting historical artifact, dating from the origins of MS-DOS as an unauthorized port (known as QDOS) of CP/M with a few trivial changes. That port was eventually bought by Microsoft, renamed to MS-DOS, and the rest is history. Most programmers form a filename by declaring a variable with a briefer name to represent the separator character, like this:

```
final String s = java.io.File.separator;
String myFile = "a" + s + "b" + s + "c.txt";
```

This helps, but does not provide 100% data file portability because it doesn't mention the Windows drive. The form of an absolute pathname differs from system to system. One approach to minimizing this is to tell the program its data filenames at runtime, either as command line arguments or as system properties.

Output

Java programs access external data by instantiating a *stream* on the data. Most physical destinations (a place to where an output stream can flow) have a class dedicated to writing output there. For example, there is a file output stream class that opens a file for writing, a piped output stream class that opens a pipe for output to another thread, a byte array output stream class that opens a connection to a byte array in memory, and so on. Similar classes exist for each individual source of input (memory, socket, file, URL, etc.). There is only a limited number of destinations for data. The most common places to write data are:

- a sequential file
- a String
- a pipe
- the system console
- an array of characters
- a URL for an HTTP GET/POST
- a random access file
- an array of bytes
- a socket

Some of these destinations have their own dedicated class whose constructor returns a stream. Other destinations have a getOutputStream() method that will hand you back a stream to write into. Either way, the stream object hides the low-level details of how the data is accessed, and just lets you get to it. After the information stream is opened, some other class is usually wrapped on top to actually transfer the data.

What Is a Wrapper?

Wrapping an object means accessing its features through some other object, known as the "wrapper.' The wrapper object will augment or improve the features available from the first object. You use the wrapper exclusively, and it in turn will invoke the first object methods as it needs them. Wrapping is widely used in the Java I/O library. In the real world, you might "wrap" a sprinkler with a hosepipe so you get the functionality of water transmission through the hose, with the value-added feature at the end of distributing it in fine drops to irrigate your lawn.

As a programming example, say you had a class that takes ordinary text and prints it out as really nice reports, with page numbers and justified margins, etc. Suppose you also had a second class that translates French text into English text. You could design the second class so that it "wrapped" the printing class.

The wrapper class would get a stream of French text and translate it into English, as before. Then it would automatically send the results directly on to the wrapped class, where they would be turned into a professional quality printed document. The net effect would be a couple of classes that worked together to turn French text into nicely-printed English documents. You would only need to learn the interface for the wrapper class, since you would invoke all your methods on the wrapper object.

There is even a code idiom for wrapper classes. They are written with a constructor whose argument is the object they will wrap. So, first you instantiate the object that will be wrapped:

```
NicePrinter wrappedObject = new NicePrinter();
```

then you instantiate a wrapper object, passing the to-be-wrapped object as an argument.

```
FrenchToEnglish wrapper = new FrenchToEnglish( wrappedObject );
```

Behind the scenes, the wrapper object will save a copy of the thing it's wrapping, and you only deal with the wrapper from that point on. When you call a wrapper method, it will do its work and then pass the results on for further processing as appropriate to the wrapped object it saved.

```
wrapper.setAsInput("Les Miserables");
wrapper.translate();
// automatically sends the translation into the wrapped object
// causing an English translation to get printed nicely.
```

Clearly, these fictitious FrenchToEnglish and NicePrinter classes have only a loose affinity. The wrapped/wrapper classes in Java I/O are much more tightly coupled. The java.io class that knows how to get data from a file is a "can be wrapped" object. The java.io class that knows how to interpret a data stream as binary values is a "can wrap" object. Put them together, and the wrapper can interpret a stream of binary data from a file.

You can layer several wrappers on top of each other. You deal only with the outermost one, but each does its own special value-add and sends the bits on to the next one. Wrapping is a design pattern that is also known as the "Decorator" pattern.

The additional wrapping classes provide logical operations, like binary I/O, printable I/O, encryption, or compression. You use the wrapping classes the same way and call the same methods regardless of whether the underlying I/O is to a socket, file, keyboard, URL, pipe, array, etc. This provides the benefit of a uniform API. Wherever you are transferring the data, you will use methods of the same two or three classes. The disadvantage is that you have to instantiate objects from two or three different classes to get anything done.

Originally, Java only had stream classes, and the streams only operated on bytes of data. However, characters in Java are two bytes wide, and byte-oriented I/O did not properly cope with internationalization. So a wider type of stream was introduced in JDK 1.1 specifically for character-based I/O. Reader classes are able to get Unicode character input two bytes at a time. Writer classes are able to

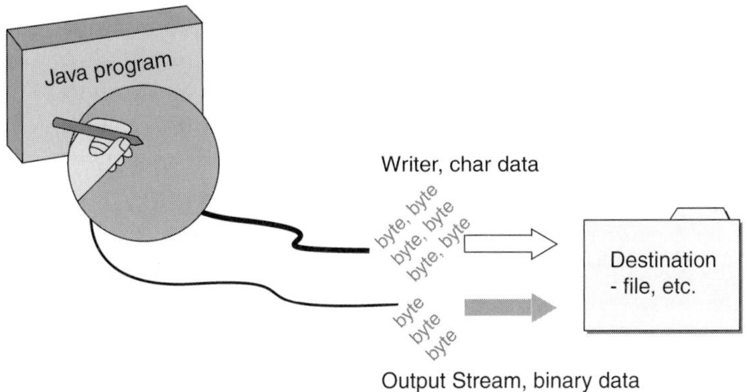

Figure 13–2 Your program outputs data into a stream or writer.

do Unicode character output two bytes at a time, as shown in Figure 13-2. Input and output streams operate on data one byte at a time.

Writers are used when you want to output Unicode data, and output streams are used when you want to output ASCII or binary data. Readers are used when you want to read Unicode data, and input streams are used when you want to read ASCII or binary data. Readers and Writers are intended to replace byte-sized character I/O streams. They do the same job as Streams, and have a very similar API. In summary, Streams operate on bytes, while Readers/Writers operate on double-byte characters and therefore handle internationalization properly. We'll start by looking at character Writers, then we'll look at byte output Streams.

Outputting Double-byte Characters

All Writer classes output double-byte Unicode characters. Most operating systems expect characters to be one byte long, so you will only use Writers when you need the internationalization features that Unicode offers (e.g., you need to represent Cyrillic letters), or if you intend to later read the strings back in for further processing.

All Writer classes have five basic write() methods for transferring 16-bit characters. The many subclasses of Writer add more methods, but you can count on these five methods in every writer. You can write a single character, or the characters from an array, or a String, or a range of characters from an array or String. Here are the signatures of the Writer output methods:

```
public void write(int);
public void write(char[]);
public void write(char[], int from, int len);
public void write(java.lang.String);
public void write(java.lang.String, int from, int len);
```

They are methods promised by the abstract class Writer, and all java.io classes with "Writer" in their name have them. You use Writers for outputting internationalizable text and numbers that some person will read, as opposed to binary or ASCII or object values for further computer processing.

First you choose whether you want printable internationalizable output or byte output. The former means you use a Writer, the latter means you use an OutputStream. Next you decide where you want to send the output. If you originally chose a Writer, you will now choose one of these Writer subclasses accordingly (see Table 13-2).

The class FileWriter is by far the most common place to send chars with a Writer. That class opens a connection onto a file. Its constructors are shown in Table 13-2. Some of the constructors take an argument that is a File or FileDescriptor object. File or FileDescriptor objects are merely ways of referring to a file without using its string name.

An example line of code that instantiates a FileWriter for a file called "\jj4\example.txt" is

```
FileWriter myFW = new FileWriter( "\\jj4\\example.txt" );
```

You have to double the backslash when it appears in a string because the backslash is also the escape character in a string. For example, "\n" is a newline and "\t" is a tab. The mistake of choosing the MS-DOS pathname separator character as the string escape happened because everyone on the original Java design team was a hardcore Unix whacker. None of them had ever written much for

Table 13–2 Choose the Writer Class Based on the Output Destination

Send Output To:	java.io Class	Constructors
A **file**	FileWriter	FileWriter(String fileName) throws IOException FileWriter(String fileName, boolean append) throws IOException FileWriter(File file) throws IOException FileWriter(File file, boolean append) throws IOException FileWriter(FileDescriptor fd)
A **char array** in your program	CharArrayWriter	CharArrayWriter() CharArrayWriter(int initialSize)
A **String** in your program	StringWriter	StringWriter() StringWriter(int initialSize)
A **pipe** to be read by a PipedReader in another thread	PipedWriter	PipedWriter() PipedWriter(PipedReader sink)

DOS, and none of them realized that backslash already had an established use on that platform.

That line of code above opens a connection to the destination file, and gives you the basic writing methods. There is no separate "open" method. Note that the constructor can throw an exception, so you need to place the statement in a "try" statement.

Writer classes output Unicode (16-bit) characters, but most operating systems only support 8-bit characters by default. To cope with this, you can define a character set that specifies how Unicode will be turned into bytes. The simplest such character set mapping is "discard the high order bytes," and this is the usual default for the file system. We'll take a longer look at character sets in the next chapter. If you are using an 8-bit (ASCII or Latin-1) codeset and you don't care about internationalization, don't bother with Writers at all. Do all your I/O in bytes with OutputStreams.

Wrapping a Writer

Those five "write" output methods common to every Writer class (listed at the start of this section) are very spartan. Therefore, you usually "wrap" the destination Writer class with another Writer class that has more output methods. You wrap a class around the Writer by passing the Writer as an argument to the wrapping class's constructor. Here's an example that wraps a PrintWriter around the FileWriter we declared a few lines back:

```
// myPrt wraps myFW
PrintWriter myPrt = new PrintWriter(myFW);
```

The PrintWriter class is the one with the methods that actually transfer data to the Writer destination as printable strings. When you call a PrintWriter method, the data goes through to the destination writer that it is wrapped around, in this case the FileWriter.

Methods of java.io.PrintWriter

```
public class java.io.PrintWriter extends java.io.Writer {
   public PrintWriter(java.io.Writer);
   public PrintWriter(java.io.Writer,boolean);
   public PrintWriter(java.io.OutputStream);
   public PrintWriter(java.io.OutputStream,boolean);
   public void flush();
   public void close();
   public boolean checkError();

   public void print(boolean);
   public void print(char);
   public void print(int);
   public void print(long);
   public void print(float);
   public void print(double);
   public void print(char[]);
   public void print(java.lang.String);
   public void print(java.lang.Object);

  public void println();
   // there are also println versions of all the above print methods, e.g.
  public void println(boolean);
   // and so on ... through to...
  public void println(Object);

  public void write(int);
  public void write(char[]);
  public void write(char[], int from, int to);
  public void write(java.lang.String);
  public void write(java.lang.String, int from, int to);
}
```

There is a print() method for most primitive types, and also a println() method that follows the output with the end of line sequence for that platform. There is no `print (byte)` because byte-oriented output is done with an Output-Stream, not a Writer. The print methods are all implemented by calling the write methods. These write methods override similar methods in the parent Writer, and suppress IOExceptions. No methods in PrintWriter throw IOException. You can

call the method `checkError()` to see if an I/O error occurred at some earlier point. The API designer should have named that method "`isError`" to follow the standard naming conventions, by the way.

As an aside, all the print methods are implemented in terms of the five basic write methods. Here is java.io.PrintWriter's print(int) method in full:

```
public void print(int i) {
    write(String.valueOf(i));
}
```

Writing everything in terms of the five basic write methods makes it very easy to implement wrapping. When you call myPW.print(i), that routine calls myPW.write(i) and that calls the write method of the object passed in to the constructor. The delegation continues along the line until the write request has been through all the wrappers and reaches an object that does the operation directly on a file or string in memory, etc.

Here is the code to create a file and write printable numbers and strings into it.

```
FileWriter myFW = null;
try {
        myFW = new FileWriter( "\\jj4\\dogs.txt" );
} catch(IOException x) { System.err.println("IOExcpn: " + x); }

PrintWriter myPW = new PrintWriter( myFW );
int i =101;
myPW.print( i );
myPW.println(" Dalmatians");
myPW.close();
```

Notice the close() method in PrintWriter. Even though there is no separate open for files, all I/O stream classes have a close method. You should develop the habit of closing each stream as you are done with it. Java does not automatically flush and close streams just because you stop writing to them. Failing to close an output stream may leave it with some data not yet flushed to the underlying device. You should also close input streams when you are done with them, as a matter of good programming practice. Streams take up some OS resources, of which there is a limited quantity. By closing a stream when you are finished with it, you allow the JVM to give the file descriptor and buffers back to the OS. Also, for pipes/sockets/URLs, closing allows the other end of the connection to see an end-of-file, and therefore is able to gracefully terminate instead of waiting for an event that may never happen.

Other Writer Wrappers

As Figure 13-3 suggests, there are two other writer classes that you can wrap around another Writer. You can wrap a BufferedWriter around it. Or you can create your own subclass of FilterWriter, and wrap that around a Writer. These two classes do specialized extra processing on the stream before it gets written to its destination.

You decorate a FileWriter (StringWriter... etc.) with a BufferedWriter to improve performance. FileWriter by itself sends its output to the underlying stream as it receives it. Because of disk latency and system call context switch overhead, it's always quicker to do one 512-character transfer than 512 individual 1-character transfers. Wrapping a BufferedWriter around any Writer will achieve that efficiency by saving up smaller writes until its internal buffer is full. Buffered I/O should have been the default behavior in this package.

FilterWriter is an abstract class that you are meant to extend and override. It provides the opportunity to look at and modify characters as they are output. You could do the same thing by extending any of the other writer classes, but using this class makes your purpose explicit.

Here is an example program that post-processes the stream written into it and changes all "1"s to "2"s. A Filter can do other things like count lines, correct spelling mistakes, calculate checksums, or write an encrypted or compressed stream.

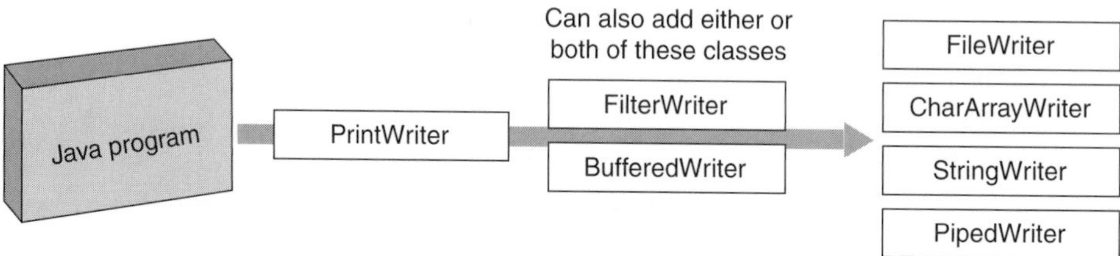

Figure 13–3 Wrapping more Writer classes.

A Filter to Replace Chars

```
import java.io.*;
class MyFilter extends java.io.FilterWriter {
      public MyFilter(Writer w) { super(w); }

      public void write(String s, int off, int len) throws java.io.IOException {
            s = s.replace('1', '2');
            super.write(s, off, len);
      }

      public void write(char[] cbuf, int off, int len) throws IOException {
            String s= new String(cbuf);
            this.write(s, off, len);
      }
}
```

The lesson to take away from this is what a small amount of code is needed for such a large amount of functionality. Here is the code that uses the above filter. Try compiling and running it to see the results.

A Class that Uses a Filter

```
import java.io.*;
public class Example2 {

      public static void main(String args[]) {
            FileWriter myFW = null;
            try {
                  myFW = new FileWriter( "dogs.txt" );
            } catch(IOException x) { System.err.println("IOExcpn: " + x); }

            FilterWriter filter = new MyFilter( myFW );
            BufferedWriter BW = new BufferedWriter(filter);
            PrintWriter myPW = new PrintWriter( BW );
            myPW.println("101 Dalmatians");
            myPW.close();
      }
}
```

In this example, the Filter overrides two of the write() methods, but you may need to override any or all of the FilterWriter methods depending on what you are doing. The example code also wraps a BufferedWriter around the filter, just to show how it is done. The API permits the BufferedWriter and the FilterWriter to be wrapped in either order. But to get the most performance benefit, you want as much of the pipeline as possible operating on buffers of data. So put the Buffered-Writer as near to the start of the pipeline as possible (i.e., the BufferedWriter should be the outermost or next-outermost wrapper). This ensures that all wrapper objects downstream of the BufferedWriter are working with buffered data.

It's common to cascade all these constructors together, like this:

```
PrintWriter myPW = new PrintWriter(
                        new BufferedWriter(
                           new myFilter(
                              new FileWriter( "\\jj4\\dogs.txt" ) ) ) );
```

If you run the program and look at the output file dogs.txt, you will see the output has been filtered. It now contains "202 Dalmatians".

Summary of Writers

- Use a Writer when you want to output printable, internationalizable 16-bit characters
- Choose a FileWriter or one of the other three destination classes, depending on where you want the chars to go
- You can optionally wrap that in either or both of a BufferedWriter or your subclass of a FilterWriter
- Then wrap a PrinterWriter on top, and use its print methods to do the output
- Wrapping one class by another to give it additional abilities is an example of the Decorator or Wrapper design pattern.

The next section looks at output streams, which are analogous to Writers but work on a byte at a time, not a Unicode character at a time.

Outputting ASCII Characters and Binary Values

Let's admit right away that this section is really about the output of binary values and 8-bit characters, of which the ASCII characters are just a subset. The full 8-bit character set is known as ISO 8859-1 Latin-1, but no one has heard of that and everyone has heard of ASCII, hence the heading above. Both ASCII and 8859-1 are listed in Appendix C so you can review them.

We'll first take a look at how to output binary values. Contrast the character output of the previous section with the binary output of this section. Character output is intended to be read by people, whereas binary output is intended for further processing by computers. The character representation of a number varies in length depending on the size of the number. The binary representation of a number is a fixed length: 4 bytes for an integer, 8 bytes for a long value. Just to make a point, the number 29,019 can be represented in a computer in several ways, as shown in Table 13-3.

Table 13–3 The Number 29,019 Stored as Three Different Types

Type	Description	Hexadecimal Value	How It Looks When Printed
String	successive double-byte characters	0032 0039 0030 0031 0039	29019 or 2 9 0 1 9 (if your design has a bug)
Array of ASCII bytes	successive bytes	32 39 30 31 39	29019
int	four byte binary integer	0000715B	q[

Notice that the binary form of a number is not directly printable. Some bytes may happen to contain printable ASCII values (I chose this example so some do), but they don't show the digits of the number. Note also that if you write Unicode into a file and then print that, you'll usually get strange extra spacing because the OS print routines typically don't know about Unicode and will find unexpected extra bytes everywhere.

The output stream classes are used when you don't want a double-byte character form. The API is very similar to that of the Writer classes. As with Writers, you decide where you want to send the output, and choose one of the classes accordingly (see Table 13-4).

Table 13–4 Choose the Output Stream Class Based on the Output Destination

Send Binary Output To:	java.io Class	Constructors

A file	FileOutputStream	public FileOutputStream(java.lang.String) throws java.io.FileNotFoundException;
		public FileOutputStream(java.lang.String,boolean) throws java.io.FileNotFoundException;
		public FileOutputStream(java.io.File) throws java.io.FileNotFoundException;
		public FileOutputStream(java.io.File,boolean) throws java.io.FileNotFoundException;
		public **FileOutputStream**(java.io.FileDescriptor);

A **byte array** in your program	ByteArrayOutputStream	public **ByteArrayOutputStream()**; public **ByteArrayOutputStream**(int);
A **pipe** to be read by a PipedInputStream in another thread	PipedOutputStream	public PipedOutputStream(java.io.PipedInputStream) throws java.io.IOException; public **PipedOutputStream**();

There isn't an output stream to write to a String, because you should use a Writer class, not a stream class, for that. There are also a couple of output destinations that you connect to using a method call to get the stream, rather than a constructor. As shown in Table 13-5, that is how you get a stream that writes into a socket or a URL. Sockets and URLs are treated differently because they can be read as well as written. The random access file can be open for reading and writing simultaneously too, and it also gets special treatment, as described in the next chapter.

Table 13–5 Choose the getOutputStream() Method Based on the Destination

Send Output To:	Class	Method in That Class to Get an Output Stream
A **socket**	java.net.Socket	public OutputStream **getOutputStream**() throws java.io.IOException;
A **URL**	java.net.URLConnection	public OutputStream **getOutputStream**() throws java.io.IOException;

Using the three classes or the two methods outlined, we can get an output stream that writes bytes into a file, a socket, a URL, a pipe, or a byte array. Writing to a URL takes a little bit of URL-specific setup (you have to open a connection, create a connection object, configure the server to allow writing, etc.), but the other four destinations are very easy to use.

Basic OutputStream Methods

All Output Streams have these three basic output methods. You can write a single byte, or the bytes from an array, or a range of bytes from an array. Here are the signatures of these output methods:

```
public void write(int b);
public void write(byte[]);
public void write(byte[], int from, int len);
```

The first method accepts an int argument, although you might expect a byte. This is a concession to reduce the amount of casting you may otherwise sometimes need to do. Whatever size of value you send in, only the least significant byte will be output.

These methods are promised by the abstract class OutputStream. All java.io classes with "OutputStream" in their name have these. You use OutputStreams for outputting bytes or binary values, not Unicode characters or objects. As with the Writer classes, you are expected to wrap another class around your Output Stream. One possible wrapper is a PrintStream class. Wrap that around a FileOutputStream or socket output stream, etc., when you wish to write printable bytes such as ASCII values. Another possible wrapper is the DataOutputStream class. Use DataOutputStream when you wish to do binary I/O. DataOutputStream has these output methods to write numbers in binary.

java.io.DataOutputStream for Binary Output

```
public class java.io.DataOutputStream
        extends java.io.FilterOutputStream
                implements java.io.DataOutput {
 // constructor
   public DataOutputStream(java.io.OutputStream);
   public final void writeBoolean(boolean) throws java.io.IOException;
   public final void writeByte(int) throws java.io.IOException;
   public final void writeShort(int) throws java.io.IOException;
   public final void writeChar(int) throws java.io.IOException;
   public final void writeInt(int) throws java.io.IOException;
   public final void writeLong(long) throws java.io.IOException;
   public final void writeFloat(float) throws java.io.IOException;
   public final void writeDouble(double) throws java.io.IOException;
   public final void writeBytes(java.lang.String) throws java.io.IOException;
   public final void writeChars(java.lang.String) throws java.io.IOException;
   public final void writeUTF(java.lang.String) throws java.io.IOException;

   public void flush() throws java.io.IOException;
   public synchronized void write(int) throws java.io.IOException;
   public synchronized void write(byte[], int, int) throws java.io.IOException;
   public final int size();  // returns number-of-bytes written so far
}
```

You will use DataOutputStream when you want to output numbers in binary format for later processing by another program. There is a write method for all primitive types, and also for Strings. Depending on which method you use, Strings will be written as 16-bit Unicode chars (writeChars), as 8-bit bytes discarding the high-order byte of each char (writeBytes), or in the UTF-encoded format where characters are 1-3 bytes in length (writeUTF) and preceded by a 16-bit length field. If you're not sure what to use, you should write Strings using the writeBytes method. Or use a PrintStream instead. You use a PrintStream if all you need to do is output printable ASCII bytes.

When you wrap several classes, only write from the outermost one. Otherwise, your I/O may get mixed up due to internal buffering. You will use PrintStream when you want to output ISO 8859-1 text and numbers in readable format for reading by a person, but you do not need internationalization. The class java.io.PrintStream has the following methods:

java.io.PrintStream for Printable Output

```
public class java.io.PrintStream extends java.io.FilterOutputStream {
  public PrintStream(java.io.OutputStream);
  public PrintStream(java.io.OutputStream,boolean autoFlush);
  public PrintStream(java.io.OutputStream,boolean,String encoding) throws

java.io.UnsupportedEncodingException;
  public void print(boolean);
  public void print(char);
  public void print(int);
  public void print(long);
  public void print(float);
  public void print(double);
  public void print(char[]);
  public void print(java.lang.String);
  public void print(java.lang.Object);

  public void println();
  // there are also println versions of all the above print methods, e.g.
  public void println(boolean);
  // and so on ...

  public void flush();
  public void close();
  public boolean checkError();
  public void write(int);
  public void write(byte[], int, int);
}
```

Use PrintStream to write ASCII bytes. Use PrintWriter when you need to write internationalizable Unicode characters. All characters printed by a PrintStream are converted into bytes using the platform's default character encoding, or the encoding given as an argument String to the constructor. Some examples of this are at the end of the next chapter.

System.in, out, and err

On all Unix operating systems, and on Windows, three file descriptors are automatically opened by the shell that starts every process. This is even true on the Mac with OS-X (because OS-X is based on the Mach variant of Unix). The file descriptor convention is so common because it is a part of the C language API. File descriptor '0' is used for the standard input of the process. File descriptor '1' is used for the standard output of the process, and file descriptor '2' is used for the standard error of the process.

These three standard connections are known as "standard in," "standard out," and "standard err" or error. Normally, the standard input gets input from the keyboard, while standard output and standard error write data to the terminal from which the process was started. Every Java program contains two predefined PrintStreams, known as "out" and "err." They are kept in Java.lang.System, and represent the command line output and error output, respectively. There is also an input stream called System.in that is the command line input. This is also referred to as console I/O or terminal I/O.

Anytime you have written System.out.println("foo = " + foo); you have already used a PrintStream, maybe without knowing it. See? It's easier than you thought!

You can redirect the standard error, in, or out streams to a file or another stream (such as a socket) this way:

```
System.setErr(PrintStream err);
System.setIn(InputStream in);
System.setOut(PrintStream out);
```

Stdin and stdout are used for low volume interactive I/O. Stderr is intended for error messages only. That way, if the output of a program is redirected somewhere, the error messages still appear on the console.

Writing a Binary File

Here is some sample code to create a file and write binary numbers into it.

```
FileOutputStream myFOS = null;
try {
      myFOS = new FileOutputStream( "numbers.bin" );
      DataOutputStream myDOS = new DataOutputStream( myFOS );
      myDOS.writeInt(29019 );
      myDOS.writeInt(3);
      myDOS.writeInt(5);
      myDOS.writeInt(67);
} catch(IOException x) { System.err.println("IOExcpn: " + x); }
```

If you look at the "numbers.bin" output file with an editor that can display the contents of a file in hexadecimal, you will see four, four-byte ints there containing the values written. Later in this chapter, we'll develop the code to dump the contents of a file that way.

Instead of a DataOutputStream or a PrintStream, you can layer an ObjectOutputStream and write Java objects from your program out to disk or across the net on a socket. There's a longer explanation of object I/O in the next chapter.

Output Stream Wrappers

At the beginning of the chapter, we saw how a Writer could have a BufferedWriter and/or a subclass of FilterWriter interposed between the FileWriter (or other destination) and the PrintWriter. Output Streams can be wrapped in the same way to provide more functionality. You can wrap any or all of these output streams onto your original OutputStream:

- BufferedOutputStream
- Your subclass of FilterOutputStream
- OutputStreamWriter
- java.util.zip.ZipOutputStream
- java.util.zip.GZIPOutputStream
- java.util.jar.JarOutputStream
- javax.crypto.CipherOutputStream
- java.io.ObjectOutputStream
- various others in the release, and which you write yourself.

The OutputStreamWriter class converts an OutputStream class to a Writer class, allowing you to layer any of the Writer classes on top of that. It provides a bridge from the 8-bit byte world to the 16-bit character world. The main motivation for doing so is that you can also specify the character set when you construct an OutputStreamWriter. Please review the next chapter for more information on character sets. It's not something frequently used.

The CipherOutputStream will encrypt the stream that it gets and write the encrypted bytes. You have to set it up with a Cipher object (and a key). There is more detail in the online API documentation.

The zip, gzip, and jar output streams will compress the bytes written into them using the zip, gzip, and zip algorithms, respectively. Jar format is identical to zip format, but with the addition of a manifest file listing the names of other files in the archive. An example of writing an archive of several files in Zip format is shown in the next section.

The ObjectOutputStream class allows you to save an object and all the objects it references. You can wrap this class around any of the other output streams and send the object to a file, to a socket, down a pipe, etc. The next chapter shows an example of ObjectOutputStream in use.

Example of Outputting a Zip File

Zip is a multifile archive format popularized by the PC but available on almost all systems now. The zip format offers two principal benefits: it can bundle several files into one file, and it can compress the data as it writes it to the zip archive. It's more convenient to pass around one file than twenty separate files. Compressed files are faster and cheaper to download or e-mail than their uncompressed versions. Java Archives (.jar) files are in zip format.

Support for zip and gzip files was introduced with JDK 1.1. GZIP, an alternative to ZIP widely used on Unix, uses a different format for the data and can only hold one file (not a series of them).

Java has classes that will compress and expand files into either the gzip or the zip format. If you wrote a file out in zip format, you have to read it back in that way too. The same holds for gzip format. The formats are not interchangeable. If you have a choice, opt for zip over gzip because it does more and is much more widely used.

Files aren't the only possible destination for zip streams (or any output, compressed or otherwise). You can equally send streams through a socket to another computer across the Internet, put them in a String or byte array for later retrieval, or send them through a pipe to another thread. The following is an example program showing how three files can be put into a zip archive. After running this program, compare the size of the zip archive with the sum of the sizes of the three files. Text strings compress well, binary data less so.

Writing a Zip Archive

```
import java.io.*;
import java.util.zip.*;
public class Example4 {

    // writing a zip archive
    static ZipOutputStream myZOS;

    public static void main(String args[]) throws IOException {
        myZOS = new ZipOutputStream (
                        new BufferedOutputStream (
                            new FileOutputStream("code.zip") ) );
        writeOneFile("Example1.java");
        writeOneFile("Example2.java");
        writeOneFile("Example3.java");
        myZOS.close();
    }

    static void writeOneFile(String name) throws IOException {
        ZipEntry myZE = new ZipEntry(name);
        myZOS.putNextEntry(myZE);

        BufferedReader myBR = new BufferedReader(
                                        new FileReader(name) );
        int c;
        while((c = myBR.read()) != -1)    // read a char until EOF
            myZOS.write(c);               // write the char we just read
        myBR.close();
    }
}
```

Executing this program will create a zip archive called code.zip. Each file in a zip archive is represented by an object called a ZipEntry. You can unpack it and recover the original source files with a Zip Input Stream, or use any of the standard Zip tools like winzip or Java's jar command.

Summary of Output Streams

- Use an Output Stream when you want to output ASCII or binary values
- Choose a FileOutputStream or one of the getOutputStream methods, depending on where you want the chars to go
- You can optionally wrap that in an arbitrary number of OutputStream filters, buffers, compressors, encoders, etc.
- Then wrap a DataOutputStream on top, and use its write methods to output numbers in binary.

A very common mistake in Java is to use binary I/O where Unicode or ASCII I/O was intended. The numeric values transferred will not usually be human readable, and you'll get a different length of data and a different value of data than you were expecting. The character values transferred will be fine because an ASCII character has the same bit representation whether it was written using an ASCII method or a binary method.

Let's finish this section by looking at how Java copes with platform differences in I/O and data. Table 13-6 shows some I/O-related platform differences. The rightmost column shows the approach Java takes to minimize these differences.

Table 13–6 Platform Differences in I/O

	MS Windows	Unix	Apple Mac	Java Feature
end of line characters	`\r\n`	`\n`	`\r`	`System.getProperty ( "line.separator" )`
filename separator	`'\'`	`'/'`	`':'`	`java.io.File.separator`
pathnames	*volume*`:\b\c\d` *or* `\\`*host*`\`*share*`\c\d`	`/a/b/c/d`	*volume*`:b :c:d`	pass pathname to program as an argument
data byte order	little-endian	varies with hardware	big-endian	big-endian, see text in next chapter

The end-of-line sequence is different on different platforms. Most of the time it doesn't matter. You can write out a "\n" character and platforms will interpret it correctly. If you have some legacy code that requires the actual end-of-line sequence, you can obtain it with the following method call:

```
String actualEOL = java.lang.System.getProperty("line.separator");
```

That statement will put the EOL sequence used by this platform into the variable. The println() methods of PrintWriter and PrintStream also output the EOL sequence of the specific platform. The I/O API often allows a file to be identified in two parts: the directory it is in, and the filename. That allows you to split off the platform-sensitive directory pathname from the comparatively portable filename string.

Input

The classes to do input are mostly the flip side of the output classes we have already seen. Java programs access external data by instantiating a *stream* on the data source. Each place from which an input stream can flow has a class dedicated to getting that kind of input. Input is read from a stream of data representing the file, pipe, socket, memory array, or whatever. If you want to read 16-bit characters, you use a Reader class. If you want to read binary bytes or ASCII, you use an input stream.

Inputting Double Byte Characters

As usual, first decide between binary and character I/O, then choose your class based on where the data is coming from. For reading double-byte character data, you will use one of the Reader classes shown in Table 13-7. Note the symmetry with the Writer classes.

Table 13–7 Chose the Reader Class Based on Where the Input Comes From

Get Input From:	java.io Class	Constructors
A **file.**	FileReader	FileReader(java.lang.String) throws java.io.FileNotFoundException; FileReader(java.io.File) throws java.io.FileNotFoundException; FileReader(java.io.FileDescriptor);
A **char array** in your program. You read from the array passed to the constructor.	CharArrayReader	CharArrayReader(char[]); CharArrayReader(char[],int from,int to);
A **String** in your program. You read from the String passed to the constructor.	StringReader	**StringReader**(String s)
A **pipe** that is written by a PipedWriter in another thread.	PipedReader	PipedReader() PipedReader(PipedWriter source)

There are only four places from which you can read chars with a Reader, and FileReader is by far the most common. That class opens a connection onto a file. The constructors are shown in the table above. The constructor takes an argument that is the String pathname to the file, or a File object or FileDescriptor object.

Basic Reader Methods

All Readers give you at least these three somewhat basic input methods:

```
public int read()
public int read(char[] cbuf)
public int read(char[] cbuf, int from, int len)
```

These read into, respectively, a single character, an array of characters, and a range in an array of characters. The call will not return until some data is available to read, although it won't necessarily fill the array. The return value will be -1 if the Reader hits end of file (EOF). This is why the single char call returns a 32-bit int, even though it only reads a 16-bit character. The high-order 16 bits in the return value allow you to distinguish EOF from a character read. Those bits will be zero when a character is read, and 0xFFFF when EOF is reached. Test the return value for equality with -1 to see if you reached EOF.

An Input Problem Rears Its Ugly Head

At this point, from general symmetry, you are probably expecting to "wrap" another class on top of these Readers. That class will probably be called PrintReader, and it will have all the convenient methods for reading a String and returning a short, an int, a float, a boolean, etc. Bzzzt! Sorry, the design falls apart here. There is no such class as PrintReader. Not only that, there is no class that *can* give you the desired feature of being able to read back in exactly the same number values as were output using PrintWriter. The problem is an algorithmic one. Numbers in printed format vary in length, so your code has no way of telling where one number ends and an immediately adjacent starts. For example, if you use PrintWriter to print two ints like this into a file:

```
myPW.print(293);
myPW.print(19);
```

The file will contain the string "29319", but if you try to read those numbers back in from that file, because of the variable length, there is no way of telling where one int ends and the next one starts. No program in any language can deduce whether the ints were originally 2 and 9319, or 29 and 319, or 293 and 19, or 2931 and 9. This problem does not arise with binary output, because all the binary types (short, int, float, etc.) have a fixed known size. This "where does a string of digits end?" problem is the reason that the XML language (see Chapter 28 on XML) always marks the end of a field with a closing tag.

Confused by Number Formats, by ASCII, Unicode, Binary?

It *is* confusing until you understand the differences. You might find it helpful to review the different formats shown in Table 13-3 earlier in the chapter.

The best you can do when reading printed numbers is to read characters until you hit something that can't be part of a number (e.g., a space), then assemble a number out of the characters that preceded it. It's common to break up such files with end-of-line sequences, and it's convenient to be able to read a line at a time and tokenize (bundle together the groups of) the characters on that line.

You really need something more than reading individual characters though, so a kludgey little hack has been devised. A readLine() method has been placed in class BufferedReader. You can wrap a BufferedReader around a FileReader, which you probably want to do anyway for the performance, and then read lines from it. Each line comes into your program as a String with the end-of-line sequence removed. You can then tokenize the line however you like to recover individual values. Here's an example of reading a line that way.

```
import java.io.*;
public class Example4 {

    public static void main(String args[]) {
        FileReader myFR = null;
        try {
            myFR = new FileReader( "\\jj4\\dogs.txt" );
        } catch(IOException x) { System.err.println("IOExcpn: " + x); }

        BufferedReader myBR = new BufferedReader(myFR);

        try {
            String in = myBR.readLine();
            System.out.println(in);
        } catch(IOException x) { System.err.println("IOExcpn: " + x); }
    }
}
```

Another approach is to write all numeric strings into fixed length fields, say, 20 characters long. Then you can always read in fixed length input. Another approach is to avoid reading/writing printable data; instead, do it all with binary byte streams. Input is certainly messier than output.

Reader Wrappers

There is the usual variety of wrapper classes that can wrap a Reader, shown in the Figure 13-4.

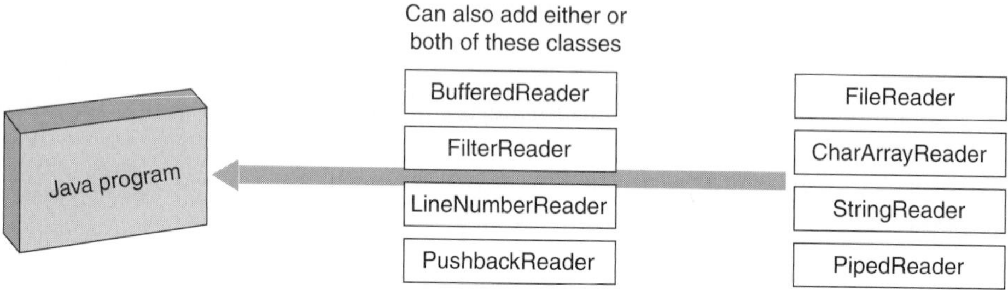

Figure 13–4 Wrapping the Reader classes.

Classes That Wrap Readers

The classes that wrap a Reader are:

- **BufferedReader**. This class can provide a performance boost, and also has a readLine() method. The BufferedReader needs to wrap the class that actually accesses the data (e.g., the FileReader or whatever). Other classes may be layered on top of the BufferedReader, too.
- **FilterReader**. You subclass FilterReader, and your overriding methods allow you to see and modify individual characters as they come in—before the rest of your program sees them.
- **LineNumberReader**. This class keeps track of the line number count on this stream. You can find out the input line you are currently on by calling getLineNumber(). This class doesn't really offer enough value to justify its existence. It was written to support the first Java compiler and included in the API for no good reason.
- **PushbackReader**. This class maintains an internal buffer that allows characters to be "pushed back" into the stream after they have been read, allowing the next read to get them again. The default buffer size is one character, but there is a constructor that lets you specify a larger size. You might use this if you were assembling successive characters into a number and you come to a character that can't be part of a number. You will push it back into the input stream so it can be ignored, but kept available for the next read attempt.

Inputting ASCII Characters and Binary Values

You choose an input stream when you want to bring bytes into your program. As with Readers, you decide where you want to read from, and choose one of the InputStream classes accordingly (see Table 13-8).

Table 13–8 Choose the Input Stream Class Based on the Source of the Input

Read Binary Input From:	java.io Class	Constructors

A **file**	FileInputStream	public FileInputStream(java.lang.String) throws java.io.FileNotFoundException;
		public FileInputStream(java.io.File) throws java.io.FileNotFoundException;
		public FileInputStream(java.io.FileDescriptor);

A **byte array** in your program	ByteArrayInputStream	public ByteArrayInputStream(byte []); public ByteArrayInputStream(byte [], int from, int len);
A **pipe** to be read by a PipedOutputStream in another thread	PipedInputStream	public PipedInputStream(java.io.PipedOutputStream) throws java.io.IOException; public PipedInputStream();
A StringBuffer object	StringBufferInputStream	*this class has been deprecated, don't use it.*

As before, you connect to socket and URL input streams using a method call, rather than a constructor. The method getInputStream() returns an input stream connected to the network resource, as shown in Table 13-9.

Table 13–9 Choose the getInputStream() Method Based on the Source of the Data

Read Input From:	Class	Method in That Class to Get an Input Stream
A **socket**	java.net.Socket	public InputStream **getInputStream**() throws java.io.IOException;
A **URL** connection	java.net.URLConnection	public InputStream **getInputStream**() throws java.io.IOException;

Using the constructors or method calls we can get an input stream that reads bytes from a file, a socket, a URL, a pipe, or a byte array. Once you have your input stream of whatever variety, it has certain basic methods available.

Basic InputStream Methods

All InputStreams give you at least these three somewhat basic input methods:

```
public int read()
public int read(byte[] b)
public int read(byte[] b, int from, int len)
```

These read into, respectively, a single byte, an array of bytes, and a range in an array of bytes. The call will not return until some data is available to read, although it won't necessarily fill the array. The return value will be -1 if the InputStream hits end of file (EOF). This is why the single byte call returns a 32-bit int, even though it only reads a 8-bit byte. The high-order 24 bits in the return value allow you to distinguish EOF from a byte read. Those bits will be zero when a data byte is read and 0xFFFFFF when EOF is reached.

The ByteArrayInputStream allows you to take data from a byte array in your program using the read() methods rather than array indexing. There is a new package in JDK 1.4 called java.nio. This package supports methods that write out an array full of data to a stream with one statement. (See Chapter 14 for an example.)

All java.io classes with "InputStream" in their name have a few other methods, too, like close(), available(), and skip(). They are methods promised by the abstract class InputStream. To harp once more on the theme that is stressed throughout this chapter: you use InputStreams for reading bytes or binary values, not Unicode characters or objects.

If those three basic read() methods aren't enough, you will wrap another class around your Input Stream. The most common wrapper is a DataInputStream class to read binary bytes. Anything written with a DataOutputStream can be read back in by a DataInputStream. The DataInputStream class has these methods for binary input.

Methods of java.io.DataInputStream

```
public class java.io.DataInputStream
    extends java.io.FilterInputStream implements java.io.DataInput {
  public DataInputStream(java.io.InputStream);
  public final int read(byte[]) throws java.io.IOException;
  public final int read(byte[], int, int) throws java.io.IOException;
  public final void readFully(byte[]) throws java.io.IOException;
  public final void readFully(byte[], int, int) throws java.io.IOException;
  public final int skipBytes(int) throws java.io.IOException;
  public final boolean readBoolean() throws java.io.IOException;
  public final byte readByte() throws java.io.IOException;
  public final int readUnsignedByte() throws java.io.IOException;
  public final short readShort() throws java.io.IOException;
  public final int readUnsignedShort() throws java.io.IOException;
  public final char readChar() throws java.io.IOException;
  public final int readInt() throws java.io.IOException;
  public final long readLong() throws java.io.IOException;
  public final float readFloat() throws java.io.IOException;
  public final double readDouble() throws java.io.IOException;
  public final String readLine() throws java.io.IOException;  // deprecated
  public final String readUTF() throws java.io.IOException;
  public static final String readUTF(java.io.DataInput) throws java.io.IOException;
}
```

As you can see, there is a read method for all primitive types, e.g., readInt() to read an int. A line of 8-bit bytes can be read into a String using the readLine() method, but this has been deprecated because it lacks proper byte-to-double-byte conversion. You can also read a string that was written in the UTF-encoded format where characters are 1-3 bytes in length (readUTF() method). The UTF format string is preceded by a 16-bit length field, allowing your code to scoop up the right amount of data. Notice that, although there is a DataOutputStream.writeChars(), there is no DataInputStream.readChars(). You have to read chars one at a time, and you decide when you have read the entire string.

A Word About IOExceptions

Let's say a few words on the subject of IOExceptions. If you look at the runtime source, you'll see that there are a dozen I/O-related exceptions. The most common I/O-related exceptions are:

FileNotFoundException EOFException InterruptedIOException UTFDataFormatError

These are all subclasses of IOException. InterruptedIOException was supposed to be raised when you called the interrupt method of a thread that was blocked on I/O. It didn't work very well, and we'll look at the replacement in the next chapter.

The name EOFException suggests that it is thrown whenever EOF (end of file) is encountered, and that therefore this exception might be used as the condition to break out of a loop. Unhappily, it can't always be used that way. EOFException is raised in only three classes: DataInputStream, ObjectInputStream, and RandomAccessFile (and their subclasses, of course). The EOFException would be better named UnexpectedEOFException, as it is only raised when the programmer has asked for a fixed definite amount of input, and the end of file is reached before all the requested amount of data has been obtained.

EOFException is not a universal alert that the normal end of file has been reached. In FileInputStream or FileReader, you detect EOF by checking for the -1 return value from a read, not by trying to catch EOFException. So if you want to use an EOFException to terminate a loop, make sure that the methods you are using will throw you one. The compiler will generally warn you if you try to catch an exception that is not thrown.

FileNotFoundException is self-explanatory. UTFDataFormatException is thrown when the I/O library finds an inconsistency in reading some UTF data.

Example

Here is some sample code to read a file and dump its contents in hexadecimal. The read method of FileInputStream returns -1 when it reaches EOF, so we use that to terminate the "get more input" loop.

```
// This program hex dumps the contents of the file
// whose name is given as a commandline argument.
import java.io.*;
public class Dump {

    static FileInputStream myFIS = null;
    static FileOutputStream myFOS = null;
    static BufferedInputStream myBIS = null;
    static PrintStream myPOS = null;

    static public void main(String[] arg) {
        if (arg.length==0) {
            System.out.println("usage: java Dump somefile");
            System.exit();
        }
        PrintStream e = System.err;
        try {
            myFIS = new FileInputStream( arg[0] );
            myFOS = new FileOutputStream( arg[0] + ".hex" );

            myBIS = new BufferedInputStream(myFIS);
            // the "true" says we want writes flushed to disk with each newline
            myPOS = new PrintStream (
                            new BufferedOutputStream(myFOS), true);
            myPOS.print("Hex dump of file " + arg[0]);
            int i;
            while ( (i=myBIS.read()) != -1 ) {
                dump( (byte) i );
            }
        } catch(IOException x) {
            e.println("Exception: " + x.getMessage() );
        }
    }

    static private long byteCount = 0;

    static private void dump(byte b) {
        if (byteCount % 16 == 0) {
            // output newline and the address every 16 bytes
            myPOS.println();
```

(continued)

```
            // pad leading zeros in address.
            String addr = Long.toHexString(byteCount);
            while (addr.length() < 8) addr = "0" + addr;
            myPOS.print( addr + ":" );
        }

        // output a space every 4 bytes
        if (byteCount++ % 4 == 0) {
            myPOS.print("  ");
        }

        // dump the byte as 2 hex chars
        String s = Integer.toHexString( b & 0xFF );
        if (s.length()==1) s = "0" + s;
        myPOS.print( s.charAt(0) );
        myPOS.print( s.charAt(1) + " " );
    }
}
```

If you look at the "numbers.txt" output file with an editor that can display the contents of a file in hexadecimal, you will see four four-byte ints there containing the values written. Here is the beginning of the output you get from running this program on its own class file (it will vary with different compilers):

```
Hex dump of file Dump.class
00000000:  ca fe ba be  00 03 00 2d  00 8e 0a 00  2f 00 45 09
00000010:  00 46 00 47  07 00 48 0a  00 03 00 49  09 00 2e 00
00000020:  4a 07 00 4b  07 00 4c 0a  00 07 00 45  0a 00 07 00
00000030:  4d 08 00 4e  0a 00 07 00  4f 0a 00 06
```

The first int word of this class file is 0xCAFE 0xBABE. The first word of all Java class files is 0xCAFE 0xBABE. It is what is known as a "magic number"— a special value put at a special place in a file to confer the magic ability to distinguish this kind of file from any other. It allows Java tools like the JVM to check that they have been given a class file to execute against. If you are going to put a special value there, you might as well use one that is easy to recognize and remember!

We wrap the FileInputStream in a BufferedInputStream as described in the next section. The program would work just as well without buffering, but may be slower for large input files. In JDK 1.4, the default size of a buffer in this class is 0.5KB. That's *much* too small. For large inputs, you should do some measurements and think about moving this into the megabyte range.

Input Stream Wrappers

We have seen several times how a basic I/O class can be wrapped or "decorated" by another I/O class of the same parent class. So it should be no surprise that an InputStream can have a BufferedInputStream and/or a subclass of FilterInputStream interposed between the FileInputStream (or other data source) and the DataInputStream.

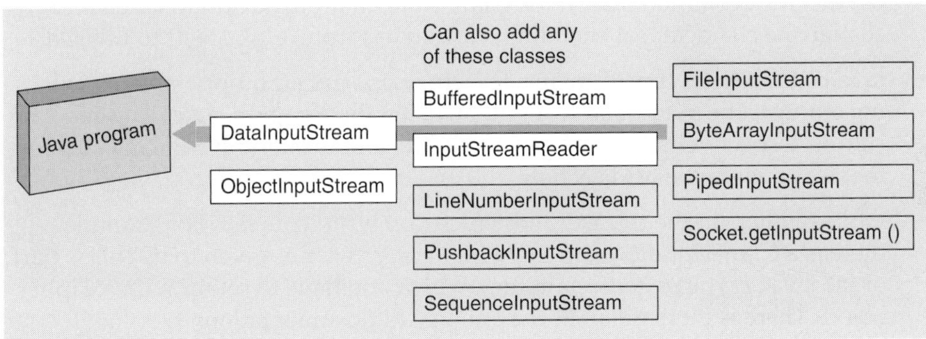

Figure 13–5 Classes that wrap Input Streams.

There are quite a variety of InputStreams that can decorate the basic access classes. Figure 13-5 shows some, but by no means all, of the most popular classes. You can wrap any or all of the following output streams onto your original InputStream:

- **BufferedInputStream**. This class must directly wrap the input source (e.g., the FileInputStream) to get the most performance benefit. You want the buffering to start as early as possible. Wrap any other classes around the buffered input stream.
- **Your subclass of FilterInputStream**. You will extend the class and override some or all of the read methods to filter the data on the way in.
- **LineNumberInputStream**. This class keeps track of the number of newlines it has seen in the input stream.
- **PushbackInputStream**. This class allows an arbitrary amount of data to be "pushed back" or returned to the input stream where it is available for re-reading. You might do this when you are trying to assemble a number out of digits in the input stream and you read past the end of the number.

- **SequenceInputStream**. This class provides the effect of gluing several input streams together, one after the other, so that as one stream is exhausted you seamlessly start reading from the next. You might use this when your data is spread across several data files with a similar format.
- **InputStreamReader**. This class converts an InputStream class to a Reader class, allowing you to layer any of the Reader classes on top of that. It provides a bridge from the 8-bit byte world to the 16-bit character world when you have an input stream and want a Reader. Remembering that the Reader methods are poor at processing anything with more structure than a character, the most common reason for going from an input stream to a Reader is to change the character set encoding—to convert from, e.g., ASCII to EBCDIC.
- **java.util.zip.GZIPInputStream**. The zip, gzip, and jar output streams will uncompress the bytes read from them, using the zip, gzip, and zip algorithms, respectively. An example of reading and expanding a file in GZip format is shown in the next section.
- various others in the release, and which you write yourself. For example, there is a CipherInputStream that will decrypt what is given to it. This is part of the javax.crypto extension library, which you have to set up with a Cipher object. There is more detail in the online API documentation.

At the very end of the chain of wrapped classes you generally have either a DataInputStream or an ObjectInputStream. The ObjectInputStream class allows you to read back in an object and all the objects it references. You can wrap this class around any of the other input streams, and read the object from a file, a socket, up from a pipe, etc. An example of object I/O is shown in the next chapter.

GZIP Files and Streams

The word "GZip" means GNU Zip. The GNU organization (a loose organization of expert programmers founded at MIT by Richard Stallman) has specified a simpler variant of a ZIP format that has become popular on Unix. It compresses its input by using the patent-free Lempel-Ziv coding. Gzip compressed format can only hold a single file, not an archive or directory of files, as with PK-ZIP. If you have several files, you must use the Unix "tar" utility to bundle them up into a single file first, then use the GZip Unix utility to compress that one file. Unpacking is the reverse of this. Here's the simplest example code to unpack a GZip file.

```
//  Expand a .gz file into uncompressed form
//  Peter van der Linden, August 2001

import java.io.*;
import java.util.zip.*;
public class expandgz {

    public static void main (String args[]) throws Exception {
        if (args.length == 0) {
            System.out.println("usage:  java expandgz  filename.gz");
            System.exit(0);
        }
        GZIPInputStream gzi = new GZIPInputStream(
                                    new FileInputStream( args[0] ));
        int to = args[0].lastIndexOf('.');
        if (to == -1) {
            System.out.println("usage:  java expandgz  filename.gz");
            System.exit(0);
        }
        String fout = args[0].substring(0, to);
        BufferedOutputStream bos = new BufferedOutputStream(
                                    new FileOutputStream(fout) );
        System.out.println("writing " + fout);

        int b;
         do {
            b = gzi.read();
            if (b==-1) break;
            bos.write(b);
        } while (true);
        gzi.close();
        bos.close();
    }
}
```

Executing this program will expand the gzip file whose name (e.g., abc.gz) is given on the command line. There is a corresponding GZIPOutputStream class that you can use to write a file into compressed gzip form. It would have been better for everyone if the GNU folks had not invented a new format, but just reverse-engineered zip. The Unix world wasn't paying enough attention to the PC world back in those days.

Suggested Use of Input Streams

- Use an Input Stream when you want to input binary values or ASCII text.
- Choose a FileInputStream or one of the getInputStream methods, depending on where you want the bytes to come from.
- You can optionally wrap that in an arbitrary number of InputStream filters, buffers, expanders, decoders, etc. Then wrap a DataInputStream on top, and use its read methods to do the input. Use ObjectInputStream if you are reconstituting objects rather than reading data.
- If you use a buffer, it should directly wrap the FileInputStream so that as much as possible of the "pipeline" of classes is buffered.

Further Reading

Here are some online resources for more information on other I/O packages:

Image I/O	*java.sun.com/products/java-media/jai/whatis.html* *industry.java.sun.com/javaone/99/event/0,1768,661,00.html* API docs at, e.g., file://c:/jdk1.4b/docs/api/index.html (click to package javax.imageio)
Speech	White paper at *java.sun.com/marketing/collateral/speech.html* Programmer's guide at *java.sun.com/products/java-media/speech/forDevelopers/jsapi-guide/Preface.html*
Logging	Overview at *java.sun.com/j2se/1.4/docs/guide/util/logging/overview.html* API docs at, e.g., file://c:/jdk1.4b/docs/api/index.html (click to package java.util.logging)
Communication ports	See the home page at *java.sun.com/products/javacomm/* The home page has a pointer to a user guide.
Printing	Be careful not to mistakenly read information on the older print APIs. *java.sun.com/printing/* API User Guide: *java.sun.com/j2se/1.4/docs/guide/jps/spec/JPSTOC.fm.html* API docs at, e.g., file://c:/jdk1.4b/docs/api/index.html (click to package javax.print). The API docs contain a small printing example.

Exercises

1. Measure the difference between buffered and non-buffered I/O operating with 10K 1-byte writes and one 10KB write, repeated 10,000 times in a loop. Draw a graph to illustrate your results. How do the results change with a buffer size of 128KB, 256KB, 512KB?
2. Modify the program that does a hex dump of a file so that it also outputs any printable bytes in a set of columns to the right of the hex dump on each line. Print the character if it has a printable form, and print a "." if it does not. This ensures that lines are the same length and columns line up.
3. Write a Java program whose output at runtime is an exact duplicate of the program's source code. The shortest Java program to do this is about a page of code.
4. Write a program that prints a table of printable ISO 8859-1 characters and their bit patterns.
5. Repeat the previous exercise using only the I/O class RandomAccessFile.
6. Rewrite the hex dumper utility to use one or more Filter classes. The first filter can turn binary bytes into the equivalent printable hex characters. The second filter can insert the addresses and newlines at appropriate points.
7. Rewrite the decss utility (see below) in Java. For extra credit, look up the algorithms on the web to actually carry out the decryption of an encoded DVD stream, and write Java code to do that. Does it run quickly enough to decode and play in real time? Explain why or why not.

Some Light Relief—The Illegal Prime Number!

By now everyone is familiar with DVDs—originally an acronym for "Digital Video Disc," later changed to "Digital Versatile Disk" for pointless marketing reasons. DVDs are similar to CD-ROMs in many ways, with a crucial difference that DVDs can hold about 4.7GBytes, or about seven times as much data as a CD. The tracks and the bits in the tracks are packed closer together on a DVD, which is why DVD players can read CDs but not vice-versa. If you use a suitable compression technology, you can actually squeeze up to 133 minutes of high resolution video with several soundtracks and subtitles onto a DVD. The compression is essential, and the movie industry uses the MPEG-2 algorithm that was designed for this purpose, and which provides 40-1 compression. The more efficient MPEG-4 (DivX) compression, which provides another fivefold reduction, is also being introduced.

However, since the movie industry doesn't want to be Napstered (have their content ripped off and broadcast for free on the Internet), they encrypt the MPEG-2 files using an algorithm called the Content Scrambling System or CSS. If you do a directory listing of a DVD, you'll see some large .VOB files. These are Video OBjects, a fancy name for content scrambled .MPG2 files. Every maker of DVD players on the planet is supposed to license the decryption algorithm from the DVD Copy Control Association (DVD-CCA) for a fee, and they impose several restrictions on the player. DCC-CCA is believed to be a subsidiary of Matsushita, the company mainly responsible for the development of DVD and CSS. Some of its restrictions take away rights that consumers have long enjoyed under copyright law. They seem more geared towards controlling what consumers can do, rather than dealing with problems of rip-offs and piracy.

So what are the restrictions that licensed DVD players have to impose? CSS encryption allows the DVD industry to force region restrictions into all DVD players. There are six geographic regions (North America, Europe, etc.) and in 1999 they added a seventh for DVDs intended for airplanes. A player in region one will refuse to play disks labelled as belonging to any other region. Region restrictions allow the movie industry to sell the same DVD at different prices in different markets. It prevents any DVDs you buy on business trips outside your region from being played on your home system. The CSS encryption also prevents you from fast-forwarding past the copyright warning or advertisements or any other content the producer wants you to see. You can sell commercials for a much higher price if people cannot skip past them. Some people speculate that CSS is also paving the way for more restrictions such as DVDs with a limited lifetime or limited number of viewings. The movie industry blows a lot of smoke about CSS preventing large scale piracy, but CSS does nothing whatever to prevent pirates from copying DVDs. Its only effect is enforcing use limitations on end consumers.

For a long time, there was no software to play DVDs available for Linux. If you had a shelf full of DVDs that you had bought, you could play them all on your tv or Windows box, but because of the CSS restrictions, not on your Linux or Solaris system. The CSS restrictions were the equivalent of a book publisher enforcing a restriction that you could read a book under incandescent lighting but not under fluorescent lighting or daylight. No one in the Linux community had the means to pay the "CSS tax" to the DVD-CCA. Then, in October 1999, a nameless German hacker reverse-engineered CSS. The source code to decrypt DVDs was published on the web by a 15-year-old boy from Norway. The program was called "deCSS" because it reverses CSS, turning the encrypted files into ordinary MPEG-2 files.

There then followed an extraordinary game of "whack-a-mole" as the DVD-CCA and the Motion Picture Association of America (MPAA) tried to chase the source code around the web and sue it out of existence. That game continues today. As far as we know, American laws do not apply in Norway, but the 15-year-old boy was hauled off by the foolish Norwegian police who also seized his PC and his cell phone. The cell phone was a lucky guess on the part of the cops, because he did actually have a back-up copy of the source stored in it (cell phones these days are effectively quite powerful computers, and many cell phones contain a JVM).

The U.S. movie industry had the foresight (and the impudence) to get a law passed so that it is illegal to write, publish, possess, or run code like deCSS. The Digital Copyright Millennium Act (DMCA) made it illegal to circumvent a "technological protection measure" put in place by the copyright owner. That means the deCSS program is illegal. Write a program to play a DVD that you own, and you could go to jail! The DCMA is a poorly-constructed law, written by the movie industry to advance its own interests at the expense of consumers. It will eventually be replaced by something more sensible but it all takes time. This is not theoretical. A Russian software developer was arrested under the DCMA by FBI agents in Las Vegas in July 2001 one day after he publicly pointed out copyright protection weaknesses in Adobe software.

Hackers started to vie with each other for the most imaginative way to publish the deCSS code. America has very strong guarantees concerning freedom of speech, and there are long-standing precedents saying that printed text (even source code) counts as speech. Programmers embedded the code in JPEG files, put the algorithm in plain English, and one person even wrote the deCSS steps in the form of a *haiku* (Japanese poetry)! There is a whole gallery of these deCSS publications at *www.cs.cmu.edu/~dst/DeCSS/Gallery/* (assuming it hasn't been sued off the net yet).

My absolute favorite deCSS code exists in the form of a prime number. Computer scientist and number theory fan Phil Carmody found a prime number which expresses the deCSS code! Phil felt strongly that the Motion Picture Association was acting in bad faith, and to oppose this he wanted to make sure that the DeCSS code was archived somewhere beyond the reach of the law. Somewhere where the number would be allowed to be printed because it had some property that made it publishable, independent of whether it was "illegal" or not. Phil had done a lot of work with prime numbers and prime number proving. It can't be illegal to possess a prime number, can it? Or can it? Basic common sense says no, but the DCMA says yes!

Phil took the deCSS source file, which contains about 100 lines of C code, and gzipped it to make it smaller. That resulted in a binary file about 600 bytes long. Then Phil considered the file as, not a 4-byte integer or an 8-byte long integer, but a ~600-byte binary super-long integer, and he looked for a small number he could append so that the whole thing would be a prime number. In character terms, say the code gzipped to the string "100," Phil was looking for an odd number suffix like "9" that would make the whole string (in this case "1009") a prime number. That kind of search is quick and easy to program.

Number theory told Phil that his chances were about 1 in 1,600 of finding a one or two byte suffix that would make the entire number prime. There wasn't a one byte suffix, so he went on to look for a two byte suffix. Even though the chances were very slim, he found one! If he had not found one, he would have simply gone on to test longer suffixes and change variable names in the code until eventually a prime number was reached. The resulting prime number is shown below. It is 1,401 digits long.

The Illegal Prime Number!

4856507896573978293098418946942861377074420873513579240196520736
6869851340104723744696879743992611751097377770102744752804905883
1384037549709987909653955227011712157025974666993240226834596619
6060348517424977358468518855674570257125474999648219418465571008
4119086259716947970799152004866709975923596061320725973797993618
8606316914473588300245336972781813914797955513399949394882899846
9178361001825978901031601961835034344895687053845208538045842415
6548248893338047475871128339598968522325446084089711197712769412
0795862440547161321005006459820176961771809478113622002723448272
2493232595472346880029277764979061481298404283457201463489685471
6908235473783566197218622496943162271666393905543024156473292485
5248991225739466548627140482117138124388217717602984125524464744
5055834628144883356319027253195904392838737640739168912579240550
1562088978716337599910788708490815909754801928576845198859630532
3823490558092032999603234471140776019847163531161713078576084862
2363702835701049612595681846785965333100770179916146744725492728
3348691600064758591746278121269007351830924153010630289329566584
3662000800476778967984382090797619859493646309380586336721469695
9750279687712057249966669805614533820741203159337703099491527469
1835659376210222006812679827344576093802030447912277498091795593
8387121000588766689258448700470772552497060444652127130404321182
6101035911864766629638584950874484973734768614208805294 43

Here's a little Java program that takes a large number stored as a string (such as the one above, hint, hint), turns that string into a super-long binary integer, and then writes that out as a gzip file. You can easily write a Java program like the example shown earlier in this chapter to expand it into a C source code file. But remember, it is illegal to have or compile or run such a source code file under American law prevailing since 1998.

Converting a Number to Binary and Writing to a File

```
// Convert a big number into binary and write it out
// Peter van der Linden, June 2001

import java.io.*;
import java.math.*;
public class togz {

    static String illegalPrime =
"4856507896573978293098418946942861377074420873513579240196520736" +
"plug the rest of the number in here... ";

    static BigInteger b = new BigInteger(illegalPrime);
    static final BigInteger two_five_six = new BigInteger("256");

    static byte[] result = new byte[illegalPrime.length()];

    public static void main (String args[]) throws Exception {
        BigInteger d_r [];

        if (b.isProbablePrime(5))
            System.out.println("b is probably prime (good)");
        else System.out.println("b is probably not prime (bad!)");

        int i=0;
        do {
            d_r = b.divideAndRemainder(two_five_six);
            b = d_r[0];    // the multiple
            result[i++] = (byte) d_r[1].intValue(); // the remainder
        } while ( b.compareTo( two_five_six ) = 0);

        result[i] = (byte) b.intValue();

        System.out.println("writing bytes.gz");
        FileOutputStream fos = new FileOutputStream("bytes.gz");

        DataOutputStream dos = new DataOutputStream(fos);
        for (int j=i; j0; j--) {
            dos.writeByte( result[j] );
        }
        fos.close();
    }
}
```

Run winzip on the resulting .gz file to unpack it, and voila, you become eligible for a prison sentence of up to 20 years. What's wrong with this picture? The CSS descrambler that you get is just three or four utility routines, not a main program. To play DVDs on your Linux, Mac, Solaris, or even Windows box, you'll need to download the software from one of several open source DVD players. I like the one at *www.videolan.org*.

Alternatively, if you like putting things together by hand, you can do a websearch for "vobdec," which is an open source utility that lets you discover the title keys on the encrypted DVDs that you own. If you have the title key you can run the `efdtt` utility (do another websearch) to turn the encrypted MPEG stream into a clear one and just point it at your favorite player.

Finally, you can try rewriting any of these in Java for fun. Just don't blame me if the FBI knocks on your door with an MPAA warrant and seizes your debugger. Illegal code! The very idea! Next thing you know, they'll be declaring t-shirts illegal.

Chapter 14

Advanced Input Output

- Random Access File
- Reading from the Keyboard
- Running Commands and Getting Output from Them
- Formatted String Output
- Writing Objects to Disk
- New I/O Package
- Memory Mapped I/O
- File Locking
- Charsets and Endian-ness
- Exercises
- Some Light Relief—The Illegal T-Shirt!

I-O!
I-O!
It's off to work we go!
I-O, I/O, I/O.

This chapter follows on from the basic I/O chapter and provides information on more advanced I/O techniques in about a half-dozen sections, mostly independent. The section on the new I/O package (in JDK 1.4 with the name java.nio) is needed to understand the three new features of pattern matching, file locking, and character sets. You can read other sections in any order, or indeed skip the entire chapter now and return when you need information on any one of these topics.

Random Access File

Until now we have seen how input and output is done in a serial mode. However, sometimes we want to be able to move around inside a file and write to different locations, or read from different locations, without having to scan all the data. Traveling in a file stream in such a manner is called "random access."

Java has a random access file class that can do these operations. This is not an indexed sequential file or a direct access file of the kind supported by data processing languages. Those two techniques require the creation and maintenance of special indexes to address the file. The class java.io.RandomAccessFile does not use indices, but lets you access a file as though it were an array of bytes. There is an index or pointer that says where the next read or write will take place. You get the value of the index with the method getFilePointer(). You set the file pointer with the method seek() giving an argument that is the absolute offset into the file. When you set the file pointer, the next access will take place at the offset indicated. Because of the way operating systems store file contents, moving around in a file does not necessarily involve inefficient reading and rereading.

class java.io.RandomAccessFile

```
public class RandomAccessFile implements java.io.DataOutput, java.io.DataInput {
  public RandomAccessFile(java.lang.String,java.lang.String) throws
     java.io.FileNotFoundException;
  public RandomAccessFile(java.io.File,java.lang.String) throws java.io.FileNotFoundException;
  public final java.nio.channels.FileChannel getChannel();  // used for locking file
  public final java.io.FileDescriptor getFD() throws java.io.IOException;
  public native int read() throws java.io.IOException;
  public int read(byte[], int, int) throws java.io.IOException;
  public int read(byte[]) throws java.io.IOException;
  public final void readFully(byte[]) throws java.io.IOException;
  public final void readFully(byte[], int, int) throws java.io.IOException;
  public int skipBytes(int) throws java.io.IOException;
  public native void write(int) throws java.io.IOException;
  public void write(byte[]) throws java.io.IOException;
  public void write(byte[], int, int) throws java.io.IOException;

  public native long getFilePointer() throws java.io.IOException;
  public native void seek(long) throws java.io.IOException;
  public native long length() throws java.io.IOException;
  public native void setLength(long) throws java.io.IOException;
  public native void close() throws java.io.IOException;

  public final boolean readBoolean() throws java.io.IOException;
  public final byte readByte() throws java.io.IOException;
  public final int readUnsignedByte() throws java.io.IOException;
  public final short readShort() throws java.io.IOException;
  public final int readUnsignedShort() throws java.io.IOException;
  public final char readChar() throws java.io.IOException;
  public final int readInt() throws java.io.IOException;
  public final long readLong() throws java.io.IOException;
  public final float readFloat() throws java.io.IOException;
  public final double readDouble() throws java.io.IOException;
  public final java.lang.String readLine() throws java.io.IOException;
  public final java.lang.String readUTF() throws java.io.IOException;
  public final void writeBoolean(boolean) throws java.io.IOException;
  public final void writeByte(int) throws java.io.IOException;
  public final void writeShort(int) throws java.io.IOException;
  public final void writeChar(int) throws java.io.IOException;
  public final void writeInt(int) throws java.io.IOException;
  public final void writeLong(long) throws java.io.IOException;
  public final void writeFloat(float) throws java.io.IOException;
  public final void writeDouble(double) throws java.io.IOException;
  public final void writeBytes(java.lang.String) throws java.io.IOException;
  public final void writeChars(java.lang.String) throws java.io.IOException;
  public final void writeUTF(java.lang.String) throws java.io.IOException;
}
```

You instantiate a random access file with a mode string that says whether you plan to read the file or both read and write it. The mode string is "r" for reading, and "rw" for reading and writing. Throughout Java I/O, although there is a notion of closing files, there is no notion of opening a file. More precisely, the instantiation of a file object automatically opens the file for I/O. When you open for read/write access, if the file does not exist, it is created. Following is an example of opening a random access file, seeking to the end, and then writing some more data. You should run this program and check that you get the expected output. When you run the program repeatedly, you will find it is appending to its output file.

```
import java.io.*;
public class Raf {
   public static void main(String args[]) throws IOException {
      RandomAccessFile myRAF = new RandomAccessFile("myfile.dat", "rw");
      myRAF.seek( myRAF.length() ); // append to end of file
      myRAF.writeInt(5);
      myRAF.writeInt(0xBEEF);
      myRAF.writeBytes("at end.");
      myRAF.close();
      System.out.println("file myfile.dat written ok");
   }
}
```

RandomAccessFile doesn't fit very well into the rest of the I/O framework, but nonetheless provides some useful features, including being able to read a line of data, which you can then break up into tokens. There are exampies of tokenizing lines of data from a different context in the next section.

Reading from the Keyboard

Java is missing some basic terminal input routines. If you want to do interactive I/O, you are supposed to do it with a GUI. If you insist on doing interactive I/O from the command line, you have to piece together your own support using several classes. Your pieces will operate on the terminal I/O objects System.in and System.out.

Output to the terminal is just the ordinary stream output we have already seen. But input suffers from the problem that there is no "raw" I/O in Java. In other words, there is no way to look at individual characters as they are typed. The only way to get input characters from the terminal is a line at a time, after the user has pressed carriage return (newline, enter, or whatever it is labelled on your keyboard). When you have an entire line, use java.util.StringTokenizer or java.io.StreamTokenizer to split the input up into strings. The tokenizer classes look for particular characters in strings and break them into smaller strings around that character. You can use them to split a comma-separated list like "eggs, bread, apples, lemons" into four individual strings.

Let's go back to System.in and see how we can assemble numbers out of the characters we know how to read in. After tokenizing into a String that just contains one number, we use various conversion methods to convert the string to float, int, etc. In all cases, we have to know in advance what type we are reading in. We need to know what to expect because the methods for reading a boolean, an int, a floating-point number, and so on, are all different.

Follow this process:

- Wrap an InputStreamReader on System.in. This gives us a Reader class on which we can layer other Readers.
- Wrap a BufferedReader on the InputStreamReader. This gives us a method that reads an entire line, allowing us to get all the text as a String when the user presses Return.
- Wrap a java.util.StringTokenizer on the String just read in. Call the nextToken() method to extract the first group of nonspace characters. This makes the input format a little more forgiving by removing trailing and leading whitespace.
- Finally, use the parseXxx method, found in the wrapper classes for the primitive types, to extract a value of the expected type. For example, use Boolean.parseBoolean(someString) to get a true/false value.

The combination of classes needed to read from the keyboard is painful, to say the least. It is a major wart on Java's mostly reasonable claim to simplicity. This book comes with an easy keyboard input class called EasyIn. You can find it on the CD. It uses the techniques shown here to read values from the keyboard.

Table 14-1 shows how to read values from the keyboard and get them into a primitive type in your program.

Table 14–1 Reading from the Keyboard

Preliminary Declarations

```
import java.io.*;
import java.util.*;
...
InputStreamReader is = new InputStreamReader( System.in );
BufferedReader br = new BufferedReader(is);
...
String s = br.readLine();
StringTokenizer st = new StringTokenizer(s);
```

Primitive Type	Code to Read It from System.in
char	int i = is.read(); // -1 denotes EOF char c = (char) i;
String	String s = br.readLine();
boolean	boolean bo = new Boolean(st.nextToken()).booleanValue();
int	int i = Integer.parseInt(st.nextToken());
byte	byte by = Byte.parseByte(st.nextToken());
short	short sh = Short.parseShort(st.nextToken());
long	long lo = Long.parseLong(st.nextToken());
float	float fl = new Float.parseFloat(st.nextToken());
double	double db = new Double.parseDouble(st.nextToken());

Note: Each statement or group of statements must either have an exception handler wrapped around it, or the method must declare that it throws an IOException. See the example below.

For the sake of completeness, here is the full code to prompt for and read an int value from the command line.

```
import java.io.*;
import java.util.*;
public class ReadIn2 {
    public static void main(String f[]) {
        int i=0;
        char c;
        InputStreamReader is = new InputStreamReader( System.in );
        BufferedReader br = new BufferedReader(is );
        StringTokenizer st;
        try {
          System.out.print( "int: ");
          System.out.flush();
          String myline = br.readLine();
          st = new StringTokenizer(myline);
          i = Integer.parseInt(st.nextToken());
          System.out.println( "got: " + i );
        } catch (IOException ioe) {
          System.out.println("IO error:" + ioe ); }
    }
}
```

Most programmers would agree that this is excessively complicated for a simple thing like interactive I/O. When Java 1.0 came out, I filed a bug against the I/O library on this topic and included in the bug report my suggested fix: the code for a new class that supported simple keyboard I/O. Alas, all efforts were in vain, for the Sun division formerly known as Javasoft made it clear that the lacuna (gap) had a low priority, and that you should do interactive I/O using a GUI, not the command line.

Running Commands and Getting Output from Them

This section explains how to execute a program from Java and read the output of that program back into your application. Just as a reminder, there are two limitations. First, untrusted applets are not allowed to do this (for security reasons). Second, the use of OS commands in your code destroys portability. If you can live within these limitations, there are four general steps to executing a program from your Java program.

1. Get the object representing the current runtime environment. A static method in class java.lang.Runtime does this.
2. Call the exec method in the runtime object, with your command as an argument string. Give the full path name to the executable, and make sure the executable really exists on the system. The call to exec() returns a Process object.
3. Connect the output of the Process (which will be coming to you as an input stream) to an input stream reader in your program.
4. You can either read individual characters from the input stream, or layer a BufferedReader on it and read a line at a time as in the code below.

Many books use the example of getting a list of files in a directory, even though there is already a Java method to do that in class File. The following code will return an array of Strings, one string for each file name in the directory:

```
File f = new File(".");
String myFiles[] = f.list();
```

The file with the magic name of "." is used on many operating systems to refer to the current working directory. We will use a different example here. We will execute a command in our Java program to make a file read-only. On Linux or other Unix, the command used would be "/bin/chmod +r", on Windows we use the "attrib +R" command as shown in the code below.

Executing the Attrib Command from Java

```
import java.io.*;
public class ReadOnly {
   public static void main(String args[]) {
      try {
        Runtime rt = Runtime.getRuntime();  // step 1
        String cmd =
          "c:\\windows\\command\\attrib.exe  +R " + args[0];
        Process prcs = rt.exec(cmd);        // step 2
        InputStreamReader isr =             // step 3
          new InputStreamReader( prcs.getInputStream() );
        BufferedReader in =
          new BufferedReader( isr );        // step 4.
        String line;
        System.out.println("have set to read-only");
        while (in.ready()) {
          System.out.println(in.readLine());
        }
        // Clean up
        prcs.waitFor();
        in.close();
      } catch(Exception e) { System.out.println(e); }
   }
}
```

This program uses a class inside java.lang called Runtime, which does a couple of runtime-related things. The main use is to provide a way to execute other programs, but it can also force garbage collection or finalization and tell you how much total memory and free memory is available within the JVM (not the system as a whole).

The exec() method returns an object of class Process. That object allows you to get the in, out, and err streams from a process, and to wait for it to complete. You'll often see the lines of code reduced by directly wrapping the classes on each other, like this:

```
prcs = Runtime.getRuntime().exec(cmd);
in = new BufferedReader(
      new InputStreamReader( prcs.getInputStream()));
```

That replaces the lines commented as steps 1,2,3, and 4 in the example. The attrib program that we have executed here doesn't produce any output, but we show how you can read lines from the InputStream for programs that do produce output. The waitFor() method lets the native program complete before the Java program continues on.

You can run the program and check the results with

```
c:\ javac ReadOnly.java
c:\ java ReadOnly somefile
have set to read-only
c:\ dir /ar

 Volume in drive C has no label
 Volume Serial Number is 0D2B-14DC
 Directory of C:\JJ4\ch14io

SOMEFILE                6 08-24-01 7:56a somefile
         1 file(s)          6 bytes
         0 dir(s)     978.20 MB free
```

The "ar" option tells "dir" to only show files with the read-only attribute.

Note that there are half a dozen other versions of the Runtime.exec() method taking different arguments. These arguments can specify environment variables and the new working directory for the subprocess. Please refer to the API guide for the full list.

Limitations on Running Processes

We already mentioned that an untrusted applet does not have permission to run executables. The Runtime.exec methods do not work well for special processes such as native windowing processes, daemon processes, Win16 or DOS processes on Win32, or shell scripts. In other words, many of the most useful things don't work! You can expect to run a non-graphics program and that's about it. There are other problems, too:

- Most platforms provide limited buffer size for standard input and output streams. It might be as small as 1 or 2Kbytes! If you do not promptly write to the input stream and read from the output stream of the subprocess, you may cause that subprocess to block and even deadlock. The same problem is often seen with Piped I/O, and it seems like everyone has to find out this limitation the hard way.
- The created subprocess is not started in an interactive shell, and so it does not have its own terminal or console. All its standard I/O (i.e., in, out, error) will take place to/from the parent process. The parent process uses the three streams (Process.getOutputStream(), Process.getInputStream(), Process.getErrorStream()) to feed input to and get output from the subprocess.
- Another implication of not running the program in an interactive shell is that the exec method does not have the ability to look for executables in the search path that your shell (or command interpreter) knows about. You should provide the complete path name for the command. This also means you cannot use commands that are built into a shell unless you explicitly call a shell as the program you wish to run (DIR and DEL are two Windows commands that are actually implemented by the shell). On Windows you can do a "find" for files with a ".exe" suffix to see which programs you can run.
- You will only be able to communicate with programs that use standard in, out, and err. Some programs like xterm open a new tty, or a GUI. These programs cannot be used as you would wish.

When you add all these restrictions together, plus the fact that a program that invokes an OS command or other program is often not portable, the usefulness of the approach can be limited.

Formatted String Output

The previous chapter showed how to write binary data such as ASCII or Unicode characters. That leads directly to the next requirement. How do we control the format of the numbers that are output? How do we specify that we want exactly two decimal places for floating-point numbers? "Format" in this section means "appearance on the printed page." Some support for formatted output was introduced with JDK 1.1, and it uses the classes in the package java.text. The package contains classes to help with collation (sorting order), formatting numbers and dates, and program messages to users. Formatting a number allows localization to Western, Arabic, or Indic numbers, as well as specifying such things as the number of decimal places.

A class called java.text.DecimalFormat has a constructor that takes a string which is a template for the format you want. You get back a DecimalFormat object and call its format() method, passing in your number. The method is overloaded for doubles and longs, so you can call it with any kind of primitive type number. Here's an example:

```
DecimalFormat df = new DecimalFormat( "#0.00;#0.00CR");
System.out.println( df.format( -1.267) );
```

The output will be:

```
1.26CR // the output
```

The format string you pass to the constructor will be made up of the symbols shown in Table 14.2. The symbols will indicate the significant digits, where to put the sign, and how positive numbers differ from negative numbers, and so on. You assemble the individual chars into a string and invoke the DecimalFormat constructor with it. That gives you back an object with a method that will format numbers in that style.

Table 14–2 Some Symbols Used in a Format String

Symbol	Meaning
0	A digit
#	A digit, with zero being dropped (not shown as a space)
.	Where the decimal point goes
,	Where the grouping separator goes
-	The default prefix indicating a negative number
%	Multiply by 100 and show as a percentage
;	Separates positive and negative formats in the format string

You can put two of these formats together separated by a semicolon. The first format will then be used for positive and zero numbers, and the second format will be applied to negative numbers. Some useful, complete format strings are shown in Table 14-3. As a reminder, you pass the string to the constructor of DecimalFormat, and you get back an object whose format() methods will turn any binary value into a formatted string. The class java.text.DecimalFormat is designed for common uses; for very large or small numbers, you should use a format that can express exponential values. Here is an example of using the number format class to get numbers printed with two decimal places. Notice that if rounding is needed, we have to do it ourselves. The format just truncates, though it would be a good idea to add a format character that says "round this digit in that direction."

Table 14–3 Some Typical Format Strings

Format String Used in Constructor	Meaning	Data	Output Result
"##0.00"	At least one digit before the decimal point, and two after	1234.567 0.256	1234.56 0.25
"#.000"	Possibly no digits before the point, three after	1234.567 0.256	1234.567 .256
",###"	Use thousands separator and no decimal places	1234.567 0.256	1,234 0
"0.00;0.00-"	Show negative numbers with sign on the right	ˆ27.5	27.5ˆ

Here is a program that demonstrates the use of DecimalFormat.

```
import java.io.*;
import java.text.*;
// write binary data as formatted characters
public class exformat {
   public static void main(String f[]) {
      double db[] = { -1.1, 2.2, -3.33, 4.444, -5.5555, 6.66666};
      DecimalFormat df = new DecimalFormat( "#0.00;#0.00CR" );
      for (int i=0; i<db.length; i++) {
         System.out.println( df.format( db[i]) );
      }
   }
}
```

Running this code gives the output shown next. The symbol CR (credit) used for negative numbers is a common business usage.

```
% java exformat
1.10CR
2.20
3.33CR
4.44
5.55CR
6.66
```

A comment in the DecimalFormat class warns that the normal use is to get a proper format string for a specific locale using one of the methods such as getInstance(). You may then modify it from there (after testing to make sure it is a DecimalFormat). They are suggesting that the proper usage is something like this:

```
NumberFormat nf = NumberFormat.getInstance( myLocale );
if (nf instanceof DecimalFormat) {
      ((DecimalFormat) f).setDecimalSeparatorAlwaysShown(true);
}
String result = nf.format( mydouble );
```

In other words, the format in which a number is printed may need to take account of the locale (geographical region). The "decimal separator" is what the Java locale folks call the decimal point. In some parts of Europe, a decimal point is a "." and in other parts it is a "," so formatting a number is bound up with internationalization and localization. Another choice is whether the decimal point appears when an integer is being formatted. Should 123 display as "123" or "123."? The previous code will cause the latter.

How Many Digits Are Output?

The Java Language Specification (section 20.10.15) says that when you output a double or float as a character string, by default it should print as many decimal places as are necessary to ensure that the number can be read back in without loss of precision. There must be at least one digit to represent the fractional part, and beyond that as many more digits as are needed to uniquely distinguish the argument value from adjacent values of type double. That could be up to 15 digits! See *www.javasoft.com/doc/language_specification/index.html* to read the specification online.

Before JDK 1.1, the floating-point output routines output six decimal places at most. From JDK 1.1 on, you get floating-point output that ensures exactly that value can be read back in again, which sometimes leads to what looks like an excessive number of decimal places being printed. When you use a NumberFormat class, you get neater output, but you lose the ability to read the number back in with the same exact value it had when output.

You Can Also Format Dates

As well as DecimalFormat, there is a java.text.DateFormat class. This gives you fine control over the formatting and parsing of Dates. The formatting styles include FULL, LONG, MEDIUM, and SHORT, which control how much the date is abbreviated ("Sept" vs. "September"). The fields can be made to appear in different orders, and in numbers or text strings. The online API has a full description of date formatting.

Writing Objects to Disk

We've already seen how to write out strings, ints, doubles, etc., in both printable and binary forms. It may surprise you to learn that you can also write out, and later read back in, entire objects. When you serialize (write out) a single object to a data stream, it automatically saves the object, namely, all its instance data. If any of these non-static fields reference other objects, those objects are serialized too. That way, when you later deserialize (restore) the object, you get back the object and all its member fields pointing to all the things they pointed to before—everything needed to reconstitute the original object.

For example, if you serialize one element of a doubly-linked list, everything it references, and everything the references reference, and so on, will be saved. For an element of a doubly-linked list, that means the elements on each side of it, and the elements on each side of those (one of which is the original element—that doesn't get written out twice), and so on until the entire list has been written to disk.

The point of including everything that your object connects to, and all the things they connect to and so on, is to ensure that you can use those objects with the same state and contents that they had when you originally wrote them out. Doesn't this swell up the size of what you're writing until it's as big as your entire program? Objects contain references to their member fields, but members tend not to back reference the object of which they are a field. That means the links mostly go one way, and so serialized objects in practice remain a manageable size.

It's quite powerful to be able to do I/O on an entire graph of objects with one simple method call. If an object can be written to a stream, it can also be sent through a socket, compressed, encrypted, read out of a socket on another host, backed up onto a file, and later read back in again and reconstituted.

To make an object serializable, all you need do is make its class implement the Serializable interface. The interface java.io.Serializable doesn't have any methods or fields. It is an example of the Marker Interface design pattern. The purpose of requiring a class to implement an empty interface is to identify to other programmers and to the runtime library that it can be serialized. Here is a class that can be serialized:

```
package java.util;
public class Date implements java.io.Serializable { ...
```

Here is how you can serialize a Date object, and save it in a file:

```
// first create the file
FileOutputStream fos = new FileOutputStream("serial.bin");
ObjectOutputStream oos = new ObjectOutputStream ( fos );

// create a Date, and write it out
java.util.Date d = new java.util.Date();
oos.writeObject(d);
```

You can go on to write many more objects into the ObjectOutputStream. You need to be aware of the types that you are writing, so that you can cast them correctly back to their original type when you read them in again. Here is how you would read a serialized object back in again:

```
FileInputStream fis = new FileInputStream("serial.bin");
ObjectInputStream ois = new ObjectInputStream ( fis );

Object o = ois.readObject();

java.util.Date savedDate = (java.util.Date) o;
```

It usually comes as a very pleasant surprise to people to see that serialization is so easy! When you read an object back in, it has the type of Object. You need to cast it back to what it actually is. Casting is type-safe in Java; you cannot force an object into a class it doesn't belong to. A ClassCastException is raised if you try that. In the example, we really are reading in a Date, and so the cast takes place without a problem. If you put the above lines in a main program and add a couple of println's for the date before and after serialization, you will see output like this:

```
javac Serial.java
java Serial
date before serialization: Mon Sep 10 13:34:12 PDT 2001
date after serialization: Mon Sep 10 13:34:12 PDT 2001
```

The important thing here is that the Date object survived its journey out into the filesystem, and came back in with the same value. Reading and writing objects is thankfully very simple. It is extensively used in Remote Method Invocation (RMI), and Chapter 18 walks through a practical example. There is no difference between serializing a Java library object and one of your own objects. You can serialize a String or an array, and arrays are treated just like objects.

If a class is serializable, so are its subclasses (any interfaces of a parent are always inherited by the child). You can make a class serializable even if its parent isn't as long as the parent has a no-arg constructor and the child takes responsibility for restoring any parent context that wasn't serialized.

Serializing and Security

Java object serialization was developed as an enabler for two other technologies: RMI and Java Beans. When serialization was still in the design stage inside Sun, there was a great deal of debate about whether Java could allow serialization as the default setting. In other words, classes would have to opt out of allowing it, rather than opt in.

After a lot of soul-searching, it was decided that programmers must take some explicit step to indicate that a class can be serializable (namely, we have to state that the class implements Serializable). The reason is that there are security implications to serializing a class.

If you serialize something like a file descriptor, someone could edit the file containing it and change some of the fields. When the file descriptor is read back in and deserialized, it will now be pointing at a different entry in the OS file descriptor table, perhaps something outside the table altogether. Even though the exploit took place using native code, it would detract from the overall high level of security that Java enjoys.

So designers need to consider the security aspects when they make a class serializable. What happens if some field is given a different value while the object is in a file? Perhaps some kind of validation can be done after the object is read back in. Fields can be cross-checked for consistency with other data. You can also take complete control over the serialization process by doing it yourself. You take this approach by implementing the Externalizable interface and providing bodies for the two read and write methods therein.

Another step to improving the security of your serialized objects is to use the "transient" keyword. Any data field that is marked "transient" will not be written out when the class is serialized. You can often mark it "private" as well. A transient field is one that has a value that depends on some current state that will not be saved. For example, "current_speed" would be transient. You can also use the transient keyword to prevent the writing out of a field that is sensitive, such as "salary." If you do that, you will need to find some other way to restore the value after you have deserialized the object, perhaps by reading it from a secure database.

Some entire classes are not capable of being serialized. One such example is java.lang.Thread. Threads consist largely of Java code, but they also have a significant native code part. Each Java thread has two stacks: one for Java code and one for C code. The native stack of a thread is not managed by Java, but by native code. The Java runtime doesn't know much about the native stack of a thread, and cannot save it. Thus, trying to serialize a thread will not be successful.

We already mentioned that only instance data is saved, not static data. You don't need to save the instructions in the methods of an object; that information is exactly what a class file is. So to successfully deserialize an object and use it, perhaps on another host, its class file must be accessible in the new environment.

XML Support Class

Just as I/O for ordinary types can be printable or binary, so too can objects be serialized into binary form or (incredibly) printable form. One of the main purposes of XML is to represent binary data in printable form. XML is described at length in the last chapter of this book, and the one sentence summary of it is, "*XML is a portable way of storing data items in character form surrounded by tags that say what type each item is.*"

The Java 1.4 release includes a class that lets you serialize objects into XML form! The documentation says that this is intended solely for Java beans. For your other classes (they say) you should continue using java.io.ObjectOuputStream. Those of us who like the advantages of XML will be the best judge of what to use where!

Here's an example of object persistence using XML:

```
import java.beans.*;
import java.io.*;
public class serial {
    public static void main(String args[]) throws Exception {
        java.util.Date d = new java.util.Date();
        FileOutputStream fos = new FileOutputStream("serial.xml");
        XMLEncoder xe = new XMLEncoder( fos );
        xe.writeObject(d);
        xe.close();
    }
}
```

After running the program, file serial.txt contains these lines:

```
<?xml version="1.0" encoding="UTF-8"?>
<java version="1.4.0-beta" class="java.beans.XMLDecoder">
  <object class="java.util.Date">
    <long>992802893720</long>
  </object>
</java>
```

XML makes a terrific serializable format for objects. I hope that Sun eventually removes the restriction and approves its use for all classes. The main reason for the restriction is to maintain backwards compatibility with all the code that uses the earlier binary format.

New I/O Package

JDK 1.4 introduced a package called java.nio. "Nio" stands for "new I/O," and the package and subpackages support some features not previously well-provisioned in Java. Some months before the JDK 1.4 beta shipped, the chief designer of the new Java APIs told me that his wife had attended a Java programming course. She came back thoroughly disenchanted with interactive I/O and told her husband (the chief Java API designer, remember) that he had to fix it. So I was optimistic that the new I/O would simplify interactive I/O. Alas, even the clearest of instructions between spouses are sometimes misunderstood. New I/O does nothing for interactive I/O. Supposedly printf- and scanf-like features will come in JDK 1.5. New I/O offers these four features:

- A non-blocking I/O facility for writing scalable servers
- A file interface that supports locks and memory mapping
- A pattern-matching facility based on Perl-style regular expressions
- Character-set encoders and decoders

Instead of building these on top of streams or file descriptors, these features are implemented using two new concepts: channels and buffers. A *channel* is a connection to something that can give or receive data, such as a file or a socket. You can think of it as a "conduit" where you pour in or siphon out data. Because a channel connects to an underlying physical device, it can do things relating to the device like support read/writes or provide file locks. There are channel classes specialized for files, for sockets, for pipes, and so on. You may think of a channel as an alternative to a stream. It has fewer fancy features (no wrapper classes), but it may have higher performance.

When to Use Channel I/O

Channel I/O is an alternative to basic stream I/O. Channels are similar to input or output streams, but allow the use of mapped I/O.

Channel I/O also supports non-blocking I/O and it can be faster than stream I/O. Perhaps Sun will reimplement the Java classloader using channels. Finally, if you need to do file locking or use a different character set from the default on your OS, channels provide an easy solution.

The second new concept in java.nio is the *buffer*. The right way to understand a buffer is to think of it like a big array in memory that holds the data transferred in from a channel. Just like an array, a buffer can only hold things that are all the same type. So you can have a byte buffer, a char buffer, a short, double, float, and int buffer. If your file contains a mixture of floats and ints, you can pull them out

of a Byte Buffer. Byte Buffer has methods to get and put all the primitive types except boolean.

The whole idea behind the Buffer class is to have a region of memory which can be accessed from both native code and Java at the same time, and that region has some special characteristics in the native code world. Buffer is a kind of "native" array—native code can access it directly, and Java can use method calls to get its hands on the contents. The use of buffers isn't limited to I/O. They are currently under consideration for use in Java3D to perform coordinate and texture updates on objects directly, without having to copy data to auxiliary memory.

Because a buffer is essentially an area of memory, it can do things relating to memory, like clear its contents, support read/write or read-only operations, give you a range of elements, and tell you how many data elements it contains. The following sections describe some features of java.nio and how to use them.

Multiplexed Non-blocking Server I/O

Channels have their own package at java.nio.channels. The package contains classes called DatagramChannel, SocketChannel, and ServerSocketChannel, among others. The single critical feature that channels offer, and that classes DatagramSocket, Socket, ServerSocket do not, is the ability to do I/O without blocking the thread.

The class java.nio.channels.SelectableChannel supports non-blocking I/O using what is called "selector-based multiplexing." Blocking I/O means that the I/O method does not return until the data transfer has taken place. If there is no input to read yet (because of network delays or because the user didn't type it yet), the entire thread will be blocked from continuing further. That's bad in terms of resource consumption. Simple non-blocking I/O, also known as "asynchronous I/O," means that you make the method call and it schedules the data transfer to take place at some future point, then returns almost immediately. No threads are blocked waiting.

Simple non-blocking I/O is helpful, but you can still burn up a lot of unproductive cpu time asking each descriptor if it is ready for more I/O yet. Selector-based multiplexing avoids this waste. It essentially says "monitor all these socket channels, and let me know when the next one of them is ready with data to transfer." The verb "to multiplex" means "to transmit several messages over the same medium all at the same time." Many different TV stations are multiplexed onto the cable of cable TV. The multiplexed part of selectors is that several data transfers may be underway at once, and the runtime system scans for pending data on the whole set of channels.

We won't review multiplexed I/O in depth, except to say that it provides the same kind of scalable I/O support as the select() system call available on all server operating systems. When select() is called, it blocks until one of a given set of socket descriptors is ready for reading or writing, or a timeout expires (whichever comes first).

To use multiplexed I/O in Java, first you get the channel from a socket. Then you register one or more channels with a Selector object, getting back a key. Finally, you do a select() on the Selector object. That waits until it can return a collection of keys that are ready for data transfer. Why is it OK for select() to block, but not other I/O methods? Because select() has a timeout feature. If no I/O becomes ready within so many milliseconds, the call returns. Also, you may be doing a select to get input from twenty sockets, but only one thread is blocked, not twenty.

Even if multiplexed I/O sounds involved, it is familiar to those who have used it in libraries for other languages. The additional objects of a key and a selector add a little more flexibility to the design. Multiplexed, non-blocking I/O is much more scalable than thread-oriented, blocking I/O. This new Java feature provides non-blocking I/O for writing scalable servers.

Recovering from Blocked Server I/O

Channels support non-blocking I/O; they also make it easier to recover from blocked I/O. Server-based systems need to be reliable and scalable, but their threads can hang because of congestion, file mounting problems, or other remote access issues. Servers need the ability to get rid of threads that are "stuck" in network I/O. Scalability generally means that you assign a new thread to process each incoming request. That thread will be allocated to a socket, and that socket consumes a file descriptor. The system and each process have limited quantities of file descriptors. The idea is that the request comes in on a socket, where a thread serves it with any necessary I/O, database access, etc. The thread returns the answer to the client, then the thread and socket terminate and are reclaimed for further use.

All I/O in Java up to JDK 1.3 is synchronous or "blocking." When you execute a read or write instruction in Java, the method does not return until the data has been safely passed along. If there is a delay in the user response or the operating system or network, such that the data transfer cannot complete, then that thread hangs (waits indefinitely). When a thread becomes non-responsive for any reason, those file descriptors stay unavailable, eventually dragging down performance by reducing the number of sockets available to handle requests.

Some system designs rely on sockets *not* being consumed in this way. The designers of Java originally provided a method called interrupt() in class Thread. If some other thread called the interrupt() method of a Thread that was blocked, it was supposed to break out of the hang and get an InterruptedIOException while leaving the stream open for further attempts. Unfortunately, it turns out that the Windows API does not have any way to implement this that is both efficient and reliable. The interrupt method never worked well.

Instead, programmers used the workaround of closing the file descriptor or handle that was not responding to the I/O request. That unwedged the thread at the cost of leaving the I/O in an unknown state. The cost is generally acceptable. The most common reason to interrupt a thread is to ask it to shut down. If you plan to shut the thread down anyway, you might as well discard any socket in an unknown state and recover by opening a new connection.

Channels officially provide the close-on-interrupt semantics that were in widespread unofficial use before. Any time you need to break threads out of blocking I/O operations, you should use a channel. You can either close the channel of a blocked thread, causing it to receive an AsynchronousCloseException, or you can call the interrupt() method of a thread that is blocked on channel I/O, thus closing the channel and delivering a ClosedByInterruptException to the blocked thread. File channels are always safe for use by multiple concurrent threads. Channels correctly support asynchronous interruption and closing.

Getting and Using a File Channel

There are several classes that support channels, but we'll only talk about FileChannels here. The network kinds of Channel (Datagrams and Sockets) are similar, but support slightly fewer operations because it doesn't make sense to lock sockets (they are inherently single-user). You get a FileChannel by calling the getChannel() method upon an instance of one of the classes FileInputStream, FileOutputStream, or RandomAccessFile in the java.io package.

```
RandomAccessFile raf = new RandomAccessFile("C:\\data.txt", "rw");
FileChannel myFileChannel = raf.getChannel();
```

The channel you get back is connected to the underlying physical file, and it will be open for read access in the case of FileInputStream, or for write access in the case of FileOutputStream. In the case of RandomAccessFile, the channel will be open for reading, or reading-and-writing,to match the mode that the random access file was instantiated with. In the code fragment above, you'll be able to read from and write into the channel to file c:\data.txt.

Once you have a file channel, there are several methods to read it into a buffer, or write it out from a buffer. The channel connects to the underlying file, while the buffer provides a place in memory to put the bytes. We'll finish up this summary of channels, then move on to buffers in the next section.

Channels also have methods to transfer data to and from another channel, to apply exclusive access locks to a file, and to map the file into memory. Mapping a file into memory is an advanced OS technique that uses the virtual memory subsystem to bring some or all of a file into the address space of a process. File mapping is an alternative to the read and write system calls used by streams. It is explained with an example a little later.

Here is the signature of a FileChannel method that reads from the channel (and hence from the file that the channel is connected to) into a byte buffer:

int read(ByteBuffer dst) throws IOException

You would use it like this:

```
ByteBuffer myBB = ByteBuffer.allocate(1024);
bytesRead = myFileChannel.read(myBB);
```

Channels, maps, and buffers maintain a notion of their "current position," just as file streams do. Bytes are read starting at this channel's current position, and then the position is updated with the number of bytes actually read. That number could be zero if nothing was read, or -1 to indicate that the channel has reached the end of stream. As with streams, you can "mark()" the current position to remember it, and then invoke reset() to return to that position later, and get the same input again (a fairly useless feature).

Here is the signature of a FileChannel method that writes from a byte buffer into the channel, and hence into the file that the channel is connected to:

int write(ByteBuffer src) throws IOException

It writes a sequence of bytes from the given buffer to the channel. It returns the number of bytes written, which may be zero. You would use it like this:

```
ByteBuffer myBB = ByteBuffer.allocate(1024);
// operations to put data into the byte buffer
myBB.put( ...  // we'll cover these soon
myBB.flip();  // changes over to writing the buffer
int bytesWritten = myFileChannel.write(myBB);
```

These lines of code write the bytes from the buffer through the channel into a file. Channels also support "scatter" reads into several buffers one after the other, and "gather" writes from several buffers into one channel. Scatter/gather I/O is convenient for certain protocol exchanges of fixed length messages. It also helps the kernel to use several small buffers instead of one big one.

What if you want to do filtering on the contents of a channel by wrapping additional classes, as we saw with the Reader/Writer and Streams classes? You cannot do that directly with a channel, but you can obtain a reader/writer/stream corresponding to a channel and then go on to wrap that in the usual way. The utility class java.nio.channels.Channels has half a dozen static methods that have the effect of converting each way between a channel and a Reader or a Writer or an InputStream or an OutputStream.

Buffers

You will create buffers either by an allocate method call, or by wrapping an existing array (or string for a character buffer) to form a buffer with the array contents, or by getting a buffer back from a channel map. You don't use a constructor to get a buffer: its a hint that there is a lot more going on here than mere object allocation. Here's a sample line that obtains a 1Kbyte buffer for you:

```
ByteBuffer bb1 = java.nio.ByteBuffer.allocate(1024);
```

Here's how you wrap an array to get a buffer that is filled with the contents of the array:

```
byte [] myByteArray = {0x11,0x22,0x33,0x44,0x55,0x66,0x77};
ByteBuffer bb2 = java.nio.ByteBuffer.wrap( myByteArray );
```

The wrapping is another example of the wrapper design pattern. A byte buffer can do pretty much all the things an array can do, and a few things of its own. As we saw above, you can write from a buffer into a channel, and thus into a file, pipe, or socket like this:

```
int count = fc.write(bb2);
```

This is very powerful. You can write an entire data array in two or three statements with no looping! Here's the entire program to read a file into a buffer:

Read a File Using a Channel and a Buffer

```
import java.io.*;
import java.nio.*;
import java.nio.channels.*;
public class MyBuffer {
   public static void main(String[] a) throws Exception {
      // Get a Channel for the file
      File f = new File("email.txt");
      FileInputStream fis = new FileInputStream(f);
      FileChannel fc = fis.getChannel();
      ByteBuffer bb1 = java.nio.ByteBuffer.allocate((int)f.length());
      // Once you have a buffer, you can read a file into it like this:
      int count = fc.read(bb1);
      System.out.println("read "+ count + " bytes from email.txt");
      fc.close();
   }
}
```

Other Buffer Methods

Once your buffer is loaded with data from a channel, how do you access that in your program, and can you change the buffer? There are several kinds of operations upon buffers. They are as follows:

- After reading into a buffer you need to rewind() it, to reset the position mark to the beginning. If you are about to start writing or getting from the buffer after a series of reads or puts, you need to call the flip() method.
- get() and put() methods that read and write the next single data item, e.g.,

```
byte b = bb1.get(); // gets the next byte
Double d = bb1.getDouble(); // gets the next 8 bytes into a double
ByteBuffer result = bb1.putChar('X'); // puts a char into the buffer
```

Gets and puts are done at the current index position in the buffer, and move the position immediately past what was just transferred. All the putSomething() methods are optional. They will only be supported if the underlying operating system supports this operation on a buffer.

There are get() and put() operations for these types: byte, char, double, float, int, long, and short. Notice that you read bytes into a buffer, but are able to get() and put() larger pieces of data. As always, you have to know the types of data that are stored in your files. A program cannot figure that out from looking at the bits.

- Absolute get() and put() methods that read and write a datum at a given offset, e.g.,

```
bb1.put(319, (byte) 0xF); // puts this byte at offset 319 in the buffer
bb1.putLong(256, 1234567890L); // puts this long at offset 256 in the buffer
```

- Bulk get() methods that transfer a sequence of bytes from this buffer into a byte array, e.g.,

```
byte[] destination = new byte[2048];
bb1.rewind();
bb1.get( destination ); // fills the array from the buffer
```

You should avoid unnecessary copying of data for performance reasons. Work directly with the buffer where possible.

- Bulk put() methods that transfer contiguous sequences of bytes from an array into this buffer, e.g.,

```
byte[] b2 = { 1,2,3,4,5,6,7,8,9,0xA };
bb1.put(b2);
```

  You can also "wrap" an array around a buffer. That causes the buffer to be filled with the contents of the array. Unlike put(), it also causes further changes to either of the buffer or the array to be reflected in the other. One way to implement this is to relocate the buffer to occupy the same storage as the array.

```
byte[] b3 = { 1,2,3,4,5,6,7,8,9,0xA };
bb1.wrap(b3);
```

  The buffer's capacity changes to match that of the wrapping array.

- Methods for allocating, compacting, duplicating, and extracting a subrange of ("slicing") a buffer.

View Buffers

Channels can only read from or write into a byte buffer. Even if the underlying file contains ints or longs, a channel cannot write into an int buffer. However, after you have read in the bytes, you can open a *view buffer* that is a differently-typed interpretation of the underlying byte buffer. A view buffer is simply another buffer whose content is backed by the byte buffer. Changes to the byte buffer's content will be visible in the view buffer, and vice versa; the two buffers' current position and sizes are independent.

Here is how you get a view buffer that interprets its data as floats:

```
bb1.rewind(); // need to move buffer index back to beginning
FloatBuffer myFB = bb1.asFloatBuffer();
```

There are corresponding as*Something*Buffer() methods for the types char, short, int, long, and double. View buffers have a couple of advantages compared with the type-specific get and put methods described above. A view buffer is indexed in terms of the size of its values, not individual bytes. If you execute `myFB.put(8, 3.14159F)`, it will make the 8th float in the buffer (bytes 56 to 63), not the 8th to 11th bytes, have the value of pi. A view buffer also provides bulk get and put methods for its type, as shown in the following complete program.

A Bulk Transfer from a Buffer to an int Array

```
import java.io.*;
import java.nio.*;
import java.nio.channels.*;
public class Buffer2 {
  public static void main(String[] a) throws Exception {
    // Get a Channel for the file
    FileInputStream fis =
             new FileInputStream("numbers.bin");
    FileChannel fc = fis.getChannel();
    ByteBuffer bb = java.nio.ByteBuffer.allocate(400);
    // fill the buffer from the file
    int count = fc.read(bb);

    bb.rewind(); // need to move buffer index back to start
    IntBuffer ib = bb.asIntBuffer();
    // bulk get into an int array
    int[] myIntArray = new int[50];
    ib.get( myIntArray );
    for (int i=0; i<5; i++) {
      System.out.println( "arr["+i+"]="+ myIntArray[i] );
    }
    fc.close();
  }
}
```

If you compile and run this program, you will see printed the first few values in the file numbers.bin. Create the file first and put any junk in there. The contents are brought into the program with a channel that is read into a byte buffer. The byte buffer is rewound and then overlayed with an int view buffer. An int array is then filled with data from the int view buffer in a single get operation. Finally, the first five ints in the array are printed. You should compare them with the values you get by reading numbers.bin with a data input stream. Depending on what is in the file originally, you will see output like this:

arr[0]=2003461731
arr[1]=1751280235
arr[2]=1986164595
arr[3]=1986947691
arr[4]=1646294541

There is one further note about buffers. You may have noticed that the first example, MyBuffer.java in the buffer section, used a file called "email.txt" that obviously contained characters. When we read it in, these characters ended up in Java 8-bit bytes, not in Java 16-bit characters. What if we wanted to move each single ASCII byte in the file into a Java double-byte char? It turns out that this is now simple to do automatically.

Once you have the data from your file in a byte buffer, you can specify a new encoding and decode it from one buffer into another. The last section of this chapter is a lengthy description of character set encodings and the order in which bytes may appear. Here is the code that reads ASCII characters from a file, and ensures that they end up in Java Unicode double-byte chars:

```
// Get a Channel for the source file
FileInputStream fis = new FileInputStream("email.txt");
FileChannel fc = fis.getChannel();

// Get a Buffer from the source file
MappedByteBuffer bb =
   fc.map(FileChannel.MapMode.READ_ONLY, 0, (int)fc.size());

Charset cs = Charset.forName("8859_1");
CharsetDecoder cd = cs.newDecoder();
CharBuffer cb = cd.decode(bb);
```

These lines are part of a complete example presented later.

Memory Mapped I/O

Let us return to the topic of memory-mapped I/O. We stated that file channels/buffers are an alternative to reads/writes on streams. Memory-mapped I/O is an alternative to both, implemented as a refinement to channels/buffers. The whole point of mapped I/O is faster I/O. When transferring large amounts of data, mapped I/O can be faster because it uses virtual memory to make the file contents appear in your address space. It takes some initial setup and puts more work on the VM subsystem, but mapped I/O avoids the extra copying into your process data buffers required by normal I/O.

When you read with a stream, the OS reads from the disk into a buffer owned by the device driver and then moves the contents from kernel space to your buffer in user space. Memory mapping only needs a couple of bits twiddled in the VM system to say "that disk page is part of this process address space." So why doesn't everyone use mapped I/O all the time? Kernel whackers do, and the rest of the world is still hearing about the feature. Also, it's not part of the ANSI C API, which is one of the most widely used I/O APIs.

Mapped memory is also known as shared memory. As well as offering performance improvements for larger files, it can be used for bulk data transfer between cooperating processes that all map in the same file. These processes don't even have to be on the same system, as long as the same file is visible to each. Mapped files were first used in Multics, the 1960s operating system that came to a sticky end, but which was the stepfather of Unix (and thus the ancestor of Linux, MaxOS X, and Solaris, too). Even the name "Unix" was a pun by Brian Kernighan on the name "Multics."

When you do a map operation on a FileChannel to map a file into memory, your return value is a mapped byte buffer that is connected to the file. The runtime system is expected to use the operating system features for memory mapping. The result is that when you write in the buffer, that data appears in the file. If you read from the buffer, you get the data that is in the file. Everyone is familiar with the way an operating system can read an executable file and make the instructions appear in the address space of a process. Mapped I/O does essentially the same thing for data files. The signature of FileChannel's map method is:

```
MappedByteBuffer map(int mode, long position, int size)
   throws IOException;
```

The position argument is the offset in the file where you want the mapping to start. This will usually be offset zero, to start at the beginning. The size is the number of bytes that you want from the file. This will usually be myFile.length() to get the whole thing.

The mode argument is one of FileChannel.MapMode.READ_ONLY,

FileChannel.MapMode.READ_WRITE, or FileChannel.MapMode.PRIVATE, for read-only, read-and-write, or copy-on-write mapping. Copy-on-write is a variation of read-and-write mapping that says "if any process changes the content of this map it gets its own private copy with its change; everyone else can carry on sharing the unchanged version." It's mostly used in systems programming to share data pages of executables, and I suppose there was little reason to hide the semantics from Java, even though it's not something used much by applications.

Here's an example of mapping a FileChannel and, hence, the underlying File into memory:

```
File f = new File("data.txt");
FileInputStream fis = new FileInputStream(f);
FileChannel fc = fis.getChannel();

MappedByteBuffer mbb = fc.map(FileChannel.MapMode.READ_ONLY, 0, (int) f.length() );
```

Note that file lengths are given in a long, but that you can only map an int's worth of memory (2GByte) in any one map, so you must make sure the map size argument is typed as an int. We do that here by using the cast "(int)". If the physical memory available to your JVM cannot hold all the file, the virtual memory subsystem will bring in pieces of it as needed without you doing anything, or even being aware of it.

A MappedByteBuffer is also termed a "direct" buffer. A direct byte buffer may also be created by invoking the allocateDirect factory method of this class. The buffers returned by this method typically have somewhat higher allocation and deallocation costs than non-direct buffers. So direct buffers should only be used for large, long-lived buffers that are subject to the underlying system's native I/O operations. The code that follows shows a file being written using a channel and buffer. Then the same file is read back in using mapped I/O. The data is compared with what was written, and it had better match.

Mapped I/O Example import java.io.*;

```
import java.nio.*;
import java.nio.channels.*;
public class MyMap {
  public static void main(String args[]) throws Exception {
    FileOutputStream fos = new FileOutputStream("ints.bin");
    FileChannel c = fos.getChannel();
    ////////////// write using channel and buffer //////////
    ByteBuffer bb = ByteBuffer.allocate(40);
    IntBuffer ib = bb.asIntBuffer();  // this is a view
    // fill the buffer
    for (int i=0; i<10; i++)  ib.put(i);
    // write the buffer full of ints to the channel and thus file
    c.write(bb);
    c.force(true);  // commit to disk
    c.close();
    ////////////////////// read back using mapped I/O //////////
    // read back loads of ints into a channel
    FileInputStream fis = new FileInputStream("ints.bin");
    c = fis.getChannel();
    MappedByteBuffer mbb = c.map(FileChannel.MapMode.READ_ONLY, 0, 40);
    // int num = c.read(mbb);  // you don't read a mapped buffer!
    System.out.println("byte buff capacity: " + mbb.capacity() );
    System.out.println("byte buff position: " + mbb.position() );
    System.out.println("byte buff    limit: " + mbb.limit() );
    for (int i=0; i<10; i++)  {
      int j = mbb.getInt();
      if (j != i) System.out.println("data mismatch: "+i+","+j);
    }
    System.out.println("Read the ints back from file ok");
  }
}
```

Many details of memory-mapped file behavior are inherently dependent upon the underlying operating system, and so they are not specified in Java.

File Locking

As we saw in the threads chapter, sometimes you have two things going on at once in a program, and to keep them straight you may need to stop them from doing the same thing together. This situation can occur in file handling. An example would be a data file that several programs want to update at the same time. Let's say the last record in the file contains the total of all the other records in the file. When a program updates the file, it first writes the new data value, then it reads the current total, adjusts it for the new value, and writes it back. If another program should happen to come along at just the wrong time, both programs may read the old total, then they will both update it, but one update of the total will overwrite the other. Result: two data changes, but only one change to the total, so the file is now inaccurate.

One way to avoid this situation is to use threads and synchronize them on some suitable object. That only works when all the threads trying to update the file are running in one JVM. Many applications cannot accept that limitation, which is where file locking comes in. Using the new FileLock class introduced in JDK 1.4 as part of package java.nio, the programmer can lock part or all of a file for exclusive access.

As a reminder, a method called getChannel() has been added to each of the FileInputStream, FileOutputStream, and RandomAccessFile classes. Invoking the getChannel() method upon an instance of one of those classes will return a file channel connected to the underlying file.

Once you have the FileChannel object for a file, you call its lock() or tryLock() method. Lock is a blocking call— it won't return until it has the lock, or the channel is closed, or the thread interrupted. The method tryLock() is not a blocking call. It returns at once, whether it got the lock or not. The return value from both these calls is a FileLock object or null. Both of these methods have variants that let you provide arguments to specify that a region of the file (rather than the whole thing) is locked. That allows finer control over how much different processes stay out of each others way, with consequently better performance.

Here is an example program that repeatedly tries to acquire a lock. When it gets the lock, it prints a message saying so, and sleeps for two seconds to simulate doing some work with the file. It then releases the lock. It sleeps a further third of a second and does the whole thing over again.

```
import java.io.*;
import java.nio.channels.*;
public class Lock {
  public static void main(String[] a) throws Exception {
    // Get a Channel for the file
    FileInputStream fis = new FileInputStream("data.txt");
    FileChannel fc = fis.getChannel();
    while (true) {
      // Try to get a lock
      FileLock lock = fc.tryLock();
      if (lock !=null) {
        System.out.println("got lock");
        Thread.sleep(2000);  // simulate some work
        lock.release();
      }
      Thread.sleep(333);
    }
  }
}
```

If you compile this lock program and run several different copies of it at the same time, you will see messages indicating that the locks have been acquired and released.

Note: When using JDK 1.4 beta, this program does not work on Windows 95 or 98, presumably because some patches are missing from either JDK 1.4 beta or Windows. Nor does it run on Linux yet. The program operates correctly on Windows NT 4.0.

The file-locking API maps directly onto the native locking facility of the underlying operating system. Thus, the locks held on a file are visible to all programs that have access to the file, regardless of the language in which those programs are written.

Whether or not a lock actually physically prevents another program from accessing the content of the locked region is system-dependent and therefore unspecified. The native file-locking facilities of some systems are advisory, meaning that programs must cooperate to observe a known locking protocol in order to guarantee data integrity. On other systems native file locks are mandatory, meaning that if one program locks a region of a file, then all other programs are prevented from accessing that region in a way that would violate the lock. To ensure consistent and correct behavior across platforms, all programmers should treat the locks provided by this API as if they were advisory locks.

The old approach (before JDK 1.4) to file locking involved creating a file. Creating a file is an atomic operation on all operating systems. If two processes try to create the same file at the same time, only one of them can succeed. That fact was used as an interim solution for real locking. Going forward, you should use the java.nio features.

Charsets and Endian-ness

A character set, also known as an "encoding," is the set of bit patterns used to represent a set of characters. ASCII is one popular encoding. EBCDIC is a family of character sets with regional variations used on IBM mainframes. Unicode is a third encoding. Before describing the character sets available to Java, we need to explain "big-endian" and "little-endian" storage conventions.

Big-endian Storage

Endian-ness refers to the order in memory in which bytes are stored for a multi-byte quantity. The term is a whimsical reference to the fable *Gulliver's Travels*, in which Jonathan Swift described a war between the Big-Endians and the Little-Endians, whose only difference was in where to crack open a hard-boiled egg. It was popularized in the famous paper, "*On Holy Wars and a Plea for Peace*" by Danny Cohen, USC/ISI IEN 137, dated April 1, 1980. It's a cool paper, well worth reading, and you can easily find it on the web if you search.

All modern computer architectures are byte-addressable, meaning every byte of main memory has a unique address. If you store a multibyte datum in several successive addresses, should the most significant byte of the datum go at the highest address or the lowest address? Big-endian means that the most significant byte of an integer is stored at the lowest address, and the least significant byte at the highest address (the big end comes first). In other words, if you have an int value of 0x11223344, the four bytes:

```
0x11, 0x22, 0x33, 0x44
```

will be laid out in memory as follows:

```
base address +0:  0x11
base address +1:  0x22
base address +2:  0x33
base address +3:  0x44
```

on a big-endian system. The SPARC, Motorola 68K, and the IBM 390 series are all big-endian architectures. Big-endian has the advantage of telling if a number is positive or negative by just looking at the first byte.

Little-endian storage

Little-endian contrasts with this by storing the *least* significant byte of an integer at the lowest address, and the highest byte at the highest address (the little end comes first). The number is "the other way up." On a little-endian system the same four bytes will be arranged in memory as follows:

```
base address +0:  0x44
base address +1:  0x33
base address +2:  0x22
base address +3:  0x11
```

The Intel x86 is a little-endian architecture, as was the DEC VAX. Little-endian has the advantage of telling if a number is odd or even by just looking at the first byte.

Java uses big-endian ordering when it processes data, regardless of the platform it is on. Big-endian is also known as "network byte order" because the fundamental Internet TCP/IP standard is defined to use big-endian. The only time endianness is an issue is when you are trying to read data that was written by a non-Java program on a PC. Then you have to remember to swap multibyte values on the way in, or wrap a buffer around an array, as explained shortly.

Supported Encodings

Table 14-4 shows some popular encodings. Every implementation of the Java platform from JDK 1.4 on is required to support these standard charsets. For character sets that include multibyte characters, endianness is an issue.

Table 14–4 Required Encodings

Name	Size	Description
US-ASCII	7 bits	The American Standard Code for Information Interchange
ISO-8859-1	8 bits	The problem with ASCII is that it is the *American* Standard Code, and has no provision for accented characters. ISO-8859-1 contains the 7-bit ASCII character set, and the eighth bit is used to represent a variety of European accented and national characters. ISO 8859-1 is shown in an appendix at the end of this text.
UTF-8	8-24 bits	A UCS Transformation Format is an interim code that allows systems to operate with both ASCII and Unicode. "UCS" means Universal Character Set. In UTF-8, a character is either 1, 2, or 3 bytes long. The first few bits of a UTF character identify how long it is. • ASCII values (less than 0x7F) are written as one byte. • Unicode values less than 0x7FF are written as two bytes. The first byte starts with 110. • Other Unicode values are written as three bytes. The first byte starts with 1110. The second or third bytes of a multibyte sequence start with the bits set to 10. UTF is a hack best avoided if possible. It complicates code quite a bit when you can no longer rely on all characters being the same size. However, UTF offers the benefit of backward compatibility with existing ASCII-based data, and forward compatibility with Unicode data. There are several variations of UTF to accommodate byte order.
UTF-16BE	16 bits	Sixteen-bit UCS Transformation Format, big-endian byte order.
UTF-16LE	16 bits	Sixteen-bit UCS Transformation Format, little-endian byte order.
UTF-16	16 bits	Sixteen-bit UCS Transformation Format, byte order identified by an optional byte-order mark. When writing out data, it uses big-endian byte order and writes a big-endian byte-order mark at the beginning.

You gain the use of one of these encodings by passing a string containing the desired encoding as an argument to the constructor of OutputStreamWriter (for output) or InputStreamReader (for input). Recall from the previous chapter that these two classes provide a bridge between the world of 8-bit characters and the world of 16-bit characters.

What actually happens is that the bit patterns you have in your program are potentially changed in length and content, according to the encoding you specify. If you are reading in ISO 8859 single byte characters, and mention that as the encoding, each one will be expanded to two bytes as it is read into Java Unicode characters. Here's an example program that writes character values using an explicit encoding.

Using a Specific Character Set

```
// Write chars using UTF-Big Endian encoding
// Peter van der Linden, August 2001
import java.io.*;
import java.util.*;
public class Codeset {
  public static void main (String args[]) throws Exception {
    FileOutputStream fos = new FileOutputStream("results.txt");
    OutputStreamWriter osw = new OutputStreamWriter(fos, "utf-16be");
    char data[] = { 0x11, 0x22, 0x33, 0x44, 0x55, 0x66, 0x77,
                    0x88, 0x99, 0xAA, 0xBB, 0xCC, 0xDD, 0xEE };
    osw.write( data );
    osw.close();
  }
}
```

If you run this program and try "utf-16be" and other character sets, you will see results as shown in Table 14-5.

Table 14–5 Character Set Results

Charset name	Output	Notes
data written	11,22,33,44,55,66, 77,88,99,AA,BB,CC, DD,EE	This is the data that is written using the various encodings.
"US-ASCII"	n/a	It's illegal to try to write 16-bit characters when you have specified a 7-bit encoding. The results are unspecified.
"ISO-8859-1"	n/a	It's illegal to try to write 16-bit characters when you have specified an 8-bit encoding. The results are unspecified.
"UTF-8"	11,22,33,44,55,66, 77, C2,88,C2,99,C2,AA, C2,BB,C3,8C,C3,9D, C3,AE	The first few bits of a UTF character identify how long it is.
"UTF-16BE"	00,11,00,22,00,33, 00,44,00,55,00,66, 00,77, 00,88,00,99,00,AA, 00,BB,00,CC,00,DD, 00,EE	Sixteen-bit UCS Transformation Format, big-endian byte order. Big-endian is network byte order.
"UTF-16LE"	11,00,22,00,33,00, 44,00,55,00,66,00, 77,00 88,00,99,00,AA,00, BB,00,CC,00,DD,00, EE,00	Sixteen-bit UCS Transformation Format, little-endian byte order
"UTF-16"	FE,FF,00,11,00,22, 00,33,00,44,00,55, 00,66,00,77 00,88,00,99,00,AA, 00,BB,00,CC,00,DD, 00,EE	Sixteen-bit UCS Transformation Format. The initial FE, FF is the byte-order mark signifying big-endian.

Consult the release documentation for your implementation to see if any other charsets are supported. Table 14-6 lists some popular encodings that may be supported on your system. There are literally dozens and dozens of other encodings.

Table 14–6 Other Popular Encodings

Name	Size	Description	Code for letter 'A'
windows-1252	8 bits	The default file.encoding property for most of Windows is "cp1252." Microsoft diverged from the standard ISO 8859-1 Latin-1 character set (which is shown in an appendix at the end of this book) by changing 27 characters in the range 0x80 to 0x9f, and called the result Code Page 1252. Complicating the situation, under Windows the shell uses a different encoding set to the rest of the system. It uses an older encoding for compatibility with MS-DOS. The shell uses either code page cp850 or cp437. To find out what code page is being used by the command shell, execute the DOS command "chcp" and see what it returns.	0x41
Unicode	16 bits	The problem with 8859_1 is that it can represent only 256 distinct characters. That's barely enough for all the accented and diacritical characters used in western Europe, let alone the many alphabets used around the rest of the world. Unicode is a 16-bit character set developed to solve this problem by allowing for 65,536 different characters. Strings in Java are made up of Unicode characters.	0x0041
EBCDIC	8 bits	The Extended Binary Coded Decimal Interchange Code is an 8-bit code used on IBM mainframes instead of ASCII. It was originally intended to simplify conversion from 12 bit punch card codes to 8-bit internal codes. As a result, it has some horrible properties, like the letters not being contiguous in the character set. EBCDIC is really a family of related character sets with country-specific variations. An EBCDIC chart is shown later in this chapter in Table 14-7.	0xC1
ISO/IEC 10646	32 bits	This is the Universal Character Set. There are two forms: UCS-2 and UCS-4. UCS-2 is a 2-byte encoding, and UCS-4 uses a 4-byte per-character encoding. This enormous encoding space is divided into 64K "planes" of 64K characters each. The ISO people want everyone to think of Unicode as just a shorthand way of referring to Plane Zero of the complete 4-byte ISO/IEC 10646 encoding space. Unicode, in other words, is UCS-2, which is a subset of the full UCS-4. They call this the "Basic Multilingual Plane" or BMP.	0x00000041

Byte-Swapping Binary Data

The character sets only affect character I/O. You cannot apply an encoding to do automatic endian-swapping of binary data. But if you are using Java to read little-endian binary data, i.e., binary data that was written by a native program on a PC, you need to do this byte-swapping. We use the buffer class introduced in JDK 1.4. In Java 1.4, you can fill a buffer directly from a file, then pull values out of it with your choice of endian-order. To byte-swap a buffer, use code like this:

```
FileInputStream fis = new FileInputStream("ints.bin");
FileChannel c = fis.getChannel();
ByteBuffer bb = ByteBuffer.allocate(40);
int num = c.read(bb);

bb.rewind();
bb.order(ByteOrder.LITTLE_ENDIAN);

Float f1 = b.getFloat();
```

Summary of Charsets

- Most native file systems are based on 8-bit characters.
- Streams automatically handle the translation to Unicode strings used internally in Java.
- You get the right thing by default.
- If you want something different, you can ask for it.

Exercises

1. (Random Access Files) Create a data file that contains ten ints and a long. The long value holds the total of the ints. Write a program that repeatedly checks the total is correct, chooses one of the ten ints at random, changes it to a random value, and updates the total.
2. (Reading from the keyboard) Explain why there is no "parseBoolean()" method.
3. (Serialization) Write a program that creates a java.util.Vector object and adds various arrays to it. Serialize the Vector to a file. Read the Vector back in, and write the code to check that it contains the same contents that it had when written out. Modify the serialized file to give one of the arrays different content. (Hint: strings are easy to update in a file.) Check that your program detects the change.
4. (Channels, Buffers) Write a program that has two threads. One thread should engage in continual I/O using a channel. It should contain a handler for ClosedByInterruptException and AsynchronousCloseException. The other thread should call the interrupt method of the first thread. Put the whole thing in a loop and run it overnight. Is it reliable enough that it is still running in the morning? Is your operating system reliable enough to cope with this?
5. (Channels, Buffers) Write a program to measure the difference in performance between I/O through a direct (mapped) buffer and a non-direct buffer. Your program should output a 512KByte array of ints 1,000 times in a loop to the same random access file. Is the performance of input any different? Account for any differences.
6. (Channels, Buffers) Take the example program that shows memory-mapped I/O for an input file and modify it so that the output is done by mapped I/O too.
7. (Locking) Take the program written for the random access file exercise. Run two copies of the program and demonstrate that the total quickly goes awry.
8. (Locking) Update the program in the previous exercise to protect the file by locking it. Run several copies of the program overnight to show that it works correctly.
9. (Locking) Update the program in the previous exercise so that it locks only the regions of the file that it is going to update: the random int and the total field. Measure the performance of this code and compare it with the code from the previous exercise. Is it faster or slower? Account for any performance differences.
10. (Encodings) Write a program that prints a neat table of EBCDIC and ASCII characters and their associated bit patterns.
11. (Encodings) Write a codeset program to write out data in all the standard encodings and confirm how the bytes are swapped with the different character sets.

Some Light Relief—The Illegal T-Shirt!

The story so far: The light relief in the previous chapter described how the Motion Picture Association of America, combined with a shadowy Japanese-controlled organization known as the DVD-CCA, were furiously trying to stuff the toothpaste of DVD decryption back into the tube of secrecy. Their efforts were aided by a bad U.S. law known as the 1998 Digital Millennium Copyright Act.

The DCMA is not the first piece of bad law affecting the Internet. The Communications Decency Act lasted less than a year before the U.S. Supreme Court struck it down as unconstitutional in 1997. The DMCA is a bad law because it tilts the balance between consumers and copyright holders too heavily toward copyright holders. Many kinds of ordinary legal uses of DVDs, such as playing them with your DVD player of choice on the computer of your choice, have become effectively illegal under the DMCA.

Every once in a while, common sense collides with the law. It's not quite the irresistible force meeting the immovable object because the law always yields to common sense in the long run. But it can be pretty entertaining in the short run. Take a look at the picture of this t-shirt (Figure 14-1).

Figure 14–1 Wear a t-shirt; go to jail!

The t-shirt contains a few lines of C code on the back, and is being sold by a New Jersey company called Copyleft. You can buy one of these t-shirts from their website at *www.copyleft.net*, but you better hurry. The DVD Copy Control Association (DVD-CCA) is suing Copyleft to try to drive this t-shirt off the market!

The dispute centers around those few lines of C code on the back of the shirt. They are just regular lines of C code, looking like this:

```
void CSSdecrypttitlekey(
        unsigned char *tkey,
        unsigned char *dkey) {
    int i;
    unsigned char im1[6];
    unsigned char im2[6]={0x51,0x67,0x67,0xc5,0xe0,0x00};

    for(i=0;i<6;i++)
         im1[i]=dkey[i];

    CSStitlekey1(im1,im2);
    CSStitlekey2(tkey,im1);
}
```

So why all the fuss? The answer lies in a vicious struggle over money, trade secrets, and a new U.S. copyright law affecting DVDs. DVDs (i.e., video films stored on high capacity CDs) hold ordinary MPEG-2 files that have been encrypted. The encryption is called the Content Scrambling System, or CSS. The DVD industry makes a lot of noise implying that CSS helps with protection against pirates. But, shiver me timbers mateys, the CSS encryption has no effect at all on piracy. Pirates just copy the entire disk bit-for-bit and resell them. DVD players don't have any way to tell if the same bits are coming from a genuine DVD or a pirated copy.

The CSS encryption is there to give the DVD industry control over how you play back the titles you bought. If the bits are encrypted, they can only be played on a DVD player that is approved by the DVD industry. The industry can then enforce all kinds of restrictions, from not being able to fast forward past the trailers and adverts at the beginning, to not being able to play DVDs from other countries, to refusing to play content that has gone out of copyright and should therefore be freely available.

The movie and publishing industry has quite a history of rewriting copyright laws to favor itself. The period of copyright protection was originally up to 28 years from date of creation. By the 1920s the law afforded a maximum of 56 years of copyright protection. This period was expanded to 75 years in 1976, after strenuous lobbying from the Walt Disney corporation concerned about losing exclusive rights to the material created by the grandfathers of current employees. Even

Table 14–7 ASCII and EBCDIC Codes

Dec	Hex	ASCII		EBCDIC	
0	00	NUL	Null	NUL	Null
1	01	SOH	Start of Heading (CC)	SOH	Start of Heading
2	02	STX	Start of Text (CC)	STX	Start of Text
3	03	ETX	End of Text (CC)	ETX	End of Text
4	04	EOT	End of Transmission (CC)	PF	Punch Off
5	05	ENQ	Enquiry (CC)	HT	Horizontal Tab
6	06	ACK	Acknowledge (CC)	LC	Lower Case
7	07	BEL	Bell	DEL	Delete
8	08	BS	Backspace (FE)		
9	09	HT	Horizontal Tabulation (FE)		
10	0A	LF	Line Feed (FE)	SMM	Start of Manual Message
11	0B	VT	Vertical Tabulation (FE)	VT	Vertical Tab
12	0C	FF	Form Feed (FE)	FF	Form Feed
13	0D	CR	Carriage Return (FE)	CR	Carriage Return
14	0E	SO	Shift Out	SO	Shift Out
15	0F	SI	Shift In	SI	Shift In
16	10	DLE	Data Link Escape (CC)	DLE	Data Link Escape
17	11	DC1	Device Control 1	DC1	Device Control 1
18	12	DC2	Device Control 2	DC2	Device Control 2
19	13	DC3	Device Control 3	TM	Tape Mark
20	14	DC4	Device Control 4	RES	Restore
21	15	NAK	Negative Acknowledge (CC)	NL	New Line
22	16	SYN	Synchronous Idle (CC)	BS	Backspace
23	17	ETB	End of Transmission Block (CC)	IL	Idle
24	18	CAN	Cancel	CAN	Cancel
25	19	EM	End of Medium	EM	End of Medium
26	1A	SUB	Substitute	CC	Cursor Control
27	1B	ESC	Escape	CU1	Customer Use 1
28	1C	FS	File Separator (IS)	IFS	Interchange File Separator
29	1D	GS	Group Separator (IS)	IGS	Interchange Group Separator
30	1E	RS	Record Separator (IS)	IRS	Interchange Record Separator
31	1F	US	Unit Separator (IS)	IUS	Interchange Unit Separator
32	20	SP	Space	DS	Digit Select
33	21	!	Exclamation Point	SOS	Start of Significance
34	22	"	Quotation Mark	FS	Field Separator
35	23	#	Number Sign, Octothorp, "pound"		
36	24	$	Dollar Sign	BYP	Bypass
37	25	%	Percent	LF	Line Feed
38	26	&	Ampersand	ETB	End of Transmission Block
39	27	'	Apostrophe, Prime	ESC	Escape
40	28	(	Left Parenthesis		
41	29	)	Right Parenthesis		
42	2A	*	Asterisk, "star"	SM	Set Mode
43	2B	+	Plus Sign	CU2	Customer Use 2

with the 1976 extension, the copyright on Mickey Mouse would expire on January 1 2004, so in the late 1990s Disney went back for another helping. Congress obligingly rolled over again and retroactively extended copyright another 20 years through the Sonny Bono Copyright Term Extension Act of 1998. Some time in the 2010s, the industry will surely want to reduce consumer rights even further and try to write itself an infinite lifetime on copyright. Even patents, flawed as they are, have a much more limited lifetime.

There are rights other than those of content producers at stake here. America has very strong guarantees concerning freedom of speech, and there are long-standing precedents saying that printed text (even source code) counts as speech. When Copyleft printed the deCSS code on a t-shirt, nobody seriously thought they'd be sued over it. Of course, the suit is really aimed at discouraging programmers from spreading knowledge about deCSS, and from playing their DVDs with software that hasn't been approved by the DVD-CCA.

The DVD industry won't achieve those goals. You can't legislate knowledge out of existence. This is the same nonsense that the U.S. government tried a few years ago, classifying some forms of encryption software as "munitions" and thereby regulating their export under the same rules as machine guns, tanks, and artillery pieces. That software ban lasted right up until the time it collided with the need to put encryption in browsers as an enabler for e-commerce. One possible outcome is that the DMCA will be found unconstitutional (i.e. contrary to the most fundamental principles of U.S. law). But until that happens, you can order your illegal t-shirt from Copyleft. Wear it with pride—you're striking a blow for freedom of speech, for consumer rights, and for running whatever code you like on your own computers.

See also these websites:

- *www.toad.com/gnu/whatswrong.html*
- *eon.law.harvard.edu/openlaw/DVD/dvd-discuss-faq.html*
- *www.opendvd.org*

Table 14-7 shows the ASCII codes and corresponding EBCDIC values.

Table 14–7 ASCII and EBCDIC Codes *(cont.)*

Dec	Hex	ASCII		EBCDIC	
44	2C	,	Comma		
45	2D	-	Hyphen, Minus Sign	ENQ	Enquiry
46	2E	.	Period, Decimal Point, "dot"	ACK	Acknowledge
47	2F	/	Slash, Virgule	BEL	Bell
48	30	0	0		
49	31	1	1		
50	32	2	2	SYN	Synchronous Idle
51	33	3	3		
52	34	4	4	PN	Punch On
53	35	5	5	RS	Reader Stop
54	36	6	6	UC	Upper Case
55	37	7	7	EOT	End of Transmission
56	38	8	8		
57	39	9	9		
58	3A	:	Colon		
59	3B	;	Semicolon	CU3	Customer Use 3
60	3C	<	Less-than Sign	DC4	Device Control 4
61	3D	=	Equal Sign	NAK	Negative Acknowledge
62	3E	>	Greater-than Sign		
63	3F	?	Question Mark	SUB	Substitute
64	40	@	At Sign	SP	Space
65	41	A	A		
66	42	B	B		
67	43	C	C		
68	44	D	D		
69	45	E	E		
70	46	F	F		
71	47	G	G		
72	48	H	H		
73	49	I	I		
74	4A	J	J	¢	Cent Sign
75	4B	K	K	.	Period, Decimal Point, "dot"
76	4C	L	L	<	Less-than Sign
77	4D	M	M	(	Left Parenthesis
78	4E	N	N	+	Plus Sign
79	4F	O	O	|	Logical OR
80	50	P	P	&	Ampersand
81	51	Q	Q		
82	52	R	R		
83	53	S	S		
84	54	T	T		
85	55	U	U		
86	56	V	V		
87	57	W	W		
88	58	X	X		

Table 14–7 ASCII and EBCDIC Codes *(cont.)*

Dec	Hex	ASCII		EBCDIC	
89	59	Y	Y		
90	5A	Z	Z	!	Exclamation Point
91	5B	[	Opening Bracket	$	Dollar Sign
92	5C	\	Reverse Slant	*	Asterisk, "star"
93	5D	]	Closing Bracket	)	Right Parenthesis
94	5E	^	Circumflex, Caret	;	Semicolon
95	5F	_	Underline, Underscore	¬	Logical NOT
96	60	`	Grave Accent	-	Hyphen, Minus Sign
97	61	a	a	/	Slash, Virgule
98	62	b	b		
99	63	c	c		
100	64	d	d		
101	65	e	e		
102	66	f	f		
103	67	g	g		
104	68	h	h		
105	69	i	i		
106	6A	j	j		
107	6B	k	k	,	Comma
108	6C	l	l	%	Percent
109	6D	m	m	_	Underline, Underscore
110	6E	n	n	>	Greater-than Sign
111	6F	o	o	?	Question Mark
112	70	p	p		
113	71	q	q		
114	72	r	r		
115	73	s	s		
116	74	t	t		
117	75	u	u		
118	76	v	v		
119	77	w	w		
120	78	x	x		
121	79	y	y		
122	7A	z	z	:	Colon
123	7B	{	Opening Brace	#	Number Sign, Octothorp, "pound"
124	7C	|	Vertical Line	@	At Sign
125	7D	}	Closing Brace	'	Apostrophe, Prime
126	7E	~	Tilde	=	Equal Sign
127	7F	DEL	Delete	"	Quotation Mark
128	80		Reserved		
129	81		Reserved	a	a
130	82		Reserved	b	b
131	83		Reserved	c	c
132	84	IND	Index (FE)	d	d

Table 14–7 ASCII and EBCDIC Codes *(cont.)*

Dec	Hex	ASCII		EBCDIC	
133	85	NEL	Next Line (FE)	e	e
134	86	SSA	Start of Selected Area	f	
135	87	ESA	End of Selected Area	g	g
136	88	HTS	Horizontal Tabulation Set (FE)	h	h
137	89	HTJ	Horizontal Tabulation with Justification (FE)	i	i
138	8A	VTS	Vertical Tabulation Set (FE)		
139	8B	PLD	Partial Line Down (FE)		
140	8C	PLU	Partial Line Up (FE)		
141	8D	RI	Reverse Index (FE)		
142	8E	SS2	Single Shift Two (1)		
143	8F	SS3	Single Shift Three (1)		
144	90	DCS	Device Control String (2)		
145	91	PU1	Private Use One	j	j
146	92	PU2	Private Use Two	k	k
147	93	STS	Set Transmit State	l	l
148	94	CCH	Cancel Character	m	m
149	95	MW	Message Waiting	n	n
150	96	SPA	Start of Protected Area	o	o
151	97	EPA	End of Protected Area	p	p
152	98		Reserved	q	q
153	99		Reserved	r	r
154	9A		Reserved		
155	9B	CSI	Control Sequence Introducer (1)		
156	9C	ST	String Terminator (2)		
157	9D	OSC	Operating System Command (2)		
158	9E	PM	Privacy Message (2)		
159	9F	APC	Application Program Command (2)		
160	A0				
161	A1				
162	A2			s	s
163	A3			t	t
164	A4			u	u
165	A5			v	v
166	A6			w	w
167	A7			x	x
168	A8			y	y
169	A9			z	z
170	AA				
171	AB				
172	AC				
173	AD				
174	AE				

Table 14–7 ASCII and EBCDIC Codes *(cont.)*

Dec	Hex	ASCII		EBCDIC	
175	AF				
176	B0				
177	B1				
178	B2				
179	B3				
180	B4				
181	B5				
182	B6				
183	B7				
184	B8				
185	B9			`	Grave Accent
186	BA				
187	BB				
188	BC				
189	BD				
190	BE				
191	BF				
192	C0				
193	C1			A	A
194	C2			B	B
195	C3			C	C
196	C4			D	D
197	C5			E	E
198	C6			F	F
199	C7			G	G
200	C8			H	H
201	C9			I	I
202	CA				
203	CB				
204	CC				
205	CD				
206	CE				
207	CF				
208	D0				
209	D1			J	J
210	D2			K	K
211	D3			L	L
212	D4			M	M
213	D5			N	N
214	D6			O	O
215	D7			P	P
216	D8			Q	Q
217	D9			R	R
218	DA				
219	DB				

Table 14–7 ASCII and EBCDIC Codes *(cont.)*

Dec	Hex	ASCII	EBCDIC	
220	DC			
221	DD			
222	DE			
223	DF			
224	E0			
225	E1			
226	E2		S	S
227	E3		T	T
228	E4		U	U
229	E5		V	V
230	E6		W	W
231	E7		X	X
232	E8		Y	Y
233	E9		Z	Z
234	EA			
235	EB			
236	EC			
237	ED			
238	EE			
239	EF			
240	F0		0	0
241	F1		1	1
242	F2		2	2
243	F3		3	3
244	F4		4	4
245	F5		5	5
246	F6		6	6
247	F7		7	7
248	F8		8	8
249	F9		9	9
250	FA			
251	FB			
252	FC			
253	FD			
254	FE			
255	FF			

Chapter 15

Regular Expressions, Collections, Utilities

We come now to a most important part of Java: the java.util and related packages that provide utilities for your code to use. Some of these utilities, like the regular expression support we start the chapter with, are very algorithmic in nature. Other utilities are more concerned with providing data structures for your programs to use.

There are a dozen or so standard data structures in software: the linked list, the hash table, the binary tree, and so on. Java provides some of these directly as library classes, and makes it easy for you to implement any others you want in a consistent manner. These data structures hold collections of objects, and the library is known as the Java Collections Framework.

The chapter finishes with a brief look at some older, but still useful, data structure classes in Java, as well as some other utilities. Most of the rest of this book is devoted to explaining more Java libraries and showing examples of their use. Let's get going with regular expressions and pattern matching.

Regular Expressions and Pattern Matching

This section uses the I/O features described in the previous chapter and describes the regular expression pattern-matching feature that was introduced with JDK 1.4.

If you have ever typed "dir *.html" to see all the html files in a directory, you have used a regular expression for pattern matching. A regular expression is just a string that can contain some special characters to help you match patterns in text. In this case, the asterisk is shorthand for "any characters at all." The name "regular expression" was coined by American mathematician Stephen Kleene who developed regular expressions as a notation for describing what he called "the algebra of regular sets."

JDK 1.4 introduced a new package called java.util.regex that supports the use of regular expressions. Using the classes in that package you can answer questions like "does this kind of pattern occur anywhere in that string?," and you can split strings apart and change their contents. These sorts of operations are very useful in several different contexts: in doing web searches (you can use regular expressions in many search engines), in filtering email (discard email where the "From:" line matches well-known spanners), and all kinds of text-manipulation tasks. Source code editors usually have a way to search using regular expressions. If you don't know how to do pattern-matching in the editor you use to edit programs, you aren't reaching your full potential as a programmer. Plus, it's a great way to beguile other programmers who look over your shoulder.

There's lots of good news about regular expressions in Java. First, the regular expression "language" (the way you form regular expressions, the special symbols and their meaning) is very similar to that used by Perl. There are a few obscure things supported by Java that Perl 5 doesn't support, and vice versa. Java is less forgiving about badly-formed expressions. But if you already know Perl, there's less to learn about Java pattern matching. If you don't already know Perl, your Java regex knowledge will get you jump-started.

Best of all, Java regular expressions are simple. There are only three classes in the package, and one of those is an exception! Well, you can't really judge the complexity of a library by the number of classes it has, but regular expressions are straightforward. Pattern matching is important, and we'll cover it in some detail here.

The class java.util.regex.Pattern is used to specify the pattern that you want to try to match in some String you have. You invoke the static method called "compile, passing in the pattern string of ordinary characters and special characters. The method compile() hands you back a Pattern object on which you invoke the matcher() method feeding it some input to obtain a java.util.regex.Matcher object. Matcher has a number of useful methods for matching, splitting up, and replacing parts of input strings.

So two of your classes are Pattern and Matcher. The final class is the exception PatternSyntaxException. That exception is thrown if you provide a faulty regular expression to Pattern.compile().

Under the covers, the Pattern.compile() method builds a tree to represent the regular expression. Each node in the tree represents one component of the regular expression. Each node contains the code that will do a comparison on an input string and give an answer about whether it matches that part of the pattern or not. It is similar to the work an ordinary compiler does to turn source code into executable code, so "compile()" is a reasonable name for the method. The programmers could have made a constructor available. The use of a static method called compile() to return an instance is a hint that there is a lot more work going on here than memory allocation and initialization.

Watch out—patterns very quickly become very hard to read.

Matching a Pattern

Just as you don't directly instantiate a Pattern object, you don't directly instantiate a Matcher. You get an instance of the Matcher class by calling the matcher() method of your Pattern object. Then you send it input from anything that implements the CharSequence interface. String, StringBuffer, and CharBuffer implement CharSequence, so they are easy to pattern match. If you want to match patterns in a text file, this is also easy to do using the new Channel I/O feature. You get the Channel for the file, then you get a Buffer from the Channel. Character Buffers implement the CharSequence interface. If you need to pattern match from some other source, you can implement the CharSequence interface yourself (it's small and easy).

Once you have a Matcher object, it supports three different kinds of match operations:

- The **find()** method scans the input sequence looking for the next sequence that matches the pattern.
- The **matches()** method tries to match all the input sequence against the pattern.
- The **lookingAt()** method tries to match some or all of the input sequence, starting at the beginning, against the pattern.

Forming Patterns

A regular expression, or pattern, is a string that describes the kind of thing you want to match. Most letters represent themselves. If you compile a literal pattern of "To: pvdl@aaa.com", it will match exactly those letters in that order. If you have a file containing old email, you could use this pattern to find all the email addressed that way.

Once you have compiled a pattern and have a Matcher object, you can invoke its find() method to look for the next occurrence of the pattern in the input. You can then call its group() method to get back the input sequence that was matched by the previous match operation. The code looks like this:

```
Pattern p = Pattern.compile("To: ted@sun.com");
Matcher m = p.matcher( someBuffer );
while (m.find())
    System.out.println("Found text: "+m.group());
```

The find() method returns a boolean saying if it found the next occurrence of the pattern in the input. The group() method returns a string containing the most recent part of the input to match. If you provide a main program and run the code on a file containing my email, it will print out the matches with output like this:

```
Found text: To: ted@sun.com
Found text: To: ted@sun.com
```

The following sections will use this example data file of email. This contains five email messages, each of which starts with "From:" and continues until the next "From:".

Sample Email Data File

```
From: aaa@sun.com
To: bbb@sun.com
Subject: weather
The weather is fine today.
From: aaa@sun.com
To: ccc@sun.com
 Hello
From: aaa@sun.com
To: ddd@xyz.com,eee@home.com
Subject: no change!
--[booo!]
Weather still fine!
   He said he was a British Subject: born in London
From: aaa@sun.com
To: bbb@sun.com
Subject: Help - no rain.
We are in a drought,
   Bill.
From: aaa@sun.com
To: BBB@SUN.COM
Subject: SHIFT KEY
HELP! SHIFT KEY IS STUCK _ BILL
```

The following sections will use this program as a framework for trying different patterns. The pattern line is marked in bold. If you want to experiment with the different patterns shown, this is the line to update. This program and the data file above are on the CD.

Sample Pattern-Matching Program

```
import java.util.regex.*;
import java.io.*;
import java.nio.*;
import java.nio.charset.*;
import java.nio.channels.*;
public class Extract {
    public static void main(String[] args) throws Exception {
        // Create a pattern to match comments
        Pattern p = Pattern.compile("To: bbb@sun.com");

        // Get a Channel for the source file
        FileInputStream fis = new FileInputStream("email.txt");
        FileChannel fc = fis.getChannel();

        // Map a Buffer in from the data file, and decode the bytes
        MappedByteBuffer bb =
            fc.map(FileChannel.MapMode.READ_ONLY, 0,
                                                  (int)fc.size());
        Charset cs = Charset.forName("8859_1");
        CharsetDecoder cd = cs.newDecoder();
        CharBuffer cb = cd.decode(bb);

        // Run some matches
        Matcher m = p.matcher(cb);
        while (m.find())
            System.out.println("Found text: "+m.group());
    }
}
```

Running the program gives this output:

```
java Extract
Found text: To: bbb@sun.com
Found text: To: bbb@sun.com
```

These three lines of code may be unfamiliar:

```
Charset cs = Charset.forName("8859_1");
CharsetDecoder cd = cs.newDecoder();
CharBuffer cb = cd.decode(bb);
```

They specify how the bytes in the file are to be translated into characters as they are brought into the buffer. The earlier examples we have seen of mapped I/O just took bytes from the file and put them into bytes in the buffer. In this case, we get an object that represents the ISO 8859 Latin-1 character set (shown in Appendix C). Using that object we get a decoder object. The decoder object has the ability to "decode" or translate bytes into double-byte characters. 8859 is a single byte character set, and the translation will turn each byte in the file into two bytes in the buffer, the most significant byte of which is zero. There is more about character sets and encodings in the second I/O chapter.

Range

The pattern "To: ted@sun.com" won't find all email to Ted, though. Email is supposed to be delivered whether the domain part of the address is in upper or lowercase. That pattern just matches lowercase. As frequently happens with regular expressions, there are several different ways of writing a pattern. We can make the pattern ignore letter case by passing a flag when we compile the pattern, as here:

```
Pattern p = Pattern.compile("To: bbb@sun.com",
                    Pattern.CASE_INSENSITIVE );
```

Another way to achieve the same effect is to use a range. When the Pattern object sees square brackets, it tries to match one of the characters inside them. If we want to match "sun" without regard to case of the first letter, we could use this pattern:

```
"[Ss]un"
```

The pattern in one pair of square brackets matches one character. You can use a hyphen to indicate a range of characters (hence the name for this feature). These two patterns will both match any single digit:

```
"[0123456789]"
"[0-9]"
```

To match exactly two digits "00" to "99" we could use "[0-9][0-9]".

A powerful feature of the range function is the ability to match "anything but" the list of characters in the range. If the first character in a range is "^" (caret), it means "match any character *except* the ones that follow." So to extract the "To:" lines for everyone except names that start with "j" we could use this pattern:

```
"To: [^j]"
```

Similarly, "`[^ ]`" matches any character other than a space, and "`[^0-9]`" matches any one character that is not a digit. If you need to match against one of the special characters like square bracket or caret, you can "escape" them in the string. You escape a special character (treat it literally) by putting two backslashes before it in the string. It would be one backslash, but the rules of Java strings take precedence over the rules of regular expression patterns here. To get one backslash in a Java string, you have to escape it with its own backslash.

This Is Really Goofy

The backslash character '\' is used in Java Strings to escape certain characters, i.e., give them some different meaning. For example, "n" in a String just means the letter lowercase n. But "\n" tells the compiler that the linefeed character, ASCII 0x0A, should be substituted. Similarly, "\r" means that you get a carriage return, ASCII 0x0D. Since backslash has this special meaning, to get a backslash in a String you have to escape the backslash itself. (JLS 3.10.6)

As a result, every time you want literally one backslash in a Java String, you have to write two. We have already seen how this means rewriting all pathnames for Windows:

```
String myFileName = "\\jj5\fmdone\\15.2.fm";
```

Well, it also means rewriting many pattern-matching strings when you place them in Java Strings. The meta-character to match a digit is \d, or in a String:

```
String matchDigit = "\\d";
```

Obviously, this is really goofy. You might blame Dennis Ritchie, who popularized this "backslash means escape in a string" protocol in C, except C was laid down in 1970. You could blame Seattle Computer Products, who created DOS and made backslash the pathname separator, apparently in ignorance of C and Unix. Or you can blame Larry Wall, who invented Perl. Or blame James Gosling, who reused C's string escape convention in Java. Or just live with it.

Ranges can be used to match literal strings. But we are often in a situation where we want to match a string that conforms to some pattern. The email subject line, for example, starts with "Subject: ", then has any kind of text at all, and ends with an end of line character. For matching a pattern that includes some arbitrary text, we use meta-characters.

Single-Character Metacharacters

Suppose we want to match the Subject line of email. We want a pattern to match "Subject: *anything*" on one line. We will use the *metacharacter* "." (dot) that matches any single character. There are other metacharacters, besides dot, that match a single character. They are shown in Table 15-1.

Table 15–1 Pattern Metacharacters

Metacharacter	Written in a Java String	Single Character Matched	Express with a Range
`.`	`"."`	Any character	*n/a*
`\d`	`"\\d"`	A digit	`[0-9]`
`\D`	`"\\D"`	A non-digit	`[^0-9]`
`\s`	`"\\s"`	A whitespace character	`[ \t\n\x0B\f\r]`
`\S`	`"\\S"`	A non-whitespace character	`[^\s]`
`\w`	`"\\w"`	A character that can be part of a word	`[a-zA-Z_0-9]`
`\W`	`"\\W"`	A character that isn't part of a word	`[^\w]`

We use "." to match any character. We also need to apply a *quantifier* that says how many times to do this. The quantifier "*" means "any number of times." It applies to whatever immediately precedes it. Putting together the "match any character" dot with the "any number of times" quantifier, our pattern to match the subject line of email is:

```
"Subject: .*"
```

This matches up to the end of a line because, by default, the dot does not match line terminator characters. If you put that pattern into a suitable program, and run it, you get output like:

```
Found text: Subject: weather
Found text: Subject: no change!
Found text: Subject: Born in London
Found text: Subject: Help - no rain.
Found text: Subject: SHIFT KEY
```

If you look back at the email.txt file, you'll see that the "Born in London" text is not actually a subject line. We fix that in a later section.

Quantifiers

There are other quantifiers, too, that can express different amounts of repetition. Table 15-2 shows some quantifiers that specify the number of times a particular character or pattern should match. In this table, "X" represents any pattern.

Table 15–2 Quantifiers

Pattern	Meaning
`X?`	X, zero or one time
`X*`	X, zero or more times
`X+`	X, one or more times
`X{n}`	X, exactly n times
`X{n,}`	X, at least n times
`X{n,m}`	X, between n and m times

You can group patterns in parentheses to indicate exactly what is being repeated. So "(\\w*: \\w*)*" will match any number of sequences that consist of wordcharacters-colon-space-wordcharacters. This is a pattern for email headers. And don't be fooled by the name "word character." It only matches a single character, not an entire word. If you want it to match a word, you have to use a quantifier to repeat it, as in the email example just given.

All quantifier operators (+, *, ?, {m,n}) are greedy by default, meaning that they match as many elements of the string as possible without causing the overall match to fail. In contrast, a reluctant closure will match as few elements of the string as possible when finding matches. You can make a quantifier reluctant by appending a '?' to the quantifier. There is an example that uses a reluctant quantifier coming up later on.

Capturing Groups and Back References

Another use for parentheses is to represent matching subpatterns within the overall pattern. These subpatterns are called *capturing groups*, and you can retrieve them independently from the matcher for use in your code. You can also refer to one of these capturing groups later in the expression itself with a backslash-escaped number. A backslash followed by a number is always interpreted as a back reference. The first backreference in a regular expression is denoted by \1, the second by \2, and so on. So the expression: "([0-9]+)==\1" would match input like "2==2" or "17==17." Remember to double those backslashes when you want to put them in a Java string!

Back references let you match against patterns that contain *Readers Digest* style junk mail. If you've never had one of these letters, they try to personalize it by repeating your name and other details they have on file about you. A typical phony letter would read like this:

> Dear Peter,
> Excuse us for caring, Peter, but we just wanted to ask you who would
> look after your family at 123 Main Street, if anything should happen to you, Peter?
> Life insurance is not that expensive, Peter, and surely the family is worth it.
> Please contact us for more details, Peter.

A pattern that would match against this would be:

```
Pattern p = Pattern.compile(
          "^Dear (\\w+),$"      // matches "Dear name,"
          + "(^"                //   any number of lines
          +   ".* \\1.*"
//   each line has the name we captured in group 1.

          + "$)*"               //   end line
        , Pattern.MULTILINE );
```

As you can see, patterns very quickly become difficult to read. This pattern matches the greeting and then up to the first line not containing the name. The important things in the Reader's Digest example is the expression in parentheses on the first line (the parens make it a capturing group), and the "\\1" on the third line of the pattern which is a back reference to capturing group 1. The back references are numbered according to the order in which their opening parenthesis appears. Capturing groups can nest inside each other.

Whenever you use parentheses, the bracketed part of the pattern becomes a capturing group (there is a way to turn that off). The method Matcher.group(int i) returns the input sequence captured by group i during the most recent match. So to extract the actual name, and print it, we would add this code:

```
Matcher m = p.matcher( someBuffer );

if (m.find()) {

   System.out.println("Letter personalized for: " + m.group(1));

   System.out.println("line from letter: " + m.group(2));
}
```

Group 1 is the name. The call to group(2) will return the String "Please contact us for more details Peter," since that is the most recent match of all the lines that the group captured.

Anchors

Returning to our email example, the pattern "Subject: .*" will also find non-subject lines, where there is text like this:

```
How to be a British Subject: marry into the Royal Family.
```

That's not an email subject line, but it contains characters that match our pattern. If we really only want Subject lines, we need to be able to specify that the pattern only matches something at the beginning of a line. To do this we use a set

of metacharacters called "anchors"—they anchor the pattern to a particular place. Table 15-3 shows some anchor characters and how they affect matching. In this email example anchoring the pattern to the beginning of a line is still not enough. The pattern could occur in the body of an email message at the beginning of a line. To get this exactly right, you will need to match on the whole message, and distinguish headers from the body. It is set as an exercise at the end of the chapter.

Table 15–3 Anchor Characters

Anchor	Effect
`^`	The beginning of a line (also needs the multiline flag)
`$`	The end of a line (also needs the multiline flag)
`<`	The beginning of a word
`>`	The end of a word
`\b`	A word boundary
`\B`	A non-word boundary
`\A`	The beginning of the input
`\Z`	The end of the input but for the final terminator, if any
`\z`	The end of the input

Notice that the anchor for the beginning of a line is a caret. Don't get confused by the fact that caret is also used in ranges with a different meaning. There are so many metacharacters needed that it's inevitable that a few would be reused. We can anchor our email subject search to the beginning of a line with a pattern like this:

```
"^Subject: .*"
```

By default, the expressions for beginning and end of line don't do that! They only match the beginning and end of the input. You must set a pattern flag for multiple lines, as we did previously for letter case. The multiline flag will cause pattern matching to extend across line boundaries in the input. Here is how you can set the pattern and a couple of flags in one statement:

```
Pattern p = Pattern.compile("^Subject: .*$",
              Pattern.MULTILINE | Pattern.CASE_INSENSITIVE );
```

The flags are actually integer constants, and you "or" them together to combine their effect, as shown in the previous line of code.

Alternation

Let's make this example more realistic by writing a pattern to extract a series of entire email messages. A mail message is defined to be everything between one

"From:" at the start of a line, and the next one. There is a method in Pattern that splits an input sequence into pieces that are separated by the pattern. It returns an array of Strings, and is perfect for this purpose. The code to use it looks like this:

```
Pattern p = Pattern.compile("^From:", Pattern.MULTILINE);
String[] messages = p.split( someBuffer );
```

That should split our file into strings, each of which contains one message. However, the method split has some bugs in the JDK 1.4 beta release, so it provides a reason to look at a couple of other topics relating to pattern matching. The first one is alternation, and it involves the " | " (vertical bar) meta character. The second topic is how do you say "anything except this word"?

When you place a " | " in a pattern, it means "or". The pattern will match if either the left side of the " | " or the right side matches the input. That's all there is to alternation! You can use parentheses to group the alternate things more explicitly if needed. There is no corresponding "and" feature, because you get that effect by writing two subpatterns one after the other. So "XY" means "match an X followed by a Y," while "X | Y" means "match if you see either an X or a Y."

Word Negation

The next topic we will cover in this section is how to match the negation of a word. Ranges provide an easy way to match the negation of a single character. There is no built-in support for negation ("everything but") of an entire word. Most people's first guess at a pattern to exclude all lines that start with "From" is "^[^F][^r][^o][^m]".

This doesn't do what you want! It matches everything where the first character is not an "F", *and* the second character is not an "r", *and* the third character is not an "o", and so on. Because these "not equal to" conditions are "anded" together, if you have a word for which *any* of these letters-and-positions is a F... or .r.. or ..o. or ...m, e.g. "**F**rob" or "g**r**in" or "sh**o**t" or "glu**m**" you will find that the pattern rejects that line overall as a match.

You have to hand-create the idiom of "exclude this word" from other primitive operations that are available. To extract complete email messages, we want to start with a "From:" at the beginning of a line, and go up to but including the next "From:" at the beginning of a line.

One way to express this is with a pattern in three parts: a "^From:" matched literally, then an "everything except a '^From'", then a "^From:" or an end-of-input (using alternation). The code looks like:

```
Pattern p = Pattern.compile(
"^From:.*$"          // first "From:"
+ "(^.*$)*?"          // anything, over several lines
+ "^(?=From:|\\z)"   // second "From:" or end of input
, Pattern.MULTILINE);
```

The "?" in pattern "*?" is the "reluctant quantifier" that we mentioned earlier. It matches zero or more times reluctantly, i.e., if there is another way to interpret this match, that other part of the pattern is preferred. Similarly, the "?=From" is a special construct that provides a match with lookahead. The matching characters are not regarded as part of the captured group. Finally, the " | \\z" causes a match on either the "From" or the end of input.

One place where regular expressions can be used to good effect is in the accept method of the class javax.swing.filechooser.FileFilter. The class java.io.File has a method: File[] listFiles(FileFilter filter). You can write a class implementing FileFilter and supply the only method there, accept(File). You can put your file selection logic in there, and base it on desired filename patterns.

Metawords

There are also metawords that match entire categories, as seen in Table 15-4.

Table 15–4 POSIX Character Classes

(US-ASCII only)	Meaning
`\p{Lower}`	A lowercase alphabetic character: [a-z]
`\p{Upper}`	An uppercase alphabetic character:[A-Z]
`\p{Alpha}`	An alphabetic character:[{lower}{upper}]
`\p{Digit}`	A decimal digit: [0-9]
`\p{Alnum}`	An alphanumeric character: [{alpha}{digit}]
`\p{Punct}`	Punctuation: one of !"#$%&'()*+,-./:;<=>?@[\]^_`{|}~
`\p{Graph}`	A visible character: [\p{Alnum}\p{Punct}]
`\p{Print}`	A printable character: [\p{Graph}]
`\p{Blank}`	A space or a tab: [\t]
`\p{Cntrl}`	A control character: [\x00-\x1F\x7F]
`\p{Xdigit}`	A hexadecimal digit: [0-9a-fA-F]
`\p{Space}`	A whitespace character: [\t\n\x0B\f\r]

All of the state involved in performing a match is in the matcher, so many matchers can share the same pattern. But matcher objects are not thread-safe, and one matcher should not be invoked from different threads at the same time.

Finally, the JDK comes with an example program that searches for regular expressions in files. This program is also a Unix utility known as "grep," which stands for "Globally search for Regular Expression and Print." A much simplified version of the program follows. Please review it carefully, as it provides an excellent non-trivial practical example of the use of regular expressions.

Java Grep Program

```
// Search a list of files for lines that match a given regular-expression
// pattern.  Demonstrates NIO mapped byte buffers, charsets, and regular
// expressions.
import java.io.*;
import java.nio.*;
import java.nio.channels.*;
import java.nio.charset.*;
import java.util.regex.*;
public class Grep {
   public static void main(String[] args) {
        if (args.length < 2) {
            System.err.println("Usage: java Grep pattern file...");
            return;
        }
        doCompile(args[0]);
        for (int i = 1; i < args.length; i++) {
            File f = new File(args[i]);
            try {                    CharBuffer cb = mapInFile(f);
               grep(f, cb);
            } catch (IOException x) {
               System.err.println(f + ": " + x);
            }
        }
    }
    // Charset and decoder for ISO-8859-15
    private static Charset charset = Charset.forName("ISO-8859-15");
    private static CharsetDecoder decoder = charset.newDecoder();
    // Pattern used to separate files into lines
    private static Pattern linePattern = Pattern.compile(".*\r?\n");
    // The input pattern that we're looking for
    private static Pattern pattern;
    // Compile the pattern from the command line
    //
    private static void doCompile(String pat) {
      try {
          pattern = Pattern.compile(pat);
      } catch (PatternSyntaxException x) {
          System.err.println(x.getMessage());
          System.exit(1);
      }
    }
    // Use the linePattern to break the given CharBuffer into lines,
    // applying
```

```
    // the input pattern to each line to see if we have a match
    private static void grep(File f, CharBuffer cb) {
        Matcher lm = linePattern.matcher(cb); // Line matcher
        Matcher pm = null;    // Pattern matcher
        int lines = 0;
        while (lm.find()) {
            lines++;
            CharSequence cs = lm.group();  // The current line
            if (pm == null)
                pm = pattern.matcher(cs);
            else
                pm.reset(cs);
           if (pm.find())
                System.out.print(f + ":" + lines + ":" + cs);
            if (lm.end() == cb.limit())
                break;
        }
    }
    // Search for occurrences of the input pattern in the given file
    private static CharBuffer mapInFile(File f) throws IOException {
        // Open the file and then get a channel from the stream
        FileInputStream fis = new FileInputStream(f);
        FileChannel fc = fis.getChannel();
        int size = (int)fc.size();
        MappedByteBuffer mbb = fc.map(FileChannel.MapMode.READ_ONLY, 0,
                                                                   size);

        // Decode the file into a char buffer
       CharBuffer cb = decoder.decode(mbb);
       return cb;
    }
}
```

That concludes the discussion of regular expressions. We now describe the very important Collections API.

Collections API

As we mentioned earlier, there are a dozen or so basic data structures in software: the linked list, the hash table, the binary tree and so on. Java provides the most important of these (including all three mentioned) in a set of library classes, jointly known as the Java Collections Framework.

You do two basic things to any Collection data structure: you add objects into it, and then you can later go through it and process those objects, perhaps updating or removing some of them. There are umpteen other secondary operations too.

Most texts launch into an involved and highly-detailed description of the individual data structures at this point. You can quickly get overwhelmed with low level information on weakly-referenced hash maps, or abstract sequential lists. Instead, lets take a look at some characteristics of groups of things, and some examples.

We collect a number of objects together because we have some interest in dealing with them as a group. The objects frequently all belong to the same class or one of its subclasses, but they don't have to. An individual object in a collection is termed an "element."

As shown in Figure 15-1, the top-level box, labeled "collection of individual things," is represented by an interface in Java. The boxes underneath represent concrete classes that implement the interface. The idea is that you choose whichever of the *concrete classes* has the same qualities as your data. If your data needs

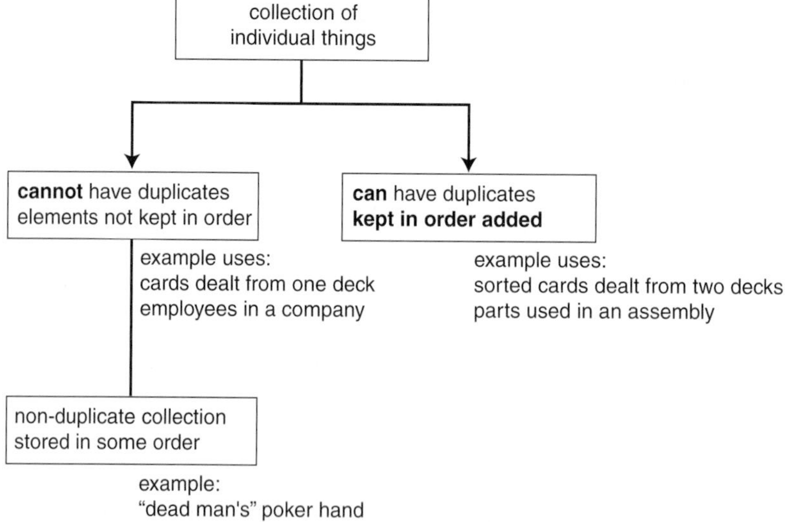

Figure 15–1 Collection characteristics.

to be kept in sorted order, use TreeSet. If your data can contain duplicate elements, use one of the Lists. But you only ever process the data using methods promised in the *interface*. That way, everyone who reads your code will know what the methods do, and if your algorithm ever changes, it is easy to substitute a different collection class for the present one.

Java 1.1 and earlier had Vector, Hashtable, and arrays as ways of storing many related objects, but there was no commonality in how you stored and retrieved from those classes. Arrays use indexing, Vector has the elementAt() method, and Hashtable uses get() and put().When you tried to write some code that operated on a data structure, it could either work on arrays, or on Vectors, or on Hashtable, but not all three. Collections fix this.

The class java.util.Collection is just an interface that defines a dozen or so methods for adding to, removing from, and querying a data structure. Now all the individual java.util data structures (and others that *you* write) can implement this interface, and everyone adds and retrieves data with the same method signatures. Collection looks like this:

```
public interface java.util.Collection {
    // basic operations
    public int       size();
    public boolean isEmpty();
    public boolean contains(Object element);
    public boolean add(Object element);
    public boolean remove(Object element);
    public Iterator iterator();

    // bulk operations on an entire collection
    public boolean addAll(Collection c);
    public boolean removeAll(Collection c);
    public boolean retainAll(Collection c);
    public boolean containsAll(Collection c);
    public void    clear();

    // put the collection into an array
    public Object[] toArray();
    public Object[] toArray(Object a[]);

    // a reminder that you may need to override these
    public boolean equals(Object o);
    public int       hashCode();

}
```

Let's take a closer look at the methods that Collection promises. All of the basic methods should be self-explanatory, with the possible exception of iterator(), which we will get to shortly.

Add() and remove() will add or remove the argument element and return true if that operation changed the Collection. In other words, if you try to remove something that is not in the collection, no exception is thrown, but the method call returns false. If the argument object actually was part of the collection, that element is removed from it and the method returns true. If you try to add something that is already in the collection, the result depends on what kind of collection it is. Some collections allow duplicate elements, and will add it again quite happily. Other collections do not allow duplicates. They will notice that they are already holding the element, and will return false to indicate that the operation did not change the collection.

The retainAll() method essentially does set intersection. It goes through this Collection and compares it with the Collection passed as the argument. It keeps all the elements that are in both collections and removes the others from this Collection.

The addAll() method adds all the elements of the argument collection to this collection. The removeAll() method removes all elements from this collection that are also contained in the argument collection. After this call returns, this collection will hold no elements in common with the argument collection.

All concrete Collection classes have a constructor that takes a Collection as an argument. There is no way for the interface to specify the existence of these constructors. It's just a generally accepted protocol. This constructor allows you to get a view of an existing Collection in one of the other Collection data structures. No cloning takes place. Collections only ever hold references to objects, so it is quick to sort or add or remove elements just by rearranging pointers.

There is a helper class, `Collections`, that consists exclusively of static functions to do useful things to a Collection argument (get the maximum element, reverse a collection, sort it, do a binary search, etc.). We come back to that later with an example. Next we'll take a look at the way you add elements to any collection, and how you can use an iterator to visit all the elements.

Adding to a Collection

One of the concrete classes that implements Collection is `java.util.HashSet`. This class is actually the "cannot have duplicates" box in Figure 15-1. You might want to write its name on Figure 15-1. It is implemented using a Hash table, and it acts like a Set, hence HashSet. Here is the code that shows how you would populate a HashSet Collection object and invoke some common methods on it:

```
Collection c = new HashSet();

for(int i = 1; i <= 5; i++)
    c.add( new Double(i));

if ( c.isEmpty() )
    System.out.println("c is empty");

boolean added;
added = c.add( "Charles Dickens");
added = c.add( new Date() );
System.out.println("c has " + c.size() + " elements");
```

Only Use Methods from the Collection Interface

This example uses the concrete class java.util.HashSet, which implements the java.util.Collections interface. HashSet stores the elements in a hash table. Notice how the *only* mention of the concrete class is in the instantiation:

```
Collection c = new HashSet(); // YES!
```

All other references and method calls use the interface, not the class.

```
HashSet c = new HashSet(); // NO!
```

Your code should follow this pattern too. It makes the code more readable, because the only methods you can call are those of the interface. It gives you more flexibility if you later need to use a different kind of collection class.

If you put those statements in a main routine and add an "import java.util.*" at the top of the class, you'll be able to compile and run the program with this result:

```
javac Example.java
java Example
c has 7 elements
```

Notice that this (strange) collection contains five Double objects, a String, and a Date object. You can store completely unrelated objects in a collection, as long as the collection doesn't have a notion of sorted order as one of its characteristics. Some subclasses of collection do keep their elements in sorted order, and some don't.

If you try to store a mixed number of objects like this into a collection that likes to hold its objects in order, you will end up comparing, e.g., a Double to a String and it will throw a ClassCastException. Later we'll see how to teach the class the way in which we would like such a comparison done. Before reading about that, let's take a look at iterators.

public interface Iterator

Iterator is an interface that allows you to visit (iterate over) all the elements in a collection without having to know all the details about how or where they're stored.

The interface java.util.Iterator replaces the earlier attempt to do the same thing, java.util.Enumerator ("I" comes after "E" in the alphabet, Iterator replaces Enumerator in the language). The names are shorter in Iterator ("next()" versus"nextElement()"). Iterator provides a safe way to remove an element that you have just arrived at, whereas Enumerator does not have this feature.

The Collection interface promises that each implementing class will have a method like this:

```
public Iterator iterator()
```

The method iterator () returns an object that fulfills the Iterator (with a capital "I") interface. As an aside, the obvious implementation for iterator() is to use an inner class to implement an Iterator, local to the method and possibly anonymous.[1] The Iterator interface looks like this:

```
public interface java.util.Iterator {
     public boolean hasNext();
     public Object next();
     public void remove();
}
```

The Iterator allows you to visit all the elements in some collection object. For an array, iteration is simply going from a[0] to a[n-1], but for a binary tree a little more effort is needed. The Iterator interface allows that effort to be encapsulated, kept in the Collection, and hidden from user classes.

1. If that sentence seemed like mumbo-jumbo, please review Chapter 9 on inner classes and tackle the collections questions in the exercises at the end of this chapter.

The method next() returns the next element of the iteration. If there is no next element, it will throw the exception NoSuchElementException. When you visit an element with next(), you can then call remove() on it to delete it from the collection, if you wish. This is much simpler than having every individual Java programmer trying to implement remove() for a linked list or whatever the structure is, for themselves.

The hasNext() allows you to test whether there is a next element in the collection. The methods next() and hasNext() are defined to be robust. You can call them in any order, and they are not tied to each other at all. The method hasNext() can be called multiple times without moving to the next element, and it will return the correct answer.

Assume we are using the Collection created in the previous example. We can work our way through each element with code like this:

```
Collection c = new HashSet();

//  code to fill the collection, omitted.

for(Iterator i = c.iterator(); i.hasNext();  )
    System.out.println("object " + i.next() );
```

With the contents set up in the previous example, the output will be:

```
object a string
object 3.0
object Mon Oct 08 20:52:52 PDT 2001
object 4.0
object 2.0
object 1.0
object 0.0
```

Notice how the objects are not at all in the order in which we added them, or in numeric or any other obvious order. Some collections put the objects into a natural sorted order as you add them, while others use an order that suits the way they store objects. Still other collections keep the elements in the order in which you add them to the collection.

HashSet is one of the collections that uses an order that suits itself, hence the elements come out in a seemingly funny order. To see why, you have to understand how hash tables work, and in particular what is going on with the methods equals() and hashcode() that are defined in java.lang.Object, and hence present in every Object. We defer this discussion to a little later in the chapter. Let's go on to look at another class that implements Collection: LinkedList.

List, LinkedList, and ArrayList

One of the concrete classes that implements Collection is java.util.LinkedList. This class is actually the "can have duplicates" box in Figure 15-1. I suggest you write its name on that figure. It's just a plain old "Data Structures 101" doubly-linked list. You provide each object that will be stored as data in a list element, and the library class does the work of linking the elements together in a list. You start by instantiating an empty LinkedList, then anything you add is put on the list as a new element.

The class LinkedList implements List which implements Collection. The exact parent-child relationship of interfaces is shown in Figure 15-2.

The interface java.util.List adds about another ten methods to the elementary data access methods specified in java.util.Collection. The additional methods are:

```
public interface java.util.List extends java.util.Collection {
    public boolean addAll(int, Collection);
    public Object get(int);
    public Object set(int, Object);
    public void add(int, Object);
    public Object remove(int);
    public int indexOf(Object);
    public int lastIndexOf(Object);

    public java.util.ListIterator listIterator();
    public java.util.ListIterator listIterator(int index);
    public java.util.List subList(int from, int to);
}
```

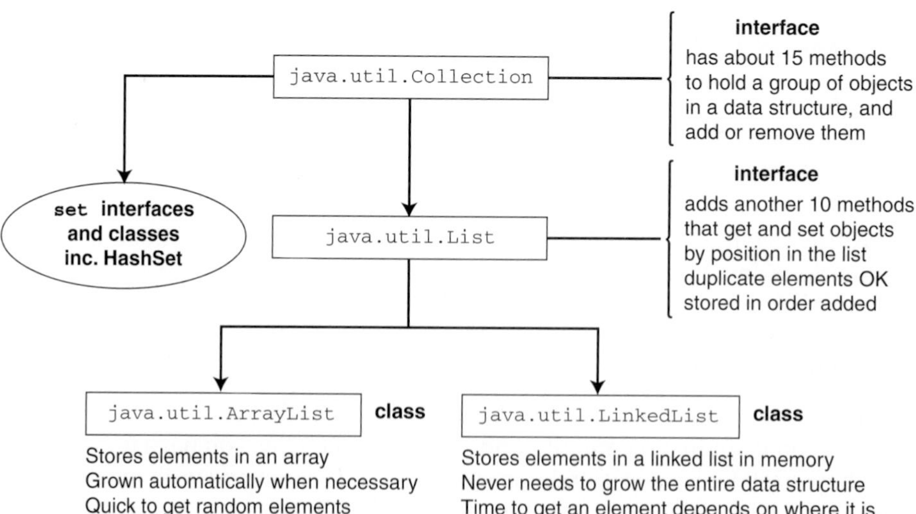

Figure 15–2 Interface relationship.

Most of these methods let the programmer access elements by their integer index (position in the list), and search for elements in the list. Unlike sets, lists allow duplicate elements. Say you owned a store, and wanted to record each item as it is sold so that you know what you need to re-order. A list would be a good choice for this kind of collection. As you make each sale, sa,y for a 21-inch Sony color tv model ABC-1, a new element representing that product is added to the list. If you sell ten of them during the day, there will be ten such records on the list.

A HashSet would not be a good choice for this collection, because after you have added the first ABC-1 record to the collection, no additional duplicates representing subsequent sales can be added. You can work around that by entering the item once and updating a count of purchases made for each item. However, it illustrates the difference between collections that allow duplicates and those that don't.

The subList() method returns a new list that points to the elements in the first list between the *from* argument, inclusive but not including the *to* argument. Lists start at element zero, just like arrays.

Note the two listIterator() methods. The first one obtains a ListIterator starting at the first element in the collection. The second one gets a ListIterator starting at the position specified by the int argument. A ListIterator is a subinterface of Iterator, and promises these methods:

```
public interface java.util.ListIterator extends java.util.Iterator {
    public boolean hasNext();
    public Object next();
    public boolean hasPrevious();
    public Object previous();

    public int nextIndex();
    public int previousIndex();

    public void remove();
    public void set(Object);
    public void add(Object);
}
```

A ListIterator allows you to iterate backwards over a list of objects as well as forwards. If you want to start at the end of the list, create a ListIterator passing an argument of list.size(). Then a call to list.previous() will return the last element, and you can keep going back through previous objects.

Unlike an Iterator, a ListIterator doesn't have a current element. The position of the ListIterator always lies in between two elements: the one that would be returned by a call to coll.previous(), and the one that would be returned by a call to coll.next().

The remove() and set() methods operate on the element returned by the most recent next() or previous(). The set() method replaces that element by the argument element. The remove() method removes that element from the list.

Here is the code for iterating backwards through a list:

```
Collection c = new LinkedList();
// code to add elements, omitted

List coll = (List) c;
ListIterator li = coll.listIterator( coll.size() );

while( li.hasPrevious() ) {
    Object o = li.previous();
    // do something with the element o
}
```

Let's run over a List example using a class that represents a hand of four cards. First, we write an interface that has constants for the suit and rank of each card. For convenience in output, we hold them as strings:

```
interface CardConsts {
  final String[] deck = {
    "spd_ace", "spd_king", "spd_queen", "spd_jack", "spd_10", "spd_09",
    "hrt_ace    "hrt_king", "hrt_queen", "hrt_jack", "hrt_10", "hrt_09",
    "clb_ace", "clb_king", "clb_queen", "clb_jack", "clb_10", "clb_09",
    "dmd_ace", dmd_king", "dmd_queen", "dmd_jack", "dmd_10", "dmd_09" };
}
```

We've left off the values 8 to 2, but you can add them when you try this example. Now we declare a class that holds four cards, and inherits these constants by implementing the interface. This code shows how you would populate a Collection of objects stored in a LinkedList.

```
import java.util.*;
  public class Hand implements CardConsts {

    Collection coll = new LinkedList();

    public Hand(String c[]) {
       for(int i=0; i< c.length; i++)
           coll.add( c[i] );
    }

   public static void main(String[] args) {
       String[] example = { "spd_king",
       "dmd_10", "clb_9", "spd_king" };

       Hand h = new Hand( example );

       System.out.println("list:   " + h.coll);

   }
}
```

You'll be able to compile and run the program with this result:

```
javac Hand.java
java Hand
coll:  [spd_king, dmd_10, clb_09, spd_king]
```

Like any class, Collection classes have a toString() method. If you invoke toString on a Collection containing Strings, it will print them out between square brackets, as above.

Notice that card 0 and card 3 in this hand are both the King of Spades (we must be dealing from two decks, or the player is cheating). Lists are quite happy holding duplicate elements. Other collections are not able to hold the same element more than once in the collection, and we will look at some of those later in the chapter.

One useful thing that we will want to do to our cards is sort them into order. The helper class java.util.Collections contains a static method that sorts a List. Here's how we invoke it, and the result:

```
Collections.sort( (List) h.coll);
System.out.println("lexi:  " + h.coll);

coll:  [spd_king, dmd_10, clb_09, spd_king]
lexi:  [clb_09, dmd_10, spd_king, spd_king]
```

Comparable and Comparator

You might wonder how the Collections class is able to sort a List: how does it know how elements are compared with each other? The answer is that you tell it. You tell Collections or anyone who is interested how your class is ordered by implementing one of two available interfaces:

- `java.lang.Comparable`—implement this interface when there is a single obvious natural ordering for the objects.

  ```
  public interface java.lang.Comparable {

      public int compareTo(java.lang.Object rhs);

  }
  ```

  The compareTo() method will compare this object with the argument, and return a negative int if this is less than rhs. If the two objects are equal, zero is returned. If this is greater, the method returns a positive integer.

  String implements Comparable, with a natural ordering of alphabetic. They call it "lexicographic order," rather than "alphabetic order," because lots of string values are digits, punctuation, or other non-alphabetic characters.

- `java.util.Comparator`— implement this interface when there are several equally good orderings for the objects. Create one Comparator for each ordering you want to offer.

```
public interface java.util.Comparator {

   public int compare(Object lhs, Object rhs);

   public boolean equals(Object comp);

}
```

  The compare() method returns a negative, zero, or positive int, for <, equal, > exactly like Comparable's compareTo().

  The equals() method is a tricky one. It is used to check two Comparators (not the objects they are comparing) to see if they are the same. If the Comparators are the same, and your List is already in the order of one of them, you don't need to sort it again. You can usually leave this method out and let your Comparator inherit the equals() method from Object.

Any class implementing one of these interfaces must be very careful to keep the normal mathematical properties expected of comparisons. If a equals b, and b equals c, then it is expected that a equals c. Further, a should equal a, and the method should be consistent with its own or any parent object's equal() method. The API documentation has a lengthy discussion of this topic.

A Common Optimization Is Wrong!

A common technique for comparing one quantity with another, returning the result as a negative/zero/positive quantity, is to use subtraction:

```
public int compareTo(int lhs, int rhs) {
    return (lhs-rhs);
}
```

So, if you were comparing 7 and -3, the answer is 7 - -3, or +10, which is positive, indicating that 7 is indeed bigger than -3. You get a three-way comparison in one line of code. This technique is widely used and is independent of programming language. It works as long as the operation fits in 32 bits, but disasterously returns the wrong answer when the subtraction overflows.

Recall from Chapter 5 that ints don't give an overflow exception, except for division by zero. The result just rolls over like an odometer. If you subtract two numbers that cause such a rollover, you may get the wrong answer. Here's an example using bytes, where it is easier to see what's going on.

```
byte lhs = -3;
byte rhs = +127;

String hex1 = Integer.toHexString(lhs).substring(6);
System.out.println("lhs: " + lhs + " is 0x" + hex1);
String hex2 = Integer.toHexString(rhs);
System.out.println("rhs:" + rhs + " is 0x" + hex2);

byte result = (byte) (lhs - rhs);
String hex3 = Integer.toHexString(result);
System.out.println("subtraction:  " + result + " is 0x" + hex3);

if (result > 0)
  System.out.println("result positive, so "
            + lhs +" seems greater than "+ rhs);
```

Running the code gives this result:

```
lhs: -3 is 0xfd
rhs:127 is 0x7f
subtraction:  126 is 0x7e
result positive, so -3 seems greater than 127
```

You can only compare using subtraction when you are certain the values cannot overflow, or when the operands are unsigned as with type char.

Let's implement a comparator for our hand of cards class. This comparator will put Strings that represent cards in order of the cards' rank, ignoring suit.

```
class CardComparator implements java.util.Comparator {

    private int toNumber(String s) {
        if (s.equals("ac")) return 14;  // aces high
        if (s.equals("ki")) return 13;
        if (s.equals("qu")) return 12;
        if (s.equals("ja")) return 11;
        try {
            return Integer.parseInt(s);
        } catch (NumberFormatException e) {
            throw new RuntimeException("bad card value: "+s);
        }
    }

    public int compare(Object o1, Object o2) {
        String c1 = (String)o1, c2 = (String) o2;
        String rank1 = c1.substring(4); // ac, ki, qu, ja, 10...
        String rank2 = c2.substring(4);

        int value1 = toNumber(rank1);
        int value2 = toNumber(rank2);
        return value2 - value1;  //  reverse order - highest card first
    }
}
```

This code should be pretty clear. The compare() method extracts the two characters that represent the rank of the card, and uses a toNumber() method to turn them into an int in the range 2...14. Because we know the range will never overflow, we can safely do a subtraction comparison. Reversing the order of the subtraction reverses the comparison, which reverses the sort, which makes the order "highest cards first."

We can do a sort based on this Comparator by passing it to the Collections sort() method, where it will be called back as needed:

```
CardComparator cc = new CardComparator();
Collections.sort( (List) h.coll,  cc);
System.out.println("sort:  " + h.coll);

// results:
list:  [spd_king, dmd_10, clb_09, spd_king]
lexi:  [clb_09, dmd_10, spd_king, spd_king]
sort:  [spd_king, spd_king, dmd_10, clb_09]
```

Why compare and compareTo Have Different Arguments

You may wonder why Comparator.compare takes two Object arguments, where Comparable.compareTo takes a "this" and one Object argument. The reason is that Comparable is used for natural order, so it is unique for each class. Therefore, the method it promises might as well be put in the class directly.

Comparator is used to give any order you like, so there may be several Comparators for a given class. At most, one of these could go into the class itself (further ones would be disallowed because you cannot have multiple methods with the same signature in the same class).

It is, therefore, convenient to implement Comparator with a separate class, perhaps nested, rather than making it a method of the class you are comparing. Once it is not a method of the class you are comparing, the "this" no longer refers to objects you are comparing, and you have to explicitly pass those objects as two arguments.

The comparison methods have different names to emphasize the difference between the interfaces.

The class java.lang.String has a Comparator, as well as implementing Comparable. The Comparator will do a case-insensitive comparison. It is implemented as a static nested class that is private inside the String class:

```
private static class CaseInsensitiveComparator
                    implements Comparator, java.io.Serializable {
        public int compare(Object o1, Object o2) {
          // 20 lines of code, omitted
        }
}
```

Then, also inside String, the Comparator is instantiated and made publicly available as part of String's API:

```
public static final Comparator CASE_INSENSITIVE_ORDER
                        = new CaseInsensitiveComparator();
```

It allows you to do a case-insensitive comparison of Strings.

The Collections Helper Class

As we mentioned above, there is a "helper" class that contains about 50 static methods and nested classes that operate on or return a Collection.

```
public class Collections extends Object {
    public static final Set EMPTY_SET;
    public static final List EMPTY_LIST;
    public static final Map EMPTY_MAP;

    public static void sort(List);
    public static void sort(List, Comparator);
    public static int binarySearch(List, Object);
    public static int iteratorBinarySearch(List, Object);
    public static int binarySearch(List, Object, Comparator);
    public static int iteratorBinarySearch(List, Object, Comparator);
    public static void reverse(List);
    public static void shuffle(List);
    public static void shuffle(List, Random);
    public static void swap(List, int, int);
    public static void fill(List, Object);
    public static void copy(List, List);
    public static void rotate(List, int);
    public static boolean replaceAll(List, Object, Object);
    public static int indexOfSubList(List, List);
    public static int lastIndexOfSubList(List, List);
    public static List nCopies(int, Object);
    public static List list(Enumeration);

    public static Object min(Collection);
    public static Object min(Collection, Comparator);
    public static Object max(Collection);
    public static Object max(Collection, Comparator);
    public static Collection synchronizedCollection(Collection);

    public static Set synchronizedSet(Set);
    public static SortedSet synchronizedSortedSet(SortedSet);
    public static List synchronizedList(List);
    public static Map synchronizedMap(Map);
    public static SortedMap synchronizedSortedMap(SortedMap);

    public static Set singleton(Object);
    public static List singletonList(Object);
    public static Map singletonMap(Object, Object);
    public static Comparator reverseOrder();
    public static Enumeration enumeration(Collection);
}
```

About half of the methods provide further List operations, including sorting and searching. These operations are not needed for Sets because there is a subtype of Set that is defined to be held in sorted order. The API documentation has the full description of each of these methods.

ArrayList implements List. We now return to another class that implements List. ArrayList is a concrete class that implements the `List` interface using an array as the underlying type. The ArrayList class should be thought of as an array that grows as needed to store the number of elements you want to put there.

When you want to put your data in a List, ArrayList is always an alternative to LinkedList. The main reason for choosing one over the other is performance.

- An ArrayList offers immediate access to all its elements (they are stored in an array, remember). You can only reach a LinkedList element by starting at one end or the other of the list, and traversing all the intervening elements.
- A LinkedList lets you add a new element very quickly. The time to add an element to an ArrayList is normally quick, too. But when the array is full, adding another element causes a new bigger array to be allocated and the old one copied over into it. LinkedList does not have that drawback.

The ArrayList class has the following public methods, in addition to those promised by the list interface:

```
public class java.util.ArrayList implements
      java.util.List, java.util.RandomAccess,
      java.lang.Cloneable, java.io.Serializable {
  public ArrayList();       // constructors
  public ArrayList(int size);
  public ArrayList(Collection c);

  public void trimToSize();
  public void ensureCapacity(int size);

  public Object clone();
}
```

You don't access ArrayList elements with the array brackets "[]," instead, you use the List methods to get and set the elements at particular indices.

To cut down on incremental reallocation, you can tell the constructor how many elements the array should allow for initially. The default allocation is ten elements, or 10% more than the size of a Collection you pass to the constructor, in the JDK 1.4 release.

Threads and Collections. The ArrayList class is a replacement for the JDK 1.0 class java.util.Vector. However, all the methods of Vector are synchronized, while none of the new Collection classes are. If multiple threads access an ArrayList or any Collection, they must all synchronize on some external shared object when one of the threads updates the list. The Collections class contains the hooks to do this.

```
Collection sl = Collections.synchronizedList( myList );
```

will wrap a List or any Collection, and provide a mutual exclusion lock. The lock can be any object; the class designer used the obvious one of the synchronized collection itself.

When a thread wants to call a Collection method, most of them have a wrapper to provide synchronization automatically. You can see this code in the nested class that handles synchronized collections in the Collections class in the runtime library:

```
public int size() {
         synchronized(mutex) {return c.size();}
}
```

The iterator() method is not so protected, and you must only call it from a block that is synchronized on the wrapped object.

```
synchronized(sl) {
    Iterator i = list.iterator(); // Must be in synchronized block
   while (i.hasNext())
       foo(i.next());
}
```

The iterator() method is treated separately because iteration is potentially a lengthy task. The programmer has to write it carefully to avoid stalling other threads for long periods of time.

Some data structures, such as HashSet, support *fail-fast* iterators. A fail-fast iterator notices if another thread is trying to change a collection that you are iterating through and throws a `ConcurrentModificationException` rather than corrupt your data.

It is fail-fast in the sense that you learn of the logic error as soon as it happens, not at some undetermined future time when the data no longer adds up. This clever piece of design is implemented by keeping a note of the size of the collection. The saved count is compared with the actual count for operations like add() and remove(). If they do not match, then some other part of your code has modified the collection outside the iterator, which is not allowed.

The Arrays Helper Class. Just as we saw the Collections helper class a few pages back, there is also a helper class called `Arrays`. It provides related services for arrays and can also give you back an array of Objects as a List. The class `Arrays` looks like this:

```
public class java.util.Arrays {
     public static List asList(java.lang.Object[]);

     public static int binarySearch(byte[], byte);
     public static boolean equals(byte[], byte[]);
     public static void fill(byte[], byte);
     public static void fill(byte[],int from, int to, byte);
     public static void sort(byte[]);
     public static void sort(byte[], int from, int to);

     // the same six methods binarySearch(), equals(), two
     // kinds of fill(), two kinds of sort, are repeated
     // for arrays of each primitive type, except boolean.
     // They are also supported for arrays of Object

     // signatures omitted here for brevity ...
}
```

The methods are shown here for byte arguments. The Arrays class also has corresponding methods for arrays of all primitive types (except Boolean) and for Object arrays.

The class java.util.Arrays thus allows you to:

- sort an array or part of an array into natural order, or use a comparator in the case of an Object array
- compare the contents of one array against another. Two arrays are considered equal if they contain the same number of elements, and the elements at the same position are equal. Two null array references are equal, as well.
- do a binary search on an array that has previously been sorted, and
- fill an array or part of an array with a specified value.

The arguments to sort() and fill() that are two ints are used to designate a range within the array where you wish the operation to occur from and to. It follows the same protocol that we saw in the subList() method of the List interface. The *from* argument is inclusive, but the *to* argument is excluded. So if you ask for a binary sort from 0 to 9, the elements 0 to 8 of the array will be sorted.

Set, HashSet, and SortedSet

One of the concrete classes that implements Collection is java.util.HashSet. We briefly visited HashSet at the beginning of this section on Collections, and now it is time to expand on it a little. This class is actually the "cannot have duplicates" box in Figure 15-1. You may want to write its name on the figure. It's just a plain old "Data Structures 101" hash table.

You provide each object that will be stored as data in the hash table, and the library class does the work of maintaining the table and putting the elements in the right places. You start by instantiating an empty HashSet, then anything you add is put in the table. If an object is already in the table, it won't be added again.

The class HashSet implements Set which implements Collection. The exact parent-child relationship of interfaces is shown in Figure 15-3.

The interface java.util.Set does not add any methods at all to the elementary data access methods specified in java.util.Collection. It is written as a separate interface to help document and represent the design of the Collections Framework. It shows the symmetry between classes that are Sets, and classes that are Lists.

As a reminder, the Collection interface, and thus the Set interface, looks like this:

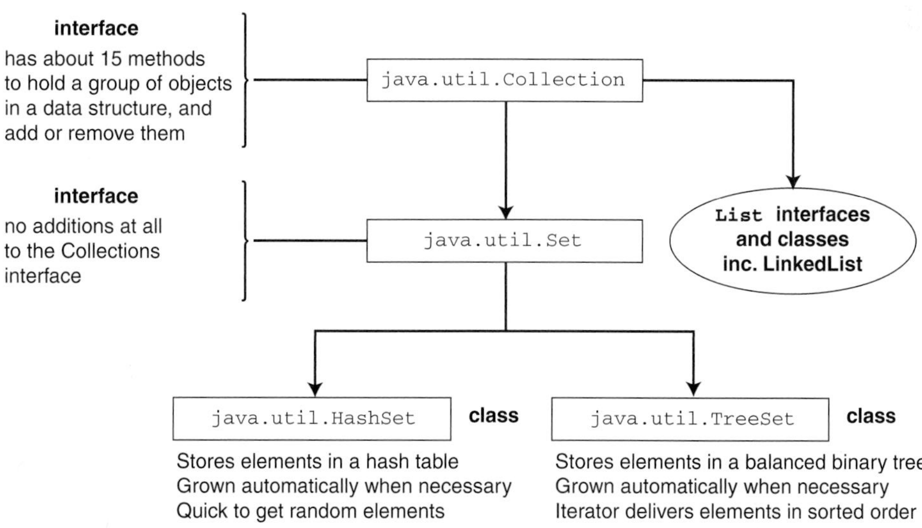

Figure 15–3 HashSet relationship.

```
public interface java.util.Set extends Collection {
     // basic operations
     public int size();
     public boolean isEmpty();
     public boolean contains(Object element);
     public boolean add(Object element);
     public boolean remove(Object element);
     public Iterator iterator();

     // bulk operations on an entire collection
     public boolean addAll(Collection c);
     public boolean removeAll(Collection c);
     public boolean retainAll(Collection c);
     public boolean containsAll(Collection c);
     public void clear();

     // put the collection into an array
     public Object[] toArray();
     public Object[] toArray(Object a[]);

     // a reminder that you may need to override these
     public boolean equals(Object o);
     public int hashCode();

}
```

A Set is *a collection that has no duplicate elements.* The interface represents the mathematical concept of a set, as applied in set theory. It is easy to calculate the intersection of two collections, or take the set difference between this set and another. An example of a set is the set of all colors that a system can display on its monitor. Here is how we would calculate the intersection of two collections:

```
String red = "red";
String green = "green";
String blue = "blue";
String magenta = "magenta";
String yellow = "yellow";

// populate first collection
Collection hs1 = new HashSet();
hs1.add( red );
hs1.add( green );
hs1.add( blue );
hs1.add( magenta );

// populate second collection
Collection hs2 = new HashSet();
hs2.add( red );
hs2.add( green );
hs2.add( yellow );

// intersection is the things that are in hs1 and in hs2
Collection intersect = hs1;
intersect.retainAll(hs2);

System.out.println("hs1       :  " + hs1);
System.out.println("hs2       :  " + hs2);
System.out.println("intersect:  " + intersect);
```

Running this code results in this output:

```
hs1       :  [blue, magenta, green, red]
hs2       :  [green, red, yellow]
intersect:  [green, red]
```

Similarly, the set difference, or "exclusive or" of two sets is calculated by:

```
Collection xor = new HashSet(hs1);
xor.addAll(hs2); // xor is now the union of set 1 and 2

Collection and = hs1;
and.retainAll(hs2);      // and is now the intersection of set 1 and 2

xor.removeAll(and);      // remove the "and" elements, to get an xor set.
System.out.println("xor       :  " + xor);

// output is
hs1       :  [blue, magenta, green, red]
hs2       :  [green, red, yellow]
intersect:  [green, red]
xor       :  [blue, magenta, yellow]
```

We should note that these methods (addAll(), retainAll(), and removeAll()) are promised by the Collection interface, so you can use them on any Collection data structure including linked lists, not just on sets! The Collection framework is very powerful, and will save you many hours of programming once you master it.

You would use a HashSet when you have a collection that is not going to have duplicates and you want fast retrieval. Throughout these collections examples we've been using String objects because they are particularly easy to print out and show what's happening, but you can, of course, store any objects in a Collection.

`TreeSet`. The fourth and final concrete Collection class in the JDK is the TreeSet class. This class is a set (i.e., collection of arbitrary elements), and it has the additional feature that the elements are kept in a way that makes it easy to fetch them in ascending order of elements.

TreeSet automatically sorts an element into its correct place in the collection whenever you add it! The sort order will either be the natural order for the class, as expressed by Comparable, or the order defined by a Comparator that you pass to the constructor. When you get an Iterator for a TreeSet, it is guaranteed to deliver the elements in this order.

A TreeSet collection is implemented by ("has a") a TreeMap behind the scenes. TreeMap in turn uses a red/black tree as its data structure. If you haven't met red/black trees yet, they are a variety of binary tree that is always kept balanced.

TreeSet works just like HashSet, but it takes a little extra work to keep everything in sorted order. Therefore, you will choose TreeSet when the ordering of the elements is important to you, and HashSet otherwise. There's no sense in incurring a performance penalty if you don't need to.

TreeSet has a few additional methods of its own, relating to the fact that it keeps elements in order. The extra features it offers, over and above Collection, are:

```
public class TreeSet extends AbstractSet
          implements SortedSet, Cloneable, java.io.Serializable {
    public TreeSet(); // constructors
    public TreeSet(Comparator);
    public TreeSet(Collection);
    public TreeSet(SortedSet);

    public SortedSet subSet(Object from, Object to);
    public SortedSet headSet(Object lessThan);
    public SortedSet tailSet(Object gte);

    public Comparator comparator();
    public Object first();
    public Object last();
    public Object clone();
}
```

The methods first() and last() obviously return you the lowest and highest element currently in the collection. The method headSet() returns a view of this Collection, containing only elements that are strictly less than the argument object. The method tailSet() returns a view of elements that are greater than or equal to the argument object. The method subSet() returns a view into the collection that holds only objects starting at the from object inclusive, and going up to but not including the to object.

The four constructors of TreeSet shown above will instantiate, respectively, an empty TreeSet, an empty tree set that will use this comparator, a TreeSet containing the elements in this collection, and a TreeSet containing the elements in this SortedSet. SortedSet is an interface that is only implemented by one class in the JDK: TreeSet. It is there so you can use it if you extend the framework with your own classes and designs.

Reforming Objects into a Different Collection. Harking back to our hand of cards example, we can change our Hand of cards class from using a LinkedList to using an ArrayList with just one line of code, as long as we only invoke methods using the List interface, not from the LinkedList object. If we change this single line

```
Collection coll = new LinkedList();
```

to this line

```
Collection coll = new ArrayList();
```

the class will now be based on an ArrayList. Everything else will work as before.

We can also get a view of an existing collection by using the "collection constructor." Each collection class has a constructor that takes an existing collection as an argument, and returns a view of that collection loaded into its own data structure. This is all done using references to objects, so it's quick and efficient. If you change fields in the original collection, those changes are seen by the new view, which is usually what you want. Here's how we could get a HashSet view onto our LinkedList of cards:

```
HashSet hs = new HashSet( h.coll );
System.out.println("hash:  " + hs);
```

The hs object now contains the objects that were in the linked list. The hs object is a HashSet, and so will not add the same object into itself twice. Sure enough, the result of executing the print statement shows that the duplicate element for the king of spades was ignored:

```
list:  [spd_king, dmd_10, clb_09, spd_king]
lexi:  [clb_09, dmd_10, spd_king, spd_king]
sort:  [spd_king, spd_king, dmd_10, clb_09]
hash:  [dmd_10, clb_09, spd_king]
```

Here's how we can hold the cards in a TreeSet and order them according to the comparator we defined earlier:

```
Collection ts = new TreeSet( cc );
ts.addAll( h.coll );
System.out.println("tree:  " + ts);
```

First, we create an empty set specifying that we want to use the cc Comparator (from the earlier code example). Then we add the existing collection into that set. Finally, we print out the results to see:

```
list:  [spd_king, dmd_10, clb_09, spd_king]
lexi:  [clb_09, dmd_10, spd_king, spd_king]
sort:  [spd_king, spd_king, dmd_10, clb_09]
hash:  [dmd_10, clb_09, spd_king]
tree:  [spd_king, dmd_10, clb_09]
```

As expected, the tree printout shows the cards arranged in order of rank. The ease of changing implementations here really shows the power of Collections. When you create your own data structures, you should think about having them implement one of the Collections interfaces, so that they will be interchangeable and present a similar API to all Java programmers. The Framework contains several abstract classes that are starting points for your own data structure classes.

Getting Arrays In and Out of Collections. Collection has a couple of signatures for methods that will flatten all the elements of a data structure into an array of Objects to provide compatability with older APIs that use arrays. The returned array is either one it allocates, or one you pass to it as an argument. If the argument array is not big enough to hold the collection, it will ignore it and return you an array that is big enough.

There is an idiomatic way of getting the array back and casting it to the correct type in one line. This example uses class java.util.Date, further described at the end of the chapter. Date holds timestamps of date and time. Say you have a collection, c, that holds lots of Date objects. Here's the one-liner to bring them into an array:

```
Date d[] = (Date[]) c.toArray( new Date[0] );
```

You can cast to arrays, just as to any object type, and that's the meaning of "`(Date[])`" right after the assignment operator. The method toArray() is defined to return an Object[], and this cast tells the compiler that the expression to its right will actually be the Date[] subtype of Object[]. The compiler allows the assignment, but plants code to check it at runtime.

Cool Coding in Collection

All the collection classes that come with the JDK support the toArray() method, but in truth it's only there for compatibility with older APIs that used arrays. You don't do a lot of conversion back and forth between collections and arrays. But if you do, it's very convenient to get back an array of the right subtype from toArray(). That way, you don't need to cast each array element before use.

The toArray() method has a rule that the runtime type of the returned array will be the same type as the argument array. We pass in a zero length Date() array just to provide the type information! The method signature promises an Object array, but the method body actually sends back an array of the Date subtype of Object. If the collection, c, holds any objects that are not Dates, an ArrayStoreException will be thrown.

Think about that for a moment. How does it know which subtype to return? It is implemented using reflection. Very cool! The code is:

```
public Object[] toArray(Object a[]) {
        int size = size();
        if (a.length < size)
            a = (Object[]) java.lang.reflect.Array.newInstance(
                            a.getClass().getComponentType(), size);
```

That last line reads as "get me a new array instance of the same element type as "a" really is." The cast to "Object()" is not needed. Reflection does not qualify for much mention in this text because it is not generally used in application programming. Reflection allows you to query existing variables and declare new ones of whatever type you want. It is used to good effect here in a library class. It is also used in writing database drivers, and in implementing component software environments.

How Do You Choose Between Sets, Lists, Maps, Stacks, and Others?

You choose the data structure according to what you want to do with the data. If you are trying to store key/value pairs, some kind of map is indicated.

If you have a collection of data and there might be some duplicate entries (e.g., you are tracking the first names of everyone in your department), you could use some kind of list. If there are no duplicates and you want to be able to get elements out in sorted order (e.g., you are storing employees' length of service), you could use a TreeSet.

If you are implementing a pocket calculator and want to be able to read and evaluate expressions, a stack is the natural data structure. A stack is trivial to implement in terms of a linked list. A queue is trivial to implement in terms of a linked list.

Being a programmer means understanding what kind of access, storage order, restrictions, and cost different data structures have. That is independent of Java. All programmers in any language need to be familiar with common data structures.

Summary of Collections.

- JDK 1.2 introduced support for Collections, also known as "container classes." There are two basic interfaces that extend `Collection` in different directions, Set and List.
- A List is a collection that has an order associated with its elements. That order is the order in which the elements were added to the collection. There does not need to be any logical relationship between elements.
- The List interface is implemented by two concrete classes, LinkedList and ArrayList. LinkedList is a doubly-linked list. The time to access elements depends on where they are in the list, but there is no overhead to growing or shrinking the collection. ArrayList is a list stored as an array. It provides quick access to any element, but it is expensive to grow or shrink the array.
- A Set is a collection that never has any duplicate objects. Unlike a mathematical set, the objects may come in some order, but it is not the order in which you add them to the collection.
- The Set interface is implemented by two concrete classes, HashSet and TreeSet. HashSet is a set backed by hash table. It is quick to add and retrieve elements, but the elements are in no particular order. TreeSet is a set backed by a red/black tree. The elements are kept in sorted order, so it costs more to insert them.

There are a couple of well-defined ways to express the order in which objects are compared. We also saw two helper classes for collections and arrays. These support some very useful sorting and extraction utilities for collections and arrays. It's possible to flatten any collection into an array, although you'll probably never need to.

All of these features together make up the Collections Framework, and there is one additional piece to it, which we will review in the next section. So far, all these data structures have dealt with individual objects. There is another interface backed by concrete classes that you can use to process pairs of key/values together. This is the Map interface.

Map, HashMap, and TreeMap

Map is a data structure interface that connects keys and values. Each key has at most one associated value. Some examples of key/value pairs would be driver's license number and licensed driver, username and password, ISBN and book title. The first of each of these pairs is a key for uniquely retrieving the second. The most obvious way of storing a Map is as a two-column table, and you can get fancier from there.

The interface provides three views onto its collection of keys/values. You can see the map as a collection of keys, or as a collection of values, or as a collection of key/value pairs. Once you have these collections back, you can invoke the standard Collection method to get an iterator and visit all the elements.

The order of a map is defined as the order in which the iterators on a map's collection views return their elements. Some Map implementations, like the TreeMap class, make specific guarantees as to their order; others, like the HashMap, do not. The Map interface looks like this:

```
public interface java.util.Map {
     public java.util.Set keySet();           // get keys
     public java.util.Collection values();    // get values
     public java.util.Set entrySet();         // get mappings

     public boolean containsKey(Object);
     public boolean containsValue(Object);

     public Object get(Object key);
     public Object put(Object key, Object value);
     public void putAll(java.util.Map);

     public Object remove(Object);
     public boolean isEmpty();
     public int size();
     public void clear();
     public boolean equals(Object);
     public int hashCode();

     public static interface java.util.Map.Entry {
          public Object getKey();
          public Object getValue();
          public Object setValue(Object);
          public boolean equals(Object);
          public int hashCode();
     }
}
```

The keys, values, and mappings are returned as collections so that you can easily compare entire maps to one another, and answer questions like "does this map have all the keys that are in that map?" or "does this map have any values in common with that map?" You answer these kind of questions by using the set difference, intersection, and union operations that we have already seen for collections.

If you have a class that implements map, you can iterate over all its mappings like this:

```
Set s = myMap.entrySet();
for(Iterator i = s.iterator(); i.hasNext(); ) {
```

The set returned by entrySet() is a collection of objects that belong to the static nested interface `java.util.Map.Entry`. You can then get an iterator for that Set, and each object that it returns will be a (thing that belongs to a class that implements) Map.Entry. You can invoke any of the methods promised in the nested interface on that returned object. You can get each key in turn, or get/set each value in turn.

```
    // nested inside the iterator for loop, above
    Map.Entry me = (Map.Entry) i.next();
    Object ok = me.getKey();
    Object ov = me.getValue();
}
```

To review, the objects ok and ov represent a single entry in the Map. The object ok is the key that maps to value ov. We got the entry set from the Map, the iterator from the entry set, and the key and value from a next() value in the iteration.

Maps and their concrete subclasses are part of the Collections Framework, but they are not in themselves collections. You can get pieces from them that are collections, but Map is not a subinterface of Collection.

In the next section, we'll look at a couple of concrete classes that implement Map. Before we do that, we'll briefly outline how hash tables work, and what it means for you in practice.

What Is a Hash Table?

A hash table is a data structure that stores keys/values like an ordinary table, but offers fast retrieval. A symbol table in a compiler is often maintained as a hash table. When a name is first read in from the source program, it is *hashed*, or converted to a table index—say, 379—by an algorithm designed to spread the hash keys around the table. It is then entered in the table at location 379 along with its value (the unhashed name, type, scope, etc.).

Then, when you get the same name again, it is hashed, and the same result, 379, is used as a subscript for immediate access to all its details in the hash table. It is marvelous that a hash table is a library data structure in Java!

If two or more elements hash to the same index value, the extra ones are stored in a linked list, hanging off that table entry.

Why is a hash table better than just maintaining a sorted list or vector? Because hashing is fast, and sorting is slow.

Now the purpose of the method hashCode() in class java.lang.Object should be clear. It ensures that every single object in the system has a hashcode, and thus can be put in a hash table without further work on your part. The hashcode is a 32 bit int, and the hash table algorithm will typically reduce it modulo the size of the table, and take the remainder as an index value.

The hashcode returned by Object.hashCode() looks like the address of the object in virtual memory, which is a good way of ensuring that unique objects have unique hashcodes. That's fine for many classes, but not so fine for others. There are some classes where objects can be unique (i.e., at different memory addresses) but still be equal.

String is an example of a class with that property. I may have a String object that holds the value "mudflap". For all purposes, the content of the string should be used to determine equality to some other String, not the unique memory address. I want any other string with those characters to compare equal. Therefore, the Object.hashCode() isn't very useful for String, and the String class should override it.

String does override Object.hashCode(), and it replaces the method with one where the hashcode is calculated based on the characters in the string. The algorithm takes each character in the String and multiplies it by 31 to the power i, where i is the character offset within the String. It sums all these values to get the hash for a given string. (Another way of looking at this is that, loosely, it converts the String to a base 31 int.)

String also overrides java.lang.Object.equals() and replaces it with an equality test that looks at content, not address. There is a rather large pitfall here that you must be careful to avoid. You must always make sure that you override equals() and hashCode() in pairs, and you must make sure they are implemented in mutually compatible ways. If two objects compare equal, then their hashCodes must have the same value too.

If you fail to follow these precautions, then any use of Maps on your object will give undefined values. You may know all the places that you use maps in your own code, but it's hard to be aware of when the runtime library is using a Map on your behalf.

HashMap Implements Map

The class java.util.HashMap implements the Map interface. It uses a hash table to minimize the searching on every lookup and it implements Map, hence, the name HashMap. You should now use this class where formerly you might have used JDK 1.0's Hashtable.

HashMap is a supremely useful class. Hash tables allow you store together any number of key/value pairs. Instead of storing items with index values 0, 1, 2, 3, as you would in an array, you provide the key to be associated with the object. Then in the future, you need provide only that key again, and voila, out pops the right object.

Here are the public members of HashMap, over and above what is promised by the Map interface that it implements:

```
public class java.util.HashMap
     implements Map, Cloneable, java.io.Serializable {

    public HashMap(int size, float load);
    public HashMap(int size);
    public HashMap();
    public HashMap(Map);

    public Object clone();
}
```

It has four constructors and a public clone() method. The size and load arguments to the constructors specify the initial size (number of elements) of the table, and the fraction of the table which can become full before it is reallocated to a bigger size. As a rule of thumb, a load factor of 0.75 seems to work quite well, and this is the default that the library uses. The last constructor does what you'd expect: constructs a new map with the same mappings as the given map.

HashMap has fail fast iterators, and is not synchronized. If you have several threads running, or several iterators in one thread, you will need to wrap it with a synchronization object. We saw an example of this earlier for List. The class Collections has a corresponding wrapper for Maps:

```
Map sm = Collections.synchronizedMap( myMap );
```

Then the iterators must be used in synchronized blocks as before.

Here is some example code that uses a hash map to hold a company phone book containing names and corresponding extension numbers:

```
import java.util.*;
public class example  {
    // the Map!
    Map phonebook = new HashMap();

    // constructor
    public example(String n[], String nums[]) {
       for(int i=0; i< n.length; i++)
           phonebook.put( n[i], nums[i] );
    }

   public static void main(String[] args) {
       // data
       String [] names = { "Bill", "Terry", "Sandy", "Rohit" };
       String [] extns = { "4873", "4810", "3769", "0" };

       // get an instance of this class
       example ex = new example( names, extns );

       // dump out the map
       System.out.println("map:  " + ex.phonebook);

       // get the mappings
       Set s = ex.phonebook.entrySet();

       // iterate over the mappings
       for (Iterator i = s.iterator(); i.hasNext(); ) {
           Map.Entry me = (Map.Entry) i.next();
           Object ok = me.getKey();
           Object ov = me.getValue();
           System.out.println("object " + me );
           System.out.println("key " + ok );
           System.out.println("value " + ov );
       }
   }
}
```

Running the program results in this:

```
% java example
map:  {Rohit=0, Terry=4810, Bill=4873, Sandy=3769}
object Rohit=0
key Rohit
value 0
object Terry=4810
key Terry
value 4810
object Bill=4873
key Bill
value 4873
object Sandy=3769
key Sandy
value 3769
```

You can see that the collection of key/value pairs has been stored into a HashMap and can be retrieved on demand.

`TreeMap.` The final Collections framework class to review here is java.util.TreeMap. This class has the same relationship to HashMap that TreeSet has to HashSet. In other words, TreeMap implements the Map interface, and its underlying data structure is a red/black tree.

TreeMap takes some extra cycles to do its work of inserting and retrieving keys in the tree, but it will produce its keys in sorted order on demand. If you have no need to see the keys in sorted order, use HashMap instead. In the context of our phone directory example, we may well wish to have the keys in order, as this would be useful if we wanted to output the office phone directory in alphabetic order of names.

Here are the public members of TreeMap, over and above what is promised by the Map interface that it implements:

```
public class java.util.TreeMap
    implements SortedMap, Cloneable, java.io.Serializable {
     public TreeMap();   // constructors
     public TreeMap(Comparator);
     public TreeMap(Map);
     public TreeMap(SortedMap);

     public Comparator comparator();
     public Object firstKey();
     public Object lastKey();
     public Object clone();

     public SortedMap headMap(Object);
     public SortedMap tailMap(Object);
     public SortedMap subMap(Object, Object);
}
```

The TreeMap class has four constructors which work in the obvious way. The first one creates an empty TreeMap. The second constructor creates an empty TreeMap that will use the Comparator passed as an argument. The third creates a TreeMap out of the elements in the given Map. The fourth constructor creates a TreeMap out of the elements in the given SortedMap.

A SortedMap is a subinterface of Map. TreeMap is the only current implementor of SortedMap. It is the interface that promises all the other methods of SortedMap that are over and above those promised by Map. The other methods will get you the comparator that is in use, or null if the TreeMap is using natural order. The firstKey() and lastKey() methods return the lowest and highest keys in the Map, respectively.

The method headMap() returns a view of this Map containing only elements that are strictly less than the argument object. The method tailMap() returns a view of elements that are greater than or equal to the argument object. The method subMap() returns a view into the Map that holds only objects starting at the from object inclusive, and going up to, but not including, the to object.

As an example use of TreeMap is the phone directory program, modified to use a TreeMap by changing one line. Some of the output has also been reduced here, as it should be clear enough to see what is happening.

```
import java.util.*;
public class example  {

    // the Map!
    Map phonebook = new TreeMap();

    // constructor
    public example(String n[], String nums[]) {
       for(int i=0; i< n.length; i++)
           phonebook.put( n[i], nums[i] );
    }

   public static void main(String[] args) {
       // data
       String [] names = { "Bill", "Terry", "Sandy", "Rohit" };
       String [] extns = { "4873", "4810", "3769", "0" };

       // get an instance of this class
       example ex = new example( names, extns );


       // dump out the entire map
       System.out.println("map:  " + ex.phonebook);

       // get the mappings
       Set s = ex.phonebook.entrySet();

       // iterate over the mappings
       for (Iterator i = s.iterator(); i.hasNext(); ) {
           Map.Entry me = (Map.Entry) i.next();
           System.out.println("object: " + me );
           Object ok = me.getKey();
           Object ov = me.getValue();
       }
   }
}
```

The output of running this program is:

```
map:  {Bill=4873, Rohit=0, Sandy=3769, Terry=4810}
object: Bill=4873
object: Rohit=0
object: Sandy=3769
object: Terry=4810
```

Most of the time you won't be querying a Map for all its mappings. Most of the time you'll have a key and want to look up the corresponding value using this method:

```
public Object get(Object key);
```

Or you'll be putting pairs into the table using this method:

```
public Object put(Object key, Object value);
```

Other Utility Classes

That brings us to the end of the Java Collections Framework, and we now round out the chapter with a description of some other utility classes you may wish to use. As always, you should browse the Javadoc html files for this package.

BitSet. This class maintains a set of bits that are identified by the value of an integer, like an array index. You can have up to about 2 billion individual bits in a set (if you have enough virtual memory), each of which can be queried, set, cleared, and so on. The bit set will increase dynamically as needed to accommodate extra bits you add to it.

```
public BitSet();  // constructor
public BitSet(int N);  // constructor for set of size N bits

public void or (BitSet s); // OR's one bit set against another.

public void set (int i); // sets bit number i.

public int size(); // returns the number of bits in the set.
```

Stack

The Stack class maintains a Last-In-First-Out stack of Objects. You can push (store) objects to arbitrary depth. The methods are:

```
public Object push(Object item);   // add to top of stack.

public Object pop();   // get top of stack.
```

In addition, there are three other methods not usually provided for stacks:

```
public boolean empty(); // nothing on the stack?

public Object peek();    // returns top Object without popping it.

public int search (Object o); // returns how far down the stack
// this object is (1 is at the top), or -1 if not found.
```

The author of this class made an interesting mistake. He made Stack a subclass of Vector, so that he would get the vector behavior of allowing unbounded input. He failed to notice that it meant all the methods of Vector would be available in Stack—including inappropriate methods like `removeElementAt()` to pull something out of the middle of a vector. So Stack does not guarantee Last-In-First-Out behavior. Hans Rohnert from Germany pointed this out in email. As Hans put it, it is not true that Stack "is a" Vector, rather it should "have a" Vector in which to store.

The usual way to "hide" unwanted methods from a base class is to override them with private versions, empty versions, or versions that throw a runtime exception. In this case, `Vector.removeElementAt(int)` is final, and final methods can't be overriden. Never call `removeElementAt()` on your stack, and you'll stay out of trouble.

Some of these early 1.0 utility packages were written very quickly by skilled programmers who were more interested in getting the code working than achieving a perfect design. It's easier to find flaws in code than it is to write faultless software. Pointing out the occasional blemish is done in the spirit of learning, not as a criticism of the work of others.

The java.math API

The java.math package is simple to understand and use. It was added to JDK 1.1 for three reasons. First, for use in the java.security Digital Signature Algorithm interfaces. Second, to complete the support for all SQL types used in database programming and to allow arithmetic on types larger than long and double. If you do database programming, you'll be comfortable with the two classes java.math.BigDecimal and java.math.BigInteger which can represent the SQL types DECIMAL and NUMERIC. Third, even if you don't use cryptography or database programming, you can still use these classes for arithmetic on numbers of arbitrary size.

As the names suggest, BigInteger deals with integers of unbounded size, and BigDecimal deals with unbounded numbers with fractional parts. BigDecimal is essentially BigInteger with some extra code to keep track of the scale (where the decimal point is). If you want to manipulate a number that takes a megabyte to store all its decimal places, you can. BigInteger provides versions of all of Java's primitive integer operators and all relevant static methods from java.lang.Math. Additionally, BigInteger provides operations for modular arithmetic, greatest common divisor calculation, primality testing, prime generation, single-bit manipulation, and a few other odds and ends.

Here's an example of BigInteger used to perform a calculation that is listed in the 1989 *Guinness Book of World Records* under "Human Computer:"

```
BigInteger bi1 = new BigInteger("7686369774870");
BigInteger bi2 = new BigInteger("2465099745779");
bi1 = bi1.multiply(bi2);
System.out.println( "The value is "+ bi1 );
```

When compiled and run, the correct answer appears:

```
The value is 18947668177995426462773730
```

BigInteger naturally does it quite a lot faster than the human record holder who took 28 seconds. Here's an example of BigDecimal used to round a number with many decimal places of precision.

```
BigDecimal bd1 = new BigDecimal( java.lang.Math.PI );
System.out.println( "The value is "+ bd1 );

int digsrightofradix = 4;
bd1 = bd1.setScale(digsrightofradix, BigDecimal.ROUND_HALF_UP);
System.out.println( "The value is "+ bd1 );
```

When compiled and run, the output is this:

```
The value is 3.141592653589793115997963468544185161590576171875
The value is 3.1416
```

The true value is 3.1415926535 8979**32**3846 2643383279 5028841971 693993751, so you can see that our value of pi is wrong in the 16th decimal place.

This is because we got the value from a double, and that's the limit on accuracy for doubles (refer back to Chapter 4 if you don't remember this). If we calculate pi from a formula using BigDecimal, we can get arbitrary precision.

Class BigDecimal also contains many other options for rounding numbers. Don't confuse the big numbers available from package java.math with the generalized math and trig operations available in class java.lang.Math.

Calendar Utilities

Java Is Year 2000 Compliant

Java is Y2K compliant in release JDK 1.1.6 and later, including JDK 1.2. The official statement is at URL *www.sun.com/y2000/cpl.html*. Prior to the 1.1.6 release there were some corner case bugs that had to be fixed.

The JDK 1.0 support for dates was poorly designed. With the benefit of hindsight, it might have been better to throw it out and start over again, but backwards-compatibility was seen as the more important goal. In JDK 1.1 most of the constructors and methods of java.util.Date class were deprecated and other classes were provided to offer better support for time zones and internationalization.

The classes specifically related to date/time are summarized below:

- The class `Date` represents a specific instant in time with millisecond precision.
- The class `Calendar` is an abstract class for converting between a `Date` object and a set of integer fields such as year, month, day, and hour.
- The class `GregorianCalendar` is the only concrete subclass of `Calendar` in the JDK. It does the date-to-fields conversions for the calendar system in common use.
- The class `DateFormat` is an abstract class that lets you convert a `Date` to a printable string with fields in the way you want (e.g., dd/mm/yy or dd.MMM.yyyy).
- The class `SimpleDateFormat` is the only concrete subclass of `DateFormat` in the JDK. It takes a format string and either parses a string to produce a date or takes a date and produces a string.
- The class `TimeZone` is an abstract class that represents a time zone offset and also figures daylight savings time adjustments.
- The class `SimpleTimeZone` is the only concrete subclass of `TimeZone` in the JDK. It is what defines an ordinary time zone with a simple daylight savings and daylight savings time period.

Not only was date/time support poorly designed, it was poorly implemented and full of bugs. The good news is that many of the bugs were corrected in 1.1.4 and 1.1.6. As of JDK 1.2, all of the common problems have been corrected. This part of the JDK is maintained by IBM.

Deprecated Interfaces

Compatibility between releases is a major goal of JavaSoft's. In most cases this works very well, but there are a small number of cases where an API has had to be changed. When an API is replaced by a different one, JavaSoft assures software compatibility by leaving the old API in place and marking it as "deprecated."

To deprecate something means to disapprove of it. Deprecated features will eventually be removed from the API. When you compile a program that uses a deprecated API, the compiler will issue a single line error message, like this:

```
% javac foo.java
Note: foo.java uses a deprecated API.  Recompile with "-
deprecation" for details.
1 warning
```

The purpose of this warning is to tell you that you are using an old interface that has been replaced. The warning will not cause compilation to fail, but it reminds you that the class will eventually be removed from the JDK and you need to bring your code up to date. Only one deprecation warning is issued for a compilation, even if you use dozens of outmoded classes or methods. To view the full list of deprecated features that you have used, compile like this:

```
% javac -deprecation foo.java
foo.java:4: Note: The constructor java.util.Date(int,int,int)
has been deprecated.
Date d1 = new Date(97,12,2);
              ^
Note: foo.java uses a deprecated API.
Please consult the documentation for a better alternative.
3 warnings
```

This tells you the deprecated feature, in this case it is one of the constructors in java.util.Date. You then look at the source code to see the suggested replacement. In this case, that piece of code refers you to java.util.Calendar. The Calendar class is the replacement for some methods in the Date class.

You can instantiate Date with no arguments to represent the current moment.

```
Date now = new Date();
```

You used to be able to provide arguments (year, month, day, hour, etc.) to say "build me a Date that represents this date/time." That use is now deprecated and you should use the class GregorianCalendar instead.

Java uses a 64-bit long to represent an instant in time. The value is interpreted as "milliseconds since Jan 1 00:00:00, 1970." The scheme is sufficient to represent dates from 292,269,053 B.C. to A.D. 292,272,993 (64 bits covers minus 9,223,372,036,854,775,808 to plus 9,223,372,036,854,775,807 milliseconds). But note that prior to JDK 1.2, a GregorianCalendar will not accept values earlier than 4716 B.C. The class Date should really be thought of as "Instant" or "Timestamp."

Calendar and GregorianCalendar

The class Calendar translates between an instant in time and individual fields like year, month, day, hour, etc. Date used to do this, but it did it in a way that didn't properly internationalize, so those methods have been deprecated.

Calendar also knows about time zones, and hence things like summertime. The time zone information has a class of its own: TimeZone. DateFormat class provides elementary Date formatting.

Calendar is an abstract base class, which is meant to be overridden by a subclass that implements a specific calendar system. It's a dumb approach: it makes the common case of simple date processing un-obvious. Most of the world uses the Gregorian calendar (named after the Pope who established it in 1582). Excessive generality in a design is as bad as (or worse than) excessive rigidity.

The class java.util.GregorianCalendar extends Calendar and provides more methods. Since Calendar is an abstract class, and the parent of GregorianCalendar, I recommend that you simply use GregorianCalendar all the time. Here is how you would get a date of a particular value:

```
GregorianCalendar g = new GregorianCalendar(61,7,13);
```

That represents the day the Berlin wall was constructed, August 13, 1961, in the European central time (ECT) zone. A better way to construct that date is to first set the correct time zone, then set the date.

```
TimeZone z_ect = TimeZone.getTimeZone("ECT");
GregorianCalendar g = new GregorianCalendar(z_ect);
g.set(61,7,13);
```

Note that (incredibly stupidly) months are in the range 0 to 11, and years are represented by the four-digit year less 1900. If you don't specify a time zone, GregorianCalendar defaults to the time zone where the program is running. For example, for a program running in Japan, the default is Japanese standard time (JST). A list of all time zones can be found by looking in the source for java.util.TimeZone.java.

You can pull the individual values out of a date like this:

```
int year = g.get(Calendar.YEAR);
int month = g.get(Calendar.MONTH);
int date = g.get(Calendar.DATE);
int day = g.get(Calendar.DAY_OF_WEEK);
```

You can also check if one date is before or after another date. There is no simple way to get the amount of time between two dates. There are two "helper" classes: TimeZone and SimpleTimeZone. Again, SimpleTimeZone is a concrete subclass of TimeZone, and can be used exclusively. You can create a time zone object for any time zone you want, and then pass it to GregorianCalendar so it will work with values in that time zone.

```
TimeZone z_ect = TimeZone.getTimeZone("ECT");
GregorianCalendar g2 = new GregorianCalendar(z_ect);
g2.set(89, 10, 9, 19, 0); // Berlin Wall Down  Nov 9 1989 7pm
g2.set(89, Calendar.NOVEMBER, 9, 19, 0); // better
```

You can do simple date/time formatting with static methods from the class java.text.DateFormat, as the example below shows:

```
public static void main( String[] args ) {
     Date d = new Date();
     String s1 = DateFormat.getDateInstance().format( d );
     String s2 = DateFormat.getTimeInstance().format( d );
     String s3 = DateFormat.getDateTimeInstance().format( d );

     System.out.println("Date is " + s1 );
     System.out.println("Time is " + s2 );
     System.out.println("DateTime is " + s3 );
}
```

The program fragment runs to produce this:

```
Date is Nov 10, 1998
Time is 7:55:23 PM
DateTime is Nov 10, 1998 7:55:23 PM
```

You can also parse or convert a string into a DateFormat using that class. With methods from java.text.SimpleDateFormat more flexible parsing and formatting is available. You provide a format String argument to the constructor in which different letters represent different fields of a date (day, hour, year, A.M. or P.M., etc.) and the style you want to see them in. Then you call the format() method with your date as the argument, and it passes it back as a String of the requested form.

```
import java.text.*;
import java.util.*;
public class df {

     public static void main( String[] args ) {
          SimpleDateFormat df1 =
           new SimpleDateFormat("yyyy-MM-dd hh:mm:ss.S");
          SimpleDateFormat df2 = new SimpleDateFormat("dd-MMM-yy");
          String startdatetime = "1998-11-10 19:23:27.0";
          try {
               Date d = df1.parse(startdatetime);
               String s = df2.format( d );
               System.out.println("Date is " + s );
          } catch (ParseException pe) {
               System.out.println("ParseException " + pe );
          }
     }
}
```

When you run that code, a String is parsed to get a Date, and then the Date is parsed to get a String in a different format. The resulting output is:

```
Date is 10-Nov-98
```

To parse/format other date and time fields, refer to Table 15-5. The number of times a pattern letter is repeated whether the short or long form of a text field is used. If there are at least four pattern letters, e.g., "EEEE," the long form will be used ("Tuesday"). Otherwise, the short form (if there is one) will be used. For a number field, e.g., "SSSSS," the field will be zero-padded to that amount. Year is handled specially; a field of "yy" means truncate the year to two digits.

The class SimpleDateFormat is in package java.text rather than java.util because it is mostly concerned with internationalized and localized ways of formatting the date.

There is a great deal more information and code examples on dates/times/time zones in the Java FAQ that is on the CD. The database crowd fixed update a little in java.sql.Date by overriding java.util.Date, and making it just deal with dates, not times as well. That's another possibility for you to use.

Table 15–5 SimpleDateFormat

Symbol	Meaning	Presentation	Example
G	era designator	(Text)	AD
y	year	(Number)	1996
M	month in year	(Text & Number)	July & 07
d	day in month	(Number)	10
h	hour in A.M./P.M. (1-12)	(Number)	12
H	hour in day (0-23)	(Number)	0
m	minute in hour	(Number)	30
s	second in minute	(Number)	55
S	millisecond	(Number)	978
E	day in week	(Text)	Tuesday
D	day in year	(Number)	189
F	day of week in month	(Number)	2 (2nd Wed in July)
w	week in year	(Number)	27
W	week in month	(Number)	2
a	A.M./P.M. marker	(Text)	PM
k	hour in day (1-24)	(Number)	24
K	hour in A.M./P.M. (0-11)	(Number)	0
z	time zone	(Text)	Pacific Standard Time
'	escape for text	(Delimiter)	
''	single quote	(Literal)	'

Other Utilities

Random

This is a class to provide pseudo-random numbers. We call them "pseudo-random" rather than random because the source of bits is an algorithm. To the casual observer it looks like a random stream of bits, and for most applications we can pretend that they are. The numbers aren't really random, though, and sequences tend to get stuck in repetitive cycles after a large number of iterations.

If you just quickly want a random number between 0.0 and (just less than) 1.0, then package Math has a method random, which is just a wrapper for instantiating Random one time and then supplying values. You would call it like this:

```
double d = Math.random();  // 0.0 .. 1.0
```

How to Look at the API of a Class

You can run javap on a fully qualified classname to list the methods in the class. The class java.util.Random (below) was listed this way:

```
% javap java.util.Random
```

The class Random has:

```
public class java.util.Random implements java.io.Serializable {
     public java.util.Random();
     public java.util.Random(long);

     public boolean nextBoolean();
     public void nextBytes(byte[]);
     public int nextInt();
     public int nextInt(int);
     public long nextLong();

     public float nextFloat();
     public double nextDouble();

     // a Gaussian distribution has mean 0.0, standard deviation 1.0.
     public synchronized double nextGaussian();
     public synchronized void setSeed(long);
}
```

The nextGaussian() provides numbers symmetrically distributed around zero, and successively unlikelier to be picked the further away from zero you get. If we collected a group of these numbers and plotted them, they would form the shape of a bell curve. The algorithm used here for taking random values from a Gaussian

distribution is from *The Art of Computer Programming* by Donald Knuth (Addison-Wesley, 1994: Section 3.4.1, Algorithm C).

You can instantiate Random with or without a seed. Here it is with a seed:

```
java.util.Random r = new java.util.Random(344L);
```

If you don't give it a seed, it uses the current reading from the day/time clock (the millisecond part of this is going to be pretty close to random). If you choose to supply the seed, you will get the same series of random numbers every time you supply that same seed. This is useful in testing and debugging code.

To get a random int value in a certain range (say, 0 to 5) to simulate the cast of a die, you would use:

```
int myturn = r.nextInt(6);
```

The method nextDouble returns a value between 0.0 and 1.0. To get a random double value in a certain range (say, 0.0 to 100.0) to simulate a percentage, you would scale it up with multiplication:

```
   double mypercent = r.nextDouble() * 100.0;
```

StringTokenizer

The fundamental idea of StringTokenizer is to instantiate it with a string, and it will then break that string up into islands of characters separated by seas of white space. If you gave it the string "Noel Bat is a fossil," successive calls to nextToken would return the individual strings "Noel" followed by "Bat" then "is" then "a" then "fossil" then a further call would throw the NoSuchElementException.

Actually, you can specify the delimiters for the substring, and they don't have to be white space. One of the constructors allows for new delimiting characters to be set and also takes a boolean saying whether the delimiters themselves should be returned. The representative methods are:

```
public  StringTokenizer(String words_to_breakup); // constructor

public  StringTokenizer(String words_to_breakup,
                        String delimiting_chars,
                        boolean return_delims); // constructor

public boolean hasMoreTokens();

public String nextToken();
```

You may have noticed that tokenizing a string is a pretty similar operation to enumerating all the elements in it. The StringTokenizer class does in fact implement the Enumeration interface and provide bodies for hasMoreElements() and nextElement(). They are alternatives to the token methods and return exactly the same objects. In the case of nextElement, the return type is Object, not String, but the Object it returns is a String. The StringTokenizer is simpler than the StreamTokenizer we met earlier. StringTokenizer just breaks things up into Strings. StreamTokenizer does this and also tries to classify them as things like numbers and words.

How to Time Your Code

Here's how you can time your Java code:

```
long start = System.currentTimeMillis();
     :   // do the work here
     :
long stop = System.currentTimeMillis();
System.out.println("time: " + (stop-start) + "millisecs");
```

Observer and Observable

These two are a matched pair. Together they provide a general interface for one thread to communicate a state change to another. We'll start with Observer because it is simpler.

Observer is an interface that looks like this:

```
public interface Observer {
     void update(Observable o, Object arg);
}
```

Any object that wants to look at (observe) something else asynchronously can declare that it is an observer and provide its own body for update. The update() method is just a callback, so let's give an example of use. When you ask an image file to load, the method returns at once and in the background (as soon as it's sure you want it) starts reading the file off disk. That incoming file is an observable event. The thread that asked to load it is an observer.

When the thing that it's looking at has something to communicate, it will call update. Since the observer might be keeping an eye on several observable objects, update needs to be told which of them is calling it. That is the purpose of the first argument. The second argument is an object to permit just about anything at all to be passed in. The body of update will do whatever needs doing when that observable object says, "Look at me."

When reading a JPEG file, for example, there will be a number of times when there is enough information to call observer.update(). It may be called when the image file header has been read, when we have decoded enough to know the height of the image, when we know the width, and when the entire transfer has been completed.

Now let's take a look at Observable. The class Observable is intended to be extended by classes you write. The key methods that Observable provides are:

```
public synchronized void addObserver(Observer o);
// this is how an Observer registers its interest
// with the Observable thing.

protected synchronized void setChanged();
// only subclasses have the privilege of saying something
// observable has changed.

public void notifyObservers();
public void notifyObservers(Object arg);
```

If the *changed* flag is true, then these two routines call the update() method of all Observers. It's done this way (with an extra flag) so the observable thing has precise control over when notification really takes place.

Observer/observable is another example of a design pattern. You can think of it as an alternative, more general, version of a wait( )/notify( ). Like wait/notify, observer/observable is always used with threads. Unlike wait/notify, observer.update( ) is called rather than just allowed to contend for the lock.

There are also methods to delete one or all Observers, and set, clear, or query an internal "changed" flag that an Observer may look at.

Note: Having justified Observer and Observable in terms of loading image files, you should be aware that image loading actually uses its own special version of Observer, called ImageObserver. It works in exactly the same way as Observer and it's unclear why the general mechanism was defined only to be passed over in favor of a special purpose implementation for image files.

One common use of Observer/Observable is in sending a message from a dialog window back to its parent Frame. The parent implements Observer; the dialog class contains an Observable object and a method to return the text. Then, when the dialog captures some relevant information, it sets its own changed bit and calls notifyObservers().

Properties

Java has a platform-independent way to communicate extra information at runtime to a program. Known as *properties*, these do a job like environment variables. Environment variables aren't used because they are too platform-specific. A programmer can read the value of a property by calling getProperty() and passing an argument string for the property in which you are interested.

```
String dir = System.getProperty("user.dir");
```

A long list of predefined properties appears in the file java/lang/System.java and in Table 15-6. Some properties are not available in applets for security reasons. You can also define a property on the command line when you invoke the program like this:

```
java -Drate=10.0 myprogram
```

That value "10.0" will be returned as a string when querying the property "rate." It can then be converted to a floating-point number and used as a value in the program. In this case, it's an alternative to a command line argument, but with the advantage that its value is visible everywhere, not just in main.

Table 15-6 lists the predefined properties guaranteed to have a value on every Java client. There are others, too.

Table 15–6 Predefined Properties

Property Name	Explanation	Visible in Applet
`java.version`	Version number of the Java system	yes
`java.vendor`	Vendor specific string	yes
`java.vendor.url`	Vendor URL	yes
`java.home`	Java installation directory	no
`java.class.version`	Java class version number	yes
`java.class.path`	Java classpath	no
`os.name`	Operating System Name	yes
`os.arch`	Operating System Architecture	yes
`os.version`	Operating System Version	yes
`file.separator`	File separator ("/" on Unix)	yes
`path.separator`	Path separator (":" on Unix)	yes
`line.separator`	Line separator ("\n" on Unix)	yes
`user.name`	User account name	no
`user.home`	User home directory	no
`user.dir`	User's current working directory	no

Most programs don't need to access these properties at all. But when they do, it's nice to be able to do it in a platform-independent way.

java.util.Properties

You will be happy to hear that there is a java.util class to help you read in and process properties. The `java.util.Properties` class is really just an instance of HashTable with a few extra methods wrapped around it. The concept of properties is in some other languages, too, like Lisp and Forth. The Java system comes with a whole set of predefined properties holding information about the implementation.

This utility class has two purposes: First, it allows a property table to be read in and written out via streams. Second, it allows programmers to search more than one property table with a single command. If you don't need either of these benefits, then just use a HashMap instead of a Properties table. Typical methods are:

```
public String getProperty(String key);

public synchronized void load(InputStream in)
     throws IOException;
// reads key/value pairs in from a stream, stores them in this

public synchronized void save(OutputStream out, String header);
// writes the key/value pairs out as text
// the header is just a comment string you provide to label
// the property table. The current date is also appended.
```

To put entries in a Properties object, just use the put(Object key, Object element) method inherited from HashTable. So that you don't feel obliged to start adding to the predefined system property table, there's a feature that allows you to provide an existing properties table to a constructor. This creates an empty properties list that you can populate. Whenever you do a getProperty, it will search your table. If nothing is found, it will go on to search the table provided to the constructor. Here is an example:

```
Properties sp = System.getProperties();
Properties mytable = new Properties(sp);
mytable.list(System.out);
```

The first line gets the standard predefined properties table. The second line piggybacks it onto a second Properties table that we create and can fill with a call like mytable.put (propertyname, propertyvalue). When we do a lookup in mytable, it will look up first in mytable and then in the system properties table. The third line prints mytable out (intended for debugging, but it's not clear why you can't just use the save() method). The method public String getProperty(String key, String default) will return the default String if there is no entry for this key in the table.

Note on the Java Native Interface

The Java Native Interface is an API that allows you to make calls into C and C++ programs from Java. You can also make calls into any other programming language that follows the C calling and linking conventions. Non-Java code is referred to as native code, hence, it is a native interface.

If you use the JNI, you tie your code to a single platform and operating system, losing the major benefit of Java. The JNI should be used only as a last resort. Most programs don't need it and won't use it.

Readers who want to put JNI into practice can browse the JavaSoft web page for an introduction to JNI. Use the search facility on the home page at *java.sun.com*, and look for "JNI." But do avoid the use of native methods if you can.

Further Reading

The book *Mastering Regular Expressions* by Jeffrey E. F. Freidl (published by O'Reilly & Associates, Inc.) is generally regarded as one of the best studies on the topic. Be forewarned that most of the book uses Perl as its example language. If you are interested enough to want to play around with Perl, you should visit the *www.perl.com/* website where you can find tutorials and download a free copy of the software. O'Reilly sponsors the Perl website, and they also support a corresponding "Java in the Enterprise" website at *www.onjava.com/*. They have some good Java articles and other resources.

See *developer.java.sun.com/developer/technicalArticles/releases/1.4regex/* and *www.meurrens.org/ip-Links/java/regex/#intro* for more on Java regular expressions.

Exercises

1. (Patterns, easy) Do a web search to find out all the pieces that can make up a URL in its full generality. State what these pieces are. Write a pattern-matching program that checks URLs for validity (e.g., no embedded spaces, etc). Show the output of your program when run on both good and bad URLs.

2. (Patterns, medium) An email message consists of an arbitrary number of headers, then a blank line, then the body of the text. The headers all have a label followed by a colon, a space, and some optional text all on one line. The "From:" and "To:" headers are required, and come first in that order. The pattern would start something like this:

```
Pattern email = Pattern.compile(
                "^From: .*$"        // "From" line
              + "^To: .*$"          // "To" line
```

Write the rest of a pattern to match an email message, and use capturing groups to separate the individual parts. Don't forget to make this a multiline pattern.

3. (Patterns, harder) Write a pattern that matches the Java regular expressions presented in this text. This is several days work. Run your meta-pattern matcher on all the Java regular expression strings shown in this chapter. Account for any that it does not accept.

4. (Collections) Here is the outline of a class that provides access to its data structure through an iterator. Write the iterator.

```
class storage {

    private Object[] data = new Object[256];

    // don't allow access to anything not yet stored
    private int nextEmptySlot = 0;
    private int i=0;
```

```
    public Iterator iterator() {
       // returns a class that iterates over the data array
       return new Iterator() {
       // insert the body of the inner class here
       // 3 methods: remove(), hasNext(), next()
      };
    }
}
```

5. (Collections) Take the storage class from the previous question and add all the code necessary to make it implement the Collection interface. Limit on the number of objects in the collection, and hence the size of the array to 128 elements. Throw an UnsupportedOperationException if someone tries to add element number 129.

6. (Collections) Take the storage class from the previous question and remove any limit on the number of data items held in the collection. If you try to add an element when there is no more room in the array, then allocate a new, larger array, and use System.arraycopy() to fill it with the contents of the old array. Hint: Add the extra code in a subclass that overrides the methods of the parent class. That way, you simply inherit all the things that you do not need to change.

7. (Collections) Write two more comparators for the playing cards held as Strings. One comparator should take account of suit as well as rank. The other comparator should implement the rule that one-eyed Jacks (the Jacks of Hearts and Spades) are wild—worth more than any other card. Write some data to demonstrate that your comparators work.

8. (Collections) In 1876, cowboy Wild Bill Hickok was shot from behind and killed while playing poker in a saloon in Deadwood, South Dakota. Legend has it that he died holding two black aces and two black eights with a nine of diamonds. Accounts differ about the fifth card, but this low poker hand of two black pairs, aces over eights, has been known since then as the "dead man's hand." Wild Bill had two other claims to fame: he was the boyfriend of Calamity Jane, and he toured with Buffalo Bill Cody's wild west show. Look up on the web the rankings of poker hands, and write a comparator that orders two objects each representing a poker hand of five cards.

9. (Math, medium) Convince yourself that the nextGaussian() numbers form a bell curve by writing a program to actually do it. *Hint:* You'll find it easier to plot a graph using ASCII text if you generate the values first, save them, and sort them into order before plotting the values. Do you know any data structures that can help with storing and sorting?

Some Light Relief—Exchanging Apples and Crays

There's an old story to the effect that "the people at Cray design their supercomputers with Apple systems, and the Apple designers use Crays!" Apart from this being a terrific example of recurring rotational serendipity (what goes around, comes around) is there any truth to it?

Like many urban legends, this one contains a nugget of truth. In the 1991 Annual Report of Cray Research, Inc., there is a short article describing how Apple used a Cray for designing Macintosh cases. The Cray is used to simulate the injection molding of the plastic enclosure cases. The Mac II case was the first Apple system to benefit from the modeling, and the trial was successful. The simulation identified warping problems which were solved by prototyping, thus saving money in tooling and production. Apple also uses their Cray for simulating air flow inside the enclosure to check for hot spots. The Cray house magazine reported that the Apple PowerBook continues to use supercomputer simulations. (Cray Channels, Spring 199, pp.10-12 "Apple Computer PowerBook computer molding simulation").

The inverse story holds that Seymour Cray himself used a Macintosh to design Crays. The story seems to have originated with an off-the-cuff remark from Seymour Cray himself, who had a Macintosh at home and used it to store some of his work for the Cray 3. Common sense suggests that the simulation of discrete circuitry (Verilog runs, logic analysis, etc.), which is part of all modern integrated circuit design, is done far more cost-effectively on a large server farm than on a microprocessor. Cray probably has a lot of supercomputer hardware laying around ready for testing as it comes off the production line.

It's conceivable that a Macintosh could be used to draft the layout of blinking lights for the front of a Cray, or choose some nice color combinations, or some other non-CPU intensive work. A Macintosh is a very good system for writing design notes, sending email, and drawing diagrams, all of which are an equally essential part of designing a computer system.

The good folks at Cray Research have confirmed in a Cray Users Group newsletter that they have a few Macs on the premises. So, while it's extremely unlikely that they run logic simulations on their Macs, we can indeed chalk it up as only-slightly-varnished truth that "the people at Cray design their supercomputers with Apple's systems, and the Apple designers use Crays," for some value of the word "design!"

Part

3

Server-side Java

Chapter 16

Servlets and JSP

- WHY USE SERVLETS?
- RELEASES AND VERSIONS
- INSTALLING THE TOMCAT SOFTWARE
- RUNNING THE EXAMPLE SERVLETS
- PORTS AND PROTOCOLS
- THE HTML TO INVOKE A SERVLET
- A SERVLET AND ITS REQUEST/RESPONSE
- SERVLET REQUEST
- RESPONSE TO A SERVLET REQUEST
- WRITING YOUR OWN SERVLET
- SERVLET OPERATING CYCLE AND THREADING
- JAVA SERVER PAGES
- JAVA BEANS IN SERVLETS AND JSP
- FURTHER READING
- EXERCISES
- SOME LIGHT RELIEF—THE JAVA-POWERED TOASTER

When Java was originally released in 1995, much of the "buzz" was about applets. People were captivated by browsers that could run executable code on a client browsing a page. Even today, no other technology can do this in a secure way. But applets soon became a civilian casualty of the "Browser Wars" as Microsoft battled Netscape. Over time, developers shifted their focus from applets to running Java on the server-side. Java on web servers is now one of the "sweet spots" of Java technology.

This chapter describes the two key Java technologies that are used in server-side Java: servlets and JSP. The first of these, servlets, is a way for a browser to cause a program to run on the server. The server calculates something, probably accesses a database, and sends HTML output back to the browser on the client. In a nutshell, that is the architecture of all web-based e-commerce systems, from

Amazon.com to E-Trade.com to the Zdnet.com online store. These are applications where the end-user interface is provided by a web browser, and the back-end logic runs on a server.

Servlets look set to become the new way for a browser to get a web page from a program (not a file) on the server. The old way used an interface called CGI, and your scripts would be written in Perl or Visual Basic or some other language. With servlets, your code is written in Java. There is a size/complexity tradeoff here: small scripts (less than a couple of pages) can be written at the drop of a hat and are well suited to Perl or PHP. There are a great many web tools used today, as shown in Table 16-1.

Table 16–1 Microsoft Web Tools and Corresponding Competitive Products

Microsoft Product	Multi-platform Alternative
Windows 2000	Linux, Solaris
Visual Basic, VC++, C#	Java, C, C++, Perl
IIS (Internet Information Server)	Apache Web server
ASP	JSP, PHP
SQLServer	many - PostgreSQL, mySQL, Oracle, DB2, etc.
ODBC	JDBC
ActiveX	Java Beans
MTS (Microsoft Transaction Server)	EJB (Enterprise Java Beans)
Office	StarOffice (freely downloadable from Sun)

The larger and more complicated your code, the more you will benefit from using a Java servlet. If you need to access a database, you can use Java's JDBC library. If you need threading or network libraries, Java has them. If your code needs to run with permissions-based access control, Java supports this. Instead of a mixture of different tools and libraries, you can write the whole thing in one consistent language. Perhaps the biggest advantage is that servlets free you from being tied to one kind of hardware or one software vendor. Because of Java's portability, you can easily move to more capable hardware as your processing needs increase. Your servlet code can be run by any servlet server. It's easy to add new capacity and leave the software unchanged.

The second technology we will visit in this chapter is called "Java Server Pages," modelled after the ColdFusion technology invented by the Allaire company of Boston, Massachusetts. Allaire now makes a Java servlet and JSP execution environment known as JRun that can be plugged into any web server. Allaire's ColdFusion product was copied by Microsoft and given the name ASP—"Active Server Pages." ColdFusion, ASP, and JSP are all ways of mixing ("embedding") programming statements, scripts, and components in web pages on the server side. When the server gets a request for the page, it executes the programming statements, and sends to the browser the fixed HTML plus the HTML dynamically generated by executing the embedded code. If you are familiar with ASP, you can pick up JSP in a few minutes. To put it another way, JSP looks a lot like fragments of Java code, but embedded in an HTML page.

An ordinary page of HTML is static. Each time the server sends it out, it sends the exact same bytes. The only way it changes is if someone updates the HTML file with an editor. But many kinds of information change dynamically: stock prices, the weather, seats available on a flight, amount of inventory on hand, account balance, contents of an online shopping cart, and so on. Servlets and JSP are a great way to get this dynamic information into a web page. The pages that the user sees are calculated by general purpose programs that can reference and update databases as part of serving the request.

For small programs, JSP is simpler than a servlet. Servlets require the programmer to write Java code to output all the HTML (the fixed part and the dynamically varying part) along with all the headers that a web server adds automatically. JSP allows a programmer to write down the fixed HTML as HTML. You write Java code fragments that create the dynamically varying HTML, and you don't need to bother with generating the HTML headers. Because you write the fixed HTML directly and literally, JSP is (in theory) a good way to keep separate the dynamic and static parts of your web page.

In practice, it takes some discipline to prevent your JSP programs from becoming hard to maintain. JSP doesn't have any extra capabilities compared with servlets, and indeed JSP is usually implemented in terms of servlets.

Both servlets and JSP are big topics, covered at book length elsewhere. In this chapter we map out the territory and get the first examples of each working. The goals are to show you how to write basic servlets, and to cover the key points of server-side Java. This chapter can be worked through in an afternoon, and gives you enough information to interview for an entry-level job on an e-commerce project. After you master the basics here, you can go on to get deeper knowledge from Robert Burdick, et al., *Professional JSP*, 2d ed., 2001, Wrox Press Ltd., Birmingham, UK.

Portability and Common Sense

Web-based software decouples the server from the clients and lets them run independently. When you choose your server development software thoughtfully, you can keep your options open for the future. If your development team doesn't pay attention to this, you might start a new project with Active Server Pages, and condemn the software to only ever run on a single platform, a single operating system, and a single chip architecture.

Mike Keating, a systems analyst in Storrs, Connecticut, explained, "IIS, ASP, VB, COM, MTS were convenient to use because they were preinstalled on our systems, or integrated easily, so I used them when I started building web applications a few years ago." When the organization became interested in the Linux server operating system for reasons of cost, stability, and performance, the price of Window's convenience became evident: none of the existing web applications could run on the Linux platform.

"Having our web applications locked to the NT platform is a big headache," Mike commented. "We're trying to get off Microsoft-only solutions as quickly as we can. By using Java, if we change our server OS again in the future, we can still run our applications on any platform that supports Java—which is pretty much everything."

"If anyone is evaluating Java-based technology against Microsoft-only software, don't think 'it can't happen to me' - you may very well find yourself some day in the near future wishing you paid more attention to platform independence. We're writing new projects in Java and rescuing our stranded applications as resources permit." Even if your company will only ever be a Microsoft shop, you can avoid the trauma of periodic Microsoft upgrades by using Java. People who tried to keep applications running while changing from MS-DOS to Win 3.1 to Win 95 to NT 4 know all about this.

Why Use Servlets?

Server-side web programming is well established on the web. It lets you build systems with a client part that can run in a browser on any computer, with any operating system, at any time, from anywhere in the world. The HTTP protocol provides a framework for communicating with a server where all the real work is done. The server-side code may do load-balancing to move incoming requests to the system best equipped to handle them. The server code can access/update your database and process any data using the most up-to-date information. It does this in a safe way. The client cannot call server routines directly. It can only send over HTTP requests saying what it wants, so opportunities to subvert the server are more restricted than when everything runs on one physical system. You still need to code defensively as people may try to access your page in a way which could make the server spend all its time trying to service their request.

Client/server programming was popular even before the web went mainstream, and bringing the two together was a natural marriage. CGI—the "Common Gateway Interface"—was the first attempt to get dynamic content into web pages. CGI got the job done, but it had security and performance problems. CGI implementations often start up an entire new process to run a script. It doesn't have to be done that way, but in practice it usually is. Servlets are loaded into memory once, and stay around ready to handle all future requests. So there can be a big performance advantage to using servlets. It also means that servlets can choose to hold system resources (such as a database connection) between requests. Since opening and closing a database connection is a lengthy operation, this is another win for servlets.

Servlets make it easier to separate the business logic used to generate results from the HTML that displays those results. JSP takes that one step further. Separation of logic from presentation has benefits. It's an enabler for the use of component software (Java Beans, described in a later chapter). Component software lets a system designer deploy the same code to handle a transaction whatever the origin is: web-based, online transaction, or batch processing. We're getting into Enterprise-level software issues here, but it delivers consistency and code reuse.

Servlet technology replaces the family of server plugins such as the Netscape API, CGI, or the Microsoft ISAPI, none of which are standardized or multiplatform like the JavaServer API is. Servlets today are the most popular choice for building portable interactive web applications. Add-on software to run servlets are available for Apache Web Server, iPlanet Web Server, Microsoft IIS, and others. Servlet containers can also be integrated with web-enabled application servers such as BEA WebLogic Application Server, IBM WebSphere, iPlanet Application Server, and others.

People are currently driving the technology even further with a technique called "ASP" or Application Service Provision. Don't confuse Application Service Providers with "Active Server Pages." ASP is all about extending the benefits of client/server systems to all kinds of application software. The idea is that instead of buying software and installing it locally on your PC, you rent access to the software at the ASP site. Instead of running a spreadsheet locally, the program executes on a server at the ASP site and sends you the equivalent data for display on your screen. Ideally, you won't see much difference between using an ASP and running your programs locally, but the total cost of ownership is lower. The ASP takes care of all the system administration tasks, data backup, etc., and your PC is just used as a communications device to reach the ASP. You don't even need an expensive heavyweight PC. You can use any number of cheap or portable or wireless devices to connect to the ASP. Servlets are ideal for use in an ASP, providing a simple way to connect clients to server processing.

The ASP model has some compelling advantages, but it is still a work-in-progress. If you think this sounds like a rerun of X-Windows or Citrix technology, you are right, but the web aspect adds a significant new dimension (the ability to run from any computer, any OS, anywhere). Nobody yet knows when or even whether Application Service Providers can deliver on the early promise, but there are a number of smart people working hard to make it happen.

Releases and Versions

By agreement with Sun Microsystems, the reference implementation for servlets and JSP is maintained by the Apache Software Foundation. The Apache web server is an open source project, and by far the most widely-used web server in the world. You can look up more information about the Apache Software Foundation at *www.apache.org*. Apache uses the project name "Jakarta" for their Java-specific work.

The servlet library is part of the Enterprise Edition of Java, but must be downloaded separately if you are using the Standard Edition. The servlet design underwent some rapid evolution at first with a number of versions and releases, but it has settled down now. Tables 16-2 and 16-3 spell out the details, so you can relate everything to other versions you may have heard about. At the time of this writing (2001), the most up-to-date version of the servlet API is version 2.3, and that is used in this chapter. Check the Apache website listed below for any later version and download and use that in preference. This technology is mature enough that there won't be any drastic changes in future revisions.

The main product of Apache's Java-based Jakarta project is a servlet-and-JSP container known as Tomcat. Tomcat can run standalone as a servlet server, or it can be added on to most other web servers to process any Java requests. Tomcat was based on an earlier program known as "JServ" (in case you hear that term used somewhere). A "servlet container" is the new name for what older books refer to as a "servlet engine." It simply means the software framework within which servlets execute. We will use Tomcat as the container throughout this chapter. Tomcat is used because it is the reference implementation for servlets, and because it is available for free download and use. It is written in Java, so you can get it running on any computer with an up-to-date JVM.

Table 16–2 Server/Servlet Versions

Servlet Container	Version Number	Compatible with This Version of the Java API
JServ	ver 1.1.3	Servlet 2.0, JSP 1.0
Tomcat	ver 3.2.1	Servlet 2.2, JSP 1.1
Tomcat	ver 4.0	Servlet 2.3, JSP 1.2

The servlet and JSP specifications have changed as people got practical experience with the technology. JSP 1.0 allowed the use of Java beans. JSP 1.1 added support for custom JSP tags. The Servlet specification 2.3 introduced filters that allow you to do preprocessing on an http request before the servlet gets it. There are additional products that combine Java and web servers at the Apache website, and it is worth visiting *jakarta.apache.org* to review these for yourself.

Table 16-3 lists a glossary covering all the new terms, so you can refresh your memory or refer back to it as needed.

Table 16–3 Glossary

Term	Definition
Apache	The Apache Software Foundation is a volunteer organization which has produced the most popular web server in the world, and made it available for free download. Their website is *www.apache.org*
Ant	A utility that accompanies Tomcat, used when Tomcat has to compile some servlet code automatically. Ant is a Java-based build utility that works out the correct dependency order in which to compile each file. It works cross-platform, unlike non-Java based tools.
Catalina	The servlet container (engine) part of Tomcat version 4.
CGI	The Common Gateway Interface was the first server-side scripting technology. It specifies how the server should execute a script when a particular web page is referenced. CGI scripts can be written in different languages, and Perl is a popular choice.
cookie	A cookie is a few bytes of information that the server asks the browser to store on the client and return on demand. This token can be used to keep track of what the client has already seen, whether they have already given a password, and other information about the current session with the server.
HTTP	Hyper-Text Transfer Protocol. The vocabulary and standard way in which a browser and a server take turn to exchange information with each other.
Jakarta	The part of the Apache Software Foundation that focuses on Java server technology, and maintains the Java part of the Apache website. It has the Tomcat software as its centerpiece.
Jasper	The JSP server part of Tomcat.
JServ	An early implementation of the Java Servlet API from the Apache Software Foundation. It has been replaced by the Tomcat project.
JSP	Java Server Pages is a technology that allows programmers to mix together programming statements and HTML in web pages. The statements are executed and replaced with their output when the page is referenced. This server-side scripting approach was pioneered by Allaire's ColdFusion product on Windows.
Servlet	A servlet is any Java class that implements the javax.servlet.Servlet interface. It is executable by any compliant servlet container. The most common form of servlet is an HTTP servlet that responds to browser requests.
Tomcat	An open source servlet-and-JSP engine, written in Java, from the Jakarta project of Apache. Tomcat also includes a rudimentary web server making it easy to use for development (you don't need to set up a separate web server).
post	A request made by a browser that will upload user-entered data to the server and get back a new page. The contents of the new page will be calculated on the fly by the server.
get	Similar to post, except the browser or server may return a cached version of the page rather than calculating it anew.

Installing the Tomcat Software

This section describes how to download and install the Tomcat servlet web server software. There is a "servlet runner" utility available from Sun that works like the appletviewer. It provides just enough context to execute your specialized web code. We could use the servlet runner, but it does not support JSP. Further, it is good experience to try installing and configuring a real web server.

To get started on your first servlet, go to the "servlets" directory on the CD that comes with this book. You can get there easily by browsing the index.html file at the top level on the CD, then just click on the servlets link. Create a top level directory on your disk called "tomcat" and copy the file "jakarta-tomcat-4.0-b3.zip" from the CD into that disk directory. If there is a later version at the Apache website *jakarta.apache.org*, use that instead. Unpack the file. You can use WinZip, or the Java "jar" utility with these commands

```
cd c:\tomcat
jar -xf jakarta-tomcat-4.0-b3.zip
```

The "-b3" in the pathname indicates we are using the beta-3 release of Tomcat version 4.0 here. Definitely switch to the FCS (First Customer Shipment, i.e., the real release) version when it is available at the Apache website. Don't deploy beta software in production systems. The jar command shown above will create a directory tree under your "server" directory, containing the Tomcat software. Give the top of this newly created tree a simpler name in the "8.3" form that works best with Windows. If you fail to do this renaming, the beta version of the Tomcat software may have problems finding files later. The renaming is:

```
cd c:\tomcat
move jakarta-tomcat-4.0-b3  4beta3
```

Now set or update these shell variables so that Tomcat can find the Java compiler, and the Java compiler can find the servlet jar file. On a Windows system, the autoexec.bat file is one convenient place to do it. Or, you can create a new batch file just for setting up Tomcat. The commands to set them on Windows look like:

```
set TOMCAT_HOME=c:\tomcat\4beta3
set JAVA_HOME=c:\jdk1.3
set CLASSPATH=c:\tomcat\4beta3\common\lib\servlet.jar;.
```

Note: The commands shown are for Windows. Make adjustments if you are using Unix, Linux, etc. That servlet.jar file has been moving around to different directories in recent beta releases, so check where it actually is located and use that pathname. That allows your programs to compile against the servlet libraries.

Be careful to get this right. You may already have a JAVAHOME variable; Tomcat needs a JAVA_HOME (with the underbar). You may already have a CLASSPATH variable, in which case you want to add to it, not replace it. If you set these variables in a batch file, make sure you execute it.

Download the Servlet Specification, Too

The process described above downloads and installs the Tomcat software and the Javadoc API web pages. That's enough to get the examples in this chapter running. You can now read the API documentation by browsing either of these URLs. The http one will only work when you have the Tomcat server running on your system, of course.

```
http://localhost:8080/servletapi-javadoc/index.html
```

or

```
file://c:/tomcat/4beta3/webapps/ROOT/servletapi-javadoc/index.html
```

It's a good idea to keep a browser window open and pointing at this resource as you read through the rest of the chapter. As we describe a class, look at it online to see all the methods and fields.

There is one more documentation file to download. It is the "Java Servlet 2.3 Specification." You might have to search for it on the Sun Java website. I found a link at:

```
http://java.sun.com/aboutJava/communityprocess/first/jsr053/index.html
```

It is a 1.6 Mb PDF file that is the servlet specification. It has a tutorial flavor to it, and contains a little documentation for configuring Tomcat. (See Chapter 9 of the specification). It is good to see that some parts of server configuration are standardized. You do not need to read it immediately, but it makes a good sequel to this chapter if you want more detailed information.

Running the Example Servlets

The next step is to try running Tomcat on one of the example servlets that accompany it. First shut down any other web servers that you have running on your system, so they don't interfere with this example. Then go to the main Tomcat directory with this command:

```
cd c:\tomcat\4beta3
```

Tomcat will run as a stand-alone web server, which is very convenient for development. It can also be configured to run as an adjunct to most other web servers and to handle the servlet/JSP requests. That's useful for deployment, and we won't get into it here. Issue the command to start Tomcat as a stand-alone server:

```
bin\startup
```

Pitfall with Starting and Stopping Tomcat!

For security reasons, you should not leave a web server running on your system where outsiders may see it. There is a corresponding shutdown script in "bin/shutdown."

```
cd c:\tomcat\4beta3
bin\shutdown
```

That shutdown script must be invoked when you have finished with Tomcat, and you must shut it down cleanly. You may also need to shut down Tomcat and restart it each time you recompile a servlet (this need can be changed by configuring Tomcat).

The startup and shutdown scripts have a horrible weakness—they use relative pathnames and so can only be invoked from the top level Tomcat directory. Make sure you are in the `$TOMCAT_HOME` directory before issuing the startup or shutdown commands.

After a second or two, a new window will appear saying that it is "Starting service Tomcat-Standalone." This means your system is now running a servlet capable web server. Tomcat serves web pages to requests that come through port 8080, so start a browser and give it the URL `http://localhost:8080`.

Pitfall with Windows Command Interpreter

A common problem on Windows is running out of environment space for shell variables. You will see an error message to that effect when it happens. Luckily, it is easy to increase the space.

Right-click on the shortcut you use to get a command line prompt, choose "properties," select the memory tab, and change the "Initial environment" setting from auto to something larger like 4096. If you use the MS-DOS command from the Start menu to get your command line, you can find the shortcut by right-clicking the Start button and choosing "Open," then double click on the "Programs" folder, and right click on "MS-DOS prompt."

You can use the name "localhost" or the special IP address "127.0.0.1" that means "this system." Or if your computer has a DNS name, you can equally use that in the URL. If you have installed and set up everything correctly, your browser will display a page as shown in Figure 16-1.

If you don't get this page served to you, something in your configuration is not set up correctly, so start again from the beginning (and check the website for this book *www.afu.com*, in case there is an update to the errata sheet).

Click on the "Servlet Examples" link displayed in your browser, and you will bring up a new page that has the top half-a-dozen examples of servlet-related things you want to do, along with a skeleton of the source code that implements them. This demonstrates that you can successfully run the example servlets on your system. After you have read the basic example here, you can return to this URL and find sample code for the following:

- getting the http headers of this request
- reading the parameters passed with an HTTP "get" request
- setting and retrieving a cookie
- creating and examining session information

We cover the first two of these in this chapter. Cookies and sessions should be studied with the online Tomcat examples. We'll now cover the material that you need to understand how servlets work. All this information might look somewhat involved, but writing servlets and JSP is easily done. My next door neighbor is a hardware engineer. Hardware engineers normally have terrible trouble with software, but she was able to teach herself how to program servlets. And you can learn it too, just as easily.

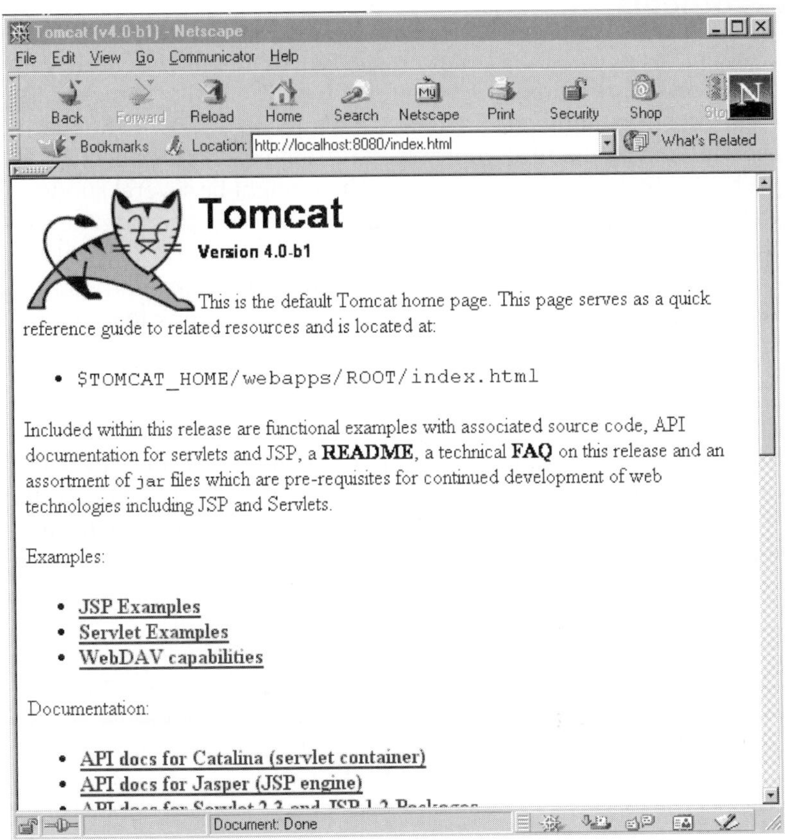

Figure 16–1 Setting up Tomcat

Review servlet and JSP Javadoc API web pages.

One of the links displayed in the default Tomcat home page is the *"API docs for Servlet 2.3 and JSP 1.2 Packages."*

It's a good idea to keep a browser window open on that page, and review each class as it is mentioned in the rest of this chapter.

Ports and Protocols

Computers on an Internet network are uniquely identified by something called an "IP address." IP addresses are stored as a group of either 32 bits (IP classic) or 128 bits (IP version 6), but binary numbers are hard for people to deal with. So the network protocols allow you to give a computer a hostname, and to collect a group of related hosts into hierarchical domains. There might be several subdomains within a domain, which is written in the form with dots separating the subdomains like this: "engineering.sun.com." Domain Name Servers (DNS) contain tables that translate between IP addresses and names within a domain. If you know a computer's IP address or DNS name, you can send anything to it: mail, ftp commands, http requests, and so on.

When you send something to a computer, the IP address specifies which computer it must go to. You also need to specify which application should receive the data. This is done with a "port number." A port in this context is a software service implemented by the operating system, not a hardware concept like the serial port or parallel port. Hardware or software, they all do the same job: provide a channel for data to enter or leave the computer. A few common port numbers and their associated applications are shown in Table 16-4.

Table 16–4 Example Port Numbers and Their Standard Applications

Port Number	Standard Application	Description
80	HTTP connections	The Hypertext Transport Protocol used between browsers and servers
8080	Servlet requests in Tomcat	The port used by the Java servlet server from the Apache group
20 and 21	FTP connections	The File Transfer Protocol used to move files between systems
23	telnet	Supports remote login from one computer to another
25	smtp	The Simple Mail Transfer Protocol
79	finger	Displays information about all the users logged into a computer
119	NNTP	The Network News Transfer Protocol used to send Usenet articles

The way you read or write data to a port is with a socket. Sockets were a Unix innovation, but are so useful that every OS now has a software library that supports use of sockets. Programmers can create a socket that sends data to a particular port on a particular host, or one that waits for data to come in on a particular port on the localhost computer. In Java, you use input and output streams on

sockets just as though you were processing a file. These libraries are found in the `java.net` package. The class `java.net.ServerSocket` lets your program accept incoming data by spawning off a thread with a socket that you can read from. The class `java.net.Socket` lets you send data to another computer, or read data that is coming into the local host. The Java libraries for sockets are much, much better designed and easier to use than the C libraries.

Servlets can be used to service any request that is made via a socket, not just web page requests. Servlets can be written to respond to any protocol, not just HTTP. You can write a servlet that sits on port 21, talks File Transfer Protocol, and takes care of FTP requests. A servlet that talks something other than HTTP is called a "generic servlet" and it will extend the class `javax.servlet.GenericServlet`. The vast majority of servlets are used to serve web requests. These are known as "http servlets," and they extend the class `javax.servlet.http.HttpServlet`. We will go into the details soon.

A web browser is just a program that sends requests to the HTTP port on a server and displays the data that the server sends back. A basic web browser that doesn't also try to be a newsreader/mail client/HTML editor/instant message service/etc., can be written in a hundred lines of code (assuming you have a GUI component that renders HTML, which Java does). A web server is just a program that waits for incoming requests on the HTTP port, and maps those into sending the contents of local files back to the requestor. One basic web server was written by the very talented programmer Jef Poskanzer in only 200 lines of code! Jef makes it available on his website at *www.acme.com*. Part of developing into a better programmer is reading code from others, so I encourage you to look at it. It's on the CD that comes with this book, along with other interesting material. We also write the world's smallest web server in Chapter 17.

The computer science term "protocol" means "an agreement on how to talk to each other." Browsers and servers talk to each other using HTTP, HyperText Transfer Protocol. The browser starts the conversation, and then each end takes its turn to say something. It goes back and forth over the net like a game of tennis. An http request from a browser is replied to with a response from the server. A commercial web server is multithreaded and typically dealing with many clients (browsers) at any moment, but is either reading a request or sending the response to each. The key concept of servlets is that when you browse a particular page, it causes the servlet to run. The servlet does whatever processing you coded, and then writes some HTML to represent the answer. The web server sends that newly-generated HTML back to the browser for display. Just as with a regular HTML page, a servlet can be invoked many times. A servlet can cope with several concurrent requests, and it may call another servlet or forward the original request to it for processing.

All this somewhat involved material is just to give you the background information. Writing servlets and JSP is actually relatively simple.

The HTML to Invoke a Servlet

This section describes the HTML that will be displayed on the client and cause a servlet to run on the server. The most common way for a browser to invoke a servlet is via an HTML form in a web page. An HTML form starts with the `<FORM>` tag and ends with the `</FORM>` tag. If the web server allows you to see that directory, you can also invoke a servlet by browsing the URL that points to the location of the servlet. There is no rule against it, but it is not common for an applet to invoke a servlet. There's an exercise at the end of the chapter inviting you to write a servlet that can send over and accept back a high score file for a game. Servlets don't have to serve HTML. They can send files of any kind, or anything that the client knows how to process. But most servlets are invoked by an HTML form.

People typically place a number of input `<INPUT>` tags inside their `<FORM>`. An HTML input tag puts some kind of simple GUI component on the browser screen, and scoops up any data the user enters. An input tag has a TYPE attribute, a NAME attribute, and often other attributes like SIZE too. (Reminder: attributes are the *name=value* pairs that live inside tags to provide extra information). The TYPE attribute says what kind of a GUI control this is: a checkbox, radio button, textfield, etc. The input tag as a whole defines a GUI component that allows the user to enter data on the web page. One of the input tags will have a TYPE attribute of "submit." Pressing that causes the entire form, with all the data the user typed in, to be sent over to the server.

Figure 16-2 shows an example of an HTML form, some INPUT tags, and the web page they generate. You should create a web page with the HTML shown here, and confirm that you can browse it, enter data, and press the submit button.

There are about 10 different GUI input types, but the most often used are *text, radio, checkbox*, and *submit*. For a complete list of all the input types and other attributes, do a web search on "HTML, form, guide." To make it all line up nicely on the screen, everything inside a form is often put in an HTML table.

Now we come to the question of how and where the browser sends the data from the form. The form tag will always have two attributes (omitted in Figure 16-2, for simplicity) that specify how and where the form data goes. These attributes are called *"action"* and *"method."* There are also additional possible attributes, to give the whole form a name, and to say how the data should be encoded before it is sent to the server. The default values are fine for these. An example of a complete form tag would be

```
<form  action="/servlet/petform"   method="post">
```

```
<center><h2>Choosing a pet</h2> </center>

<form ...some attributes... >
<h4>Preferred weight (lbs): </h4>
    <input type=text  name=weight  size=3>

<h4>Number of legs: </h4>
   <input type=radio  name=legs value=0>
      0 legs <br>

   <input type=radio  name=legs value=4 checked>
      4 legs <br>

   <input type=radio  name=legs value=notsure>
      other number  <p>

<input type=submit value="send pet data">
</form>
```

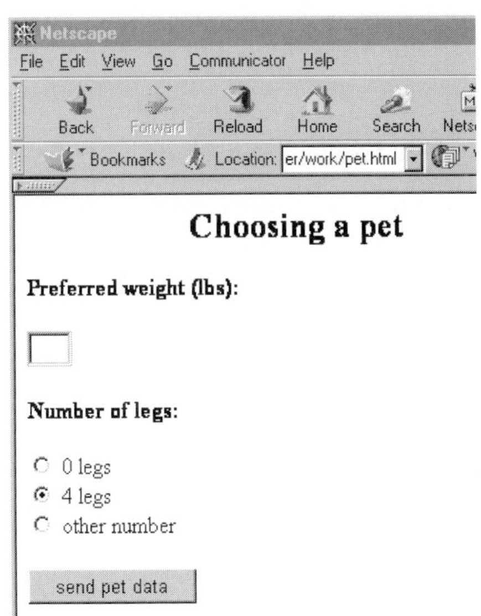

Figure 16–2 HTML example form.

The *action* attribute gives the URL for the script or servlet that will process the data. It doesn't need to be an URL on the same server that served the form. It doesn't need to be a full URL. It can be a partial URL that is based on the page already being served. The *method* attribute specifies the HTTP approach that the browser should use when sending over the data. The two possibilities are "GET" and "POST." In HTML, attributes *may* be enclosed in quotation marks. In XML (which we'll meet in Chapter 27) attributes *must* be enclosed in quotation marks. So you may as well get into the habit now.

Reams of pages have been written about using POST versus GET in an HTML form. Originally, GET was used to ask for a file from the server, and POST was used to send data to the server. Today, either can be used to transmit form data to a server-side application. The differences boil down to this:

- POST passes the form data to the server as a series of fields in the body of the HTTP request. GET sends the data appended to the URL as a query string, like this

  ```
  http://www.yahoo.com/stocks.htm?somename=somevalue
  ```

  Since the GET data is actually added onto the end of the URL string, the user can bookmark it, and submit the same data later by going to the bookmark. This is why search engines often use GET. As it is part of the URL, the user can also see it and play around with it, which you may not want.

- GET is limited to a small amount of text data that can be appended to the address (less than 255 characters). POST handles an arbitrary amount of text and binary data and does not show up as part of the address URL. Many web servers log URLs. If you don't want your logs to contain sensitive user data (like account names and passwords), you *must* POST it.
- GET responses can be cached anywhere along the way—by your browser, by your company's proxy server, or by the web server. With POST, the page request is required to go through all the caching layers to the server and extract the data again. So POST should be used when the servlet is counting accesses, or making a charge to see the page, or controlling who can see the page.

You will typically "post" form data to a servlet. If you are sending data to a web servlet by some other means, you need to send the data according to the HTTP protocol. The HTTP protocol defines the contents of HTTP *requests* and *responses*. The user does not see all the text that makes up an HTTP request sent to the browser. All they see is the URL in the location field at the top of the browser. But the browser also assembles several other text strings, specifying extra administrative details that will help the server answer. These are known as "header fields." All of this together forms the "HTTP request," as shown in Figure 16-3.

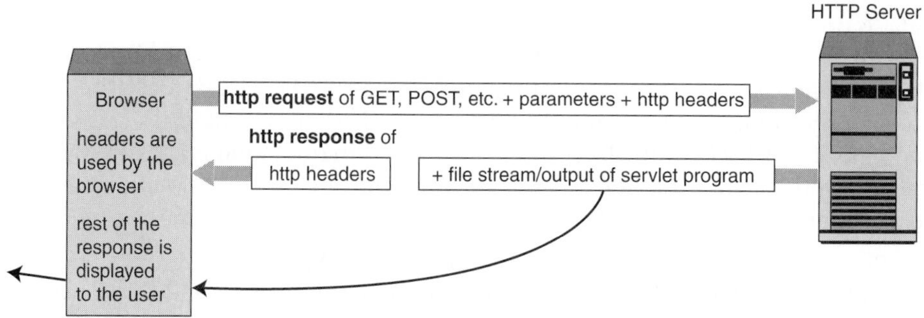

Figure 16–3 An HTTP request and response.

The browser sends requests, and the server sends back responses.

The header information, together with the HTML body forms the "HTTP response." The browser deals with what the headers tell it to do, and displays the rest of the response on the screen for the user to read. Some of the HTTP headers defined in RFC2616 are shown in Table 16-5.

Table 16–5 HTTP Headers

Header	Purpose
`Content-Encoding`	This header tells the browser that the content has been encoded for transmission, so the browser knows it has to change it back before displaying it. The content might be zip compressed, for example.
`Content-Language`	This header specifies the language in which the content is written. The value is one of the language codes laid down by RFC 1766, e.g., "`en`" (English), "`en-us`" (North American dialect), etc.
`Expires`	This header specifies the time when the content is considered out of date, and hence should no longer be cached.
`Connection`	This header can have a value of "`keep-alive`" when persistent connections are being used, or "`close`" when they are not.

We will only use forms to send data in this chapter, avoiding the rarer techniques of applets or browsing the servlet URL directly. When you use a form, your browser automatically provides any necessary headers for the HTTP request. If you want to get more details on headers that can appear in an HTTP request or response, the best resource is RFC 2616 (the Internet standard for HTTP) available at *www.rfc-editor.org*. You will need this information if you craft an HTTP request or response by hand in a program.

A Servlet and Its Request/response

In this section we will present the skeleton of a servlet, and also look at the objects that it uses to learn about a request and send a response. We will start by restating that a servlet is really just like any other Java program, but one that (like an applet) has a special context in which to run. In the case of an applet, the context is a web browser sandbox. In the case of a servlet, it runs inside a web server engine, termed the "container."

You create your servlet by extending one of the javax.servlet classes, and overriding one or more of the methods in it with your own code. There is some configuration or conventions that tell the servlet container where your servlet is and what URL should invoke it. The servlet container will call your overriding methods when a certain URL is requested, and pass in parameters that encapsulate (have all the information about) those events. Again, this is very similar to the way applets work.

The skeleton of an http servlet looks like this:

```
public class MyServlet extends javax.servlet.http.HttpServlet {

    public void init() { ... }
    public void doGet() { ... }
    public void doPost() { ... }
    public void destroy() { ... }
}
```

This code is simplified slightly by leaving off the method parameters and the exceptions they can throw. They are shown a couple of paragraphs later. The init() method is called only once when the class is first loaded. You would use this for one-time initialization, such as opening a connection to a database. The destroy() method is also called only once when the servlet is unloaded. This method is used to free any remaining resources or do final housekeeping on shutting down. If you don't have any special startup or shutdown code, you don't need to override these methods.

The doGet() or doPost() methods are the ones that do the work of the servlet. Obviously, doGet() is called when the HTML form used a "get" method, while doPost() is invoked by a form with a "post" method. There are other less important do*Something*() methods, too, corresponding to the other things that an HTML form may do. For example, there are other methods that can be overridden for less common HTTP requests like DELETE. You can review these in the source file HttpServlet.java that is part of the servlet kit.

The doGet() and doPost() methods take the same parameters: an `HttpServletRequest` and an `HttpServletResponse`. Both of these are interfaces, and all these doSomething() methods will get passed objects that implement the interfaces. You call methods on the `HttpServletRequest` to find out what the browser is asking for exactly. There's a method you call to get a PrintWriter from the `HttpServletResponse`, and you write your resulting plain text, HTML, image file, audio file, or Javascript using it. What you write gets sent back to the browser. It's as simple as that.

The actual signature of the doPost routine in `javax.servlet.http.HttpServlet` is:

```
protected void doPost(javax.servlet.http.HttpServletRequest req,
                      javax.servlet.http.HttpServletResponse resp)
              throws javax.servlet.ServletException, java.io.IOException;
```

The method `doGet()` has the same parameters and can throw the same exceptions. Note that the two routines are labelled as "protected," meaning that they can only be called by routines in the same package or in a subclass. That makes sense. It is probably not meaningful for your servlet to be called other than to process an http request. If it *is* meaningful to invoke your doPost() routine otherwise, then your system design probably needs some refiltering, perhaps to split out a chunk of the common code into a Java bean.

Servlet Request

Part of a request and part of a response will be the HTTP headers and the parameters. Headers are the bookkeeping information supplied automatically by the browser or server, stating things like the locale and the version of HTTP in use. Parameters are provided by the user and passed in the query string or in the form data. A parameter name is whatever the html form designer called it. It is legal for parameter or headers to have several values, usually in a comma-separated list. You need to be alert to this possibility in your code.

Let's take a look at the classes that implement response and request objects to see what information comes and goes. We'll start with the java class that represents an HTTP request. Tomcat will create an object that implements this interface to hold all the data in the incoming request. Tomcat will then invoke your servlet, and pass the request object to it as an argument.

These methods are just the highlights of an HTTP servlet request object. There are about 20 get*Something*() methods in HttpServletRequest, and another 20 in its parent, ServletRequest, allowing all information in the request to be retrieved.You will invoke these methods (shown in Table 16-6) on the `javax.servlet.http.HttpServletRequest` parameter, as shown in the example coming up.

Notice that some of these methods return Enumeration objects, rather than the newer Iterator object that was intended to replace Enumeration and was part of JDK 1.2. This is for backwards compatibility with existing servlet code.

Table 16–6 Key Methods of **javax.servlet.http.HttpServletRequest**

Method	Purpose
`getHeader(String s)`	Returns the first value of the header whose name you provide, or null if there isn't one of that name.
`getHeaderNames()`	Returns an Enumeration of all the header names in this request.
`getHeaders (String s)`	Returns an Enumeration of all the values of the header whose name you provide, or an empty Enumeration if there isn't one of that name. Some headers, such as Accept-Language, can be sent by clients as several headers each with a different value rather than sending the header as a comma-separated list.
`getIntHeader (String s)`	Used when you want to pull an integer out of the headers. String s is the name of the header. It will return the int value of the header, or throw a NumberFormatException, or return -1 if there is no header with this name.
`getParameter (String s)`	Returns the value of the parameter whose name you provide, or null if there isn't one.
`getParameterValues (String s)`	Works like getParameter(), but is used when the parameter can have several values, e.g., it may be a set of checkboxes or a multiselection list. It returns an array of String containing all the values.
`getParameterNames()`	Returns a java.util.Enumeration object containing all the parameter names in this request.
`getServerName()`	Returns the hostname of the server that received the request.
`getCookies()`	Returns an array of the cookies that came with this request. A cookie is a few bytes of data that the server sends to the browser and gets back in later requests, allowing the server to keep track of the client.

Response to a Servlet Request

Tomcat will also pass your servlet one of these response objects as an argument. The object has lots of methods that let you give values to its fields. You send back the actual data by writing to a print writer that you get from the response object. Table 16-7 shows the most frequently called methods of your response object, the HTTP servlet response.

Table 16–7 Key Methods of `javax.servlet.http.HttpServletResponse`

Method	Purpose
`getWriter()`	Returns a PrintWriter that will get written with the data part of the servlet response.
`setHeader(String n, String v)`	Adds a response header with the given name and value.
`setDateHeader(String s, long d)`	Adds a response header with the given name and time value.
`setIntHeader(String s, int v)`	Adds a response header with the given name and int value.
`addCookie(Cookie c)`	Adds the specified cookie to the response.
`setStatus(int sc)`	Set the status code for this response.
`setContentType (String s)`	Sets the response's MIME content type.
`setContentLength (int size)`	Sets the Content-Length header of the response.

You will invoke these methods on the `javax.servlet.http.HttpServletResponse` parameter, as shown in the example coming up. There are about 20 methods in HttpServletResponse and its parent class, ServletResponse, allowing just about any field to be set and returned to the browser. There are about 20 static final variables giving names to each of the status codes. You should review the Javadoc descriptions of these classes.

There are about a dozen HTTP headers, but you can ignore them unless you need the special effects that they cause. The content type is the only one you need to set. You can also look a few pages further on in this chapter where we write a JSP program to echo the headers received from the browser. That shows you some typical headers.

Writing Your Own Servlet

Here is the code for a servlet that can process the HTML form that we created in the previous section. We're going to send a reply that suggests a suitable pet based on the weight and leg count the user submitted. Make sure that your CLASSPATH has the servlet.jar file in it, as shown in the section "Installing Tomcat."

```
import javax.servlet.*;
import javax.servlet.http.*;
import java.io.*;
import java.text.*;
import java.util.*;

public class PetServlet extends HttpServlet {

    private String recommendedPet(int weight, int legs) {
        if (legs ==0) return "a goldfish";
        if (legs ==4) {
           if (weight<20) return "a cat";
           if (weight<100) return "a dog";
        }
        return "a house plant";
    }

    public void doPost(HttpServletRequest req,
                       HttpServletResponse resp )
        throws ServletException, IOException {

        // get the input field values
        int petWeight = 0, petLegs = 0;
        try {
          petWeight = Integer.parseInt(req.getParameter("weight"));
          petLegs = Integer.parseInt(req.getParameter("legs"));
        } catch (NumberFormatException nfe) {
          petWeight=petLegs=-1; // indicates that we got an invalid number
        }

        resp.setContentType("text/html");

        PrintWriter out = resp.getWriter();

        out.println(" <html> <body> <h1>Recommended Pet</h1> <p>");
        out.println("You want a " + petLegs + "-legged pet weighing "
                    + petWeight + "lbs.");

        String pet = recommendedPet(petWeight, petLegs);
        out.println("<P> We recommend getting <b>" + pet );
        out.println("</b> <hr> </body> </html> ");

        out.close();
    }
}
```

Note the line that says "`resp.setContentType("text/html").`" It is putting some standard information in the HTML headers that are sent back to the browser. We have to provide the minimal set of headers for the HTTP response. If you are going to set any headers, make sure you do it before you start writing the content of the response. A common content type is "text/plain" for ordinary character files, and "text/html" for HTML files. It refers to the MIME encoding of the strings that follow. MIME encoding is a way of turning arbitrary binary files into ASCII and labelling what the data represents. MIME was developed so that binary files like JPEG images could be mailed around more easily, and it is equally useful for HTTP transactions. MIME is an abbreviation for "Multipurpose Internet Mail Exchange," and is laid down in RFCs 1521 and 1522 if you want to look it up. In this example you don't need to set any other headers.

There are two versions of HTTP: 1.0 and 1.1. If you use any contemporary browser you get support for 1.1, which is good, but a lot of people out there are not using modern browsers. Among other improvements, HTTP 1.1 allows clients to send more requests to the server on the same socket that it just used. That saves time if you're getting some more content on the same web page, e.g., if you are displaying some HTML with image files. Normally, the client knows when it has got all the content because the server ends by breaking the socket connection. But if the server tells the client how many bytes are in the current response body, the client can count them as they arrive and will know when the server has sent everything and is ready for another request on this socket.

So it's good practice to set a header giving the length of the content part of each response when you know it. You can do that by assembling all the content in a ByteArrayOutputStream before sending it. ByteArrayOutputStream grows automatically as needed. Write everything to a ByteArrayOutputStream. After you have written all the data, call the `size()` methodof the `ByteArrayOutputStream` to find out how much you wrote, and do a `setContentLength()`. Finish up by doing a `response.getOutputStream()` and passing that as an argument to the ByteArrayOutputStream's `writeTo()` method. You don't have to copy anything anywhere. The code fragment that follows illustrates this approach. Needless to say, you must have completely finished writing any headers before you start writing the content of the response.

Keeping Track of Content Length

```
ByteArrayOutputStream ba = null;
    private void writeBytes(String s) throws IOException {
        byte buf[] = s.getBytes();
        ba.write(buf);
    }
    public void service(HttpServletRequest req,
                        HttpServletResponse resp )
        throws ServletException, IOException {
        resp.setContentType("text/html");
        // How to calculate content length
        ba = new ByteArrayOutputStream();
        writeBytes("<P> some text <HR> ");
        resp.setContentLength(ba.size());
        OutputStream out = resp.getOutputStream();
        ba.writeTo(out);
        out.close();
    }
}
```

Three further tips. First, always close the output stream when you are not going to write any more to it. Second, examine your exception handling, and try to express any problem in terms of an appropriate HTML status code if there is one. The HTML status codes are static int constants that can be found in interface `javax.servlet.http.HttpServletResponse`. Third, each servlet container has some way to log unexpected situations. Find out what that way is for your web server, and write log records as part of running each servlet.

Now compile and run this servlet. You can put this first example source file anywhere, but for simplicity and convenience I recommend that you put the source file and its class file in the same directory along with the examples that come with Tomcat. If you do this, no other configuration of Tomcat is needed. And Tomcat configuration is more difficult than it needs to be because of its confusing directory names and scarce tutorials. The pathnames you need to use and other information are shown in the Table 16-8. It's very finicky! So double check that you have used the exact names shown here.

Apache and Tomcat are great web-serving engines: free, open source, widely-used. Their weakness is that the information needed to configure them is not very accessible. Every web server is going to have its own configuration rules, and some are easier than others. Make sure you have set the environment variables listed at the beginning of this chapter, then complete the example by compiling the source file in the directory specified below, setting up the HTML, starting the Tomcat server, and finally browsing the URL for this servlet. Set all the pathnames up according to the table below. This re-uses the existing Tomcat "examples" directory, and you don't need to create or configure anything additional.

Table 16–8 Pathnames to Execute Your Servlet

Purpose	Value
Servlet source file	`$TOMCAT_HOME\webapps\examples\WEB-INF\classes\petservlet.java`
When compiling, your $CLASSPATH must include (the path may differ on non-Windows platforms).	`$TOMCAT_HOME\bin\servlet.jar`
Command to compile the servlet	`javac petservlet.java`
Form html file	`$TOMCAT_HOME\webapps\examples\servlets\petform.html`
HTML tag that invokes the servlet	`<form action=/examples/servlet/petservlet method=post>`
browse this URL to run	`http://127.0.0.1:8080/examples/servlets/petform.html`

Note the last two entries in this table. The HTML tag has the singular "servlet," and the URL has the plural "servlets." This inconsistency is a bit of a "newbie hurdle" but it won't exist for real servlets that you deploy. They will be placed in a different directory and will have a descriptor (entry in a file) that tells the container about them. We've avoided that here so there is less to do to get the example running.

On some Windows systems, using the name "localhost" in a URL will cause the computer to try to connect to the network to find a DNS server. It's fine to let that proceed.

The petservlet produces a result in the browser as shown in Figure 16-4.

Figure 16–4 Result of the petservlet.

Servlet Development and Debugging Tips

Debugging a servlet presents some new challenges because the servlet container may not provide a lot of support. Tomcat allows you to set a variable in its configuration file for each servlet that represents the "debugging level" from 1 to 10. The higher the number, the more events that are logged.

Another possibility is to use print() statements, but since the container probably doesn't have a console window, you need to use System.setOut() to redirect the output to a file. This affects the whole JVM. Turn it off before production use. Another choice is to learn and use the debugger that comes with your IDE, and do your preliminary testing in that environment rather than in a real web server.

If a servlet hits an unhandled exception, the container will typically pass the Java runtime error message back to the client. That's meaningful while you are debugging a system, but should be avoided in deployed systems. You can find out the call chain at the point where an exception is handled by putting this in your code:

```
try { ...
} catch (Throwable ex) {
       ex.printStackTrace();
}
```

That stack trace will go to System.err—you probably want to redirect it somewhere useful (depending on the container.) Alternatively, you can specify a PrintWriter to send the trace to.

Finally, servlet expert Jon Skeet suggests thinking about servlets from the browser's point of view. Jon offers the following advice. A browser doesn't know there's a servlet behind the scenes; it's just talking to a web server. This simplifies program creation and debugging, because you can apply all your HTML knowledge when designing servlets.

You can design the user interface, putting in dummy static data where necessary, and then write your servlet so that it outputs the HTML you've written, along with any images needed. Each request only gets one response, so to get a page with two pictures on it, there are three requests. First, the browser requests the HTML for the page, e.g., index.html. Second, when it gets the HTML, it notices that there are two img tags, so it requests each of the images. As far as the servlet programmer is concerned, these are all independent requests. With HTTP/1.1, they may come on the same connection, but that doesn't affect you. The servlet should just write each image or page as it's requested.

Frames are similar to images—there's one request for the frameset, then one request per frame. Stick to the idea that each HTML page you've written corresponds to one request, and everything will work like a charm.

Servlet Operating Cycle and Threading

Servlets typically have the operating cycle, as shown in Figure 16-5.

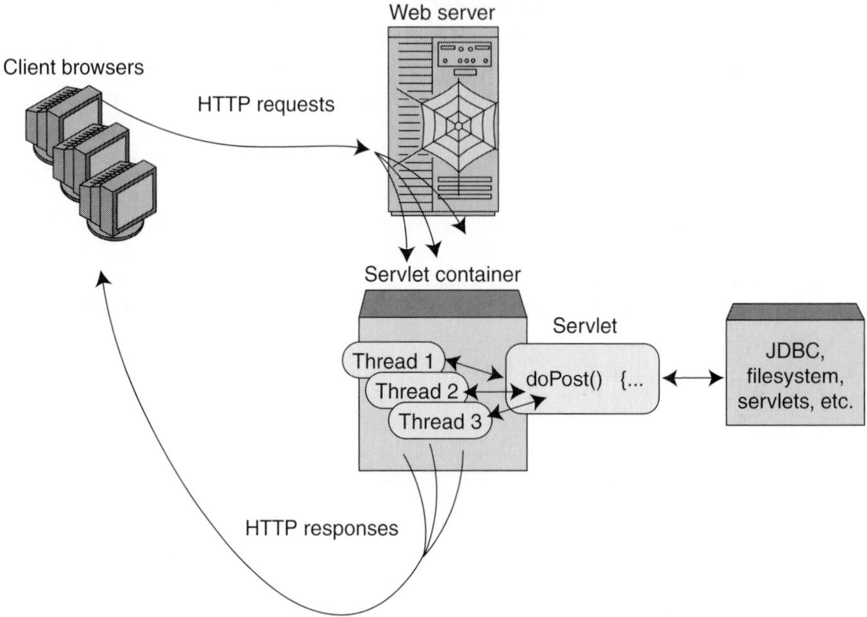

Figure 16–5 Operating cycle of a servlet.

The sequence of events in a servlet's lifetime is:

1. The servlet container starts up, and at some point constructs an instance of the servlet and calls its `init()` method. The `init()` method is only called once. Not once per request, not once per session, but once at the beginning of the servlet's lifetime. The `init()` method is a good place to put code to open a database connection.
2. Unlike, say, a GUI, there is no background thread always running code in the servlet. The servlet instance object just stays ready in memory, waiting for a request. This makes servlets very efficient. Eventually, a request comes to the web server, and the web server passes the request to the servlet container.
3. The servlet container instantiates a new thread to process the request. Note that the container does not instantiate a new servlet object. The newly created thread representing the request calls the `doPost()` method (or whatever is appropriate for this request) of the existing instance of your servlet.

The servlet can access a database, the filesystem, other servlets, etc. It creates the HTTP response which the container returns to the client. Thread-per-request makes servlets scalable and high performance.

4. Repeat steps 2 and 3 for each request. Eventually the web server will be requested to shut down. At that point, the servlet's destroy() method is called. Then it is a candidate for garbage collection and finalization. A servlet instance will also be destroyed if you have set things up so that newer versions of a servlet are loaded automatically.

Servlets typically run on multithreaded servers and instantiate a new thread for each incoming request. This is the usual way that servers process incoming requests on a socket—create a new thread for each request for service. The use of threads means that two requests might be executing in your servlet code at the same time. Your code will need to synchronize access to any resources that are shared. This will include resources like instance variables, database connections, and static data. If you don't properly synchronize access to instance data, you will run into trouble with data race bugs.

Consider a servlet that accesses a database and puts data in an instance variable of the servlet. If two requests come in together and you are unlucky with scheduling, it could happen that request A gets its data out of the database, but it is overwritten in the instance variable with B's data from the database before A can use it. Then the servlet returns B's data to both A and B, confusing everyone. Chapter 11 on advanced thread topics explains synchronization in more detail.

Performance Tip

Synchronization is costly in terms of time, and drags down performance. The fastest approach is to avoid instance variables, and thus the need for synchronization in your servlets (and other code too). Instead nest all your variables inside any method (i.e., make them local variables), and pass them as parameters as needed.

Each thread has its own stack, and local variables are allocated on that stack. That means that variables local to a method are separate for each thread and never need to be synchronized. Any objects they create are still on the one heap, but as long as the instantiations are done inside a method and you don't do anything to explicitly cause them to be shared, then these don't need to be synchronized either. But you must always synchronize access to data that is visible in more than one thread.

There is an alternative to making your servlet thread-safe. You can declare that it implements javax.servlet.SingleThreadModel, like this:

```
public class petservlet extends HttpServlet
                    implements javax.servlet.SingleThreadModel {
```

When you implement this interface, the servlet container queues up HTTP requests so that only one thread at a time is executing in your servlet. However, the container may create multiple instances of your single thread model servlet, so you still have to worry about synchronizing class (static) data. Normal servlets only have one instance per context per container (according to the 2.2 specification) but can have many threads in that one instance. Generally speaking, SingleThreadModel should be avoided as an unnecessary drag on performance, unless there are special reasons to use it. One reason would be when you know you will never have many concurrent requests. In this case, the simplest code will use the single thread model, making the database connection an unsynchronized instance variable.

There is not much more to servlets than this. The topics outside the scope of this chapter are cookies, setting a session, security, filtering, and redirecting the request to another servlet. All of these are covered at length in the Servlet version 2.3 Specification which can be downloaded from the Sun website. Although they call it a specification, and it's more than 200 pages long, it's easy to read and worth taking a look at. You can find it at *java.sun.com/products/servlet/index.html*.

A cookie is a morsel of tasty data that a server sends back to the clien and can retrieve on demand. It allows the server to retain some state information for each of its clients. The information is typically something like, "what pages has the user seen?" or "has this user given the password yet?" A session is a way for the server to identify a user across more than one page request. You would use a session to conduct an entire e-commerce transaction, with all the different pages for choosing goods, submitting credit card numbers, and so on. Cookies are often used to maintain session information. Readers who want to know more about these two matters can look at the examples in the sample code that comes with Tomcat. Start Tomcat running and then browse the URL `//127.0.0.1:8080` to see these pages.

Windows Shortcuts

You can create Windows shortcuts to start and stop Tomcat. These can be on the desktop or under the Start menu (or both). Here's how you do it:

1. Right-click on the MS-DOS prompt shortcut and choose "copy," then right click and choose "paste."
2. Right-click on the copy and choose "rename." Rename the copy to "tomcat start."
3. Right-click on the shortcut and select "Properties" -> "Program" tab.
4. Type in the new name, such as "Tomcat 4.0."
5. Change the "Cmd line" to: "C:\tomcat\4beta3\bin\startup.bat" (or whatever matches the release).
6. Change the "Working" (directory) to: C:\tomcat\4beta3.
7. Change the "Batch file" to: C:\autoexec.bat.
8. Select "Minimized" for the Run property, and select the "Close on exit" checkbox.
9. Choose a new icon by clicking on "Change Icon...." I like the racing car.
10. Click on the "Memory" tab and check that the "initial environment" value is 4096.

Press "OK" to save your changes to this shortcut. You can create a similar shortcut to stop Tomcat.

Java Server Pages

We will conclude this tour of server-side Java with a description of Java Server Pages (JSP), and an example JSP program. One way of understanding JSP is to say that JSP is ASP, without the restriction to Windows only. Another way of understanding it is to say that JSP programs are a variant on ordinary servlets, where some of the simple tasks are automated for you. In fact, the container implements JSPs by automatically translating them into the equivalent servlet which is then run in the usual way.

An ordinary unchanging web page contains HTML (plus Javascript perhaps). A servlet is a compiled Java program. A JSP program is a hybrid of these two. It lets you mix individual Java statements in with your HTML code. The Java code will be executed on the server when the page is browsed, and it will provide some dynamic content to the page. You might do some calculations, or put something in a loop. Your JSP Java code fragments are padded out to make a complete servlet. This servlet is automatically compiled for you by the JSP container when the page is browsed. As with servlets, JSP code is compiled once and loaded into memory on first use. A developer will typically browse all the JSP pages when deploying a system, so that there is no "first time through" time penalty of compilation for the users.

A large part of a servlet is "boilerplate," meaning text that is the same in all servlets. The class declaration, the method signatures, and so on are needed to make sure your code compiles, but they are the same in every servlet. JSP eliminates all that standard context. It is provided for you automatically. This can dramatically shorten the amount of code you need to write, and also makes it simple enough for non-programmers to produce JSP.

JSP uses special tags to separate the Java from the HTML. The JSP opening tag is "<%" and the closing tag is "%>". The opening tag "<%" might be followed by another character such as "!" or "@" or "="to further specialize its meaning. A very brief example here will show you best. These lines in a JSP file:

```
<b> current time is:
    <%=  new java.util.Date() %>
</b>
```

will produce a line of output like this when you browse the jsp page:

current time is: Mon Feb 19 18:37:23 PST 2001

Note that it may take 30 seconds or so to appear because the container has to compile your JSP file the first time you browse it. When you browse the same file a minute later without changing anything, the resulting page will show a different time, demonstrating that the JSP provides dynamic page content. Second and later references give results much more quickly as the container keeps the compiled class file for future use. If the automatic JSP compilation results in compiler error messages, these will be sent back to the client for display in the browser.

The piece that is new is the second line in the JSP file. It starts with the tag "<%=" which means "evaluate the Java expression that follows, convert it to String, and write it to the HTML output." Other JSP tags have their own meaning, as shown in Table 16-9:

Table 16–9 JSP Tags and Meanings

Start of JSP Tag	Meaning of JSP Tag
`<%`	Everything up to the closing tag "%>" is java code (blocks, statements, declarations, etc.).
`<%=`	Evaluates the Java expression that follows, converts it to String, and writes it to the HTML output. Ends with "%>".
`<%!`	This is a Java declaration which is inserted into the body of the servlet where it is available to all methods in the servlet.
`<%@`	This tag can be followed by one of several different strings, such as "method," "import," "implements," "extends." These are followed by a string that specifies the name for a Java method, package, interface, etc. This tag affects the generated Java, rather than the HTML it will output.
`<jsp: useBean ...\>`	Has a list of attributes that specify a Java bean to invoke, and parameters to pass to it. Note that it ends with "\>". This tag uses the XML conventions.

As a further example, the following JSP code echoes back all the headers that the page received. Note that there are some variables predefined within JSP for the coder's convenience. The response PrintWriter is "out," the HttpServletRequest is "req," and the HttpServletResponse is "resp."

First Example of JSP

```
<html>
<body bgcolor="white">
<h1>The Echo JSP</h1>
<%   java.util.Enumeration eh = request.getHeaderNames();
     while (eh.hasMoreElements()) {
          String h = (String) eh.nextElement();
          out.print("<br> header: " + h );
          out.println(" value: " + request.getHeader(h));
     }
%>
</body>
</html>
```

You should type this in and try running it using the pathnames shown in Table 16-10. Make sure Tomcat is running when you try this program, otherwise there is nothing to handle the request!

Table 16–10 Executing Your JSP

Purpose	Value
JSP source file	`$TOMCAT_HOME\webapps\examples\jsp\echo.jsp`
JSP class file	generated automatically for you.
Your $CLASSPATH	You do not need to set this for JSP, but it doesn't hurt if you leave it set pointing to the servlet.jar file.
Browse this URL to run	`http://127.0.0.1:8080/examples/jsp/echo.jsp`

Since we aren't sending across any parameters, we don't need to invoke the JSP with a form, and we can just directly browse the JSP file itself. If you have connected up everything correctly, there will be a small pause while Tomcat automatically generates a servlet for the JSP and compiles it. Then you should see something like Figure 16-6 appear in your browser.

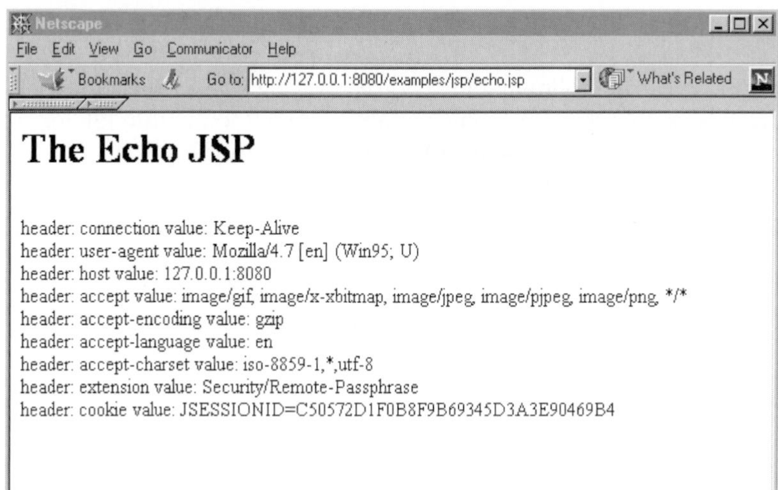

Figure 16–6 Results of browsing your JSP file.

A browser doesn't know if there's a servlet, JSP, or static web page at the other end of the URL. These are the kind of headers that the client sends with any request. The headers will vary slightly on different systems and browsers. It is possible to shorten this JSP example by using the JSP tag that automatically does the output, as shown in this next JSP example.

Second Example of JSP

```
<html>
<body bgcolor="white">
<h1>The Echo 2 JSP</h1>
<%   java.util.Enumeration eh = request.getHeaderNames();
     while (eh.hasMoreElements()) {
         String h = (String) eh.nextElement();
%>
         <br> header: <%=  h  %>
              value: <%=  request.getHeader(h) %>
<%
     }
%>
</body>
</html>
```

JSP code can become messy if you are not careful, as this example shows. Tangled messes seem much more common than nicely separated code. People have put effort into additional servlet-based technologies such as WebMacro (www.webmacro.org), Enhydra (xmlc.enhydra.org), and Velocity (jakarta.apache.org/velocity) to try to enforce the separation more cleanly. If you are working with JSP, you should look into these packages.

To help deploy all the files to your application server, you may create a Web Archive (WAR) of your JSPs. A war file is just like a jar file with the addition of a "/WEB-INF" directory and a "web.xml" file that describes the application to Tomcat. You can use the "jar" tool that comes with the JDK to create it. The file format is the same, but a different extension name was chosen to highlight the different uses of a .jar and a .war file. A .jar file contains a set of classfiles that can be placed in a classpath. It might also be double-clickable, containing everything including a GUI needed to run an application. A .war file contains servlet and JSP classfiles that can only be run in the context of a web server.

The Tomcat server has a configuration directory at `TOMCAT_HOME\conf`. In there you will find a `web.xml` file that can configure Tomcat for web-related issues (like the MIME types it understands), and an example `server.xml` file that configures it with information about your servlets.

The configuration file uses XML, which is a human-readable form that looks a bit like lots of new HTML markup tags. Chapter 28 has more information on XML. You will find that you need to stop and start Tomcat again so that it can pick up changes in your servlets. You can change the configuration file so that it always looks for a newer version classfile before running a servlet. This is called making the servlet reloadable, but there is a large performance cost to this feature, so you want to turn it off after your development is complete. You can add other details to the configuration file, like the servlet names and the URLs that correspond to them. If you stick to the pathnames shown in this chapter you can get it all running without the additional distraction of mastering a Tomcat configuration though. The most important thing is to put your compiled code under the directory `c:\tomcat\webapps\ROOT\WEB-INF\classes\`. The directory structure under that must match the package hierarchy of your code (see Table 16-11). If you are getting a few examples working without using a named package, the classes can go right into that directory.

Table 16–11 Where to Put Files with Tomcat

Purpose	Value
Directory for .jsp and .html files	`\tomcat\webapps\ROOT`
Directory for .class files	`\tomcat\webapps\ROOT\WEB-INF\classes`
Then access pages as:	
JSP page	`http://localhost:8080/my.jsp`
HTML page	`http://localhost:8080/myservlet.html`
Servlet URL	`http://localhost:8080/servlet/myservlet`

Java Beans in Servlets and JSP

This chapter wouldn't be complete without pointing out the role of Java beans on the server side. Java beans are software components, namely well-specified "modules" which do a specific job and can easily be reused in many applications. Microsoft makes extensive use of software components under the product name ActiveX, often for some visual or GUI feature. For example, a programmer might write a piece of code that can display a set of numbers as a pie chart. That routine is very suitable for turning into a software component, making it available to any program on the system.

The point of JSP is to use lots of Java beans that cover your business processes. You might have one bean that encompasses everything you can do with a customer record, another for an order, a third for a payment transaction. JSP lets you easily glue these beans together in a web-based display framework. JSP has a special tag that lets web pages on the server easily interact with beans with hardly any "glue" code needed. People call this a "tag library." Here's an example of the tags that connect a JSP page to a Java bean that manages database access.

```
<%@ page language="java" import="java.sql.*" %>

<jsp:useBean id="db" scope="request"
  class="com.afu.database.DbBean" />

<jsp:setProperty name="db" property="*" />
```

You use the same beans (the same logic) for your non-web-based processing so you have the advantages of consistency, familiarity, and software reuse. The combination of Java beans and JSP is dealt with at length elsewhere, so we will note that it is a major use of JSP and leave it at that.

The main reason for using JSP is that it allows web developers to quickly build web pages that interface to enterprise systems. The JSP tags let HTML designers tie web information into corporate business logic contained in Java objects without having to learn all about Java object-oriented programming. A separate, smaller programming team can create libraries of software components. Then web designers can use those libraries by writing markup tags that they are familiar with. Use of "tag-libraries" are one of the cornerstones of JSP. JSP thus provides a rapid prototyping framework for building two tiers (the client and the front-end server) of an N-tier distributed system.

Servlets can act as a middleware gateway to existing legacy systems, providing an easy way to "webify" your current systems. Furthermore, since all the code is on the server (not the client), when you want to update your application you just roll the code out to a few servers and your entire user base gets the newest code at once.

Further Reading

When you start to write servlets on a regular basis, you might want to check the website *www.revusky.com*. At that site, skilled Java programmer Jonathan Revusky has made available some free tools for improving and simplifying your Java code. One of the tools is "Niggle"—an easy-to-use framework for building robust web applications.

If you are interested in a more detailed study of servlets, download and read the Java Servlet 2.3 Specification from the *java.sun.com* website. Although its title is "Specification," it actually contains some good explanations of the details of servlets. Marty Hall's book, *Core Servlets and JavaServer Pages* (Prentice Hall, 2000), is also recommended.

If you want to know what kind of web server a site is running, or you want to see the market share of different webservers, look at *www.netcraft.com*. Finally, the website *www.servlets.com* is a great resource for programmers writing servlets and JSP code.

Exercises

1. Modify the petform servlet so that it includes the content length in its response.
2. Write a servlet that sends back to the client (for display) all the parameters and HTTP request headers that it received. Have the servlet get enumerations of all the headers and all the parameters, and echo them back to the client.
3. Write a Java Server Page that handles our "pet selection" form.
4. Earlier in this chapter, we showed an HTML form that invoked a servlet. It's actually possible to write a servlet or JSP that delivers that form as well as responding to it. When the servlet is invoked by a URL, it should respond with the HTML representing the form for pet selection. When the servlet is invoked by submitting the form, it should make the pet selection. That keeps everything relating to pet selection in one file, possibly easing maintenance. You can tell if a form was submitted by doing a requestParameter() on any of the argument names, like this: `String formSent = request.getParameter("legs")`. If the string comes back null, there wasn't a form submitted (or at least that argument was not filled in), so the servlet must have been invoked with a URL reference; the service routine should then generate the form. Otherwise, the servlet should send back the HTML with the pet selection. Write a JSP file so that it delivers the pet selection form in this way, and responds to it too.
5. Write an applet/servlet combination that writes/displays a high score file for a game. You might want to integrate this with one of existing games on the CD.
6. (Extra credit) Read RFC 2616 (the Internet standard for HTTP) available at *www.rfc-editor.org*. Use that information to write a very simple web server in Java that can list directories and serve plain text and HTML files. It should use a ServerSocket to accept requests, read the requests, and then send back the appropriate information. Use a property file to configure the web server (e.g., the root directory that it will serve, etc.). Ignore sessions, cookies, headers, etc. This can be done in 200-300 lines of Java.

Some Light Relief—The Java-Powered Toaster

First prize for the "most entertaining Java application of 2001" goes to Robin Southgate. For his final year project as an Industrial Design student at Brunel University, England, Robin designed and built a bread toaster. Not just any toaster though. Robin's toaster is powered by a Java program that dials a weather service, retrieves the forecast, and singes the outlook onto the toast. Examples of the toast are shown in Figure 16-7.

Toast on a sunny day

Toast on a rainy day

Figure 16–7 Java-powered Toaster

Robin's design integrates a standard domestic toaster with the TINI microcontroller from Dallas Semiconductor. The TINI (Tiny InterNet Interface) is a $20 microcontroller chip set that supports an incredible software development platform. TINI contains a Java virtual machine, a web server, and a TCP/IP network stack running on top of a real time operating system, all in less than half a Mbyte of flash RAM. You program the chip and control I/O to its peripherals completely in Java. The peripherals can include ethernet, a parallel port, a wireless network interface, as well as the usual RS232 serial port and I2C bus.

Robin modified the toaster so that it works automatically. When a piece of toast is put in, the microcontroller wakes up and dials out through a modem on the serial port to remotely access the weather information. The Java code then condenses the forecast into a choice between "sunny," "overcast," "rain," or "snow," and chooses the appropriate baffle to move in front of the toast heater element. The baffle is made of polytetrafluorethylene (more commonly known as "teflon" or PTFE) which is both food-safe and heat resistant at toaster temperatures. The baffle has a hole in the shape of the weather icon, exposing that area of the toast to more radiant heat than adjacent masked areas. The toast pops up in about 30 seconds with the weather icon burned onto it.

When he started on the project, Robin appealed to the TINI engineering mailing list for advice. About half the engineers made a lot of fat-headed suggestions, like using cocoa powder for toner to print on the bread. Another proposed using a CO2 laser to reduce cooking time into the 1-2 second range. They just didn't seem to be taking the project seriously. Other engineers could see the value of Java-powered toast, and gave Robin guidance on how he could refine his design.

The project involved sensing toaster operation, communicating with a remote site, decoding the data returned, moving the baffles, and controlling the toaster element. The protoype shown in Figure 16-8 needed special attention to switch the high current for the heating element safely. TINI is an excellent choice for this kind of embedded design. It has a built-in serial port that can trivially drive an external modem. There are readily available modules to monitor current, temperature, baffle position, and to switch loads. A key element with all projects is to build and debug the new design in stages rather than trying the whole thing at once. And of course, all the programming was done in Java.

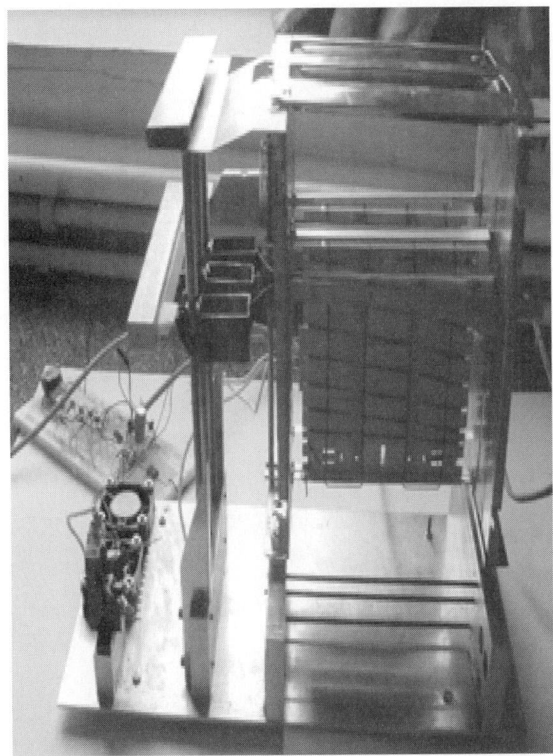

Figure 16–8 Java-powered toaster.

See *www.dalsemi.com* for more information on the amazingly capable Java products from Dallas Semiconductor. As one engineer on the mailing list concluded, "when it comes to domestic appliances for toast-related processing, Java has the biggest appetite."

If, like me, you have often wondered what a Java program to control a weather-forecasting toaster looks like, here is the answer. It is just the regular "put bit patterns into ports" that comprises most embedded programming, but expressed in Java quite neatly.

```
//  The toaster main control program

import java.util.*;
import java.io.*;
import com.dalsemi.onewire.*;
import com.dalsemi.onewire.adapter.*;
import com.dalsemi.onewire.container.*;
import com.dalsemi.onewire.container.OneWireContainer.*;
import com.dalsemi.onewire.utils.*;
import com.dalsemi.onewire.utils.Address;

public class WeatherSwitch {

    public static void main(String args[]) {
         // details omitted...
         // contact server, get forecast
         // translate it into a command for the Switch.
    }

    public static void Switch2405(byte[] ID) {
       // "ID" is a byte array of size 8 with the address
       // of a part we have already found.
       // "access" is a DSPortAdapter
       DSPortAdapter access = new TINIExternalAdapter();
       int i=0;
       OneWireContainer05 ds2405 =
                    (OneWireContainer05) access.getDeviceContainer(ID);
       ds2405.setupContainer(access,ID);
       byte state[] = {}; // declare variable first, we'll assign it below

       try // catch exception {
         state = ds2405.readDevice();
       } catch (Exception e) {};

       // I know that the 2405 only has one channel (one switch)
       // and it doesn't support 'Smart On'
       boolean latch_state = ds2405.getLatchState(0,state);
       System.out.println("Current state of switch: "+latch_state);
       System.out.println("Current output level:" +
                                             ds2405.getLevel(0,state));
       if (!latch_state) {
           System.out.println("Toggling switch");
           ds2405.setLatchState(0,!latch_state,false,state);
           try {
               ds2405.writeDevice(state);
               state = ds2405.readDevice();
               latch_state = ds2405.getLatchState(0,state);
           } catch (Exception e) {};

           System.out.println("Current state of switch: "+latch_state);
           System.out.println("Current output level:"
                                            +ds2405.getLevel(0,state));

       }
    }
```

Chapter 17

Networking in Java

"If a packet hits a pocket on a socket on a port,
and the bus is interrupted and the interrupt's not caught,
then the socket packet pocket has an error to report."

— Programmer's traditional nursery rhyme

The biggest barrier to understanding Java networking features is getting familiar with network terms and techniques. If you speak French, it doesn't mean that you can understand an article from a French medical journal.

Similarly, when you learn Java, you also need to have an understanding of the network services and terminology before you can write Internet code. So this chapter starts with the basics of TCP/IP networking, followed by a description of Java support.

There is a lot of knowledge in this chapter. After the TCP/IP basics, we'll develop some socket examples. We'll see how a client gets services from a remote server using sockets. Then we will look at server sockets to see how incoming connections are accepted. Our first example will merely print HTTP headers. We will add to it little by little until it is a complete multithreaded HTTP web server. Finally, we will show how to use new I/O channels with server sockets.

Everything You Need To Know about TCP/IP but Failed to Learn in Kindergarten

Networking at heart is all about shifting bits from point A to point B. We bundle the data bits into a packet, and add some more bits to say where they are to go. That, in a nutshell, is the Internet Protocol or IP. If we want to send more bits than will fit into a single packet, we can divide the bits into groups and send them in several successive packets. The units that we send are called "User Datagrams" or "Packets." Packets is the more common term these days.

User Datagrams can be sent across the Internet using the User Datagram Protocol (UDP), which relies on the Internet Protocol for addressing and routing. UDP is like going to the post office, sticking on a stamp, and dropping off the packet. IP is what the mail carrier does to route and deliver the packet. Two common applications that use the UDP are: SNMP, the Simple Network Management Protocol, and TFTP, the Trivial File Transfer Protocol. See Figure 17-1.

When we send several pieces of postal mail to the same address, the packages might arrive in any order. Some of them might even be delayed, or even on occasion lost altogether. This is true for UDP too; you wave goodbye to the bits as they leave your workstation, and you have no idea when they will arrive where you sent them, or even if they did.

Uncertain delivery is equally undesirable for postal mail and for network bit streams. We deal with the problem in the postal mail world (when the importance warrants the cost) by paying an extra fee to register the mail and have the mail carrier collect and bring back a signature acknowledging delivery. A similar protocol is used in the network work to guarantee reliable delivery in the order in which the packets were sent. This protocol is known as Transmission Control Protocol or "TCP." Two applications that run on top of, or use, TCP are: FTP, the File Transfer Protocol, and Telnet.

What Is Your IP Address?

On Unix workstations, you can run the "ifconfig" (interface configuration) program to find out your IP address.

On WIndows 9x, you can run WinIPCfg to get the same information. Type this in a command tool:

```
c:\> winipcfg
```

It will popup a window that lists the host name, IP address, subnet mask, gateway, and even the MAC address of your network card.

The MAC (Media Access Control) address is the address on the network interface card burned in at manufacturing time. It is not used in TCP/IP because, unlike IP addresses, it lacks a hierarchy. To route packets using MAC addresses, each router would need a list of every MAC address in the world.

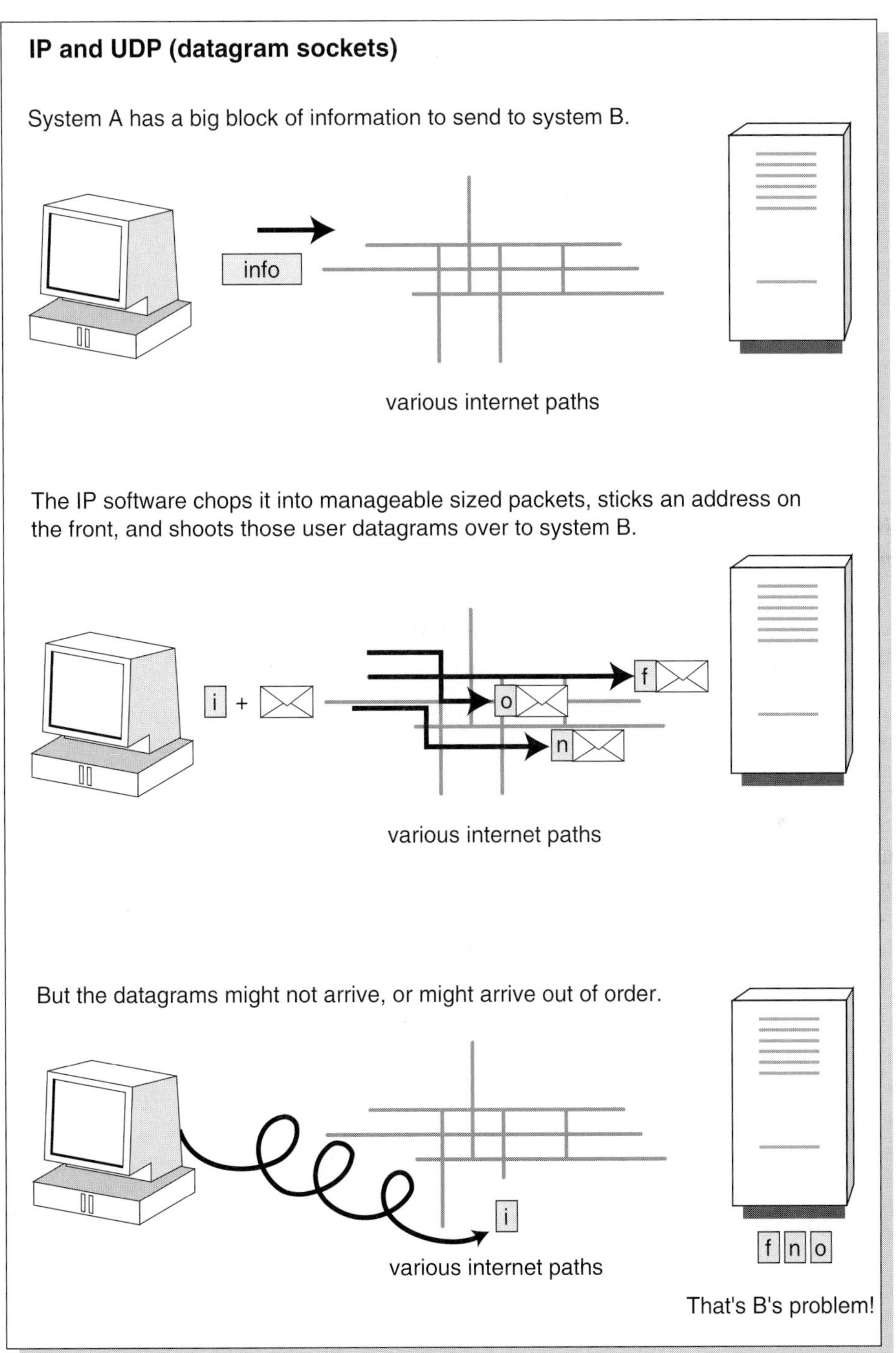

IP and UDP (datagram sockets)
System A has a big block of information to send to system B.
info
various internet paths
The IP software chops it into manageable sized packets, sticks an address on the front, and shoots those user datagrams over to system B.
i +
f
o
n
various internet paths
But the datagrams might not arrive, or might arrive out of order.
i
various internet paths
f n o
That's B's problem!

Figure 17–1 IP and UDP (datagram sockets).

TCP uses IP as its underlying protocol (just as UDP does) for routing and delivering the bits to the correct address. The "correct address" means the IP address; every computer on the Internet has an IP address.However, TCP is more like a phone call than a registered mail delivery in that it supports an end-to-end connection for the duration of the transmission session. It takes a while to set up this stream connection, and it costs more to assure reliable sequenced delivery, but the cost is usually justified. See Figure 17-2.

The access device at each endpoint of a phone conversation is a telephone. The access object at each endpoint of a TCP/IP session is a socket. Sockets started life as a way for two processes on the same Unix system to talk to each other, but some smart programmers realized that they could be generalized into connection endpoints between processes on different machines connected by a TCP/IP network. Today, every operating system has adopted IP and sockets.

IP can deliver the following via socket connections:

- Slower reliable delivery using TCP (this is termed a *stream socket*)
- Faster but unguaranteed delivery using UDP (this is a *datagram socket*)
- Fast raw bits using ICMP (Internet Control Message Protocol) datagrams. They are not delivered at all, but ask the remote end to do something or respond in some way.

ICMP is a low-level protocol for message control and error reporting. It uses IP packets, but its messages are directed at the IP software itself and don't come through to the application layer. Java doesn't support ICMP and we won't say anything more about it.

Socket connections have a client end and a server end, and they differ in what you can do with them. Generally, the server end just keeps listening for incoming requests (an "operators are standing by" kind of thing). The client end initiates a connection, and then passes or requests information from the server.

Note that the number of socket writes is not at all synchronized with the number or timing of socket reads. A packet may be broken into smaller packets as it is sent across the network, so your code should *never* assume that a read will get the same number of bytes that were just written into the socket.

The most widely used version of IP today is Internet Protocol Version 4 (IPv4). However, IP Version 6 (IPv6 or IPng) is also beginning to enter the market. IPv6 uses 128 bit addresses, not 32 bit, and so allows many more Internet users. IPv6 is fully backward compatible with (can process packets sent using) IPv4, but it will take a long time before IPv4 is displaced by v6. IPv4 is supported with hardware-based routing at wire speed on 2.5Gb links. IPv6 currently uses software routing.

An IPv4 feature called "Network Address Translation" (NAT) has reduced the pressure to move to v6. A few years ago, it looked like we were going to run

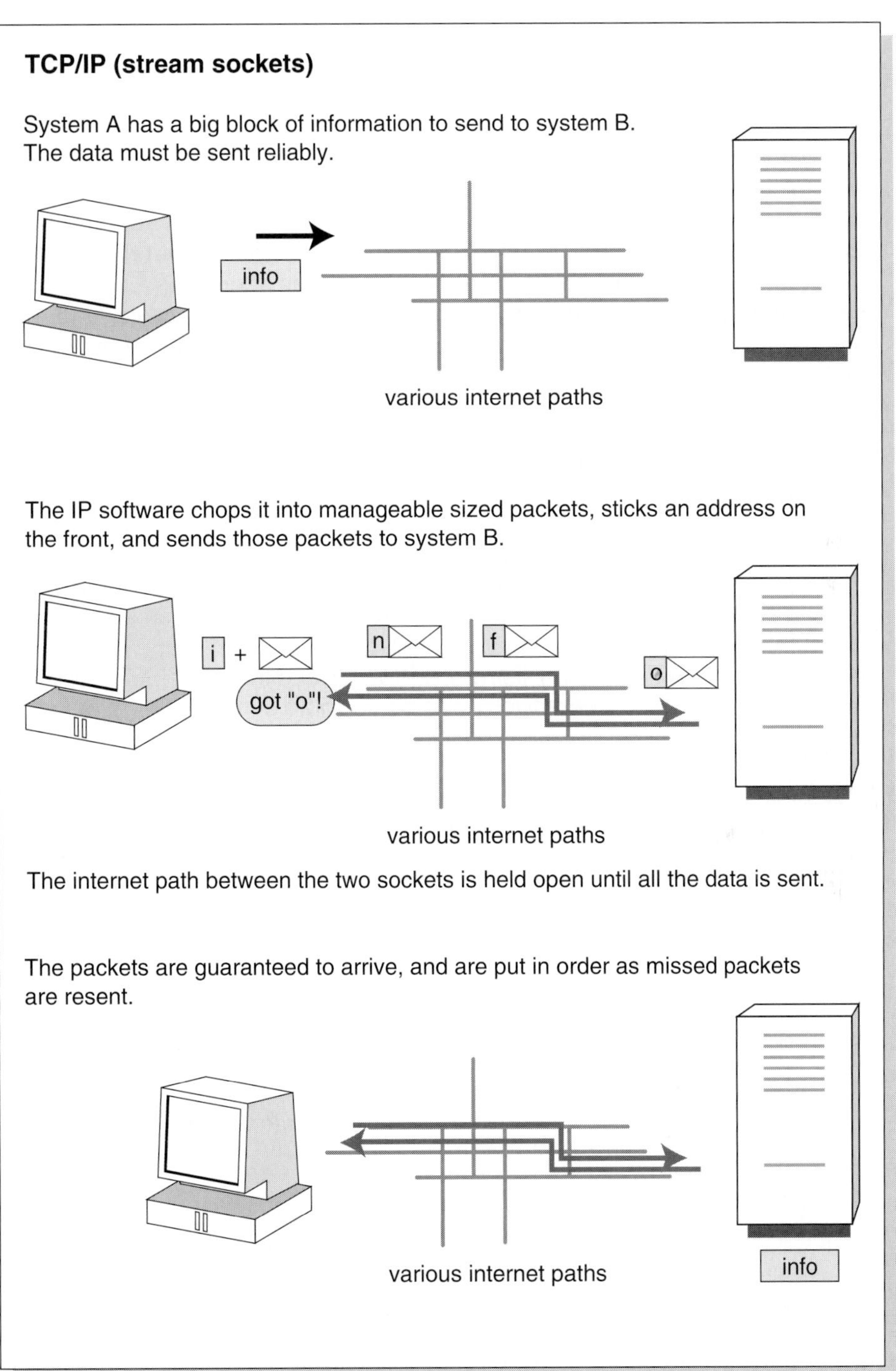

TCP/IP (stream sockets)
System A has a big block of information to send to system B.
The data must be sent reliably.
info
various internet paths
The IP software chops it into manageable sized packets, sticks an address on the front, and sends those packets to system B.
i
+
n
f
o
got "o"!
various internet paths
The internet path between the two sockets is held open until all the data is sent.
The packets are guaranteed to arrive, and are put in order as missed packets are resent.
various internet paths
info

Figure 17–2 TCP/IP (stream sockets).

out of IP addresses. Today NAT lets your big site have just one assigned address, which you use for the computer with the internet connection. You use any IP address you like for the computers on your side of the firewall. You may be duplicating numbers that someone else uses behind their firewall, but the two systems don't interfere with each other. When you access the internet, NATS translates your internal IP address into the externally visible one, and vice versa for incoming packets. From outside, it looks like all your traffic is coming from your computer that runs NATS.

Looking at a Packet Traveling over the Net

Packets are moved along by routers, which are special-purpose computers that connect networks. Every IP packet that leaves your system goes to a nearby router which will move the packet to another router closer to the destination. This transfer continues until finally the packet is brought to a router that is directly connected to the subnet serving the destination computer.

Routers maintain large configuration tables of what addresses are served by what routers, what the priorities are, and what rules they should use for security and load balancing. These tables can be updated dynamically as the network runs.

Windows has a program that lets you trace a packet's movement between routers. Here's the output from a sample run, tracing the route between my PC and java.sun.com. Unix has a similar program, called "traceroute."

```
c:\> tracert java.sun.com
Tracing route to java.sun.com [192.18.97.71]over a maximum of 30 hops:
 1     93 ms     95 ms     95 ms  sdn-ar-008carcor001t.dialsprint.net
[63.128.147.130]
 2     94 ms    100 ms   100 ms  sdn-hr-008carcor001t.dialsprint.net
[63.128.147.129]
 3     99 ms    100 ms     95 ms  sdn-pnc1-stk-4-1.dialsprint.net
[207.153.212.49]
... and so on to ...
 12    164 ms    170 ms    160 ms  sun-1.border3.den.pnap.net
[216.52.42.42]
13  166 ms 160 ms   161 ms  java.sun.com [192.18.97.71]
Trace complete.
```

This shows that it takes 13 "hops" for packets to travel from my PC to Sun's Java website. The program sends three test packets and notes the round trip time in milliseconds to reach each successive router. It works by sending out packets with brief time limits, and gradually increasing it until the first router gets it, and then the next, and so on. As each router replies, objecting to the timed-out packet, traceroute can figure out the hop time for each step. Traceroute is good for determining network connectivity.

Here it tells us that overall packets travel from me to Java-HQ in under a fifth of a second.

There! Now you know everything you need to use the Java networking features.

What's in the Networking Library?

If you browse the network library API, you'll find the following classes (there are a few other classes, but these are the key ones):

- `Socket` — This is the client Socket class. It lets you open a connection to another machine, anywhere on the Internet (that you have permission).
- `ServerSocket` — This is the server Socket class. ServerSocket lets an application accept TCP connections from other systems and exchange I/O with them.
- `URL` — The class represents a Uniform Resource Locator—a reference to an object on the web. You can create a URL reference with this class.
- `URLConnection` — You can open a URL and retrieve the contents, or write to it, using this class.
- `HttpURLConnection` — The class extends URLConnection and supports functions specific to HTTP, like get, post, put, head, trace, and options.
- `URLEncoder/URLDecoder` — These two classes have static methods to allow you to convert a String to and from MIME x-www-form-urlencoded form. This is convenient for posting data to servlets or CGI scripts.

The class DatagramSocket supports the use of UDP packets. We don't deal with UDP here because it is much less widely used than TCP. Most people want the reliability feature that TCP offers. Ironically, the widespread use of subnets using directly connected switches (instead of shared ethernet) has made UDP much more reliable, to the point where people are using it on LANs instead of TCP, and getting performance *and* reliability.

Let me try that last sentence again. When we started extensive networking in the late 1970s, ethernet was the medium of choice. You strung a single ethernet cable down a corridor and workstations physically attached to the net by tapping into the cable. That meant that all the network traffic was visible to all the workstations that used that cable. It was electronically noisy and slow. Today, nearly everyone uses 10baseT or 100baseT wiring. The number is the speed in Megabits, and the "T" part means "Twisted pair." There is a twisted pair wire from your workstation directly to the switch that controls your subnet. No other workstation shares your twisted pair wiring. Result: faster performance, less electronic noise, and more reliable subnets, leading to greater confidence using UDP.

TCP/IP Client/Server Model

Before we look at actual Java code, a diagram is in order showing how a client and server typically communicate over a TCP/IP network connection. Figure 17-3 shows the way the processes contact each other is by knowing the IP address (which identifies a unique computer on the Internet) and a port number (which is a simple software convention the OS maintains, allowing an incoming network connection to be directed to a specific process).

What Is a Socket?

A socket is defined as "an IP address plus a port on that computer."

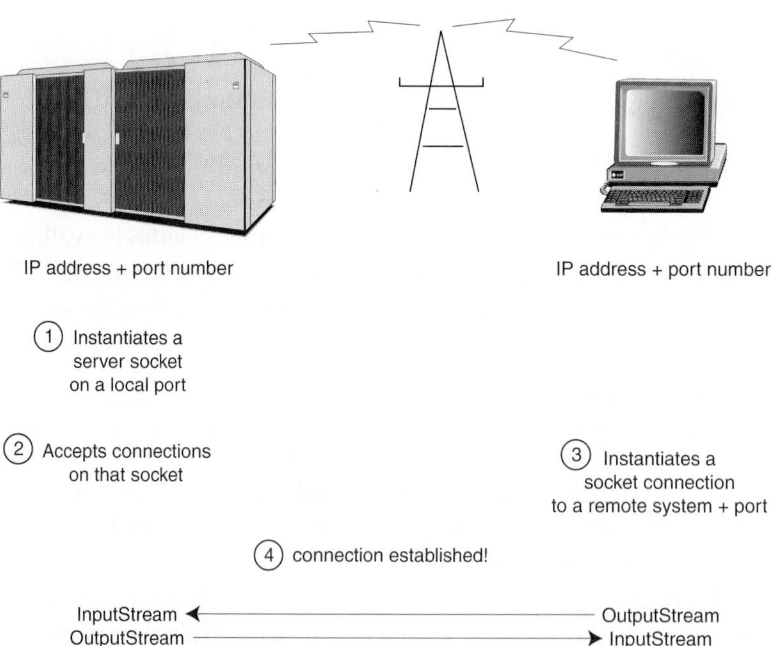
IP address + port number
IP address + port number
1 Instantiates a server socket on a local port
2 Accepts connections on that socket
3 Instantiates a socket connection to a remote system + port
4 connection established!
InputStream
OutputStream
OutputStream
InputStream

Figure 17–3 Client and server communication using a TCP/IP connection.

An IP address is like a telephone number, and a port number is like an extension at that number. Together they specify a unique destination. As a matter of fact, a socket is *defined* as an IP address and a port number.

The client and server must agree on the same port number. The port numbers under 1024 are reserved for system software use and on Unix can only be accessed by the superuser.

For simplicity, network socket connections are made to look like I/O streams. You simply read and write data using the usual stream methods (all socket communication is in 8-bit bytes), and it automagically appears at the other end. Unlike a stream, a socket supports two-way communication. There is a method to get the input stream of a socket, and another method to get the output stream. This allows the client and server to talk back and forth.

Almost all Internet programs work as client/server pairs. The server is on a host system somewhere in cyberspace, and the client is a program running on your local system. When the client wants an Internet service (such as retrieving a web page from an HTTP server), it issues a request, usually to a symbolic address such as www.sun.com rather than to an IP address (though that works, too).

There will be a Domain Name Server locally (usually one per subnet, per campus, or per company) that resolves the symbolic name into an Internet address.

The bits forming the request are assembled into a *datagram* and routed to the server. The server reads the incoming packets, notes what the request is, where it came from, and then tries to respond to it by providing either the service (web page, shell account, file contents, etc.) or a sensible error message. The response is sent back across the Internet to the client.

All the standard Internet utilities (telnet, rdist, FTP, ping, rcp, NFS, and so on) operate in client/server mode connected by a TCP or UDP socket. Programs that send mail don't really know how to send mail—they just know how to take it to the Post Office. In this case, mail has a socket connection and talks to a demon at the other end with a fairly simple protocol. The standard mail demon knows how to accept text and addresses from clients and transmit it for delivery. If you can talk to the mail demon, you can send mail. There is little else to it.

Many of the Internet services are actually quite simple. But often considerable frustration comes in doing the socket programming in C and in learning the correct protocol. The socket programming API presented to C is quite low-level and all too easy to screw up. Needless to say, errors are poorly handled and diagnosed. As a result, many programmers naturally conclude that sockets are brittle and hard to use. Sockets aren't hard to use. The C socket API is hard to use.

The C code to establish a socket connection is:

Horrid C Sockets

```
  int set_up_socket(u_short port) {
    char   myname[MAXHOSTNAME+1];
    int    s;
    struct sockaddr_in sa;
    struct hostent *he;

    bzero(&sa,sizeof(struct sockaddr_in));     /* clear the address */
    gethostname(myname,MAXHOSTNAME);           /* establish identity */
    he= gethostbyname(myname);                 /* get our address   */
    if (he == NULL)                            /* if addr not found... */
        return(-1);
    sa.sin_family= he->h_addrtype;             /* host address */
    sa.sin_port= htons(port);                  /* port number */

if ((s= socket(AF_INET,SOCK_STREAM,0)) <0)     /* finally, create socket */
        return(-1);
    if (bind(s, &sa, sizeof(sa), 0) < 0) {
        close(s);
        return(-1);                            /* bind address to socket */
    }

    listen(s, 3);                              /* max queued connections */
    return(s);
  }
```

By way of contrast, the equivalent Java code is:

```
ServerSocket servsock = new ServerSocket(port, 3);
```

That's it! Just one line of Java code to do all the things the C code does.

Java handles all that socket complexity "under the covers" for you. It doesn't expose the full range of socket possibilities, so Java avoids the novice socketeer choosing contradictory options. On the other hand, a few recondite sockety things cannot be done in Java. You cannot create a raw socket in Java, and hence cannot write a ping program that relies on raw sockets (you can do something just as good though). The benefit is overwhelming: You can open sockets and start writing to another system just as easily as you open a file and start writing to hard disk.

A "ping program," in case you're wondering, is a program that sends ICMP control packets over to another machine anywhere on the Internet. This action is called "pinging" the remote system, rather like the sonar in a ship "pings" for submarines or schools of fish. The control packets aren't passed up to the application layer, but tell the TCP/IP library at the remote end to send back a reply. The reply lets the pinger calculate how quickly data can pass between the two systems.

The Story of Ping

If you want to know how quickly your packets can reach a system, use ping.

```
c:\> ping java.sun.com
Pinging java.sun.com [192.18.97.71] with 32 bytes of data:
Reply from 192.18.97.71: bytes=32 time=163ms TTL=241
Ping statistics for 192.18.97.71:
    Packets: Sent = 4, Received = 4, Lost = 0 (0% loss),
Approximate round trip times in milli-seconds:
    Minimum = 160ms, Maximum =  169ms, Average =  163ms
```

This confirms that the time for a packet to hustle over from Mountain View to Cupertino is about 0.16 seconds on this particular day and time. "TTL" is "Time to Live." To prevent infinite loops, each router hop decrements this field in a packet, and if it reaches zero, the packet just expires where it is.

The most used methods in the API for the client end of a socket are:

```
public class Socket extends Object {
    public Socket();
    public Socket(String,int) throws UnknownHostException,
                                java.io.IOException;
    public Socket(InetAddress,int) throws java.io.IOException;

    public java.nio.channels.SocketChannel getChannel();
    public InputStream getInputStream() throws IOException;
    public OutputStream getOutputStream()
                                throws IOException;

     public synchronized void setSoTimeout(int) throws SocketException;
     public synchronized void close() throws IOException;

    public boolean isConnected();
    public boolean isBound();
    public boolean isClosed();
    public boolean isInputShutdown();
     public boolean isOutputShutdown();

     public boolean shutdownOutput() throws IOException;
     public boolean shutdownInput() throws IOException;
     public static void setSocketImplFactory(
                                          SocketImplFactory fac);
}
```

The constructor with no arguments creates an unconnected socket which you can later `bind()` to a host and port you specify. After binding, you will `connect()` it. It's easier just to do all this by specifying these arguments in the constructor, if you know them at that point.

The `setSoTimeout(int ms)` will set a timeout on the socket of ms milliseconds. When this is a non-zero amount, a read call on the input stream will block for only this amount of time. Then it will break out of it by throwing a java.net.SocketTimeoutException, but leaving the socket still valid for further use.

The `setSocketFactory()` method is a hook for those sites that want to provide their own implementation of sockets, usually to deal with firewall or proxy issues. If this is done, it will be done on a site-wide basis, and individual programmers won't have to worry about it.

The socket API has one or two dozen other get/set methods for TCP socket options. Most of the time you don't need these and can ignore them.

A Client Socket in Java

This section shows a simple example of using a socket to communicate with another computer. You should type this code in and try it. If you haven't done much network programming, you'll find it a gleeful experience as you network with systems around the planet, and even in space. The space shuttle has a TCP/IP connection to Mission Control, but the spoilsports at NASA keep its address secret.

There is an Internet protocol known as Network Time Protocol or NTP. NTP is used to synchronize the clocks of some computers. Without periodic sync'ing, computer clocks tend to drift out of alignment, causing problems for times they need to agree on, like email and file timestamps. NTP is pretty fancy these days, but a simple part of the protocol involves making a socket connection to a NTP server to get the time.

Our example program will open a socket connection to an NTP server and print out the time it gets back. The way a client asks for the time is simply to make a socket connection to port 13 on an NTP server. Port 13 is the Internet standard on all computers for the time of day port. You don't have to identify yourself or write some data indicating what you want. Just making the socket connection is enough to get the server to give you an answer. Java does all the work of assembling the bytes into packets, sending them, and giving you an input stream with the bytes coming back from the server.

Here is a Java program that connects to an NTP server and asks the time:

```
import java.io.*;
import java.net.*;
public class AskTime {

    public static void main(String a[]) throws Exception {
        if (a.length!=1) {
            System.out.println("usage:  java AskTime <systemname> ");
            System.exit(0);
        }

        String machine = a[0];
        final int daytimeport = 13;
        Socket so = new Socket(machine, daytimeport);
        BufferedReader br =
               new BufferedReader( new InputStreamReader(
                         so.getInputStream() ) );
        String timestamp = br.readLine();
        System.out.println( machine + " says it is " + timestamp );
    }
}
```

The program expects the name of an NTP server to be passed to it on the commandline. There are about 200,000 NTP servers on the Internet. Several national standards organizations allow reading the time via NTP. Table 17-1 gives some addresses for the service.

Table 17–1 Some Global Timeservers

Organization	NTP Server	IP Address
Silicon Graphics Inc., Mtn. View, CA, USA	clock.sgi.com	192.48.153.74
Physikalisch-Technischen Bundesanstalt, Germany	ptbtime1.ptb.de	194.95.250.35
Mass Inst. Technology, USA	tick.mit.edu	18.145.0.30
US Naval Observatory, Washington, DC	tock.usno.navy.mil	192.5.41.41
Univ. of Adelaide, Australia	ntp.adelaide.edu.au	129.127.40.3
Inet Inc., Seoul, Korea	time.nuri.net	203.255.12.4

These servers come and go. Do a web search on "NTP server" for a current list. When you run the program, giving a hostname as argument, you see this:

```
% java AskTime ntp.adelaide.edu.au
ntp.adelaide.edu.au says it is Wed Oct 17 23:20:32 2001
```

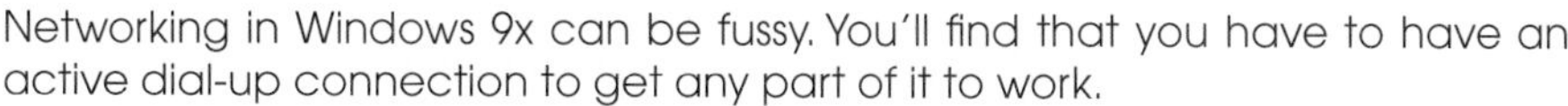

TCP/IP on Windows

Your Java network programs are going to work only if you are using a computer that has an IP address and a connection to a TCP/IP network.

On a Unix workstation, TCP/IP support is a standard part of the operating system. On Windows 95, you'll need to have the TCP/IP protocol stack (library) installed.

Networking in Windows 9x can be fussy. You'll find that you have to have an active dial-up connection to get any part of it to work.

You can even provide the IP address instead of the server name, and the program will work equally well.

This program demonstrates how easy it is to open a socket connection to a port on another computer using the Java networking library. It's just flat out impressive to write a dozen lines of code that can ask a computer anywhere on the planet to tell you the time. Maybe there's something to this Internet thing, after all.

Sockets are used in client or in server mode. The program above is an example of the client use of socket. The client side initiates the contact. It is like knocking on a door or calling a phone number and starting a conversation with whoever answers.

The server side is just sitting there, waiting on a socket until someone shows up to ask for something. We will show how to write a server socket a little later in the chapter. The next topic is another example of how a client can obtain a service by opening a socket connection and writing to it. The example here is sending email, by writing to the mailserver port which (as another Internet standard) lives on port 25.

Sending Email by Java

As our next example, let's write a Java program to send some email. Email is sent by socketed communication with port 25 on a computer system. All we are going to do is open a socket connected to port 25 on some system that is running a mail server and speak "mail protocol" to the sendmail demon at the other end. If we speak the mail protocol correctly, it will listen to what we say, and send the email for us.

The following below requires an Internet standard mail (SMTP) program running on the server. If your server has some non-standard proprietary mail program on it, you're out of luck. You can check which program you have by telnetting to port 25 on the server, and seeing if you get a mail server to talk to you.

There are two wrinkles to this approach. First, it became common for spammers to steal time on other people's mailservers to relay their spam. As a result, most mail servers are now selective about who they accept a connection from. You won't be able to get mailers around the world to talk to you, just your ISP mail server. Second, Java now has a mail API with a somewhat higher-level interface, so you don't need to understand individual mail commands. But the point here is to show some give and take over a socket connection. Again, this example shows the client end of the socket connection.

The code to send email is:

```
import java.io.*;
import java.net.*;
public class email {

  public static void main(String args[]) throws IOException {
     Socket sock;
     DataInputStream dis;
     PrintStream ps;

     sock = new Socket("localhost", 25);
     dis = new DataInputStream( sock.getInputStream());
     ps = new PrintStream( sock.getOutputStream());

     ps.println("mail from: trelford");
     System.out.println( dis.readLine() );

     String Addressee= "linden";
     ps.println("rcpt to: " + Addressee );
     System.out.println( dis.readLine() );

     ps.println("data");
     System.out.println( dis.readLine() );

     ps.println("This is the message\n that Java sent");
     ps.println(".");
     System.out.println( dis.readLine() );

     ps.flush();
     sock.close();
  }
}
```

Running this program will send email to the addressee. Many of the Internet services are like this one. You set up a socket connection and talk a simple protocol to tell the server at the other end what you want.

Note that the main() routine has been declared as throwing an Exception. This is a shortcut, permissible in development, to save the necessity of handling any exceptions that might be raised. It only works because exceptions are not considered part of the signature of a method. In production code, it is important to catch and handle any exceptions.

You can find all the Internet Protocols described in documents in *Request For Comments* (RFCs), the format in which they were originally issued, available online at: *www.internic.net/std*. The mail RFC is RFC821.txt.

You can find all the WWW protocols described in documents linked to from the URL *www.w3.org/pub/WWW/Protocols/*. A careful study of some of these documents will often answer any protocol questions you have.

You can find more information on the Java mail API at *java.sun.com/products/javamail/*.

If you write a simple Swing GUI around this mail-sending code, you've written a mailer program! It's not that hard to get the RFCs for the POP3 and IMAP[1] protocols and write the code to read and display incoming mail, too.

1. POP3 is "Post Office Protocol 3," and IMAP is "Internet Mail Access Protocol," different standards for the client end of mail systems. POP3 downloads mail and keeps it on the client. IMAP keeps the mail on the server, which is more convenient if you read it from several different computers.

A Server Socket in Java

This section shows a simple example of creating a *server* socket to listen for incoming requests. We could write the server side of a simple NTP server, but let's try something a little more ambitious. It should be fairly clear at this point that HTTP is just another of the many protocols that use sockets to run over the Internet.

A web *browser* is a client program that sends requests through a socket to the HTTP port on a server and displays the data that the server sends back. A basic web browser can be written in a couple of hundred lines of code if you have a GUI component that renders HTML, which Java does.

A web *server* is a server program that waits for incoming requests on the HTTP port and acts on those to send the contents of local files back to the requestor. It can be implemented in just a few dozen lines of code.

Security of Network Programs—A Cautionary Tale!

Be very careful when you start developing networked programs on your computer. Before you try it at work, check if there is a company policy about network use. You can get fired for doing the wrong thing!

The problem is that any server sockets you create may be visible more widely than you intended. If you are running this at home, and you are not using a firewall, your server socket will be visible to the entire net. That's like leaving the front door of your home wide open.

When I was developing the HTTP server in Java for this chapter, I left it running on my PC to test it. Someone's automated port scanner script soon noticed my server, made an unauthorized connection to it, and issued this HTTP command:

```
GET /scripts/..%%35c../winnt/system32/cmd.exe?/c+dir HTTP/1.0
```

This is an attempt to break out of the scripts directory, run a shell, and do a "dir" to see what's on my system. Crackers will try to add their own backdoor on your computer where you'll never find it. Then they can use your system whenever it's on the net (they love cable modems) for such things as distributed denial of service attacks. My server was logging client requests, but not fulfilling them, so the nimrod was out of luck. But be careful out there; people are actively looking for systems to break into.

The example here is part of the code for a web server. This is the code that opens a server socket on the http port, port 80, and listens for requests from web browsers. We echo the requests, but don't act on them.

The code is split into two classes to better show what's happening. The first class is the main program. It instantiates a server socket on port 80 (use port 1080 if you're on a Unix system without root access). The code then does an accept() on the server socket, waiting for client connections to come in. When one does come in, the program creates a new object to deal with that one connection and invokes its getRequest() method.

```
public class HTTPServer {
    public static void main(String a[]) throws Exception {
        final int httpd = 80;
        ServerSocket ssock = new ServerSocket(httpd);
        System.out.println("have opened port 80 locally");

        Socket sock = ssock.accept();
        System.out.println("client has made socket connection");

        OneConnection client = new OneConnection(sock);
        String s = client.getRequest();
    }
}
```

There are only two new lines of code in this server program. This line:

```
ServerSocket ssock = new ServerSocket(httpd);
```

and this line:

```
Socket sock = ssock.accept(); // on the server
```

The first line instantiates a server socket on the given port (httpd is an int with the value 80). The second line does an accept() on this server socket. It will block or wait here until some client somewhere on the net opens a connection to the same port, like this:

```
clientSock = new Socket("somehost", 80); // on the client
```

At that point, the accept() method is able to complete, and it returns a new instance of a socket to the server. The rest of this conversation will be conducted over the new socket, thus freeing up the original socket to do another accept() and wait for another client. At the client end, the socket doesn't appear to change.

In a real server, the code will loop around and accept another connection. We'll get to that. Here is the second half of the code: the OneConnection class that the main program uses to do the work for a single client request.

```
import java.io.*;
import java.net.*;
class OneConnection {
    Socket sock;
    BufferedReader in = null;
    DataOutputStream out = null;

    OneConnection(Socket sock) throws Exception{
        this.sock = sock;
          in  = new BufferedReader(
          new InputStreamReader( sock.getInputStream() ) );
          out = new DataOutputStream(sock.getOutputStream());
    }

    String getRequest() throws Exception {
        String s=null;
        while ( (s=in.readLine())!=null) {
             System.out.println("got: "+s);
        }
        return s;
    }
}
```

The constructor keeps a copy of the socket that leads back to the client and opens the input and output streams. Sockets always do I/O on bytes, not Unicode chars. HTTP is a line-oriented protocol. We push a BufferedReader onto the input stream so we can use the convenient readLine() method. DataInputStream has one of those too, but it is deprecated.

If you're using a binary protocol, do everything with streams, not readers/writers. We wrap a DataOutputStream on the output side of the socket. We don't write anything in this version of the program, but we will soon develop it and start writing.

Socket Protocols

The getRequest() method reads successive lines from the socket and echoes them on the server. How does it know when to stop reading lines? This is one of the tricky things with sockets—they cannot tell the difference between "end of input" and "there is more input, but it is delayed coming through the network."

To cope with this inability to know when it's done, socket protocols use one of three approaches:

- have the client precede each message by a number giving the length of the following message. Or use some other indication to end transmission, such as sending a blank line.
- have the client close its output stream, using `sock.shutDownOutput()`. That causes the next read at the server end to return -1.
- set a timeout on the socket, using `sock.setSoTimeout(int ms)`. With this set to a non-zero amount, a read call on the input stream will block for only this amount of time. Then it will break out of it by throwing a java.net.SocketTimeoutException, but leaving the socket still valid for further use.

The third approach, using timeouts, is the least reliable because timeouts are always too long (wasting time) or too short (missing input). HTTP uses a mixture of approaches one and two.

Running the HTTP Server Program

Compile the code and then run the program. Make sure you run it on a computer that is not already running a web-server, otherwise it will find that it cannot claim port 80. If all is well, the program will print out:

```
java HTTPServer
have opened port 80 locally!
```

then it will block, waiting for an incoming request on the port. This is exactly what a webserver does: opens port 80 and waits for incoming socket connections from clients.

Loopback Address

Every computer system on the Internet has a unique IP address consisting of four groups of digits separated by periods like this: 204.156.141.229

They are currently revising and increasing the IP address specification so that there will be enough new IP addresses to give one to every conceivable embedded processor on earth, and a few nearby friendly planets. These version 6 addresses look like: 1080:0:0:0:8:800:200C:417A

One special version 4 IP address is: 127.0.0.1. This is the "loopback" address used in testing and debugging. If a computer sends a packet to this address, it is routed to itself, without actually leaving the system. Thus, this special address can be used to run Internet software even if you are not connected to the Internet. Set your system up so that the Internet services it will be requesting are all at the loopback address. Make sure your system is actually running the demons corresponding to the services you want to use.

The hostname for the loopback address is "localhost," if you are requesting services by name rather than IP address. On any system, you should be able to enter the command "ping localhost" and have it echo a reply from the loopback IP address. If you can't do this, it indicates that your TCP/IP stack is not set up properly.

Here's the interesting part. You can make that connection using any web browser! Just start up your browser and direct it to the computer where you are running the Java program. You can run your browser on a different system altogether, and give it the name of the computer running the Java program.Or, if you are running everything on one computer, the name will be "localhost," and the URL will be something like:

```
http://localhost/a/b/c/d.html
```

The rest of the URL doesn't matter since our server program doesn't (yet) do anything with the incoming request. You will see the Java server print out the message that a socket connection has been made ("got a socket"), and then print the HTTP text it receives on the socket from the browser!

```
got a socket
got: GET /a/b/c/d.html HTTP/1.1
got: Accept: image/gif, image/x-xbitmap, image/jpeg, image/pjpeg, */*
got: Accept-Language: en-us
got: Accept-Encoding: gzip, deflate
got: User-Agent: Mozilla/4.0 (compatible; MSIE 5.5; Windows NT 4.0)
got: Host: localhost
got: Connection: Keep-Alive
got:
```

These strings are HTTP headers. They are created by the browser to tell the server what file it has asked for, and they provide information about what kinds of format the browser can accept back.

A couple more points to note here. First, almost all servers uses threads. That way, they can serve the client and at the same time accept further requests. We will shortly show the code to do this. Second, these dozen or so lines of server code are at the heart of every webserver. If you add a couple of routines to read whatever file the browser asks for and write it into the socket, you have written a webserver. Let's do it.

The ServerSocket API is:

```
public class ServerSocket {
    public ServerSocket() throws IOException;
    public ServerSocket(int) throws IOException;
    public ServerSocket(int,int) throws IOException;
    public ServerSocket(int,int,InetAddress) throws IOException;

    public Socket accept() throws java.io.IOException;
    public void close() throws java.io.IOException;
    public java.nio.channels.ServerSocketChannel getChannel();

    public void bind(SocketAddress) throws IOException;
    public void bind(SocketAddress, int) throws IOException;
    public boolean isBound();
    public InetAddress getInetAddress();
    public int getLocalPort();

    public boolean isClosed();
    public synchronized void setSoTimeout(int) throws SocketException;
    public synchronized int getSoTimeout() throws java.io.IOException;
    public static synchronized void setSocketFactory(SocketImplFactory)
              throws IOException;
     public synchronized void setReceiveBufferSize(int) throws
SocketException;
    public synchronized int getReceiveBufferSize() throws SocketException;
}
```

The accept() method listens for a client trying to make a connection and accepts it. It creates a fresh socket for the server end of the connection, leaving the server socket free to do more accepts.

The bind() method is used to connect an existing socket to a particular IP address and port. You would use this when you want to use channels instead of streams for socket I/O; there's an example at the end of the chapter.

The other methods should be clear from their names. There are other methods in the API, but these are the main ones you will use.

Debugging Sockets

The little HTTPServer program we just saw can be used to help debug some server socket problems. You can see exactly what headers the browser sends you for different HTML requests. It works for other protocols too. If you make the code listen on another port, you can look at the incoming stream there.

Standing on the Corner, Watching All the Packets Go By

The server program, shown on the previous pages, will echo all the input that is sent to one socket. This is similar to the way that the FBI's controversial Carnivore program works.

Carnivore was created so that the FBI could do the online equivalent of phone tapping. It works at the more fundamental level of individual packets rather than sockets, but the principle is the same.

Carnivore is basically a packet sniffer that can be installed at an ISP and directed to copy packets that meet certain criteria (to or from a given IP address, for example). In this way, Carnivore can give the FBI a copy of all the email, all the web site visits, all the telnet sessions for a particular target over the course of a month or more. A court order is needed to authorize each use of Carnivore.

The FBI made a PR error by giving the program such an aggressive name. Law enforcement needs access to these tools to track down online fraud, network disruption, and other crimes. But they would have done themselves a favor by calling the software something calmer like "Old Packet Collector."

Another debugging technique uses the telnet program to look at incoming text to a client socket. Telnet's actual purpose is to open a command shell on a remote computer. The lines you type are sent over the socket connection, and the responses sent back the same way. However, you can tell telnet to use any port. The stream that it receives on that port will be displayed in the telnet window, and the things you type will be sent through the socket back to the server. The characters you type will be sent to the other end, but not echoed however.

Telnet is just a quick and dirty debugging technique to help you see what's going on. Figure 17-4 uses telnet to see what an NTP server is sending back. Most servers will close a socket as soon as they have given you the requested information, hence the "connection lost" pop-up window. There is also a "keep-alive" option to a socket that requests the connection be retained for expected use in the very near future. This is useful for HTTP.

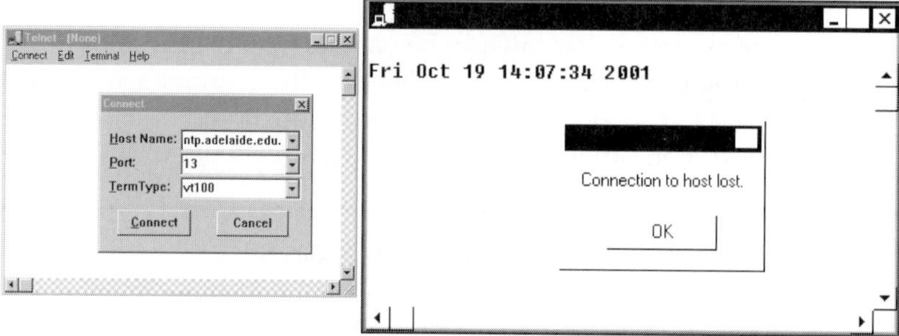

Figure 17–4 Debugging with Telnet.

These days you should avoid the use of telnet and ftp for their main purpose, as they send passwords "in the clear" to the remote socket. They are thus vulnerable to packet-sniffing by crackers at routers. Use SSH, the secure shell, instead. There is a Java implementation of SSH on the CD that comes with this book.

Using Netstat

Another useful tool for seeing what is going on with your network connection is netstat. It is available on Windows and Unix. Run netstat like this:

```
c:\> netstat
Active Connections
  Proto  Local Address        Foreign Address             State
  TCP    h:1891               images-vdc.amazon.com:80    ESTABLISHED
  TCP    h:1902               images-vdc.amazon.com:80    ESTABLISHED
  TCP    h:1426               afu.com:143                 ESTABLISHED
  TCP    h:1025               localhost:1028              ESTABLISHED
  TCP    h:1028               localhost:1025              ESTABLISHED
```

This shows all the current IP connections, the local socket, the remote socket, and the state. Netstat lets you see if you can at least make a connection to a remote system.

The "-?" option to netstat will give you a message about other options.

Finally, there's a very helpful website at *straylight.cso.niu.edu*. You can use one of their webpages (specifically, *straylight.cso.niu.edu/cgi-bin/test-cgi.cmd*) to see what is happening with your HTML pages. If you specify that web page as the "Action" value for an HTML form, when you press the "submit" button, the script will echo back to you everything that your form sent across. If this site goes

off the net, try doing a websearch for "CGI test forms". Using an echo script makes it easy to see what is going on, and hence what you need to correct.

Getting the HTTP Command

Let's add a few lines of code (in bold) to our server to extract the HTTP "GET" command that says what file the browser is looking for. We will develop this example by extending the OneConnection class. That way, we will add just the new code in the child class, and use the existing methods from the parent. The code in the new child class is:

```
class OneConnection_A extends OneConnection {


    OneConnection_A(Socket sock) throws Exception {
        super(sock);
    }


    String getRequest() throws Exception {
        String s=null;
        while ( (s=in.readLine())!=null) {
            System.out.println("got: "+s);
            if (s.indexOf("GET") > -1) {
                out.writeBytes("HTTP-1.0 200 OK\r\n");
                s = s.substring(4);
                int i = s.indexOf(" ");
                    System.out.println("file: "+ s.substring(0, i));
                return s.substring(0, i);
            }
        }
        return null;
    }
}
```

The getRequest() method now looks at incoming HTTP headers to find the one containing a GET command. When it finds it, it writes an acknowledgement back to the browser (the "200 OK" line), and extracts the filename from the GET header. The filename is the return value of the method.

The main program will need to construct the OneConnection_A object and then call its getRequest() method. From here it is a small step to actually get that file and write it into the socket.

Never Use println() with Sockets!

The println() method is defined to output the platform specific line separator. This will be "\n" on Unix, "\r" on Macs, and "\r\n" on Windows.

However, lots of TCP/IP protocols are line based, and the line is defined to end with carriage return line feed "\r\n", or just line feed "\n". So if you're on a Mac, the println method won't output something that a socket server recognizes as a complete end of line sequence.

The Mac client will do a println, which sends a "\r", and then wait for a response from the server. The server will get the "\r" and wait for a "\n" to complete the end of line sequence. Result: deadlock! Each end is waiting for something from the other. See Apple Tech Note 1157 for more on this:

developer.apple.com/technotes/tn/tn1157.html

The solution is to never use println with remote protocols on any platform. Always use explicit "\r\n" characters when writing to a socket.

Here's a new class that is a child of OneConnection_A; it adds a method to get the file of the given name and write it into the socket. Since it knows how big the file is, it might as well generate the HTTP header that gives that information.

```
class OneConnection_B extends OneConnection_A {

    OneConnection_B(Socket sock) throws Exception {
        super(sock);
    }

    void sendFile(String fname) throws Exception {
        String where = "/tmp/" + fname;
        if (where.indexOf("..") > -1)
            throw new SecurityException("No access to parent dirs");
        System.out.println("looking for " + where);
        File f = new File(where);
        DataInputStream din = new DataInputStream(
                                    new FileInputStream(f) );
        int len = (int) f.length();
        byte[] buf = new byte[len];
        din.readFully(buf);
        out.writeBytes("Content-Length: " + len + "\r\n");
        out.writeBytes("Content-Type: text/html\r\n\r\n");
        out.write(buf);
        out.flush();
        out.close();
    }
}
```

The main program will need to construct the OneConnection_B object and then add a call to its send file method. Now that our server has the ability to return files we need to build in some security. The first few lines of the method prepend the string "/tmp/" onto the filename. The code also checks that the filename does not contain the string ".." to enter a parent directory. These two limitations together ensure that the server will only return files from your \tmp directory.

The "Content-Length" and "Content-Type" are two standard HTTP headers that help the browser deal with what you send it. The blank line tells the browser that is the end of the headers and the text that follows should be displayed.

At this point you should try compiling the code, placing a test html file in the \tmp directory, and then starting the server. Browse the URL *localhost/tmp/example.html* and check that the browser displays the file correctly.

We have completed a basic webserver. That's quite an accomplishment! The next section looks at client side sockets again, in particular how to use a socket to pull information from a web page. It then shows the same task done by a URLConnection. We then describe the class that represents IP addresses and finish the chapter by making the web server multithreaded.

HTTP and Web Browsing: Retrieving HTTP Pages

Here is an example of interacting with an HTTP server to retrieve a web page from a system on the network. This shows how easy it is to post information to HTML forms. Forms are covered in more depth in the chapter on servlets, and you may want to refresh your memory on that section.

For the impatient, HTML forms allow you to type some information in your browser which is sent back to the server for processing. The information may be encoded as part of the URL, or sent separately in name/value pairs.

The Yahoo site is a wide-ranging access portal. They offer online stock quotes that you can read in your browser. I happen to know (by looking at the URL field of my browser) that a request for a stock quote for ABCD is translated to a socket connection of:

```
http://finance.yahoo.com/q?s=abcd
```

That's equivalent to opening a socket on port 80 of finance.yahoo.com and sending a "get /q?s=abcd." You can make that self same request yourself, in either of two ways. You can open a socket connection to port 80, the http port. Or you can open a URL connection which offers a simpler, higher-level interface. We'll show both of these here. Here's the stock finder done with sockets:

```
import java.io.*;
import java.net.*;
public class Stock {

    public static void main(String a[]) throws Exception {
        if (a.length!=1) {
            System.out.println("usage:  java Stock <symbol> ");
            System.exit(0);
        }

        String yahoo = "finance.yahoo.com";
        final int httpd = 80;
        Socket sock = new Socket(yahoo, httpd);

        BufferedWriter out =
               new BufferedWriter( new OutputStreamWriter(
                                    sock.getOutputStream() ) );

        String cmd = "GET /q?" +"s=" +a[0] +"\n";
        out.write(cmd);
        out.flush();

      BufferedReader in =new BufferedReader(
          new InputStreamReader( sock.getInputStream() ) );
      String s=null;
        int i, j;
      // pick out the stock price from the pile of HTML
      // it's in bold, so get the number following "<b>"
        while ( (s=in.readLine()) != null)  {
             if (s.length()<25) continue;
             if ((i=s.indexOf(a[0].toUpperCase())) < 0) continue;
             s=s.substring(i);
             if ((i=s.indexOf("<b>")) < 0) continue;
             j = s.indexOf("</b>");
             s=s.substring(i+3,j);
             System.out.println(a[0] +" is at "+s);
             break;
        }
    }
}
```

The Yahoo page that returns stock quotes contains thousands of characters of hrefs to ads and formatting information. It consists of many HTML lines like this:

```
a href="/q?s=SUNW&d=t">SUNW</a></td><td nowrap
align=center>12:03PM</td><td nowrap><b>9.55</b><
```

Luckily it's fairly easy to pull out the stock price. From inspecting the output, it's on a line with more than 25 chars. The line contains the stock symbol rewritten in upper case. The number we want is bracketed by <b> ... </b>, which is the HTML to print the number in bold face.

Given all that, running the program provides this output:

```
java Stock ibm
ibm is at 101.26
```

It was a lot more fun running this program in the year 2000. Here is the same program, rewritten to use the classes URL and URLConnection. Obviously, URL represents a URL, and URLConnection represents a socket connection to that URL. The code to do the same work as before, but using URLConnection is:

```
import java.io.*;
import java.net.*;
public class Stock2 {

    public static void main(String a[]) throws Exception {
        if (a.length!=1) {
            System.out.println("usage:  java Stock <symbol> ");
            System.exit(0);
        }

        String yahoo = "http://finance.yahoo.com/q";

        URL url = new URL(yahoo);
        URLConnection conn = url.openConnection();
        conn.setDoOutput(true);
        PrintWriter pw = new PrintWriter( conn.getOutputStream());
        pw.print("s=" + a[0]);
        pw.close();

        BufferedReader in = new BufferedReader( new InputStreamReader(
                                             conn.getInputStream()));
        String s=null, stock=a[0].toUpperCase();
        int i=0,j=0;
        while ( (s=in.readLine()) != null)  {
           if (s.length()<25) continue;
             if ((i=s.indexOf(a[0].toUpperCase())) < 0) continue;
             s=s.substring(i);
             if ((i=s.indexOf("<b>")) < 0) continue;
             j = s.indexOf("</b>");
             s=s.substring(i+3,j);
             System.out.println(a[0] +" is at "+s);
             break;
        }
    }
}
```

The main difference here is that we form a URL for the site and file (script) that we want to reference. Then we open a connection to the URL, tell it that we are going to do output to it, and write the "name=value" parameter. We finish up as before, reading what the socket writes back and extracting the characters of interest. Clearly, this program will stop working when Yahoo changes the format of the page, but it demonstrates how we can use a URL and URLConnection for a slightly higher-level interface than a socket connection. We could even go one step further and use the class HttpURLConnection which is a subclass of URL-Connection. Please look at the HTML documentation for information on these classes.

A URL can pose a security risk, since you can pass along information even by reading a URL. Requesting *www.cia.gov/cgi-bin/cgi.exe/secretinfo* passes "secret-info" along to the CGI script, for example. Since requesting a URL can send out information just as a Socket can, requesting a URL has the same security model as access to Sockets. Namely, an applet can only open a socket connection back to the server from which the applet came. Security is also the reason that an applet may not open a socket connection to any other system except its server. Otherwise, it could look at information on its subnet behind the firewall, and send it back to crackers everywhere.

If you are behind a firewall (and who isn't these days?) you will need to tell Java the details of your proxy server and port in order to access hosts outside the firewall. You do this by defining properties, perhaps when starting the code:

```
java -DproxySet=true -DproxyHost=SOMEHOST -DproxyPort=SOMENUM code.java
```

Without this, you'll get an UnknownHostException. The proxy settings are needed for both java.net.URLConnection and for java.net.Sockets. At work, your systems administrator will know the values. At home, you won't be using a proxy server unless you set it up yourself.

How to Find the IP Address Given to a Machine Name

The class java.net.InetAddress represents IP addresses and about one dozen common operations on them. The class should have been called IP or IPAddress, but was not (presumably because such a name does not match the coding conventions for classnames). Common operations on IP addresses are things like: turning an IP address into the characters that represent the corresponding domain name, turning a host name into an IP address, determining if a given address belongs to the system you are currently executing on, and so on.

InetAddress has two subclasses:

- `Inet4Address` — The class that represents classic, version 4, 32-bit IP addresses
- `Inet6Address` — The class that represents version 6 128-bit IP addresses

Your programs will not use these classes directly very much, as you can create sockets using domain and host names. Further, in most of the places where a hostname is expected (such as in a URL), a String that contains an IP address will work equally well. However, if native code passes you an IP address, these classes give you a way to work on it.

The InetAddress class does not have any public constructors. Applications should use the methods getLocalHost(), getByName(), or getAllByName() to create a new InetAddress instance. The program that follows show examples of each of these.

This code will be able to find the IP address of all computers it knows about. That may mean all systems that have an entry in the local hosts table, or (if it is served by a name server) the domain of the name server, which could be as extensive as a large subnet or the entire organization.

```
import java.io.*;
import java.net.*;
public class addr {

    public static void main(String a[]) throws Exception {

        InetAddress me = InetAddress.getByName("localhost");
        PrintStream o = System.out;
        o.println("localhost by name =" + me );

        InetAddress me2 = InetAddress.getLocalHost();
        o.println("localhost by getLocalHost =" + me2 );

        InetAddress[] many = InetAddress.getAllByName("microsoft.com");
        for (int i=0; i<many.length; i++)
              o.println( many[i] );
    }
}
```

Run it with:

```
java addr

localhost by name =localhost/127.0.0.1
localhost by getLocalHost =zap/10.0.10.175
Microsoft: microsoft.com/207.46.230.218
Microsoft: microsoft.com/207.46.230.219
Microsoft: microsoft.com/207.46.197.100
Microsoft: microsoft.com/207.46.197.101
Microsoft: microsoft.com/207.46.197.102
```

The getAllByName() method reports all the IP addresses associated with a domain name. You can see from the output above that Microsoft.com, like most big sites, is served by multiple IP addresses, on two different subnets (probably for fault tolerance). Each of those five IP addresses probably represents load balancer hardware fanning out to dozens of server nodes.

Some Notes on Protocol and Content Handlers

Some of the Java documentation makes a big production about support for extending the MIME types known to browsers. If it is asked to browse some data whose type it doesn't recognize, it can simply download the code for the appropriate handler based on the name of the datetype and use that to grok the data. This is exactly what happens with plug-ins. If you stumble across a RealAudio file, the browser prompts you to download the plug-in that can play it. Java can make this completely automatic. Or so the theory runs. It hasn't yet been used much in practice.

The theory of the handlers is this. There are two kinds of handler that you can write: protocol handlers and content handlers.

A *protocol handler* talks to other programs. Both ends follow the same protocol in order to communicate structured data between themselves ("After you," "No, I insist—after you.") If you wrote an Oracle database protocol handler, it would deal with SQL queries to pull data out of an Oracle database.

A *content handler* knows how to decode the contents of a file. It handles data (think of it as the contents of something pointed to by a URL). It gets the bytes and assembles them into an object. If you wrote an MPEG content handler, it would then be able to play MPEG movies in your browser, once you had brought the data over there. Bringing MPEG data to your browser could be done using the FTP protocol, or you might wish to write your own high performance protocol handler.

Content handlers and protocol handlers may be particularly convenient for web browsers, and they may also be useful in stand-alone applications. There is not a lot of practical experience with these handlers in Java yet, so it is hard to offer definitive advice about their use. Some people predict they are going to be very important for decoding file formats of arbitrary kinds, while other people are ready to be convinced by an existence proof.

How to Make an Applet Write a File on the Server

Everyone who writes an applet sooner or later wants to have it write a file back on the server. This is perhaps the most frequently asked question in Java. You might want the high score in a high score file, or have a guestbook that visitors to the page can sign, or count the number of HTTP requests for this page.

If you think about it, giving write access to your server system to anyone anywhere on the Internet is a very bad idea. It would be the equivalent of leaving the keys in your car with the engine running and a sign on the windshield saying, "Help yourself." One of Java's goals is to improve, not undermine, system security and so there is *no* built-in support allowing an applet to directly write to a file on a server. None! You can read a file on the server inside an applet, but you absolutely cannot directly create or write a file on the server unless the server does it for you. But all is not lost. We could write the ping program even though Java doesn't support ICMP.

How can you persuade the server to write a file for you? One possibility is to write a system demon that runs on the server 24 hours a day and listens to a specified port. When one of your applets wants to write a file, it opens a socket on that port on the server, sends commands saying what it wants to do, gives the filename, and then sends the data. This is open to abuse, though. Anyone who knows about this service could similarly connect to that port and fill up your file system with their files. You could lessen the probability of that happening if you protected the service by a password challenge.

The Linlyn Class for File Transfer

Well, what do you know? The previous paragraph is a pretty good description of the standard FTP (file transfer protocol) service. This service will frequently be running on any system that has full TCP/IP support. The standard FTP port is port 21 for commands and port 20 for data. Simply open a socket connection from your applet to port 21 on the server and you can have FTP write the files for you. Of course, you have to know the FTP commands to send, and you have to be able to deal with the password challenge.

Luckily, that work has already been done for you. The request for code to write to the server from an applet is made so frequently that I got together with my colleague, Bob Lynch, and we created the Linlyn class. (Hey, at least the name's not an acronym.) The Linlyn class does easy FTP file transfer from an applet to a server. The Linlyn class was designed with absolute ease-of-use as its foremost consideration, and a copy of it (along with a sample applet) is on the CD in the goodies directory.

The Linlyn class is published under the GNU public license for anyone to use or improve. Be advised that in its standard form you compile the userid and password as a String into the class file. That is appropriate only for use on a secure intranet, and must not be used for an applet that you publish on the Internet. It would be a simple matter, however, for you to prompt the user for the password, instead of hard-coding it in the program. Then you or anyone that you trust with your FTP password (and your credit card, car keys, wallet, etc.) can write files on your server from your applet.

A Multithreaded HTTP Server

There's one improvement that is customary in servers, and we will make it here. For all but the smallest of servers, it is usual to spawn a new thread to handle each request. This has three big advantages:

1. Foremost, it makes the server scalable. The server can accept new requests independent of its speed in handling them. (Of course, you better buy a server that has the mippage to keep up with requests.)
2. By handling each request in a new thread, clients do not have to wait for every request ahead of them to be served.
3. The program source can be better organized, as the server processing is written in a different class.

The following code demonstrates how we would modify our HTTP web server to a new thread for each client request. The first step is to make another child in the One_Connection hierarchy to implement the Runnable interface. Give it a run method that will actually do all the work: get the request, then send the file.

```
import java.io.*;
import java.net.*;
class OneConnection_C extends OneConnection_B
                      implements Runnable {

    OneConnection_C(Socket sock) throws Exception {
        super(sock);
    }

    public void run() {
      try {
        String filename = getRequest();
        sendFile(filename);
      } catch (Exception e) {
        System.out.println("Excpn: " + e);}
    }

}
```

The main program will have the server socket and it will put the accept in a loop (so that we can handle many requests, not just the first one). It will instantiate our connection class as before, turn it into a thread, and invoke its start method. The code follows:

```
public class HTTPServer4 {
    public static void main(String a[]) throws Exception {

        final int httpd = 80;
        ServerSocket ssock = new ServerSocket(httpd);
        while (true) {
            Socket sock = ssock.accept();
            System.out.println("client has made socket connection");
            OneConnection_C client = new OneConnection_C(sock);
            new Thread(client).start();
        }
    }
}
```

The code seems so brief because we have draped the functionality across several classes in an inheritance hierarchy. That was done so that the example code would be smaller and easier to present. You should try putting the code back into one or two classes. It's still only 50 or 60 lines long. This has got to be the world record for the smallest HTTP server.

A Mapped I/O HTTP Server

The final section of this chapter presents the code to use the new mapped I/O facility in a socket server. Sun distributes a sample mapped I/O socket application with JDK 1.4 beta. However, their sample application does not work on Windows 98. It hangs in the accept() statement.

I reported the bug to Sun and hope it will be fixed in the final release. It may not be: after all, mapped I/O is a server feature, and Windows 9x is not a server operating system. Anyway, as a refresher, an example of channel I/O on files would be this program that duplicates a file:

```
import java.io.*;
import java.nio.*;
import java.nio.channels.*;
import java.net.*;
class Files {

    void copyThruChannel(String fname) throws Exception {
        File f = new File(fname);
        FileInputStream fin = new FileInputStream(f);
        int len = (int) f.length();

        FileChannel fc = fin.getChannel();
        System.out.println("allocating buff");
        ByteBuffer myBB = ByteBuffer.allocate(len);
        int bytesRead = fc.read(myBB);
        myBB.flip();

        System.out.println("getting fout channel");
        FileOutputStream fos = new FileOutputStream(fname+".copy.txt");
        FileChannel fco = fos.getChannel();
        int bytesWritten = fco.write(myBB);
        fco.close();
    }

    public static void main(String a[]) throws Exception {

        Files client = new Files();
        client.copyThruChannel(a[0]);
    }
}
```

In a similar way, the code to update our HTTP server, so that it uses channel I/O, looks like this:

```
import java.io.*;
import java.nio.*;
import java.nio.channels.*;
import java.net.*;
class OneConnection_D extends OneConnection_C  {

    OneConnection_D(Socket sock) throws Exception {
        super(sock);
    }

    void sendThruChannel(String fname) throws Exception {
        File f = new File(fname);
        FileInputStream fin = new FileInputStream(f);
        int len = (int) f.length();

        FileChannel fc = fin.getChannel();
        System.out.println("allocating buff");
        ByteBuffer myBB = ByteBuffer.allocate(len);
        int bytesRead = fc.read(myBB);
        myBB.flip();

        System.out.println("getting sock channel");
        SocketChannel sc = sock.getChannel();
        int bytesWritten = sc.write(myBB);
        sc.close();
    }
}

public class HTTPServer4 {
    public static void main(String a[]) throws Exception {

        final int httpd = 80;
        ServerSocketChannel ssc = ServerSocketChannel.open();
        InetSocketAddress isa
        = new InetSocketAddress(InetAddress.getLocalHost(), httpd);
      ssc.socket().bind(isa);
        System.out.println("have opened port 80 locally!");

        System.out.println("waiting for accept");
        Socket sock = ssc.accept();
        System.out.println("client has made socket connection");

        OneConnection_D client = new OneConnection_D(sock);
        String filename = client.getRequest();
        client.sendThruChannel(filename);
    }
}
```

Note: This version is not multithreaded to keep the code focused on the issue of interest. The main routine shows how you have to open a server socket channel, then bind it to the port of interest. From here it is easy to use mapped I/O.

Further Reading

TCP/IP Network Administration, by Craig Hunt (O'Reilly & Associates, Sebastopol CA, 1994), ISBN 0-937175-82-X.

The modest title hides the fact that this book will be useful to a wider audience than just network administrators. It is a very good practical guide to TCP/IP written as a tutorial introduction.

Teach Yourself TCP/IP in 14 Days, by Timothy Parker (Sams Publishing, Indianapolis, 1994), ISBN 0-672-30549-6.

When a book starts off with an apology for the dullness of the subject material, you just know that the author has some unusual ways about him.

Unix Network Programming, by W. Richard Stevens (Prentice Hall, NJ, 1990)

The canonical guide to network programming.

Exercises

1. Extend the previous example mail program so that it prompts for user input and generally provides a friendly front end to sending mail.
2. Write a socket server program that simply returns the time on the current system. Write a client that calls the server and sends you mail to report on how far apart the time on the local system is versus the time on the current system.
3. In the previous exercise, the server can only state what time it is at the instant the request reaches it, but that answer will take a certain amount of time to travel back to the client. Devise a strategy to minimize or correct for errors due to transmission time. (Hard—use a heuristic to make a good guess.)
4. Read the API for java.net.URLEncoder and URLDecoder and write a program that encodes a string into the MIME format called `x-www-form-urlencoded`.
5. Update the multithreaded webserver so that it can also serve JPG and GIF files and correctly identify their type to the browser. You can just use the file extension as an indicator of the contents.

Some Light Relief—Using Java to Stuff an Online Poll

The email to me was brief. It just read:

```
From billg@Central Mon May  4 11:57:41 PDT
Subject: Hank the Angry Dwarf
To: jokes@Sun.COM

Hey everyone.  If you've got five seconds to spare, go to the following
url:
     http://www.pathfinder.com/people/50most/1998/vote/index.html

and vote for:
     Hank the Angry, Drunken Dwarf

This is a huge joke.  We want to try to get Hank way up there on the
People Magazine 50 most beautiful people of the year list.  As of 2:00AM,
he's already up to number 5!
```

Well, I can recognize a high priority when I see one. I put down the critical bug fix I was working on, went right to the website, and checked what this was all about.

Every year the celebrity gossip magazine *People* prints a list of "the 50 most beautiful people in the world," and this year they were soliciting votes on their web site. *People* had started the ball rolling with nominations for actors like Kate Winslet and Leonardo DiCaprio, who were in the public eye because of their roles in the Titanic movie.

People magazine gave web surfers the opportunity to write in names of people for whom they wanted to vote. A fan of the Howard Stern radio show nominated "Hank the angry, drunken dwarf" for *People*'s list. When Stern heard about Hank's nomination as one of the most beautiful people in the world, he started plugging the candidacy on the radio. A similar phenomenon took place on the Internet, and many people received email like I did. Another write-in stealth candidate widely favored by netizens was flamboyant, blond-haired, veteran pro-wrestler Ric Flair.

Hank, the angry, drunken dwarf, is an occasional guest on Stern's syndicated radio program. Hank is a 36-year old dwarf who lives in Boston with his mother and has made a name for himself as a belligerent, if diminutive, devotee of beer, tequila, and Pamela Anderson.

The *People* website soon crashed under the strain of incoming votes for Hank. When the *People* poll closed, the results were as follows:

230,169 votes	Hank the dwarf	Angry, drunken dwarf and Stern radio guest
17,145 votes	Ric Flair	25-year pro-wrestling performer
14,471 votes	Leonardo DiCaprio	High school dropout
7,057 votes	Gillian Anderson	Actress
5,941 votes	Kate Winslet	High school dropout

Hank Nassif, the angry, drunken dwarf, was officially the most beautiful person in the world, by a margin of more than 10-to-1 over the runner-up! Unhappily, *People* magazine showed their true colors at this point, ignored the clear mandate from the website, and went ahead with a cover story naming the guy who came in third as the official "most beautiful person in the world" for 1998. What a rip-off.

The Java Votebot

There were dark allegations here of automated voting programs, or votebots. I was shocked. But not too shocked to show you how to write a votebot using your new-found Java networking skills.

First, find any online poll. Lots of sites run them because they are a lot cheaper than having actual meaningful content. Let's pick on, I don't know, say, CNN.com. The goofballs in the media are always running some kind of "scientific" poll in an attempt to seem "with it" and "hip" to the latest trends and "cool slang." In October 2001, they were running a poll asking, "Is al Qaeda sending coded messages to followers via video statements?" You could answer "yes" or "no." There wasn't a box for people to respond, "This kind of inane question only trivializes serious matters, and distracts attention from the real issues".

Do a "view source" on a poll web page in your browser to see how they are submitting the results. You're probably going to want to reread the chapter on servlets to get the most out of this. The part of the HTML page that deals with the poll will probably look something like this:

```
<FORM METHOD=POST ACTION="http://poll.cnn.com/poll?1682781"
TARGET="popuppoll">
<INPUT TYPE=HIDDEN NAME="Poll" VALUE="168278">
<!-- Question 1 --><INPUT TYPE=HIDDEN NAME="Question" VALUE="1">
<SPAN class="BoxStory">
Is al Qaeda sending coded messages to followers via video statements?
<BR><BR></SPAN>
</TD> </TR>

<!-- Answer 1 -->
<TR> <TD>
<SPAN class="BoxStory"> Yes </SPAN>
</TD>
<TD align=center><INPUT TYPE=RADIO NAME="Answer168279" VALUE=1>
</TD> </TR> <!-- /end Answer 1 -->

<!-- Answer 2 -->
<TR> <TD>
<SPAN class="BoxStory"> No </SPAN>
</TD>
<TD align=center><INPUT TYPE=RADIO NAME="Answer168279" VALUE=2>
</TD> </TR>
```

So that tells us this is a simple form which is posted to URL "`http://poll.cnn.com/`," the script is called "`poll`," its argument is called "`1682781`," and the name/value posted is "`Answer168279=1`" for yes, and "`Answer168279=2`" for no. There is a hidden attribute giving the question number, too.

It doesn't matter which way you stuff this poll, the point is that a news organization needs to decide if it is in the news business or the entertainment business. Here's the program to do it:

```
// implements a votebot to stuff Internet polls
import java.io.*;
import java.net.*;
public class votebot {
    public static void main (String args[]) {
        try {
            for (int i=0; i<1000; i++) {
                URL u = new URL("http://poll.cnn.com");
                URLConnection uc = u.openConnection();
                uc.setDoOutput(true);
                OutputStream os = uc.getOutputStream();
                PrintStream ps = new PrintStream(os);
                ps.print("GET /poll?1682781p\r\n");
                ps.print("Question=1&Answer168279=2\r\n");
                System.out.print(".");
            }
         } catch (Exception ex) {
            System.out.println("Excpn: "+ex.getMessage());
         }
    }
}
```

If this doesn't work for you, there are several possible reasons. There could be a bug in the code. Or the polling site may be employing "electronic countermeasures," such as discarding multiple inputs from one IP address. Or the "poll" may in fact be completely fake and discard all input from anyone at all times.

After writing several more test programs, I reached the conclusion that the "results" of the CNN online polling are completely unrelated to the web votes cast!

Chapter 18

Remote Method Invocation

- Object Serialization
- Remote Method Invocation
- Object Communication Middleware
- Exercises
- Some Light Relief—The Origami Kamikaze Water Bomber

"There's a tomato *in every au*tomato*n."*

— Professor Rudolph's Big Book of Finite State Machines and Fruit Fancies

This chapter tells you all about Java's Remote Method Invocation feature, which is a library that supports method calls made "across the net." Why would you want to make a method call on an object that lives on some other system? Think about it this way: it's the natural evolution of client/server systems.

Sockets provide basic system-to-system communication. Classes like URLConnection and HttpURLConnection provide higher level services with specialized methods for sending HTML data. RMI generalizes this, and makes it available to any class. You may have a database on a server which is accessed via a Java program. RMI allows Java processes on client systems to call into that program, without writing everything in terms of low-level socket protocols.

It turns out that this is useful enough that people created a framework to do it before Java was popularized. That framework is known as CORBA—the Common Object Request Broker Architecture. Its designers were farsighted enough to make CORBA language independent, and Java could have just adopted CORBA for its object communication protocol. However, CORBA is a richly-featured system that can be heavyweight and complex. The Windows-only equivalent is COM+ which is now morphing into .NET. RMI is lighter weight and simpler than both of these. Sun has added some significant new software to allow cooperation and coexistence between Java and CORBA, described at the end of this chapter.

RMI is built on top of sockets, but your code only knows about Java objects. All the implementation is handled under the covers for you. As with sockets, there is a client end and a server end, with a slightly different set up for each.

Object Serialization

We covered object serialization in Chapter 14, and you may want to review this now. We saw how objects could be serialized, allowing them to be written out. Serialization basically means extracting all the values in the non-private, non-transient data fields and presenting them for output. RMI uses serialization behind the scenes to write objects into a socket to ship them between systems.

Serializing Terminology

There are some commonly used terms for serializing an object. Writing it to disk is called *swizzling* or *pickling* or *preserving* the object. People also talk about *marshalling* and *unmarshalling* an object when it is being sent somewhere.

I prefer the term *lyophilize* (pronounced "laff-alize") as it is a better description. When you pickle something, you add brine to it. Lyophilize is a term from chemistry meaning "freeze-dry." When you freeze dry something, you take the water out and just leave the dry stuff. When you lyophilize an object, you remove the code and just save the data.

Although the serialization and data transfer is done for you behind the scenes, you have to make sure that your classes have that capability. Every class that you pass into or return from a Remote object must implement java.io.Serializable.

Class Versioning

After you swizzle an object, you've got no guarantee that someone won't later update its class and recompile it. So the serializer calculates a hash value on the class and saves that as part of the swizzled object. The saved hash value from the object you bring in must match the hash value for the class in memory. This is checked when the object is read in again. If there is a mismatch, you'll get an exception like this:

```
java.io.InvalidClassException:
MyClass; Local class not compatible at
java.io.ObjectStreamClass.setClass(ObjectStreamClass.java:219)
```

How do you avoid this? With the "`serialver`" utility that comes with the JDK. You use serialver when you want to create a new version of a class, yet you want it to be Serialization-compatible with a prior version.

Rather than letting the system compute the serialVersionUID for your class, you run "`serialver`" on your old class file and it will provide you with a version id to add to the new class in a declaration like this:

```
private static final long serialVersionUID = 4021215565287364875L;
```

The first version of class doesn't need this field, but any later versions do if you are going to be serializing and deserializing them. The version id lets Java identify the classes and accept those where the serial version UID is given to it and matches what is in the serialized class. That way, if you want to let Java know that you have made a compatible change (such as adding a method), you just put the right version UID in the class.

If you think you might be updating classes which are serialized, then the simplest approach is just to include this field from the very beginning and set the version UID to whatever value you want. That way, you can manage the versioning yourself and decide when the class is incompatible with prior serialized versions. At that point, you give it a new value for the version UID, and version mismatches will be detected and rejected.

Note that when you read an object back in, after you have written it out, you do not get back the same object. You get back a different object with identical values in the data fields. But it will be at a different address, and compare as "not equal" in a reference comparison to the original object.

Remote Method Invocation

Remote Method Invocation (RMI) is a java-specific version of a CORBA framework. RMI means that an object on one system can call a method in an object somewhere else on the network. It will send over parameters and get a result back automatically. It all happens invisibly and just looks like the invocation of a local method (it may take a little longer time of course). RMI directly supports client/server systems in Java. Clients can truly make procedure calls directly to their server.

How does this differ from opening a socket to the server? It's a higher-level interface. RMI is actually built on top of sockets. A socket just lets you pass data to the server. RMI lets you call a method on the server and pass entire objects in and out. This is a big deal!

For those familiar with Remote Procedure Calls (RPC), RMI is RPC with an object-oriented flavor. It is also very simple to set up and use, compared to what it offers. Let's think about the problem for a second, look at Figure 18-1, then use that to lead into a description of how it works with a code example. What we are trying to do is allow an object in a Java program on one system to call a method in a Java program on another system. Furthermore, we want this to look as similar as possible to a method calling a method in the same program.

Not only does RMI look like RPC, it is implemented in a similar way to this established and ingenious software. We'll explain how the implementation works, but first let's walk through the client side of an actual RMI system.

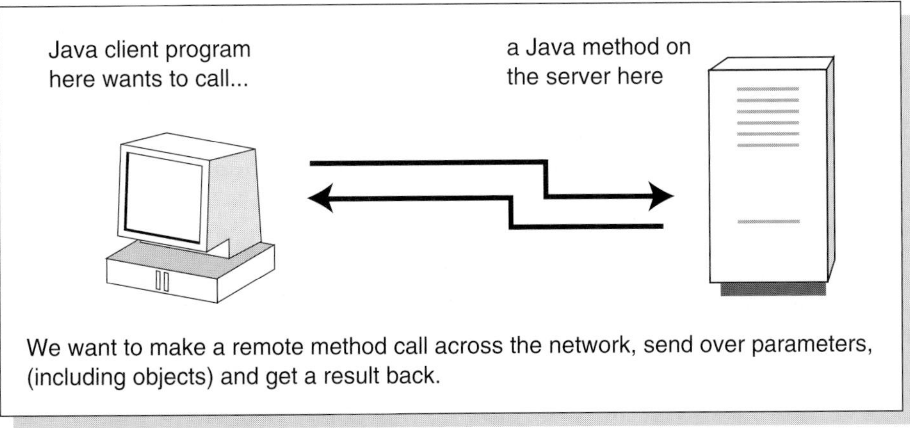
Java client program
here wants to call...
a Java method on
the server here
We want to make a remote method call across the network, send over parameters,
(including objects) and get a result back.

Figure 18–1 What RMI does.

The Client Side of RMI

Just as with sockets, HTTP, and other forms of system-to-system communication, RMI has a client side and a server side. The client side and server side have different functions and are coded differently. By the way, we should make clear that RMI is completely a library feature. There is nothing in the Java language that was added to enable RMI. You could build an RMI library for any programming language.

A major goal of RMI was that it be simple and lightweight. Client calls to remote methods should look as much as possible like calls to local methods. I think Sun has met these goals, and the designers in Sun's Boston R&D facility, where RMI was developed, deserve full credit. I always like programming languages and libraries that are easy to use and understand. That way you can devote most of your brainpower to solving the problem, not wrestling with the system.

A common computer science proverb is, "anything can be solved with one more layer of indirection," and this is the approach that RMI uses. Instead of having a object on the client, you have a interface. The interface extends the interface java.rmi.Remote and describes the server methods that you will be able to invoke. Behind the scenes at runtime, you will be provided with a real object which implements the interface and which knows how to use sockets to make the actual remote call on your behalf.

Do you remember the Network Time Protocol from Chapter 17? That's a protocol that allows one computer to ask another what the time is so that they can keep synchronized and keep file and email timestamps consistent. We wrote an NTP client using sockets, and it was a pretty small program. We will implement the client and the server ends of a time service for our RMI example.

With NTP, the client must know which server to use and what port the service is on. RMI is a little higher-level: you only need know the name of the service. To make things easier, instead of remembering dozens of pairs like "server X offers service Y" and "server A offers service B," Java RMI gathers all those pairs into a single registry. If you know the name of a service, you can ask the registry to get you the server for it.

Client programs have to know where the registry is. But if a service moves to a new server, only the registry needs to be updated, not the hundreds of clients. A client tells the registry it wants "service B," and it will get back an object that lets the client make a call on that service. This object will be something that implements both an interface describing the service and the Remote interface. It's time for that code example!

Let's keep our program honest by keeping the client and server code in separate directories. That way, they can only find one another through the class path mechanism, and not by virtue of being in the same directory. Set up two directories c:\work\server and c:\work\client.

We first have to provide an interface that describes the methods that can be called remotely. This is simple—we are just going to offer a getCurrentTime(). All remote methods must be able to throw a RemoteException, so that needs to be specified as part of the method in the interface. The interface for our time server is:

```
import java.rmi.*;

public interface TimeServerIntf extends Remote {

    public java.util.Date currentTime() throws RemoteException;

}
```

Put that code in the server directory and compile it. It is recommended that you always compile remote servers and interfaces into a named package, and not try to lazily squeak by using the anonymous package as we do here.

You may be surprised to learn that the java.rmi.Remote interface is just a "marker" interface, like Cloneable or Serializable. It has no methods or data, but simply identifies these methods as ones that can be called from a remote system.

After you have compiled the remote interface, put its class file where the client can see it. You can put its directory in the class path, or you can move the class file to the JRE library directory like this:

```
mkdir c:\jdk1.4\jre\classes
move TimeServerIntf.class c:\jdk1.4\jre\classes
```

Use the correct pathname corresponding to wherever you installed the JDK.

Next, write the Client code that looks up the service in the registry and invokes the remote method promised by the interface:

```
import java.rmi.*;
import java.util.Date;

public class TimeClient {

    public static void main(String[] args) throws Exception {
        //System.setSecurityManager( new RMISecurityManager() );
        String what = "rmi://localhost/PetesTimeService";

        TimeServerIntf t = (TimeServerIntf) Naming.lookup(what);
        Date d = t.currentTime();
        System.out.println("current time: " + d);
    }
}
```

That code should go in the c:\work\client directory that you created. Amazingly, even for a trivial service like time look-up, the RMI code is shorter than the equivalent socket code. Apart from the naming look-up to get the interface object, there is nothing at all in this code that is different from a wholly local system. It's great to have code that works the same way in the local case and when distributed across a network. Let's walk through the example.

The first line, which is commented out, installs a security manager on the client program at runtime. It is inherently insecure to load classes that are shipped to you from across the Internet. You therefore have to tell the RMI library what privileges you are going to grant this program. If you leave this line commented out, so that there is no security manager, the RMI class loader will not load any classes from remote locations. That's OK for the code we will run here because we will run everything on a local host. We'll revisit the security manager after completing the basic example.

The next line of code creates a string that looks like a URL. The string contains the hostname where the RMI registry is running and the name of the service we want to look up. Here we are going to run everything on localhost, but the registry may be on any host, such as:

```
String what = "rmi://www.afu.com:1099/PetesTimeService";
```

The ":1099" is the port number, as in other URLs. Port 1099 is the default port for RMI, but you can use any port if you specify it explicitly.

How to Learn the hostname

You can find out the name of a host computer on Unix by running the "hostname" command.

On Windows, click on the Control Panel, then Network, then the Identification tab on the tabbed pane that pops up. The entry marked "Computer name" is the host name. You can type a new value here and then reboot to give the host a new name.

The next line of code does a java.rmi.Naming.loookup() on that string.

```
TimeServerIntf t = (TimeServerIntf) Naming.lookup(what);
```

The name lookup returns a reference to the remote object. This is cast to the remote interface type, and we now have an object on which we can invoke methods that are located on other systems!

Finally, call the remote method promised by the interface in the usual way:

```
Date d = t.currentTime();
```

You may notice that Date is equally available on all systems and so does not need to be called remotely. That's true, but remember the whole purpose of NTP is to synchronize computers with some central server's version of time. That remote server may even be located in some other time zone.

Compile this code in the normal way:

```
javac TimeClient.java
```

Providing you correctly made the interface visible to the compiler, this will compile without errors. Before we can execute it, we need to implement the server, and that is the subject of the next section.

The Server Side of RMI

The server side of this time service is going to implement the method promised by the TimeServerIntf, namely:

```
public interface TimeServerIntf extends Remote {
    public java.util.Date currentTime() throws java.rmi.RemoteException;
}
```

We will start off by writing this as a local class that runs in the same JVM and then add the features that make this a remote server. Put the code in the server directory c:\work\server along with the interface that we put there earlier. Here's the basic code:

```
public class TimeServer
    implements TimeServerIntf {

   public java.util.Date currentTime() throws java.rmi.RemoteException {
        return new java.util.Date();
   }
}
```

All remote methods must be able to throw a RemoteException. The class java.rmi.RemoteException is the common superclass for about twenty individual RMI exceptions that may be raised to indicate different problems that have occurred.

The server needs some extra capabilities to be able to act as an object that clients can reach remotely. Primarily, it needs to be able to return a reference to itself which can be used from another system. This remote reference will contain an IP address, a port number, and a reference within a JVM that is local to that IP address.

The easiest way to give a server these capabilities is to make it extend the class `java.rmi.server.UnicastRemoteObject` and thus get the capabilities by inheritance. This is what the UnicastRemoteObject class is for. The name "Unicast" is meant to contrast with "Multicast," which is a concept Sun is developing to represent objects that are replicated over several servers (for improvements in fault tolerance and throughput).

As the name might suggest, the UnicastRemoteObject class implements the java.rmi.Remote interface. And thus (Ta-da!) our server class can be used whenever the Client system is expecting something that fulfills the Remote interface. So add this line to the declaration of the server class:

```
extends UnicastRemoteObject
```

If your server already extends some other class, you have two choices. The harder choice is to look at all the source code in UnicastRemoteObject and add that to your server. The easier choice is to create a simple remote proxy class. The proxy will be a Remote class, and it will offer all the services that your server does. It will implement them by making a local call to your server in the same JVM.

The server must have a no arg constructor, and this constructor must be specified as capable of throwing a RemoteException. Add this line to the server code:

```
public TimeServer() throws RemoteException {}
```

The only remaining work is for the server to have a main routine that tells the registry it is ready to go to work. That action is called "binding" with the registry. Bind() is a static method in the class java.rmi.Naming. It takes two arguments:

- a string holding the URL for the registry and service name, just as we used in the client code.
- an object of the server class.

Binding with the registry can be expressed in two lines of code, shown as follows in bold. Putting all the code together, the server looks like this:

```
import java.rmi.*;
import java.rmi.server.*;

public class TimeServer
    extends UnicastRemoteObject
    implements TimeServerIntf {

    public TimeServer() throws RemoteException {}

    public java.util.Date currentTime() throws RemoteException {
        return new java.util.Date();
    }

    public static void main(String[] args) throws Exception {
        System.out.println("Attempting to bind server...");
        TimeServer me = new TimeServer();
        Naming.bind("rmi://localhost/PetesTimeService", me);
        System.out.println("Server bound succesfully");
    }
}
```

The server tells the registry about itself with bind(). As well as bind(), there is unbind() to remove the record of a service, and rebind() to replace the record. You may want to use rebind() in your code, because that saves you from having to restart the RMI registry each time you update the server.

The name you give the service is arbitrary. Here is it called "PetesTimeService." You need to be consistent in naming, because the name is how clients find your service. You can only use characters that can appear in a URL, so don't use embedded spaces.

Compile this code in the normal way:

```
javac TimeServer.java
```

The program reaches the end of the main routine, but it does not terminate because the act of binding starts a new thread running in this process.

Creating the Server Stub and Skeleton

Quite a lot of work happens behind the scenes when a client calls a remote object. It is not possible to make the desired call directly, so we break the problem down into smaller pieces that can be done directly. We make the client call a local routine which represents the one it wants to call remotely. We call this local dummy or stand-in for the server method a *stub*. The stub is responsible for getting the incoming arguments and transmitting them over to its buddy on the server machine. It does this by opening a socket, serializing the objects, and passing the data across.

The buddy routine on the server machine is called a *skeleton* because it's just the bare bones of a routine. It doesn't do anything except unmarshal the data passed to it, and call the real server method. The procedure is then reversed to communicate the result back to the method on the client machine. And so a remote method has been invoked on one system by another, as shown in Figure 18-2.

You have to create class files for the stub and the skeleton. They are generated using the server class, and there is an "rmi compiler" that will create them. Run the tool on the server class like this:

```
rmic TimeServer
```

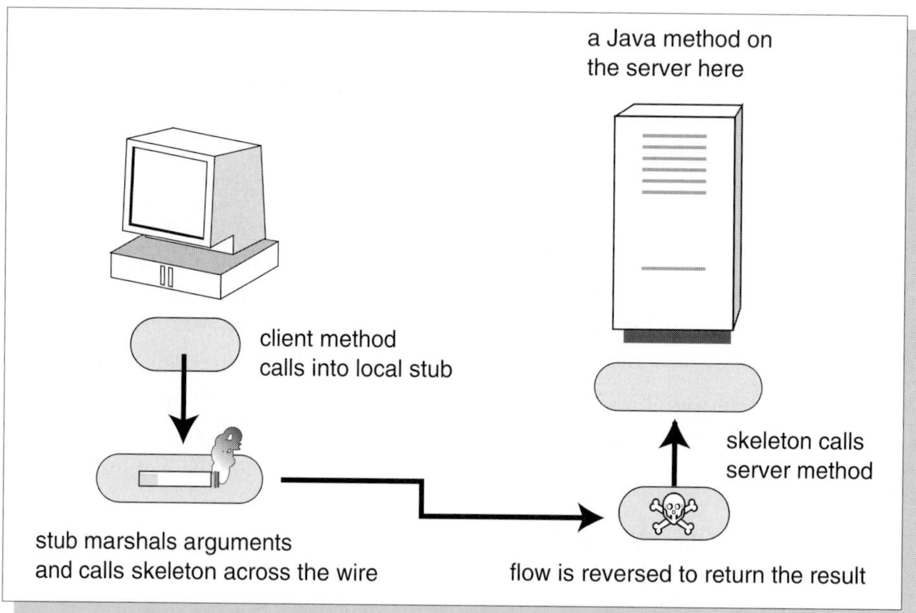

Figure 18–2 How RMI does it.

That will create the two files TimeServer_Stub.class and TimeServer_Skel.class. You can disassemble these if you're curious to see what's in them.

Decompiling Java

There are a couple of free decompilers on the CD. These decompilers take the information in a class file and try to reconstruct the source code. Often they can do a pretty good job, if the class file has not been obfuscated.

You can run the Mocha decompiler right off the CD, like this:

java -classpath e:\decompilers\mocha.zip Mocha.decompiler somefile.class

Assuming "e:" is your CD drive that recreates the source file somefile.mocha.

Try it on TimeServer_Stub.class and TimeServer_Skel.class.

After you have compiled the server and created the corresponding stub and skeleton classes, you must put the class files where the server system can find them at runtime. The easiest way to do this is to move the class files to the JRE library directory on the server like this:

```
mkdir c:\jdk1.4\jre\classes
move TimeServerIntf.class c:\jdk1.4\jre\classes
```

The stub class must go on the client and the skeleton class on the server. Use the correct pathname corresponding to wherever you installed the JDK. If you are experimenting and running everything on localhost, then you will have already created this directory.

Running the RMI Example

At last, we can run the example. We'll do it in three steps, corresponding to the registry, the server, and the client.

1. On the host where you want to run the registry, start the RMI registry.

   On Unix or Windows, in a command window, type "rmiregistry."

   You can also use the Windows command "start rmiregistry," which will start the program in the background and give you a prompt back. But you will not be able to see any error messages the program prints.

2. On the host where you want to run the server:

   On Unix or Windows, in a command window, type the command line to run the java server program, "java TimeServer."

   You can also use the Windows command "start java TimeServer" which will start the program in the background and give you a prompt back. But you will not be able to see any messages the program prints.

3. On the host where you want to run the client:

   On Unix or Windows, in a command window, type the command line to run the java server program, "java TimeClient." Again, you can use the start command to run it in the background on Windows.

Once you have all the components running, the electrons will whiz back and forth and after a few seconds the client will show output like this:

```
c:\ > java TimeClient
Attempting to find server...
Server found successfully
current time: Mon Oct 22 21:37:40 PDT 2001
```

There may also be some diagnostic output in the server program.

Logging the Server

The secret to effective debugging is using the right tools to see what is going on inside a system. Those tools can include utilities, debuggers, hex-editors, logging options, and so on.

If you start an RMI server defining this property:

```
java -Djava.rmi.server.logCalls=true TimeServer
```

it will print out all the RMI calls that it receives in the command window where you started it. This is helpful to get a better understanding of what is happening.

You don't have to start the registry as a separate, external process. You can create and run a registry thread from within your server with this line of code:

```
java.rmi.registry.LocateRegistry.createRegistry(1099);
```

Various extra cleverness takes place to support sending objects across the network, including sending the exact type of the object arguments with the data. If that class doesn't exist on the receiving side, the corresponding class object is also sent over the network and loaded into the JVM.

Adding the Client Security Manager

Let us return to the security manager that we mentioned in the client part of this example. As a matter of fact, you can install a security manager in the server as well as in the client should you so wish.

At runtime, when the client executes this statement:

```
TimeServerIntf t = (TimeServerIntf) Naming.lookup(what);
```

it will cause the stub for the TimeServer to be downloaded across the network from the server to the client. This is why the client needs a security policy: it attracts code to itself across the net and executes it. If the Server uploads code from the client (i.e., the two mutually communicate via remote objects), it should have a security policy too.

If you do not install a security manager, the RMI class loader will not load any classes from remote locations. That means the system will not run when the client and server are on different hosts. Refresh your memory on the client code that we commented out. It looked like this:

```
public class TimeClient {

    public static void main(String[] args) throws Exception {
        //System.setSecurityManager( new RMISecurityManager() );
```

By uncommenting that line of code, we cause the default implementation of an RMI Security Manager to be installed for our client code. This security manager in turn is driven by a policy file. The policy file for an individual user will typically be kept in a centralized location by the system administrator.

We discuss security policy files in Chapter 25. For now, just use the sample policy file that is shown here. It grants the client permission to connect to a range of sockets and to do DNS name resolution. The file should be called "client.txt" and it contains:

```
grant {
    permission java.net.SocketPermission
    "*:1024-65535", "connect,resolve";
     permission java.io.FilePermission "/tmp/*", "read";
};
```

The I/O permission is not needed, but is an example of granting another kind of permission: read permission on files in the /tmp directory.

The permission file looks vaguely like Java, but it isn't. For reasons best known to themselves, Sun hasn't yet caught onto the idea of using XML to express the configuration of security policy. They use this pseudo-Java syntax.

Uncomment the setSecurityManager() statement, recompile the client, and try running it *without* using the security policy file. You will find that it fails with a java.security.AccessControlException.

Now execute it like this:

```
java -Djava.security.policy=client.txt TimeClient
```

That command line defines the java.security.policy property and names the file containing the permissions we wish to grant. Now the client will run successfully. This illustrates the fine granularity of granting runtime permissions to Java applications.

A common mistake results in this error message:

```
    Unexpected exception; nested exception is:
java.io.NotSerializableException:
```

Any classes whose objects are sent remotely must implement java.io.Serializable. This is a change between JDK 1.0 and JDK 1.1.

RMI is a very powerful technique for building large systems. The fact that the technique can be described, along with a working example, in just a few pages, speaks volumes in favor of Java. RMI is tremendously exciting and it's simple to use. You can call to any server you can bind to, and you can build networks of distributed objects. RMI opens the door to software systems that were formerly too complex to build.

Jini Software

The Jini software makes extensive use of RMI. Jini is a technology for dynamically finding and connecting services automatically on a TCP/IP network. On any given subnet you can start a Jini server. When new devices or services appear on the subnet, they are able to register themselves with the Jini server ("Hey, I'm a color printer! I have these 3 methods for printing!"). Clients can look for services and connect to them dynamically. You can tell your digital camera "go and find a printer that I just plugged in, and print a contact print of all your snapshots."

Jini is emerging technology. It's one of those things that needs a killer application to showcase the benefits. That's why it's a subheading here, and not a chapter title, yet.

Object Communication Middleware

This section contains a description of some Java-related products. It provides useful background information on non-Java object software.

CORBA

If you read the object-oriented trade press, one term you may have seen more and more is CORBA. CORBA is the *Common Object Request Broker Architecture*. In a single sentence, it is a framework to let objects on one computer talk to objects on another computer, just as Unix RPC (Remote Procedure Call) lets processes talk to one another.

CORBA is a true object-oriented distributed processing framework. The "common" part means that it is not tied to any one language, or any one hardware vendor, but can interoperate among all. CORBA was designed over the course of several years in an open industry-wide process, with the main participants being the Unix hardware vendors: H-P, Sun, IBM, and DEC (now part of Compaq, which itself will soon be swallowed by H-P).

Why do you want objects on different computers to talk to each other? Because it allows you to build much more complicated and capable systems that support true distributed processing. It's not intended for a single programmer working on a lone PC. It is highly useful in a large enterprise with Terabytes of data distributed in databases on dozens of mainframe class systems.

CORBA implementations have been deployed over the last couple of years. CORBA is language-neutral, and it achieves this by having an interface language (it looks close to C) that other languages must map into.

Making CORBA language independent was a very farsighted decision on the part of the original designers, and it means CORBA and Java can work together. CORBA implementations were often deployed with C++, but with the right "glue" or interface definition language (IDL), they can talk to Java programs and supply object services across a net.

When you want objects to communicate across different systems, there are two main reasons for using CORBA instead of just using Java's RMI:

- CORBA provides an object framework that is language independent. If you're using multiple languages, or you wish to leave that option open for the future, or you want to access C++ legacy systems, CORBA makes it easy.
- The CORBA initiative started before Java, and the CORBA code is further along. CORBA ORBs are sophisticated pieces of middleware that can schedule, route, queue, and dispatch incoming object requests. System administrators can inspect queues and do load-balancing across servers.

JDK 1.2 adds a set of classes to provide ORB access and full support for talking to anybody's objects through CORBA. The release even includes a lightweight ORB, which can be replaced by your commercial ORB of choice.

The overlap between Java RMI and CORBA has been worked on extensively. Sun has now added a library that lets RMI run over IIOP (the Internet Inter-ORB Protocol allowing different CORBA implementations to talk to one another). That library makes it simpler still for Java to communicate with the existing base of distributed systems. Start up Java RMI at one end and let it talk IIOP directly to your CORBA objects—without the programmer needing to have IDL knowledge.

CORBA is a big, industrial-strength, language-independent, object communication system. Java's RMI is a smaller, simpler system that can be used when both endpoints are written in Java, or when Java needs to talk to CORBA. CORBA gives you compatibility with legacy code; Java's RMI provides simplicity of remote communication. The two are converging into a single Java solution.

IDL

IDL or *Interface Definition Language* is the way CORBA achieves language-neutrality. You describe in IDL the signature of the methods and data that CORBA will pass back and forth for you. IDL looks somewhat like C, but it is purely for describing interfaces, not writing actual programs. IDL is only for people using CORBA. Many Java systems won't see the CORBA framework directly, so many Java programmers will not need to bother with IDL.

Exercises

1. Write a small program that serializes an object of one of your classes (perhaps the class that you are writing). Write several such objects out to a file and read them back in again. Dump the hex bits in the file, and try to relate them to the original class.
2. Update the program in exercise 1 to include a serial version UID in the class. Adding a data field is regarded as an incompatible change. Can you read in the objects you formerly wrote out? Add another method to the class (a compatible change) and recompile. Can you read in the objects now? Why or why not?
3. Write an RMI server and client to simulate a stock price application. The Remote interface will contain one method

   ```
   public String getPrice(String symbol);
   ```

   The server should have a Map linking prices with (invented) values.
4. Update the program in the previous exercise so that the server queries the Yahoo stock server web page to get stock prices. The client should use RMI to talk to the server. This is a basic 3-tier e-commerce system.
5. Disassemble and print out the stub and skeleton routines for any Remote server you wrote. Add comments to the code, explaining what is happening.

Some Light Relief—The Origami Kamikaze Water Bomber

Origami is an ancient and honorable technique of delicate paper folding. It takes finesse, skill, and subtlety—so, we certainly won't be discussing *that* any further. Instead, this section explains how to make a paper airplane that takes a payload. Not only can you impress your co-workers with paper airplanes, but you can bombard them with an air delivery of confetti, glue, or shaving cream from the far side of the room. People will be talking about you for days to come, and your manager will certainly remember your achievements when the review period comes around.

One warning here: At the age of 14, I dropped a paper water bomb on the head of schoolfriend "Piffer" Tully from an upstairs classroom. He didn't see who did it, and I felt it better not to burden him by claiming responsibility. Now, 25 years later, it is probably safe to own up (ha, ha, ha, Piffer!), and also alert you to the fact that not everyone appreciates the drollness of saturation bombing by paper airplane. So, pick your targets carefully, or stick to launching blanks.

As always, observe the three cardinal safety rules when working around electronic equipment:

1. Make sure you know where the main circuit breaker is located.
2. Keep a grounding strap around your wrist.
3. Most of all, wait till your boss goes on a lunch break before starting this project.

Figure 18-3 shows you how to make the Kamikaze water bomber. There is an applet that animates these steps on the CD that comes with this book.

First, take an ordinary sheet of 8.5" by 11" paper, and make it narrower by cutting off 1.5" or so to make 7" by 11". Then follow these instructions:

Fold up the edges of the wings for better flight, and fill with payload through hole in nose. Umm, the hole in the *plane's* nose, that is. Launch and enjoy.

Origami is relaxing and fun—just the thing for unwinding after a busy day chasing electrons. If you really have a lot of spare time, check the origami models at *www.origami.vancouver.bc.ca/*. There's a praying mantis there that takes 100 steps to complete!

Begin by cutting down an 8-1.2 x 11 sheet of paper to 7 x 11 inches.

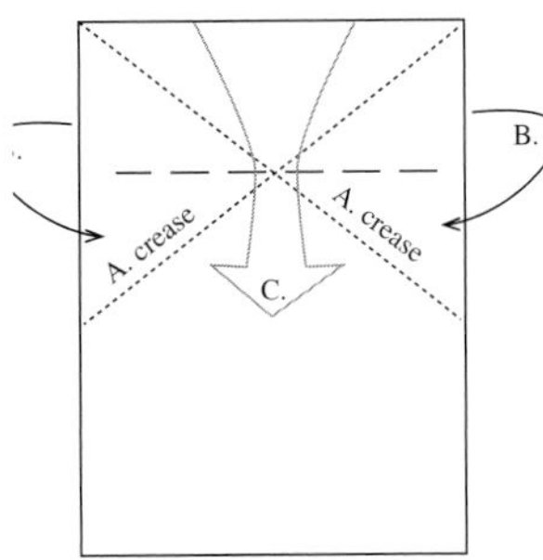

A. Fold over and crease twice
B. Bring sides in, so the 2 B's touch
C. Fold top down into triangle

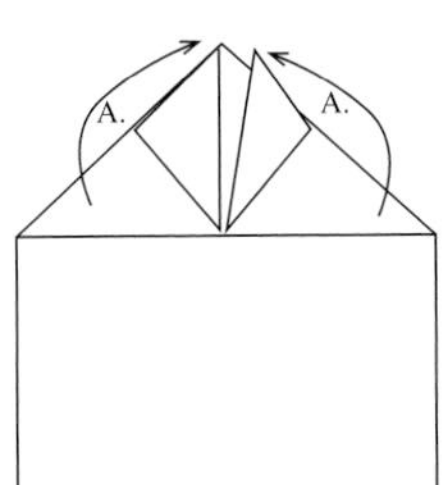

A. Fold corners up to apex

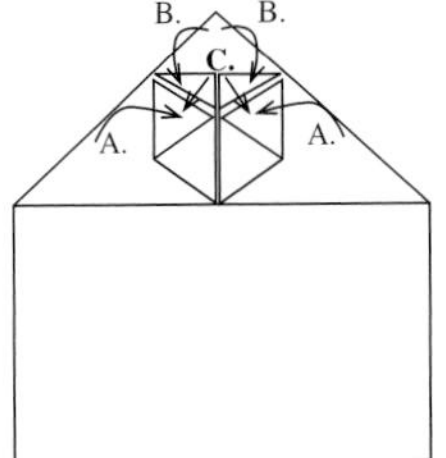

A. Fold in the side corners
B. Fold down the top corners
C. Tuckcorners of top triangle into pocket of lower triangles

NOW TURN THE PAPER OVER

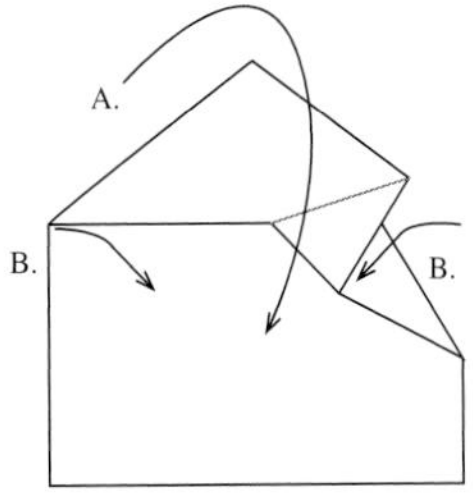

A. Foldbig triangle over and crease
B. Tuckcorners in under as you fold big triangle down again, (similar to the Valley fold done as Step 1B, the two B's come together underneath the pointed flap marked A).

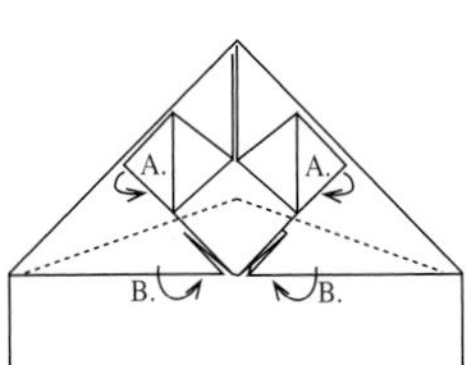

A. Tuck flaps in and behind
B. Tuck second flaps up and behind to secure and hold the first tucks

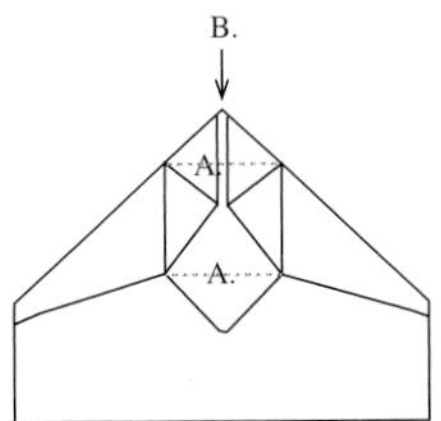

A. Firmly crease
B. Inflate by gently holding wings, pulling accordian folds & blowing into nose to expand cargo cabin
C. Fill with payload through hole in nose.

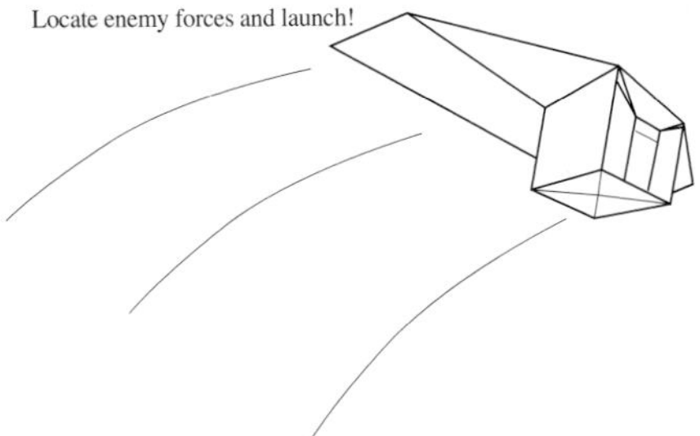

Figure 18–3 The Kamikaze water bomber.

Part 4

Client Java

Chapter 19

GUI Basics and Event-Handling

All GUI libraries have four basic areas of functionality:

- Creation of user interface "controls" or components such as scrollbars, buttons, and labels.
- Support for giving behavior to the controls by tying GUI events (like clicking on a button) to code that you write.
- Support for grouping and arranging the controls on the screen.
- Support for accessing window manager facilities like specifying which window has the input focus, reading JPEG and other image files, and printing.

Related graphics libraries also provide support for graphics operations like drawing an arc, filling a polygon, clipping a rectangle, and so on. There may even be a complete 2D drawing library, such as Java has.

For the first couple of major releases, Java supported GUI operations solely with a package called `java.awt`. The "AWT" stands for "Abstract Window Toolkit." The AWT supported the portability goals of Java. It gave user programs a common binary window interface on systems with wildly different native window systems. That's an unusual feature, like having your favorite Macintosh program run on a Windows PC and still do GUI operations. You might be wondering how it is done.

Inside the AWT runtime there are methods that you can call to pop-up a native menu, resize a window, get the location of a mouse click, and so on. Since these methods are implemented with a little bit of Java wrapping, you can call them from Java user programs. Java can thus keep track of what is happening, and then the methods call through to a native code library. The *Java bytecode* is the same on each platform, and the *native library* behind the Java runtime library is specific to each platform. The AWT code uses the underlying native (or "peer") window system to manipulate GUI objects. The AWT is a series of abstract interfaces along with Java code to map them into the actual native code on each system. This is why it is an *abstract* window toolkit: it is not tailored for a specific computer but offers the same API on all. Too much native behavior showed through and, eventually, Java moved to an all-Java GUI known as Swing. Swing uses basic native canvases, but all the rest of the behavior is implemented in Java.

At the start of the chapter we mentioned the list of services that any GUI library must support. In this chapter we will focus on one of these services: an event-handling system that notices when the user adjusts one of the components and interrupts the program to tell it what happened

You have to know how to handle the events that controls can generate before you can make sense out of the controls themselves. Event-handling is a dull but necessary prerequisite, like eating your vegetables before you can have dessert. We will deal with controls in the next chapter. The basic idea with Java GUI programs is that you do the following:

1. Declare controls. These are such things as your buttons, menus, and choices. You can subclass them to add to the behavior, but this is often unnecessary.
2. Implement an interface to supply your event handler that will respond to control activity. Your implementing class will often be an anonymous class. Using an anonymous class reduces the amount of code and puts the class declaration close to where it is used.
3. Add the controls to a container. Subclassing the container is possible but frequently unnecessary. Containers are what you display on the screen. They can hold several related controls that you want to appear next to each other on-screen. Example: a Frame can hold two buttons and a scrolling panel.

It's a challenge to explain all this. The first three topics—declaring controls, handling their events, and putting them in containers—fit together so closely that you have to understand a bit of each before you can fully understand any. They are such big topics that I've given them a chapter each and will take them serially.

All About Event-Handling

First, a few necessary words of explanation about the programming model for window systems. Unlike procedural programs in which things happen sequentially, windowing programs are *asynchronous*, meaning that things happen at unpredictable times. You never know which of the on-screen buttons, menus, frames, or other elements the user will touch next. Accordingly, a model known as *event-driven programming* is used.

In event-driven programming, the logic of your code is inverted. Instead of one flow of control from beginning to end, the runtime system sits in a "window main loop" simply waiting for user input. When the user clicks the mouse, the operating system passes it to the window manager which turns it into an *event* and passes it on to a handler you supplied earlier. This is known as a *callback*. Your handler is a *callback routine,* because the window system calls back to it when the event happens. Your event handler will deal with the graphics event and any work that is associated with it.

If a button says "press here to read the file," your code must arrange for the file to be read when called. Handling a button event just means noticing that it occurred and doing the associated action, but other events may involve some drawing on the screen. For example, dragging something with the mouse is just repeatedly drawing it under the mouse coordinates as it moves.

Threads, the Event Dispatcher, and Your Code

You will soon notice that once you put a GUI component on-screen, your program does not end. It may reach the end of the main() method, but the program as a whole does not end. This is not a new rule—it's the same old rule about a program not ending while it still has one or more threads running.

When you make a GUI component visible, a thread is started inside the Java runtime library to receive events that may be generated by that component. The underlying OS window system library is told to pass all events to this Java runtime library thread, and this thread will be responsible for dispatching the events on to your code. The fact that this thread is live prevents your program from exiting when it falls off the end of main(). So the GUI stays on the screen, and the program now runs in response to user input on the GUI.

This Java library thread is called the "event dispatching thread." It runs in your address space, in parallel with all your code, but spends most of its time blocked waiting for a GUI event. When a GUI event occurs, the event dispatching thread either consumes the event itself, or calls back to the event handler code that you wrote and registered.

Therefore, your event handlers are executed by one of the Java runtime library threads, not by one of *your* threads! One implication of this is that your event handlers will block the delivery of other GUI events, and so must be brief and quick to execute. You *never* want to undertake some time-consuming operation like reading a file in an event handler. Instead, spawn it off into a thread of its own.

GUI events are automatically added to a queue in the runtime library as they happen. The event dispatching thread empties this queue by dispatching the events to your handler code. You can actually post your own fake AWT events to this queue if you want to simulate input like key presses or mouse movements (perhaps for testing purposes). See class java.awt.EventQueue, method postEvent().

Another implication is that, since all event dispatching is handled by one library thread alone, the library can do less synchronization than would be required if many threads were running. Less synchronization equals better overall performance... as long as the synchronization is still correct.

Java Event Model

The *event model* is the name we give to the framework that turns a GUI interaction (mouse click, menu selection, button press, etc.) into a call for your code to process it. The event model can also be used for something unrelated to the GUI, like a timer going off. In other words, the event model is the design for connecting your code to any kind of asynchronous actions, termed *events*, for handling.

Obviously, the window manager can't directly call your event-handling routines because the runtime library doesn't even see your code until it is asked to run it. So, at runtime, the event model has to be told which of your routines are there to handle events.

Java originally used inheritance to tie together your code and the event model. JDK 1.1 introduced a better approach called the *delegation-based* model. Some of the Java documentation still refers to "1.1-style events," meaning the current model. To get any events, your code has to begin by telling the window system, "send those events of yours to these methods of mine." You connect the controls that generate events by registering a callback with your event-handling classes, as shown in Figure 19-1.

You register your handler code once at the beginning with the GUI object that will be generating events. After that, those events are fired to you when they occur. In particular, your handler code is called and passed the event object as an argument.

If you are not 100% clear on callbacks, go back and read that section in Chapter 8. It is *essential* that you fully understand callbacks since they form the basis of the new event-handling model.

The events that are fired (sent) from the source to the listener are simply objects passed as arguments to a method call. An event object has several data fields holding such information as where on the screen the event took place, what the event is, how many mouse clicks there were, the state of a checkbox, and so on. There is a general `java.util.EventObject` type, and all AWT events are children of that, as shown in Figure 19-2.

Figure 19–1 How events are passed in JDK 1.1.

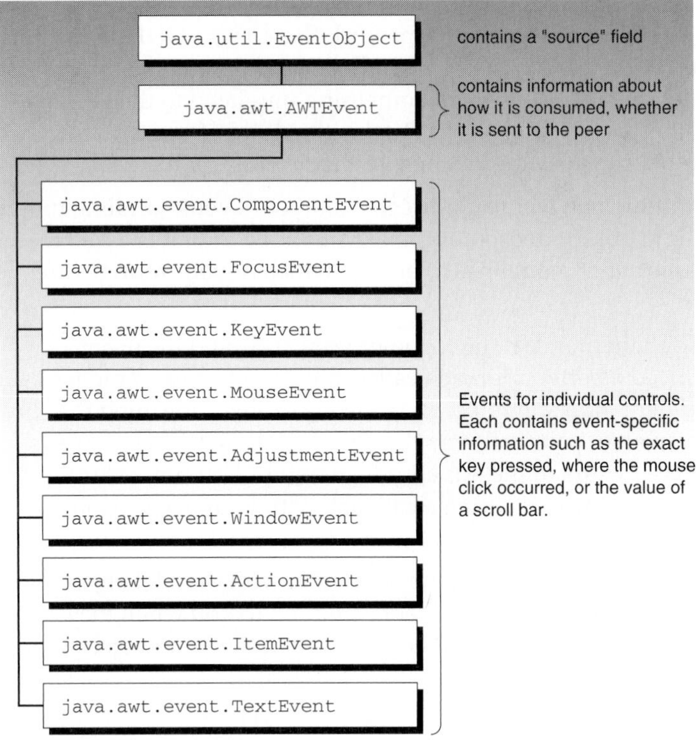

Figure 19–2 The hierarchy of event objects in JDK 1.1.

The JFrame Example

A `JFrame`, a subclass of the AWT class `Frame`, has a title string and a menu bar on which you can add several menus. Here is the code to put a `JFrame` on the screen from an application:

```
import javax.swing.*;
public class FrameDemo {
     public static void main(String[] args) {
          JFrame jframe = new JFrame("Example");
          jframe.setSize(400,100);
          jframe.setVisible(true);
     }
}
```

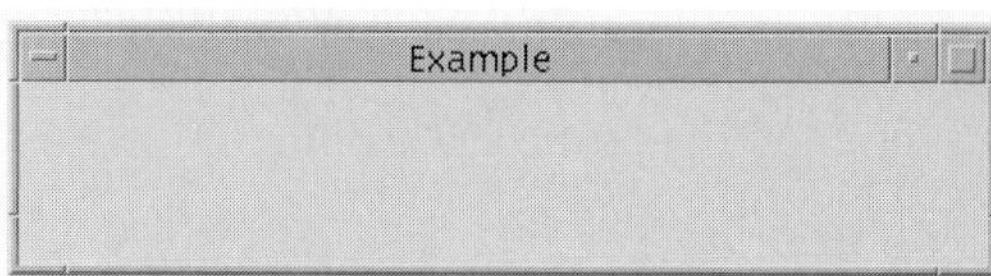

Figure 19–3 The `JFrame` is a subclass of `Frame` which is a subclass of `Window`.

Compiling and executing this program will cause a `Frame` like that in Figure 19-3 to appear on the screen. Here, we just gave it the name on the title bar of "Example." Pretty simple, yes?

Since it is a Window, JFrame is capable of receiving events generated by Windows. When you click on a Window to close it, that generates an event. If you try this with the program above, you'll notice that the JFrame goes away, but your program stays active. You have to press control-C to get out of the program. That's because you need to write code to handle the "window closing" event. The code should quit the program when it is invoked.

Let's add an event handler to our JFrame that notices when the WindowClosing event takes place. That event will be delivered when you click to close a Window.

First, I'll tell our JFrame that Window events are handled by an object that I call "mwh" here—a nice short name which is an abbreviation of "my window handler." The code appears exactly as before, and we add this one line to the main() routine:

```
jframe.addWindowListener(mwh);
```

The callback for a Window event is registered by calling the AWT method `addWindowListener`. This is a method in the `Window` superclass of JFrame that takes as a parameter an interface called `WindowListener`. Your applet must declare an instance of a class that implements the `WindowListener` interface and that will be the event handler for this button. You still have to write that class, but assuming it has the name shown below, you can instantiate an object like this:

```
myCodeToHandleWinClose mwh = new myCodeToHandleWinClose();
```

The last step is to write the `myCodeToHandleWinClose` class that implements the `java.awt.event.WindowListener` interface and provides the promised methods. The class can be in a separate file or the same one.

```
class myCodeToHandleWinClose implements WindowListener {
     public void windowClosing(WindowEvent e) {System.exit(0);}
     public void windowClosed(WindowEvent e) { }
     public void windowOpened(WindowEvent e) { }
     public void windowIconified(WindowEvent e) { }
     public void windowDeiconified(WindowEvent e) { }
     public void windowActivated(WindowEvent e) { }
     public void windowDeactivated(WindowEvent e) { }
}
```

The `windowClosing()` method of the `myCodeToHandleWinClose` class is called whenever the Window "close" choice is made. Notice that it was necessary to provide declarations for all the routines in the interface. Since we are interested only in WindowClosing, there are empty bodies for the other methods. We'll show a way of simplifying this later in the chapter.

The `WindowListener` interface (like many of the `SomethingListener` interfaces) is declared in the `java.awt.event` package. There are other event and Listeners declared in the `javax.swing.event` package. The `WindowListener` interface promises that there will be half a dozen methods with specific names. The methods will be called for different Window events now that we have delegated the task to the object "mwh" that contains the methods.

One advantage of the Java event framework is that the GUI-related code is easily separated from the application logic code. This flows from good use of OOP: Put everything in a class of its own, and declare instances of the class as needed. In that way, encapsulation works for you. If you want to change what happens on window close, you just update the class that deals specifically with it. In a non-OOP implementation, it's too easy to mix everything together, making program maintenance and testing ten times harder than it needs to be. The same event framework is used for JavaBeans (component software), as well as the AWT.

Putting the whole thing together and into our JFrame example, the code to handle the window closing event is as follows:

```
import javax.swing.*;
import java.awt.event.*;
public class CloseDemo {
     public static void main(String[] args) {
          JFrame jframe = new JFrame("Example");
          jframe.setSize(400,100);
          jframe.setVisible(true);
          myCodeToHandleWinClose m = new myCodeToHandleWinClose();
          jframe.addWindowListener(m);
     }
}

class myCodeToHandleWinClose implements WindowListener {

     public void windowClosing(WindowEvent e) {System.exit(0);}
     public void windowClosed(WindowEvent e) { }
     public void windowOpened(WindowEvent e) { }
     public void windowIconified(WindowEvent e) { }
     public void windowDeiconified(WindowEvent e) { }
     public void windowActivated(WindowEvent e) { }
     public void windowDeactivated(WindowEvent e) { }
}
```

Notice that the code inside the WindowClosing method calls System.exit() to quit the program. When you run this, you'll see the same frame as before, but when you click on the window to close it, the program will now exit gracefully. Well done! You have finished your first example of an event handler.

You may wonder, "How do I know what events there are, what interfaces deal with them, and what methods the Listener interfaces use?" Table 19-1 summarizes the answers to all three questions. You should also review the javadoc pages for classes and interfaces in package java.awt.event. The source code for the interfaces and their methods can also be reviewed in the directory $JAVA-HOME/src/java/awt/event.

The same basic framework is used by all the event handlers:

1. Write a class that implements a `SomethingListener` interface.
2. Declare an object—called, say, `myHandler`—of your class.
3. On your component, call the `add`*`Something`*`Listener(myHandler)` method.

You can shortcut the amount of code with inner classes. The next section explains how.

Table 19–1 Categories, Events, and Interfaces

General Category	Events That It Generates	Interface That the Event-Handler Implements
Mouse	Dragging, moving mouse causes a `MouseEvent`	`MouseMotionListener`
	Clicking, selecting, releasing causes a `MouseEvent`	`MouseListener`
Mouse wheel	Mouse wheel events (new in 1.4)	`MouseWheelListener`
Keyboard	Key press or key release causes a `KeyEvent`	`KeyListener`
Selecting (an item from a list, checkbox, etc.)	When item is selected causes an ItemEvent	`ItemListener`
Text Input Controls	When newline is entered causes a `TextEvent`	`TextListener`
Scrolling Controls	When a scrollbar slider is moved causes an `AdjustmentEvent`	`AdjustmentListener`
Other Controls (button, menu, etc.)	When pressed causes an `ActionEvent`	`ActionListener`
Window Changes	Open, close, iconify, etc., causes a `WindowEvent`	`WindowListener`
Keyboard Focus Changes	Tabbing to next field or requesting focus causes a `FocusEvent`. A component must have the focus to generate key events.	`FocusListener`
Component Change	Resizing, hiding, revealing, or moving a component causes a `ComponentEvent`	`ComponentListener`
Container Change	Adding or removing a component to a container causes a `ContainerEvent`	`ContainerListener`

Tips for Slimming Down Handler Code

Inner classes are intended for event handlers. They allow you to put the event-handling class and method right next to the place where you declare the control or register the callback listener. Anonymous classes are a refinement of inner classes, allowing you to combine the definition of the class with the instance allocation. Here is the code rewritten using an anonymous class:

```
import javax.swing.*;
import java.awt.event.*;
public class CloseDemo2 {

    public static void main(String[] args) {
          JFrame jframe = new JFrame("Example");
          jframe.setSize(400,100);
          jframe.setVisible(true);

          jframe.addWindowListener( new WindowListener() { // anon. class
               public void windowClosing(WindowEvent e) {System.exit(0);}
               public void windowClosed(WindowEvent e) { }
               public void windowOpened(WindowEvent e) { }
               public void windowIconified(WindowEvent e) { }
               public void windowDeiconified(WindowEvent e) { }
               public void windowActivated(WindowEvent e) { }
               public void windowDeactivated(WindowEvent e) { }
          } ); // end of anonymous class.
    }
}
```

Try compiling and running the example above. Your `CloseDemo2.java` file generates class files called `CloseDemo2.class` and `CloseDemo2$1.class`. The second of these represents the anonymous `WindowListener` inner class.

You should only use inner classes and anonymous classes where the event handler is just a few lines long. If the event handler is more than a screenful of text, it should be in a named top-level class. We have to admit, however, that the notational convenience for smaller cases is considerable—just don't get carried away with it.

There are two further refinements: making your top-level class implement the appropriate listener interface, and using an adapter class. These techniques further reduce the amount of "housekeeping code" you need to write. You'll see them in other programmers' code. I'll present them here so you can recognize the pattern.

Making a Top-Level Class into a Listener

You don't *have* to declare a separate class to implement the Listener interface. You can make any of your existing classes do the work. The code below shows an example:

```
import javax.swing.*;
import java.awt.event.*;
public class CloseDemo3 implements WindowListener {

    public static void main(String[] args) {
        JFrame jframe = new JFrame("Example");
        jframe.setSize(400,100);
        jframe.setVisible(true);

        jframe.addWindowListener( new CloseDemo3() );
    }

    public void windowClosing(WindowEvent e) {System.exit(0);}

    public void windowClosed(WindowEvent e) { }
    public void windowOpened(WindowEvent e) { }
    public void windowIconified(WindowEvent e) { }
    public void windowDeiconified(WindowEvent e) { }
    public void windowActivated(WindowEvent e) { }
    public void windowDeactivated(WindowEvent e) { }
}
```

Here you make the demo class itself implement WindowListener. The body of the class provides all the methods that WindowListener demands. When you want to add the WindowListener, you just instantiate an object of the demo class and away you go. The work is done in the main method which is static. If you were making that call in an instance method, the line would be even simpler:

```
jframe.addWindowListener( this );
```

It's a handy technique, but you're not done yet. You can make the code shorter still, as the next section explains.

Using a Listener Adapter Class

Even though you were interested only in the `windowClosing` event, you had to supply null bodies for all the methods in the `WindowListener` interface. To make things a little more convenient, a concept called *adapter classes* can be used. An adapter is one specific example of a design pattern. An adapter is the design pattern that converts the API of some class into a different, more convenient API.

In Java AWT event-handling, for some of the Listener interfaces (such as `WindowListener`), you might want to implement only one or two functions to handle the one or two events of interest, but the `SomethingListener` interface

may specify half a dozen methods. The language rules are such that you must implement all the functions in an interface even if you just give them empty bodies, as in the `WindowListener` above. The package java.awt.event provides adapters that help with the situation by allowing you to override as few methods as you like. They are:

- `ComponentAdapter`
- `MouseMotionAdapter`
- `WindowAdapter`
- `ContainerAdapter`
- `MouseAdapter`
- `FocusAdapter`
- `KeyAdapter`

These adapters are classes that provide empty bodies for all the methods in the corresponding `SomethingListener` interface. Here is WindowAdapter.java:

```
public abstract class WindowAdapter implements WindowListener {
     public void windowOpened(WindowEvent e) { }
     public void windowClosing(WindowEvent e) { }
     public void windowClosed(WindowEvent e) { }
     public void windowIconified(WindowEvent e) { }
     public void windowDeiconified(WindowEvent e) { }
     public void windowActivated(WindowEvent e) { }
     public void windowDeactivated(WindowEvent e) {}
}
```

If you can declare your event handler as a subclass of one of these adapters, you can provide only the one or two methods you want, instead of implementing all the methods in the interface. Let inheritance do the work. Another way of doing this would be to have one `Adapter` class that implements *all* the `Listener` classes with null methods for all of them. In that way, you don't have to remember all the individual adapter names. That's the way I would have done it, which is probably why I'm not on the Swing design team.

Since Java classes have only one parent, you can't use this technique if you already inherit from some other class (although you can always create a new class just to make it a subclass of some adapter). Here is an example showing how the `WindowAdapter` class is used when all you are interested in is the `windowClosing` event:

```
import javax.swing.*;
import java.awt.event.*;
public class CloseDemo4 extends WindowAdapter {

     public static void main(String[] args) {
          JFrame jframe = new JFrame("Example");
          jframe.setSize(400,100);
          jframe.setVisible(true);

          jframe.addWindowListener( new CloseDemo4() );
     }

     public void windowClosing(WindowEvent e) {System.exit(0);}
}
```

The code is much shorter and easier to understand. What could be simpler than an adapter? Well, it turns out that there is a major pitfall with adapter classes, and it's one of those awful problems that leaves you swearing at the keyboard the first time you encounter it. You'll know to check for it thereafter, but the first time is a little frustrating. I'll use KeyAdapter as an example, because you've seen enough of WindowListener. The KeyListener is an interface used to send keyboard events. A keyboard event is generated when a key is pressed, released, and typed (pressed and released). There are KeyListener methods for all three of these. For this example, let's say you are going to use an adapter because you're interested only in the keyPressed event. Let's create an anonymous class for the KeyAdapter.

When you create an inner class for an adapter class, you simply supply the one or two methods that you wish to override, like this:

```
new KeyAdapter() {
     public void keyPressed(java.awt.event.KeyEvent e)
     { System.out.println("got "+e.getKeyChar()); }
} // end anon class
```

You may, however, make a small spelling or letter case error in supplying your method, like this:

```
new KeyAdapter() {
     public void KeyPressed(java.awt.event.KeyEvent e)
     // Notice capital "K" in "KeyPressed" WRONG!
     { System.out.println("got "+e.getKeyChar()); }
} // end anon class
```

Such a spelling mistake means that your method will not override the intended method in the adapter class. Instead, you have added a new method that never gets invoked. The empty body of the correctly spelled method in the adapter class will be invoked instead, and it will do nothing. If your event handler seems to do nothing and you used an adapter, your first check should be that the method name and signature exactly matches something in the adapter class.

As mentioned at the start of the chapter, learning how to handle events is like clearing your plate of vegetables before being allowed to sit down to dessert. You've now eaten enough vegetables, so I'll wrap up this chapter with a summary.

Summary of Event-Handling

We have seen a specific example of handling the event generated by closing a Window. It can be written more compactly if you write it as an inner class or even as an anonymous class. You can junk even more unneeded code if you use an adapter class.

There are several kinds of events for the different controls: a button generates one kind of event, a text field another, and so on. To impose a little order and to split them up according to what they do, there are a dozen or so individual Listener interfaces shown in Table 19-1. They all work the same way: You write a handler class that implements the interface, and register it with the control. When the control fires an event, the method in the handler object that you registered is called.

The key points to note on GUI handling are:

- Each interface `SomethingListener` has one or more methods showing the signature of a method that is called when the corresponding `SomethingEvent` occurs.
- Your handler code implements the `SomethingListener` interface and therefore has methods with signatures that fulfill those promised in the interface.
- Each control has a method called `addSomethingListener()`. The `addSomethinglistener()` method takes a single argument, an object that implements the `SomethingListener` interface.
- Swing requires that all code that might affect GUI components be executed from the event-dispatching thread. There is a section, "Swing Threads—A Caution!," explaining what this means in the next chapter.
- You call `addSomethingListener()`, using an instance of your handler class as the parameter. This registers your object as the handler for that kind of event for that control.

The `SomethingEvent` class is a subclass of class `AWTEvent` and stores all the information about what just happened, where, and when. An object of the `SomethingEvent` class is passed to the method in the `SomethingListener` interface. It sounds more complicated than it is. The design pattern is shown in Figure 19-4.

643

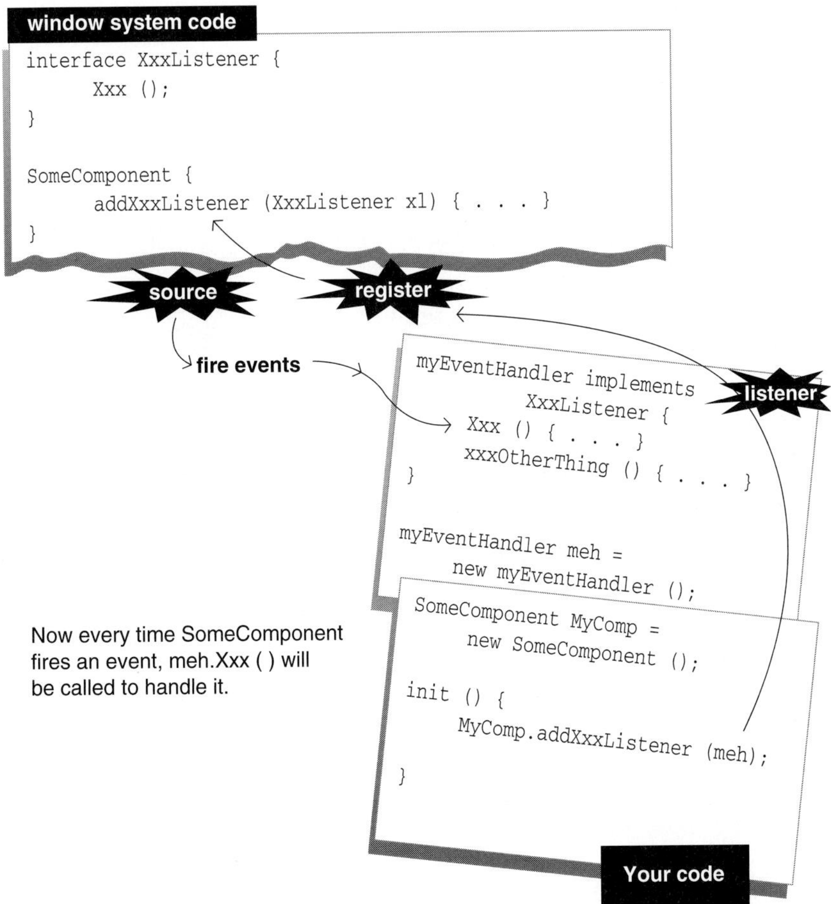
window system code
interface XxxListener {
Xxx ();
}
SomeComponent {
addXxxListener (XxxListener xl) { . . . }
}
source
register
fire events
myEventHandler implements
XxxListener {
Xxx () { . . . }
xxxOtherThing () { . . . }
}
listener
myEventHandler meh =
new myEventHandler ();
SomeComponent MyComp =
new SomeComponent ();
init () {
MyComp.addXxxListener (meh);
}
Now every time SomeComponent fires an event, meh.Xxx ( ) will be called to handle it.
Your code

Figure 19–4 Design pattern of JDK 1.1 event-handling.

You can register several handlers to receive the same single event if you wish. You can dynamically (at runtime) remove or add an event handler from a control. You add an event handler with a call like this:

```
myComponent.addWindowListener( myEventHandler );
```

You won't be too surprised to learn that the method to remove one is this:

```
myComponent.removeWindowListener( myEventHandler );
```

We won't show all the dozen or so *Something*Event classes and *Something*Listener interfaces here. You can and should look at them by typing the following:

```
javap java.awt.event.MouseEvent
```

Compiled from `MouseEvent.java`:

```
public synchronized class java.awt.event.MouseEvent
        extends java.awt.event.InputEvent
{
    public static final int MOUSE_FIRST;
    public static final int MOUSE_LAST;
    public static final int MOUSE_CLICKED;
    public static final int MOUSE_PRESSED;
    public static final int MOUSE_RELEASED;
    public static final int MOUSE_MOVED;
    public static final int MOUSE_ENTERED;
    public static final int MOUSE_EXITED;
    public static final int MOUSE_DRAGGED;
    int x;
    int y;
    int clickCount;
    boolean popupTrigger;
    public int getX();
    public int getY();
    public java.awt.Point getPoint();
    public synchronized void translatePoint(int, int);
    public int getClickCount();
    public boolean isPopupTrigger();
    public java.lang.String paramString();
    // constructor
    public java.awt.event.MouseEvent(java.awt.Component,
        int,long,int,int,int,int,boolean);
}
```

Similarly, you can check on the interface that is implemented by your handler by typing the following:

```
javap java.awt.event.MouseListener
```

Compiled from `MouseListener.java:`

```
public interface java.awt.event.MouseListener extends
        java.lang.Object implements java.util.EventListener {
    public void mouseClicked(java.awt.event.MouseEvent);
    public void mousePressed(java.awt.event.MouseEvent);
    public void mouseReleased(java.awt.event.MouseEvent);
    public void mouseEntered(java.awt.event.MouseEvent);
    public void mouseExited(java.awt.event.MouseEvent);
}
```

We don't need to show the `java.awt.event.MouseAdapter` class because it has all the same methods, only with empty bodies (of course). You should use the online browser documentation to look at the public fields and methods of all the other Events and Listeners. A full list of the events and listeners is given in the next chapter.

There are a lot of new ideas presented by event-handling, so don't worry if it doesn't all make sense now. Sleep on it, reread it, try the sample programs, and it will all come together. Get the event-handling down before moving on.

Exercises

1. Review the javadoc pages for classes and interfaces in package java.awt.event. How many classes and interfaces are there?

2. Write a program that displays a JFrame. Install a key listener and the three kinds of mouse listener on the frame. Print out each event that is received. Are you surprised at the number of mouse motion events?

3. The source code for the event interfaces and their methods can also be reviewed in the directory $JAVAHOME/src/java/awt/event. ($JAVAHOME is wherever you installed the release. On my system it is "C:\jdk1.4".)

   Take a look at MouseWheelEvent.java, which shows how support for the new mouse wheels was added in JDK 1.4. What information can a mouse wheel event convey?

4. After doing the previous exercise, design and describe the event that represents a Zap. Zaps are delivered from the new "Wendy Wand" hardware that can be pointed at any component and invoked with a wink and a shake. Zaps have a location on the screen, a Zap-strength field (wimpy, medium, stun, or to-frog), and a Zap-Color.

5. Write a program that displays a JFrame and handles Zap events. Simulate Zap events by instantiating them and posting them to the event queue. Class java.awt.EventQueue has a method postEvent() that will do this for you. Perhaps you could make a mouse click generate a Zap event in its handler.

Some Light Relief—The Mouse That Roared

If you think about it, just about everything computer-related must have been designed for the first time or done for the first time by somebody. At some point there must have been the first editor, the first debugger, the first core dump, the first disk drive.

Sometimes these events are surprisingly recent. Sometimes they are old. The term "core dump," meaning a copy of the contents of a process's memory, is pretty old. It dates back to the early 1950s when computer memories really were composed of cores. Main memory was built out of tiny ferrite rings or "cores" threaded on fine wires which could induce or reverse a magnetic polarity in the cores. Memory was literally made up of cores each holding one bit, and the contents of memory was a "core dump." Switching time was slow, but it didn't matter because processors were slow too, with cycle times in the milliseconds.

One of the computer "firsts" was the first mouse pointing device. We even know where this was launched: at the Fall Joint Computer Conference in San Francisco in October 1968. It took another 16 years before memory and graphics software got cheap enough to bring the mouse into everyday use with the 1984 Apple Macintosh.

The pioneering inventor of the mouse was computer scientist Doug Englebart (Figure 19-5), who worked at the Stanford Research Institute in Menlo Park, California. Doug (pictured here in 2001) was interested in graphical displays and ways of improving the human-computer interface. He had the idea for a hand-operated pointing device in 1964, and it took four years to bring it to fruition.

Figure 19–5
Mouse inventor Englebart.

At that time, there were no computers for personal use. Time-sharing was only just starting, and the only people with graphical displays were radar operators. Doug had to persuade managers at SRI to buy an $80,000 graphics console to support his research project. He could foresee a time when screens would replace teletypes, and computers would be cheap enough to have several at home.

The world's first computer mouse still exists (Figure 19-6). Doug brings it along to talks and shows it off. It's about the size of a house brick, and is carved out of a block of pine wood. Pieces are getting chipped off it over the years. The mouse size was determined by the internal mechanism. It uses two large potentiometers to track movements. The pots are essentially wheels that have an electrical resistance that changes as the wheel rotates. Doug wanted a sideways mouse movement of 6 inches to correspond to a complete move across the screen; 2.pi.r equals 6, so you need pots about two inches in diameter, and a case the size of a house brick to hold everything.

Figure 19–6
The first mouse.

Figure 19-7 shows the underside of the prototype mouse, clearly showing the workings.

The pot wheels are mounted at right angles to each other. As you push the mouse, the wheels rotate in proportion to the amount it moves up and along. The resistance of the pots varies, and an analog-to-digital converter turns the measurements into numbers that are sent down the cable to the computer. The computer displays those changing numbers in the form of a moving cursor. The wheels are chamfered so they turn even when pushed diagonally.

The world's first mouse had a single red button at the top right. Notice that the tail comes out of the front of the mouse, not the rear. Clearly, the first priority was to prove the concept, then improve the ergonomics. The device was named early in its development, nobody now remembers by who. With its original size, it could easily have been labeled a "cat" instead of a mouse.

Figure 19–7
The belly of the mouse.

Some later studies at Xerox PARC showed that the mouse was near optimal in terms of access time and accuracy. It is twice as good as some other kinds of pointing devices: eye tracking systems, light pens, or graphics tablets. The mouse is going to be with us for some time to come.

The new high ground in input devices is speech. You can buy several voice recognition products today, but let me tell you, they are nowhere near as good as the speaking computer on the starship Enterprise. Speech is generally a poor way of communicating with a computer. It's tiring and tiresome. You probably won't use it much where a keyboard is available, but it will be a boon to control your cell phone or pocket organizer.

The software has to improve substantially before real-time spoken I/O becomes common. That is partly a matter of boosting CPU power, which is driven by Moore's Law. At the end of 2001, the fastest Intel chip you can buy runs at 2 GHz. By 2005, it will be ten times faster at 20 GHz.

There is a Java Speech API developed under the Java Community Process as specification JSR-113. You can read more about it at *java.sun.com/products/javamedia/speech/*. There are several implementations available today to let you put speech technology into your user interfaces in a future-proof way. When better implementations using more processor power come out, you can plug them in underneath your Java code without changing a single line. That's not guaranteed to happen if you program directly to the third-party APIs. I'm still thinking about those 20 GHz cpus. That's a lot of processor power to soak up. We'd better get busy! Bridge to computer: The helm is yours.

Chapter 20

All About Applets

"People say you can't compare apples and oranges. But why not? They are both hand-held, round, edible, fruity things that grow on trees."

—*Anonymous*

Java is a fine general-purpose programming language. It can be used to good effect to generate stand-alone executables just as C, C++, Visual Basic, Pascal or Fortran can. Java offers the additional capability of writing code that can live in a web page and be downloaded and executed when the web page is browsed. Here is why is it useful to put a program in a web page and publish it on the Internet:

- Anyone, on any platform, with any version of any operating system, can run the program immediately, without installing anything (as long as the browser has Java configured).
- It is simple to run the program— just browse the web page it is on.
- An applet enables a web page to move beyond a static one-way presentation to live content that can interact with the user and with the web server. See examples at the end of the chapter, and on the CD.

Although most commercial applets are written for in-house use, and thus do not have a high public profile, applets remain an important capability of Java. If you want to write applications, write applications. If you want to write applets and put them in web pages, write applets and put them in web pages. This chapter explains how to do that.

Reminder on Java Programs

There are three different ways to run a Java executable:

- As a stand-alone program that can be invoked from the command line. This is termed an *application.*
- As a program embedded in a web page to be run when the page is browsed. This is termed an *applet.*
- As a program that is invoked on demand on a server system and that runs in the context of a web server. This is termed a *servlet.*

Applications and applets differ in the execution privileges they have and also in the way they indicate where to start execution.

Differences Between Applets and Applications and How to Convert Between Them

Many programmers are unduly worried about the differences between applets and applications. People often post questions on the Java newsgroups saying that the book they are reading focuses on one of these when they are interested in the other. The truth is that 95% of the information carries over between applets and applications. All the GUI information is common.

In fact, apart from the security restrictions on applets, each kind of execution framework can be transformed easily into the other. All the examples here can easily be rewritten as an applet or an application. The JDK demo directory has a class in file $JAVAHOME/demo/applets/GraphicsTest /AppletFrame.java that provides the framework to run an applet as an application. In application mode, AppletFrame creates a frame and puts the applet inside. You could use this class as the basis for your code. This doesn't quite take you all the way, as you still need to take care of applications that need applet services like `appletContext()`, but it does 99% of what you need.

Java Plug-In Is Now Much Easier to Use! The Java plug-in is a browser plug-in like the Acrobat PDF reader, or the VRML virtual reality viewer. Its purpose is to provide a standard JVM for applet web pages that the browser downloads.

Java Plug-in version 1.3.1_01a and later has a huge improvement. It now supports ordinary HTML applet tags. When first introduced, the Java plug-in needed a special HTML tag that said, in effect, "execute this applet using the Java plug-in rather the browser's non-standard or down-rev Java VM." This special HTML tag (the "<object>" tag) was very clumsy and offputting, and required you to update all your HTML pages. It was never very popular, and so the plug-in was never popular, and so Java applets were stuck with 1.1 features only. That's as far as the browser companies got before Microsoft fixated on "cutting off Netscape's air supply" (as one Microsoft executive put it).

Sun has found a way to get the plug-in to run applets, even when the browser has some Java support and would normally render them itself. It is done through the registry on Windows; no binary patches are involved. This is great news and could lead to a revival of applets if the news were better publicized, or if the plug-in was preinstalled on more computers. With the plug-in, your applets can use all the Java 2 features, and no special HTML is needed. The plug-in is part of the JRE, and you download it from *java.sun.com/j2se/1.4/jre/index.html*. When you install the JRE, it automatically installs the plug-in too.

After downloading the file, double-click on its icon to run the installer. The installer will add an icon for the plug-in into your control panel on Windows. You can further configure the plug-in from there, for example, to display the Java console window. Now you can happily run applets that use the latest JDK 1.4 libraries and features.

There are a number of special considerations that apply to applets. These considerations include connecting a class file to a web page, starting execution, screen appearance, parameter passing, and security. Let's take these one by one.

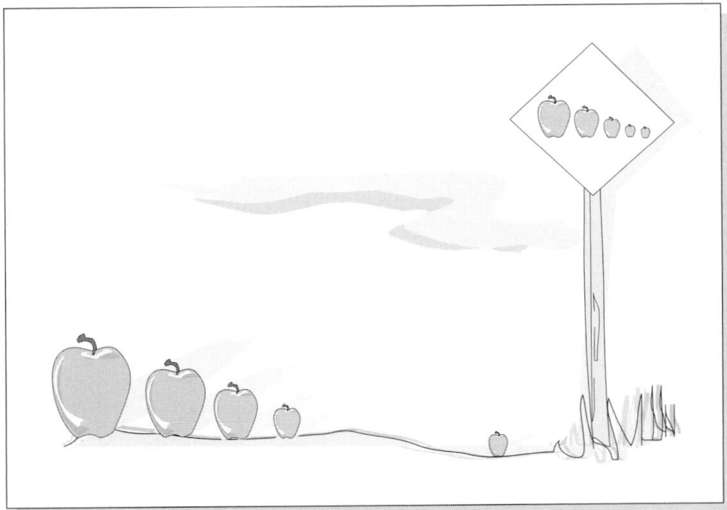

Figure 20–1 Applets come in all sizes.

Embedding a Java Program in a Web Page

As mentioned previously, an applet is a Java program that is invoked, not from the command line, but rather through a web browser reaching that page, or equivalently through the appletviewer that comes with the Java Development Kit. We will stick with using the appletviewer in this chapter because we are trying to teach the language, not the use of a browser.

The first thing to understand about applets is how they are run from a web browser. The numerous Applet methods that your applet subclasses can override follow from that.

Web browsers deal with HTML (HyperText Markup Language). There are HTML tags that say, "Set this text in bold," "Break to a new paragraph," and "Include this GIF image here." There is now an HTML tag that says, "Run the Java applet that you will find in this .class file." Just as a GIF image file will be displayed at the point where its tag is in the HTML source, so the applet will be executed when its tag is encountered. The applet will start running even if it is on a part of the page that is scrolled off the screen.

The HTML to Invoke an Applet

An example of the HTML code that invokes an applet is shown below:

```
<h1>A simple applet</h1>

<applet code=myApplet.class width=300 height=50>
               ... a bunch of optional parameters can go here
</applet>
```

The width and height fields are mandatory, and they are measured in units of pixels (dots of resolution on the computer monitor). Applets run in a GUI subclass object, either a `JApplet` (newer Swing GUI) or an `Applet` (older AWT GUI). You have to tell the browser how big a panel the applet takes up on the page.

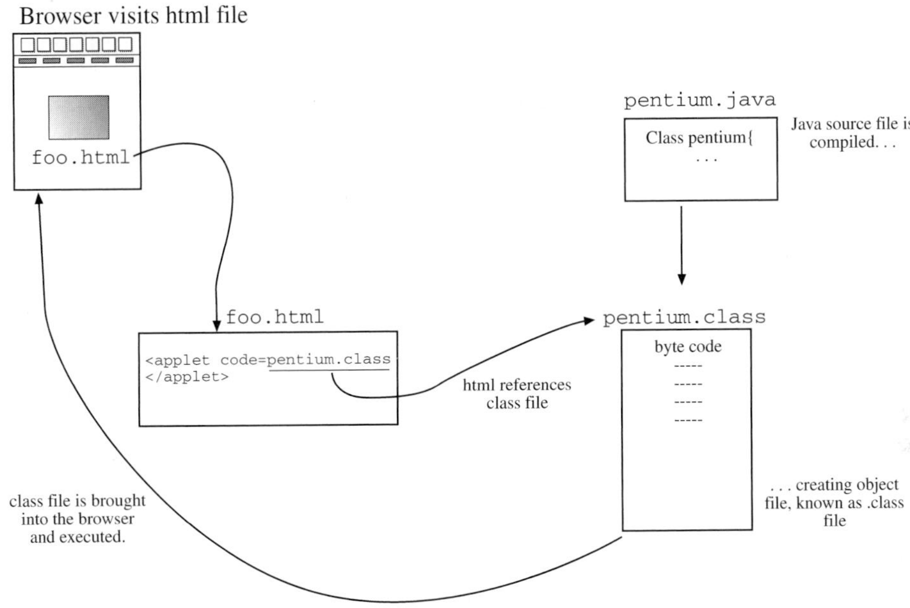

Figure 20–2 The file example.html will run here as shown.

Figure 20-2 shows how the source, bytecode, and HTML files are related, and how they are used. The classfile must be found in one of these two places:

- **remotely**, in the same directory that served up this HTML page, or at the CODEBASE defined in the HTML tag. CODEBASE specifies a different directory or URL that contains the applet's code.
- **locally on the client,** somewhere along the CLASSPATH environment variable or in the standard places the browser will look for code (varies for each browser).

Applets located on remote servers can be accessed just as easily as those stored locally.

The full list of tags that can be used for applets is listed at the end of the chapter.

Starting Applet Execution

Applets are started up in a different manner from applications, and the difference is more than just command-line versus HTML file. Applications start execution in a public function called `main()` similar to the convention used in C. Applets have a different convention, involving overriding certain prenamed functions.

The first thing to note is that an applet is a *window object* that *runs in a thread object*, so every applet will be able to do window-y kind of things and thread-y kind of things. An applet's execution starts using the thready kind of methods that we have already seen.

You always create an applet by extending the Java class `javax.swing.JApplet`, and providing your own versions of some of the methods. You can override the `start()` and `stop()` methods, but you do not call them yourself. This funny stuff exists because of the funny context in which applets live. The class is loaded once, instantiated by the browser (not you), and then subject to repeated execution as the web browser visits and revisits the page containing the applet. The diagram in Figure 20-3 shows how.

Java Applets, Browsers, and Plug-Ins

Applets have been somewhat sidelined as a technology because of the browser wars between Microsoft and Netscape. As a result, I do not know of any browsers that support Swing applets (JApplet) out of the box.

To run Swing-based applets, you will need to augment the browser with the Java plug-in. The plug-in is included with the JDK and the JRE, so you don't even need to install it separately.

The method `init()` is a good place to create GUI objects and threads. Similarly, you will only override the methods `start()` and `stop()` if you have something that actually needs to be started and stopped, namely, threads. You can usually leave `destroy()` alone.

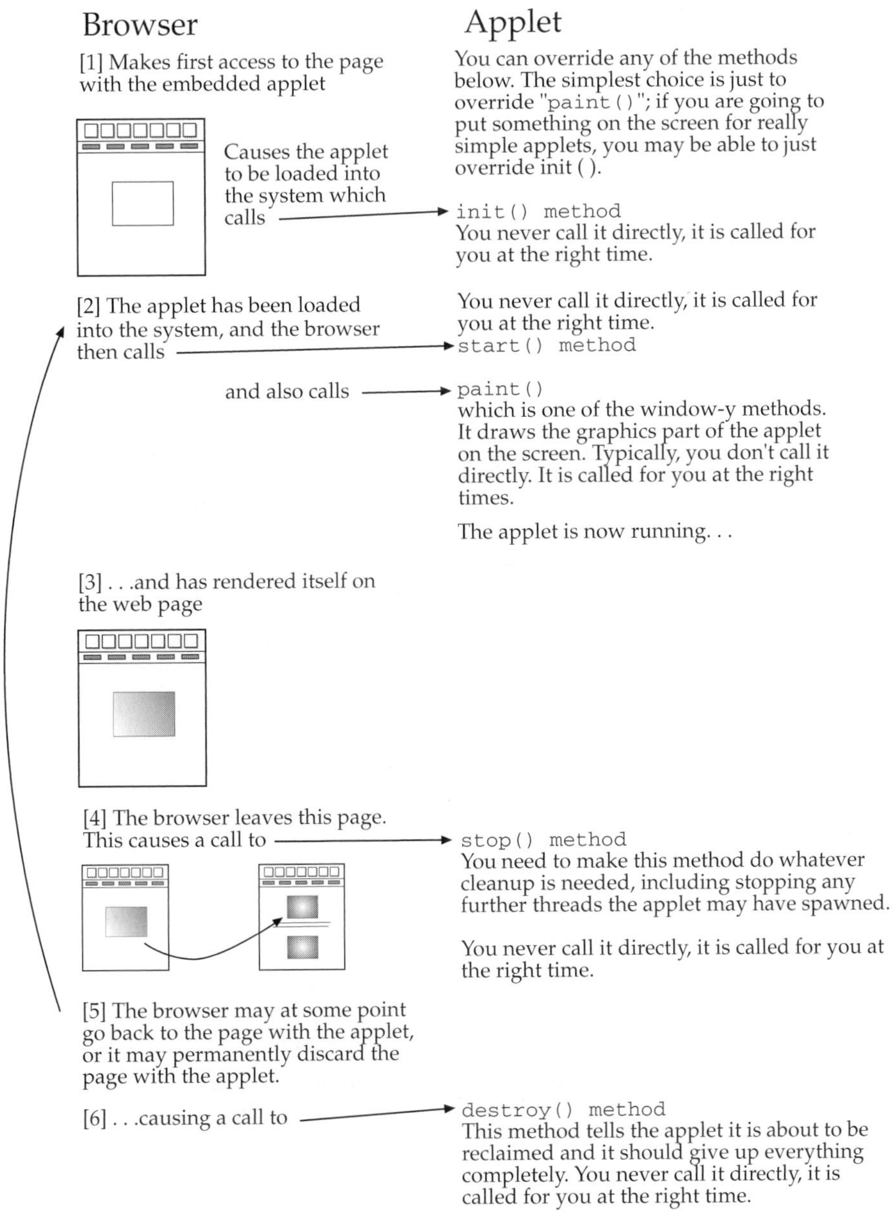

Browser

[1] Makes first access to the page with the embedded applet

Causes the applet to be loaded into the system which calls →

Applet

You can override any of the methods below. The simplest choice is just to override "`paint()`"; if you are going to put something on the screen for really simple applets, you may be able to just override init ( ).

`init() method`
You never call it directly, it is called for you at the right time.

[2] The applet has been loaded into the system, and the browser then calls →

You never call it directly, it is called for you at the right time.
`start() method`

and also calls →

`paint()`
which is one of the window-y methods. It draws the graphics part of the applet on the screen. Typically, you don't call it directly. It is called for you at the right times.

The applet is now running. . .

[3] . . .and has rendered itself on the web page

[4] The browser leaves this page. This causes a call to →

`stop() method`
You need to make this method do whatever cleanup is needed, including stopping any further threads the applet may have spawned.

You never call it directly, it is called for you at the right time.

[5] The browser may at some point go back to the page with the applet, or it may permanently discard the page with the applet.

[6] . . .causing a call to →

`destroy() method`
This method tells the applet it is about to be reclaimed and it should give up everything completely. You never call it directly, it is called for you at the right time.

Figure 20–3 Repeated execution caused by a hypertext web browser.

```
public class MyApplet extends javax.swing.JApplet {

      public void init() { ... }

      public void start() { ... }

      public void stop() { ... }

      public void paint(Graphics g) { ... }
}
```

Figure 20–4 Basic code framework of an applet.

All applets have the same basic code framework that corresponds to the life cycle shown in Figure 20-3. The framework is shown in Figure 20-4

It is most important that you override `stop()` and explicitly stop any threads in the applet. Otherwise, they will continue to run and consume browser cycles even after you leave the page. Table 20-1 summarizes the applet methods and when they are called. You do not have to have threads in your applets.

Table 20–1 Summary of Key Applet Methods

Method	Description
`void init()`	Called when the applet is first loaded into memory. Typically, you override it with one-time initialization code.
`void start()`	Called each time the browser visits the page containing this applet. Typically, you override it to start or resume any threads the applet contains.
`void stop()`	Called when the browser leaves the page containing this applet. Typically, you override it to stop or suspend any threads the applet contains.
`void paint(Graphics g)`	Will be called by the window system when the component needs to be redisplayed. You will not call this. You will override this method with your code to dynamically change the appearance of the screen.
`void run()`	This has nothing to do with applets. This is the routine in which thread execution starts, if the applet has one.

We won't use threads in applets here for simplicity. They can be used if you want. We will show them in a later chapter.

In JDK 1.2, the GUI appearance was greatly improved by a new library called the Swing library, which supplements the original AWT library. The AWT Applet class is extended by the Swing JApplet class. All the basic applet functionality still comes from the java.applet.Applet class which follows.

```
public class java.applet.Applet extends java.awt.Panel {
// lifecycle methods:
     public java.applet.Applet();
     public void init();
     public void start();
     public void stop();
     public void destroy();

// media related methods
     public java.applet.AudioClip getAudioClip(java.net.URL);
     public java.applet.AudioClip getAudioClip(java.net.URL, String);
     public java.awt.Image getImage(java.net.URL);
     public java.awt.Image getImage(java.net.URL, java.lang.String);
     public static final java.applet.AudioClip newAudioClip(java.net.URL);
     public void play(java.net.URL);
     public void play(java.net.URL, java.lang.String);

// get information methods
     public java.lang.String getParameter(java.lang.String);
     public java.lang.String getParameterInfo()[][];
     public boolean isActive();
     public java.applet.AppletContext getAppletContext();
     public java.lang.String getAppletInfo();
     public java.net.URL getCodeBase();
     public java.net.URL getDocumentBase();
     public java.util.Locale getLocale();
     public void resize(int, int);
     public void resize(java.awt.Dimension);
     public final void setStub(java.applet.AppletStub);
     public void showStatus(java.lang.String);
}
```

The `javax.swing.JApplet` class has this appearance:

```
public class javax.swing.JApplet extends java.applet.Applet
     // inherits all the Applet methods above, plus
     // about 2 dozen methods of its own relating to Swing (omitted)
     ...
}
```

Screen Appearance of an Applet

Here is an example of the minimal applet:

```
public class Message extends javax.swing.JApplet {
     public void paint(java.awt.Graphics g) {
          g.drawString("Yes!", 30, 10);
     }
}
```

An HTML suitable for this program might be this:

```
<applet code=Message.class width=200 height=100> </applet>
```

Now put it in a file called Message.html. Compile the Java program.

```
javac Message.java
```

Run it under the appletviewer with the following command:

```
appletviewer Message.html
```

A window will appear, as shown in Figure 20-5.

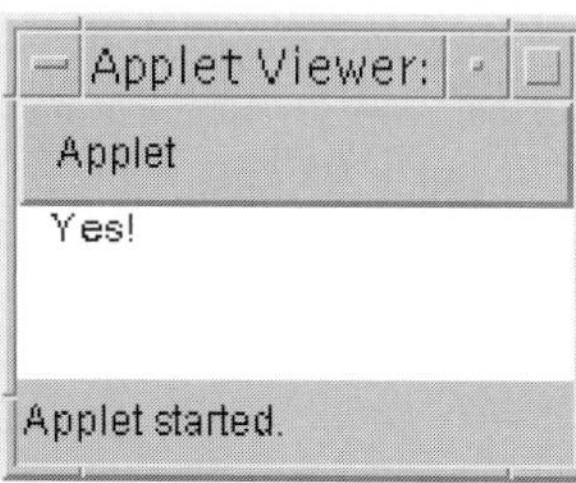

Figure 20–5
A minimal applet.

If you don't see this, step through the installation instructions again, checking that you have done everything correctly. You can also run this in your browser by directing it to browse the HTML:

```
netscape file:///home/linden/Java/Message.html
```

Because an applet is a windowing thing (we will get back to more formal terminology eventually), it does not use ordinary command line I/O that we have seen so far. Instead, it uses the facilities that are available to windows, like drawing a string at particular coordinates. The coordinate system of every window has the origin in the top-left, as shown in Figure 20-6.

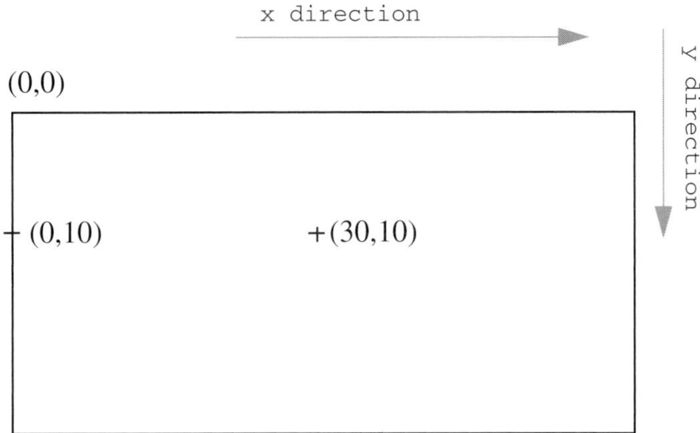

Figure 20–6 Every window's coordinates originate in the top-left corner.

Watch out: if you paint text at a y coordinate of zero, it will be painted up from there, and will not be visible. What are the other facilities that are available to windows? We will discuss these in greater depth in the later chapters that deal with the Abstract Window Toolkit. The AWT class called `Container` contains the superclass from which JApplet is (eventually) derived. Container has the method paint() which is called by the Window toolkit whenever the applet panel needs to be refreshed. By providing our own version of paint, we override Container's version.

You can look at the source for method drawString() in file java/src/awt/Graphics.java.

```
public void paint(Graphics g) {
     g.drawString("text to display", x_pos, y_pos);
}
```

The Graphics class has many methods concerned with rendering a shape, line, or text onto the screen. It will also let you select colors and fonts.

The convention throughout Java is that class names begin with a capital letter, and method names start with a lowercase letter, but subsequent words in the name are capitalized. This leads to odd-looking names like "drawString" that make it seem as though someone had a previous job writing ransom notes wItH rAndOmlY caPitALiZeD LeTteRs. ("wE HaVe yOuR MiSsinG piXeL. seNd $10K iN sMaLL BilLS. dO nOt TeLl tHe PolICe. ThEy'Re sTuPId.")

When the compiler complains that it can't find one of the library methods, your first thought should be "did I get the capitals right?" It is not always consistent in that we have MenuBar and yet Scrollbar in the window toolkit. In particular, watch out for the "instanceof" operator that uses no capitals. In cases like this, it's better to always be consistent or always be inconsistent, but not keep changing between the two.

We mentioned that some programs need to explicitly start threads, rather than have them created and started in one operation. An applet running in a web browser is one of those programs. It allows a closer fit to the "go back to a page you already visited and which is likely to still be loaded" model. That is why init() (one-time initialization) is separated from start() (called every time the page is accessed).

Speed Up Applet Development!

When you start creating applets, you usually need at least three files before anything can happen: a .java source file, a .class bytecode file, and a .html file. If you aren't careful with your naming, you'll lose track of what's where.

One suggestion (for experts only) that is useful while the code is under development is to put the HTML commands in the java source file, inside a comment, like this:

```
// <applet  code=Message.class  height=100  width=100>
// </applet>
public class Message extends javax.swing.JApplet {
    public void paint(java.awt.Graphics g) {
        g.drawString("Yes!", 10,10);
    }
}
```

It offers two advantages: First, you cut out the need for a separate HTML file (so you don't waste time flipping back and forth between HTML file and source file in the editor); and secondly, you can put the parameters for the applet right in the file with the applet code (so it's easy to check that you've got them right). Then you invoke appletviewer on the source file, like so:

```
appletviewer  Message.java
```

This works because browsers just read arbitrary text files looking for tags. They don't care if the file contains source code as well.

Browser Summary

The browser will automatically instantiate an object of your Applet subclass, and make certain calls to get it running.

You can overload some of the called methods. The methods init() and paint() are the ones you will mostly overload, unless you have threads in the applet, when you will want to overload start() and stop(), too.

Typically, you never call any of these methods. They are called for you by the window system/browser at appropriate times. As the browser visits pages and moves away from them, these predefined Applet methods are invoked.

Passing Parameters to Applets

Just as we have command-line arguments for applications, there is a similar feature for passing arguments from the HTML file to the applet it invokes. Parameters are indicated by an HTML tag of this form:

```
<param     name=namestring     value=valuestring>
```

The param tags come after the <applet> tag and before the </applet> tag. An example of some actual parameters in an applet version of the anagram program might be:

```
<applet  code=anagram.class  width=500, height=500>
    <param   name=datastring value="surfing the net">
    <param   name=wordfile   value="words.txt">
    <param   name=minsize    value="2">
</applet>
```

It does not matter if strings are quoted or not, unless the string contains embedded white space. Inside the program you call getParameter() with the name as an argument, and it returns the string representing the value. If there isn't a parameter of that name, it returns null. Here is an example:

```
String s = getParameter("minsize");
// parse to an int. int minsize = Integer.parseInt(s);
```

Notice that this follows the same conventions as `main( String argv[] )`—all arguments are passed as strings, and programmers need to do a little processing to get the values of arguments that are numbers.

To pass a double as a parameter to an applet, the HTML tag would look like this:

```
<param name=peach   value="3.1" >
```

The code to retrieve it would be:

```
String s = getParameter("peach");
double d = Double.parseDouble(s);
```

JDK 1.2 introduced a parseDouble method to create a double from a String. Before that, you had to create a double object from the String, then extract the double value from that.

Build in Debugging Help

You can put a main method in any class—even a class that runs as an applet or a class that isn't the main routine of your application. Like any other method that isn't called, it doesn't do any harm.

Some programmers recommend adding a main() routine to all classes. This main should just be a test driver to check the functionality of that class. When you are debugging your system, you'll find it most convenient to test individual classes this way. Just leave it there—it won't hurt in the finished version of the system.

Alternatively, you can use a main() routine in a different class as a different entry point to your program, allowing the program to do slightly different things depending on which class you tell the interpreter to start in. You can vary this from run to run.

You can also create a program that runs as either an applet or an application. Just add a main() method that creates a Frame for the applet to run in. Then create an instance of the applet and call its start() and init() methods.

You will need to do a little more work if your applet wants to reference anything that belongs to its parent class, because most of those fields are filled in by the browser and will be null. There's an applicet framework which does all the hard work for you available at *users.belgacombusiness.net/arci/*.

Zip Files and Jar Files

This section explains how you can group together any number of files into one zip file. There are two reasons for doing this: a small reason and a big reason. The small reason is that if you have a Java program that consists of five `.class` files, three `.jpg` files, four `.au` files, and a GIF file, that's a lot of files to remember to move onto your web server. It's much more convenient for passing the program around if you can roll all the pieces up into one large archive file, just as the Windows ZIP or the Unix tar utilities do.

The second, more important reason for grouping together lots of little files into one large file is that HTTP (the protocol used between a web server and a client browser) is an inefficient protocol. It takes a large amount of effort on both the server and client side to set up an HTTP connection. For files of just a few K, the time and effort to set up the connection can easily outweigh the time to transmit the file. And not just by a little, but by a lot. As with disk I/O, one large read of 1000 bytes is far less time and effort than the sum of 1000 small reads of 1 byte each. For an individual client, the applets arrive and start running faster. At the server end, the server can handle many more client requests at a time, and throughput rises.

JDK 1.0.2 lets you wrap up several class files in a `.zip` file using the standard PKZIP format popularized on PCs. Zip file format does two pieces of work: it shrinks individual files by compressing them, and it groups together multiple files into a single zip file archive. The compressed zip format was not supported in JDK 1.0.2, but came in the next release. We won't dwell on zip files in JDK 1.0.2 because things are better and easier in JDK 1.1.

PKZIP

PKZIP stands for Phil Katz ZIP. The zip part just means "bringing things together speedily" as a clothing zip fastener does. Phil Katz was the programmer who, several years before Java, developed the zip file format, the compression format, and `.zip` file extension and put it all in the public domain for the benefit of everyone in the industry. Java now has a built-in API to read and write zip files; some examples of this are in the first I/O chapter.

Keep Your Software in a Jar

In JDK 1.1, the format was extended to a JAR, or "Java ARchive." A jar file contains a group of files in zip format with compression turned on. Jar format is (to all intents and purposes) identical to zip format, and you can use all the zip tools to process jar files, and vice versa. You can create your own jar files by using standard WinZIP, other software, or the `jar` utility that comes with JDK 1.1. The `jar` program has a command line that looks like this in general form:

```
jar [ options ] [manifest] destination input-file [input-files]
```

The options that `jar` takes are similar to those of `tar`—the Unix tape archive utility—but the formats are different, and tar files are not used in Java. JDK 1.2 also introduced an option to update (replace a file in) an existing Jar file. To create a compressed archive of all the class files and `.jpg` files in a directory, you would use the command

```
jar cvf myJarFile.jar *.class *.jpg
```

An example of the applet tag used with a jar file follows:

```
<APPLET   ARCHIVE=myfile.jar
          CODE=myapplet.class
          WIDTH=600   HEIGHT=250>
</APPLET>
```

These lines will use an applet called `myapplet` that can be found in the jar file `myfile.jar`. You can supply several jar file names in a comma-separated list.

Removing the Contents from a Jar

As we mentioned earlier, a jar file can contain media files as well as code. The class files will be extracted automatically when the class loader sees a jar file in an applet tag such as:

```
<applet
   archive=Example.jar
   code=Example.class
   height=200 width=250>
</applet>
```

The noncode files, however, like `.gif`, `.au`, or `.jpg`, must be extracted a slightly different way. The method `getImage (getCodeBase(), image_name)`, which works for individual image files in the HTML directory, doesn't work when the file is in a jar.

This applet example shows how to pull a media file out of a jar file. The key idea is that the class loader (that brought the bytes into memory) knows where to find the Jar file. It has a method that lets you create a URL for files inside the jar (this line is shown in bold in the example). The rest of the code is the magic associated with displaying an image and is described in the chapter on graphics programming. The approach also works for `.au` (sound) files and `.gif` files.

First, create our example source file called `view.java` with this HTML and code inside it.

```
 /* <applet
       archive=view.jar    code=view.class
       width=350           height=450>
   </applet>
*/
import java.net.*;
import java.awt.*;
import java.awt.image.*;
import java.applet.*;

public class view extends Applet {
    String MyFileName = "titan.jpg";
    URL MyURL;
    Image MyImg;
    ImageProducer MyImgProd;

    public void init() {
        Toolkit tool = Toolkit.getDefaultToolkit();
        MyURL = getClass().getResource(MyFileName);
        try {
            MyImgProd = (ImageProducer) MyURL.getContent();
        } catch (Exception ex) {
             System.out.println(ex.getMessage());
        }
        MyImg = tool.createImage( MyImgProd );
    }

    public void paint(Graphics g){
        g.drawImage(MyImg, 10, 10, this);
    }
}
```

The code is on the CD under `book/ch20`. This works because an object's class knows about its classloader, and its classloader knows how and where the class file was brought in from a file.

Compile the code, and create the jar file by entering these commands:

```
% javac view.java

% jar -cvf view.jar  view.class titan.jpg
adding: view.class (in=1418) (out=781) (deflated 44%)
adding: titan.jpg (in=59698) (out=59340) (deflated 0%)
```

Then, you can run the program by using the appletviewer:

```
% appletviewer view.java
```

The applet will successfully read and execute the code from the jar file. It will then extract the JPEG file from the jar and display it on the screen, as shown in Figure 20-7.

Be careful: The appletviewer may just wait forever if you send it to look for a file that isn't there. You must make sure that your applet tags, jar name, and file names are all absolutely correct.

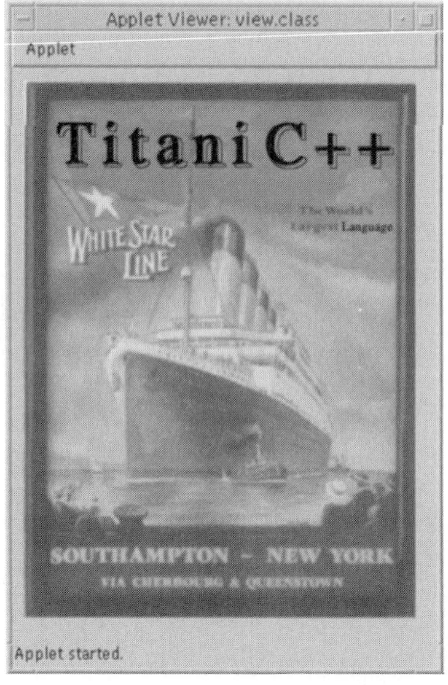

Figure 20–7
Displaying a JPEG extracted from a jar file.

Also, if you are using the programmer's shortcut of placing the HTML into the source file, then it's better to use `/*` to open a comment at the beginning, and `*/` to close a comment at the end of all the tags. The browsers and applet viewers get confused if they find `//` on lines interspersed with applet tags.

Finally, don't forget that once you put some code in a jar, it's not enough to recompile when you change something. You must also rebuild the jar file with the new `.class`; otherwise, you'll continue to get the old version of the program.

Lastly, note that `getClass().getResourceAsStream()` should be used for the Netscape 4.x browsers. Netscape has disabled getResource() under some circumstances due to their own security considerations.

Applications Can Be Stored in Jars, Too

This chapter has shown several examples of applets run from a jar file. You can also store an application in a jar file and run it without unpacking the contents. The command will execute the application contained in the jar file.

```
java -jar  MyApp.jar
```

For this to work, the manifest file in the jar file needs to say which class has the main() routine where you want execution to start. You provide this information with the Main-Class header, which has the general form:

```
Main-Class: MyMainClassName
```

Put that line of text into a file called "wheretostart.txt." When you create the jar file, ensure that the information gets put into the manifest of the jar by using the command

```
jar cmf wheretostart.txt write.jar write.class
```

Java Web Start

There is one area of browser-related Java technology that is flourishing, and that is Web Start. Java Web Start is a small piece of software "glue" installed on a client. It allows the client to get to applications via web pages. Click on a link—the web server downloads an application, and Web Start launches it locally on the client.

Why do this instead of just installing and running the application locally? Because the application is now secured and kept up to date on the server. Upgrading the application is done by replacing one copy on the server, instead of 100 copies on 100 clients.

A company can put up a web page on its intranet with links to all the authorized IT applications. Employees access all the applications they need through the centralized web server, but get all the advantages of running the application locally. The first time an application is run it has to be downloaded, but that copy is saved locally. On subsequent runs, Web Start checks that the software is still up to date and downloads any updates before starting the application.

There is a demonstration at *java.sun.com/products/javawebstart/demos.html* that lets you download the client part of Web Start, and then gives you access to five small sample applications that can be downloaded. One of the applications is an application manager that keeps track of things you ran recently or frequently. All this is written in Java, of course. The manager is shown in Figure 20-8.

If applets don't meet all your needs, but you still want the administrative ease of centrally-served applications, look into Web Start.

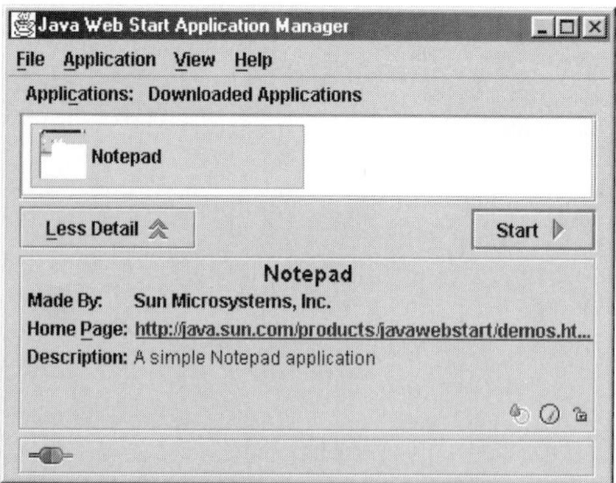

Figure 20–8 Webstart Application Manager.

HTML Applet Tags

The full list of tags that can be used for applets is:

```
<applet
     code=classfilename
     width=integer_pixels
     height=integer_pixels
     [archive=archivefile [,archivefile]]
     [codebase=applet-url]
     [vspace=integer_pixels]
     [hspace=integer_pixels]
     [align=alignment]
     [name=some_name]
     [alt="You need a browser that understands Java" ]
>
```

The applet tag can be followed by zero or more parameter tags, with the general form of attribute name/value pairs.

```
<param name=param_name  value=param_value >
```

Here is an example:

```
<param name=soundfile value=teletubbies.wav>
```

You can also put some alternate HTML here, which will only be formatted if the browser doesn't understand the applet tag. Finally, the applet ends with an "end applet" tag:

```
</applet>
```

Confusingly, letter case is not significant for any HTML tags or attribute names, but it is significant for some of the arguments they take (e.g., the name of the class file). When in doubt, make your use of uppercase and lowercase consistent.

The attributes have the following meanings:

```
code=classfilename
```

This attribute is required and names the class file that is to be executed. *Note:* This must be just a single file name, with no part of a longer path prefixed to it. So, "foo.class" is good, but "bin/foo.class" is bad.

```
width=integer_pixels
height=integer_pixels
```

These two attributes are required and say how large a space the applet takes up in the browser.

All the remaining attributes are optional.

```
archive=archivefile [,archivefile]
```

This attribute allows an applet to bundle all its class files and media files into one ZIP or jar archive. The browser will retrieve the entire file in one big transaction, rather than many slow, smaller transactions.

```
codebase=applet-url
```

This attribute allows you more flexibility where applet class files are located. You can provide a URL identifying a directory in which the browser looks for the class files this applet loads. Since it is a URL, the directory can be specified anywhere on the Internet, not just on the server or client system. If this attribute is omitted (a common occurrence), the class files must be in the same directory as the HTML file.

```
vspace=integer_pixels
hspace=integer_pixels
```

These two attributes allow you to specify the size of the blank margin to leave around the applet in the browser. These two tags and the one below are similar to the attributes of the same names used with the <IMG> tag.

```
align=alignment
```

This attribute allows you to control where the applet appears on the page. There are several possible alignment values: "left," "right," "top," and "middle" are popular choices.

```
name=some_name
```

The name provided here is associated with the applet. It can be used by other applets running on the same page to refer to the applet and communicate with it.

```
alt=some_text
```

This attribute specifies the text to be displayed in the (unlikely) event that the browser does not understand Java.

The <applet> tag was invented specifically for Java, but it is possible that people will want to download other types of executable content. It would be a poor idea to have to invent a new tag for each new type of downloadable program. Accordingly, the <embed> tag has been proposed to replace the <applet> tag. The main difference is that <embed> allows you to put a full URL on the beginning of the "class=" attribute (and it calls it "src=," not "class="). As a result, the codebase attribute would not be needed.

Exercises

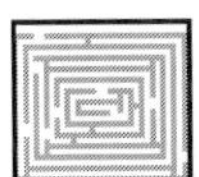

1. Make the anagram application into an applet.

2. The scheme for passing parameters to applets from HTML is very flexible and in fact allows you to pass an arbitrary number of parameters. Let's say you give your HTML parameters names that end with a number in sequence, like this:

```
<param  name=myparam1   value="some value" >
<param  name=myparam2   value="another value" >
<param  name=myparam3   value="25.2" >
```

It's then easy to concatenate a count onto the name as an argument to getParameter like this:

```
next = getParameter( "myparam"+i );
i++;
```

That way you can keep retrieving parameters until null is returned. Write a program with the two statements above in a loop to demonstrate this. Print out the value of the parameters received.

3. Write an applet that reads a file. Run it in the appletviewer and set the properties so it runs successfully. Then sign it and configure a browser to run it. You will probably want to review the security chapter first.

4. Distinguish between "init()" and "start()" in an applet.

5. Modify the Web War game to give a player six lives.

6. Modify the Web War game so that the box shapes that come at you are star shapes instead.

Some Light Relief—Three Fine Applets

In this last part of the applet chapter we'll present some real-world applets. These will give you a good idea of the results that skilled programmers can achieve with applets. For our first example, we'll zoom over to the Microprizes site created by Carl Ginnow.

Microprizes is a company that creates small game and puzzle applets. They are similar in concept to the toy prizes found in boxes of cereal. Advertisers can use Microprizes to bring customers to their web sites. Because they are small, they download quickly, and don't cost much compared to larger computer games.

Carl has a whole collection of Microprize applets at *www.microprizes.com/mpmap.htm*. I like the game called "Sparky's fun house" in which you help a chipmunk-like character navigate through a maze of conveyor belts (hey, I didn't say it made sense or anything).

Carl worked in aerospace for a while, and the laser puzzle is based on his experiences there. The whole Microprize concept is clever. People are fed up with pop-up ads, and the time is right for better ways of attracting customers to your site.

The next applet that we will review was written by programmers at NASA. You can find it at *liftoff.msfc.nasa.gov/RealTime/JTrack/Spacecraft.html*. JTrack 3D is an applet that displays a model of the planet earth, and decorates it with the paths of over 500 satellites that are in orbit. It plots the positions of the satellites in real

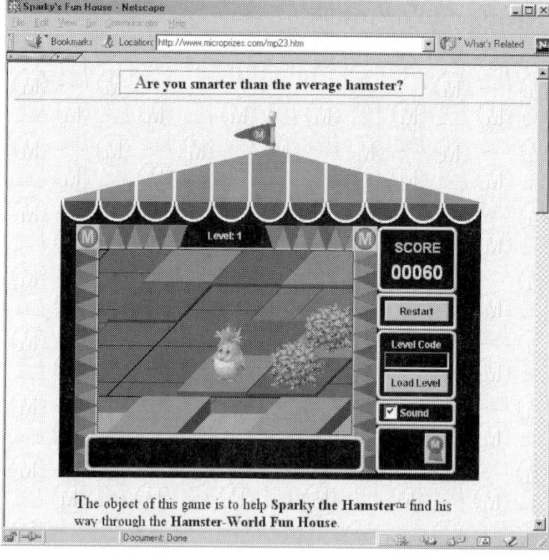

Figure 20–9
Sparky's Fun House.

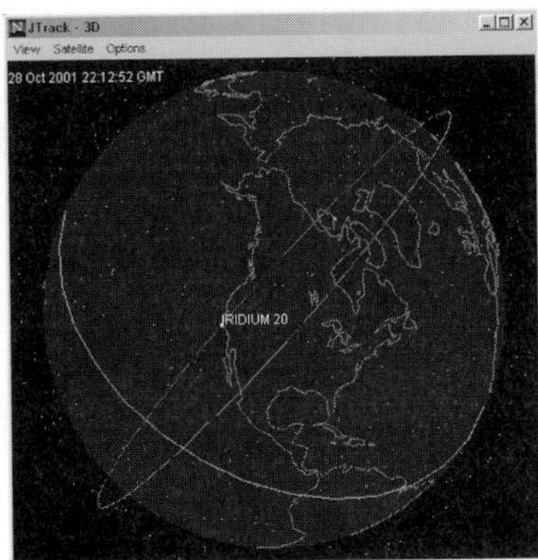

Figure 20–10
NASA's JTrack 3D.

time so you can use it to predict when one of these will be visible overhead (see Figure 20-10).

Satellites don't have any running lights, so they are only visible when they reflect the light of the sun. The best time for seeing them is just after dusk and just before dawn. That's when the sky is dark for you on the ground, but the satellite is high enough up to see the sun and reflect its light to you.

My career in satellite observation has been somewhat checkered. A few years ago, I got my family out of bed at 5 a.m. to tramp out in the middle of a field and (supposedly) watch the space shuttle pass overhead. We all arrived in the field and stared glumly overhead in the gloom. The wind sprung up and flapped at our pajamas. A light rain began to fall. After some time it was clear that I was not going to be able to produce the shuttle or anything else that compared with the attraction of a warm bed. Despite my entreaties, a withdrawal was ordered, and we never did see the shuttle, that day or any other. Perhaps JTrack will help me with more accurate data.

Each white dot is the current position of a satellite. You can click on any of them to bring up an identifying label. You can zoom in and out, and click/drag the earth to change its orientation. It's hard to describe how awesome that effect is; you just have to try it.

The JTrack 3D applet also lets you speed up real time so you can watch the orbits and the planet spin many times faster than one rotation per day.

The last applet that we'll review here is an arcade-style game called "Web Wars" (Figure 20-11). It was written by Burkhard Ratheiser who runs a games software company in Germany. Burkhard is currently completing a doctorate in biochemistry, and he has been fascinated by computer games and games programming since he borrowed his elder brother's Commodore VIC at the age of ten.

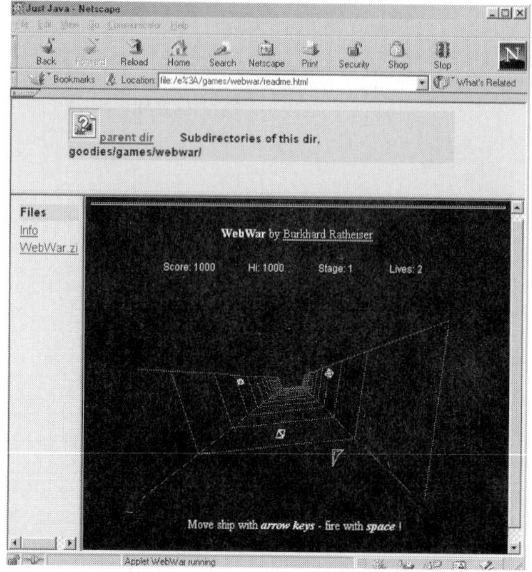

Figure 20–11
Web Wars.

Burkhard has graciously agreed to allow me to put the source code on the CD. You will find it in the "games" subdirectory.

I must admit, the first thing I usually do when I get the source code of a game is modify it to give me some extra lives so I'll have a chance of getting good at it.

The premise of Web Wars is that you are piloting a triangular craft down a channel or ditch. You can swing up to either side of the channel, but not out of it. Wireframe boxes come racing down the channel. You can shoot them down by pressing the space bar. If they collide with you, you crash and lose.

I love the physics in this game. Once you get up a level or two, the boxes start dancing towards you in graceful curves. Position your craft just right, and you can spit a straight line of ack-ack fire, and let the boxes drift across it. Hah! So perish all packages that dare to oppose the Web War Master!

You can try the Web War applet by browsing the CD that comes with this book:

file:/e:/games/webwar/readme.html

(substitute the correct letter for "e" if your CD drive is in another place).

Chapter 21

JFC and the Swing Package

- Java Foundation Classes
- All About Controls (JComponents)
- Swing Threads—A Caution!
- Swing Components
- More about Swing Components
- Further Reading
- Exercises
- Some Light Relief—The Bible Code

In Chapter 19, we saw that the basic idea behind Java GUI programs is that you:

- Declare controls. You can subclass them to add to the behavior, but this is often unnecessary.
- Implement an interface to get the event-handler that responds to control activity.
- Add the controls to a container. Again, subclassing is possible but frequently unnecessary.

That chapter explained how to handle the events that controls generate. This chapter dives into the details of the controls themselves: what they look like, how you use them, and what they do. The next chapter wraps up by describing containers and how you use them to lay out controls neatly on the screen.

Java Foundation Classes

Supporting a Java interface to the underlying native window libraries achieves the goal of making Java GUI programs highly portable, but it comes at the cost of inefficiency. Peer events must be translated into Java events before they can be handled by Java code. Worse, native libraries aren't identical on each platform, and sometimes the differences leak into the Java layer.

Example of How Native Library Behavior Leaked into the AWT

Sun never did get filename filtering working for the AWT "file selection dialog" on Windows systems. This is bug 4031440 on the Java Developer Connection at *java.sun.com/jdc*.

To support FilenameFilter, the AWT FileDialog needs to issue a callback for each file it wants to display, and you supply a FilenameFilter that can accept or reject the file. But on Win32, the FileDialog control works in a completely different way. It doesn't issue callbacks. Instead, it accepts simple wildcard patterns to match against filenames. That's a reasonable alternative to FilenameFilters, but that model isn't supported by the current Java API. As a result, AWT filename filtering never worked on Win32.

This is an example of the difficulties of trying to make a common window library above the native library. Swing solved these difficulties, since there is no reliance on native library support. The javax.swing.JFileChooser class lets the user select a file without dependence on the native components.

The Java Foundation Classes (JFC) are a set of GUI-related classes created to solve the AWT problem of platform idiosyncrasies. JFC also supports:

- A pluggable look-and-feel, meaning that when you run the program, you can choose whether you want it to look like a Windows GUI, a Macintosh GUI, or some other style.
- An accessibility API for things like larger text for the visually impaired.
- The Java 2D drawing API.
- A drag-and-drop library and an "undo last command" library.
- The Swing component set.

The Swing components (scrollbar, button, textfield, label, etc.) replace the AWT versions of these components. The AWT is still used for the other areas of GUI functionality, like layout control and printing. There's an appendix in this book that contains descriptions of the AWT components. They are simpler than the Swing components, but more basic and more bug-prone. We're describing and working with JFC from here on.

JFC is bundled with JDK 1.2 as a standard part of Java and was also available unbundled for JDK 1.1. Although it's a core library now, the "x" in the package name in JDK 1.2, `javax.swing`, reflects the fact that the package first became available as an optional extension library. There was quite a bit of churn over the correct package name for Swing, and the unbundled version for JDK 1.1 was released as package `com.sun.java.swing`. You should use Swing, rather than AWT components, in new programs you write. All browsers now support Swing through the use of the plug-in.

How Do AWT, JFC, and Swing Fit Together?

AWT (Abstract Window Toolkit) provides the totality of GUI support in JDK 1.0. It offers a basic set of GUI objects, and also supports all the other features of a Window toolkit: the ability to lay out objects, group them together, print them, and so on.

JFC (Java Foundation Classes) is a big set of libraries that adds to one part of AWT and replaces another part. JFC provides support for things that are missing in AWT, like accessibility features for the visually impaired, a 2D drawing library, and the "pluggable look-and-feel."

One of the key pieces of JFC is the *Swing component set*. The Swing GUI components (button, textfield, scrollpane, etc.) are intended to completely replace the corresponding AWT GUI components. The Swing components are better and often simpler. AWT is still needed for all the non-component services that it provides. Swing only replaces one piece of AWT.

The choices you have for GUI objects are:

JDK 1.0—AWT

JDK 1.1—AWT or the unbundled version of Swing

JDK 1.2—The core Swing package or AWT

For the sake of simplicity, I use AWT exclusively in JDK 1.0 and 1.1, and Swing in JDK 1.2 for GUI components.

The Java Foundation Classes are aimed squarely at programmers who want to build enterprise-ready software at least as good as (often better than) software built with native GUI libraries. The JFC has the additional advantage of being a lot simpler than competing window systems and producing code that runs on all systems. It is also future-proof. Your programs won't stop working on your next OS change. JFC is the most important thing to happen in user interfaces since the Macintosh operating system.

Some Terminology

In Win32, the term *control* means the group of all the GUI things that users can press, scroll, choose between, type into, draw on, and so forth. In the Unix XWindows world, a control is called a *widget*.

Neither control nor widget is a Java term. Instead, we use the term *Component*, or, when talking specifically about Swing, the *JComponent* subclass of Component. Each Swing control is a subclass of `javax.swing.JComponent`, so each control inherits all the methods and data fields of `JComponent`. JComponents are serializable, meaning the object can be written out to disk, can be read in again later, and can become an object again. They follow the rules for JavaBeans, so they can be coupled together in visual builder tools.

Heavyweight versus Lightweight Components

In AWT, all components are based on peer components. A Java AWT button really is a Win32 button on Windows. This is termed a *heavyweight component.* A *lightweight component,* like all the Swing JComponents, is one which doesn't use a peer or native component. Instead, it is drawn by Java code on a piece of the screen that already belongs to Java. It is drawn onto its container. The most important differences are:

- Lightweight components can have transparent areas in them, so they don't have to look rectangular in shape.
- Mouse events on a lightweight component are delivered to its container. So if you want a JButton to get mouse events for some reason, add the listener to the container.
- When they overlap, lightweight components are never drawn on top of heavyweight components. This is because you can't draw half of a lightweight component on one component and the other half on another. Lightweights exist wholly within their parent heavyweight component.

JavaSoft recommends that you not mix Swing JComponents with AWT components because of the poor behavior when overlapping.

This whole chapter is about explaining the Swing components and how you use them. You will build up your GUI programs using these components. The first thing to note is that the Swing components are no longer peer-based, but are written in Java and are thus consistent on all platforms. Under the AWT, a button ended up being a Win32 button on Windows, a Macintosh button on the Macintosh, and a Motif button on Unix. With Swing, the button is rendered on a little bit of screen area that belongs to some ancestor Java component, and Swing puts all the button semantics on top of that. Swing draws the button so it looks armed (ready to push), pushed, or disabled. Because the code is written in Java, the button has identical behavior no matter where it runs.

Frankly, JFC is a very big topic. There are more than three hundred classes in the Swing library alone. We'll present nine or ten individual Swing JComponents here, and provide pointers on the rest. This amounts to quite a few pages, so I recommend you read one or two in depth, then just look at the figures to get an idea of what each does. Return to the appropriate section in the chapter as you need actual code examples.

Overview of `JComponent`

Object-oriented programming fits well with window systems. The concept of making new controls by subclassing existing ones and overriding part of their behavior saves time and effort. Another similarity is the way that controls have to handle events just as objects handle messages. Method calls are equivalent to sending a message to an object, and some OOP languages even refer to a method call as "sending a message."

There is an abstract class called `JComponent`, which is the parent class for most things that can appear on screen. The basic ingredients of a GUI are all subclasses of the class called `JComponent`. `JComponent` is the superclass that holds the common information about an on-screen control and provides higher-level features common to each control, such as:

- Size (preferred, minimum, and maximum).
- Double buffering (a technique to make frequently changing components look smoother with less flickering).
- Support for accessibility and internationalization.
- Tooltips (pop-up help when you linger on a JComponent).
- Support for operating the control with the keyboard instead of the mouse.
- Some help for debugging by slowing component rendering so you can see what's happening.
- The thickness of any lines or insets around the edge of the Control.

Components correspond to "things that interact with the user" and Containers are "backdrops to put them on." The superclass of `javax.swing.JComponent` is `java.awt.Container`. And the parent of Container is java.awt.Component.

The behavior and appearance of each specific control is one level down in the subclasses of JComponent. The Swing lightweight controls can be divided up as shown in Table 21-1. We will look at just one or two components from each of these categories.

Each control has methods appropriate to what it does. The `JFileChooser` control has methods to get and set the current directory, get the selected filename(s), apply a filename filter, and so on. We'll examine these individual JComponents later in the chapter.

Table 21–1 Swing Lightweight Controls

GUI Category	Control	Swing Class Name
Basic Controls	Button	`JButton, JCheckBox, JRadioButton`
	Combo box	`JComboBox`
	List	`JList`
	Menu	`JMenu, JMenuBar, JMenuItem`
	Slider	`JSlider`
	Toolbar	`JToolbar`
	Text fields	`JTextField, JPasswordField, JTextArea, JFormattedTextField`
Uneditable Displays	Label	`JLabel`
	Tooltip	`JToolTip`
	Progress bar	`JProgressBar`
Editable Displays	Table	`JTable`
	Text	`JTextPane, JTextArea,JEditorPane`
	Tree	`JTree`
	Color chooser	`JColorChooser`
	File chooser	`JFileChooser`
	Value chooser	`JSpinner`
Space-Saving Containers	Scroll pane	`JScrollPane, JScrollBar`
	Split pane	`JSplitPane`
	Tabbed pane	`JTabbedPane`
Top-Level Containers	Frame	`JFrame`
	Applet	`JApplet`
	Dialog	`JDialog, JOptionPane`
Other Containers	Panel	`JPanel`
	Internal frame	`JInternalFrame`
	Layered pane	`JLayeredPane`
	Root pane	`JRootPane`

All About Controls (JComponents)

We now have enough knowledge to start looking at individual controls in detail and to describe the kinds of events they can generate. Almost the whole of window programming is learning about the different controls that you can put on the screen and how to drive them. This section (at last) describes some individual controls. The controls shown in Figure 21-1 are all subclasses of the general class `JComponent` that we have already seen.

These classes are the controls or building blocks from which you create your GUI. What you do with all these components is the following:

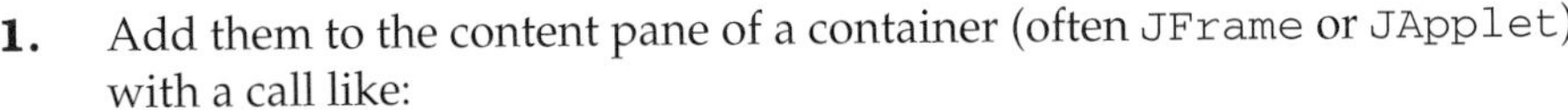

1. Add them to the content pane of a container (often `JFrame` or `JApplet`) with a call like:

   ```
   MyJContainer.getContentPane().add( myJComponent );
   ```

   The content pane is a layer within a container whose purpose is to have controls added to it. This is not well thought out. It would be better if you just added controls to a container, as you do in the AWT. Sun actually added a special check for this at runtime. If you add to a container instead of a container's content pane, it throws an exception and the message reminds you of the "right" way to do it!

2. Register your event-handler using the `addSomeListener()` method of the control. This tells the window system which routine of yours should be called when the user presses buttons or otherwise makes selections to process the event.

Fortunately, both of these activities are quite straightforward, and we'll cover them here in source code, words, and pictures. The add method can be applied to a `Frame` in an application like this:

```
JFrame jf = new JFrame();
                    ...
jf.getContentPane().add( something );
```

Or, it can be applied to the `JApplet`'s panel like so:

```
public static void init () {
     this.getContentPane().add( something );
```

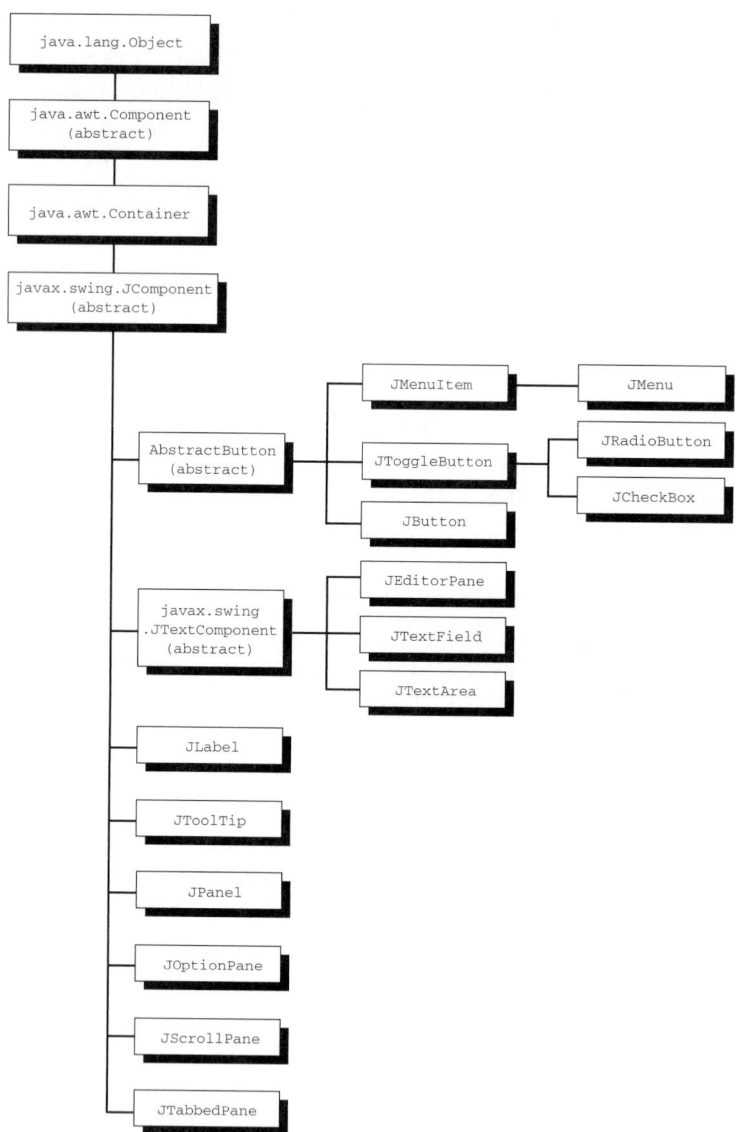

Figure 21–1 Some JComponent controls (visible GUI objects) of Java.

Recall the `Applet/JApplet` life cycle described in an earlier chapter. That discussion made clear that there is an `init()` method which each `Applet` should override. It will be called when the applet is loaded, and it is a good place to place the code that creates these GUI objects. We will use `init()` for that purpose. If you are writing an applet with Swing components, you must use JApplet (not Applet) as your parent class to ensure that all drawing and updates take place correctly.

Whenever a user operates a `JComponent` (presses a button, clicks on a choice), an event is generated. The source code for the `event` class can be seen in the `$JAVAHOME/src/java/awt/event` directory. It contains information about the coordinates of the event, the time it occurred, and the kind of event that it was. If the event was a key press, it has the value of the key. If the event was a selection from a list, it has the string chosen.

As we saw in the previous chapter, the runtime library creates one of these event objects for each occurrence of an event and queues them up on the event queue. The event dispatching thread takes event objects off the queue and calls your appropriate event handlers with the event object as an argument.

How to Display Components

Containers are the objects that are displayed directly on the screen. Controls must be added to a Container if you want to see them. The container in this example driver program is called *JFrame*. JFrame will be the main window for most of your Swing applications.

Let's create a JFrame, set its size, set it visible, tell it how to arrange JComponents that are added, and add some event-handler code to exit the program when it detects that you have clicked on the JFrame to close it. Phew! That's quite a list of tasks, so we'll split them off into a separate method. Make everything static. In this way, we can use it from the main() method, and we get the following:

```
import java.awt.*;
import java.awt.event.*;
import javax.swing.*;
public class Demo {
     static JFrame jframe = new JFrame("Example");

     public static void setupJFrame() {
          jframe.setSize(400,100);
          jframe.setVisible(true);
          jframe.getContentPane().setLayout( new FlowLayout() );

          WindowListener l = new WindowAdapter() {
               public void windowClosing(WindowEvent e) {
                    System.exit(0);}
          };
          jframe.addWindowListener(l);
     }

     public static void main(String[] args) {
          setupJFrame();
          JButton jb = new JButton("pressure");
          jframe.getContentPane().add( jb );
          jframe.setVisible(true);
     }
}
```

The JButton Component that we are trying to demonstrate is printed in bold type. The line that follows adds the JComponent to the JFrame's content pane. To cut down on the extraneous code in the pages ahead, I'll show only the statements that directly deal with the JComponent. That means I'll show only the two bold statements in the example above. You should supply all the missing code when you compile and run the examples. Next, a thread caution, then on to the first example!

Swing Threads—A Caution!

Here's a caution relating to threads. The GUI components are maintained on the screen by a thread of their own, separate to any threads that you have running in your code. This GUI thread is called the *event-dispatching thread*, and it takes care of rendering the GUI components and processing any GUI events that take place. An example of a GUI event would be a mouse click, a selection from a menu, or a keystroke on a text field.

The need for thread safety occurs in the system libraries just as much as it does in your code. To work properly, *Swing requires that all code that might affect GUI components be executed from the event-dispatching thread!*

As you know, events are handled by a callback from the window system to an event handler object you supply. That means that your event-handler code automatically executes in the event-dispatching thread, as it should. But should you try to create new GUI components in some other thread of yours, your thread will not be synchronized with runtime library data structures. Thus, the only place where you should create, modify, set visible, set size, or otherwise adjust GUI components, is in your event handler code. Otherwise, you will bring hard-to-debug synchronization problems down on your own head.

Here is an example of the natural-looking code which is erroneous:

```
public static void main (String[] args) {
    createSomeFrame(); // created in the main thread
    showThatFrame();   // shown by main thread,
    // now that first component is displayed, no more
    // code that affects components may be run from
    // any thread other than the event-dispatching thread
    createSomeOtherGUIComponent(); // WRONG!!!
}
```

There is one exception to the rule of doing GUI work only in the event-dispatching thread, which fortunately allows us to write our programs in the most natural way. You are allowed to construct a GUI in the application's main method or the Applet's init method, providing no GUI components are already on the screen from your program and providing you do not further adjust it from this thread after the GUI becomes visible. Most people obey these rules by accident, but you should know about them. For practical purposes, this means if you want to create a new GUI component in response to a GUI event, you *must* do the instantiation in the code that handles the GUI event.

If you have to do some further GUI work from one of your own threads, you can easily put it into the correct thread by using the Runnable interface. There is a Swing utility that takes a Runnable as an argument and runs it in the event dispatching thread. The code is as follows:

```
Runnable toDo= new Runnable() {
     public void run() {
          // things to do in the event-dispatching thread
          doTheWork();
     }
};
          ...
     SwingUtilities.invokeLater( toDo );
```

Be careful to follow this protocol in Swing programs! Now let's look at some Swing components.

Swing Components

JLabel

What it is: JLabel is the simplest JComponent. It is just a string, image, or both that appears on screen. The contents can be left-, right-, or center-aligned according to an argument to the constructor. The default is left-aligned. JLabel is a cheap, fast way to get a picture or text on the screen

What it looks like on-screen:

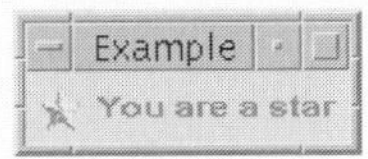

The code to create it:

```
//   remember, we are only showing relevant statements from main()
     ImageIcon icon = new ImageIcon("star.gif");
     JLabel jl = new JLabel("You are a star", icon, JLabel.CENTER);

     frame.getContentPane().add( jl );
     frame.pack(); // size the JFrame to fit its contents
```

Note the way we can bring in an image from a GIF or JPEG file by constructing an ImageIcon with a pathname to a file. Labels do not generate any events in and of themselves. It is possible, however, to get and set the text of a label. You might do that in response to an event from a different component. The constructors for JLabel are:

```
public javax.swing.JLabel(java.lang.String);
public javax.swing.JLabel(java.lang.String,int);
public javax.swing.JLabel(java.lang.String,javax.swing.Icon,int);
public javax.swing.JLabel(javax.swing.Icon);
public javax.swing.JLabel(javax.swing.Icon,int);
```

The int parameter is a constant from the JLabel class specifying left-, right- or center-alignment in the area where the label is displayed.

JLabels are typically used to augment other controls with descriptions or instructions. People often want to know how to get a multiline label (or a multiline button). There is no direct way. Either use multiple labels, or program the functionality in for yourself by extending the class `JComponent` to do what you want.

JButton

What it is: This is a GUI button. You supply code for the action that is to take place when the button is pressed.

What it looks like on-screen:

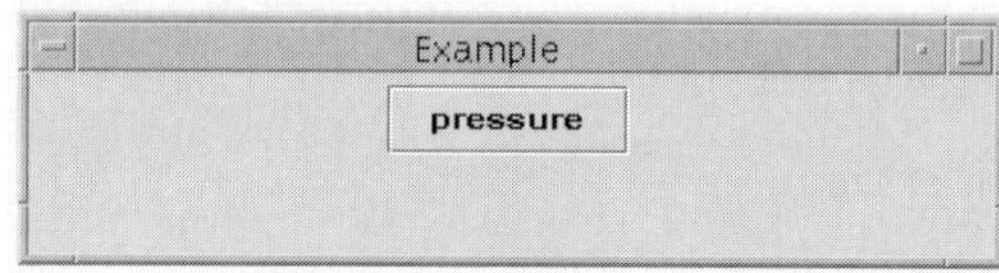

The code to create it:

```
JButton jb = new JButton("pressure");
jframe.getContentPane().add( jb );
```

The code to handle events from it:

```
jb.addActionListener( new ActionListener() {
     int i = 1;
     public void actionPerformed(ActionEvent e)
          { System.out.println("pressed "+ i++); }
     } );
```

When you press this button, the event-handler will print out the number of times it has been pressed. You can easily create buttons with images as well, like this:

```
Icon spIcon = new ImageIcon("spam.jpg");
JButton jb = new JButton("press here for Spam", spIcon);
```

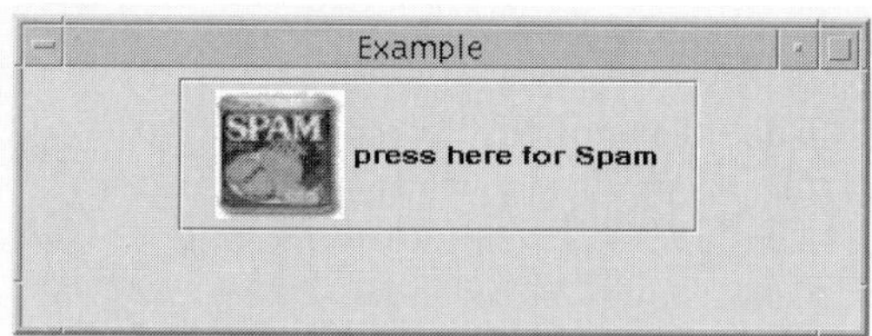

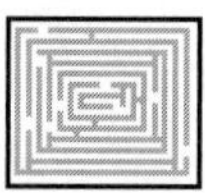

You can add a keyboard accelerator to a button, and you can give it a symbolic name for the text string that it displays. This helps with internationalizing code.

Program an "Alice in Wonderland" JFrame with two buttons, one of which makes the frame grow larger, the other smaller. The `Component` method `setSize(int, int)` will resize a `component`. (Easy—about twenty lines of code).

JToolTip

What it is: This is a text string that acts as a hint or further explanation. You can set it for any JComponent. It appears automatically when the mouse lingers on that component and it disappears when you roll the mouse away.

Tooltips don't generate any events so there is nothing to handle.

What it looks like on-screen: We'll add a tooltip to the JLabel that we showed on the previous page.

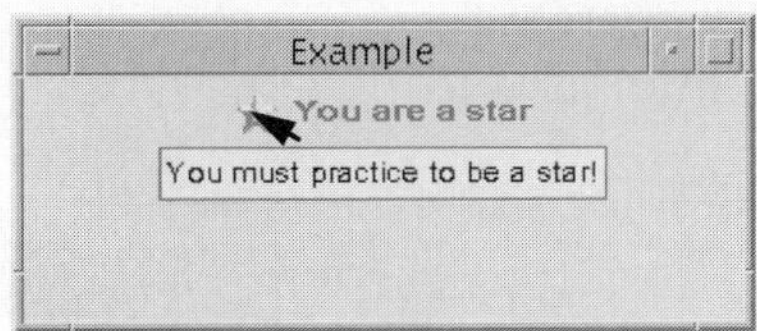

The code to create it:

```
JLabel jl = ...
jl.setToolTipText("You must practice to be a star!");
```

Notice that you don't directly create a JToolTip object. That is done for you behind the scenes. You invoke the `setToolTipText()` method of JComponent.

It's so quick and easy to create tooltips; use them generously.

JTextField

What it is: This is an area of the screen where you can enter a line of text. There are a couple of subclasses: JTextArea (several lines in size) and JPasswordField (which doesn't echo what you type in). You can display some initial text. The text is selectable (you can highlight it with the cursor) and can be set to be editable or not editable.

What it looks like on-screen:

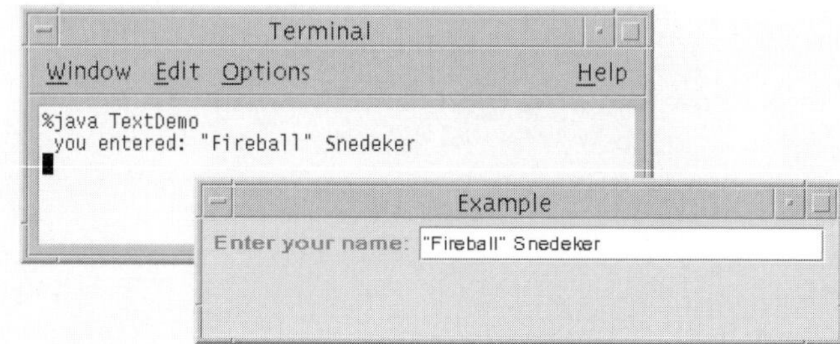

The code to create it:

```
JLabel jl = new JLabel("Enter your name:");
JTextField jtf = new JTextField(25); // field is 25 chars wide
```

The code to retrieve user input from it: Text fields generate key events on each keystroke and an `ActionEvent` when the user presses a carriage return. This makes it convenient to validate individual keystrokes as they are typed (as in ensuring that a field is wholly numeric) and to retrieve all the text when the user has finished typing. The code to get the text looks like this:

```
jtf.addActionListener( new ActionListener() {
     public void actionPerformed(ActionEvent e)
     {  System.out.println(
          " you entered: " + e.getActionCommand() ); }
     } );

Container c = jframe.getContentPane();
c.add( jl );
c.add( jtf );
```

In this example, running the program, typing in a name, and hitting carriage return will cause the name to be echoed on system.out. You should write some code to try implementing a listener for each keystroke.

JCheckBox

What it is: A checkbox screen object that represents a boolean choice: pressed, not pressed, on, or off. Usually some text explains the choice. For example, a "Press for fries" JLabel would have a JCheckBox "button" allowing yes or no. You can also add an icon to the JCheckBox, just the way you can with JButton.

What it looks like on-screen:

The code to create it:

```
JCheckBox jck1 = new JCheckBox("Pepperoni");
JCheckBox jck2 = new JCheckBox("Mushroom");
JCheckBox jck3 = new JCheckBox("Black olives");
JCheckBox jck4 = new JCheckBox("Tomato");
Container c = jframe.getContentPane();
c.add( jck1 ); c.add( jck2 ); // etc...
```

The code to retrieve user input from it: Checkbox generates both `ActionEvent` and `ItemEvent` every time you change it. This seems to be for backward compatibility with AWT. We already saw the code to handle ActionEvents with Button. The code to register an `ItemListener` looks like this:

```
jck2.addItemListener( new ItemListener()
{ // anonymous class
     public void itemStateChanged(ItemEvent e) {
          if (e.getStateChange()==e.SELECTED)
               System.out.print("selected ");
          else System.out.print("de-selected ");
          System.out.print("Mushroom\n");
     }
} );
```

In this example, running the program and clicking the "Mushroom" checkbox will cause the output of `selected Mushroom` in the system console.

Handlers in real programs will do more useful actions as necessary like assigning values and creating objects. The ItemEvent contains fields and methods that specify which object generated the event and whether it was selected or deselected.

JPanel

What it is: There was (and is) an AWT component known as `Canvas`. It is a screen area that you can use for drawing graphics or receiving user input. A `Canvas` is usually subclassed to add the behavior you need, especially when you use it to display a GIF or JPEG image. A `Canvas` contains almost no methods. All its functionality is either inherited from `Component` (setting font, color, size) or from functionality you add when you extend the class.

Everyone expects there to be a JCanvas replacing Canvas, just as JButton replaces Button, JFrame replaces Frame, and so on. There is no JCanvas. The AWT component Canvas was just like the AWT component Panel, except Panel was also a container. The Swing version of Panel, JPanel, does double duty. It replaces both Canvas and Panel.

To draw on a JPanel, you may want to supply your own version of the method `paintComponent(Graphics g)`. To do that, you need to extend the class and override the `paintComponent()` method[1] for this `Container`. That gives you a Graphics context—the argument to `paintComponent()`—which is used in all drawing operations. The many methods of Graphics let you render (the fancy graphics word for "draw") lines, shapes, text, etc., on the screen.

A simpler alternative for simpler drawings is to use JLabel to create the picture and add it to JPanel as shown in the following code.

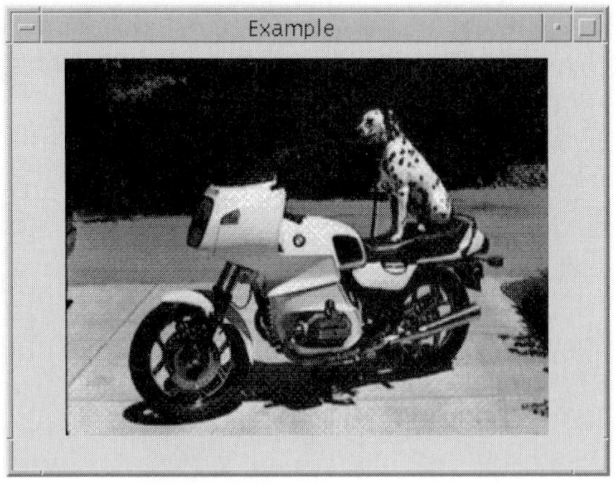

I like this picture because it looks the same in black and white as it does in color.

Figure 21–2 JPanel replaces Panel and Canvas.

1. A more descriptive name for the `paintComponent()` method would be `how_to_draw_me()`.

The code to create it: Figure 21-2 results from running the following code:

```
class MyJPanel extends JPanel {
     JLabel jl = new JLabel(new ImageIcon( "bmw.jpg"));
     { add(jl); // instance initializer just for fun

          addKeyListener( new KeyAdapter() {
               public void keyPressed(KeyEvent e) {
                    char c = e.getKeyChar();
                    System.out.println("got char "+c);
               }
          } );
     }
}

...

     public static void main(String[] args) {
          setupFrame();
          MyJPanel mjp = new MyJPanel();
          jframe.getContentPane().add(mjp);
          jframe.setVisible(true);
          mjp.requestFocus();
     }
```

I have also added a KeyListener for the JPanel here. That allows you to make keystrokes on top of the JPanel and have the callback take place for each one individually. All you do is echo the characters to prove you got them. With the picture backdrop and the capture of individual keystrokes, you have the basics of a computer game right there. There are a couple of real computer games on the CD.

You have to request the focus for a component before key events will be sent to it, and the component has to be visible at the time you do that.

`JRadioButton` and `ButtonGroup`

What it is: JRadioButtons are used when you have a group of checkboxes and you want a maximum of one of them to be selected. This was done with a `CheckboxGroup` in the AWT, but the design has been cleaned and simplified in Swing. JRadioButton, JCheckBox, and JButton are now subclasses of AbstractButton and have common consistent behavior, can be given images, can be embedded in menus, and so on.

The term "radio buttons" arises from the old manual station selection buttons in car radios. When you pressed in one of the buttons, all the others would pop out and be deselected. `ButtonGroups` work the same way.

What it looks like on-screen:

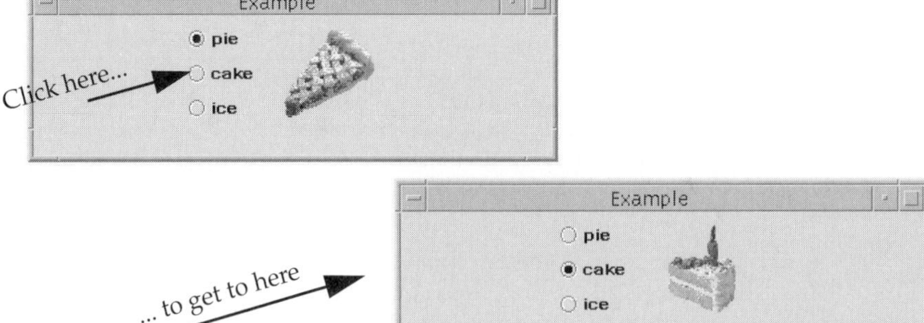

On Windows, mutually exclusive checkboxes are round, while multiple selection checkboxes are square. This is one of those "look and feel" differences between window systems.

The code to create it: This example shows some more sophisticated things you can do in your event-handler. In this example, we have a JLabel with a picture of the choice. In the event-handler, we set the label to correspond to the RadioButton choice.

The ButtonGroup class automatically takes care of arming the previous radio button when you press another.

```
// JRadioButton code
     final JLabel piclabel
          = new JLabel(new ImageIcon( pieString + ".gif"));

     /** Listens to the radio buttons. */
     class RadioListener implements ActionListener {
          public void actionPerformed(ActionEvent e) {
          // getting the event causes update on Jlabel icon
          piclabel.setIcon(
               new ImageIcon( e.getActionCommand()+".gif"));
          }
     }

     JRadioButton pieButton = new JRadioButton(pieString);
     pieButton.setMnemonic('b');
     pieButton.setActionCommand(pieString);
     pieButton.setSelected(true);

     JRadioButton cakeButton = new JRadioButton(cakeString);
     JRadioButton iceButton = new JRadioButton(iceString);

     // Group the radio buttons.
     ButtonGroup group = new ButtonGroup();
     group.add(pieButton);
     group.add(cakeButton);
     group.add(iceButton);

     // Register a listener for the radio buttons.
     RadioListener myListener = new RadioListener();
     pieButton.addActionListener(myListener);
     cakeButton.addActionListener(myListener);
     iceButton.addActionListener(myListener);

     // Put the radio buttons in a column in a panel to line up
     JPanel radioPanel = new JPanel();
     radioPanel.setLayout(new GridLayout(0, 1));
     radioPanel.add(pieButton);
     radioPanel.add(cakeButton);
     radioPanel.add(iceButton);

     jframe.getContentPane().add(radioPanel);
     jframe.getContentPane().add(piclabel);
     jframe.setVisible(true);
```

JOptionPane

What it is: This is a utility pane that can pop up some common warning and error messages. It's as easy to use as JToolTip, and it works the same way. You don't instantiate it directly, but you call a method to make it happen.

What it looks like on-screen:

The code to create it: The method to show a JOptionPane takes four arguments:

- A parent frame (null means use a default). The Pane appears below its parent.
- The thing to display. It can be a String or an icon or a JLabel or other possibilities that are converted to String and then wrapped in a JLabel.
- The title String to put on the Pane title bar.
- The type of message, like `ERROR_MESSAGE`, `WARNING_MESSAGE`, or `INFORMATION_MESSAGE`.

```
Icon s = new ImageIcon("spam.jpg");
JLabel jl = new JLabel("Are you getting enough?", s,JLabel.CENTER);

JOptionPane.showMessageDialog( null, // parent frame
                   jl,   // Object to display
                   "Plenty of spam", // title bar message
                   JOptionPane.QUESTION_MESSAGE );
```

The code to retrieve user input from it: No input comes back from this component. When the user clicks on the button, the Pane is dismissed automatically. There are a great many choices and methods that fine-tune this JComponent to let you convey exactly the nuance of information you want.

JScrollPane

What it is: Of all the JComponents, this one is probably my favorite. It works so hard for you with so little effort on your part.

A JScrollPane provides a scrollable view of any lightweight component. You just instantiate a JScrollPane with the thing you want to scroll as an argument to the constructor. Then set the ScrollPane's preferred size with a method call, add it to your container, and you're done! This is so much easier than messing around with individual and highly buggy scrollbars that we had in JDK 1.0.

By default, a scroll pane attempts to size itself so that its client displays at its preferred size. Many components have a simple preferred size that's big enough to display the entire component. You can customize a scroll pane with many refinements on how much to scroll, which of the scroll bars to show, custom decorations around the sides, and so on. The visible area in the Pane is called the "viewport."

What it looks like on-screen:

The code to create it: In this code, we put the JPanel subclass that we created earlier into a JScrollPane.

```
MyJPanel mjp = new MyJPanel();
JScrollPane jsp = new JScrollPane( mjp );
jsp.setPreferredSize( new Dimension(150, 150));
jframe.getContentPane().add(jsp);
```

The code to retrieve user input from it: You won't need to interact with your scroll pane very frequently, as it does so much of the right thing by default. However, you can implement the `Scrollable` interface if your enthusiasm extends to wanting to get callbacks for individual clicks on the scroll bars.

JTabbedPane

What it is: A Tabbed Pane is a component that lets you economize on-screen real estate. It simulates a folder with tabbed page dividers. You have a series of "tabs" (labels) along the top, associated with Components on a larger rectangular area beneath. By clicking on a tab label, you bring its associated component to the front. We'll show an example using the JEditorPane and the JPanel we already saw.

What it looks like on-screen:

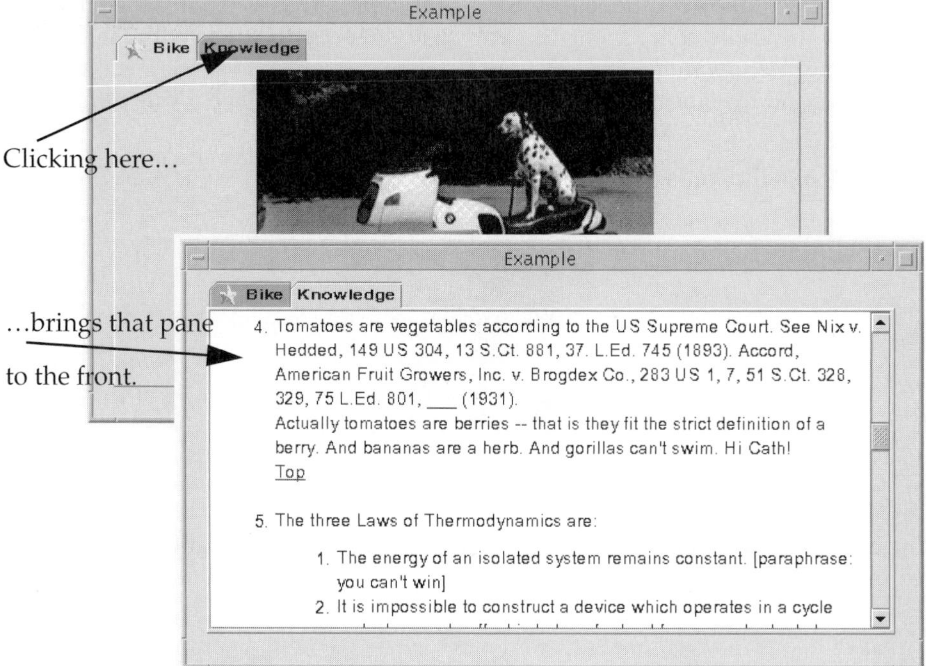

You can make the tabs appear on any of the four sides of the TabbedPane. You can have even more than one row of tabs, but the human factors of that are so appalling that Sun corrected it in JDK 1.4. When you have multiple rows, any tab that's clicked moves to the bottom row of tabs. As a result, clicking on some tabs causes all of them to change places. To prevent this, you can pass an argument to the constructor saying that you want tabs to scroll, not to wrap, when you exceed a line.

The code to create it:

```
// set up the editor pane, as before
     JEditorPane jep =null;
     try {
          jep = new JEditorPane( "file:///tmp/know.html" );
     } catch (Exception e) {System.out.println("error: "+e); }

     jep.setEditable(false); // turns off the ability to edit
     JScrollPane jsp = new JScrollPane( jep );
     jsp.setPreferredSize( new Dimension(550, 250));

// set up the JPanel, as before
     MyJPanel mjp = new MyJPanel();
     jframe.getContentPane().add(mjp);

// create a tabbed pane and add them to it.
     JTabbedPane jtp = new JTabbedPane();
     ImageIcon ic = new ImageIcon("star.gif");
     jtp.addTab("Bike", ic, mjp,
                "1989 BWM RS100/1996 Dalmatian Annie");
     jtp.addTab("Knowledge", null, jsp, "who knew?");

     jframe.getContentPane().add(jtp);
     jframe.setVisible(true);
}
```

The method to add a tab and the Component together takes four arguments:

```
public void addTab(String title,
                   Icon icon,
                   Component component,
                   String tip)
```

The title is the phrase to put on the tab. The icon is a little picture with which you can decorate the phrase. For example, on the "Bike" pane I use a star, and on the "Knowledge" pane I use null to signify no picture. The third parameter is the component that you want associated with that tab. The final parameter is a String representing tooltip text that you get for free with this component.

JEditorPane

What it is: This is a very powerful JComponent! JEditorPane allows you to display and edit documents that contain HTML, Rich Text Format, or straight Unicode characters. It formats the text and displays it.

What it looks like on-screen:

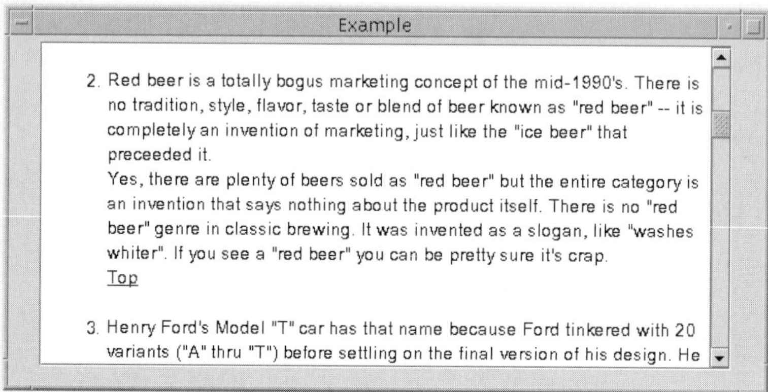

You can load the component from a URL or from a String containing a URL as shown below, or from the contents of a String itself. In the following example, the JEditor pane is placed in a ScrollPane so it displays and scrolls well.

The code to create it:

```
JEditorPane jep =null;
try {
     jep = new JEditorPane( "file:///tmp/know.html" );
} catch (Exception e) {System.out.println("error: "+e); }

jep.setEditable(false); // turns off the ability to edit
JScrollPane jsp = new JScrollPane( jep );
jsp.setPreferredSize( new Dimension(550, 250));

jframe.getContentPane().add(jsp);
```

Notice how trivial it is to display an HTML file and to wrap a JScrollPane around it. JEditorPane is a subclass of the less specialized JTextComponent.

Let's quickly review the match between components and events (Table 21-2).

Table 21–2 Components and Events

Component	Event Handler Interface	Method(s) the Interface Promises
JButton JMenu JMenuItem JRadioButton JCheckBox	`ActionListener`	`public void actionPerformed(ActionEvent e);`

Component	`ComponentListener`	`public void componentResized(ComponentEvent);`
		`public void componentMoved(ComponentEvent);`
		`public void componentShown(ComponentEvent);`
		`public void componentHidden(ComponentEvent);`

Container	`ContainerListener`	`public void componentAdded(ContainerEvent);` `public void componentRemoved(ContainerEvent);`
Component	`FocusListener`	`public void focusGained(FocusEvent e);` `public void focusLost(FocusEvent e);`
JButton JMenu JMenuItem JRadioButton JCheckBox	`ItemListener`	`public void itemStateChanged(ItemEvent e);`

Component	`KeyListener`	`public void keyTyped(KeyEvent e);`
		`public void keyPressed(KeyEvent e);`
		`public void keyReleased(KeyEvent e);`

Component	`MouseListener`	`public void mouseClicked(MouseEvent e);`
		`public void mousePressed(MouseEvent e);`
		`public void mouseReleased(MouseEvent e);`
		`public void mouseEntered(MouseEvent e);`
		`public void mouseExited(MouseEvent e);`

Table 21–2 Components and Events *(cont.)*

Component	Event Handler Interface	Method(s) the Interface Promises
Component	MouseMotionListener	public void mouseDragged(MouseEvent e);
		public void mouseMoved(MouseEvent e);
JTextField	ActionListener	public void actionPerformed(ActionEvent e);
Dialog	WindowListener	public void windowOpened(WindowEvent e);
JDialog		public void windowClosing(WindowEvent e);
Frame		public void windowClosed(WindowEvent e);
JFrame		public void windowIconified(WindowEvent e);
Window		public void windowDeiconified(WindowEvent e):
JWindow		public void windowActivated(WindowEvent e);
		public void WindowDeactivated (WindowEvent e);

More about Swing Components

Table 21-2 named all the significant JComponents, and there were about forty in all (including all the subclasses of subclasses). We've presented, briefly, some of the more important ones here. That's certainly enough to get you started writing GUI programs. To keep the book to a manageable size, however, and still fit in all the other information, we don't show all of them.

Here are some pointers on how to find out more about the other components when you're ready to. The first resource is the good (if somewhat fluid) online tutorial on Java generally, and Swing in particular, that Sun Microsystems maintains at *java.sun.com/docs/books/tutorial/ui/swing/*.

The second resource is the Swing section of the Java Programmers FAQ that is on this CD and is also online in a more up-to-date form at *www.afu.com*. The FAQ has lots of nuggets of information about Java problems that everyone initially encounters. It gives advice on solutions and workarounds.

The third resource is to buy or borrow a book that examines JFC, including the Swing components in depth. These books are frequently intimidating in size. One such book that I like is Kim Topley's *Core Java Foundation Classes* (Prentice Hall, New Jersey, 1998, ISBN 0-13-080301-4). It weighs in at over 1,100 pages, so be prepared to put in a few evenings and weekends.

Debugging Lightweight Components

JComponent supports a method to help the implementation team debug the Swing library, but you can use it, too. You can call the following:

```
RepaintManager.currentManager(yourContainer.getRootPane()).
            setDoubleBufferingEnabled(false);
anyJComponent.setDebugGraphicsOptions( options );
```

The first statement turns off double buffering for the container your component is in. The "options" parameter on the second statement is an int which is 0 to switch debugging off, or contains any of these flags OR'd together:

DebugGraphics.FLASH_OPTION // flash the component as it is accessed

DebugGraphics.BUFFER_OPTION // show the offscreen graphics work

DebugGraphics.LOG_OPTION // print a text summary of graphics work

The flash option is pretty spectacular and allows you to see lightweights being drawn.

Finally, I have the same advice that Obi-Wan gave Luke Skywalker on his quest to defeat the forces of evil: *Use the source*. The Java platform is almost unique among commercial products in that the complete source code for the runtime library is distributed with the system. If you installed the compiler in C:\jdk1.4fcs, then the source is in C:\jdk1.4fcs\src.jar. Jar (Java archive) files have the same format as zip files, so you can unpack it by using `unzip src.jar`. That will put the Swing source files into the C:\jdk1.4fcs\src\javax\swing directory.

Having the source is a triple blessing. You can read the code to find out how something works and what features it offers (the code is heavily commented). You can recompile the code with more of your own debugging information, and use that instead of the standard runtime library (not everyone will want to tackle this, but in fact, it is trivial to use the "update" option to jar to replace a single class file in rt.jar). You will also be exposed to the ideas, style, and designs that are used by the best Java programmers in the world. The best programmers in the world learn from each other by reading each other's code. Now you have this opportunity, too. Seize it.

I really like Swing. It passes the golden rule of software: It's simple to do simple things. Just be aware that all the components have many more features than are presented here and you can get some very sophisticated effects when you start combining them and using them to full advantage.

Further Reading

The first Java website that you visit should be Sun's at *java.sun.com*. But the Java website that you visit most frequently should be the Java Lobby at *www.javalobby.org*.

The Java Lobby is an independent group representing Java developers. Led by software entrepreneur Rick Ross, the Lobby has more than 50,000 members. It is a great place for thoughtful discussion and late-breaking news on Java. You can even get advice on coding. The Java Lobby is a great resource and membership is free.

Exercises

1. Review the javadoc-generated description of the javax.swing.SwingUtilities class. Write a program that demonstrates the use of two of the utilities in that class.
2. Add the JEditorPane that can render html to some code that can make a socket enquiry in the HTTP protocol. Create a basic web browser in less than 150 lines of code. You can do this in one evening, and spend the rest of the year adding refinements to it.
3. Review the class java.awt.Robot. It is intended to generate native system input events for test programs. Instead, use it to develop an automatic player for Web Wars (hard) or Minesweeper (easier).
4. This code will grab a screen image.

```
Robot ro = new Robot();
Toolkit t = Toolkit.getDefaultToolkit();
final Dimension d = t.getScreenSize();
Rectangle re = new Rectangle(d.width, d.height);
final Image image = ro.createScreenCapture( re );
```

Look up Image I/O in the next chapter, and write code to turn this into a JPG or GIF file.

Some Light Relief—The Bible Code

A couple of chapters back, the Light Relief section ended with a praying mantis (origami), so I'll continue the religious theme with a description of the Bible code. The concept of "Bible codes" was something that became popular in 1997, helped by a mass marketed book on the subject. It's a completely bogus idea that there are hidden strings in the first five books of the Bible, and these hidden strings foretell the future.

The hidden strings, or *Bible codes,* are supposedly found by looking at individual characters of the Bible, starting at some offset, and taking every Nth letter thereafter to form a phrase. It works much better with a Bible in Hebrew because the classic written form of that language does not have any vowels. Hence, you can construct many possible phrases depending on which vowels you choose to put in and where you choose to end a word. "BLLGTS" can be interpreted as "Boil leg & toes" or "Be a li'l gutsy" or even "Bill Gates."

When you find a Bible "code" you frequently find other related phrases around it. Of course, you can often find clouds in the sky that have shapes that look like animals, and the reason is exactly the same: people tend to see what they want to see. There's a huge amount of sky and clouds to look at, and you can always find something if you look at enough random stuff.

I thought it would be fun to write some Bible code software in Java, so I put it on the CD. There's a program in \bible that you can run to search for arbitrary patterns in the Bible (a copy of the King James Version is also on the CD). See Figure 21-3 for the results when I set it to search for the string "Java"—a place and language unknown in biblical times.

As you can see, it has found the word along with other astonishing and highly meaningful phrases ("knowledge of Java, a great blessing, bit, net"). You can run the program for yourself and find other phrases of your choice.

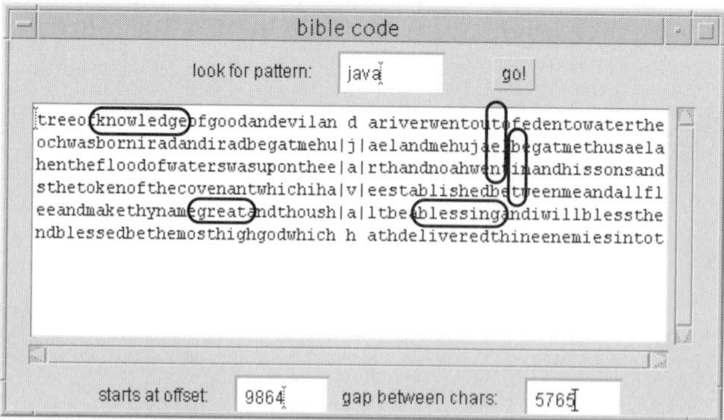

Figure 21–3 Bible code says "Java a great blessing!"

One of the promoters of the Bible code concept challenged his critics to find hidden messages in non-Bible texts like *Moby Dick*. He thought there weren't any. He was dead wrong!

You will find that *Moby Dick* contains predictions for the deaths of Indira Gandhi, President Rene Moawad of Lebanon, Martin Luther King, Chancellor Engelbert Dollfuss of Austria, Leon Trotsky, Sirhan Sirhan, John F. Kennedy, Robert Kennedy, and Princess Diana, among others! Figure 21-4 shows the Diana prediction from *Moby Dick*.

"Lady Diana, Dodi, foolishly wasted, mortal in these jaws of death!" The two likeliest conclusions follow. Either Herman Melville was the Supreme Creator of the Universe and he encoded Bible code style predictions in *Moby Dick* as well as in the Bible. Another option is that the notion of hidden messages encoded in revered works is a bunch of nonsense put about by some people who should know better. I don't know about you, but I'm going with the simpler of the two explanations. Let me add that the meaninglessness of the codes doesn't impugn the origin of the Bible. It just says that people can be wrong when they try to project their own interpretations onto any text.

Take a look at the CD directory bible\MobyDick for details. There's a copy of Moby Dick there, along with the Bible code software to search it. I'd like to find out what hidden messages there are in the Sherlock Holmes books. This is what programmers do when they have too much time on their hands.

```
Applet Viewer: mobycodeapp.class
Applet
look for pattern: ladydiana   go!  stop!

limmeroflightcomeintotheroomfr o munderthedoorlordsavemethinks
eandallthoughinslightmotionsti|l|lmaintainsapermanentobliquity
othestheareabeforethehousewasp|a|vedwithclamshellsmrshusseywor
atithedartedtheironrightoverol|d|bildadsbroadbrimcleanacrossth
fandherbreadandnottobefoolishl|y|wastedwhereforehehadnofancyfo
ngiftedwithsuchwondrouspoweran|d|velocityinswimmingastodefyall
kingsentimentintarandblubberch|i|ldeharoldnotunfrequentlyperch
eralrageandhatefeltbyhiswholer|a|cefromadamdownandthenasifhisc
rossagainsttheskywasitnotsoodo|n|miguelthouchilianwhalemarkedl
gimmortalinthesejawsofdeathinv|a|inwehailedtheotherboatsaswell

starts at offset: 70576   gap between chars: 37310
Applet started.
```

Figure 21–4 Bible code links Lady Di and Dodi.

Chapter 22

Containers, Layouts, and AWT Loose Ends

We're now two-thirds of the way through our tour of JFC and Swing. This chapter completes the topic by presenting some containers and an explanation of how you use them to lay out your components neatly on the screen. We give some information on a couple of topics that are related to the window system generally. And we present a practical example showing how easy it is to make mistakes in threaded code.

Pluggable Look and Feel

Let's start off the chapter with something that, while not unique to Java, is certainly not otherwise widely-available. I'm referring to the *Pluggable Look and Feel* or *PLAF* as it is usually abbreviated. By default, a Swing program has the *Metal* look and feel, which is a look and feel designed especially for Java. You can easily change that so a program has the look and feel of Windows, the Macintosh, or of Motif. PLAF means that you, the programmer, can add a few extra lines of code to allow users to select which look and feel they want anytime they run your program, regardless of what operating system is running underneath.

The Pluggable Look and Feel is a big win for software portability. Not only do your Java programs run everywhere, but they can even look the same everywhere. This is a great boon for users who have become comfortable with a program on one particular platform. Now that same knowledge and familiarity can be retained regardless of the execution environment.

As a programmer, you might share my opinion that the look and feel of a window system is not the most important topic in software today. The fact remains that, for some users, it *is* an important topic. Those users buy the software that pays the wages that keep us employed.

Figure 22-1 is an example of the kind of differences you see on different window systems. The three panels show the same controls in three different "looks and feels." The top panel is the Metal look and feel. If you choose to have your GUIs display in Metal, your programs will have a consistent look regardless of the operating system or window libraries. The second panel has the Motif look and feel. The lines are so delicate and thin that some of them don't reproduce completely on this screen capture. The bottom panel is the basic Windows look and feel. Pay no attention to the relative sizes of fonts and, hence, buttons. That can all be resized to suit the program. The difference is in how much shading appears around a button, how thick the dot is in a selected radio button, whether components are given a 3D look, and so on.

Here's the really cool thing: there is only one program here! And they are all running on a Windows PC. When you select one of those JRadioButtons, it transforms the program to display in that style. I started up three copies of the pro-

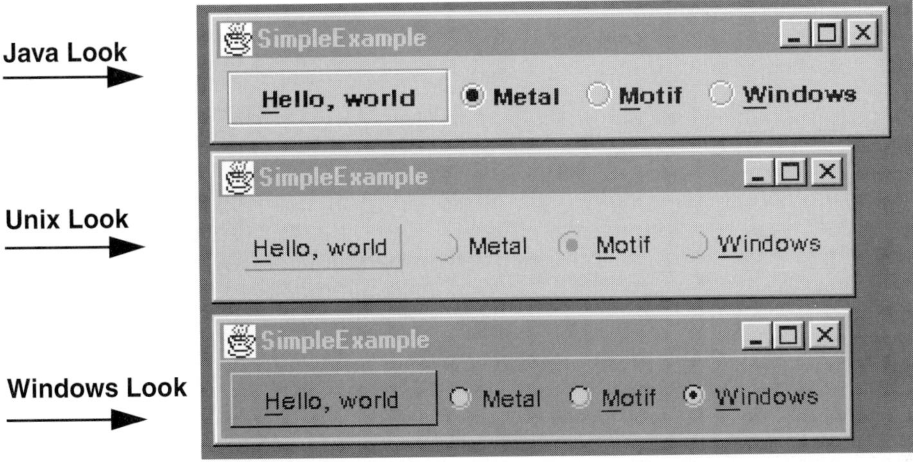

Figure 22–1 A Pluggable Look and Feel (PLAF).

gram, chose a different look and feel in each, put them next to each other, and took a screen snapshot. This is less than 150 lines long, and the key area is a couple of lines. It declares the JComponents and a listener for the radio buttons. The listener has the code (shown below) that does the magic. That's all there is to it!

```
String metalPLAFName = "javax.swing.plaf.metal.MetalLookAndFeel";
String motifPLAFName = "com.sun.java.swing.plaf.motif.MotifLookAndFeel";
String winPLAFName = "com.sun.java.swing.plaf.windows.WindowsLookAndFeel";
String lnfName = e.getActionCommand();
try {
     UIManager.setLookAndFeel(lnfName);
     SwingUtilities.updateComponentTreeUI(frame);
     frame.pack();
} catch (Exception exc) { ...
```

This program is distributed as part of the JDK, and you can find it in $JAVA-HOME/demo/jfc/SimpleExample/src/SimpleExample.java.

Model/View/Controller Architecture

You may hear people talk about the *Model/View/Controller*, or *MVC*, architecture of Swing. MVC is a design pattern or framework originally developed by Professor Trygve Reenskaug at Xerox PARC in 1978. The purpose of MVC was to provide convenient GUI support in Smalltalk.

Model/View/Controller is used extensively in Swing. For the basic components, you don't notice it. For more complicated components like JTree and JTable, you need to know a little about it. A one-line summary of MVC is "Rather than having one big class for each JComponent, different GUI responsibilities have been split out into different classes." MVC makes the Platform Look and Feel possible, or at least a lot simpler.

Basically, the *model* contains your data, the *view* is the graphical representation, and the *controller* is responsible for the interaction between the other two. As an example, think of a program that keeps time and displays it as part of a user interface desktop. The Model will be the part of the program that reads the real-time clock, turns it into hours and minutes, and adjusts for timezone. There is only one model, but there can be multiple views of it. One view would be a display in the form of a clock with hands. Another view would be a digital display of hours, minutes, and seconds. A third view would be a clockface with Roman numerals. The controller is any "glue" code connecting the model and its views.

In practice, the controller and the view are often put in the same class. Swing initially kept them separate, but realized it was easier to let the model and views talk to each other directly. Model and views are separate, though.

There are a couple of methods in the library to let you force the look and feel to match the system on which you are running. Here's the code to do that:

```
UIManager.setLookAndFeel(UIManager.getSystemLookAndFeelClassName());
```

Here's the code to force a program to use the common Metal look:

```
UIManager.setLookAndFeel(UIManager.getCrossPlatformLookAndFeelClassName());
```

Since the look and feel is rendered by Java code, not by use of native libraries, it is feasible to have any look and feel on any platform. Microsoft and Apple, however, have chosen not to grant permission for their look and feel to be used on other platforms. The Java FAQ has some information about how the runtime system checks this, and how you can influence it.

All About Containers

We come now to the third of the three ideas common to all Java GUI programs: grouping together controls and arranging them neatly by adding them to a container.

Controls, Containers, Component...Where Will It All End?	
Here's the way to tell these three similar-sounding names apart!	
Control	This is not a Java term. This is the PC term for what is called a widget in the Unix world. It's a software element on the screen, like a button or a scroll bar.
Container	These are screen windows that physically contain groups of controls or other containers. You can move, hide, or show a Container and all its contents in one operation. Top-level containers can be displayed on the screen. Non top-level containers have to be in a top-level container to be displayed.
Component	This is a collective name for Controls and Containers. Since they have some common operations, Component is their common parent class. Swing's JComponents are a subclass of Component.

We've seen this when we added the JComponents to the content pane of a JFrame, and the JFrame showed up on the screen. The piece that is new is that a container can have different *layout policies* for where components go on the screen when you add them. A layout policy might be, "Add components from left to right across the container. When you reach the right-hand margin, start a new line of them." Another layout policy might be, "Components can go to the north, south, east, west, or in the center of the component. You have to tell me where you add one." There are a number of classes, called *Layout Managers*, that implement layout polices like these. We are going to describe them at length in this chapter. Before we do, we'll look at Containers a bit more closely.

The Container Class Hierarchy

The previous chapter described many controls of JDK 1.2. Now let's take a look at the Containers that hold them. The class hierarchy for containers is shown in Figure 22-2. Notice that most of the Swing containers are not JComponents, but are specializations of existing AWT containers.

On the following pages, we will outline these containers, suggest typical uses, and show code examples. `Container` is the class that groups together a number of controls and provides a framework for how they are positioned on the screen.

`Container` has fields and methods to deal with the following:

- The layout manager used to automatically position controls.
- Forcing the layout to be done.
- The thickness of any lines or insets (*Borders*) around its edges.
- Adding a `ContainerListener` for `ContainerEvents`.
- Adding, removing, and retrieving a list of any of the controls.
- Size (current, preferred, minimum, and maximum).
- Requesting the keyboard focus.
- A `paint()` routine that renders it on the screen.

The AWT class called `Container` is the superclass for components whose purpose is to hold several controls. A `Container` is essentially a rectangular portion of the screen that allows you to treat several individual controls as a group. You don't display a control directly; you add it to a `Container`, and it is the container that is displayed.

`Container` also has methods to get and set many attributes and to add and remove `Components` from itself. Containers must have either their `pack()` method called or have their initial size set before they will show up on the screen. Set their size by using the following:

```
public void setSize(int width, int height)
```

The units are pixels (dots on the screen). Since a `Container` is a subclass of `Component`, it also has all the `Component` fields. You can and should review the `Container` methods by running `javap java.awt.Container`.

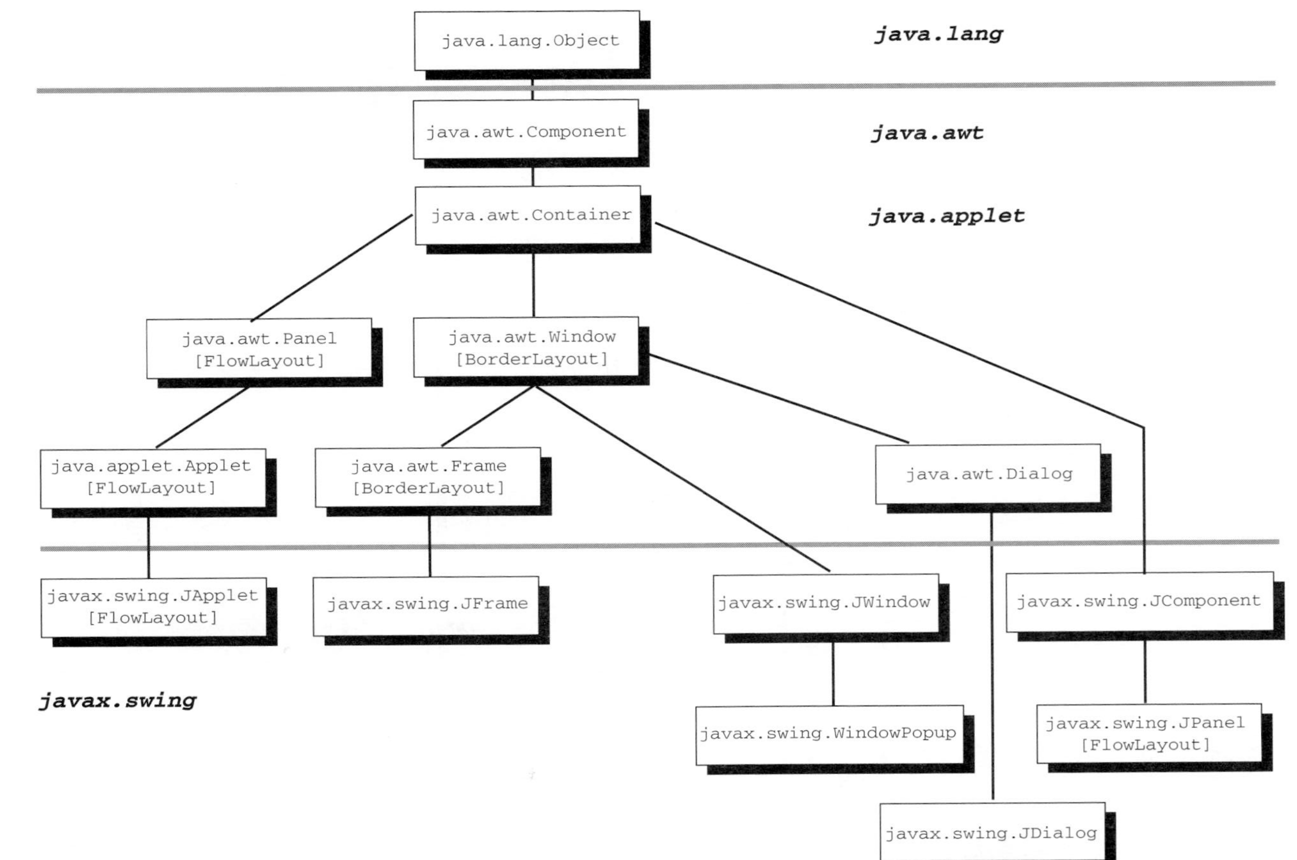

Figure 22–2 Class hierarchy of containers.

When you have finished adding or changing the components in a Container, you typically call the first three of these methods on the Container.

```
myContainer.invalidate();  // tell AWT it needs laying out
myContainer.validate();    // ask AWT to lay it out
myContainer.show();        // make it visible

myContainer.pack();        // squeeze it down smaller
```

These methods aren't needed if you are just adding to an applet, but you will need to use them in your more complicated programs.

What's in a Swing Container?

In this section, we look at what a Swing container has that an AWT container doesn't, and why you must use a Swing container to contain Swing components. Most of it comes down to the difference between lightweight and heavyweight components and making lightweight components work properly.

You add a component to an AWT container with a statement like:

```
myAWTContainer.add(myAWTComponent)
```

Swing containers are different. They have several layers, as shown in Figure 22-3. The different layers are used for different effects.

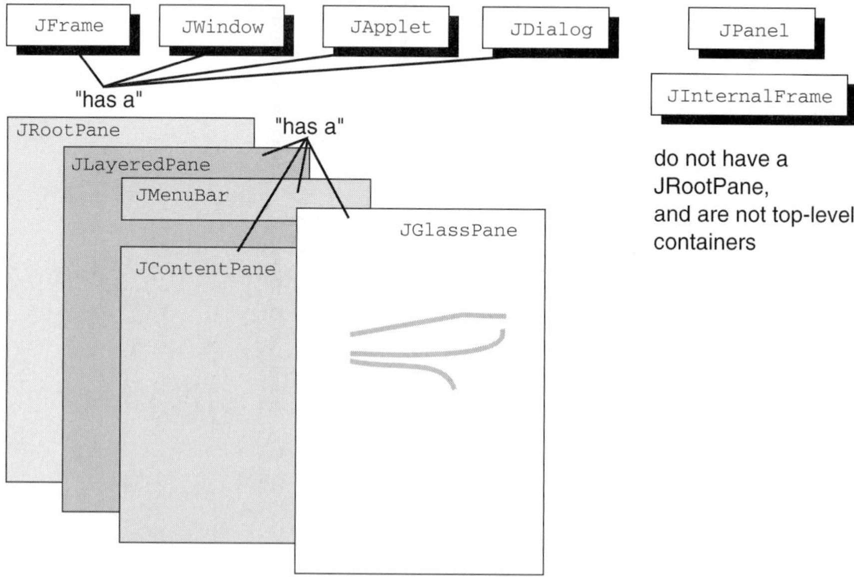

Figure 22–3 Layers of Swing containers.

The *JRootPane* is the data structure that holds all the various other panes that Swing containers have. The *JLayeredPane* manages the JMenuBar and the content pane. It also maintains a notion of z-order (which components are on top of other components within the container). It has several default depth ranges, including one for floating toolbars, one for modal dialogs, one for things being dragged, and so on. The JLayeredPane does the right thing by default, but also allows you to "get under the hood" and set things explicitly where you want them.

The *JContentPane* is the object within a Swing container to which you add your JComponents and set layout policies. The default layout policy is border layout. Border layout components are added around the four edges and in the center of the container. The *JMenuBar* is an object that keeps track of any menus associated with the container. In many cases there won't be any.

The *JGlassPane* is a transparent pane that lays over everything and allows you to intercept mouse events or draw over the whole container without getting distracted by the components within it, if you so wish.

A JPanel is a lightweight container whose purpose is to be drawn on, and to group controls together. The Swing containers have methods to get and adjust these individual pane layers. We saw many times in the previous chapter how you add components to a Swing container. You add them to the container's content pane:

```
mySwingContainer.getContentPane().add(child);
```

Now we'll look at some individual Swing containers.

JFrame

A `JFrame` is a window that also has a title bar, a menubar, a border (known as the inset), and that can be closed to an icon. JFrame is the Swing version of Frame. You should avoid mixing Swing and AWT controls and containers.

We've seen the code to create, resize, and show a JFrame throughout the previous chapter. That was done as an application, but frames can also be displayed from an applet. When you create a `JFrame`, it is not displayed physically inside the applet or other Container but is a separate free-floating window on the monitor.

A JFrame is a specialization of Frame in the Swing package. It has more refined default behavior on closing the Frame, and it adds a number of methods for getting the different "layers" of a Swing container. Following is how you associate a file containing an icon with a Frame so that when you close the Frame, it collapses to the icon.

```
// load the image from a file Toolkit
Toolkit t = MyFrame.getToolkit();
Image FrameIcon = t.getImage(filename);
MyFrame.setIconImage(FrameIcon);
```

The file name should point to a GIF or JPEG file that is the icon you want to use. Typically, this image will be thumbnail-sized, 32 × 32 pixels or so.

Other Ways to Bring in an Image

We saw in the previous chapter that it is convenient to use ImageIcon to import an image file into a Java program. Here are the constructors for ImageIcon:

```
// constructors of ImageIcon
public javax.swing.ImageIcon();
public javax.swing.ImageIcon(java.awt.Image);
public javax.swing.ImageIcon(java.awt.Image,java.lang.String);
public javax.swing.ImageIcon(java.lang.String); // a filename
public javax.swing.ImageIcon(java.lang.String,java.lang.String);
public javax.swing.ImageIcon(java.net.URL);
public javax.swing.ImageIcon(java.net.URL,java.lang.String);
public javax.swing.ImageIcon(byte[]);
public javax.swing.ImageIcon(byte[],java.lang.String);
```

Once you have an ImageIcon, you can retrieve the image from it with the following:

```
Image myImage = myImageIcon.getImage();
```

JPanel

A `JPanel` is a generic container that is always in some other container. It does not float loose on the desktop, as `JWindow` and `JFrame` do. A JPanel is used when you want to group several controls inside your GUI. For example, you might have several buttons that go together. Adding them to a Panel can treat them as one unit, display them together, and lay them out on the screen under the same set of rules (more about this later).

Note that the Swing JPanel isn't descended from the AWT Panel. They still fulfill the same kind of role: to be a generic non-top-level container. By being a JComponent, JPanel can also provide other support not present in AWT. It can provide automatic double buffering and the accessibility help. Double buffering is a technique that uses more memory to obtain flicker-free updates to components that are being updated frequently on the screen.

Applet and JApplet

Applet is a subclass of Panel. This means that applets come ready-made with some GUI features. JApplet is the Swing subclass of Applet. We've seen applets many times now. Figure 22-4 shows another one.

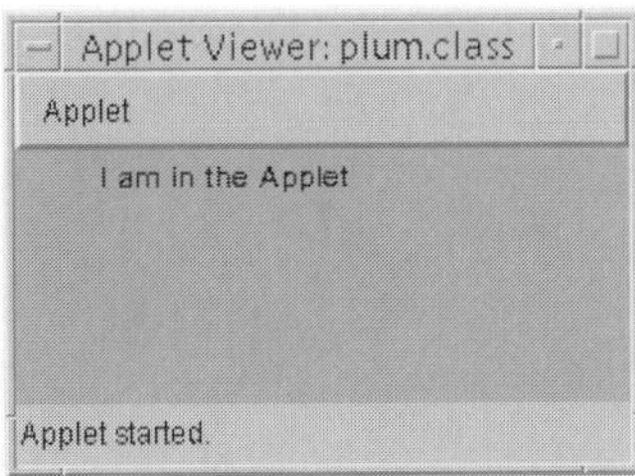

Figure 22–4
Another applet.

Here is the code that created that applet:

```
// <applet code=plum.class height=100 width=200> </applet>

import java.awt.*;
import javax.swing.*;

public class plum extends JApplet {

    public void init() {
       setBackground(Color.green);
       resize(250,100);
    }

    public void paint(Graphics g) {
       g.drawString("I am in the Applet", 35,15);
    }
}
```

As with Panel and JPanel, JApplet adds some Swing conveniences and is required when your applet consists of Swing components. Since JApplet is a subclass of Applet, it has all the Applet methods described on the next page.

One advantage of an applet over an application for a GUI program is that you can start adding and displaying components without creating an underlying backdrop. With an applet, one already exists.

Here are some popular methods of Applet:

```
public URL getDocumentBase() //the URL of the HTML page
                              // containing the applet
public URL getCodeBase() //the URL of the applet code

public String getParameter(String name)
public void resize(int width, int height)

public void showStatus(String msg)
public Image getImage(URL url) //bring in an image
public Image getImage(URL url, String name)

public static AudioClip newAudioClip(URL url) // NEW in 1.2
public AudioClip getAudioClip(URL url) //bring in a sound file
public void play(URL url)
```

These four methods are for the stages in the applet life cycle:

```
public void init()
public void start()
public void stop()
public void destroy()
```

As you can see, Applet has several methods that deal with sounds and pictures. For both of these, it uses an URL to pinpoint the file containing the goodies. You can now obtain an audio clip from an URL with a static method. That means you can do it in an application, not just in an applet. You do not have to do anything special to make an Applet retrieve media from its server over the Internet—it is a built-in method. An URL can locate something that is local to your system or anywhere on Internet.

The DocumentBase referred to in the first method is simply the directory containing the HTML page that you are currently visiting. Similarly, the CodeBase is the directory that contains the applet you are currently executing. For security purposes, the machine with the codebase is regarded as the server. Often, these two directories will be the same, but since the codebase is an URL, it can be anywhere on the Internet. The source for Applet can be seen in $JAVA-HOME/src/java/applet/Applet.java and for JApplet in $JAVAHOME/src/javax/swing/JApplet.java.

`Window` and `JWindow`

This container is a totally blank window. It doesn't even have a border. You can display messages by putting Labels on it. Typically, you don't use `Window` directly but instead use its more useful subclasses, `Frame` and `Dialog`. The Swing class JWindow is really only there to help with pop-up menus.

Windows can be modal, meaning they prevent all other windows from responding until they are dealt with (e.g., dismissed with a checkbox). `Window` has a few methods for bringing it to the front or back, packing (resizing to preferred size), or showing (making it visible).

For security purposes, the browser typically makes sure any `Window` or subclass of `Window` originating from an untrusted applet contains a line of text warning that it is an "untrusted window" or an "applet window." This message ensures the applet user is never in any doubt about the origin of the window. Without this clear label, it would be too easy to pop up a window that looked like it came from the operating system and ask for confidential information to send back to the applet server.

Now that we've met containers, we are ready to move on to the next section and tackle layouts!

Another Debugging Tip

If you ever want to see what components are in a Java GUI, you can press control + shift + F1.

These three keys will dump out on system.error the text representation of the components that are on the screen. You will see results like this:

```
java.awt.Frame[frame0,0,0,500x275,layout=java.awt.FlowLayout,
resizable,title=bible code]
  java.awt.Label[label0,130,32,98x24,align=left,text=look for pattern:]
  java.awt.TextField[textfield0,233,29,76x31,text=,editable,selection=0-0]
  java.awt.Label[label1,314,32,20x24,align=left,text=   ]
  java.awt.Button[button0,339,32,31x24,label=go!]
  java.awt.TextArea[text0,20,65,459x175,text=,editable,selection=0-
0,rows=10,columns=62, scrollbarVisibility=both]
  java.awt.Label[label2,67,248,91x24,align=left,text=starts at offset:]
  java.awt.TextField[textfield1,163,245,69x31,text=,editable,selection=0-0]
  java.awt.Label[label3,237,248,121x24,align=left,text=gap between chars:]
  java.awt.TextField[textfield2,363,245,69x31,text=,editable,selection=0-0]
```

It's a bit of a "brute force" technique, but it's nice to know about.

Layout in a Container

Here in Figure 22-5 is a frame to which we have added several controls. They are positioned automatically as we add them.

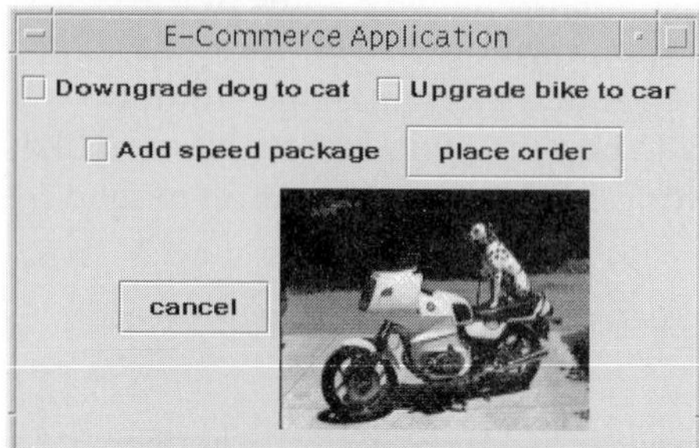

Figure 22–5
Arranging controls on the screen.

The code for this is on the CD in the directory containing all the other AWT programming material. Problem: The end result doesn't look very professional because nothing is neatly aligned. Solution: Layout managers!

Layout Managers are classes that specify how components should be placed in a Container. You choose a layout manager for a Container with a call like this invoked on the content pane:

```
setLayout( new FlowLayout() );
```

We'll look at six layout managers: the five that are part of AWT and a sixth one that comes with Swing. The first and most basic layout manager is FlowLayout.

FlowLayout

Figure 22-6 is the same code as above using FlowLayout and with the JFrame pulled out wide to the right.

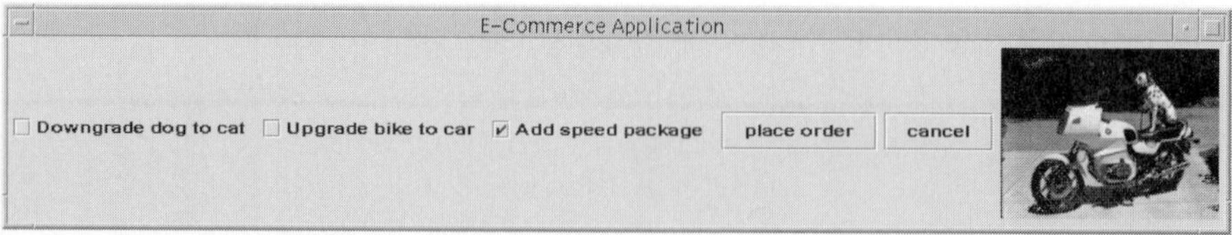

Figure 22–6 In this applet, buttons are positioned left to right and centered.

A flow layout means that Components are added left to right, keeping them centered in the Container and starting a new line whenever necessary. When you resize the applet, components might move to a new line. There are possible "left" and "right" arguments to the constructor to make the components be left- or right-justified instead of centered, as shown here:

```
setLayout (new FlowLayout (FlowLayout.RIGHT));
```

Most of the layouts allow you to specify the gap in pixels between adjacent components by specifying the values to the constructor. One FlowLayout constructor looks like this:

```
public FlowLayout(int align, int hgap, int vgap);
```

Our first example on the previous page was actually a FlowLayout, too. As we made the JFrame less wide, it folded the flowing line of Components with the result seen there.

This is the code that sets a flow layout on a JFrame:

```
myJframe.getContentPane().setLayout( new FlowLayout() );
```

Some layout managers adjust their components to fit the container, and some layout managers just lay out components unchanged. `FlowLayout` doesn't change the sizes of contained components at all. The `BorderLayout` tells its enclosing container the size to allow for each control by invoking the `preferredSize()` methods of each control. Other layout managers (`GridBagLayout` and `GridLayout`) force the components to adjust their size according to the actual dimensions of the container.

Every component has methods to getMinimumSize(), getPreferredSize(), and getMaximumSize(). These methods inform layout managers how much they can adjust the size of a component to fit the layout. You can extend a component and override one or more of these methods to change the behavior. Or you can use the setter versions of the methods, shown later in the example accompanying Figure 22-11.

Following is the code used to generate Figure 22-6 and the following two examples (commenting and uncommenting code as needed).

```
import java.awt.*;
import java.awt.event.*;
import javax.swing.*;
public class BorderDemo {
     static JFrame jframe = new JFrame("E-Commerce Application");

     public static void setupjframe() {
          jframe.setSize(400,400);
          jframe.setVisible(true);
// jframe.getContentPane().setLayout( new FlowLayout() );
     jframe.getContentPane().setLayout( new BorderLayout(10,7) );
// jframe.getContentPane().setLayout( new GridLayout(3,2, 10, 7));
          WindowListener l = new WindowAdapter() {
          public void windowClosing(WindowEvent e){System.exit(0);}
          };
          jframe.addWindowListener(l);
     }

     public static void main(String[] args) {
          setupjframe();
     // JCheckBox jck1 = new JCheckBox("Downgrade dog to cat");
          JCheckBox jck2 = new JCheckBox("Upgrade bike to car");
          JCheckBox jck3 = new JCheckBox("Add speed package");
          // p.add( jck1, "North" ); //max. 5 components
          Container p = jframe.getContentPane();
          p.add( jck2, "East" );
          p.add( jck3, "South" );

          JButton jb1 = new JButton("place order");
          p.add( jb1, "North" );
          JButton jb2 = new JButton("cancel");
          p.add( jb2, "West" );

          JLabel jl = new JLabel(new ImageIcon( "bmw.jpg"));
          p.add(jl, "Center");
          jframe.pack();
     }
}
```

Grid Layout

Figure 22-7 shows the same code with a one-line change to give it a grid (m-by-n) layout.

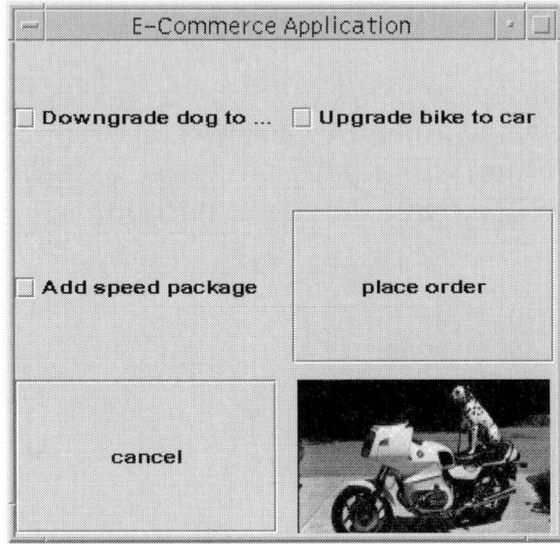

Figure 22–7
A grid layout puts things in equally-sized boxes starting from the top-left.

In the constructor you specify the number of rows and columns, like this:

```
int rows=7, cols=3;
setLayout( new GridLayout(rows, cols) );
```

That creates seven lines on a grid that is three boxes wide.

Grid layouts are simple and somewhat rigid. One thing that always surprises and annoys programmers is the way the components change in size to match the grid size. Compare the size and shape of the buttons here with those in the previous layout. To avoid this, add a component to a panel, and add the panel to the container with the grid layout.

This is the code that sets a grid layout on a JFrame:

```
jframe.getContentPane().setLayout( new GridLayout(3,2, 10, 7) );
```

The "3, 2" are the rows and columns. The "10, 7" are the horizontal gap and the vertical gap in pixels to leave between components.

BorderLayout

The third popular type of layout is BorderLayout. As the name suggests, you can put four components around the four edges of the Frame, with a fifth component taking any remaining space in the middle. The default layout for a Window and its subclasses Frame and JFrame is BorderLayout. You can set a border layout in a ContentPane with a line like this:

```
setLayout( new BorderLayout() );
```

You then add up to five widgets, specifying whether they go at the north (top), east (right), and so on. The same application with a one-line change to use BorderLayout looks like that shown in Figure 22-8. Note the size of the buttons.

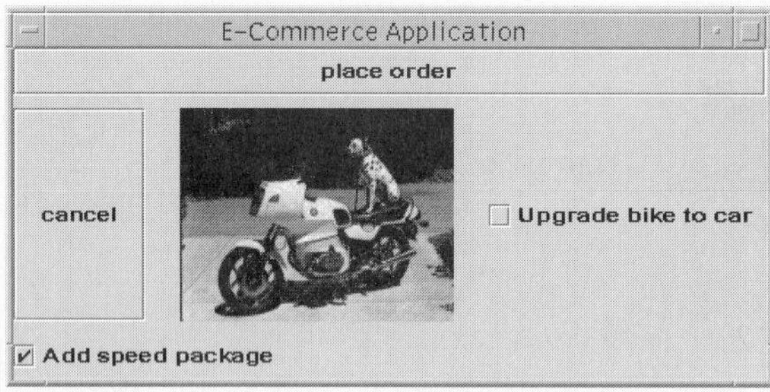

Figure 22–8 Frame using BorderLayout.

It's obviously inconvenient to have a maximum of five widgets, and that brings us to the real way layouts are used. There probably isn't a single layout manager that will do exactly what you want. Instead, group related components onto panels, and then add the panels to a Frame, using another layout manager. We'll explain how this works using BoxLayout, introduced with Swing. This is the code that sets a border layout on a JFrame:

```
jframe.getContentPane().setLayout( new BorderLayout(10, 7) );
```

Again, the "10, 7" are the horizontal and vertical gaps. This is the code for a component to Container with a Border Layout:

```
myFrame.getContentPane().add( myComponent, "East" );
```

The directions can be "North," "South," "East," "West," and "Center."

There are two important points to note with BorderLayout. First, you have to set BorderLayout before adding components. Otherwise, you mysteriously see nothing (this isn't true, however, for the other two layout managers). Second, letter case is significant when setting the position. For example, you can't use "north" instead of "North."

BoxLayout

A fourth kind of layout manager is BoxLayout, named because of its ability to align a group of components horizontally or vertically, as shown in Figure 22-9.

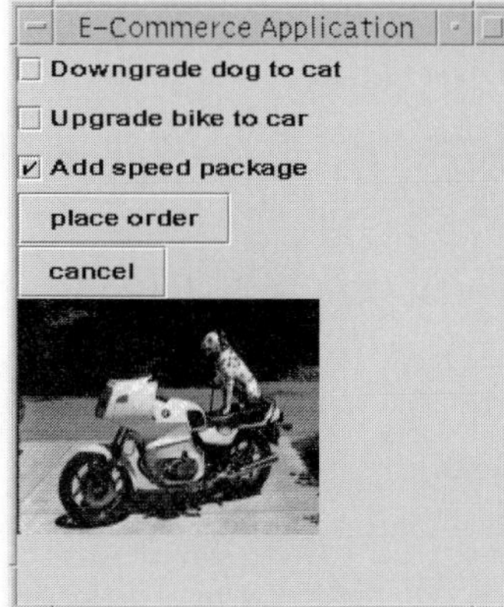

Figure 22–9
A screenshot using BoxLayout.

The code to apply a BoxLayout to a Container looks like this:

```
Container c = jframe.getContentPane();
c.setLayout( new BoxLayout(c, BoxLayout.Y_AXIS));
```

Note that, unlike the other layout managers, this one takes the content pane as an argument as well as being invoked on the content pane. The second argument says whether to stack vertically (as here) or horizontally, `BoxLayout.X_AXIS`.

You add components exactly the same way as in the previous layout managers:

```
JButton jb1 = new JButton("place order");
p.add( jb1 );
```

Box layout gives us the ability to, say, stack all the radio buttons on one panel, the Jbuttons on another panel, and add them to a Frame in three columns with grid layout or border layout. Let's try that.

Combining Layouts

Figure 22-10 shows the results of putting the three radio buttons on their own panel, putting the two buttons on their own panel, then adding the two panels and the Jlabel to the Frame with a border layout. Already this is starting to look

Figure 22–10 A screen capture using several layouts.

more normal. The size, shape, and positioning of the components won't fly all over the place when you resize the frame.

Here's the important part of the code to produce the above results:

```
JPanel p1 = new JPanel();
p1.setLayout( new BoxLayout(p1, BoxLayout.Y_AXIS));
JCheckBox jck1 = new JCheckBox("Downgrade dog to cat");
JCheckBox jck2 = new JCheckBox("Upgrade bike to car");
JCheckBox jck3 = new JCheckBox("Add speed package");
p1.add( jck1 );
p1.add( jck2 );
p1.add( jck3 );

JPanel p2 = new JPanel();
p2.setLayout( new BoxLayout(p2, BoxLayout.Y_AXIS));
JButton jb1 = new JButton("place order");   p2.add( jb1 );
JButton jb2 = new JButton("cancel");    p2.add( jb2 );

JLabel jl = new JLabel(new ImageIcon( "bmw.jpg"));

Container c2 = jframe.getContentPane();
c2.add(jl, "Center");
c2.add(p1, "West");
c2.add(p2, "East");
jframe.pack();
```

That layout can still be improved in a couple of ways. You can:

- Move the radio buttons in from the edge of the panel. This can be done by adding a *border* to the panel. The following code adds a ten-pixel border all around the component:

  ```
  JPanel p1 = new JPanel();
  p1.setBorder(BorderFactory.createEmptyBorder(10, 10, 10, 10));
  ```

- Make the two buttons the same length by setting the maximum size of the shorter button to the preferred (or regular) size of the longer button, like this:

```
JButton jb2 = new JButton("cancel");
jb2.setMaximumSize( jb1.getPreferredSize() );
```

- Add a bit of spacing between the buttons, by adding a blank area, as follows:

```
p2.add(Box.createRigidArea(new Dimension(0, 15)));
```

- Box is a helper class for BoxLayout.
- Finally, we can add a border around the panel on which the buttons are located, as follows:

```
JPanel p2 = new JPanel();
p2.setBorder(BorderFactory.createEmptyBorder(14, 14, 14, 14));
```

Put it all together and you have quite a pleasing and professional looking GUI, as shown in Figure 22-11.

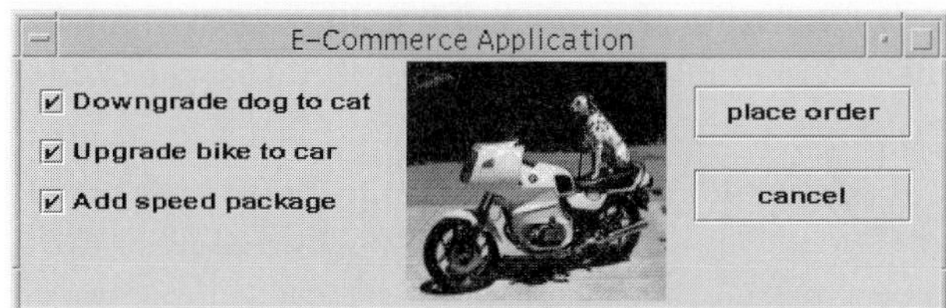

Figure 22–11 Adding multiple elements to a layout.

The only thing that is at all new is the `BorderFactory.createEmptyBorder(14, 14, 14, 14)` call. A *factory* is a class that can create other classes and return them to you. Here, it will send you some instance of a border class, possibly shared if you're using the same kind of border in two places. I've only scratched the surface of the many ways you can improve alignment and appearance in Swing. Although there are many more features available to the expert, the features we have reviewed will serve your basic needs.

Other Layout Managers

AWT has a CardLayout manager. It does exactly the same thing as a tabbed pane, but without the finesse. There's no reason to use CardLayout now that we have tabbed panes.

The final kind of AWT layout manager is GridBagLayout, which is a variation of GridLayout. Rather than force you to fit components one per grid position, it allows you to let a component take up the space of several adjacent grid positions. It uses a series of constraints and weights to work out what goes where.

GridBagLayout is excessively complicated for what it does, and I recommend helping it fall into disuse by not bothering with it. If you really want to spend time on GridBagLayout, there is a tutorial about it online at *java.sun.com/docs/books/tutorial/uiswing/layout/using.html.*

JDK 1.4 introduced the SpringLayout class. It provides layouts that are similar to absolute positioning of Components, but also supports the helpful feature of resizing appropriately to changes in container size or component fonts (which absolute positioning does not support). SpringLayout is intended to be used by tool-builders who implement IDEs. It gives them a way to let programmers drag-and-drop components where they want them to show the preferred layout appearance by example. SpringLayout (like GridBagLayout) does its work using Constraints objects that specify preferred, maximum, minimum, and current values for where it is relative to its neighbors. You probably won't code SpringLayout explicitly in your programs.

Most of the use of GridBagLayout and SpringLayout comes from programmers who use IDEs like Visual Cafe or SuperCede. The layout code is generated automatically, and programmers don't have to wrangle it by hand (unless they later try to fix it up without the visual tool). It's just drag-and-drop-and-hope.

Layouts are useful and provide automatic component resizing when you resize the container. You probably won't find any one layout that does exactly what you want. The solution is to divide your Panels and Frames into subpanels, use an appropriate layout manager for each panel, and then display the different panels together in a single frame. You may then use borders and boxes to hone the results. Skilled programmers can write their own layout managers. AWT contains enough power for you to do that. You might consider it if you're trying to match the look and feel of some existing custom application. In Java, you can write your own look and feel, not just layout, if you care to go down that path.

Finally, you always have the option of setting a null layout manager and positioning controls at absolute coordinates using `public void setLocation(int x, int y)`. It is almost always better to use a layout manager than to use absolute positions. It's less work for you, and the GUI will look better when run on different platforms. An absolute layout that looks good on one platform frequently looks terrible on another platform.

A Subtle Thread Bug

Thread code is hard to write correctly. The simple demo program presented in Chapter 1 has a latent thread bug. Recall that the code looks like this:

```
public void paint(final Graphics g) {
  g.setFont(font);
  g.setColor(colors[i]);
  g.drawString(messages[i], x, y);
 }
...
public static void main(String[] args) {
  ... i = ++i % 4;
```

In the main() method, we write variables x, y, i. The AWT calls the paint() method of the frame from the event dispatching thread ("please do a paint" events are posted to the event queue just like any other event). The paint method reads variables x, y, and i. But main() and paint() are called from different threads.

In other words, it is possible that while main() is executing, the runtime can context-switch out that thread in the middle of some statement, and allow the AWT thread to run instead.

In particular, if the expression "i = ++i % 4;" was interrupted after the increment, but before the modulo, then we could index the array with the value 4, and get an ArrayIndexOutOfBoundsException.

To make this bulletproof we *must* lock the variables for exclusive access before manipulating them:

```
public void paint(Graphics g) {
  g.setFont(font);
  synchronized (lock) {
    g.setColor(colors[i]);
    g.drawString(messages[i], x, y);
  }
}
```

and do a similar thing in the main method.

It might take months of running this program before it failed. Or it might fail the first time you tried it. Or the first time you tried it on a multiprocessor. Race condition bugs like this are very hard to reproduce, to debug, and to find. Avoid them by carefully examining variables that are read and written. If the activities are in different threads, you must lock them for exclusive access in both places.

Tying up the Loose Ends

At this point, we have dealt with events, components, and containers both in summary and in depth. There are just a few other topics to cover to conclude the chapter.

JDK 1.4 Image I/O

Java at last has an API for image I/O, allowing you to read and write files in several popular formats both locally and across the net. It's nicely-designed and extensible so that as new formats appear they can quickly be supported by Java.

Java 1.4 beta Image I/O supports reading GIF, JPEG, and PNG formats. GIF is not supported for writing because it uses LZW compression, the algorithm for which is encumbered by a patent held by Unisys (which expires in June 2003). Unisys has indicated that it thinks it holds some other patents that continue its ownership of GIF.

PNG is "Portable Network Graphics," a newer standard intended to replace GIF, and not encumbered by patents. You can read about the formats (any format, in fact) at *www.wotsit.org*.

There are five packages in Java Image I/O, but most of them are concerned with the implementation and plugability of new support. You will probably find that the class `javax.imageio.ImageIO` contains static methods to do all the simple things you need. You can read a jpg file into an Image with these two lines!

```
File f = new File("c:\images\myimage.jpg");
BufferedImage bi = ImageIO.read(f);
```

It is equally easy to write out an image in PNG or JPEG format. If you refer back to the previous chapter, we showed code to do screen capture into an object of type java.awt.Image. When you have one of these, check if it is the BufferedImage subclass. You can write BufferedImages to a file with these lines:

```
BufferedImage bi = (BufferedImage) myImage;
File f = new File("c:\images\myimage.jpg");
ImageIO.write(bi, "jpg", f);
```

Once you have something as an Image, you can easily get its graphics context and draw on it:

```
Graphics2D big = bi.createGraphics();
big.setPaint(Color.red);
big.drawString ("Date: Oct 2001", 20, 20);
```

Those lines of code let you put a date or other caption in the top left of your digital photos.

The javax.imageio package contains the basic classes and interfaces for reading and writing thumbnails and for controlling the image reading process (ImageReader, ImageReadParam, and ImageTypeSpecifier) and the image writing process (ImageWriter and ImageWriteParam). It also supports conversion between formats (ImageTranscoder).

There is more information about Java 1.4 Image I/O online at *java.sun.com/j2se/1.4/docs/guide/imageio/spec/apps.fm1.html.*

Games programmers will love the "full screen exclusive mode" of JDK 1.4. It lets the programmer suspend the windowing system and write directly into video memory, and hence onto the screen. Because you are writing directly to memory rather than through many layers of GUI software, it is very fast, although it lacks the features of a window system.

A similar mode is available using Microsoft's Direct-X library, which is widely used by games programmers. Now games programmers can get the performance they need, and the future-proofing/portability of Java code too. Full-screen exclusive mode is handled through a java.awt.GraphicsDevice object. For a list of all available screen graphics devices (in single or multi-monitor systems), you can call the method getScreenDevices on the local java.awt.GraphicsEnvironment().

The Toolkit

A `Component` method called `getToolkit()` returns a reference to the toolkit. The name *toolkit* just means "a bunch of generally useful window-related things" and is the "T" in AWT. Once you have a `Toolkit`, you can call any of its methods, which can do the following:

- Set things up for printing the screen.
- Get information about the screen size and resolution.
- Beep the keyboard.
- Get information about the color model in use.
- Get information about font size.
- Transfer data to and from the system clipboard.
- Set the icon image of the Frame.

For example, `java.awt.Toolkit.getDefaultToolkit().getScreenSize()` returns a `java.awt.Dimension` object, which has ints representing height and width. As usual, you can view all the methods by typing `javap java.awt.Toolkit`.

JFC introduced the ability to transfer data to and from the system clipboard and to drag-and-drop components. The topics are a bit outside the scope of this book, but you can find the source files in $JAVAHOME/src/java/awt/datatransfer and dnd, respectively, and a tutorial online at *java.sun.com/docs/books/tutorial/dnd/index.html.*

Printing the Screen

Java's world view of printing is a little strange. It regards the purpose of printing as being to transfer GUI content onto paper. Most people think that printing is about transferring the content of files onto paper with neat margins and fonts. Once you understand that Java printing means rendering frames and panels onto paper instead of the screen, some of the features become clearer. If you really want to print files, bring them up in a GUI or use the OS-specific commands.

Java support for printing has evolved over the years, and JDK 1.4 introduces the third variation on a printing API. JDK 1.0 had no support for printing. JDK 1.1 offered some basic low-resolution printing to a printer based on the class PrintJob. JDK 1.2 introduced the java.awt.print package, and the ability to print anything that can be rendered on the screen. It uses callbacks: the application provides information on the components that it wants printed. The printing system will call back to the paintComponent() method when it is read to print. Instead of passing it a Graphics context that relates to the screen, it passes one that will eventually get sent to the printer. There's a certain convenience for everyone in this approach. It makes it easy for the printing subsystem to print pages repeatedly or in a different order. Just as the window system can call on any component to repaint itself at anytime, the printing system has the same ability, and callbacks provide it.

JDK 1.3 added two new classes giving finer control over properties of a print job (like destination or number of copies) and attributes of a printed page (like paper size, orientation, and quality).

JDK 1.4 implements JSR006, the unified printing API. It is unified in the sense that it will allow printing on all platforms, including the Java 2 Micro Edition. It builds on the JDK 1.2 print API, and has a new package, javax.print. That package lets you discover and select print servers. In JDK 1.4 you also get improved formatting options, and there is an interface for plug-ins, so third parties can provide their own plug-in printing services.

Setting up a print job JDK 1.2-style is a little elaborate. This is how it is done:

- First, you get the Toolkit.
- From the Toolkit, you get a `PrintJob`.
- From the `PrintJob`, you get a `Graphics` object, called, say, `go`. Since this is a regular graphics object, you can do all the things with it that you can do with any graphics object, including drawing in it directly with the kinds of statements that you typically use inside `paint()`, like `drawString()`.

- Then, you call `printAll(go)`. This method will pop up the native printing dialog. Every component has a `print()` method that just calls its `paint()` routine by default. You can override these as needed for special effects.
- Finally, invoke dispose on `go`, and invoke `end()` on the PrintJob.

Yes, I know. This all seems to have been designed with the "principle of most astonishment" in mind. The code looks like this:

```
import java.awt.*;
import java.awt.event.*;
import javax.swing.*;

public class exprint extends JFrame {

     Image si;
     public exprint(Image i) { this.setSize(200,200); si=i;}
     public void paint(Graphics g) { g.drawImage(si,0,0,this);}

     public static void main(String args[]) {

          Image i =Toolkit.getDefaultToolkit().getImage("RSM.jpg");
          exprint f = new exprint(i);
          f.show();
          f.printMe();
     }

     public void printMe() {
          Toolkit t = getToolkit();
          PrintJob pj = t.getPrintJob(this, "my printing", null);
          Graphics pg = pj.getGraphics();
          printAll(pg);
          pg.dispose();
          pj.end();
     }
}
```

The third argument to `getPrintJob` is a property table you supply that can be used for such things as specifying the printer to use. A null reference works here.

This kind of printing allows you to put anything that you can see on your screen onto your printer. If all you want to do is print text, you don't need to get so elaborate. Just write it to a file, and print the file.

The standard print properties are shown in Table 22-1.

Table 22–1 Print Properties

Print Property	Description or Effect
`awt.print.destination`	Can be "printer" or "file"
`awt.print.printer`	Name of printer to use
`awt.print.fileName`	Name of the file to print
`awt.print.numCopies`	Number of copies to print
`awt.print.options`	Options to pass to the print command
`awt.print.orientation`	Can be "portrait" or "landscape"
`awt.print.paperSize`	Can be "letter," "legal," "executive," or "a4"

The defaults are destination=printer, orientation=portrait, paperSize=letter, and numCopies=1.

Running the code will pop up a print dialog box as shown in Figure 22-12.

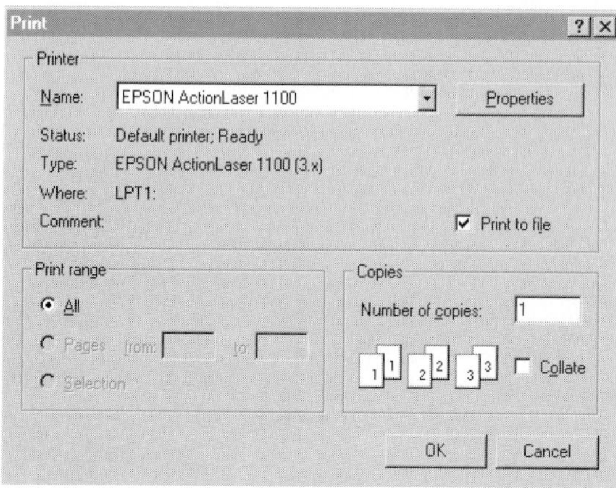

Figure 22–12 Print dialog box.

Changing Cursor Appearance

In JDK 1.0.2, the cursor could be set only for a `Frame`. In JDK 1.1, this restriction was lifted, and the cursor can now be set for each individual `Component`. The cursor is the little icon that moves about the screen tracking the mouse movements. There are fourteen different cursor icons shown in Table 22-2.

Table 22–2 Fourteen Cursor Icons

Appearance	Name
Eight different directions for resizing	Cursor.SW_RESIZE_CURSOR, etc.
One default cursor	Cursor.DEFAULT_CURSOR
One crosshair cursor	Cursor.CROSSHAIR_CURSOR
One text cursor	Cursor.TEXT_CURSOR
One busy waiting cursor	Cursor.WAIT_CURSOR
One hand cursor	Cursor.HAND_CURSOR
One move cursor	Cursor.MOVE_CURSOR

Some of these icons are shown in Figure 22-13.

Arrow	Busy	Resize	SizeEast	Text	CrossHair

Figure 22–13 Some of the many cursor icons.

The cursor appearance can be set for any component with the following method:

```
public synchronized void setCursor(Cursor cursor)
```

For example, to set the hand cursor, use the following:

```
this.setCursor(new Cursor(Cursor.HAND_CURSOR) );
```

There is a `getCursor()` method, too. There is no way in JDK 1.1 to supply your own bitmap for a custom cursor, though obviously this is a reasonable thing to want to do. Custom cursors arrived in JDK 1.2 with the following toolkit method:

```
Cursor createCustomCursor(Image cursor, Point hotSpot, String id)
        throws IndexOutOfBoundsException
```

You must override that method, and then call `setCursor()`.

How to Simulate Multibutton Mice

Here, as a further example, is the code to show which mouse button has been pressed. This applet will run on Macintoshes, MS Windows, and Unix (one-,two-, and three-button mice systems, respectively). It will allow you to generate events from button two and button three, even on single-button mice.

How the AWT Smooths over Hardware Differences

Where there are big differences in window toolkits, Java adopts conventions to smooth over those differences. For example:

- Macs have one button on the mouse.
- PCs have two buttons on the mouse (left and right).
- Many Unix systems have three buttons on the mouse (left, right, and center).

Java deals with this hardware difference by adopting the convention that all mice have three buttons. If the GUI invites a user to "click on the right button," a one-button mouse user can simulate it by holding down the META key while clicking. The following code is an example.

```
//<applet code=exmouse.class height=100 width=200> </applet> import
java.applet.*;
import java.awt.*;
import java.awt.event.*;

public class exmouse extends Applet {

     public void init() {
          addMouseListener( new MouseAdapter() {
          public void mouseClicked(MouseEvent e) {
               if ((e.getModifiers() & InputEvent.BUTTON1_MASK)!= 0)
                    System.out.println( "button1 pressed" );
               if ((e.getModifiers() & InputEvent.BUTTON2_MASK)!= 0)
                    System.out.println( "button2 pressed" );
               if ((e.getModifiers() & InputEvent.BUTTON3_MASK)!= 0)
                    System.out.println( "button3 pressed" );

               if ((e.getModifiers() & InputEvent.ALT_MASK) != 0)
                    System.out.println( "alt held down" );
               if ((e.getModifiers() & InputEvent.META_MASK) != 0)
                    System.out.println( "meta held down" );
               }
          } // end anon class
          ); // end method call
     }
}
```

If you hold down the ALT key while you click button one, you will get a mouse button two event. If you hold down the META key while you click button one, you will get a mouse button three event.

On a two-button mouse system, clicking the left button will result in the following output:

```
button1 pressed
```

Holding down the ALT key while clicking the same left mouse button will result in this output:

```
button2 pressed
alt held down
```

How do you know which is the ALT key and which is the META key? Often one or both of these is marked on the keyboard. The META key is just as often not marked or is marked as something else. Use a bit of experimentation.

Exercises

1. Take the MyFrame program that demonstrates the thread bug and update it to reproduce the race condition more easily. Change the arithmetic that updates variable i into two statements, and put a sleep() or a yield() statement between them. Observe the failure.

2. Update the MyFrame program to remove the race condition by making the reading and writing of the variables mutually exclude each other. Test your code by running it on a version of the program that quickly reproduces the race condition failure.

3. Write a small Java program to capture the screen, display it in a scroll panel inside a frame, and allow the user to trim the size of it. Write the cropped region out to a file on request. Allow the user to choose any output file format that the Image I/O library on that platform supports.

4. Write a program that uses Image I/O to display a thumbnail display of all the GIFs, JPGs, and PNGs in a directory. Let the user select one, and display that full size in a new window. Allow the user to change the size of it, crop a region, and save it in a new format. This is the very beginning of a general-purpose Java image editing application.

Some Light Relief—Sky View Cafe: A High Quality Applet

For the end piece in this chapter, I want to introduce you to the Sky View Cafe program and its author, Kerry Shetline. Sky View Cafe is an astronomy applet, but even if you have no interest in astronomy, it's a terrific showcase for the very professional graphics effects that a careful programmer can achieve.

In case you are interested in astronomy, I'll mention that Sky View Cafe displays many types of astronomical information, and is particularly easy to use. It shows star charts, rise and set times for the Sun, Moon, and planets, Moon phases, orbital paths of the planets in 3-D (I love animating that one!), a perpetual calendar with astronomical events, lunar and solar eclipses, the moons of Jupiter and Saturn, and more besides. See Figure 22-14 for the main screen.

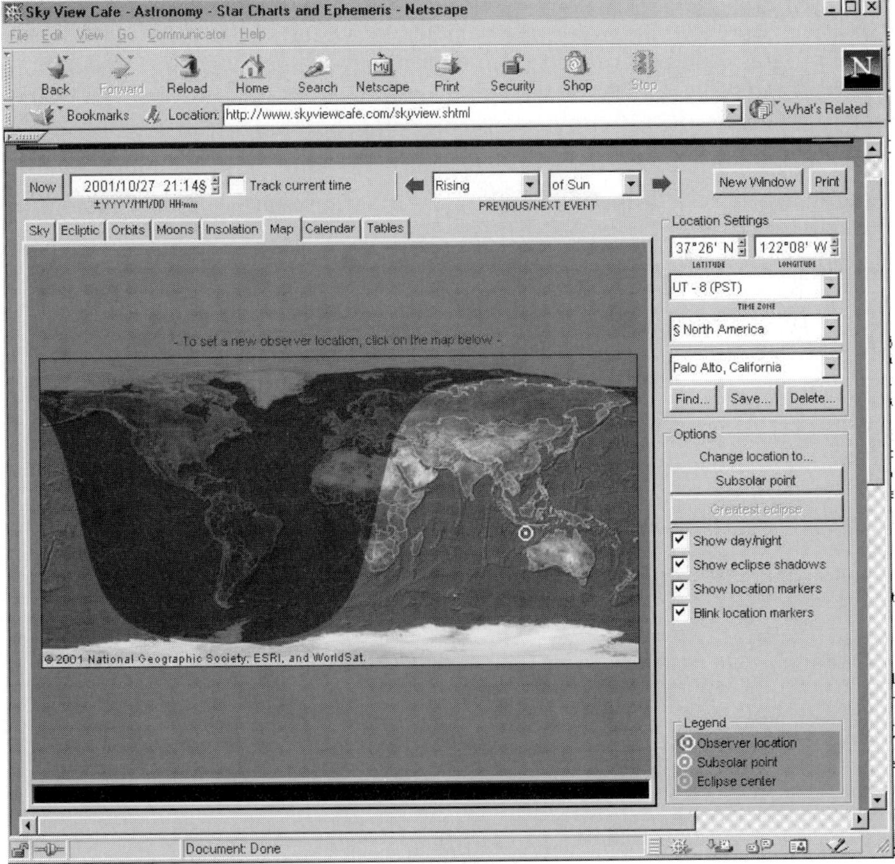

Figure 22–14 The Sky View Cafe astronomy applet.

That shows the half of the world that is in darkness and the half that's in daylight at this moment. It's a funny shape because the world is round and flattened out into an unrolled cylinder on the screen. You can see that the Antarctic is enjoying 24 hours of daylight at the moment.

The first thing to do is to click on the map to tell the program where you are on the planet. That makes the night sky maps accurate for your position. Instead of clicking, you can look up your city name by pressing the find button on the right hand side. Since ordinary applets can't write locally, it will tell the server to set a client side cookie, saving your location for future runs. Now you can select one of the other tabs on the tabbed pane. Printing is done in a very clever way: it causes a showDocument(), which brings up a new browser containing the thing you want printed. Then you use the browser's print command! Clever—and it avoids much tricky code.

We won't run through all the features of Sky View Cafe here. Part of the fun is exploring it for yourself. Kerry has a strong background in writing "what if" software that makes it easy to try things and easy to back out of them. He started professional programming writing programs for that excellent magazine, *Creative Computing* (long since defunct, alas). Later, Kerry worked in C++ for seven years. He has used Java for the last three years, and points out that he can get more done more quickly in Java; his programs run on all computers and operating systems.

Following is a code snippet from the class that represents our solar system:

```
package org.shetline.astronomy;

import java.util.*;
import java.io.*;
import org.shetline.util.*;
import org.shetline.math.*;

public class SolarSystem extends MathUser implements AstroConstants
{
   protected HeliocentricPlanets     planets = null;
   protected EclipticBody            moon = null;
   protected Pluto                   pluto = null;
   protected String[]                planetNames;

   // Result in days per revolution.
   //
   public double getMeanOrbitalPeriod(int planet)
   {
      if (planet < MERCURY || planet > PLUTO)
         return 0.0;

      // Convert degrees per Julian century into days per revolution.
      return 100.0 * 365.25 * 360.0 / elems[planet - MERCURY][0][1];
   }
```

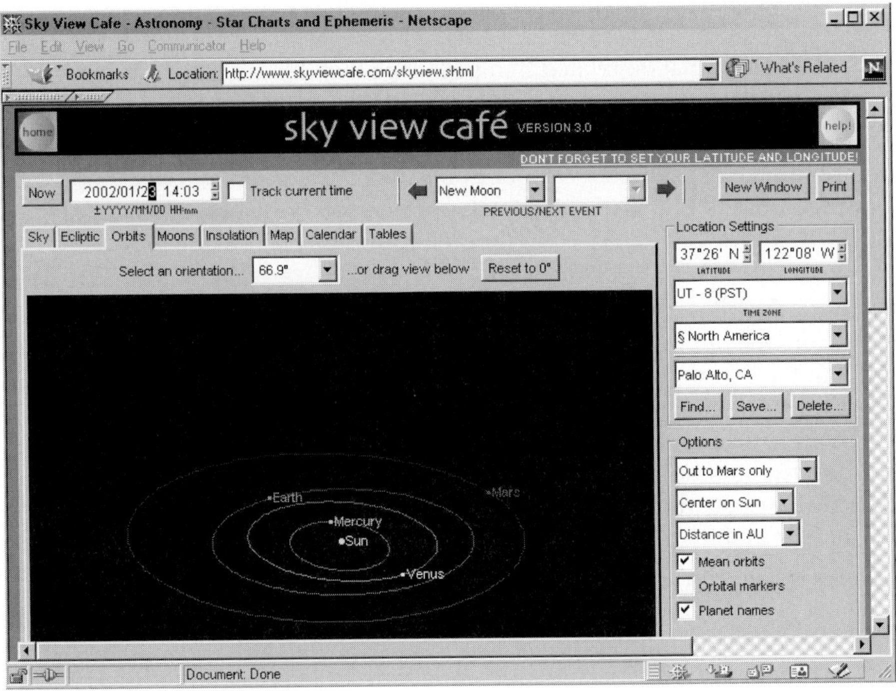

Figure 22–15 Moving model of the solar system.

This code implements, in part, one of the Sky View Cafe features that I really like: the animated model of the solar system known as an Orrery. It's the third tabbed pane, the one marked "orbits." Pressing it brings up a display showing the paths of the nine planets, including earth, that orbit our star. You can adjust the angle from which you're viewing the solar system by dragging on it (see Figure 22-15).

If you highlight a single digit in the "date" field up at the top left, and then press the spinner (one of a pair of small arrows to the right) to adjust the date, you can advance the model by that amount (minute, hour, day, month, year, decade, etc.). When you do this, the planets move in their orbits correspondingly. If you keep the spinner pressed, it keeps incrementing time, and keeps moving the planets around. Beautiful!

The name "Orrery" (for a moving model of the solar system) comes from the Earl of Orrery (a small place in Ireland) who paid a clockmaker to build him one in 1712. The device was created by George Graham, so it really should be a "Graham."

Kerry explained how he designed and coded Sky View Cafe. You have to have a strong interest in the subject area that you're programming. It helps to look for other programs that do related things. Maybe they'll have some good ideas you can re-implement, or have some bad ideas that you can avoid.

Newsgroups can provide helpful information, and Sun hosts some Java-specific newsgroups at the Java Developer Connection at *developer.java.sun.com*. Kerry also urges programmers to read the Javadoc-generated API documentation for each library class they want to use. There's lots of information in there, but it won't do you any good unless you read it.

You need to think ahead when you write any class. Try to imagine how it might be reused somewhere later, and write it accordingly. Don't build in knowledge about the current context, but pass it in as parameters. Perhaps the class can be generalized by making it abstract, and then subclassing it to provide more detail. Kerry is a firm supporter of early prototyping for GUI code. Get a basic framework running reliably so that you can see how your ideas work in practice. Add to this framework in gradual steps. Avoid a development style where you are coding for months without having enough to test or run.

An important feature of Sky View Cafe is the amount of effort that went into making it a well behaved applet. Although it's big at around 375Kb (one minute to download on a phone line), it has been crafted to run in just about any browser, and to avoid many known browser bugs. The code is all in JDK 1.1 for this reason. Kerry develops on a Macintosh using the CodeWarrior IDE., and tests on almost all platform/browser revision combinations.

Sky View Cafe was a labor of love, and it took Kerry about 18 months of hobby project time (evenings and weekends) to bring it to this state. Too many open source projects reach version 0.8, and the programmer loses interest. Sky View Cafe is now at version 3.0 with 4.0 under development, and it is open source shareware. Kerry has generously published the source so others can learn from his work, and he invites people to register if they find the program useful. The current versions of Sky View Cafe source and executable are on the CD that comes with this book. Take a look! The source and applet are also online at the website *www.shetline.com*.

Part

5

Enterprise Java

Chapter 23

Java Beans in Theory

Java beans is the architecture for component software in Java. It's a pretty big topic, so we'll cover it in two chapters. This chapter explains the theory: what component software is, how it is used in Java, what software tools are used and when. The chapter concludes with a summary of Enterprise Java Beans, which is the use of component software to construct server-side systems rather than client applications.

The next chapter provides a program specification for two Java beans. It then walks through creating these components and integrating them. A bean info class is developed for each of the two beans. Beans are all about three things: properties, events, and methods. The bean info class describes these three qualities of the bean to a visual design tool. Chapter 24 concludes with a small amount of additional material on specialized features of the beans model. This chapter is a prerequisite for getting the most out of the following chapter.

Unhappily, a large number of the beans white papers, books, and tutorials in existence are dense and impenetrable. They fall into the classic pitfall of presenting material which is "clear only if already known." The situation is made worse because, like much software, beans tend to be a little abstract. Throw in the confusing new terminology and the multistage lifecycle, and you have a recipe for something obscure and ponderous.

To remedy the situation we will go step by step. We'll start with a description of components in general. Next, a refresher on events, followed by an outline of the code conventions for beans. Then we'll look at the proof-of-concept design-time tool called the Beanbox. We won't present any beans code in this chapter, but we will walk through a full example of how beans are integrated in the beanbox. That knowledge will be used in the next chapter, where we gradually develop two practical beans.

What Is Component Software?

If you are already familiar with the power of software components, perhaps through using one of the Windows-based tools like Visual Basic Extensions or Delphi, then you can safely skip over this first section. Otherwise, read on for an introduction to a powerful new technique that is widely used in the Microsoft Windows world, and emerging on Unix and the Mac.

Programming is one of the few professions where each piece of work starts more or less from first principles. When programmers are assigned to a new project, the design and coding often begins with literally a blank sheet of paper. By the time you have completed half a dozen projects, you can recognize similar situations and perhaps create some application-specific libraries. But that is often the extent of code sharing and reuse.

Imagine if plumbers worked that way. Think what it would mean if every job required the plumber to laboriously handcraft each pipe, bolt, and valve. Plumbing jobs would take a lot longer and be much more costly. Thankfully, plumbers buy their supplies ready made, and a lot of plumbing simply involves using standard pipes and joints to connect big preassembled components such as garbage disposals, dishwashers, and water heaters. Programming is still catching up with plumbing in this respect. Component software is an attempt to use software building blocks larger than "individual lines of code."

In general, with most programming languages, there are two approaches for organizing and arranging executable code. The code can either be set up as an executable program (e.g., an application, an applet, or a servlet). Or it can be a library that implements some API and contains many related classes and methods. Component software is a third approach, with some aspects that are like "executable program" and some that are like "library." Component software strives to combine the reusability of a library with the customized specialization of an individual program.

To look at it another way, when you use a large library (like Swing) sometimes you only use a handful of pieces from it. What if there were some way to bundle up just the code that has a single well-defined purpose, and quickly use it in several different programs without having to code it in line-by-line? What if you had a component editor which allowed you to add, move, and join together classes instead of "lines of code"? Coming from the Windows world, which places a heavy emphasis on GUI tools, component software relies on some kind of visual tool to assemble the units. Software components are intended to bring these three good things to your software products:

- widespread reuse of code
- simplicity of component integration via visual tools, leading to
- higher overall productivity for code development

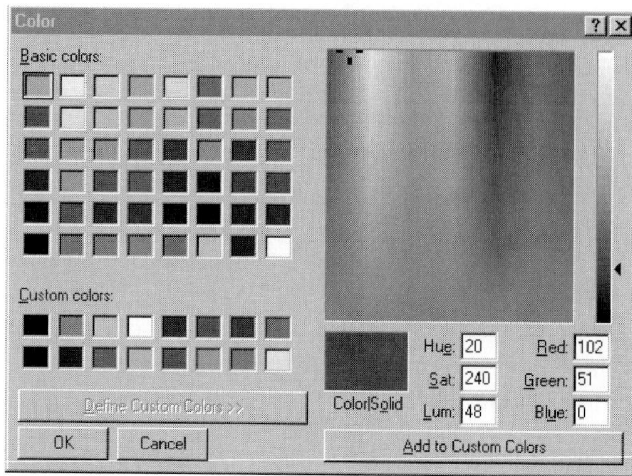

Figure 23–1 A "color chooser panel" makes a good software component.

So what makes a good candidate to be a software component? Essentially, it is any self-contained piece of code with a well-defined function that you might use in several programs, and frequently with a GUI representation. For example, Figure 23-1 shows a "color chooser panel" that displays a matrix of different shades and allows the user to click on the color needed— a great candidate to be a software component.

This is the color chooser used on Windows 98, and you can't tell from running the program whether this actually is implemented as a component or not. Regardless, it's an example of the kind of self-contained functionality that makes a good component. A color chooser panel is written once, and can be turned into a software component by following some simple coding conventions which we will see later. The component can then be integrated with any of your programs that need to process colors by dragging and dropping in a visual builder tool. Components can be created out of several simpler components. This color chooser clearly uses simpler components like Button, TextField, Cursor, and Canvas. Most components also belong to a library, allowing you the choice of using a visual builder tool, or explicitly writing the lines of code to instantiate and invoke the functions you need.

Once you get used to it, the visual way can be quick. However, there is no free lunch. It takes perhaps twice the effort to write a software component and build in the flexibility. Generally speaking, the easier it is to customize and use a given software component, the more work it takes to implement it. Another factor to consider is that Java beans are not as easy to learn as some other parts of Java. There isn't a single overall design philosophy, the way there is with, e.g., JDBC. Java beans (or more accurately, the bean info classes that accompany them) are built out of an obscure mixture of arbitrary rules, conventions, and language features. One programmer compared creating Java beans to "trying to build a space shuttle out of kitchen utensils for a child to operate." So grab your egg whisk, spatula, and space helmet, and let's get going.

What Is a Java Bean?

A Java bean is an individual software component written in Java. The definition of a Java bean from one of Sun's white papers follows. To let a class be a Java bean you follow a few simple naming conventions, or you may prefer to write a "bean info" class that accompanies your bean and explicitly describes its interfaces. The bean-related framework is in the `java.beans` and `java.beans.beancontext` packages. A bean context is a logical container for several beans, allowing them to be nested in a hierarchy (beans within beans).

Definition of a Java Bean

A Java bean is a reusable software component that can be manipulated visually in a builder tool. Any Java class functions as a bean by following a few easy coding conventions:

- important fields have "get" and "set" methods
- the class is serializable
- the class has a no-arg constructor (which can be explicit, or implicit because you left off all constructors)

These are preferred guidelines more than absolute requirements. You can equally well provide the necessary information by writing a BeanInfo class to accompany and describe your bean.

Here is a minimal Java bean:

```
public class SmallestBean {}
```

Here is a small, useful, complete Java bean:

```
public class MyButton extends javax.swing.JButton {
    public MyButton() {  // no-arg constructor
        super("press for service");
    }
}
```

Note that the simple definition means just about every existing class is a Java bean automatically! Another advantage is that, unlike all other component architectures, Java beans are not tied to just one platform. Because they are written in Java, they run on all computers. Component software as currently practiced with Visual Basic is limited another way, too. VB components are most often used for GUI controls. Java has taken software components much further. With an architecture known as Enterprise Java Beans (EJB), the beans model has grown up to encompass sophisticated business algorithms completely unrelated to visual presentation. Enterprise Java Beans (EJB) is the recommended approach to server-side Java components. We summarize EJB at the end of this chapter.

The Visual Basic variety of component software (developed by Alan Cooper and purchased by Microsoft) has been very successful. There are many companies that make a living solely from selling VBX (Visual Basic eXtensions) components. They often do pretty well, right up to the time Microsoft decides to bundle that kind of component with VBX. There are some companies selling Java beans, too, but they do not have the volume of VBX today. On the other hand, the Java components are more useful because they can be used on more than one platform, and they have much greater capabilities (network, security, multimedia, threading, etc.).

Some Commercial Java Beans

There are Java beans for sale at these places, among others:

```
http://www.javabeanstore.com/
http://jars.developer.com/jars_resources_javabeans.html
http://www.getobjects.com/Components/components.html
http://www.desaitech.com/mindex.html
```

You will find you can buy source or binary forms of beans at reasonable prices to do popular tasks. Beans are available for charting and graphing, date/time processing, animations, ftp, cryptography, database access, and more.

Several VB companies are now offering migration tools to automate the conversion of VB to Java. See

```
http://www.halcyonsoft.com/service/service-vb.asp
http://www.blackdirt.com/
http://www.diamondedge.com/
```

Although VB components (and the ever-changing framework names of OLE, COM, ActiveX, DNA, and now .NET) are widely used, they have a limited area of best applicability: the creation of small to medium GUI applications that are restricted to Windows platforms. Java beans go way beyond this, bringing the benefits of component software to every tier of an N-tier system, and particularly to server-side programming.

Java beans come in two varieties: visual and non-visual. All visual beans extend the class `java.awt.Component` or one of its subclasses. Non-visual beans don't extend the `java.awt.Component` class and don't have a GUI element at runtime, but are still manipulated visually at design time. All server-side software components are non-visual beans. An example of a server-side component would be a bean to access a database. The bean knows how to set up a connection with a database, send in queries, and get back data. Any program to which you add this bean instantly becomes database-capable! IBM gives away a similar bean that connects to an Excel spreadsheet.

You should use beans when you anticipate that the benefits (the amount of code customization and reuse) will more than offset the cost (the extra work involved in coding that flexibility and following the bean protocols).

Properties and Events

Software components must have simple well-defined public interfaces that allow access to everything they do. Most of the Java beans conventions are intended to help with this. Beans have *properties* that store and let you change characteristics of the bean. A property is any characteristic of a bean that can be given an initial value after the bean is written and before the bean is used. Properties customize the appearance or function of a bean. They are things like what font should be used, what size on the screen it is, and so on. A property of a bean is really just a data field in the bean class, with public getter and setter methods.

Too much literature comes at beans all wrong. It focuses on properties, when it should be focusing on what beans do, namely:

- Bean A changed one of its field values, and it needs to tell bean B about it.
- Bean A has a GUI interaction that should cause a method in bean B to be invoked.
- Bean A wants to change one of its field values, and it needs to ask bean B if it's OK.

Beans communicate with each other using events. The three tasks above are all implemented by one bean sending an event, and another bean receiving it and reacting to it. Some beans generate events, some beans handle events, and some do both. The bean has no way of knowing at coding time what it will be connected to. All it has to do is generate and handle appropriate events. Beans should be like Lego bricks: you can buy any Lego kit anywhere and be confident that it will be compatible and interoperate with all your other Lego sets.

Coding Time, Design Time, Runtime

There is a very important distinction between *coding time* (when a skilled programmer writes the bean), *design time* (when someone uses a visual tool to customize beans and connect them to other beans), and *runtime* (when the user runs the integrated program containing the components). Visually connecting existing components doesn't need a lot of programming skill, and the task may be done by web page developers rather than programmers.

Figure 23-2 shows the three stages in the life of a bean.

It's important to have a solid appreciation of the three different stages in the life of a bean. Certain tasks can only be done at certain times. The three stages, along with what you do in each, are:

1. **Coding time.** During coding time, your best programmers will be writing the java bean software components. They will establish the properties, methods, and events that allow beans to be configured and to pass data to each other. Writing a bean is mostly like writing any program, but you typically want to make far more of the behavior configurable. In addition, you can make things more polished by providing extra classes giving bean information to the design time visual tool.
2. **Design time.** Design time is when web programmers, or even knowledgeable users, run some kind of visual component integration tool to "glue" beans together. They will set the initial defaults for bean properties, choose among the configuration possibilities, and draw connections for data, methods, and events for beans. Design time is a mixture of programming and systems integration. You don't actually write any lines of code, but the visual tool will generate plenty on your behalf, to implement the connections you have made. There's an example of this later in the chapter. The final output from design time is an assembly of software components in the form of a jar file.
3. **Runtime.** At runtime, the users will execute the jar file that contains the finished, customized components. They will see the behavior that was chosen for them at design time, among all the behaviors that were implemented at coding time.

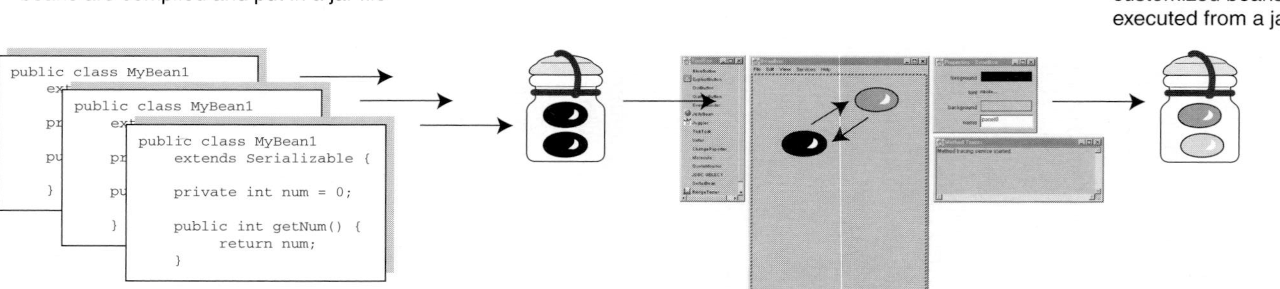
1. Coding time
beans are compiled and put in a jar file
public class MyBean1
public class MyBean1
public class MyBean1
extends Serializable {
private int num = 0;
public int getNum() {
return num;
}
2. Design time
beans are customized using property sheets,
connected using events, and written out to a jar file
3. Runtime
customized beans are
executed from a jar file

Figure 23–2 The life cycle of beans.

Refresher on Events

You absolutely must have a good understanding of events and event handling to understand how to write beans. Bean events are just like ordinary window system events. As a refresher, we use events to communicate between two different parts of a program. One part of the program has things happening asynchronously (i.e., at irregular and unpredictable intervals), such as a key in a GUI being pressed. The thing that is happening is called the "event," and the code where it happens is the "event generator." Pressing a key on the keyboard generates an event. Clicking on a button generates an event. Moving the mouse generates an event. A timer expiring is an event. Another part of the program has some code that needs to hear about the events and handle them.

The operating system calls a routine in the java runtime library when an event happens. How do we get the runtime library to call your event-handling routine? The runtime library is not compiled with your code, and has no knowledge of it. The same problem arises with beans. In general, different beans are not going to be compiled, and should have no knowledge of each other. Yet we need to connect them together somehow. Beans use events to solve this problem (see Figure 23-3).

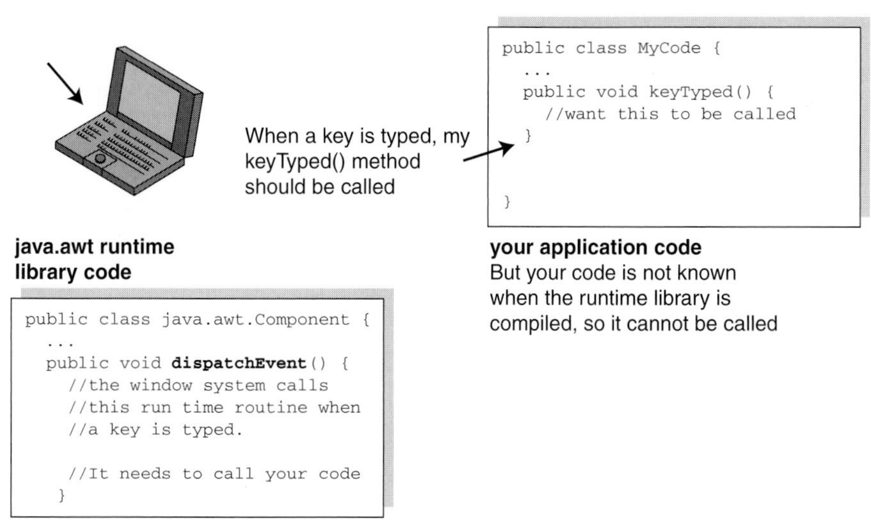
public class MyCode {
...
public void keyTyped() {
//want this to be called
}
}
When a key is typed, my keyTyped() method should be called
java.awt runtime library code
your application code
But your code is not known when the runtime library is compiled, so it cannot be called
public class java.awt.Component {
...
public void dispatchEvent() {
//the window system calls
//this run time routine when
//a key is typed.
//It needs to call your code
}

Figure 23–3 Problem: How to get them to connect.

The same solution to this problem is used in both cases (window system code and beans code). A piece of your code is interested in being told about each event as soon as it happens, and each time it happens. This piece of code is going to "handle" or process the events. It is called the event handler, and there may be several of them for any event. This code will implement an interface called ZzzzListener, where "`Zzzz`" is a word describing the event generator in some way. AWT has KeyListener, ActionListener, WindowListener, FocusListener, etc. The interface will have a method or methods that say, in effect, "`zzzzHappened().`"

The event generator will have a method called `addZzzzListener()`. That method takes a parameter that is a `ZzzzListener` interface. Anyone that wants to get the events must first register their event handler with the event generator by calling its add listener method (see Figure 23-4). The event generator will save a reference to all the listeners that register. Then, each time the event happens, it will call them back to say "the event just happened."

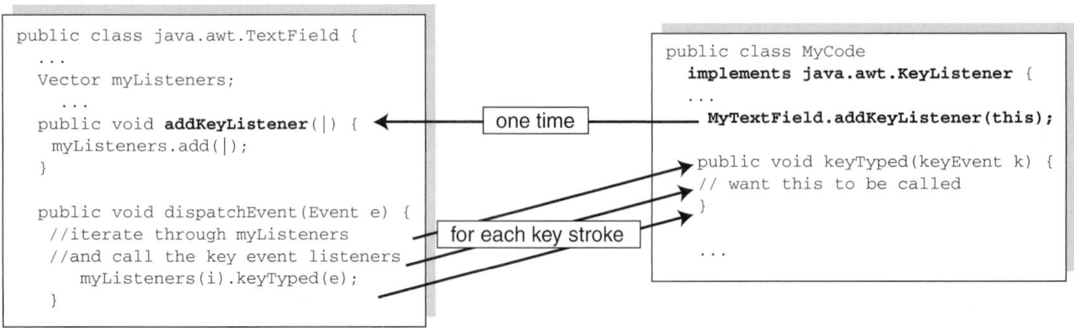

Figure 23–4 Solution: Register your code at runtime.

In regular event programming, an event handler will register itself with the event generator by calling the generator's `addZzzzListener()` method. The handler must pass in an object that implements the methods promised in the `ZzzzListener()` interface (often itself, or it could be a nested class). With beans, we strive to eliminate knowing the details of any other bean, so the event handlers in one bean don't add themselves directly to the list of Listeners in the event generator bean. Instead, a designer will use the design tool to connect an event listener bean to an event generator bean. The tool creates some "glue" code that will execute at runtime and call the add listener method.

At runtime, the generator has a collection of listeners that have registered their interest in listening to this event. Each time a Zzzz event occurs, the generator goes through that list and calls the appropriate method in the object that the handler sent over as a parameter.

Bean Conventions

The Java Bean architecture and the design tools expect your bean classes to follow the get/set/is conventions for fields and the methods that operate on them. The standard bean naming conventions are best shown by examples:

- an int property called "myValue" is set (assigned a value) by a method with this signature:

  ```
  public void setMyValue(int i)
  ```

- the value of an int property called "myValue" is obtained by a method with this signature:

  ```
  public int getMyValue()
  ```

- a boolean property called "`moreData`" can also use this form of name in place of `getMoreData()`, allowing it to read more fluently in `if` statements and expressions:

  ```
  public boolean isMoreData()
  ```

There is a letter case inconsistency here which is defined not to be a problem. Following the rules in the Java Language Specification, class names start with a capital letter, data fields start with a lower case letter, and the first letter of each word in an identifier is capitalized. That means that the property "`myValue`" corresponds to methods "`setMyValue()`" and "`getMyValue()`" even though they actually differ in letter case. The beans specification has a special rule that says, effectively, "yeah, we know, but we're going to define that these things match." The alternative would have been to introduce a new keyword or two, and nobody wanted to do that.

All the Swing GUI controls have been written to follow the simple code conventions that allow a class to act as a bean. So all Swing components are beans. The examples above use boolean and int types, but the same naming pattern is used whatever the type of the property. Some of the Sun literature refers to this naming convention as a "design pattern." It's a pattern in the sense of a template, applied to method names. But the term "design pattern" has already been taken for something else (pre-packaged algorithms for common situations), so Java beans should have called it something else. As well as this get/set convention, you need to be very careful to choose meaningful names for your methods. The names show up in the bean application builder, and are one of the key ways that bean integrators figure out what the method does.

Serialization

Beans needs to be persistent (i.e., you can write them out to a disk file) so that an application builder can save work in progress. In JDK 1.3 and earlier, beans are written to disk using the standard object serialization in class `java.io.ObjectOutputStream`. As a refresher, a class indicates that its state can be saved by implementing the serialization interface, like this:

```
public class MyComponent implements java.io.Serializable { ...
```

That interface does not have any methods so there is no further work to do, except possibly adding the keyword "transient" to any fields that don't need to be saved. These will be the fields that are always recalculated before use (like "current speed") and other kinds of transient data.

We don't need to write "implements serializable" with any Swing components that we make into beans. All Swing components are subclasses of java.awt.Component which implements serializable. When a parent class implements an interface, all child classes inherit the methods and hence that capability. Sometimes people write "implements Serializable" anyway, for emphasis.

From JDK 1.4, beans are written out in XML form to serialize them (more about this later).

The next section describes how to install and run the BeanBox, which is a rudimentary design time tool. You don't *create* a bean in the beanbox—you *connect* existing beans. The section will show you how to connect some existing demo beans that come with the beanbox. In the next chapter, we will use this knowledge to connect the beans we develop ourselves.

Install the Beanbox

The next few pages sidetrack from beans in order to introduce the visual tool we will be using at design time. The java.bean package has been part of the JDK since Java 1.1, but you also need some application builder software to experiment with beans. Most Java IDEs, such as Sun's Forte, Borland's JBuilder, IBM's Visual Age for Java, or Symantec's Visual Cafe, include bean builder software.

Try Forte

There are many excellent IDEs that support Java beans. One well-regarded IDE is the Forte product, which is available for downloading from *java.sun.com.* If you want to step up to something better than the beanbox, Forte is a good choice.

Forte comes in several versions of increasing features and price. The entry level version (the community edition, known as "Net Beans") is both open source and free. Forte also has good support for bean development. It needs a lot of memory, at least 256MB, to run well. If you don't have that much memory on your system, you'll need to consider IDEs with a smaller footprint. The Java Programmers FAQ (on the CD that accompanies this book) lists several.

Rather than present any one of the dozens of IDEs available, we will download and use the very basic and free "Beanbox" from Sun. The beanbox is a rudimentary design time visual integration tool for beans. It has enough functionality to show the bean concept, but it has not been kept up to date (it does not serialize beans using XML, for example). The beanbox does roughly the same job for Java beans that the appletviewer does for applets. It provides a quick, simple way to see them running. To get started on your first bean, go to

```
http://java.sun.com/products/javabeans/software/bdk_download.html
```

and download the Bean Development Kit version 1.1 (or later). You can download it as a zip file, or as a Windows-only .exe file which can be executed to do the installation automatically. If using Windows, download the .exe file version and install the BDK into disk directory `c:\bdk1.1`.

Pitfall with BDK installation!

To avoid a bug, the BDK software must not be installed in a Windows directory with a space in the filename. Therefore, do *not* install it in the default location offered by the installer of `"C:\Program Files\BDK1.1"`! Instead, install the BDK to `c:\bdk1.1`

If you fail to heed this warning, the beanbox will hang when it tries to automatically generate and compile adapter classes that connect your beans.

After choosing the installation directory, the installer will prompt you to select which Java runtime environment to use. Any JRE of release JDK 1.2 or greater is fine. If the installer does not offer you any JVMs to choose from, use "find" on your system to find a file called "java.exe" and use the latest version of that.

Some of the advanced IDEs available today make little distinction between coding time and design time. They provide plenty of visual support for both. They offer forms and templates that will automatically generate events and event handlers, and put them in the right place. Once you master an environment like this, you can be very productive. I've avoided using such an IDE in this chapter because it would hide what is going on, and you'll be a better beans programmer if you understand what is going on. Unlike these other IDEs, the beanbox doesn't help you code beans at all. Its purpose is to let you initialize and connect beans at design time, and provide a basic test environment to run them.

Run a Demo Bean

The next step is to use the beanbox on one of the example beans that accompany it. It is traditional to use the juggler bean. The juggler bean displays several gifs in rapid succession to present an animated demonstration of juggling. Go to the beanbox directory and start the beanbox with these commands:

```
cd c:\bdk1.1\beanbox
run
```

The run.bat script updates your class path to include bean libraries and will bring up the beanbox with its four windows shown in Figure 23-5. There is also a run.sh script for people using Unix.

The narrow left-hand window labeled "ToolBox" has a list of all the beans the beanbox currently knows of. The largest window, labelled "BeanBox," is where we will manipulate beans, and make connections between beans. You will click on a bean in the Toolbox window, and then click on the beanbox to transfer the bean to the box and start working on it.

The upper window on the right side, labelled "Properties - BeanBox," will show a list of the properties (loosely, the public fields) of the bean. When you first start up the beanbox, no other beans are loaded, and it shows four properties of itself: background and foreground color, panel name, and panel font. (That's right, the beanbox is written in 100% pure Java, runs on all platforms, and is itself a bean!)

The lower window on the right-hand side, labeled "Method Tracer," is a recent addition to the beanbox. The method tracer is intended to provide a proof of concept of bean debugging support through tracing the flow of control. We don't use it here, and suggest you move it out of the way by selecting "Services | Hide Method Tracing" from the menu along the top of the beanbox.

Loading a Bean into the Beanbox

When you start the beanbox, it will load all the jar files that it finds in the directory `c:\bdk1.1\jars`. The beanbox will then display all the beans from those jar files in the lefthand "toolbox" window. The beanbox comes with about one dozen demonstration beans, sadly none of them tutorial in nature. These beans will appear in the toolbox window when you start the beanbox. You transfer a bean to the beanbox by clicking on it in the "toolbox" window. The cursor will change to a crosshair. Move it over to the beanbox, click again, and a copy of the bean will appear in the beanbox.

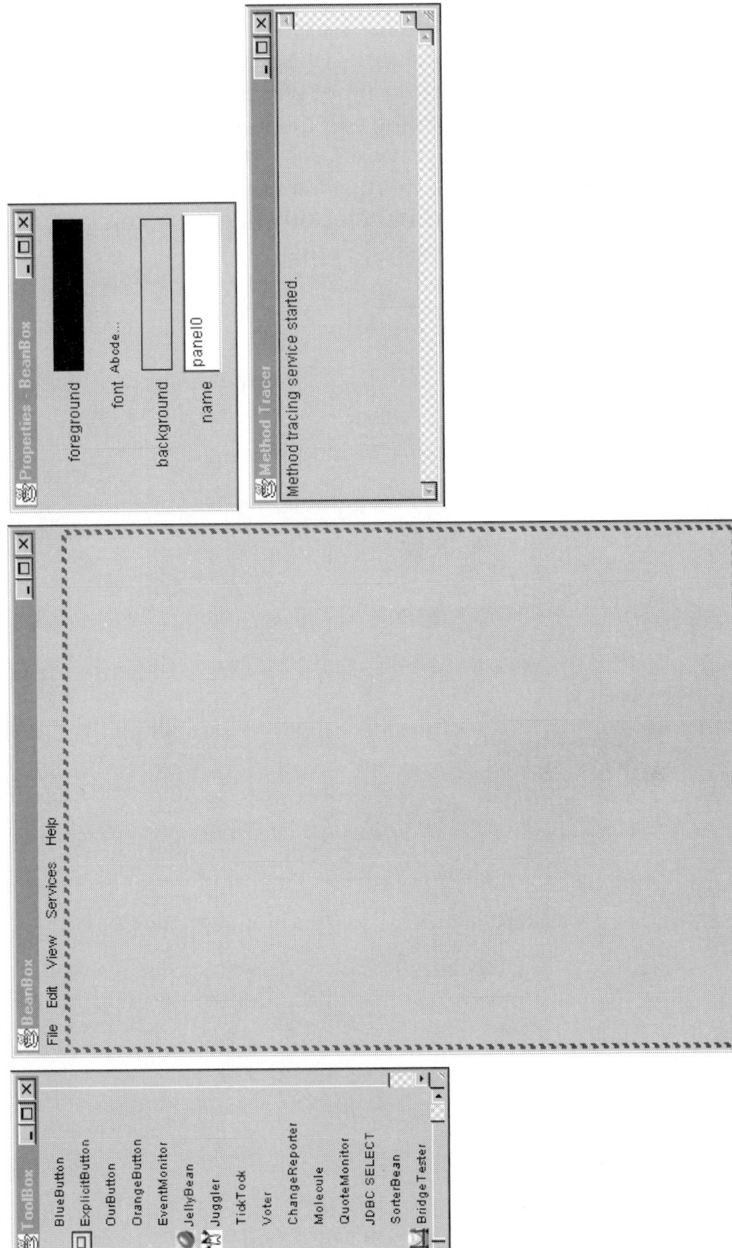

Figure 23–5 The beanbox.

The new copy of the bean will have a crosshatched border in the beanbox. That indicates which bean has the focus (the active component in a GUI is said to "have the focus," meaning that user input will be directed to it). This is the bean to which editing operations from the edit menu will be applied. You can drag the highlighted bean around to a new position by click-and-dragging on the cross-hatching. Figure 23-6 shows the "juggler" demo bean after an instance has been dropped on the bean box. There are some other beans in this beanbox, too, but only the juggler has the cross-hatched border.

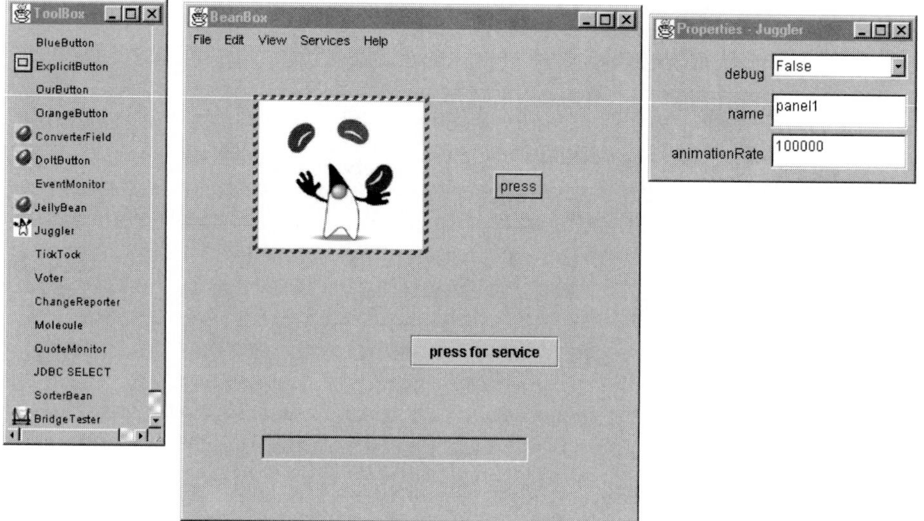

Figure 23–6 The cross-hatched border shows the bean with the focus.

Customizing Bean Properties

The beanbox is a design time tool. After coding some beans, put the jar files containing them in a directory known to the bdk, and transfer several of the beans to the beanbox. In the beanbox you can then select the beans one by one, and customize their properties using the properties sheet shown on the right of Figure 23-6.

The property sheet shows that the juggler bean has three properties called "debug," "name," and "animation rate." You can give the highlighted bean new values for these properties by typing them on the property sheet window. These new values will change the appearance or behavior of the bean. The new values that you give to these properties will be carried forward to runtime. The bean will start running with these initial values. Note that you can edit bean properties *only* when the bean is surrounded by cross-hatching in the beanbox. That's all there is to customization.

Try it. You'll see that a small number (less than 100) makes the animated frames fly by. The "animation rate" property represents the number of milliseconds between frames. Speed it up to 1, and then keep an eye on the image. Pauses and discontinuities in the animation represent garbage collection or other work your system is doing. Enough of the fun, let's get back to work. Set the animation rate at 10,000 so it is less distracting. Next, we will connect a button component to stop the animation entirely. This will be our first example of integrating two beans. Stopping/starting animation is a service that the juggler bean offers, and we just need to find a way to connect a button to it.

Connecting a Button to a Method in Another Bean

This section walks you through the steps to connect a button push event to a method in another bean. After you make this design time connection, each press of that button at run time will cause the method in the other bean to be called. We want to avoid building any knowledge of one bean into the other at coding time. We certainly don't want the method to be called directly by name from another bean. The whole idea is to keep things as flexible as possible by allowing arbitrary beans to be joined after coding time wherever it makes semantic sense. These beans could be created at different times by different people without any knowledge of each other, and we still expect them to fit together.

The beanbox design tool uses a combination of menu choices and mouse movements (tracked by red lines) to make the connections between beans. The finished integrated beans are delivered from the beanbox in the form of a jar file that can be run as an applet.

The first step is to bring the "OrangeButton" bean from the toolbox into the beanbox, and leave it highlighted by clicking near its border. You can move beans about in the box by clicking and dragging on the cross-hatched border. Next, click on the "Edit" menu at the top of the beanbox. That displays a drop-down menu with a list of things you can do with this bean, including cut, copy, paste, and "Events," which leads to a pull-right menu, as shown in Figure 23-7.

The Events menu selection lists all the events that the highlighted component has said it can generate. Select the only choice on the button push menu, and the beanbox will now look like Figure 23-8.

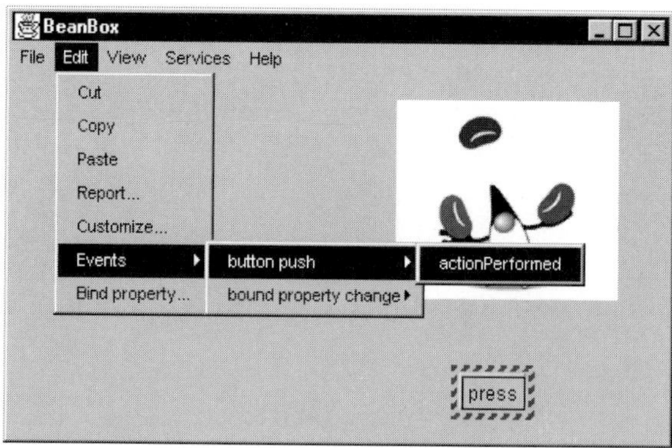

Figure 23–7
Connecting an event.

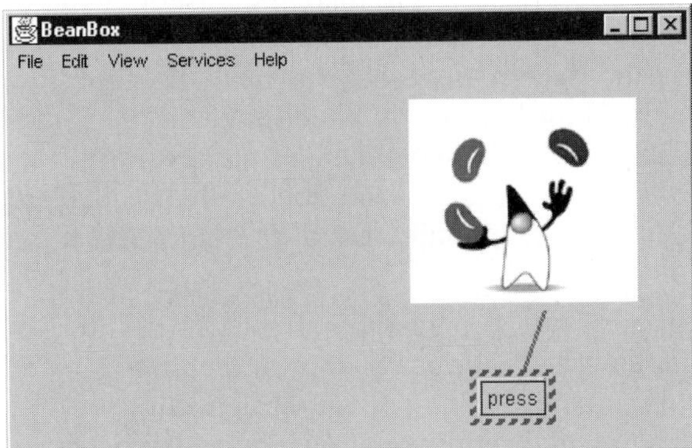

Figure 23–8
Connecting an event.

The red line represents the event we are trying to connect. It starts at the component that generates the event, and follows the mouse as we move it around. Decide to which component you would like to send this event, and click on its border. If you make a mistake, you can cancel and start again. When you have successfully chosen the destination java bean, you will get a pop-up window as shown in Figure 23-9.

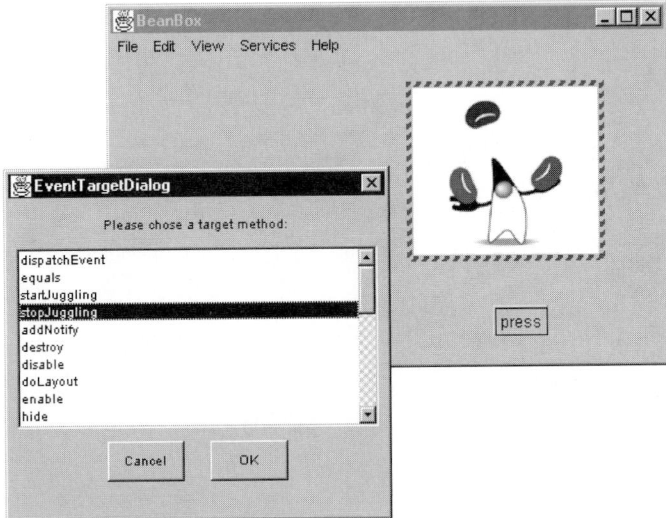

Figure 23–9 Connecting an event.

The Event Target Dialog (as this pop-up is known) displays a list of methods that are candidates to be called when the button push event is delivered to the juggler bean. Not all methods are candidates. Only those that have the right signature will be shown in the dialog. And the bean coder better have picked names that suggest clearly what the methods do, because the method names are your only guide to the semantics until you read the documentation for this bean. Here we can see a method called "stopJuggling." Highlight it and click "ok" to dismiss the dialog.

A new pop-up window will briefly appear to inform you that the beanbox is "generating and compiling an adapter class." The beanbox is automatically generating some "glue" code to make the connection that will allow an event to be sent between these two beans. The pop-up will disappear within a few seconds and you are free to press the button and stop the picture of the Tooth Fairy from juggling.

After that, highlight the orange button again, and use the property sheet editor to change its label to "stop juggler." Voila! You have connected two beans by an event from one bean causing a method call in the other. Now add another button, give it a pink color in the property sheet, relabel it as "start," and connect it to the startJuggling method.

Looking at the "Glue" Code

The beanbox automatically generates and compiles a small amount of glue code at design time to integrate your beans together. The code boils down to an additional class that provides an event handler in one bean and has it call a method in the same bean. When bean A sends the event, the handler in bean B gets it and invokes its parameterless method. It's that easy.

The glue code doesn't change any of your code, but is an additional class on the side. Beans should not know anything about other beans, but the glue code can have that knowledge. You can see the generated classes in directory

```
\bdk1.1\beanbox\tmp\sunw\beanbox
```

Here is typical glue for a button press event:

```
// Automatically generated event hookup file.
package tmp.sunw.beanbox;
import ConverterField;
import java.awt.event.ActionListener;
import java.awt.event.ActionEvent;
public class ___Hookup_171141f68c
    implements java.awt.event.ActionListener, java.io.Serializable {
    public void setTarget(ConverterField t) {
        target = t;
    }
    public void actionPerformed(java.awt.event.ActionEvent arg0) {
        target.validateAndMultiply();
    }
    private ConverterField target;
}
```

This class will be an add-on to the event handler class, our juggler bean. In this case, the entire event handler part is automatically generated, so the juggler bean does not even have to know what kind of events other beans might send. We could just as easily connect the juggler actions to key strokes in a textfield. That's one of the exercises at the end of the chapter.

When a button event comes in, the hookup class's action performed method is called, and that invokes the juggler routine we really want called. This is just the classic idiom of "pass an object to the constructor, save the reference to it, and later invoke one of its methods." You should have seen this idiom a few times before, and you'll see it a lot again in your object-oriented programming career.

The final step is to choose "File | Make Applet..." to prove that you can save your work and run it outside the beanbox. Accept the default destination that the Make an Applet panel offers you. When it has finished generating and compiling the applet code, you can cd to the destination and run your software components by entering these commands

```
cd \bdk1.1\beanbox\tmp\myapplet
appletviewer myapplet.html
```

You should see exactly what you constructed in the beanbox, but running as an applet rather than in a design tool. It is not particularly convenient that the beanbox will turn your components into an applet. A stand-alone executable jar file would be much more useful. An applet output form was chosen for ease and speed of beanbox implementation by the Sun programmers. Applets already have a graphical context within which they execute; for a stand-alone executable, that would have to be specified and provided somehow. Sun doesn't intend you to use the beanbox for anything except quickly checking that your components can snap together.

You are now a wizard of visual programming.

The beanbox is a crude design time tool, but you can see that visual programming is easy. The next chapter shows the low-level details needed to make it all work well. Specifically, we will look at the bean information classes that accompany your beans, and help provide information to the design time tool. This is a good place to take a break. The remainder of the chapter describes more sophisticated uses of beans that you may later engage with.

Activation Framework and Infobus

There are two software packages that provide additional support for beans: the Java Activation Framework, and the InfoBus. You can write much java bean software without ever needing either of these, but they are available when you want them. The Activation Framework lets your code determine the type of an arbitrary piece of data, discover the operations available on it, and instantiate an appropriate bean to perform those operations. For example, if one of your programs expected an arbitrary data stream and actually got a stream of MPEG data, the activation framework would let your code identify the data as MPEG. From that type, your code could locate and instantiate an object that will play the movie.

Java Activation Framework

The Java Activation Framework is currently packaged as a standard extension to Java, meaning it is not bundled with the JDK. Sun intends to fold this functionality into a future release, probably JDK 1.5. In the meantime, you install it by downloading the file activation.jar from *java.sun.com* and placing it somewhere in your classpath. The activation framework is part of a larger, improved specification for beans known as the "Glasgow specification." Glasgow includes three parts in all:

- the Java Activation Framework
- runtime containment and services protocol allowing nested beans
- an interface allowing Java programs to easily tie into native drag 'n drop

There is a specification beyond Glasgow known as Edinburgh. Edinburgh is the next specification of the Java Beans component architecture. It looks like Edinburgh is generally adding more services and more complicated services rather than changing existing practices (good!). The city names Glasgow and Edinburgh were suggested by project leader Larry Cable. Larry noticed that Microsoft was in the habit of naming releases after cities: Win95 was code-named Chicago, NT 4.0 was Daytona, and the infinitely-delayed object-oriented version of NT was called Cairo. Tongue in cheek, Larry proposed that they name the next four EJB releases after cities in the home countries of the four lead developers in the JavaBeans team. For once, marketing listened to engineering, and Larry says he really learned a lesson about making goofy suggestions to marketing. The first EJB release is the Glasgow release, the second the Edinburgh release, and these will be followed by Nice and Barcelona releases. The most recent information on Edinburgh is on the Sun website at *java.sun.com*.

Infobus

Infobus is a way for beans to communicate data more directly with each other. It was developed by the Lotus folks at IBM and given back to Sun to advance the cause of Java. Infobus classifies beans as "data providers" or "data consumers." Data providers access data from some native source, such as a DBMS, spreadsheet or flat file, and move the data onto the InfoBus. Data consumers retrieve data from the bus for analysis or visual display. Splitting producers from consumers lets applications be independent of their data. For example, a charting bean need not understand SQL or JDBC in order to access DBMS data. The InfoBus specification gives these beans a set of interfaces to share and exchange data at runtime.

After you have read the next chapter, you may wonder how the Infobus differs from bound properties. After all, bound properties are used to communicate data changes between two beans. The InfoBus adds the features needed for more dynamic data interchange. Bound properties are not really intended for things like sending an entire file from one bean to another. Infobus can step up to that task with ease. Infobus support is bundled with BDK 1.1.

Limitations of Beans

The Java bean model works well, but visual beans have been held back by nagging and seemingly trivial inconsistencies between the native look-and-feel and Swing's emulation of it. Back in the last century, I filed several bugs with Sun on this topic for things like Java ignoring Windows control panel settings for system-wide font size and color preferences. Most of these bugs are addressed in JDK 1.4, but those incompatibilities, plus the JVM start-up time, has made Java a less attractive choice for GUI applications. And that has delayed the acceptance of beans for visual programming. Fix that JVM start-up time, Sun! It can be done by making the JVM always resident in memory, and threaded to handle multiple Java programs at once.

There are other limitations which Sun is also addressing. Java beans have limited ability to find out about their neighbors in the design tool. Sun added a concept called the "bean context" to allow beans to get more information. This support is placed in a package called `java.beans.beancontext`, and consists of ten or so classes and as many interfaces. Bean context improves the situation but doesn't take it all the way yet. You still don't have any way for beans to tell each other where they are located on the screen relative to each other. You want to know that information when you have a number of similar components (like number entry field) laid out on a panel and communicating with each other (as in a calculator or spreadsheet).

These drawbacks only apply to visual beans. The Java bean model has found more widespread use on the server side, as described in the next section.

Enterprise Java Beans (EJB)

Enterprise Java Beans (EJB) extend the Java bean component architecture to include the services and framework used in large-scale server-side applications. It is not part of the Java 2 Standard Edition, but is distributed with the Java 2 Enterprise Edition. A typical use of EJB appears in Figure 23-10. This shows where EJB components work in a multitier system.

So what is EJB all about? EJB is the specification for an industry-standard framework that supports the features common to most multitier systems. Enterprise-level multitier applications usually need system features like transaction support, naming services, and persistence. These features don't add anything to your application logic, but they are needed to make it run correctly. EJB is a kind of framework that factors out and provides all these services in a standard form which is easy to integrate into your code.

In the past people had to laboriously reimplement these services over and over again as part of each application. Or implementors could fill their code with calls to proprietary libraries, using an application server such as IBM's WebSphere or BEA's WebLogic. This has the advantage of moving the system's programming into a product supported by someone else, but it also has the disadvantage of tying the code to someone else's API (and different application servers have different APIs).

The EJB specification does the same job as application server middleware, and indeed is usually implemented as a thin layer on top of an existing applica-

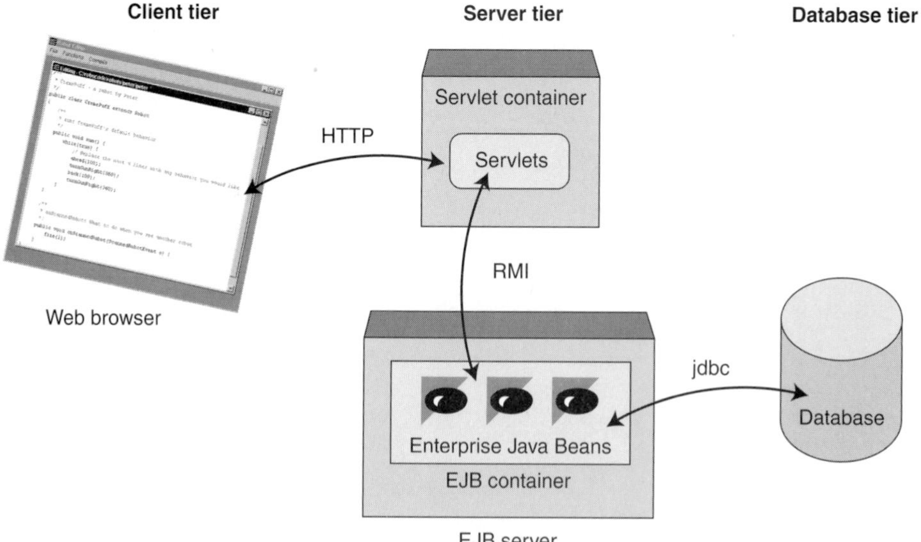

Figure 23–10 EJB components in a multitier system.

tion server product. The situation is very similar to the way ODBC support mushroomed. Microsoft defined a single library called ODBC that was a C API for database access. Every database vendor in the world quickly provided a library that implemented ODBC access to its own products. If a customer decided to change database vendors, it was (in theory) as simple as relinking the code with the ODBC library from the new vendor. The EJB specification provides the same kind of common interface layer to application servers and services. EJB is middleware, where middleware is defined as "anything that connects a program to its data, such as a TP monitor, a database, or an OLTP (Online Transaction Processing) framework."

What Is an Application Server?

Application servers are a relatively new idea, appearing in the mid 1990s. You can think of them as being a logical outgrowth or evolution of an Online Transaction Processing library. They provide a framework for quickly building and deploying an e-commerce system or other kinds of web-based applications.

Building a multitier web-based system is more challenging than building a simple client/server system. An applications server eases the task by managing and recycling scarce system resources, such as processes, threads, memory, database connections, and network sessions on behalf of the applications. Some application servers even do load-balancing to distribute application processing across multiple servers.

Just as an applet needs a framework in which to execute (either a browser or the applet runner), EJB is run in a framework known as a container. The EJB container runs in an EJB server, and the EJB server is typically part of an application server (omitted from Figure 23-10 for clarity). An application server combines traditional online transaction processing support with the new distributed objects technology. The goal is to let programmers quickly assemble the pieces of code that change and put them in a stable framework that supports the common library services.

The Enterprise Java services form a layer over existing infrastructure services. Enterprise Java Beans technology enhances and simplifies popular systems such as CORBA or DCOM. By accessing the applications server through EJB, organizations can avoid yet another incompatible set of middleware technologies. Clearly, EJB is aimed at the largest kind of web systems with the most demanding requirements. Why not just use servlets? For some systems you can. But as soon as you need full transaction support, servlets can't help you. You can get transaction support by using JDBC to access a database, which means adding another server tier to your system. EJB components are intended for systems that need to communicate across multitier environments. If you're not doing this, you don't need EJB.

Using EJB in an Application Server

An application server provides access to infrastructure services such as naming, directory services, transactions, persistence, and security. The EJB specification can be regarded as a single common, portable, Java interface to all the different application servers. Enterprise Java Beans allow programmers to add their applications logic in component-sized chunks.

Modern large-scale web software designs thus follow these steps:

1. The only software on the client should be GUI-displaying software. All non-GUI code moves to the server. This ensures that code updates need only be rolled out to 30 servers, rather than 3,000 client desktops.
2. Write the non-GUI business-logic code as EJB components. That provides the benefits of component software.
3. Use an Application Server accessed via EJB for common framework services.

The result is portable, scalable, reusable, quickly-deployed web systems. EJB has been through a 1.0 release, a 1.1 release, and has now evolved to version 2.0, which can be downloaded from Sun's website (see the URL in the Further Reading section). Table 23-1 summarizes details on a few application servers that support EJB at various levels.

Table 23–1 Some EJB Servers

Organization	Product	Website	Comments
JBoss Group	jboss	www.jboss.org	Open source EJB server. Allows technology deployment at zero capital cost.
Allaire Group	JRun	www.allaire.com	Free evaluation. From the company that developed Cold Fusion (ASP). Allows technology evaluation at zero cost.
Orion	Orion App Server	www.orionserver.com	The fastest J2EE-based application server.
IBM	WebSphere	www.ibm.com	One of the biggest supporters of Java, and this is its EJB application server.
BEA	WebLogic	www.bea.com	Software company whose main product line is focused here.
Borland	App Server	www.borland.com	Has an easy-to-use and easy-to-cluster reputation.
Netscape	iPlanet Server	www.netscape.com	Part of a suite of server-side software enablers. Created in partnership with Sun.
Pramati Technologies	Pramati Server	www.pramati.com	Well integrated with many server-side tools.

There are many more companies with application server products; Table 23-1 is to give you an idea of the industry-wide support for EJB. Most of the major vendors—including IBM, Oracle, Sybase, Netscape, and BEA Systems—have participated in specifying the Enterprise JavaBeans standard. These vendors are in the process of upgrading their products to be compatible with the latest revision of the Enterprise Java Beans specfication. When you evaluate these products, you'll want to compare features like supported platforms, supported browsers, supported databases, EJB revision level, training aids, scalability, and availability of vendor consulting.

The only vendor of any significance that is not adapting its server products to support Enterprise Java Beans is Microsoft. The Microsoft Transaction Server (MTS) could be updated to support Enterprise Java Beans components. That would be useful for Microsoft's customers, but it would not be useful for Microsoft itself. The Java portability message would undermine Microsoft's strategy of tight integration to Windows-only. Instead of EJB, Microsoft is offering developers application systems based on its COM+ component model (now rebranded to .NET). MTS will provide a container system for .NET server components, with transactional and security services similar to those provided in Enterprise Java Beans servers but restricted to one platform.

EJB Summary

The first EJB containers have been implemented by mapping the component to the underlying vendor-specific infrastructure. These infrastructure services cover such features as distributed communication services, naming and directory services, transaction services, messaging services, data access and persistence services, and resource-sharing services. EJB provides a common interface to access them. Programs written using EJB can execute using any application server running on any operating system on any hardware.

Further Reading

You can find example beans, many with source, by doing a websearch or by visiting *www.javashareware.com*.

IBM is encouraging the spread of Java beans by offering a large number of them for free download at the alphaWorks JavaBeans repository *www.alphaworks.ibm.com/alphaBeans*.

IBM gives away an open source bean to access Excel spreadsheets on Windows only at *oss.software.ibm.com/developerworks/opensource/excel/index.html*. If you write your own bean to make an RMI connection you can siphon that Excel data from/to anywhere that has a JVM.

The Java Bean and EJB specifications are on Sun's website at *java.sun.com/products/javabeans/docs/*. IBM also has some good online presentations on EJB, which you can find at *www106.ibm.com/developerworks/java/library/whatareejbs/part1/* and *www6.software.ibm.com/developerworks/education/ejb/index.html*. Sun has a white paper on EJB for managers at *java.sun.com/products/ejb/white/white_paper.html*.

Sun has a three-part tutorial on Java beans on the developer part of its website at *developer.java.sun.com/developer/onlineTraining/*. You need to register with them to access this part of the website, but it is free to register, and you can choose how much spam you want them to send you. Unfortunately, I have yet to find a Java Beans book that I can recommend.

Exercises

1. Take the "Tooth Fairy" (Duke) juggler bean that comes as a demo with the beanbox and add and connect two more buttons to the beanbox. One button should cause the juggler to hide itself (become invisible) and the other should cause it to become visible again. Visibility is a standard property of JComponent, so it is straightforward to connect button actions to that property of any JComponent in the beanbox.

2. Connect the juggler bean "stop" and "start" actions to keystrokes in two textfields, instead of two buttons. When a character is typed in one field, the juggler should stop. A character typed in the other field should make the juggler animation resume. Note: You will need to read ahead in Chapter 24 to find the steps for getting an ordinary textfield into the beanbox. You don't need to add any code to the textfield for this exercise.

Some Light Relief—Furby's Brain Transplant

The smash hit toy of Christmas 1998 was Furby. Furby was designed by Californian toy inventor Dave Hampton. Part of Dave's motivation to develop Furby was a reaction against the previous "virtual pet," the Japanese Tamagotchi. Tamagotchis are bland, inert lumps of plastic. Dave knew he could do better, and he created a fur-covered toy that sings, farts, and wobbles—sometimes all at once. No kid could resist that. In 1998, Furby sold over two million units, and they were actually being rushed by air from mainland China factories to satisfy U.S. market demand! Toys have a limited life. Furby was red hot in 1998, warm in 1999, and by 2000 you could buy one for $9.99 in Target.

Furby is an animated doll about 7 inches high. It looks like a Gremlin from the 1984 movie of that name, and toy distributor Hasbro had to settle an infringement claim from Warner Brothers. Inside, Furby is packed with a rich assortment of devices. It has a microphone, a loudspeaker, infrared transmitter/receiver, light detector, speech generation chip, CPU, EEPROM, and RAM. It has a motor and various cams to animate ears, eyes, body, etc. Obviously, it was imperative to take one of these apart and reprogram it for more useful tasks.

Unfortunately, at some point in the past, Furby architect Dave Hampton had been rudely surprised by "potty-mouth Barney," and he was determined that no one would pull the same stunt with Furby. There was another reason to make it difficult to reverse-engineer Furby: to prevent other toy companies from copying the technology. The world of children's toys is (apparently) a cutthroat, rapacious, dog-eat-dog world, where intellectual property is Napstered on a daily basis, and only the strong survive. The main defense against reverse-engineering Furby was a brittle epoxy shell that completely encased Furby's CPU, ROM, RAM, audio data, and the I/O interfaces such as driver transistors and an analog-digital convertor.

The epoxy made it impossible to clamp a logic analyser onto the CPU, read the bus traffic, and dump out the control program. It is impossible to chip or grind off the epoxy without destroying the components underneath. Certain U.S. government labs are equipped with the right acids and neutralizers to break into equipment like this. But I don't know anyone at the CIA or NSA, and this didn't seem like the right project to introduce myself. Furby's software and sound data is not accessible for reading, writing, disassembly, replacement, or even examination. There are no exposed data/address buses, interrupt lines, or I/O lines other than those that directly drive the peripherals. Conclusion: Reprogramming Furby would require junking the existing CPU and fitting another CPU and memory—effectively, a Furby brain transplant.

So I issued the "Hack Furby" challenge from my website at *www.afu.com* (where I also keep the Java Programmers FAQ). The Hack Furby challenge offered a cash prize for the first person to reverse-engineer Furby or retrofit it with a different CPU. It was similar to challenges issued in the early days of aviation. Almost all the early aviation milestones—Bleriot's flight across the channel, Alcock and Brown across the Atlantic, Lindbergh's solo Atlantic crossing—were in response to a cash challenge, and I felt sure that computer engineers were no less motivated. This was no easy task and almost a year passed by before a winner claimed the prize.

The challenge was finally met by Jeff Gibbons, a talented Canadian computer consultant working for Motorola. Jeff chose the Intel 8051 processor to drive Furby because of the vast amount of free support tools and low cost hardware available. The 8051 is an 8-bit CPU that's been around for about 20 years, and that fully meets the time-honored Intel processor tradition of "ignore all design suggestions from the software guys." Jeff architected and built replacement circuit boards that fit into the existing space in Furby, after you junk the epoxy-protected boards. The new circuit boards carry the 8051, EEPROM, 1Mbyte RAM, an RS232 port, a power regulator, an amplifier, a digital-analog converter, and tons of support hardware. This was an incredible achievement on Jeff's part. He essentially designed and built a complete general-purpose computer system in four months of evenings and weekends.

After Jeff produced the working hardware, I wrote the first draft of the "Furby Programmer's Reference Manual" which is on the CD with this book, and online at Jeff's site at *www.furbyupgrade.20m.com/*. For a while, Jeff was also selling kits from that site. For well under $100 you can convert your Furby into a TV remote controller, a speaking clock, a pocket calculator, or anything else that will run on a 20MHz processor and a little over 1Mbyte of RAM. Furby can be programmed in assembler or in C, and you download the program through a tether cable to the serial port on a PC. Clearly, the next step is to get a JVM running on Furby, and bring up Java 2 Micro Edition on Furby. Put a telnet connection on the serial port, and we're really cooking.

For legal and policy reasons, I can't show you a picture of a modified Furby in this book. You've no idea how easily those toy moguls take offense. But if you hustle over to *www.afu.com/furby* you can feast your eyes on all the "stripped and re-chipped" Furby pictures that anyone could want.

This whole project was done under GPL, the Gnu Public License, which means we openly published all the schematics, results, software, etc. Some of this material is on the CD, and the rest is on Jeff's website. The goal is to enable volunteers to carry the project forward. So if you know a lot about embedded systems and are trying think of what to do with all your plentiful spare time, perhaps Java-powered Furby could be in your future.

The last word should come from Furby himself. I did the FCC compliance testing on the Furby prototype "borrowing" some time in one of the hardware labs at work. FCC testing measures the amount of electronic interference that a product generates. It has to be lower than certain limits to comply with FCC rules. In the photo here, Furby is on the lower TV screen, on a table on a large turntable, executing all his motions and new vocabulary. The upper TV screen shows the very sensitive "bow tie" antenna 6 meters away which sweeps for electromagnetic radiation as Furby revolves. The oscilloscope on the right graphs the radio frequencies that Furby transmits in every direction. There was a lot of unwanted radio wave leakage, known as noise, coming out of hacked Furby. The chief engineer of the lab came in unexpectedly, listened to Furby chirping and jabbering away, and sized up what I was doing in his lab. Then he glanced at the measurements (Furby failed FCC parts A and B) and grunted, "Noisy little critter, ain't he?"

Chapter 24

Java Beans in Practice

In this chapter we develop two independent Java beans then integrate them using the beanbox. We'll start with the program specifications for what we want our two Java beans to do. That's the eventual goal we are aiming at, and we will get there in steps. We'll write as much as we can of our two components without using anything specific to beans. Then we will add the beans conventions and support framework piece by piece until we have a full working example. You'll want to refer to the example in Chapter 23 for reminders on how to use the beanbox. At each step we will make clear what problem we are trying to solve, and how the code we added helps us get there.

The Specification for Two Beans

You will get the most benefit if you can work along on your computer as you read. Type in the code as it evolves, compile and run it in the beanbox, and you'll quickly get a good understanding of how this all works. Here is the specification for the first of two Java beans that we will develop in this chapter. These beans are independent software components. We will develop the code for them, and then integrate them in the beanbox.

Specification for "ConverterField" Component

This code will allow floating point numbers to be entered and displayed on a screen. If a user types some characters that don't represent a floating point number and then hits "enter" on the keyboard, the field should turn red to indicate the error. The bean always knows whether it has a valid number on the display or not, and it publishes this information to any bean that is interested. The display will turn back to white when the characters represent a valid double number. The font size and style should be chosen at design time. The ConverterField will look like this:

27.5

As well as storing the number that is displayed, the component will also store a hidden constant value that represents a "conversion rate," e.g., the conversion rate for "inches to centimeters" is 2.54. The conversion rate for "dollars to pounds sterling" is 0.698 (June 2001).

The stored constant conversion rate can only be set at design time, not at runtime. At runtime, when it gets an event from another bean, the ConverterField will multiply the value in its display by its conversion constant, and display the new, converted result. Note: It's unrealistic to have a currency converter that doesn't allow the rate to be updated at runtime. We'll address that limitation in the exercises at the end of the chapter.

The point of component software is to write self-contained chunks of code that do a single thing well. Then any of the class files can be snapped together to form a bigger system. Beans must do all their communication using events or the bean framework. That way, any bean can be connected with any other bean that agrees on the events sent. Beans should not have any dependencies on or knowledge of each other at coding time. Of course, you can usually write the same classes, and probably more quickly, if you let them reference each other directly. But then they are not beans. By avoiding dependencies at code time, you make your beans more flexible and general-purpose.

The second bean that we will develop is much simpler (has much less behavior). It will be a button that will tell some other component that it is time to "do" something. Hence, we call it a "DoIt" button. The specification follows.

Specification for the "DoItButton" Component

The DoItButton is mostly an ordinary button. The purpose of the button is to give the end user a way to initiate some action. When pressed, the button informs another component that it must do something. At design time the label on the button can be set to some text. The designer will choose some text that documents what constant has been given to the ConverterField. For example "*Press to convert feet to inches,*" or "*Enter $ amount, £ (pound) rate is 0.698*" are helpful labels for the DoItButton.

convert feet to inches

We will connect the DoItButton to the ConverterField at design time. Then at runtime pressing the button will cause the conversion calculation to occur. The button background color should be settable at design time. The font style and size should be settable at design time.

The button must disappear from the screen if the user enters an invalid number in the ConverterField. This is allegedly to prevent users from trying to do a conversion on something that isn't a number. When the user corrects the text of the ConverterField, this button will reappear on the screen. (Making components appear and disappear will probably cause confusion in a GUI. The real reason for this part of the specification is to visibly show how something happening in one bean can cause something to happen in another bean.)

The Code for the ConverterField Bean

From reading the specification, here are the parts of the ConverterField. We can write almost all these pieces immediately without needing any component features. For one piece we need to learn more about beans. The pieces of the code that we can write are shown below, interleaved with explanations of what they do. Here are the properties that our specification calls for:

Properties of the ConverterField Bean

`ConverterField`	• conversion rate value • font size and style • whether the display is currently a valid number

The `ConverterField` class should clearly be based on `javax.swing.JTextField`, since that supports entering and displaying text. In JDK 1.4, we could use the new `javax.swing.JFormattedTextField`, which adds the hooks for automatically formatting arbitrary kinds of values. However, it is overkill for what we want here, so we'll stick with `JTextField`.

```
import javax.swing.*;
import java.awt.Color;
import java.awt.event.*;
public class ConverterField extends javax.swing.JTextField
        implements KeyListener {
    public ConverterField() {  // no-arg constructor
       super("0", 16);  // default display is 16 digits long
       setBackground(Color.white);
       addKeyListener(this);
    }
```

We can easily write some code to do the "validate as a number" action. The code gets the string from the text field, tries to parse it as a double length floating point number, and sets the background of the text field to either white (valid) or red (invalid).

```
    public void validateNumber() {
    // gets a double from the text field, and
    // sets the textfield color to red if invalid.
    String s = this.getText();
    try {
        n = Double.parseDouble(s);
          // success -- n holds the number
        setBackground(Color.white);
        setValidNum(true);
    } catch (NumberFormatException nfe) {
          // failed to parse TextField as number
          // set background to red!
        setValidNum(false);
        requestFocus();
        setBackground(Color.red);
        n = Double.NaN;
    }
}
private double n;
```

We want to validate the text field when the user hits "enter." How do we know when that happens? We will make the component be a listener for keystrokes that take place over it. When "enter" is pressed, we will call the validate number method. We provide methods for all three methods in the key listener interface, even though we only use one of them. The work takes place completely in this class and has no impact on other beans.

```
public void keyPressed(KeyEvent e) {}
public void keyReleased(KeyEvent e) {}
public void keyTyped(KeyEvent e) {
  // ConverterField generates these events, and
  // validates the number when user hits "enter".
    if (e.getKeyChar() == KeyEvent.VK_ENTER) {
        validateNumber();
    }
}
```

We need to keep track of the "rate" property and acquire its initial value from the property sheet editor. The design tool will have the ability to set and change the value of properties without requiring any coding on your part. So the code to implement a rate property is this:

```
// holds the rate that we will multiply with the TextField
// the rate will be set at design time, and doesn't change
private double rate = 1.0;
public double getRate() {  return rate; }
public void setRate(double d) {
    rate = d;
    this.setText( "rate set to " + Double.toString(d) );
}
```

We need to keep track of whether the text in the display represents a valid number or not. In fact, this should be a boolean property of the component. Let us call it "validNum." That also fixes the names of the getter and setter methods because of the naming conventions. When validNum changes from true-to-false or false-to-true, we need to be able to make other beans aware of it somehow. The button is going to use that property change as a command to hide or reveal itself.

```
private boolean validNum = true;
public boolean isValidNum() {  return validNum; }
public void setValidNum(boolean b) {  validNum = b; }
```

We can write the routine that validates the number in the text field and does the multiplication. We already saw in the previous chapter how to use the beanbox to connect a button to another bean such that a button press triggers some action in the other bean. That is how we will get the button press to cause the validate and multiply in this bean. There is no code to add to the ConverterField class. The beanbox will create it for us.

```
public void validateAndMultiply() {
    // we do this when another bean tells us to.
    validateNumber();
    if ( !(isvalidNum()))  return;
    n = n * rate;
    setText( Double.toString(n) );
}
```

Pretty much all the other needed characteristics (such as font) can be inherited from the parent class. A complete listing of the `ConverterField` class is at the end of the chapter. Take a moment to look it over. Every reader who has got this far in the book already has the ability to write this ConverterField code and other code like it. We have created 99% of a Java bean without having to learn a single new thing.

There is one tiny part of ConverterField that is beans-specific, and that we have not been given the information to write yet. We have not yet seen how to write the code that informs other beans that the validNum property has changed. As you probably guessed, this will be done by sending an event from ConverterField each time validNum changes between valid and invalid. There will be an expanded explanation later in this chapter, but for now note that a property in one bean that is connected to another bean is known as a "bound property."

The beanbox will take care of generating the event handler and registering beans as listeners for the property. There is a special event type that represents a change in value of a bean property. It is known as a PropertyChangeEvent, and the class is part of the java.beans package. The visual design tool will automatically generate Java code for other classes that express interest in listening for the PropertyChangeEvent for the ConverterField validNum property. The programmer must manually write the code (in the bean with the property) to fire the event when the property changes. The obvious place to put the code is in the method that sets the property. This code is shown in bold below.

```
public void setValidNum(boolean newVal) {
    boolean oldVal = validNum;
    firePropertyChange( "validNum", oldVal, newVal);
    validNum = newVal;
}
```

You do not have to check if the old and new values are actually different because firePropertyChange does that for you. The method firePropertyChange() is part of all Swing components, by virtue of being present in javax.swing.JComponent. The ConverterField bean is now 100% complete.

Summary of ConverterField Bean

Let's summarize what we did in this section. We created the ConverterField class based on JTextField. We added a method to read the string from its text field and check if it is a valid floating point number, setting the textfield background to various colors accordingly. We made the class a key listener, so that the text field can be validated based on each character entered.

The program specification told us the bean must have three properties. In our implementation, one of them is inherited from the parent class, and we wrote code to implement the other two. The validNum property uses a boolean set by the validate routine. An alternative and equally good approach would have it call the validate routine.

Finally, the specification makes it clear that the validNum property is going to be bound to other beans. So, in the only bit of beans-specific code in this example, we added some code to make ConverterField fire an event when the validNum property changes. That is the ConverterField bean finished and 100% complete. And the good news is that the DoItButton is even simpler than this.

The Code for DoItButton Bean

The DoItButton specification makes clear the properties of the component.

Properties of the DoItButton Bean

`DoItButton`	• label on button • font size and style • background color of the button • whether the button is visible or invisible

Here are the tasks we need to code for the DoItButton:

- The `DoItButton` class should clearly be based on `javax.swing.JButton`, since that gives us the button behavior we want.
- `JButton` has methods to keep track of label, font, and color. These properties can be customized using the property sheet, without any code needed in the class.
- We already saw in the previous chapter how to use the beanbox to connect a button to another bean so that a button press triggers some action in the other bean. That is how we will get the button press to cause the validate and multiply in the ConverterField bean. There is no code to add to the DoIt button class. The beanbox will create it for us.

- JButton has methods to keep track of whether a button is visible or invisible. We haven't yet seen how to connect a property (validNum) to a property (the "visible" property) in some other bean. We know how to make the button disappear. You can make any Swing component disappear by setting its "visible" property to false. We haven't yet seen how to do that when the ConverterField decides that the validNum property has changed to invalid. In fact, the beanbox can make this connection between the two beans and automatically generate the glue code, just as with the button press. So there is no code impact here.
- All other needed characteristics are inherited from the parent class.

  The DoItButton code looks like this:

```
import javax.swing.*;
public class DoItButton extends JButton {
    public DoItButton() {
        super("press for service");
    }
}
```

As we go on to develop these two classes into Java beans, you may be surprised to learn that no further changes or additions whatsoever are needed in DoItButton. That is our finished Java bean right there. That is a formidable statement about the lightweight, non-intrusive nature of Java component software.

It's easy enough to compile these two classes in the usual way. The next task to tackle is how to put them in a jar file and get them into the beanbox. We will show that in the next section. We still need to write the two bean info classes that accompany these beans and describe them to the visual design tool. That makes up the rest of the chapter as we gradually develop the bean info code. You should recompile, re-jar, and retry each time to see the effect of each change.

Compile, Jar, and Load Classes into Beanbox

The next task is to compile these two bean classes and put them in a jar file along with a manifest file. Then move the jar file to the jars subdirectory of the BDK and start the beanbox. Here are the steps to get your beans and related classes into the beanbox.

We need a way to bundle all the classes, images, audio files, etc., that make up a bean and pass them around in one file (exactly like a zip archive). Fortunately, there is already something that does that: a jar file.

Beans are Best Carried Around in Jars

(I have been waiting a long time for the chance to make that pun.) When you have written and compiled your beans, use your favorite editor to create an ASCII text manifest file that contains two lines for each class that is a bean and that you want to show up in the beanbox. The lines give the filename of the class file and state that it is a Java bean. Here is the content of the manifest file for our example.

Beans manifest file, e.g., mybeans.mf

```
Name: ConverterField.class
Java-Bean: true

Name: DoItButton.class
Java-Bean: true
```

Be sure to have a blank line between each bean and to include a carriage return at the end of the last line. Next, put the classfiles and any other resources that your beans will use (other classes of yours, gif files to represent a bean as an icon for display in the design tool, etc.) into a jar file, along with this manifest file. If you called this manifest file "mybeans.mf," the jar command would look like:

```
jar cfvm  mybeans.jar   mybeans.mf   *.class  *.gif
```

"jar" is one of the java utilities in the JDK, like "java" and "javac." So you need to make sure the JDK bin directory containing those executables is in your path. The mysterious "cfvm" string is the options to the jar program:

c = create a new jar file

f = the name of the output file is supplied on the command line

v = do the work in verbose mode

m = the name of the manifest file is supplied on the command line

Make sure that your jar filename and your manifest filename appear on the command line in the same order as their option switches, i.e., if "f" appears before "m" in the options, the jar filename must come before the manifest filename in the rest of the command line. This pitfall catches people again and again. The jar code should really be made a bit more robust by Sun.

It's a good idea to use the "v" (verbose) option so that the jar tool prints out the name of each file it processes. That lets you check that it is dealing with the files that you intended. Now move the jar file to the jars subdirectory of the BDK, or load it using the "file | load jar" menu item on the beanbox window.

```
move mybeans.jar  c:\bdk1.1\jars
```

Now start the beanbox again:

```
cd c:\bdk1.1\beanbox
run
```

You should now see the names of your beans from the manifest file appear in the ToolBox window. At this point, you should experiment with connecting events and methods as we did with the juggler bean in the previous chapter.

Bean Icons

It's a good idea to provide icons that represent your beans at design time. The visual aspect is a big part of component software. The best way to make the association between a GIF icon file and a Java class would be in the manifest file that describes the contents of the jar file where they are all stored. After all, that's where you provide the information about whether a given class is a bean at all. Unfortunately, one of the beans designers decided it should instead be done in the bean info class.

The bean info class is the subject of most of the rest of the chapter. You will typically code a bean info class for each of your beans to provide information about the bean at design time. Your bean info class can contain a method called getIcon( ) that the design tool invokes to retrieve an icon file and turn it into an image. An example of the getIcon method in a bean info class follows. The design tool passes in a parameter saying what size and shade icon it would like, and the method tries to provide it.

```
public java.awt.Image getIcon(int iconKind) {
 if (iconKind == BeanInfo.ICON_MONO_16x16 ||
     iconKind == BeanInfo.ICON_COLOR_16x16 ) {
     java.awt.Image img = loadImage("JellyBeanIconColor16.gif");
     return img;
 }
 if (iconKind == BeanInfo.ICON_MONO_32x32 ||
     iconKind == BeanInfo.ICON_COLOR_32x32 ) {
     java.awt.Image img = loadImage("JellyBeanIconColor32.gif");
     return img;
 }
 return null;
}
```

Just add this method to your bean info classes and change the filename string to a gif file that you have. Some icon gif files can be found in the directories under `c:\bdk1.1\demo\sunw\demo`. Icon gif files can be in color or black and white, either 32 pixels or 16 pixels square. There are large numbers of icon gifs available for free download on the web. Sun has made a number of them available for free download at *developer.java.sun.com/developer/techDocs/hi/repository/*. You can also reuse the gif files that come with the beanbox for your own programs, as I have done here with the jellybean icon.

You should type this code in, put it in a class called ConverterFieldBeanInfo, compile it, jar it with a manifest, and then load it into the beanbox, as shown in the previous section. You should see that your bean is now represented by a small icon in the toolbox window of the beanbox. In the next section, we will add several more methods to the ConverterFieldBeanInfo class to provide more information about the bean to the design tool.

The Bean Info Class

Let's consider the features a software component architecture needs to offer so it can allow code to be manipulated visually. These are the requirements:

- The visual builder tools must be able to look at a bean class file and *know what fields and methods it has,* and what the parameters and return type are. With this knowledge, the tool can connect one bean with another.
- The tools must be able to *configure the appearance or behavior of a bean,* typically by setting new initial values or defaults. An example would be setting the text on a button. We dealt with this in the previous chapter, under "customization."
- The tools should be able to *save an instance of a bean object* to a disk file, and later restore it with the same state and values. For example, once we have decided what text will appear on a button, we need to keep that information. That will allow the tool to remember new defaults and settings that are given to beans. Customized components can be saved and loaded from the beanbox file menu.

These three requirements are design time needs. The computer science terms for them are *introspection, customization,* and *persistence,* respectively. In this section you will see how to write a bean info class that accompanies your bean into the beanbox, and fulfills the first requirement by publishing the bean internal details to the visual design tool. You do not *have* to write a bean info class. Some or all of the information can be derived by the Java runtime system and the visual design tool using introspection. However, it's good practice to provide a bean info class to help with the discovery of properties and other class information.

Note: *No further code needed for the beans.* To avoid confusion, we emphasize that both our bean classes are 100% complete at this point. All further code that appears in this chapter (with the sole exception of revisiting firePropertyChange) relates to the Bean Info classes for the beans at design time, not the beans themselves.

A bean info class for each of your beans makes the design time task much easier. Instead of the visual builder tool showing absolutely every method, property, and event that meets its criteria, it can just display the ones you mentioned in the bean info class. The bean info class is also the place where you mention any icon GIF file that you would like to be associated with the bean in the toolbox window.

If you do not provide a bean info class, the tool will make its best guess about what the properties are. Without a bean info class, the property sheet window for ConverterField when you load it in the beanbox will look like Figure 24-1. These are all the properties of `ConverterField`, its parent `JTextField`, `JTextField`'s parent, and so on, all the way back to `java.lang.Object`.

In many cases you will want to let every property in the inheritance chain be customizable at design time. To make this example easier to follow, we will code a ConverterField BeanInfo to restrict the properties to just the ones we are going to

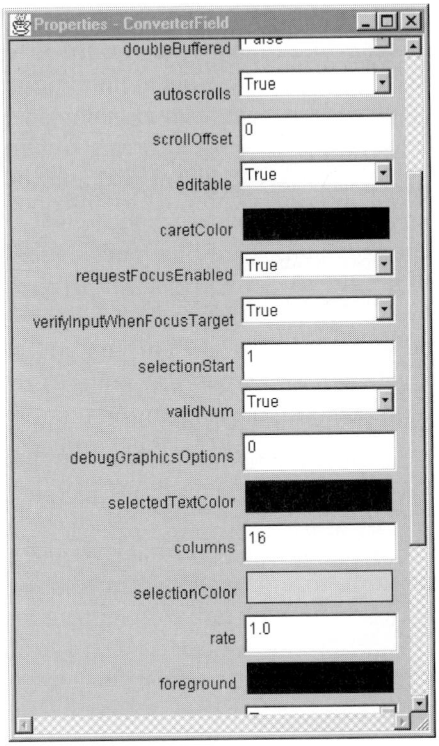

Figure 24–1
Properties of ConverterField *without* a BeanInfo class.

use directly. We do the same thing for `DoItButton` properties in the `DoItButtonBeanInfo` class. We write descriptors explicitly mentioning only the font, label, background color, and visible properties.

This section builds up to a complete bean info class for each of our beans. Bean info classes are always named as "the name of your class" with "BeanInfo" appended. If you call your bean XxxxBean, then the info class will be XxxxBean-BeanInfo. So here, the info classes will be called `ConverterFieldBeanInfo` and `DoItButtonBeanInfo`.

Bean info classes have to provide the eight methods promised by the `java.beans.BeanInfo` interface. The simplest way to do this is to extend the `java.beans.SimpleBeanInfo` class which is provided for this purpose. It implements all eight methods with no-ops saying "I don't have any info on that." You then provide versions of the methods you want to implement. Your methods will override the corresponding ones in SimpleBeanInfo. Following are the methods promised by the BeanInfo interface, and implemented by SimpleBeanInfo. The method names are highlighted in bold type; the return types are to the left of the method names.

How to Write BeanInfo

```
public interface java.beans.BeanInfo {
    public static final int ICON_MONO_32x32;  // other icon consts omitted
    public java.awt.Image                    getIcon(int);
    public java.beans.BeanDescriptor         getBeanDescriptor();
    public java.beans.EventSetDescriptor[] getEventSetDescriptors();
    public int                               getDefaultEventIndex();
    public java.beans.PropertyDescriptor[] getPropertyDescriptors();
    public int                               getDefaultPropertyIndex();
    public java.beans.MethodDescriptor[]  getMethodDescriptors();
    public java.beans.BeanInfo[]            getAdditionalBeanInfo();
}
public class java.beans.SimpleBeanInfo implements BeanInfo {
    // same 8 methods, returning empty or null info
    ...
}
  ...
//---------------------------------
  ...  then in other files, your code is:
public class ConverterFieldBeanInfo
         extends java.beans.SimpleBeanInfo { ...
      ... getPropertyDescriptors() { ... }
      ... getBeanDescriptor() { ... }
}



public class DoItButtonBeanInfo
                extends java.beans.SimpleBeanInfo { ...
      ... getPropertyDescriptors() { ... }
      ... getBeanDescriptor() { ... }
}
```

Descriptor Classes

Beans are all about three things: properties, events, and methods. You will write descriptor objects to hold information about the bean properties, events, and methods for the design tool. You will put these descriptor objects in the bean info class for each bean. The descriptor classes are all part of the `java.beans` package, and you should review the javadoc-generated HTML pages in your browser. The classes are named PropertyDescriptor, EventSetDescriptor, and MethodDescriptor. There are other descriptors, too: BeanDescriptor and ParameterDescriptor.

Be clear about this point: The BeanInfo classes are solely to help with connecting beans at design time. Never put any of your processing logic into a bean info class, and remember that the BeanInfo class has finished its job after running at design time.

A descriptor sounds like it might be complicated. Luckily, it is not. A more familiar and accurate name would be Description, and that's exactly what these classes do. Descriptors just gather together some strings and other data describing the properties, methods, events, and more of your bean. The details include:

- the class that we're providing information on
- a string giving the name of the property, method, event, etc.
- other related information specific to the kind of descriptor it is. For example, event descriptors also keep track of the type of listener. Method descriptors allow you to supplement the information with parameter descriptors and so on.

Let's say your bean has a property called rate. That property will be described using an object of class `java.beans.PropertyDescriptor`. You call a constructor, passing the property name ("rate") and your bean class (`ConverterField.class)` as arguments. That instantiates the property descriptor object for this property of this bean. You write descriptors for all the interesting attributes of your bean, and declare them in your bean info class for that bean. You don't have to construct a descriptor object for every single thing that a bean contains—create them only for the things that you want to be visible at design time.

The visual tool will invoke methods in your bean info class at design time to get data structures that correspond to your bean class. That, along with introspection, tells the design tool what to display to the person connecting these beans. The beans introspection API is built on top of reflection mechanisms introduced with JDK 1.1. Reflection provides classes and interfaces for obtaining information about classes, methods, and fields loaded in the JVM. The class `java.beans.Introspector` uses classes in package `java.lang.reflect` to learn about the properties, events, and methods supported by a target Java Bean.

No information on reflection or introspection is provided here because it is only useful to programmers writing specialized software like bean development tools, or debuggers, or database drivers. It is enough to know that Java has support for discovering at runtime the kinds of methods, fields, and parameters that objects have, and even for generating parameters of the right type and invoking methods dynamically. This is what the beanbox uses the bean info for.

We'll write the descriptors for the properties of our class, put them in an array, and make the array be returned as the value of the, e.g., `getPropertyDescriptors()` method that we will override in our extension of the `java.beans.BeanInfo` class. I did warn you that this topic can be a little abstract! Here's the same information in Figure 24-2, and then we'll look at it in code.

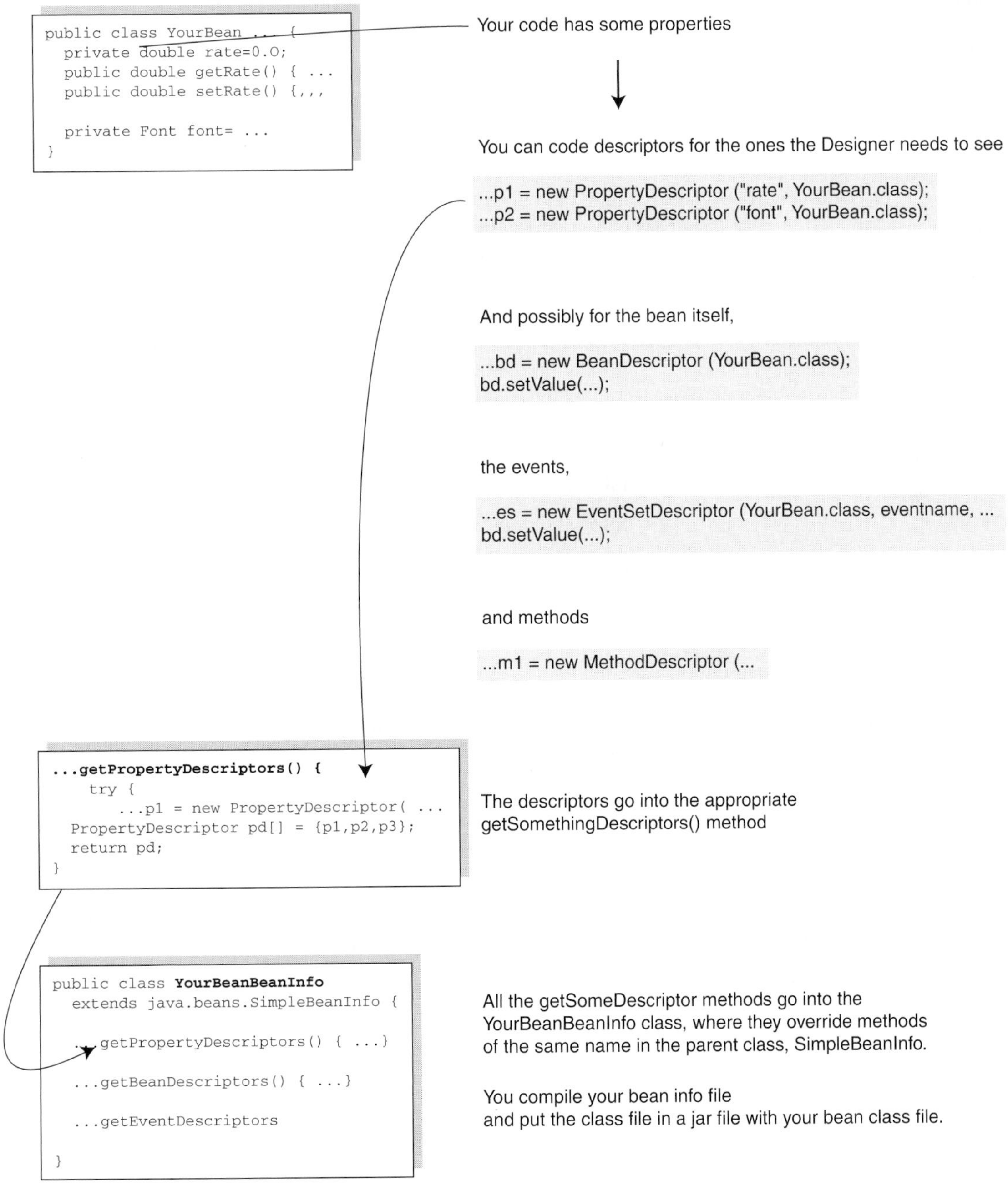

```
public class YourBean ... {
  private double rate=0.0;
  public double getRate() { ...
  public double setRate() {,,,

  private Font font= ...
}
```

Your code has some properties

You can code descriptors for the ones the Designer needs to see

```
...p1 = new PropertyDescriptor ("rate", YourBean.class);
...p2 = new PropertyDescriptor ("font", YourBean.class);
```

And possibly for the bean itself,

```
...bd = new BeanDescriptor (YourBean.class);
bd.setValue(...);
```

the events,

```
...es = new EventSetDescriptor (YourBean.class, eventname, ...
bd.setValue(...);
```

and methods

```
...m1 = new MethodDescriptor (...
```

```
...getPropertyDescriptors() {
    try {
        ...p1 = new PropertyDescriptor( ...
  PropertyDescriptor pd[] = {p1,p2,p3};
  return pd;
}
```

The descriptors go into the appropriate getSomethingDescriptors() method

```
public class YourBeanBeanInfo
  extends java.beans.SimpleBeanInfo {

  ...getPropertyDescriptors() { ...}

  ...getBeanDescriptors() { ...}

  ...getEventDescriptors

}
```

All the getSomeDescriptor methods go into the YourBeanBeanInfo class, where they override methods of the same name in the parent class, SimpleBeanInfo.

You compile your bean info file and put the class file in a jar file with your bean class file.

Figure 24–2 How descriptors are declared in a Bean Info class.

Properties

The word "property" comes directly from the Microsoft Windows world. It means some characteristic or default value of the bean that we will be able to set in the visual tool when we customize the bean. Customization is a very important part of component software, and you want to give bean integrators maximum freedom. The properties that our specification calls for are outlined in Table 24-1.

Table 24–1 Properties of the Two Beans

Bean	Properties
`ConverterField`	• conversion rate value • font size and style • whether the display is currently a valid number
`DoItButton`	• label on button • font size and style • background color of the button • hide/reveal the button when another component says to

Some properties (like button label) will be visible on the screen, and some (like the rate value) are not. Some things are visible at runtime, but are not customizable at design time, so they are not properties. The color that ConverterField displays on error (red) is an example of a field that we chose not to make customizable. The visual tool typically has a separate window that lists all the properties, and lets you edit their values. This window is known as a "property sheet," a "property editor," or a "property sheet editor."

The bean info class explicitly tells the visual tool what properties should be displayed on the property sheet. Here is the bean info code to do that for the ConverterField.

Describing the Properties in a BeanInfo Class

```
import java.beans.*;
public class ConverterFieldBeanInfo extends SimpleBeanInfo {
   public PropertyDescriptor[] getPropertyDescriptors() {
     try {
       PropertyDescriptor rate =
          new PropertyDescriptor("rate", ConverterField.class);
       PropertyDescriptor font =
           new PropertyDescriptor("font", ConverterField.class);
       PropertyDescriptor validNum =
           new PropertyDescriptor("validNum", ConverterField.class);
       PropertyDescriptor props[] = {rate, font, validNum};
       return props;
     } catch (IntrospectionException e) {
            throw new Error(e.toString());
     }
   }
}
```

Whenever you have to identify the class you are dealing with for the design tool, you use the `java.lang.Class` object. There is an object of that type for every class, and one way to get it is by invoking the `getClass()` method on any class or interface. The code above uses the equivalent and more convenient "`.class`" suffix that can be appended to the name of a class or object to get the same information.

Weird Exception Handling

Note the idiomatic exception handling in the BeanInfo classes, borrowed from the examples that Sun supplies. The method will throw an exception at design time if your descriptions are not accurate. You should send the exception back to the invoker. However, none of the methods in BeanInfo is defined to throw exceptions, so you cannot introduce them in the signature of your overriding methods. But you want to get that exception back to the caller! What you do is get the string from the original exception; `e.toString()` is used here, but `e.getMessage()` might be better.

Then construct a new Error instance using the String and send that back to the caller. The class java.lang.Error represents a serious runtime problem that a reasonable application should not even try to catch. So a method is not required to declare in its throws clause any subclasses of Error that might be thrown during its execution.

The bean design here for exceptions is certainly a little suspect. PropertyDescriptor is returning us an Exception which we turn into an Error in order to evade the need for declaring the exceptions. It would have been better to define `getPropertyDescriptors()` as able to throw an `IntrospectionException`. This appears to be an oversight on the part of Sun's software engineers.

Back to Descriptors

You can and should provide descriptors for the interesting fields that you have from your parent class. In the DoItButton example, all the property fields come from the parent class. The source code for all the files in the example is on the CD, and listed at the end of the chapter.

After doing the compiling and jar creation mentioned earlier, start up the beanbox program, load your jar, and click your ConverterField bean into the beanbox window (see Figure 24-3). You will see that the property sheet window contains just these three properties, along with GUI controls for setting them. This is the result of the bean info code shown in the previous code example.

Next, click the DoItButton into the beanbox. Highlight the DoItButton bean, and change some of its properties. Give the button label a bold typeface and a pink background, for example.

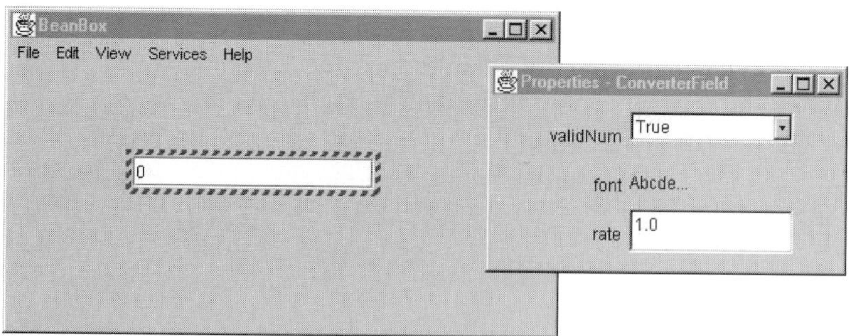

Figure 24–3 Properties of ConverterField *with* our BeanInfo class.

Bound Properties

So far we have just been dealing with simple properties, but there are some variations on the theme. A simple property is the basic variety of property, which represents a single value. This could be an object such as the font used, or the background color, or the pathname to a datafile, or it could be a primitive value like a desired number of decimal places of precision, or the visibility status of a component.

Some properties are better represented by an array, not a single value. Say our converter field was modified to hold 25 different rates, perhaps representing conversion rates for the dollar against 25 different currencies on a particular day. It would be convenient to make rate be an array of double, rather than a double. This is termed an *indexed property,* but a better name would be an *array property.* With this kind of property, you need accessor methods to get/set the whole array, as well as individual indexed elements.

```
double[] getRate()
double getRate(int indx)
void setRate(double rates[])
void setRate(int indx, int rate);
```

Apart from the index, an indexed property works exactly like a simple property.

So far we have just been dealing with simple properties that only affect their own class. But the whole point of component software is to make it easy for components to communicate state information to each other. The easiest way to do this is to use our old friend, the event.

There are two slight twists we can give a property concerning the way it affects other beans. We can "bind" a property to some similar property in another class. And we can "constrain" a property so that you can't change its value without getting agreement from all the other beans that are tracking it. These two operations (changing a field in one bean to keep it consistent with a field in another bean, and letting some beans veto a proposed change in another bean) are felt to happen frequently enough that they are given special support in the beans component framework.

In other words, a property can be:

- **a bound property**—the property has a number of customers that need to hear the new value when it changes. This is done by sending an event to everyone who has registered as a listener. (A better name would be a *"keep in sync"* or *"make same change"* property.) If you explicitly write the listeners, then your code can take an arbitrary action based on the change to the bean property. If you don't code the listeners, then the design tool will provide them for you, and they will simply make the same change in the property you are bound to.

- **a constrained property**—the property is a "bound" property, but one that also sends an event message *before* it changes value as well as *after*. You might like to think of this as an *"agree to change"* property. The listeners have the ability to refuse the proposed property value change. One place to use this kind of property is when the bean is collecting values, and listeners are in a better position to validate the values for consistency and accuracy. If a listener judges that some proposed new value for a property is invalid, it can prevent the change. An example would be a bean that represents "withdrawal transaction" and another bean that represents "account balance." The second bean may veto a proposed withdrawal if it exceeds the amount in the account.

All the properties in our beans are private fields, but we provide public accessors, effectively making them public. Obviously, in order to be useful to other classes, a property must be public.

Practical Example of a Bound Property: validNum

The next part of the specification to implement in our beans is the part that says the button should disappear when the text field contains a string that is not a valid double, and reappear when the user corrects it. All Swing components have a `setVisible(boolean b)` method that makes them disappear or reappear according to the argument. That method follows the property naming convention, and indeed is already a boolean-valued property of `JButton` and, hence, of `DoItButton`.

If you refer back a few paragraphs, you'll see that we made `validNum` a boolean property of `ConverterField`. The validNum property keeps track of whether the String in the text field represents a double length floating point number. A string like "3.1412" does represent such a number, whereas a string like "3 eggs" does not.

So all we have to do is make `DoItButton.visible` track and move in lockstep with `ConverterField.validNum`, and we will automatically get our "button is only visible when display holds a number" behavior for free! It turns out that it is quite common for one property to need to track another in a different bean. And that is exactly what bound properties are for. We'll make sure that `visible` is mentioned as a property in the `DoItButtonBeanInfo` class. We'll also set an attribute saying that this is a bound property in `ConverterFieldBeanInfo`. You should add this line to the `ConverterFieldBeanInfo` after the existing line shown:

```
PropertyDescriptor validNum = ...   // no change to this line
validNum.setBound(true);        // add this line
```

That code in the bean info class will give you the menu item in the beanbox, as shown in Figure 24-4.

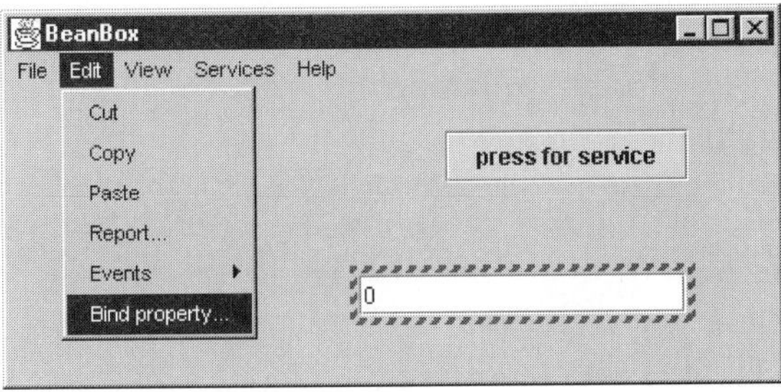

Figure 24–4 The effect of myProperty.setBound(true) in the bean info class.

When you select "Bind property" on the menu, another pop-up appears. This pop-up lets you specify the name of the source property that is being bound. Here you will choose "validNum" (see Figure 24-5).

The purpose of a bound property is to communicate changes between two beans. When the bound property changes at runtime, an event is sent to every bean that it was bound to at design time. Here we are using it to keep two boolean properties consistent. But the receiving beans can take whatever action is appropriate for their specification: execute a method, update a file, delete a record, spell check a document—anything.

By providing bean info saying that this property is bound in bean A, we make it show up on the beanbox "edit" menu item when bean A is highlighted. After you have selected the source property that you are binding, the stretchy red line

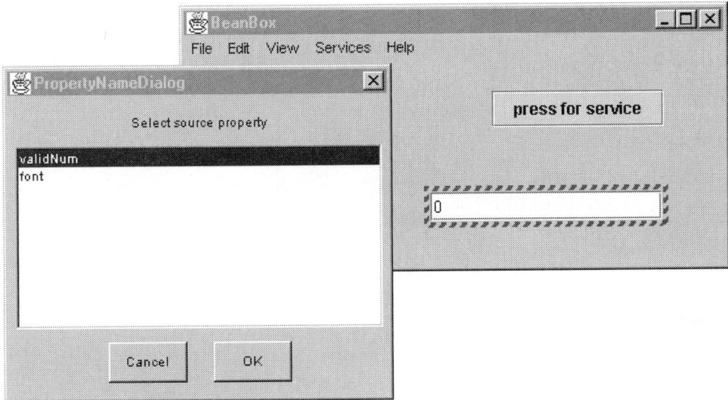

Figure 24–5 Selecting "bind property" in the beanbox edit menu.

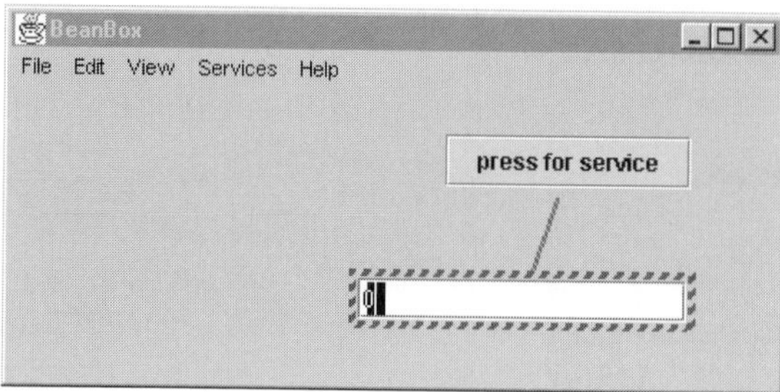

Figure 24–6 Choosing bean B that bean A property will be bound to.

appears. You stretch the red line to the component containing the property you want to bind to. A dialog will then pop up, allowing you to choose the receiving component.

When you choose the receiving component, a fourth dialog panel pops up to allow you to select the receiving property that you are binding to. The source property and the destination property that it is bound to must be assignment compatible (capable of being assigned directly to one another). With reference to Figures 24-6 and 24-7, bean A is the ConverterField, and bean B is the DoItButton.

"Under the hood" bound properties are implemented by the sending bean firing a PropertyChangeEvent to all receiving beans. The visual design tool will automatically generate Java code to listen for the PropertyChangeEvent that signifies a change in the bound property. The programmer must manually write the code (in the bean with the bound property) to fire the event when the property changes.

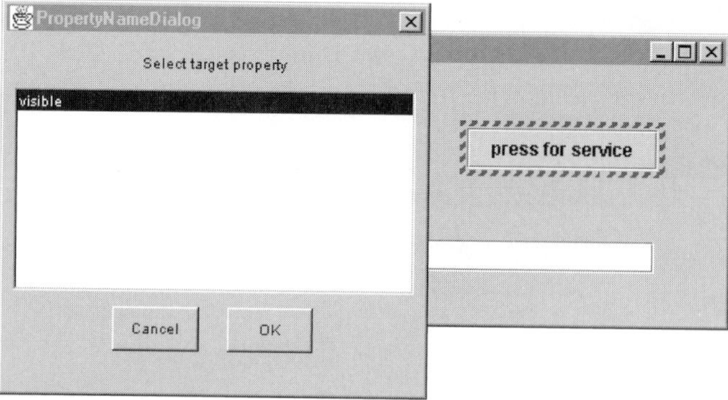

Figure 24–7 Choosing the property in bean B that bean A property is bound to.

That is easily done by putting the event firing code in the setter method for this property. A rule for get/set methods is that all changes to properties must be done using these methods, even if a class has the ability to assign to the field directly. Earlier, we saw the code needed in ConverterField to make it fire property changes. This architecture comes together so neatly you really have to admire it. The code is:

```
public void setValidNum(boolean newVal) {
    boolean oldVal = validNum;
    firePropertyChange( "validNum", oldVal, newVal);
    validNum = newVal;
}
```

There are several overloaded versions of `firePropertyChange()` in class `java.beans.PropertyChangeSupport`. The signatures are:

```
void firePropertyChange( PropertyChangeEvent evt );
void firePropertyChange( String propname, Object oldVal, Object newVal);
void firePropertyChange( String propname, int oldVal, int newVal);
void firePropertyChange( String propname, boolean oldVal, boolean newVal);
```

According to the documentation, firePropertyChange() does not fire an event if the old and new value are equal and non-null. If you pass in null instead of the old value, as in setValidNum() above, then firePropertyChange can't suppress changes that aren't really a change. For each of these invocations, a PropertyChangeEvent will be fired, even though the property is just being set to the same value repeatedly. If you *know* that users of this bean are able to cope with duplicated change events, you can send null instead of the old value, as in the ConverterField bean.

The class `javax.swing.JComponent` has several overloaded firePropertyChange methods. It has the four methods mentioned above, plus additional ones for all the other primitive types (long, byte, float, etc.). If your component is a Swing-based bean, you can call firePropertyChange directly. If your component is not a visual bean, you need to declare a PropertyChangeSupport object and invoke the firePropertyChange() methods in that. It seems to be an oversight that `java.beans.PropertyChangeSupport` does not have all the overriding versions of firePropertyChange that are present in JComponent.

Bound Properties

It may help you to remember what a bound property is if you consider the following sentence:

Whenever a bound property changes, an event is "bound to" (certain to) happen and that generated event is "bound for" (on its way to) the other beans.

The other beans being, of course, the ones containing the properties that this property is bound to. When bean A binds its property to something in bean B, the design tool says "Aha! Bean A is an event generator, and I need to register bean B as one of bean A's property change event listeners."

If you are following along online, making changes to the BeanInfo class for our two beans, recompiling and reloading the bean jar file in the beanbox, then connecting them, you should now see results. When you enter some text that is not a number in the ConverterField and tap "enter," the field turns red and the button disappears! It will reappear when you change the text to something that is a number. We bound a boolean value of validNum in ConverterField to a boolean value of visible in DoItButton. It's more common to bind identical properties (e.g., make sure two beans have the same font or background color). But as long as the types match, you can bind any properties together.

The beanbox works only with components and never shows code to you, but most of the other IDE tools treat beans as easily introspected classes and let you add code at design time. Recent versions of both JBuilder and CodeWarrior will actually pop up editable source code to hook beans together. That's a curious approach. It makes it easier for programmers to use non-bean interfaces (bad), and it makes it harder for HTML coders to use beans (also bad). At the other end of the spectrum, IBM's VisualAge is closer to the beanbox model. IBM takes beans very seriously.

Property Change Support for Non-Visual Beans

The code shown below, with some design time "glue" from the visual tool, lets one bean register as a listener with another. Something like this needs to be in all beans that have bound properties. The code was not added to our example beans above because it is automatically present for all Swing components (it is in `javax.swing.JComponent`). You must explicitly code these lines for beans that are not subclassed from Swing components.

```
private PropertyChangeSupport pcs = new PropertyChangeSupport(this);
public void addPropertyChangeListener(PropertyChangeListener p) {
        pcs.addPropertyChangeListener(p);
}
public void removePropertyChangeListener(PropertyChangeListener p) {
        pcs.removePropertyChangeListener(p);
}
```

This code is an example of the "Delegate" design pattern. It delegates the work (passes it on) to an instance of the `java.beans.PropertyChangeSupport` class. That instance then handles add and remove listener requests from other beans. You also need to use the design tool to ensure that other beans do add and remove themselves as property change event listeners to the bean with the bound property.

When you mark a property as bound in the bean info class, you are telling the visual design tool that this class will send out a property event change to all beans that have registered as listeners. There is only one property change event class that handles all properties, so you must provide a string that identifies which of the several possible bound properties in this class has changed. Use the property name as the string value. That string will be sent over as part of the property change event, as a parameter of `firePropertyChange`.

Summary: Telling Another Bean About a Change in One of Your Values

Table 24-2 summarizes how a bean that changes one of its property values will communicate that to some other bean.

Table 24–2 Bean That *Generates* the Changed Value

Purpose	Code

initial setup
(already present in JComponents)
	`private PropertyChangeSupport pcs = new`
	`PropertyChangeSupport(this);`
	`public void`
	`addPropertyChangeListener(PropertyChange`
	`Listener p) {`
	`pcs.addPropertyChangeListener(p);`
	`}`
	`public void`
	`removePropertyChangeListener(Property`
	`ChangeListener p) {`
	`pcs.removePropertyChangeListener(p);`
	`}`

send an event with the old and new changed values (needed in all beans with bound properties)	`Double oldVal = new Double(prevNum);`
	`Double newVal = new Double(num);`
	`pcs.firePropertyChange( "num", oldVal,`
	`newVal);`

Table 24-3 summarizes the code in a bean that needs to hear about a property change from some other bean.

Table 24–3 Bean That *Needs to Hear About* the Changed Value

Purpose	Code

initial setup	`class ... implements java.beans.PropertyChangeListener`
	`...`
	`// this is hooked up at design time by beanbox`
	`//`
	`someOtherBean.addPropertyChangeListener(this );`

This event handler is called each time the value changes.
You can either write an explicit property change handler, or let the default one be generated for you.
Note: The code opposite illustrates typical code in a property change handler, but is not meant to be part of the beans we are developing.
	`void propertyChange( PropertyChangeEvent e) {`
	`String s = e.getPropertyName();`
	`if (s.equals("validNum")) {`
	`Boolean B = (Boolean)e.getNewValue();`
	`setVisible( B.booleanValue() );`
	`Object oldVal = e.getOldValue();`
	`} else if (s.equals("rate") {`
	`Object newVal = e.getNewValue();`
	`double dnew = ((Double) newVal ).doubleValue();`
	`...`
	`}`

Fortunately, events in the beans world are exactly the same as events in the Java GUI world, and are generated and handled in exactly the same way. If an object is interested in something happening, it registers itself as a listener for that event with the thing that fires the event. When the thing happens, the event-causing object looks at its group of registered listeners and does a callback to each, saying in effect, “that event you said you were interested in just happened.”

Connecting a Swing Event to a Method in Another Bean

This section describes something very common: connecting an event (not a property) in one bean to a method in another bean. In this case, we want to connect the button press in DoItButton to the validate-and-multiply method in ConverterField. We have already seen how to do that in the beanbox (refer to the example that added a button to the Juggling animator bean).

The usual approach is taken to set things up in the BeanInfo files. As always, you do not have to provide a BeanInfo class. The beanbox will do introspection on the class to guess at what the events are. If you are following along with code as you read this chapter, try this example with and without providing event information in the BeanInfo class. You will see that the bean is simpler and more polished in the beanbox when you code the event set descriptor in the BeanInfo class.

The DoItButtonBeanInfo class will need an EventSetDescriptor describing the button push event, what you want it to be called on the beanbox menu, and the event it generates. The code that will be added to our DoItButtonBeanInfo class looks like this:

EventSet Descriptor Code

```
public EventSetDescriptor[] getEventSetDescriptors() {
// these are the events that this bean generates and wants to publish
    try {
      EventSetDescriptor push = new
EventSetDescriptor(DoItButton.class,
                                    "ActionEvent",

java.awt.event.ActionListener.class,
                                    "actionPerformed");
      push.setDisplayName("button push");
      EventSetDescriptor[] rv = { push };
      return rv;
    } catch (IntrospectionException e) {
            throw new Error(e.toString());
    }
}
```

You may wonder why it is an EventSetDescriptor rather than just an Event-Descriptor. The reason is that in many cases, a given group or set of events are all delivered as different method calls within a single event listener interface. For example, the standard AWT keyboard event `java.awt.event.KeyEvent` represents any of three events (key pressed, key released, and key typed), all of which are delivered via the `java.awt.event.KeyListener` interface. Therefore, programmers need to keep in mind that they are usually dealing with a set of events, and will need to implement the correct method to receive each specific event.

The ConverterFieldBeanInfo class will need a MethodDescriptor describing the method that should be made visible. The code looks like this:

```
import java.lang.reflect.*;
    ...
public MethodDescriptor[] getMethodDescriptors() {
    try {
       Method m1 = ConverterField.class.getDeclaredMethod(
                                 "validateAndMultiply", null);
       MethodDescriptor validateAndMultiply = new MethodDescriptor(m1);
       MethodDescriptor md[] = {validateAndMultiply};
       return md;
    } catch (NoSuchMethodException e) {
            throw new Error(e.toString());
    }
}
```

Make these additions to the bean info files, recompile, put into a jar, move the jar to the beanbox/jars directory, and start the beanbox up. Put these two beans on the beanbox and set the rate field to 1.15.

Hidden State

The purpose of the property sheet is to allow bean integrators to set initial values for properties. This is where we will enter our rate constant, by typing it into the field to the right of the text "rate." You can see that it is currently set to 1.0, which was the initial value in our code (refer to the listing of ConverterField.java).

We will create a "tip calculator" component. The standard tip in the western world is 15%, so to calculate the bill plus 15% our rate should be 1.15. Set this by typing into the rate field on the property sheet. If you try to type something that is not a valid string for a double, the property sheet will not pass it on to the bean.

If you, as a programmer, intend to allow designers to provide a new value for any property, you must provide an additional descriptor in the bean info class. Of course, this is almost always the case. You need to provide a descriptor for the bean as a whole and set an attribute that says that it has "hidden state," meaning you expect property changes at design time. The code you need to add to our two bean info files looks like this (the .class object will have a different name in the DoItButton bean, of course).

```
public BeanDescriptor getBeanDescriptor() {
     BeanDescriptor bd = new BeanDescriptor(ConverterField.class);
     bd.setValue("hidden-state", Boolean.TRUE);
     return bd;
}
```

The customizations are stored with the jar file that is written out of the design tool. If you fail to provide this descriptor, then the design time customizations will be lost after you leave the beanbox. It is not clear why hidden state is not assumed as the default behavior. This "hidden state" attribute was a last-minute addition right before the final release of beans, so we can only conjecture that it was for an important but obscure reason.

The Completed, Integrated Rate Calculator

Now the moment of truth. Connect the button event to the converter field validate-and-multiply routine, just as we did with the juggler bean button to the gif animator. Put a good value in the convertor field, say 60, and press the button. Check that the converter field now reads "69.0" and we're done! We've created two beans and planted them together! (See Figure 24-8.)

At this point with a real set of beans, you would write them out to a jar file ready for deployment with a client application or a servlet. The rest of the chapter fills in the gaps with a few more bean-related topics.

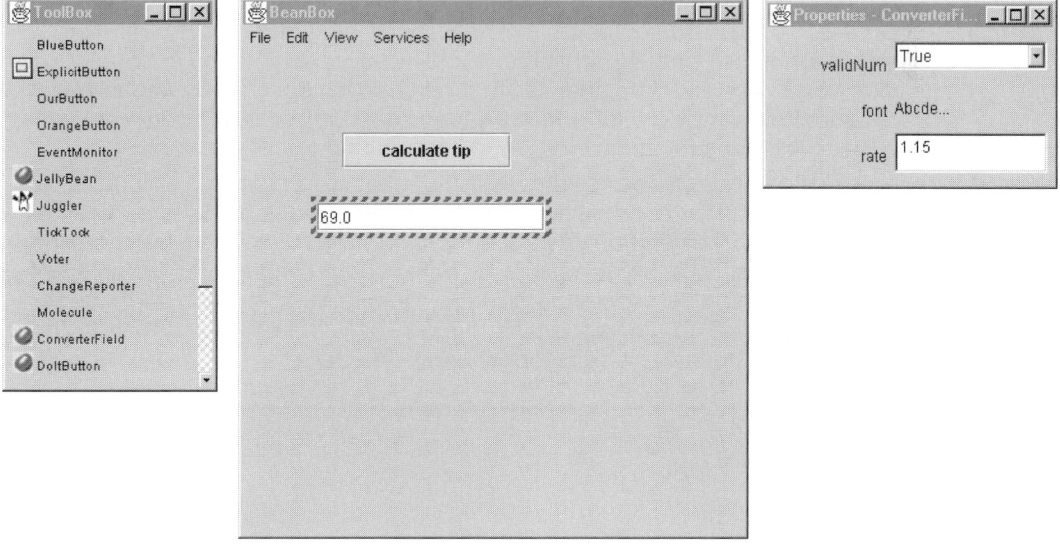

Figure 24–8 The completed beans in the beanbox.

Pitfall: Floating Point Arithmetic Has Limited Accuracy

As you play around with rate multiplications, you will very quickly observe that some numbers don't give the right result. If you multiply 100 by 1.15 in the calculator, you will see an answer of 114.99999999999 instead of 115. Floating point arithmetic, on every computer and with every programming language, is always limited in the accuracy of its results. It must be, because mathematics tells us there are an infinite number of real numbers between 0 and 1. You cannot cope with an infinite number of possibilities in a 64-bit quantity.

Instead, we limit the precision with which we store values. Doubles are good for about 14-15 significant figures. Numbers that start out with more precision than this in the real world lose it as soon as you start computing with them. Another problem is accuracy of representation. Floating point numbers are represented with base-2 (binary) arithmetic, while people do arithmetic with base-10 (decimal) numbers. Some numbers that have an exact representation in base-10 do not have an exact representation in base-2 and vice versa. For example, the decimal number 0.1 does not have an exact representation in binary format. It is stored as a number that is very, very, very close to 0.1, but differs from it by a minute quantity.

These differences sometimes show up in unexpected places in calculations. The fraction 0.15 cannot be stored to infinite precision. So the result of 114.99999999999 differs from the correct answer. The difference is less than one billionth, which is usually regarded as being "close enough for government work." However, it's a very visible difference in a text display. Some languages round numbers to six significant figures before displaying them. The inaccuracy is still there; it is just suppressed in the display.

Customizing More Complicated Properties

The beanbox's property sheet editor knows how to accept and validate several types of properties: most primitive types, and types commonly seen in Swing components like Color and Font. But builder tools cannot know how to display and edit arbitrary classes. The class java.beans.PropertyEditorManager is used here. You have to write some code that implements the PropertyEditor interface and then register it with the PropertyEditorManager. At design time, when the visual tool finds a property which it doesn't know how to edit, it will ask the PropertyEditorManager to locate a suitable editing class. If it can find a suitable editor, it will use it. Otherwise, the visual tool will issue a warning message.

Writing a PropertyEditor is nowhere near as hard as writing a general purpose editor. You only have to deal with getting and setting a few values that will ultimately be expressed in primitive types. There's a PropertyEditorSupport class that you can start from. You can choose whether to give your editor a GUI in a pop-up window invoked from the property sheet, or restrict yourself to textfields. The bean info class will have an entry in the property descriptor that references the property editor.

There's a level of sophistication beyond writing your own property editor. For a really involved bean, you might write a customizer. This is a class that displays a GUI allowing you to set any and all properties of bean in one place. It's your own custom-written alternative to editing via the property sheet. The bean info class will have an entry in its bean descriptor that mentions the customizer, so the design tool knows to invoke it. The property sheet editor is adequate for your first few beans.

Constrained Properties

Constrained properties in a bean are one step further than bound properties. The two example beans we have been developing do not use constrained properties at all. You can skip this section entirely if you just want to work through the code of the two example beans.

A bean with a constrained property will send out a PropertyChangeEvent indicating that it *wishes* to make this change from old value to new value. Listeners can veto the change by throwing an exception which is rethrown back into the first bean. The "glue" code that non-visual beans need is shown below; Swing components already have this and you should not add it.

```
private VetoableChangeSupport vcs = new VetoableChangeSupport(this);
public void addVetoableChangeListener(VetoableChangeListener v) {
        vcs.addVetoableChangeListener(v);
}
public void removeVetoableChangeListener(VetoableChangeListener v) {
        vcs.removeVetoableChangeListener(v);
}
```

The code in the bean with the constrained property will also need to fire the event, like this:

```
try {
    vcs.fireVetoableChange(propertyName, oldValue, newValue);
    // proposed change may now be made
    setXxxx( newValue );
    pcs.firePropertyChange(propertyName, oldValue, newValue);
}
catch (java.beans.PropertyVetoException pve) {
    // some bean vetoed the change
}
```

If you look in the class `java.beans.VetoableChangeSupport`, you'll see that the `fireVetoableChange()` method actually compares the old and new values, and will not fire the event if they are the same. You should be aware of this when you write your bean code. You'll also want to add a line like this to the Bean Info class for the bean with the constrained property:

```
validNum.setConstrained(true);
```

The property name used here is "validNum," and you actually want to use whatever name you gave your constrained property. Adding this line to the bean info class makes an entry for "vetoableChange" show up in the "Edit | events" menu in the beanbox. You need to make sure you connect this entry at design time to the `vetoableChange()` method of all the beans that can veto the change.

The beans that are receiving vetoable change events will have vetoable change listeners like this:

```
public void vetoableChange(PropertyChangeEvent ev)
            throws PropertyVetoException {
    Integer I = (Integer)(ev.getNewValue());
    int newVal = I.intValue();
    if (newVal < 0)
        throw new java.beans.PropertyVetoException(
            "proposed value is negative", ev );
}
```

If a listener does veto the proposed change, then the `fireVetoable Change()` method automatically fires a new event reverting everyone to the old value and then rethrows the PropertyVetoException so your code gets a crack at it. The code example above shows how to read the new value in the Listener. The old value associated with the proposed change can be read in a similar way. The code example shows how an int value is passed. The property may be any type, of course. If it is a primitive type, the appropriate wrapper must be used (here, Integer) to turn it into an object. Your code needs to make the association between the property name string, and the type of values that property stores. You can get and use the property name from the event object with these lines of code:

```
String propName = ev.getPropertyName();
if (propName.equals("visible")) { ...
```

All constrained properties should also be bound properties (so that the bean has a way to inform listeners when a value *does* successfully change). That means that the beans that listen to constrained properties must have the standard code for handling a property change event, namely something like this:

```
public void propertyChange(PropertyChangeEvent ev) {
  // check the property name
    String propName = ev.getPropertyName();
    if (propName.equals("visible")) {
          Boolean B = (Boolean)ev.getNewValue();
          setVisible( B.booleanValue() );
    }
}
```

If you are binding one property to another of the same type, you can let the code be generated for you at design time. If the property change handler needs to do anything more sophisticated, you need to write the code explicitly.

Notice the symmetry here. The bean with the constrained property will fire two property change events to make a change—one from fireVetoableChange() and then (if no one objected) one from firePropertyChange(). The beans that are listening to the constrained property will handle the first event in vetoableChange, and the second in propertyChange. In all cases, the event that is sent and handled is a PropertyChangeEvent. Don't let that confuse you.

Calling a Method in Another Bean—Don't Do It!

Writing a bean that directly invokes a method in another bean is a mistake. Tempting as it is to try to do that, beans programming requires you to give up the style of programming where objects know about other objects and their methods. You cannot directly call a method of another bean, pass in arbitrary parameters, and get back an arbitrary return value. Think about it: you (usually) need to know the name of a method to invoke it, and you need to have an instance of a class to invoke instance methods on. But you do not want to build those kinds of dependencies into your beans.

You can get exactly the same effect by using the same tools we have already seen. The bean that needs to make a call should instead send an event to the other bean. The event should contain an object representing any arguments that need to be passed across. The handler for the event should unwrap the arguments and then make the call itself on its own method. Any return value can be sent back to the would-be invoker the same way, by sending it as an event.

The event that you send across either way can be a property change event (in which case you'll probably want to make whatever provokes the need for the call be a property), or you can define your own event type by extending `java.util.EventObject`. If you create your own event type you'll also need to support add and remove listener methods for it, and to fire the custom event. You must follow the standard event naming conventions here, or the visual design tool probably won't recognize what you are trying to do. In the following lines of code we show the event-naming conventions using the fruit name "plum" where the event name should appear.

```
// visible to both beans
public class PlumEvent extends java.util.EventObject { ... }
public interface PlumListener extends java.util.EventListener {
    public void plumHappened(PlumEvent evt);
}

// in the bean sending the event, add 3 methods
    public synchronized void addPlumListener(PlumListener l) { ...
    public synchronize void removePlumListener(PlumListener l) { ...
    public void firePlumEvent(PlumEvent evt) {  ...

// in the bean receiving the event
public class SomeBean implements PlumListener {
    ...
       SendingBean.addPlumListener(this);
    ...
    public void plumHappened(PlumEvent evt) {
       this.myMethod( ... );
       ...
    }
    public void myMethod ( ...
```

The design tool will take care of planting code to actually call `addPlumListener()` when you connect the beans.

Hasn't this merely swapped a dependency on knowing a method name for a dependency on knowing an event name? Absolutely! That is the point. Anyone can send an event to anyone who has registered an interest in listening to that event. But you cannot call a method unless you have an instance of the object. In the first case, the bean that does the work has to register with the event generator. In the second case, the responsibility would be the other way around, and the identities are not known at compile time. Before leaving the topic, let us just mention that you can get instances of communicating beans. Any bean that has registered as a listener for one of your events has given you a reference to itself. Any bean that has sent you an event has given you a reference to itself, if you call the `event.getSource()` method. But you want to avoid these back doors in your beans, as they reduce flexibility and create unwanted interbean dependencies.

As an aside, the names we give events are not defined by any naming pattern. Hence, we see a variety of event names with different forms like keyTyped, actionPerformed, textValueChanged, propertyChange (not changed), and so on.

Pitfall: Swing Object Persistence Has Changed with JDK 1.4

All Swing components, like JButton, had this warning in the JDK 1.3 documentation:

Warning: Serialized objects of this class will not be compatible with future Swing releases. The current serialization support is appropriate for short-term storage or RMI between applications running the same version of Swing. A future release of Swing will provide support for long-term persistence.

That warning applies to software components that you build out of Swing components. It is saying that older components will all have to be modified for the new persistence model. The document at *java.sun.com/products/jfc/tsc/articles/persistence2/* mentions the new proposal which is part of JDK 1.4. Swing components are now written to persistent storage by transforming them into XML and writing out the XML text. The previous approach to serializing objects had the drawback that you could only be sure of reconstituting the serialized objects on the exact same implementation of the exact same Java runtime version that was used to write them out. Using XML to serialize objects removes this limitation.

A bean is written to a stream by the writeObject() method of a new class called java.beans.XMLEncoder. Similarly, a bean can be read back in by the readObject() method of class XMLDecoder. You, as a bean creator, do not invoke the methods. They will be invoked by the design time tools that you use. Chapter 28 has more information about XML. Chapter 14 on I/O shows an example of serializing an object into XML.

Exercises

1. Hide the floating point inaccuracies in the rate calculator beans by rounding results to two decimal places. This exercise lets you make a small change and then practice rebuilding the beans from first principles.

2. Modify the ConverterField so that it takes its background color from the DoItButton, i.e., make the DoItButton background color a bound property that tells ConverterField when it has changed. Make each button press cause the button to change to a new color.

3. Make the button background color property change to a new primary color after each press. Bind the color to the ConverterField as in the previous exercise, but allow the ConverterField to veto a proposed color change if it would conflict with its "red means bad data entry" convention.

4. Modify the two beans in this chapter so that users can type "s," "c," "t" on the DoItButton, and that character will replace the button label. It will also change the operation done by the ConverterField so that it provides the sine, cosine, or tangent (respectively) of the number on the display. The button should generate an event when the label changes, and the text field should listen for that event.

5. It's unrealistic to have a currency converter that doesn't allow the rate to be updated at runtime. Find and program a way to allow the rate to be updated at runtime. Hint: support a special case of text that can be typed in the ConverterField. This will allow you to input a new rate and a new label for the button.

6. Write a pocket calculator as a series of components. Don't use the usual horrible GUI design of mimicking the appearance of a physical pocket calculator with one button per number. Instead, acquire your numbers in text fields, use sliders to specify the number of decimal places in the display, and use a radiobutton list to specify the operations. To do this easily, you need properties like "I am the left operand," "I am the right operand," "I am the result field." You could also make three subclasses of your NumberField class for this purpose, and have three different beans.

Some Light Relief—Java's Duke Mascot

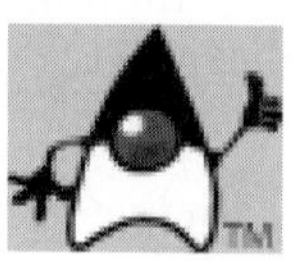

In spite of appearances, Duke is not really the tooth fairy. Duke was created in 1992 by artist Joe Palrang. Joe was working for Sun's Green project which preceeded Java when he was tasked with designing a figure to represent the user's actions in the GUI. The Green project was an early set-top box for TVs. It sat in the user's hands like a remote control and had a tiny display screen. The figure had to be small, which is why Duke is such a simple triangular shape. The hands, nose, and hat are simple visual cues to Duke's position and direction. The team wanted a visual agent that could move, turn, and look expressive. Duke was the result.

Before he was called "Duke," the figure had several other names including "tooth," "fang," and "the agent." Joe didn't like any of them, so he rechristened his creation "Duke" in vague honor of John Wayne. You can surely see the likeness to the cinematic gunslinger with the whiskey nose. The Green project came to an end without turning into a product, but the team members liked Duke and he became the mascot of the Java project that followed. Sun was pretty big on mascots at that time. You might remember "Network," the dog who graced Sun's advertising material and was brought on stage at a JavaOne conference. Network even toured Sun's Menlo Park campus once, and all us dog lovers got to pet him. He was big, woolly, and patient. He sniffed my hand to check if I had anything edible up my sleeve. I checked his neck to see if he was carrying a flask of brandy. Both of us were slightly disappointed. Network's kennel was situated outside Sun's corporate headquarters in Palo Alto for several years.

No one was quite sure what role Duke should play in Java, so he has gone in and out of the spotlight over the past few years. He appeared in early demonstration software, then disappeared for a while, and resurfaced in some Java tutorials. He now limits himself to appearances on Sun's Java website (*java.sun.com*), book covers, and live appearances at JavaOne (by a short person in a life-sized stuffed suit). Duke didn't make any live appearances for several months in the late 1990s when the costume mysteriously disappeared from its storage closet in the Javasoft office building in Cupertino. Despite heart-rending email from the manager who was supposed to look after the costume, it never resurfaced, nor was a ransom note ever found. They made up a second costume and now Duke walks again. Since there's no obvious connection with Java, the live appearances confuse a lot of people who haven't heard the early history! They wonder if Duke is a penguin, perhaps suggestive of Linux. But no, Duke is just Duke.

Complete Code Listings

DoItButton.java

```
 import javax.swing.*;
public class DoItButton extends JButton {
    public DoItButton() {
        super("press for service");
    }
}
```

DoItButtonBeanInfo.java

```
import java.beans.*;
import java.lang.reflect.*;
public class DoItButtonBeanInfo extends SimpleBeanInfo {
    public PropertyDescriptor[] getPropertyDescriptors() {
        try {
            PropertyDescriptor label =
             new PropertyDescriptor("label",
                               javax.swing.AbstractButton.class);
            PropertyDescriptor font =
             new PropertyDescriptor("font", DoItButton.class);
            PropertyDescriptor visible =
             new PropertyDescriptor("visible",
                                          java.awt.Component.class);
            PropertyDescriptor background =
             new PropertyDescriptor("background", DoItButton.class);
            PropertyDescriptor rv[] = {label, font, visible,
                                                       background};
            return rv;
        } catch (IntrospectionException e) {
            throw new Error(e.toString());
        }
    }
    public EventSetDescriptor[] getEventSetDescriptors() {
        // these are the events that this bean generates
        try {
            EventSetDescriptor push =
            new EventSetDescriptor(DoItButton.class,
                                    "ActionEvent",

java.awt.event.ActionListener.class,
                                    "actionPerformed");
            push.setDisplayName("button push");
            EventSetDescriptor[] rv = { push };
```

(continued)

```
            return rv;
        } catch (IntrospectionException e) {
            throw new Error(e.toString());
        }
    }
    public BeanDescriptor getBeanDescriptor() {
       BeanDescriptor bd = new BeanDescriptor(DoItButton.class);
       bd.setValue("hidden-state", Boolean.TRUE);
       return bd;
    }
    public java.awt.Image getIcon(int iconKind) {
      if (iconKind == BeanInfo.ICON_MONO_16x16 ||
          iconKind == BeanInfo.ICON_COLOR_16x16 ) {
          java.awt.Image img = loadImage("JellyBeanIconColor16.gif");
          return img;
      }
      if (iconKind == BeanInfo.ICON_MONO_32x32 ||
          iconKind == BeanInfo.ICON_COLOR_32x32 ) {
          java.awt.Image img = loadImage("JellyBeanIconColor32.gif");
          return img;
      }
      return null;
    }
}
```

ConverterField.java

```
/* A bean that allows the user to type a number in a text
 * field and get it multiplied by a constant on demand.
 * Peter van der Linden, May 2001, Silicon Valley.
 */
import javax.swing.*;
import java.awt.Color;
import java.awt.event.*;
public class ConverterField extends javax.swing.JTextField
           implements KeyListener, java.io.Serializable {
  // holds the rate that we will multiply with the TextField
  // the rate will be set at design time, and doesn't change
  private double rate = 1.0;
  public double getRate() {  return rate; }
  public void setRate(double d) {
      rate = d;
      this.setText("rate set to " + Double.toString(d));
  }
  private boolean validNum = true;
  public boolean isValidNum() {  return validNum; }
  public void setValidNum(boolean newVal) {
      boolean oldVal = validNum;
      firePropertyChange( "validNum", oldVal, newVal);
      validNum = newVal;
  }
  public ConverterField() {
      super("0",16);
      setBackground(Color.white);
      addKeyListener(this);
  }

  public void keyPressed(KeyEvent e) {}
  public void keyReleased(KeyEvent e) {}
  public void keyTyped(KeyEvent e) {
      // ConverterField generates these events, and
      // validates the number when user hits "enter".
      if (e.getKeyChar() == KeyEvent.VK_ENTER) {
           validateNumber();
      }
  }
  private double n;
  public void validateNumber() {
      // sets a double from the text field, and
      // sets the textfield color to red if invalid.
      String s = this.getText();
      try {
          n = Double.parseDouble(s);
            // success -- n holds the number
```

(continued)

```
            setBackground(Color.white);
            setValidNum(true);
        } catch (NumberFormatException nfe) {
              // failed to parse TextField as number
              // set background to red!
            setValidNum(false);
            requestFocus();
            setBackground(Color.red);
            n = Double.NaN;
        }
    }
    public void validateAndMultiply() {
        // we do this when another bean tells us to
        validateNumber();
        if ( !(isValidNum()))  return;
        n = n * rate;
        setText( Double.toString(n) );
    }
}
```

ConverterFieldBeanInfo.java

```
import java.beans.*;
import java.lang.reflect.*;

/**
 * BeanInfo for the ConverterField.
 */
public class ConverterFieldBeanInfo extends SimpleBeanInfo {
    public PropertyDescriptor[] getPropertyDescriptors() {
        try {
            PropertyDescriptor rate =
                new PropertyDescriptor("rate",
                                       ConverterField.class);
            PropertyDescriptor font =
                new PropertyDescriptor("font",
                                       ConverterField.class);
            font.setBound(true);
            PropertyDescriptor validNum =
                new PropertyDescriptor("validNum",
                                       ConverterField.class);
            validNum.setBound(true);
            PropertyDescriptor rv[] = {rate, font, validNum};
            return rv;
        } catch (IntrospectionException e) {
            throw new Error(e.toString());
        }
    }
    public MethodDescriptor[] getMethodDescriptors() {
        try {
            Method m1 = ConverterField.class.getDeclaredMethod(
                            "validateAndMultiply", null);
            MethodDescriptor validateAndMultiply = new
                                       MethodDescriptor(m1);
            MethodDescriptor md[] = {validateAndMultiply};
            return md;
        } catch (NoSuchMethodException e) {
            throw new Error(e.toString());
        }
    }
    public BeanDescriptor getBeanDescriptor() {
      BeanDescriptor bd = new BeanDescriptor(ConverterField.class);
      bd.setValue("hidden-state", Boolean.TRU  E);
      return bd;
    }
    public java.awt.Image getIcon(int iconKind) {
        if (iconKind == BeanInfo.ICON_MONO_16x16 ||
           iconKind == BeanInfo.ICON_COLOR_16x16 ) {
           java.awt.Image img = 1
```

(continued)

```
oadImage("JellyBeanIconColor16.gif");
            return img;
        }
        if (iconKind == BeanInfo.ICON_MONO_32x32 ||
           iconKind == BeanInfo.ICON_COLOR_32x32 ) {
            java.awt.Image img =
loadImage("JellyBeanIconColor32.gif");
            return img;
        }
        return null;
    }
}
```

Chapter 25

Java Security

- THE SANDBOX
- CODE SIGNING
- THE SECURITY MANAGER
- APPLYING THE SECURITY POLICY
- SIGNING A JAVA PROGRAM
- SOME LIGHT RELIEF—SOFTWARE ABOUT NOTHING
- FURTHER REFERENCES

The term "security" means controlling the resources of your computer system: the files, screen, peripherals, and CPU cycles. Even on a single-user PC, this is an issue because a Windows virus can destroy your data, or the system can be hijacked from over the network. Some form of security check is particularly needed with anything that is downloaded and executed automatically on your behalf. Just by browsing a web page, embedded applets are sent over and executed on your system. Without a security check an applet could, either through maliciousness or poor programming, corrupt your files or transmit the contents to points unknown.

Viruses are already too prevalent in the PC world. Viruses are today commonly spread today through MS-Word documents by using an "execute macros on start-up" feature. Windows 9x has essentially no security. In October 2001, a Gartner Group analyst advised sites that value security not to use Microsoft's IIS web server. The ActiveX framework has identification through code signing, but no security in terms of resource access permission. A malicious or even simply buggy program can access your entire system, even if you wanted only to give it read access to one specific temp directory. This security deficiency makes ActiveX (or OLE, or DCOM, or DNA, .NET etc.; whatever is Microsoft's current marketing name for its preferred method of executing programs on a remote computer) unsuitable for use across the Internet.

The point is that security on desktop computers is far from where it should be, and there are large, real costs associated with that. Any new technology needs to help move the situation back in the right direction, rather than add to the problems.

Java improves on the current situation by defining and supporting several levels of resource access control. Some of Java's security is user-configurable, and some of it (to avoid a breach of security) is not. Here's how security has been refined and extended over successive Java releases:

- All Java releases feature *language security* (strong typing, no pointer arithmetic, etc.) and *runtime type checking* of array indexes, casts, references, etc., as well as *verification* of remotely-loaded bytecode.
- JDK 1.0.2 runs applets in the *sandbox*—a restricted environment that denied applets access to client system resources like local files.
- JDK 1.1 introduced the ability to *sign* applets, meaning "provide a cryptographic assurance that the applet comes from a source you trust." Signed applets can run with the same privileges as local applications. All code is still subject to the language and runtime security features, of course.
- JDK 1.2 (i.e., the Java 2 platform) introduced the really significant security improvements. All code, regardless of whether it is local or remote, an applet or an application, can now be made subject to a *security policy* that defines how and what it can access. For example, you can give a program write access to a directory, but not read access. The policy can be set by programmers, by systems administrators, or by users.

  The *security policy* is a list of all the possible permissions available for code (read access, write access, which directories, etc.), matched with a list of the various URLs code can come from and the various organizations from which you will accept signed code. You apply aspects of the policy to bundles of classes, called *domains*. System administrators can put a central security policy in place, and users can customize it for their individual needs.
- JDK 1.3 introduced a moderate number of minor improvements, such as compatibility with Verisign's code signing certificates. Several new methods were added to the APIs.
- JDK 1.4 introduced a small number of quite significant features. Three optional packages (Java Cryptography, Secure Sockets, and Authentication/Authorization Service) were made part of the standard release. Due to

import regulations in France, Israel, and Russia preventing their citizens from having strong encryption software, the system ships with encryption of limited strength.

Finally, JDK 1.4 offers a new library that implements the Generic Security Services API, allowing Java programmers easy access to Kerberos V5 and other security mechanisms.

The Parts of Java Security. As delivered with JDK 1.4, Java security provides these features:

- A permissions and *access control* framework for code at runtime. A full example of how to use this framework appears in this chapter.

  The features are in package `java.security` and its subpackages.

- A set of classes and tools for *code signatures*. A "signature" is a digital stamp of authenticity that can be applied to a file. The signature is different for each file, and it guarantees that the bytes in the file have not changed since they were signed. The signature is generated from a key which you keep private (so no one else can forge your signature), and it can be confirmed by anyone using a key that you publish. Examples of digital signature algorithms are DSA or RSA with MD5. A full example of how to sign code is given in this chapter.

  The features are in package `java.security` and its subpackages.

- A set of classes and tools for *certificate management*. A "certificate" is a digitally signed statement from one organization or person that you trust, blessing or vouching for the public key of some other organization or person. Certificates are specified by the X.509 v3 standard, or the PGP standard.

  The features are in package `java.security.cert`

- A set of classes to *encrypt and decrypt* to and from Streams. You get an instance of a Cipher by calling javax.crypto.Cipher.getInstance("what"), giving a string argument that specifies the cipher you want. You then construct a java.io.OutputStream, and layer a javax.crypto.CipherOutputStream on it, giving the Cipher object as an argument. Writes to the CipherOutputStream will be encrypted, and the results can be read back in through a CipherInputStream.

  The features are in package `javax.crypto` and its subpackages.

- A set of packages to *authorize and authenticate* users. The classes in these packages can be used to reliably and securely identify who is attempting to execute some Java code. The authentication can be done by Kerberos, or the Java Naming and Directory service, or by an operating system feature.

  The features are in packages `com.sun.security`, `javax.security`, and their subpackages.

- A set of classes to support *message authentication* codes (MAC). A MAC gives a way to check the integrity of information stored or sent over an insecure channel. It does not keep the bits secret; it answers the question "have these bits been changed at all?" It is like a very reliable parity code. MACs are a general case of code signatures. Typically, MACs are used between two parties to validate the information arriving at one end is the same as it was when it left the other. Java uses two well-known cryptographic hash functions to support MAC: MD5 and SHA-1.

  The features are in package `javax.crypto` and its subpackages.

- A set of classes to support *secure sockets layer* networking (SSL). Secure Socket Extension (JSSE) is a set of Java packages that enable secure Internet communications. It implements a Java version of SSL (Secure Sockets Layer) and TLS (Transport Layer Security) protocols and includes functionality for data encryption, server authentication, message integrity, and optional client authentication. Using JSSE, developers can securely send data between a client and a server running any application protocol (such as HTTP, Telnet, NNTP, and FTP) over TCP/IP.

  The features are in package `javax.net` and its subpackages.

What Is Kerberos?

In ancient Greek mythology, Kerberos was a three-headed dog that guarded the entrance to the underworld and prevented mortals from gaining access. In technology, Kerberos is an authentication protocol developed at MIT that prevents unauthorized mortals from gaining access to services on TCP/IP networks.

Kerberos has a database containing everyone's secret key, and uses *tickets* to do its work. When a client wants to access a server, it asks Kerberos for a ticket. The ticket will be issued by Kerberos after checking that the client is who it claims to be. A ticket is good for multiple requests from one particular client to a particular server, until it time expires (to prevent replay attacks).

The encryption technology used to be shipped separately in an optional extension package only available in North America, due to U.S. law which made it a crime to export certain kinds of software. That law didn't prevent anyone anywhere from getting encryption technology, but it did mean they could not get it from American companies.

As an aside, the U.S. government has a hate/hate relationship with encryption software. At the drop of a hat, the director of the FBI will make speeches urging strict restrictions on crypto software (one proposal involved requiring you to give the government your secret decoding key). The proposals are generally accompanied by vague handwaving about crime and terrorism. But the handwaving is not borne out by facts. The Center for Democracy and Technology did a study of wiretaps and encryption, and discovered that of 1,190 wiretaps that were authorized in the year 2000, in 20 cases they came across some encryption, and the government was able to decode every one. A similar study of steganography (hiding messages in other files) by two University of Michigan researchers in 2001 looked at more than 2 million files on the Internet and found no coded messages at all.

The problem for the U.S. government is not that it cannot break your coded messages. The problem seems to be that if everyone uses encryption routinely, it becomes more difficult to do traffic analysis or pay special attention to encoded messages. In any event, the encryption software laws have now been relaxed a little, and JDK 1.4 now includes encryption tools that can be exported without restriction from the USA.

In this chapter we will specifically look at the sandbox, code signing, and the security manager (which is how the security policy is applied).

The Sandbox

Default Capability Differences

Note that there is a difference in default capabilities between an applet loaded from over the net and an applet loaded from the local file system. Where an applet comes from determines what it is allowed to do. An applet from over the net is loaded by the applet class loader, and it is subject to the sandbox restrictions enforced by the applet security manager.

An applet stored on the client's local disk and accessible from the CLASSPATH is loaded by the file system loader. These applets are permitted to read and write files and load Java libraries and exec processes. Local applets are not passed through the bytecode verifier, which is another line of defense against code from the net.

The verifier checks that the bytecode conforms to the Java Language Specification and looks for violations of the type rules and namespace restrictions. The verifier looks at individual instructions to ensure that:

- There are no stack overflows or underflows. That is, every path through a basic block leaves the stack pushed or popped by the same amount. Thus, you can keep track of stack depth and avoid illegal accesses.
- All register accesses and stores are valid.
- The parameters to all bytecode instructions are correct.
- No illegal type conversions are attempted.

Code Signing

An earlier chapter showed how to put Java applets into jars. The next step is to describe how jars can be used to convey the notion that the code is trusted. Since an applet can be downloaded from anywhere on the net just by browsing a URL, the default security model needs to be very strict. JDK 1.1 introduced support for signing an applet, which gives the browser the opportunity to identify who wrote the applet and then choose to let the applet access all system resources. JDK 1.2 lets you configure more precisely the resources that can be accessed by signed code.

Signing some code in a jar file is like signing a bank check. It means labeling it with a tamper-proof identifying mark saying where it came from. Don't we already know this? Doesn't it come from the URL we are browsing? The answer is that we are not sure enough to give our system away to the applet.

Applets start running by virtue of visiting a page; there need not be any visible indication that the page contains an applet. Secondly, although an applet is hosted on a page, it is not necessarily located on that page. The CODEBASE applet tag can point to a URL anywhere else on the net. Finally, with enough effort, it is possible to spoof (masquerade as) web servers. If the stakes are high enough people could do this to make a malicious or fraudulent applet appear to come from *mother.teresa.org*.

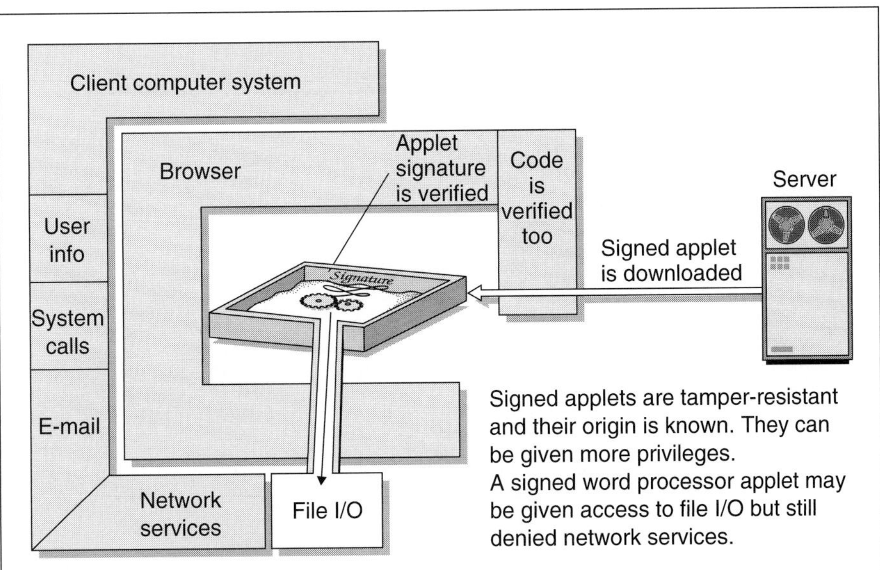

Figure 25–1 Signed applets have more privileges.

A sandbox is like a room built out of firewalls (see Figure 25-2). Applets are executed inside a sandbox by default, so they cannot access the private or vulnerable resources of your system. This is a representative but not exhaustive list of the restrictions on remotely accessed applets.

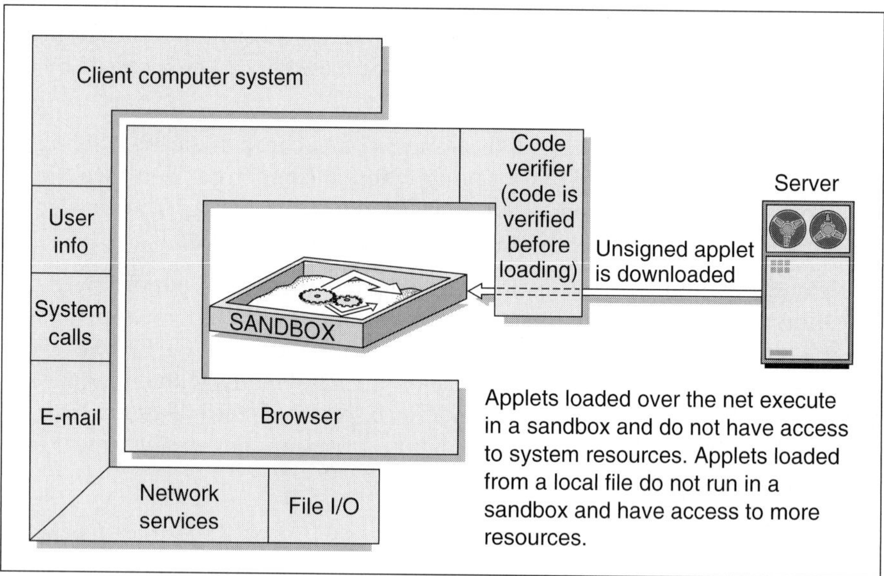

Figure 25–2 The secure sandbox.

By default, an applet accessed over the net:

- cannot read or write files;
- cannot open a socket connection, except to the server that it came from;
- cannot start up a program on your system;
- cannot call native (non-Java) code.

Applets accessed from a local file system (rather than over the net) are allowed more privileges. They can only be on your local file system with your permission, so it is presumed that you trust them (see Figure 25-3).

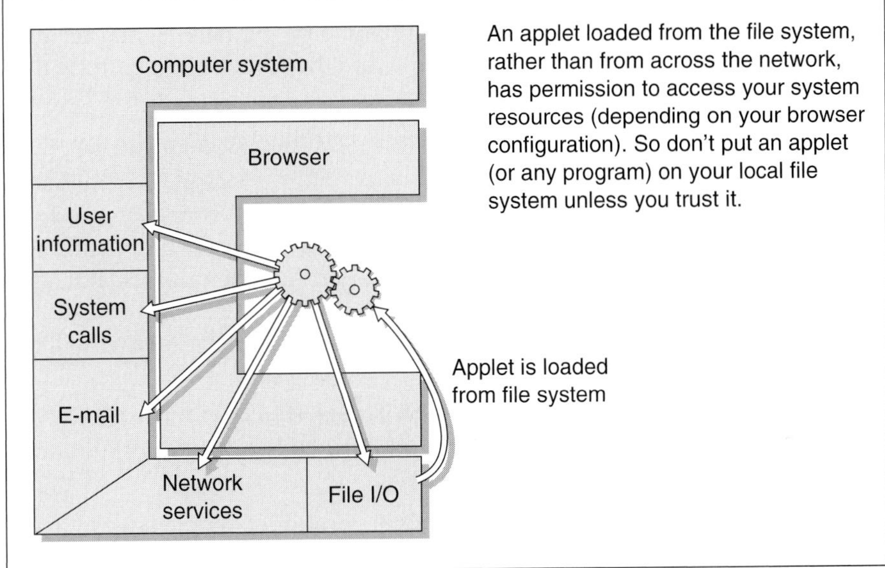

Figure 25–3 A local applet can access more resources.

We can write our signature on a check because it is a physical piece of paper. For an applet in a jar file, we add an extra file saying what the origin is. Obviously, it wouldn't be good enough just to put an ASCII text file in there saying, "Software from Honest Software Corporation," since the drug-peddling, code-encrypting, porno-terrorists that the FBI says are all over the Internet could easily forge that file on their own applets.

Instead, we use computer encryption to sign a file. Here is a summary of the basic steps:

1. Do all the one-time preparation necessary to set yourself up for encrypting files. The preparation consists of generating your code keys, registering them with the keystore database, getting yourself a digitally-signed certificate attesting to who you are, and a couple of other things. You will use the Java `keytool` utility program for all this.
2. Put all the files that make up the applet into a jar file. We have already seen how to do this in the previous section.
3. Sign the jar file. The `jarsigner` signing utility looks up your secret code in the `keystore` database and runs it over a hash of the jar file and the directives file. Then, it adds the coded result to the jar. Anyone can look at it, and anyone could change it, but if they do, the results won't match the hash value that was generated using your secret code, and the tampering will be obvious.
4. Export the public key certificate that you generated in step 1. People who wish to check your signature before running the code must import your certificate into their own keystore.
5. Put the signed applet jar file on your web page, and let people have at it.

This process makes the applet trusted. The longest part of the process is the one-time setup.

The Security Manager

All browsers install a security manager, and you can install one on your applications too. It's called by the runtime. Look at this code in the runtime library to create a FileInputStream:

```
public FileInputStream(String name) throws FileNotFoundException {
    SecurityManager security = System.getSecurityManager();
    if (security != null) {
       security.checkRead(name);
   }
   fd = new FileDescriptor();
   open(name);
}
```

Before it does anything else, the code gets the SecurityManager object for the system. If there isn't one (the reference is null), it goes ahead. However, if someone has created a SecurityManager, then its `checkRead()` method is called.

The checkRead() method will judge whether this operation is permitted or not. Perhaps it looks to see if the program is trying to read from one of several directories that it is allowed to access. Perhaps the program is only allowed to read files with a certain name, or that are newer than some date. There will be some application-specific protocol for judging whether access is permitted or not.

If it is permitted, the method does its work and returns without a problem. If the file access is not permitted (you're an ordinary applet that was just downloaded, for example), a `SecurityException` is thrown, tossing you out of the FileInputStream constructor before the object creation completes.

The SecurityManager is a built-in class in package java.lang with about a dozen methods, each of which checks access to a particular resource: threads, properties, socket connections, reading a file, and so on.

What Do All the Cryptographic Terms Mean?

We don't present a general tutorial on computer cryptography in this text. Bruce Schneier does that in his excellent book referenced at the end of the chapter, and it takes 750 pages. The pages are packed with information and stories that will keep you reading and learning.

You don't have to know how computer cryptography works in order to sign Java applets, but most readers will be very interested to find out more details. Cryptography is a truly fascinating topic, with an engaging blend of intrigue, high finance, and technical challenges. If you get caught up in it, it might even become your career!

The java.lang.SecurityManager class contains the following public methods:

```
public class java.lang.SecurityManager extends java.lang.Object {
     public java.lang.SecurityManager();
     public void checkAccept(java.lang.String, int);
     public void checkAccess(java.lang.Thread);
     public void checkAccess(java.lang.ThreadGroup);
     public void checkAwtEventQueueAccess();
     public void checkConnect(java.lang.String, int);
     public void checkConnect(java.lang.String, int, Object);
     public void checkCreateClassLoader();
     public void checkDelete(java.lang.String);
     public void checkExec(java.lang.String);
     public void checkExit(int);
     public void checkLink(java.lang.String);
     public void checkListen(int);
     public void checkMemberAccess(java.lang.Class, int);
     public void checkMulticast(java.net.InetAddress);
     public void checkMulticast(java.net.InetAddress, byte);
     public void checkPackageAccess(java.lang.String);
     public void checkPackageDefinition(java.lang.String);
     public void checkPermission(java.security.Permission);
     public void checkPermission(java.security.Permission, Object);
     public void checkPrintJobAccess();
     public void checkPropertiesAccess();
     public void checkPropertyAccess(java.lang.String);
     public void checkRead(java.io.FileDescriptor);
     public void checkRead(java.lang.String);
     public void checkRead(java.lang.String, java.lang.Object);
     public void checkSecurityAccess(java.lang.String);
     public void checkSetFactory();
     public void checkSystemClipboardAccess();
     public boolean checkTopLevelWindow(java.lang.Object);
     public void checkWrite(java.io.FileDescriptor);
     public void checkWrite(java.lang.String);
     public boolean getInCheck();
     public java.lang.Object getSecurityContext();
     public java.lang.ThreadGroup getThreadGroup();
}
```

The methods scrutinize some specific form of resource access. So checkRead(java.io.FileDescriptor) will return normally if a read may be done using this file descriptor, and throw an exception if it should not. The three methods, whose names are not self-descriptive, carry out this processing:

`checkSetFactory()`	This effectively checks whether the caller is allowed to provide his own implementation of certain network-related objects.
`getInCheck()`	Simply says whether a check is currently taking place.
`getSecurityContext()`	Returns an implementation-dependent Object which stores enough information about the current execution environment to perform some of the security checks later.

You never call these checking methods; they are called at appropriate times by the Java runtime. The calls are already in place throughout the runtime library. When a Java system first starts executing, the security manager is set to null and the only access restrictions are those imposed by the underlying operating system. In other words, anything goes.

To change the default, you can write your own class that extends SecurityManager and provide new methods to override the parent checking method for the resources you are interested in. The body of each new method contains your algorithm for deciding whether to grant access or not. It will either return or throw a security exception. Returning without throwing an exception means the access is allowed. If you install a new security manager of your own, then every resource *not* controlled in your new manager is disallowed. Following is an example that allows access to all system properties and nothing else:

```
class MySecurityManager extends SecurityManager {
     public void checkPropertyAccess(String key) {
          return;
     }
}


public class foo {
     public static void main(String s[]) {
          SecurityManager msm = new MySecurityManager();
          try {
               System.setSecurityManager(msm);
          } catch(Exception e){}
     }
}
```

A SecurityManager can be set, at most, once during the lifetime of a Java runtime. There is no way to install a new SecurityManager that includes permission to keep installing new SecurityManagers—it's a one-shot deal and cannot be replaced, changed, or overridden later on. In an application, you, the programmer, can define the level of security for your program. In an applet, the browser sets the SecurityManager and decides what processes to follow to grant or deny access. Applets must be unable to impose a new security manager.

Different browsers have imposed slightly different SecurityManager policies, and they can take into account whether an applet was loaded from a local file or from browsing over the Internet. Local files only exist on your system because you put them there, so they are presumed to have more privileges. Table 25-1 is a matrix of browser characteristics extracted from the JavaSoft site *www.javasoft.com/sfaq*.

Table 25–1 Capabilities of an Untrusted Applet

Capabilities	BP/net	BP/local	Av/net	Av/local	Applic
Read or write a file in /home/me with access control list set	no	no	yes	yes	yes
Read the user.name property	no	yes	no	yes	yes
Connect to port on client	no	yes	no	yes	yes
Connect to port on 3rd host	no	yes	no	yes	yes
Load library	no	yes	no	yes	yes
Exit(-1)	no	no	no	yes	yes
Create a pop-up window without a warning	no	yes	no	yes	yes

Key:

- BP/net: browser with a Java Plug-in, loading applets over the net
- BP/local: Browser with a Java Plug-in, loading applets from local file system
- Av/net: Appletviewer, loading applets over the net
- Av/local: Appletviewer, loading applets from the local file system
- Applic: Java stand-alone applications

The restrictions mean that an applet loaded from over the Internet:

- Can really read and write files if an access control list file permits it, and you run the applet using appletviewer.
- Cannot make network connections to hosts other than the one it came from.
- Cannot start a program on your system by using the equivalent of the system() call in C. An application or local applet can do this with the method `java.lang.Runtime.exec()`.
- Cannot load a library.
- Cannot execute native code.

The SecurityManager class provides a way to recognize trusted code so we can grant it more capabilities without jeopardizing system security.

You can configure the Sun appletviewer to read and write files on your local disk by editing the file .hotjava/properties. This file is in your home directory on Unix (note its name starts with a dot, so it is not usually visible when you list the directory). Under Windows, the files is in the root directory of the drive on which you installed Java (the file might be C:\.hotjava\properties). Note that this works for the *appletviewer only*, not other browsers like Netscape.

Then you can set the acl.read and acl.write properties to point to the files or directories that you will allow applets to read or write. For example, if I add these two lines to my ~/.hotjava/properties file (or my C:\.hotjava\properties file on Windows), then applets are allowed to read any files in /home/linden or to write to any files in the /tmp directory.

```
acl.read=/home/linden
acl.write=/tmp
```

ACL stands for Access Control List—a mainframe feature for providing fine-grained control of resources like files.

Here's an applet that you can run under Sun's appletviewer to confirm this:

```
// <applet code=show.class  height=100 width=200> </applet>
import java.io.*;
import java.awt.*;
import java.applet.Applet;
public class show extends Applet {

     public void Read() throws IOException {

          DataInputStream dis;
          String s, myFile = "show.java";

          dis = new DataInputStream(new FileInputStream(myFile));
          s = dis.readLine();
          System.out.println("line> "+s);
     }

     public void paint(Graphics g) {
          try {
               Read();
               g.drawString("Success in read", 10, 10);
     }
          catch (SecurityException e) {
               g.drawString("Caught security exception in read", 10, 10);
     }
          catch (IOException ioe) {
               g.drawString("Caught i/o exception in read", 10, 10);
          }
     }
}
```

If you need a refresher on the I/O details take a look at Chapter 13. For now, the purpose is to demonstrate that the security manager controls the resources accessed by applets and that file I/O is possible from an applet using the appletviewer.

How to Profile Java Code

This has little to do with security, and is more of a general Java tip. There is an undocumented and unsupported utility available in JDK 1.4 for profiling your programs to see where they spend their time.

You invoke the utility by using a special option on the command line:

```
java -Xrunhprof:cpu=times myprogram
```

The program will run about ten times slower than usual (which itself may cause some profiling effects) and then generate a file called java.hprof.txt in the current directory.

That report file will be thousands of lines long, even for a small program. It contains some explanatory text at the front, and then dozens of lines like this:

```
rank   self  accum    count trace method
   1 24.73% 24.73%        3  1260 java.lang.Object.wait
   2 24.65% 49.38%        2  1275 java.lang.Object.wait
   3  7.52% 56.89%   786432   756 DataBufferInt.getElem
   4  7.26% 64.15%      768   718 SampleModel.getPixels
   5  7.11% 71.26%   786432   259 BufferInt.getElem
   6  6.95% 78.22%      768   535 Model.getPixels
   7  2.45% 80.66%     1605   349 Deflater.deflateBytes
   8  1.28% 81.95%        1   363 LinearRGB16TosRGB8LUT
   9  1.21% 83.15%    65536   638 java.lang.Math.round
  10  1.16% 84.32%    65330   405 java.lang.Math.pow
```

These lines report where the program spent its time. Almost 50% of this program was spent in one of two wait routines. More information about each appears in the trace buffers numbered 1260 and 1275 that will appear earlier in the report. The times probably indicate that the program is I/O-bound.

The count column is the number of times the method was invoked. The two wait() methods were only invoked five times, but they account for half the runtime of the program. The next most time-consuming method was getElem()—some of the names have been abbreviated to fit on the page here—that was called about three-quarters of a million times and accounts for 7.5% of execution time.

Reading this profile tells you that it is going to be very hard to speed up this particular program. It spends most of its time waiting in the runtime library for data to come to it. Your best hope for speed would be to use a different algorithm.

Applying the Security Policy

The previous three sections explained how security restrictions are enforced. This section describes how a fine-grained security policy can be set up to specify exactly what the restrictions are and to which code and code signers they apply. The notion of security policies, and the tools to adjust them, has been in Java since JDK 1.2.

The one-sentence summary of Java Security Policy is, "There are a bunch of files outside the Java system that keep a record of the way application and applet classes are grouped together into domains, and the permissions associated with those domains." The security is carefully tracked by the runtime, so a less-privileged class cannot grab more permissions because it called or was called by a more powerful domain.

The way that permission is granted is by adding an entry to a policy file. Policy files exist in a couple of standard places, and users can create additional ones and specify them as a command-line argument when they start a program. The format of an entry in a policy file is a little tricky; it resembles statements in a programming language. At least the entries are in ASCII, not binary, so you don't have to use the policytool provided, and can just edit the file if you prefer. If this was designed today, the configuration would be specified in XML. Instead. it uses a pseudo-Java syntax.

Each grant entry in the policy file is of the following format, where the leading `grant` is a reserved word that signifies the beginning of a new entry. Optional items appear in brackets. The keyword `permission` is another reserved word that marks the beginning of a new permission in the entry. Each entry grants a set of permissions to the specified code source.

```
grant [SignedBy "signer_names"] [, CodeBase "URL"] {

     permission permission_class_name
       ["target_name"]   [,"action"]   [,SignedBy "signer_names"];

          // there may be a series of permission statements
};
```

Here is an example of a pretty minimal policy file. We will use this in a later chapter to grant a program the ability to connect and accept connections on sockets:

```
grant  {
     permission java.net.SocketPermission "*", "connect";
     permission java.net.SocketPermission "*", "accept";
};
```

We put that text into a file called "permit," and then start the program mentioning the permission filename like this:

```
java -Djava.security.policy=permit  MySocketProgram
```

Here is another example policy file, where I say that I will grant file read and write permission in the /tmp directory or any subdirectory of it to all applets that originate from the Sun Java site.

```
grant CodeBase  "http://java.sun.com/" {
     permission java.io.FilePermission "/tmp/*", "read,write";
}
```

So where are the standard places that a policy file can exist, and what is the list of permissions?

There is by default a single system-wide policy file, and a single-user policy file. The system policy file is by default located here:

```
$JAVAHOME\lib\security\java.policy  (Windows)
$JAVAHOME/lib/security/java.policy  (Solaris)
```

The user policy file is by default located in the user's home directory in a file called this:

```
.java.policy  (note the leading "." in the name))
```

The system makes provision for specifying a number of additional policy files, including defining the name of one as a property when you invoke the program, as shown above. This can be done for the appletviewer, too, like so:

```
appletviewer -J-Djava.security.policy=file:/foo/permit applet.html
```

The full list of permissions and subpermissions is shown in Table 25-2. The policytool software will help you navigate these, and you can see why it's useful.

Table 25–2 Important Permissions and Subpermissions in JDK 1.4

Permission Class Name	Target Name (a subpermission)	Actions
java.io.FilePermission	*filenames*	read, write, delete, execute
java.security. AllPermission	–	–
java.awt.AWTPermission	accessClipboard, accessEventQueue, showWindowWithoutWarningBanner	–
java.net.NetPermission	requestPasswordAuthentication, setDefaultAuthenticator	–
java.net. SocketPermission	–	accept, connect, listen, resolve
java.util. PropertyPermission	–	read, write
java.lang.reflect. ReflectPermission	suppressAccessChecks	–

Table 25–2 Important Permissions and Subpermissions in JDK 1.4

Permission Class Name	Target Name (a subpermission)	Actions

`java.lang.`
`RuntimePermission`
	`queuePrintJob, setFactory, setIO,`
	`modifyThread, modifyThreadGroup`
	`getProtectionDomain,`
	`setProtectionDomain`
	`readFileDescriptor,`
	`writeFileDescriptor`
	`loadLibrary.`*<library name>*
	`accessClassInPackage.`*<package name>*
	`defineClassInPackage.`*<package name>*
	`accessDeclaredMembers.`*<class name>*
		–

`java.security.`
`SecurityPermission`
	`getPolicy, setPolicy`
	`getProperty.`*<property name>*
	`setProperty.`*<property name>*
	`insertProvider.`*<provider name>*
	`removeProvider.`*<provider name>*
	`setSystemScope, setIdentityInfo,`
	`setIdentityPublicKey,`
	`addIdentityCertificate,`
	`removeIdentityCertificate`
	`clearProviderProperties.`*<provider*
	name>
	`putProviderProperty.`*<provider name>*
	`removeProviderProperty.`*<provider name>*
	`getSignerPrivateKey, setSignerKeyPair`
		–

`java.io.` `SerializablePermission`	`enableSubclassImplementation,` `enableSubstitution`	–

The next section is a step-by-step example of signing a piece of code so that it can write to the local filesystem.

Signing a Java Program

Applets are not allowed to write to the local file system by default. We will walk through the example of how we can sign an applet so that it does have that ability. It's a lengthy process the first time because you also need to create and register your cryptographic keys.

There are steps that the code signer has to do (here, linden), and steps that the code receiver has to do to run the code (here, sauceboy). You can sign any kind of Java code: applets or applications. Applets always run under the control of a security manager, but you have to provide one if you want an application to have the same level of assurance.

Step 1: Setup for Applet Signing (One-Time)

We'll start by listing the bits and pieces involved in registering yourself with the Java system as a person or organization that can sign code. Note that you can sign applications as well as applets.

- Public and private keys: Java uses public key cryptography which involves two keys, one private and one public. Anyone can use your public key, but only you know your private key. There is no practical way to discover one key from the other, but either key can turn a message into seemingly random bits, and the other key can recover it.
- Encrypting something is like translating it into Martian—the encryption key is an English-to-Martian dictionary, and the decryption key is a Martian-to-English dictionary. Only instead of Martian, we use mathematical ciphers that are a lot harder to search exhaustively.
- Certificates: Anyone can generate their own keys, and anyone can claim to be whoever they like. To provide better assurance that you are who you say you are, we use X.509 certificates (bit files) in the online world.
- The keystore database: This repository holds records of all users, their certificates, and the pairs of code keys that each has. There can be several of these files on a system. It replaces the earlier javakey database of JDK 1.1
- The `keytool` utility: You'll be relieved to hear that there is a utility to do all this key generation and database registration. It has lots of different options, but there's only one command: `keytool`.

Now that we know the players, let's go over the rules of the game shown in Table 25-3.

Table 25–3 Getting Your Keys and Register Yourself with a Keystore

Step	Action
Step 1a	Generate your pair of keys.
Step 1b	Generate or buy an X.509 certificate.
Step 1c	Register your keys and certificate in a keystore database.

When you have completed these three steps, you will be able to sign applets. Although the process may seem cumbersome, remember that these steps have to be done only once and then you can do any amount of code signing. The Java keytool utility does all three steps in one go, so it takes a large number of options to drive it.

Register Yourself and Your Keys in a Java Keystore. As we mentioned, there is only one utility, `keytool`, to do all the preparatory work, and it has many different options which you can see if you type:

```
%    keytool
keytool usage:

-certreq        [-v] [-alias <alias>] [-sigalg <sigalg>]
                [-file <csr_file>] [-keypass <keypass>]
                [-keystore <keystore>] [-storepass <storepass>]
                [-storetype <storetype>]

-delete         [-v] -alias <alias>
                [-keystore <keystore>] [-storepass <storepass>]
                [-storetype <storetype>]

-export         [-v] [-rfc] [-alias <alias>] [-file <cert_file>]
                [-keystore <keystore>] [-storepass <storepass>]
                [-storetype <storetype>]

-genkey         [-v] [-alias <alias>] [-keyalg <keyalg>]
                [-keysize <keysize>] [-sigalg <sigalg>]
                [-dname <dname>] [-validity <valDays>]
                [-keypass <keypass>] [-keystore <keystore>]
                [-storepass <storepass>] [-storetype <storetype>]
```

…and there are many more!

For more information, see the documentation online at *java.sun.com/products/jdk/1.2/docs/guide/security/spec/security-specTOC.fm.html.*

We use a command of the following form all on one line:

```
keytool -genkey -storepass password1 -keystore name1
     -alias name2 -keypass password2
```

The actual command is like the following, all on one line, remember:

```
keytool -genkey -storepass soupy99  -keystore lindenstore
          -alias linden  -keypass lime43
```

The options mean:

`-genkey`	Generates a public and private keypair in this operation.
`-storepass soupy99`	Supplies the password to access this keystore file. It is better not to enter this on the command line, as it can be snooped. If you leave it off, you will be prompted for it.
`-keystore lindenstore`	This pair of options gives a name to the keystore that you are creating or using. The name can include a pathname.
`-alias linden`	The option says how you want to refer to the particular entry containing the keys that will be generated. It gives a name to the linden keypair.
`-keypass lime43`	The option gives a password for accessing and updating the linden keypair. Again, it is better to leave it off and be prompted for it.

When you run the keytool command, you will be prompted to provide more information identifying the person or organization who owns this keypair:

```
What is your first and last name?
  [Unknown]:  Peter van der Linden
What is the name of your organizational unit?
  [Unknown]:  code grinding shop
What is the name of your organization?
  [Unknown]:  AFU (Cayman Islands) Inc.
What is the name of your City or Locality?
  [Unknown]:  Silicon Valley
What is the name of your State or Province?
  [Unknown]:  California
What is the two-letter country code for this unit?
  [Unknown]:  US
Is <CN=Peter van der Linden, OU=code grinding shop, O=AFU (Cayman Islands)
Inc., L=Silicon Valley, ST=California, C=US> correct?
  [no]:  y
```

The keytool takes a few seconds to run, and then this 1.3KB keystore file is generated:

```
% ls -l
-rw-r--r--    1 linden    staff        1351 Nov 15 14:21 lindenstore
```

Now you have a keypair within a keystore and a self-signed X.509 certificate. You are ready to sign code using it.

What Is an X.509 Certificate? To reiterate, anyone can generate their own keys, and anyone can claim to be whoever they like. To provide better assurance that you are who you say you are, we use X.509 certificates (bit files) in the online world.

X.509 is an ISO standard for computer authentication. There are companies in business simply to check your credentials and issue you an unforgeable X.509 certificate in the form of an encrypted file. Search the web looking for "X.509 certificate" for a list of vendors.

You prove who you are to a certification authority using real-world documents then show them your public key, and they issue you a certificate. An X.509 certificate is like a passport, or perhaps better because it's harder to forge. An X.509 certificate works like a notary public. You identify yourself to the notary public and sign something, and then the notary affixes an official seal to guarantee your signature.

Buying an X.509 certificate from a certification authority is more reliable for your users and will make your code accepted in more places. Generating our own certificate is good enough for this example. The certificate does the same job as a PGP fingerprint. There's a glossary for these terms online at: *java.sun.com/docs/books/tutorial/security1.2/summary/glossary.html.*

Step 2: Put All the Files That Make up the Applet into a Jar File

We saw how to put the class files and other resources into a jar file earlier in this chapter. Here is the example code we will use. It is an applet that attempts to write to a local file on the client. Untrusted applets do not have permission to write to local files.

```
/* <applet
       archive=write.jar    code=write.class
       width=120           height=75>
   </applet>
*/
import java.io.*;
import java.awt.*;
import javax.swing.*;

public class write extends JApplet {

    public void init() {
       try {
           FileWriter fw = new FileWriter("score.txt");
           fw.write("new high score: 14 \n");
           fw.close();
       } catch (Exception e) {System.out.println(e);}
  }

    public void paint(Graphics g){
        g.drawString("Try to write a file", 15, 15);
    }
}
```

Don't worry about the I/O details—that will be covered in full in a later chapter. For now, the purpose is to demonstrate that browsers control the resources accessed by applets, and that file I/O is possible from an applet when the permission is granted. Compile the applet and put the class in a jar file.

```
% javac write.java

% jar -cvf write.jar  write.class
```

The applet attempts to open a file and write to it. When you try to run the applet, it will fail with a security error. Untrusted applets are not permitted access to the client file system. After this, we will sign it and try again.

```
% appletviewer write.java
java.security.AccessControlException: access denied
(java.io.FilePermission score.txt write)
```

Step 3: Create a Signed Jar File

To sign a jar file, we use the jarsigner tool (new with JDK 1.2). A typical run might look like this:

```
jarsigner -keystore lindenstore -signedjar swrite.jar write.jar linden
```

The options are self-explanatory. The program takes an unsigned jar file and creates a signed jarfile version of it. *(Tip:* Use the same name, but prefix an "s" on the beginning.) It signs it with linden's key from the lindenstore keystore. The utility will prompt you for passwords for both the keystore and the linden keypair.

```
Enter Passphrase for keystore: soupy99
Enter key password for linden: lime43
```

You can see that the following jar files now exist:

```
-rw-r--r--    1 linden    staff        2249 Nov 15 14:24 swrite.jar
-rw-r--r--    1 linden    staff         977 Nov 15 14:18 write.jar
```

Jar files (even unsigned jar files in JDK 1.2) have an extra directory called `META-INF` that it contains "meta-information"—information about the information in the archive. The MANIFEST.MF file is a list of files to be found in the archive, in the same sense that a manifest is a list of the cargo on a ship.

Step 4: Change the Applet Tag

Now we change the applet tag in our HTML file to refer to the signed version of the jar file. We want users to reference the newly-created signed file instead of the old `.jar` file.

The new tag will look like this:

```
<applet
       archive=swrite.jar
       code=write.class
       width=120
       height=75>
   </applet>
```

Step 5: The Person Who Runs the Applet Must Import My Certificate

You now have a signed jar file swrite.jar. The runtime system of the code receiver will need to authenticate the signature when the write program in the signed jar file tries to write a file. The authentication is done using a policy file that grants the permission to this signed code.

The person (sauceboy, in this example) who is going to run this applet needs to set up a policy file that says in effect, "I am going to allow file access to code written by user linden." So sauceboy's system has to know about linden's X.509 certificate and public key. Here's how we tell it.

The signer of the code sends a copy of the certificate authenticating the public key to anyone who plans to run it. That certificate must be put into their own keystore. Here is how linden extracts the X.509 certificate from the keystore using the keytool utility:

```
keytool -export -keystore lindenstore  -alias linden  -file linden.cert
```

Again, the tool will challenge you for the password.

```
Enter keystore password:  soupy99
Certificate stored in file <linden.cert>
```

The file that holds the certificate is a binary file (bear that in mind if you e-mail or FTP it somewhere). Sauceboy must now import that into his keystore by running a command like this:

```
keytool -import -alias linden -file linden.cert -keystore sauceboystore

Enter keystore password:  sauce99
Owner: CN=Peter van der Linden, OU=code grinding shop, O=AFU (Cayman
Islands) Inc., L
=Silicon Valley, ST=California, C=US
Issuer: CN=Peter van der Linden, OU=code grinding shop, O=AFU (Cayman
Islands) Inc.,
L=Silicon Valley, ST=California, C=US
Serial number: 364f53f0
Valid from: Sun Nov 15 14:21:36 PST 1998 until: Sat Feb 13 14:21:36 PST
1999
Certificate fingerprints:
         MD5:  E8:83:20:2C:99:5E:AD:25:82:F7:28:B4:96:05:F5:8E
         SHA1: CA:EE:D3:1D:D3:A2:00:0E:E7:C8:0E:CC:8D:06:FC:76:E7:2E:6A:3D
Trust this certificate? [no]:  y
```

The certificate fingerprints can be used to check that there has been no monkey-business with the certificate. You can read the expected fingerprints on a company letterhead, or off its annual report, or confirm them by phone. Don't check them by going to the company web site, though.

Step 6: Set up a Security Policy for the User, Allowing Signed Code

The person who wishes to run the signed code (sauceboy, in this example) must now set up a policy file allowing this runtime permission. The policy file is an ASCII file that associates URLs with code signers, with code, and with permissions. You can edit the file manually, but there is a GUI utility in JDK 1.2 to help you. The utility is called policytool, so start it up by typing that name. It has the same kind of elementary look and feel as early versions of Netscape. You can't type directly into text fields; you have to select them from the menu first.

Start policytool and a main window will come up. Using the "Edit" -> "Change KeyStore" menu, type in the new keystore URL for the sauceboy keystore that we created in step 5. Note that the keystore is accessed by an URL, so it can be located anywhere on the Internet (or more likely, your private intranet). Also enter "File" -> "Save as" and enter the pathname for where you want the policy file to go. The screen will look like Figure 25-4.

That takes care of reading the contents of sauceboy's keystore. Now we need to add a policy entry for the precise permission we want to grant. Press the button marked "Add Policy Entry" to bring up the policy entry screen.

The policy entry screen has two text fields at the top, "CodeBase" and "SignedBy." If we enter a URL in the codebase field, we are saying that the permission applies to code that arrives from that codebase. Thus, you might enter "http://java.sun.com" to apply a permission to all applets that you browse on the Sun Java web site. If you leave the field blank, it means the permission you are about to specify applies to all code, regardless of where it comes from.

The second text field "SignedBy" identifies who signed the code. We need to enter the alias that we used to identify the linden certificate when we entered it into the sauceboy keystore. If you look back a couple of pages, you'll see we just used the string "linden."

"Code signed by linden" is shorthand for saying," Code in a class file contained in a JAR file, where the JAR file was signed using the private key corresponding to the public key that appears in a keystore certificate in an entry aliased by linden." Phew!

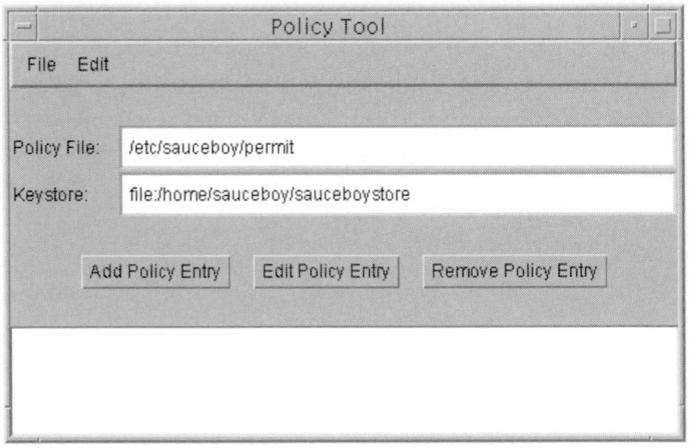

Figure 25–4 The Policy Tool utility.

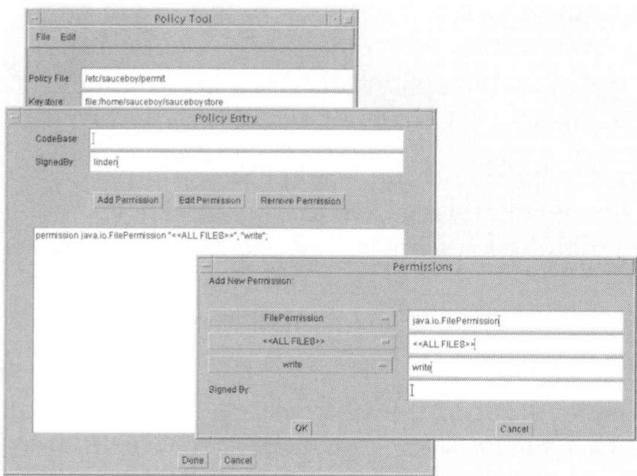

Figure 25–5
Setting up security.

You then click the "add permission" button and select the appropriate permission, what it applies to, and the level of access. The permissions are listed back in Table 25-2. The screen resembles Figure 25-5.

The "Target" is the file or directory to which you want to apply the permission. The "Action" is the kind of access: read, write, execute, delete. Finish up by clicking "Done" and saving the file.

Take a look at the policy file, and you will see something like this:

```
/* AUTOMATICALLY GENERATED ON Sun Nov 15 16:31:02 PST 1998*/
/* DO NOT EDIT */

keystore "file:/home/sauceboy/sauceboystore";

grant signedBy "linden" {
  permission java.io.FilePermission "<<ALL FILES>>", "write";
};
```

By the time this book gets into the hands of readers, more browsers are expected to support configurable applet security. One need is to be able to configure browsers to accept or refuse certain X.509 certificates. You'll want to be able to tell your browser, "Accept applets that are accompanied by certificates from these five companies, and ask me explicitly about any others."

Step 7: Run the Code Using the Policy File

The final step is to execute the code, like so:

```
appletviewer -J-Djava.security.policy=file:/etc/sauceboy/permit write.html
```

The "-J" option tells the appletviewer to pass the option that follows to the JVM.

The applet will run, and the file will be written successfully to the local filesystem.

Some Light Relief—Software About Nothing

Anyone who has had to do "booth duty" at a computer exhibition knows the problem: Software is nebulous stuff, and very hard to demonstrate. Take a compiler for example. You don't really have anything to show that is going to make people gasp in astonishment. You type a command-line, the compiler runs and creates an object file, and that's it. The problem is even worse for utility and system administration software. There's just plain nothing to see.

A software company based in southern California, Syncronys Softcorp, took this concept to the limit (and then took one step further) with SoftRAM95, a best-selling Windows product. An advertisement on page 81 of the December 1995 issue of *Wired* read:

> double click.
>
> double memory.
>
> Doubling RAM doesn't have to be hard. Install SoftRAM95 and instantly speed up Windows 95 and Windows 3.0 and higher. Run multimedia and RAM hungry applications. Open more applications simultaneously. Say good-bye to 'Out-of-Memory' messages. 4MB becomes at least 8MB. 8MB becomes at least 16MB. Get the idea? (In fact, you can get up to 5 times more memory.) SoftRAM95 works with all 386 and higher desktops and laptops. PC Novice calls SoftRAM the 'real RAM doubler for Windows.'
>
> Executive summary: Don't Run Windows Without It."

The trade press named SoftRAM95 as the hottest-selling utility for Windows 95. More than 600,000 people bought SoftRAM95 and Syncronys's stock price shot up from $.03 a share in March 1995 to $32 a share just five months later. SoftRAM95 works like this in action (see Figure 25-6).

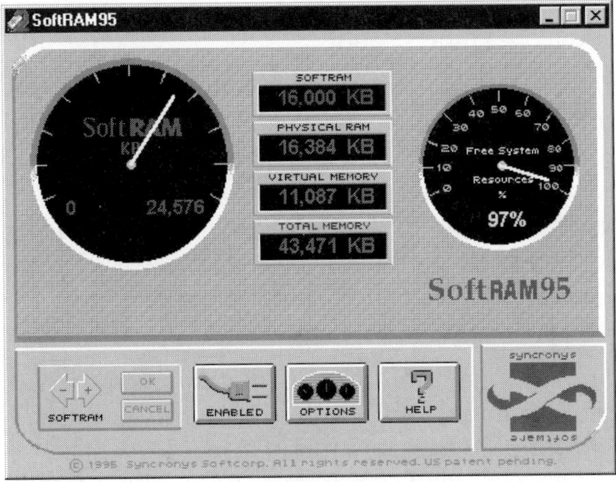

Figure 25–6
SoftRAM95: Just a pretty face.

I don't mean "SoftRAM95 *looks* like this picture in a book"— I mean "SoftRAM95 *works* like this picture in a book. It looks pretty but it does nothing." The program was on the market for several months and sold hundreds of thousands of copies before word started to get out that the emperor had no clothes.

SoftRAM95 was based on an earlier Syncronys Windows 3.1 program that also did nothing. However, it featured a really slick control panel that reported on the amount of memory present and the extra resources that the software said it was providing. The trade press was initially full of favorable reports, but careful consumers noticed that the dials read the same whether or not the Syncronys libraries were on the system, which tended to cast doubt on whether the control panel was reporting what the system was doing, or what it wanted users to *think* the system was doing.

The jig only started to unravel well after SoftRAM was a big hit in the market. Three independent tests reported that SoftRAM did not work as advertised, and in fact did not work at all. It did not speed up Windows. It did not double memory. The software did not do anything at all. *PC Magazine*'s technical editor Larry Seltzer reported, "I've never seen a product that was so devoid of value as SoftRAM. After careful testing, we found no evidence that SoftRAM95 performs any of the main functions it claims to perform."

Amazingly, the product continued to sell in boatloads, and with a list price of $79.95, Syncronys was reluctant to admit that the only effect of the software was a placebo effect. Syncronys's reseller in Germany actually sued German computer magazine, *c't*, which was the first to report that SoftRAM didn't work as advertised. At first, Syncronys circulated a favorable report done by XXCAL labs, claiming that the report "confirmed that SoftRAM95 effectively doubles Random Access Memory (RAM)." After criticism continued to mount, Syncronys issued a press release in October 1995 that admitted, "RAM compression is not being delivered to the operating system." Syncronys glossed over the critical fact that the software didn't even attempt any compression of memory, so of course it couldn't deliver anything at all to the operating system.

At last the Federal Trade Commission began to ask a few half-hearted questions of Syncronys, which announced in December 1995 that it was recalling SoftRAM and would credit or refund purchasers. Even then Syncronys didn't give up, and wrote to its distributors saying that it would soon be relaunching SoftRAM and creating a version for the Macintosh. And in June 1996 Syncronys had its lawyers warn *Dr. Dobbs Journal* over an upcoming review of SoftRAM 95. *Dr. Dobbs Journal* wasn't intimidated and went ahead and printed the truth in its August 1996 issue without further ado.

Finally, the FTC brought a complaint against Syncronys. It was settled by Syncronys agreeing "not to make representations about the performance, attributes, benefits, or effectiveness of SoftRAM, SoftRAM95, or any substantially similar product unless the representations were true and substantiated." In other words,

Syncronys siphoned millions from unwary customers, and got away clean with a slap on the wrist. In a news story reporting the consent decree, Syncronys CEO Rainer Poertner was quoted as saying that SoftRAM for Windows 3.x "always worked perfectly." I suppose it depends on your definition of "perfectly." While the program perfectly delivered a lot of cash into Syncronys's bank account, it certainly didn't deliver the memory benefits claimed for it.

Syncronys had perhaps the biggest of the best-selling programs that do nothing, but they are by no means alone in the field. Right now there is a vendor hawking "security" software that supposedly safeguards your system against hostile Java applets. They're using all the same tools to keep the software on the market: lawyers letters, favorable test reports from "independent" labs, press releases, and so on. And the software has just as much use. Hostile Java applets don't exist; because of the security measures in place from the first Java release, about the worst that a cracker can do in a Java applet is a "denial of service" attack—chew up CPU cycles that don't belong to him.

Jerry Seinfeld used to take great pride in his comedy show, saying it was "a show about nothing." Sometimes life does imitate art. Syncronys had a best-selling Windows product that bore the "Designed for Windows 95" logo that did absolutely nothing.

Addendum: In the summer of 2000, Syncronys's stock nose-dived to less than one-tenth of a cent. When I last checked their website, it had been taken over by an adult content operator. I was curious to find out who. A reverse DNS look-up showed it was being operated from an address in Yerevan, Armenia. Why am I not surprised?

Further References

Applied Cryptography, 2nd edition by Bruce Schneier. (John Wiley and Sons, New York, NY, 1996), ISBN 0-471-11709-9 (paperback).

> A wonderful book. The author has gone to considerable trouble to explain a complicated mathematical topic so that any programmer can follow it. More technical books should be written like it.
>
> There is more information on Java Security at *java.sun.com/security,* which is Sun's Java security home page.
>
> The Java documentation has some information which, if you installed the documentation, will be at file:/c:/jdk1.4/docs/guide/security/index.html.

Chapter 26

Relational Databases and SQL

In the first half of this chapter we'll look at the most widely used kind of database, the relational database. We'll examine the model for using it, and we'll introduce some of the special terms that database experts use. We will work through a couple of small examples to show the techniques that apply equally well to much larger databases. The second half of the chapter is a primer on SQL, the specialized programming language used to talk to a database and update information in it. We'll look at the way you create database tables and populate them with data. Then we'll describe the SQL statements to extract, update, and remove information from a database. SQL has its own data types and operators, presented here. All this will prepare us to use JDBC, the Java library that supports

access to databases, in the following chapter. If you are already well versed in databases and SQL, you can safely go straight on to the next chapter now.

The JDBC library is one of the most important Java libraries, right up there with the XML library and the servlet library. JDBC solves a problem that has previously been a drawback to all other database programming approaches, namely, platform lock-in. When you write your database access code in Java using JDBC, your database can easily be moved to another database vendor and another OS environment. If you outgrow the capacities of either of these, it's straightforward to trade up to a more capable platform with minimal or no changes to your software. If you want to change database vendors for any reason, your software is easily portable to the new environment.

Database programming is a central part of modern enterprise software systems. All professional programmers should understand the basics. This chapter gives you a solid grounding in programming database queries in SQL. JDBC uses SQL to do its work. We focus on SQL here and defer the Java part to the next chapter.

Introduction to Relational Databases

A database is a structured collection of data. It may be anything from a simple list of members of a sports club, to the inventory of a store, or the huge amounts of information in a corporate network. To retrieve and update data stored in a computer database, you need database management software. There are several approaches to database software architecture: relational, hierarchical, and Codasyl network. Here, we'll focus on relational databases, which have become the most widely used approach by far. They are simpler to understand, to implement, and to program.

Like so many of the best ideas in computer science (e.g., TCP/IP, HTTP, XML, ethernet, sockets, or the JVM), relational databases are based on a simple fundamental concept. The idea behind relational databases is that you can organize your data into tables. Other approaches to databases have tried to keep everything in one big repository. Having individual tables that keep the related pieces of data together simplifies the design and programming. It also adds speed and flexibility to the implementation.

What specifically do we mean by a "table"? We mean the data can be represented in tabular form with columns that all contain values of one type, and where a row holds the related data on one thing (one customer, one account, one order, one product, etc.). The table format is a logical, not a physical, organization. Under the covers, the database management software will typically store the data in indexed files and cache it in memory in tree structures when the program is running. But it will always present the appearance of tables to your programs.

Table 26-1 shows some (fictional) people, their age, favorite bands, and where they live.

Table 26–1 The "People and Music" Table

Name	Age	Lives in	Listens To
Robert Bellamy	24	England	Beatles
Robert Bellamy	24	England	Abba
Robert Bellamy	24	England	Oasis
Judith Brown	34	Africa	Muddy Ibe
Judith Brown	34	Africa	Abba
Butch Fad	53	USA	Metallica
Timothy French	24	Africa	Oasis
Timothy French	24	Africa	Nirvana
Grayham Downer	59	Africa	Beatles

There are some special database terms that go with tables. A single row of data is known as a *tuple,* or more commonly a *record* or *row.* It's effectively a set of data that belong together in some way. In our first table, the record (Robert Bellamy, 24, England, Beatles) is saying that the age, place, and music preferences are those of Robert Bellamy. The second record stores another music preference for Robert: he also listens to Abba. The name of the data in a column is called an *attribute.* Age is an attribute here. An attribute is the term for an individual field of a record.

A *domain* is the set of allowable values for an attribute. An example domain for the age attribute could be "integers between 0 and 125." The domain is a constraint on the values of the attribute. A *relation* is (informally) a table with columns and rows. The number of attributes in a relation (i.e., how many fields a record has) is called its *degree.* The number of tuples in a relation (i.e., the number of data records you have in it) is called its *cardinality.* If math scares you, you can forget this paragraph, but it's how database maestros talk to each other at conferences. We'll prefer the more widely used terms of record, column, etc. from this point.

We have special terms for all these things because they are mathematical concepts. Relational databases are based on the mathematical concepts known as set theory and predicate logic. People often think that the "relational" part of the name comes because we store related things together. Actually, it is because the architecture uses mathematical relations that say how one group of data is associated with another. There is a formal underpinning to our data manipulation, and it can be proved that certain operations will yield the correct result, are equivalent to some longer operation, and so on. To make certain that our databases remain true to the mathematics, these qualities are required to be true at all times:

- Each table has a different name from all the others in the database.
- Each column has a different name from all the others in the database.
- Each row has a different value from all the others in the table. There is no duplicate data in a table.
- Each "cell" (attribute) in a table contains exactly one value.
- The order in which the rows and columns appear has no significance. To make order be significant, you create a new column to relate two rows instead.
- Values of a column are all from the same domain, i.e., if a column starts off representing age, it doesn't suddenly change into salary halfway through a table.

Referring to Table 26-1, say we want to find all the people who live in Africa and listen to Abba. We simply look at each record and compare the "Lives in" and "Listens to" attributes, printing out the ones that match "Africa" and "Abba,"

respectively. It works well for this query, but there are some big disadvantages to storing the data all in one table. If someone moves out of the country, we have to find every record in which their name appears and update it. As we are going through the database trying to update records, we have to lock out other read attempts to stop them seeing inconsistent data. Because so much data is duplicated, our storage needs will be bigger, and all programs which run against the database will take longer. The amount of data here is very small, but keep in mind that all the sizes scale up. A company could easily have a database containing hundreds of tables, some of which have millions of rows.

The recommended approach to designing databases is to try to minimize the amount of data duplication. You try to have one relation for each kind of entity (customer, employee, order, cd catalog, shipment, etc.) and store in there only the attributes directly associated with that kind of entity, not every possible attribute it has. In this case, we will probably create a couple of tables, such as Table 26-2.

Table 26–2 The "Person" Table

Name	Age	Lives in
Robert Bellamy	24	England
Grayham Downer	59	Africa
Timothy French	24	Africa
Butch Fad	53	USA
Judith Brown	34	Africa

In Table 26-3, we store attributes called "Name" and "Music Group Name." There, each record represents a person and a group that they listen to regularly.

Table 26–3 The "Listens To" Table

Name	Music Group Name
Robert Bellamy	Beatles
Robert Bellamy	Abba
Robert Bellamy	Oasis
Butch Fad	Metallica
Judith Brown	Muddy Ibe
Judith Brown	Abba
Timothy French	Oasis
Timothy French	Nirvana
Grayham Downer	Beatles

Do you see what we have done? We have "factored out" the common data of name, age, and lives in into one table, leaving name and music group name in Table 26-3. Now when Robert Bellamy moves to the USA, that information only needs to be updated in exactly one record. The data in "Listens To" is related to the data in "Person" by matching the name attribute. If Robert stops listening to Abba, we can delete that row without also dropping Robert, his age, and his country from the database.

We will be using these tables with this data for the rest of the chapter, so you may want to turn the corner of the page down so you can easily refer back to this section. Now we dive into some low-level details for a few paragraphs. You need these terms to understand how to use SQL, so don't go on until you have understood it.

Primary and Foreign Keys

Every table must and will have an attribute (or group of attributes together) that uniquely identifies a record. This attribute or group of attributes is called the *primary key* to the table. By "uniquely identify a record," we mean that no other record has the same value for that attribute or group of attributes. The primary key to our Person table is the "Name" attribute. We can never allow two different people to have the same name in this small database, although that is an unrealistic restriction in real life. That's why banks and other agencies identify you by social security number or an account number, which is guaranteed to be unique.

In our "Listens To" table, we need both attributes to uniquely identify a record. People who like two bands are in there once for each band, so name is not unique. And since several people can listen to the same band, music group names are duplicated too. But the combination of person name plus music group name is unique. So the primary key to our "Listens To" table is both these attributes.

As well as primary keys, many tables contain foreign keys. These are attributes in one table that are a primary key in some other table. The "Listens To" table has a foreign key of Name, which is the primary key for Person. The Person table does not contain any foreign keys. Although it has the Name attribute, that is only part of the key for the "Listens To" table, not the whole key. It's called a "foreign" key because it is not a key in this table, but a table in some other place.

When you have a value of a foreign key, for instance, "Judith Brown" in the "Listens To" table, that value *must* also occur in the table for which it is the primary key. In other words, there must be a "Judith Brown" entry in the Person table. In fact, the purpose of keys is to be able to get to related data in other tables. Keys are how we navigate through the database. When the foreign key existence requirement is met, then the database is said to have *referential integrity.* You keep referential integrity in a database by being careful about the data you remove. If you drop a customer account because of lack of activity, you must also drop all references to that customer in all tables in your database. The onus is on the programmer to keep referential integrity; the database cannot do it for you. If your database lacks referential integrity, you'll get funny results when you try to extract data from more than one table together.

There are two other forms of integrity that databases need: entity integrity and database integrity. If you don't have a value for some attribute, perhaps because you are still acquiring data for that table, there is a special value called "null" that can be assigned. Null doesn't mean zero. It means "no value has yet been assigned." An expression involving null evaluates to null. We could use null in the age column, when someone does not wish to give us their age. We must never use null in any column that is part of a primary or foreign key. This is referred to as *entity integrity.* The entity integrity rule ensures that all our keys are always valid keys.

To understand *database integrity* think of an update to a database that moves money from one account to another. There will probably be a relation for each of the different accounts. You need to write a statement that deducts the money from the first account, and a second statement that adds that sum to the second account. You want to be absolutely sure that either both statements are executed or neither of them are. You never want to be in a situation where the money was deducted but not paid in to the second account. If you have a way to group statements and ensure that the whole transaction either occurs or does not occur, you can maintain database integrity.

1-Many, Many-Many Relationships

Let's say more about the relationship between a foreign key and the table where it is a primary key. That relationship can be 1-to-1, 1-to-many, or many-to-many. A 1-1 relationship says that the two things are matched exactly (it's a special case of a 1-many relationship, too). The relationship between ship and captain is 1-1. Each ship has one captain, and each captain has one ship (ignoring real world details like captains waiting for a command, etc.). As you might guess, a 1-many relationship means that one thing in this table corresponds to potentially many things in that table. Each individual ship has multiple sailors, so the ship/crew member relationship is 1-many. All the sailors on a given ship will have the same value for the "is a crewmember of" attribute. The "1" side of a 1-many relationship will be a primary key, as shown in Figure 26-1. The ship's name would be a primary key in the table of a shipping line's fleet.

Many-many relationships occur when multiple records in the first table are somehow related to multiple records in the second table. We can see what this means if we introduce a "MusicGroup" table that is a list of bands. We could store any band-specific information in it too, such as the "land of origin" for each music group. Take, for example, Table 26-4.

Table 26–4 The "MusicGroup" Table

Music Group Name	Land of Origin
Beatles	England
Abba	Sweden
Oasis	England
Metallica	USA
Muddy Ibe	Africa
Nirvana	USA

Now our database has tables that hold a many-many relationship. Some people listen to several bands, and other bands are listened to by several people. That's a many-to-many relationship between the Person and MusicGroup tables. Many-to-many relationships can't be processed directly in relational databases (though it's clearly possible to create the table). The reason is that a primary key can only link tables on a one-to-many basis. Unless you take other steps, the restriction on many-many means we cannot make direct queries based on band name (e.g., "who listens to a given band?"). That may be acceptable if you never want to make that kind of query, but you want to build flexibility into your designs, not rule it out.

Stating the many-many limitation in terms of Java code, you can think of a primary key as being like the index variable in a Java "for" loop. It lets you process the whole table without missing any rows out, or considering any primary keys twice. Many-many would be like resetting the index variable several times in the looping. Luckily, there is an easy way to get over the restriction that many-many relationships can't be processed directly. You resolve many-many relationships by adding a new table that can express the relationship in terms of two 1-many tables.

We simply need a new table that, for each band, has a record for each person who listens to it. That new table is on the "many" end of a 1-many relationship with the MusicGroup table. The new table must also have for each person, a record for each band they listen to. So the new table will also be on the "many" end of a 1-many relationship with the Person table. And that's an exact description of our existing ListensTo table! (Of course, the design was chosen with this in mind). Each name there is related to several music group names, and each music group is related to several names. You can see that Robert is associated with the Beatles, Abba, and Oasis, while Oasis is associated with Timothy and Robert.

Using the ListensTo table we represent the many-many relationship between MusicGroup and Person. We can now do the SQL equivalent of "for each MusicGroupName in MusicGroup table, find the matching MusicGroupName in the ListensTo table, and print out the person name." This new table allows us to do queries by band. To summarize, we resolve many-many relationships in a relational database by decomposing them into two 1-many relationships, adding a new table as needed.

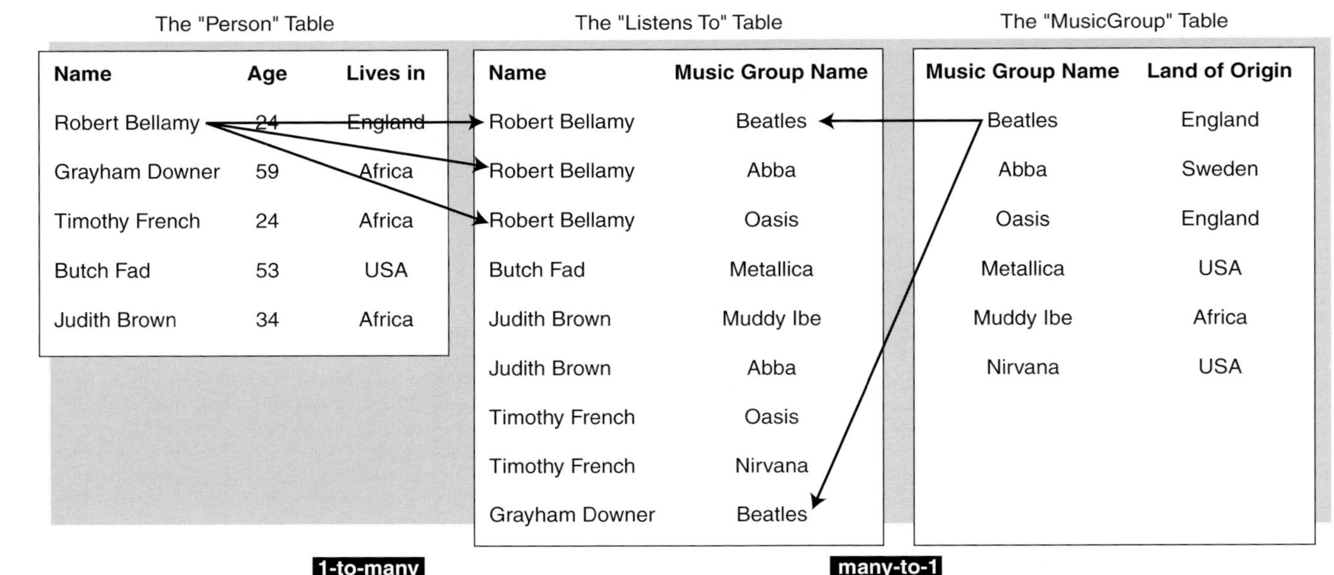

Figure 26–1 Breaking up a many-many relationship: "Many people listen to many bands."

Normal Forms

Tables need to follow a set of numbered rules known as "normal form." First normal form says that all attributes must be atomic. That means there can be no lists of items in an attribute. You can't have an attribute that is "contents of a shopping cart," because that could contain several items. Atomic means "only one, and it cannot be subdivided any further."

Second normal form says that it is in first normal form and every non-key attribute depends fully on the key. The Person table has non-key attributes of "age" and "lives in" and both of these are completely dependent on the person we are identifying by the name attribute. However, if we added a column to the table to store, say, the land of origin of the band, we would be breaking second normal form. The band's land does not depend on the primary key (the person name).

A table is in third normal form if it is in second normal form and all non-key columns are mutually independent. In the Person table, the non-key columns are "age" and "lives in." These are mutually independent because they can change without affecting the other. If we were to add a column to store "is a minor" data in Person, the table would no longer be in third normal form. Whether or not someone is a minor depends on their age, which is another attribute in the Person relation.

If you find your table designs break a normal form rule, you can always fix it by adding an extra table as we did above to resolve a many-many relationship. You may need to move columns from one table to another or to add an identification number to a couple of tables to relate records between them. Raw data can always be put into third normal form. There are additional normal forms beyond this, but third normal form is enough for most purposes. If you make sure all your tables are in third normal form, you will be able to use relational database operations on them and get the right results. A database that has been designed to be in third normal form is said to be "normalized." There's a great memory aid for the form in which you want your tables: the data in a table has to *depend on the key, the whole key, and nothing but the key.*

Relational Database Glossary

Table 26-5 is a glossary of terms that you can review and refer to as necessary. There are a few terms in here that appear later in the chapter.

Table 26–5 Relational Database Glossary

Name	Description
attribute	a column in a table, e.g., the "Name" attribute
cardinality	The number of tuples in a relation
database integrity	You maintain database integrity by grouping statements in a "transaction" that is either executed as a whole, or has no part of it executed
degree	The number of attributes in a relation
domain	The set of permissible values for an attribute
entity integrity	The requirement that key attributes never contain a null
first normal form	A table in which all attributes consist of exactly one data item
foreign key	The attribute or group of attributes in one table that form a primary key for some other table
join	An operation that combines the data in two or more tables by using foreign keys in the first table to access related data in a subsequent table. This is an "inner join" or "equijoin"
prepared statement	An SQL statement which is cached in native code form to allow faster processing
primary key	The attribute or group of attributes that together uniquely identify a record in a table
referential integrity	The requirement that all foreign keys are present in the table where they are a primary key
relation	A table in a relational database. It corresponds to a file of records
relational database	A collection of relations in third normal form
second normal form	A table is in second normal from when it is in first normal form and also every non-key attribute depends on the primary key
stored procedure	A group of related SQL statements which are kept in precompiled form, and can be invoked just like a method call
third normal form	A table is in third normal form when it is in second normal form and also all non-key attributes are independent of each other
trigger	A trigger is an SQL statement that is stored in the database, and that executes automatically when a specified event occurs in the database, such as a column update. It will usually be some kind of automatic delete, insert, or update of some other attribute
tuple	A tuple is a row of related data in a table. It is essentially a record of related data

Once we have our tables, SQL is the language we use to access and process them. The JDBC library is a way of connecting to a database, shipping it SQL statements, and getting back the results in a form that Java can process. In this section we will present a primer on SQL, showing the highlights of the language for those who have never seen it before. If you are already familiar with SQL, you can safely skip this section.

At first, every database vendor had its own special database query language. Users eventually got fed up enough to create an industry standard around IBM's SQL. There was the SQL'89 standard, followed by the SQL'92 standard, both created under the umbrella of ANSI (American National Standards Institute). SQL version 3 was published in 1999, and is known as "SQL:1999" or SQL-3. SQL is also a FIPS standard, FIPS PUB 127-2. FIPS is a Federal Information Processing Standard issued with the full weight and authority of the U.S. Government, after approval by the Secretary of Commerce. In practice, SQL is fragmented with many slightly incompatible dialects from database vendors. In this chapter we keep to the current ANSI standard and do not present any vendor-specific code. You should follow the same practice in your programs too.

Basic SQL Primer

SQL is an abbreviation for "Structured Query Language" and is a programming language in its own right. It's usually pronounced like the word "sequel" or spelled out as individual letters s-q-l. SQL is specialized for its application area, and is not used for general purpose programming. But all of the operations that you are likely to want to do to a database are built-in functions in SQL. One attractive feature of the language is that you express what you want to do in English-like text such as this. By convention, the SQL keywords are written in uppercase. They need not be.

```
SELECT name FROM Person
     WHERE lives_in = 'Africa'
     ORDER BY name;
```

In other words, you describe the results you want, not the steps to carry out to get them. This style of programming is known as "functional programming" and it contrasts with the "procedural programming" of more familiar languages like Java. Because you don't give the steps to get what you want, database implementors are free to find the most efficient way to get it. The big database companies put a lot of effort into their query optimizers, and this is one of the big advantages of SQL over earlier query languages.

The designers of SQL could have chosen to make programmers express the operations in terms of mathematical formulae or algebra, instead of words. That would make programs harder to read for many people and raise an unnecessary barrier to learning and teaching. Executing the above SQL statement on our Person table would yield a result set of:

Grayham Downer

Judith Brown

Timothy French

So far we have outlined the way a relational database stores data and extracts it from a single table. The power of the technology comes from the flexible way you can extract and combine data from several tables to create new tables. It's a little contrived to show this in a small example, so keep in mind that this works equally well on the huge datasets common in industry, and the benefits are proportionately larger.

There are four categories of SQL statement:

- CREATE and INSERT to create tables and put records into them
- SELECT to query the database and get back data that matches your criteria
- UPDATE to change the values in existing records
- DELETE and DROP to remove records and tables from the database

There is a surprisingly rich variety of options that can be added to these statements, allowing a large amount of work to be done with a few simple English phrases. JDBC issues SQL commands by putting them in a String, and passing that String to various methods in the JDBC library. So to program in JDBC we need to know what the SQL phrases look like. Or to put it another way, you don't have to learn another database language if you know SQL. So why bother with JDBC and Java at all? Because you want to do something with the data you pull out of the database: send it to a client, wrap an email around it, mark it up with XML, and so on. Java is frequently the best way to do that something.

These SQL statements are powerful, but they seem to have been designed in a way that makes it very hard to present them in an easy-to-read format! So they are shown here in terms of a template, which is annotated on the right-hand side with some additional remarks. If you try to show the formal grammar for SQL, it explodes in size and gets in the way of clarity. Even so, it's a bit of work to show the four different kinds of statement. You may want to make one quick pass through the remainder of this section, and then come back to it when you need specific information.

Creating and Populating Tables

The CREATE statement is used to create a new table, and the INSERT statement is used to add a new record to a table.

The CREATE statement has this general format:

Format of SQL CREATE Statement — **Additional Information**

```
CREATE TABLE tablename(
     colName  dataType              <— can repeat this line, separated by commas
optionalConstraint
);
```

Here is an example of the use of the CREATE statement:

Example of SQL CREATE Statement — **Additional Information**

```
CREATE TABLE Person (
        name      VARCHAR(100) PRIMARY KEY,   "PRIMARY KEY" is a
        age       INTEGER,                    constraint
        lives_in  VARCHAR(100)
);
```

This statement will create the Person table that we saw earlier in the chapter. It will have three columns called "name," "age," and "lives in." The "optional-Constraint" above means that you can add or omit a constraint to a column, giving more information about what kind of values are legal there. We have added a constraint to the "name" column, saying that this is the primary key of the table. That has the effect of making sure that records always have a non-null unique value there when the records are inserted into the table. "Not null" and "unique" are also constraints that can be applied individually.

Some datatypes that SQL understands and the corresponding Java types are shown in Table 26-6. The SQL keywords and datatypes can use any letter case. The convention is to write them all in uppercase.

Table 26–6 Some SQL Datatypes

SQL Datatype	Corresponding Java Type
`CHAR(`*n*`)`	`String, exactly` *n* `chars`
`VARCHAR(`*n*`)`	`String, up to` *n* `chars`
`INTEGER` *or* `INT`	`int`
`DOUBLE`	`double`
`DATE`	`java.sql.Date`
`TIMESTAMP`	`java.sql.Timestamp`
`BLOB`	`java.sql.Blob`
`ARRAY`	`java.sql.Array`
`DECIMAL, NUMERIC`	`java.math.BigDecimal`

The BLOB datatype means "Binary Large Object." There are also CLOBs, "Character Large Objects." SQL arrays are sequences of data. Think back to earlier in the chapter where we said that first normal form means that there are no lists of items in an attribute. There's a question of where you draw the line though. If you are recording student marks over 12 weeks of homework assignments, it's overkill to store each mark in a new record. Instead, we'll have a student/course marks record, and the course marks will be held as a fixed length array that gets updated with a new mark each week. BLOBs, CLOBs, and arrays are represented by classes in the java.sql package, and they have methods to get their values.

The CREATE statement just creates an empty table. As yet it has no records in it. We will put records in using the INSERT statement, which has this general appearance:

Format of SQL INSERT Statement | **Additional Information**

```
INSERT INTO tablename
    (colName1  ,colName2  ,colName3 ...)
    VALUES
    (value1    ,value2    ,value3 ...)
;
```

<— can provide a value for all attributes or just some

<— can repeat this line, separated by commas these values are inserted into the attributes listed

Here is an example of the use of the INSERT statement:

Examples of SQL INSERT Statement | **Additional Information**

```
INSERT INTO Person ( name, age, lives in )
    VALUES ('Robert Bellamy', 24, 'England' ),
           ( 'Grayham Downer', null, 'Africa' ),
           ( 'Judith Brown', 34, 'Africa' );
```

Note the use of single quotes to surround a String

Downer doesn't want to give his age

This statement will start to populate (fill in with data) the Person table that we saw earlier in the chapter. The values are inserted into the record in the order in which the attributes are named. The number of values given in each of the value lists should match the number of attributes in the list before the "values" keyword. SQL is very picky about the requirement that character strings be enclosed in single quotes.

Note that some database vendors have not implemented support for inserting multiple rows with one statement. So to retain maximum portability you would want to restrict yourself to adding one record per insert statement.

Querying and Retrieving Data

The SELECT statement is used to query a database and get back the data that matches your query.

The SELECT statement has this general format:

Format of SQL SELECT Statement	**Additional Information**
`SELECT`	
`Name1 ,Name2 ,Name3 ...`	*<— can mention one or more columns, or "*" for all columns*
`FROM`	
`tablename1, tableName2, ...`	*<— can mention one or more tables*
`WHERE` `conditions`	*<— the "`WHERE`" clause is optional and can be omitted*
`ORDER BY colNames` `;`	*<— the "`ORDER BY`" clause is optional and can be omitted* *It returns the data sorted by this field*

We have already seen an example of a basic select from a single table. The power of the statement arises when you select from two or more tables at once. So to find all the people in Africa in our database who listen to the Beatles or the band Fela Kuti, we could use the SQL command shown below. Numbers have been added on the left to help with commenting on the code; these will not appear in actual SQL code.

```
1    SELECT Person.name, Person.lives_in, ListensTo.music_group_name
2    FROM Person, ListensTo
3    WHERE ListensTo.music_group_name IN ( 'Fela Kuti', 'Beatles' )
4    AND Person.name = ListensTo.person_name
5    AND Person.lives in = 'Africa' ;
```

Going through the statement line by line, we can make the following observations:

Line 1 gives the columns that we want to get back in our answer. Notice that the table name can be used to qualify the column so that there is no ambiguity.

Line 2 gives the names of the tables that we will be running the query on.

Line 3 starts our "where" clause. It says which data values or rows will be returned as the answer, based on matching the criteria that follow. The first criterion is that the music_group_name must be one of those in the list given. Notice the way you can compare against a list of items in parentheses.

Line 4 adds another condition. It says that whenever we have found one of those two bands, we look for the same name in the Person table.

Line 5 is the final part of the condition. It says that the "lives in" field for that person should hold the value "Africa." Voila, we are done. Running the query produces the output:

```
Grayham Downer, Africa, Fela Kuti
Grayham Downer, Africa, Beatles
Judith Brown, Africa, Fela Kuti
```

Grayham Downer appears in the list twice because he matches the criteria twice. He listens to both the target bands. If you were sending out promotional mail based on this query, you would want to ensure that you did not send two mails to him. Database inquiries frequently have results that may seem surprising if you are not familiar with set theory. The keyword "DISTINCT" after "SELECT" will eliminate duplicate records from being returned to you. If you sent the SQL command:

```
SELECT DISTINCT Person.name
    FROM Person, ListensTo
    WHERE ListensTo.music_group_name IN ( 'Fela Kuti', 'Beatles' )
    AND Person.name = ListensTo.person_name
    AND Person.lives_in = 'Africa' ;
```

The result set will be:

```
Grayham Downer
Judith Brown
```

The significance of primary key and foreign key should now be clearer. You always use a foreign key to relate one table to another. The operation is called "join" because you are merging or joining the data in two or more tables where the data match your conditions. In this case we used person_name which is a foreign key in the ListensTo table and the primary key for the Person table. Because it is a key, that allows us to retrieve the data from Person that corresponds to the name we found in ListensTo. This kind of join is an "inner join" or "equijoin." In set theory terms, it is data that falls in the intersection of the two tables. There are also "outer joins," which get you the data that is in one table, but not the other. These are outside the scope of this basic primer.

Let's elaborate on the conditional selections. You can use all the operators shown in Table 26-7 to compare attributes.

Table 26–7 SQL Comparison Operators

Meaning	SQL Operator	Example
equals	`=`	`WHERE lives_in = 'Africa'`
greater than	`>`	`WHERE age > 39`
less than	`<`	`WHERE age < 21`
greater than or equal	`>=`	`WHERE name >= 'Brown'`
less than or equal	`<=`	`WHERE age <= 65`
not equal to	`<>`	`WHERE name <> 'Brown'`
pattern match	`LIKE`	`WHERE name LIKE '%own'`
matches any of several choices	`IN`	`WHERE age IN (18, 19, 20)`

When you compare a string for being greater than some other string, it does a lexical comparison of the characters. So the name "Crown" is greater than "Brown." The "like" operator is for pattern-matching, and uses a "%" as a wild card. The example shown in the table will match any names that end with "own." There are other operators in SQL. The name we select from a table can be a mathematical function of some column in the table. That's expressed like this:

```
SELECT COUNT(*) FROM Person;
```

That statement gives you the cardinality of the Person table. There are other functions too. Table 26-8 shows some of them. These come after the SELECT keyword, and the entire statement may also have a WHERE clause that restricts the records that are input to the function.

Table 26–8 Some SQL Functions

Meaning	SQL Function	Example
Gives the number of rows satisfying the WHERE condition if present.	`COUNT(*)`	`SELECT COUNT(*) FROM Person;`
Gives the total of the named column, for all rows that meet the condition. This examples adds the ages of people over 21 in our database.	`SUM(col)`	`SELECT SUM(age) FROM Person WHERE age 21;`
Calculates the average of the named column. This example gives the average age of the minors.	`AVG(col)`	`SELECT AVG(age) FROM Person WHERE age < 21;`
Returns the largest value in that column.	`MAX(col)`	`SELECT MAX(age) FROM Person;`
Returns the smallest value in that column.	`MIN(col)`	`SELECT MIN(age) FROM Person;`

Subquery Selections

Quite frequently you want to submit a further select on the result of a select. There are several ways to do that, one way being to nest a select statement inside another. A nested select statement is called a subquery. Here is an example of a subquery:

```
SELECT person.name FROM person
WHERE
   person.lives_in IN ('England', 'USA')
AND
   person.name NOT IN
     ( SELECT listens_to.name FROM listens_to
       WHERE
          listens_to.music_group_name = 'Beatles' );
```

The simplest way to understand subqueries is to look at them piece by piece, starting from the innermost nested one. In this case, the nested select statement is:

```
( SELECT listens_to.name FROM listens_to
  WHERE
     listens_to.music_group_name = 'Beatles' );
```

A moment's reading should convince you that this provides a result set of names of people who listen to the Beatles. So substitute that into the entire statement, and we get:

```
SELECT person.name FROM person
WHERE
   person.lives_in IN ('England', 'USA')
AND
   person.name NOT IN ( names-of-people-who-listen-to-Beatles ) ;
```

That can quickly be seen as all the people who live in England or the USA, and who do not listen to the Beatles. Be careful. Excessive use of subqueries results in SQL code that is hard to understand and hard to debug. As an alternative to subqueries you can often create, insert into, select from, and then drop temporary tables. Another alternative is to generate the queries dynamically. That is, to use one query to get the list of names, hold that in a variable, and use that variable in the second query. This will become clearer after reading the next chapter.

SELECT and all the SQL statements have even more features than are shown here, but this is enough to start writing real applications.

Result Set of a SELECT Query

We've seen informally in previous examples how the results of a SELECT statement are returned to you. The results of a query come back in the form of zero, one or more rows, and is called the *result set*. The rows in the result set can be retrieved and examined individually using something called a *cursor*. Just as a GUI cursor marks your position on the screen, a database cursor indicates the row of the result set that you are currently looking at. A cursor is usually implemented as an unsigned integer that holds the offset into the file containing your result set. It has enough knowledge to move forward row by row through the result set.

Database management systems typically provide a cursor to the SQL programmer automatically. The programmer can use it to iterate through the result set. JDBC 2 upgrades the features of a cursor available to Java. Now you can move the cursor backward as well as forward, providing the underlying database supports that. You can also move the cursor to an absolute position (e.g., the fifth row in the result set) or to a position relative to where it is now (e.g., go to the immediate previous record).

We can ask for our result set to come to us sorted by some column or columns. We achieve this by using the "ORDER BY" clause. In this case, it makes sense to use the cursor to ask for the record before the one we are currently looking at. For example, if you order by "billing price" you can go backward until you reach orders under $10. That way, you can process your most valuable orders first, and stop invoicing when the amount is smaller than the cost of processing.

SELECT Pitfalls

Here are some common pitfalls encountered when using the SELECT statement. When you hit an error in your programs in the next chapter, check if it is one of these!

- not surrounding a literal string in single quotes
- only mentioning the tables that you are extracting from in the "from" clause. You need to mention all the tables that you will be looking at in the "where" clause
- failing to specify "distinct," and thus getting duplicate values in certain columns
- failing to leave a space between keywords when creating a Java String on several lines containing SQL

Updating Values

The UPDATE statement is used to change the values in an existing record.

The UPDATE statement has this general format:

Format of SQL UPDATE Statement	Additional Information
`UPDATE tablename`	
`SET`	
`colName1=value1 ,colName2=value2 ...`	*<— can provide a value for all attributes or just some*
`WHERE`	
`colNamei someOperator valuei ...`	*<— can repeat this line, separated by AND or OR*
`;`	

Here is an example of the use of the UPDATE statement:

Example of SQL UPDATE Statement	Additional Information
`UPDATE Person`	
`SET age = 25, lives_in = 'USA'`	*Robert celebrated his birthday by moving to the USA.*
`WHERE name='Robert Bellamy' ;`	

This statement will start to populate (fill in with data) the Person table that we saw earlier in the chapter. The values are inserted into the record in the order in which the attributes are named.

Deleting Records and Tables

The DELETE statement is used to remove records from a table, and the DROP statement is used to completely remove all trace of a table from the database.

The DELETE statement has this general format:

Format of SQL DELETE Statement	Additional Information

`DELETE FROM` *`tablename`*
`WHERE`
`colName someOperator value` `...`
`;`
	<— *can repeat this line, separated by AND/OR to further refine which records get deleted*

If you forget the "where" clause, all records in the table are deleted! A table with no records still exists in the database, and can be queried, updated, etc. To get rid of all traces of a table (not a common operation in most databases), use the DROP statement.

The DROP statement has this general format.

Format of SQL DROP Statement	Additional Information
`DROP TABLE` *`tablename`* `;`	

There is frequently more than one way to write an SQL query. Some of the ways will do less work than other ways. Nowadays it is the database's responsibility to reorder queries for the best performance.

SQL Prepared Statements and Stored Procedures

Prepared statements and *stored procedures* are two different ways of organizing your SQL code and getting it to run faster. When you send an SQL statement to your database, there is an SQL interpreter that reads the statement, figures out what it means and which database files are involved, and then issues the lower level native instructions to carry it out. Depending on what the statement is exactly, it may be quite a lot of work to analyze and interpret it.

If you find that you are issuing a statement over and over again, the database will be doing a lot of work that can be avoided. The way to do this is with a prepared statement. As the name implies, the prepared statement is constructed and sent to the SQL interpreter. The output of the interpreter (the native code instructions) is then saved. The prepared statement can later be reissued, perhaps with different parameters, and it will run much more quickly because the interpretation step has already been done. Does this remind you of anything? This is exactly how Just-In-Time (JIT) Java compilers speed up execution—by compiling to native code and caching the results.

A stored procedure is a similar idea to prepared statements but taken one step further. Instead of caching an individual statement, you can save a whole series of statements as a procedure. A stored procedure will typically implement one entire operation on a database, like adding an employee to all the relevant tables (payroll, department, benefits, social club, etc.). It is typical to provide parameters to a stored procedure; for example, giving the details of the employee who is being added to the company.

The vast majority of database systems support stored procedures, but a major sticking point has been the variation in the exact syntax used. JDBC 2 solves this issue by allowing you to write stored procedures in Java. That means your library of stored procedures is now portable to all databases, which is a major step forward!

This concludes our tour of the concepts of SQL and databases, and we now proceed to the next chapter to look at how Java interfaces to all this.

Further Reading

There is a terrific SQL tutorial written by Frank Torres that includes a server-side script allowing you to submit SQL queries against a small database at *www.sqlcourse.com/*. It is worthwhile to look at this site, which is sponsored by Oracle, the world's premier database management software company. There is a follow-up advanced version of the course at *sqlcourse2.com*. Note that the SQL server at Frank's site doesn't support all of the standard SQL shown in this chapter, but it easily does enough to let you try some SQL now.

If you're interested in the emerging technology known as "object-oriented databases," there is a good paper to read at the Slashdot site. See "*Why Aren't You Using an Object Oriented Database Management System?*" by Dan Obasanjo at *slashdot.org/features/01/05/03/1434242.shtml*.

Exercises

1. Define and give examples of the following database terms: *tuple, attribute, relation.*
2. What does it mean to normalize a database design? Describe first, second, and third normal forms.
3. Review the basic SQL course at *www.sqlcourse.com/* that allows you to formulate and run SQL queries online.
4. Write an SQL statement to display the name and age of everyone in the Person table who is older than 39.
5. Write an SQL statement to display the name of everyone in the Person table who lives in a NATO country and listens to the Beatles. There are 19 member nations of the North Atlantic Treaty Organization, including the USA, UK, Canada, France, Germany, Greece, and Poland. New members join from time to time, so the roll should probably be kept in a table, rather than a set of literals.
6. What is an SQL subquery, and when would you use one?
7. Write an SQL statement to display the name of everyone in the Person table who lives in a NATO country and *does not* listen to the Beatles. Be careful to exclude people who listen to the Beatles, and also listen to other bands as well. The simplest way to do this is to use a subquery.
8. Explain, using examples, the difference between a primary key and a foreign key.

Some Light Relief—Reading the Docs

How do you tell if a user has read the software documentation? If users are anything like us programmers, it's a pretty safe assumption that they have *not* read the documentation. Time is short, and reading manuals is tedious and time-consuming. I knew someone who worked on the support desk for a large internal software application. He cut his workload by 85% using one simple technique. Whenever someone complained about a bug in the software, he asked them which page of the manual it violated before he would investigate it. Most users preferred to live with any bug rather than spend hours tunneling through the manual, and Jenkins's technique saved him a lot of bother, right up until the time he got fired.

Another way of encouraging people to read the manual is to have the program ask "Did you read the manual, answer y/n:" The program won't proceed until it gets the right answer. And neither "yes" nor "no" is the right answer. Somewhere in the manual, buried deep in an obscure paragraph, is the information that this question expects to continue: the answer "foo." But you'll only know that if you read the manual thoroughly.

Are you a student reading this chapter for an "Advanced Java" class? OK, then! Please demonstrate that you have read this chapter by writing your favorite color at the top right of the front sheet of your homework for this chapter. If blue is your favorite color, write "blue." Write "black" if you like black best, etc. Professors: see how many of your students really do the assigned reading.

Chapter 27

JDBC

In this chapter we'll build on the relational database and SQL knowledge from Chapter 26. We'll show how to download and install one of the several excellent open source Java-friendly relational databases available. This will let you run a database management system on your own computer and try the features in practice. The bulk of the chapter to describes JDBC, the Java library that supports access to databases. We'll walk through its classes and the way they are used. We will reuse the data from the previous chapter, involving a database holding the music preferences for a group of people. Finally, we'll show code to create and update a database, and give you the information needed to write more Java-database code yourself.

JDBC is made up of about two dozen Java classes in the package `java.sql`. The classes provide access to relational data stored in a database or other table-oriented form. JDBC works in a similar way to Microsoft's database access library (known as ODBC), but redesigned, simplified, and based on Java, not C. ODBC imposed a single library that let your code interface to any database. If you are familiar with ODBC, JDBC will be a snap to learn. And even if you are not, it's still pretty straightforward. JDBC works with the largest database servers and with the smallest desktop database systems, such as xBase files, FoxPro, MS Access, and mSQL. JDBC can even access text files and Excel spreadsheets using the ODBC bridge. One thing that JDBC doesn't give you, and Microsoft does, is all the forms, GUIs, and visual tools to make it trivial to put together the client interface to small or prototype databases. These kinds of tools are still a third-party opportunity in Java.

JDBC classes allow the programmer to use modern database features like simultaneous connections to several databases, transaction management, precompiled statements with bind variables, calls to stored procedures, and access to metadata in the database dictionary. JDBC supports both static and dynamic SQL (a query or update constructed at runtime). JDBC and SQL greatly simplify deployment issues, because you can now rely on the presence of a set of vendor-independent standard Java interfaces for queries and updates to your relational database.

Downloading and Installing the Software

A major goal of this chapter is to give readers the means to actually try some hands-on relational database programming. That's an ambitious goal, because relational databases are industrial-strength and industrial-sized pieces of software. Up until a few years ago, the only choice in a database management system was which of the commercial vendors would you buy from. More recently, the explosion of interest in open source software has led to a much larger number of choices, some of which require no financial outlay. Tables 27-1 and 27-2 show some popular commercial and non-commercial products and their characteristics.

There are some truly excellent databases which are available for free download over the Internet. Some of them even come with the source code, which provides additional learning opportunities. The last three in Table 27-2 are all implemented completely in Java and run on any up-to-date JVM. The first three products are only available on certain platforms.

The Mckoi database software is used as the example here because it comes with example programs, has good documentation, and is very easy to get running. Mckoi is largely the work of talented English programmer Toby Downer, backed by his employer Diehl and Associates who support the goals of the open source movement. This chapter was written using the 0.89 beta release of McKoi, and that software is on the CD. You should check the Mckoi website, download any more up-to-date release, and adapt to any changes in installation, pathnames, etc. Toby made this software open source so that others will have the chance to learn from his work. Take that opportunity! People get to be expert programmers by spending a lot of time reading code from others.

To get started, go to the Mckoi website at

```
www.mckoi.com/database
```

Click on the "latest version" link under "Download the software." You can download the zip file to your C:\ top level directory. It is less than 1.5MB in size, so it downloads quite quickly. You could instead copy the version 0.89 beta release from the CD to your disk. After the mckoi zip file is on your disk, unpack its contents using a command like this:

```
cd c:\
jar -xvf mckoi0.89b.zip
```

Table 27–1 Some Commercial Databases

Company	Product	Product Attributes	Website	Java Support
Oracle	Oracle 9i family	Supports even very large datasets, and also effective for small businesses. Available for Solaris and Windows.	www.oracle.com	full support
IBM/Informix	DB2, Informix	Large capacity, multi-platform database.	www.ibm.com	full support
Sybase	Adaptive Server IQ	Large capacity, multi-platform database.	www.sybase.com	full support
Microsoft	SQL server	Runs only on the NT line, limited by the capacity of the underlying PC.	www.microsoft.com	no vendor support
IBM/Informix	Cloudscape	A commercially-supported pure Java database that is included with Java 2 Enterprise Edition. It is the reference implementation of an embedded Java database.	www.informix.com /cloudscape	full support

Table 27–2 Some Non-Commercial Databases

Organization	Software	Product Attributes	Website	Java support
PostgreSQL	PostgreSQL 7.1	Written in C, open source, commercial support available, excellent SQL support. Supports medium to lower end large databases.	www.postgresql.org	full support
MySQL AB	MySQL 3.23	Written in C, open source, commercial support available. Supports small to medium size databases.	www.mysql.com	full support
Hughes Technologies	mSQL	Lightweight relational database, free for non-commercial use.	www.Hughes.com.au/ products/	full support
Diehl & Assoc.	Mckoi SQL database	Written in Java, open source, very easy to start using. Supports small to medium size databases.	www.mckoi.com/database	full support
Lutris Technologies	InstantDB	Written in Java, free, no source, has GUI tools. Supports small to medium size databases.	instantdb.enhydra.org	full support
FFE Software	FirstSQL/J	Written in Java, commercial support available. Supports small to medium size databases.	www.firstsql.com	full support

Jar files have the same format as zip files, so you can also use winzip or another archive extraction utility. The unzip creates a directory called mckoi0.89b containing the database management software (binaries and Java source code), some documentation, and sample programs. You must be running at least JDK 1.2 to use this database. Since Java performance has improved greatly from release to release, I recommend using the latest available JDK that is at the FCS (First Customer Shipment, after a release has finished beta testing) revision level. In Spring 2002, that was JDK 1.4. The installation guide that accompanies the Mckoi release even explains how to rebuild the source code. It is quite straightforward. You would recompile the database if you fixed a bug in its code, or if you wanted to get the performance boost of a more recent JDK release.

Make the Mckoi libraries visible to your java compiler and runtime. There are three jar files in the directory where you just extracted the release. These jar files are:

file name	contents
mckoidb.jar	The database management software
gnu-regexp-1.0.8.jar	GNU regular expression package
mkjdbc.jar	The JDBC driver software

The commands shown here to make the libraries visible to the compiler are for Windows. Make the necessary adjustments for Unix, Linux, Mac, etc. There are at least three alternative ways of making the libraries visible on a Windows system:

- Add the full pathname of the libraries to the $CLASSPATH variable in the autoexec.bat or other start-up file.
- Use the "-classpath" option to the compiler and JVM, and give the pathname to the jar file. At runtime use the "-cp /path/to/jarfile" option. The lengthy commands to compile and run can be put in a batch file.
- Move the jarfile to the ...`\lib\ext` directory of your Java runtime installation. Jar files in here are automatically regarded as part of the standard runtime library. Be careful! This directory might not be where you think it is. On my Windows system, the JDK was installed in c:\jdk1.3. However, the JRE libraries that the system actually uses for execution can be established by using the "-verbose" option on a Java run. Look for the pathnames of where the system libraries are picked up.That shows that (on my system) the JRE libraries are at `c:\program files\javasoft\jre\1.3\lib\ext` and that is where the Mckoi jar files must be put. Your system may be different.

The simplest approach is the first one. The most convenient approach is the third one. You move the library jar files to that special directory, and they are automatically found by the javac and java commands. One disadvantage is that you have to remember to copy them to the same place in any new JDK version you install.

Running the McKoi Database

The Mckoi JDBC driver has two modes of execution—embedded and client/server mode. In embedded mode, the JDBC driver starts the database engine within the current Java Virtual Machine when your program causes the driver to get loaded. Embedded mode is designed for standalone applications that need database functionality. It is "embedded" in the sense that the database is linked to your image as one big program at runtime.

In client/server mode, the JDBC driver uses TCP/IP to communicate with a Mckoi database server running on a remote machine.

For the purposes of this chapter, you can execute the database and sample programs in embedded mode. Embedded mode is slightly simpler to get running as it only involves one computer. If you use the software in a production system, use client/server mode because that supports the use of the JDBCQueryTool or other application using the database while your program is running.

To use embedded mode, simply make the jar files visible in your class path as described above. To use client/server mode, start the database server with this command:

```
java -jar mckoidb.jar
```

Then use this kind of URL for the JDBC connection: "`jdbc:mckoi://host[:port]/`" where host is a DNS hostname, and port is a non-default port that you have configured McKoi to use.

Running the Example Code

The next step is to try running one of the example database programs that accompany the release. Go to the demo directory with this command:

```
cd c:\mckoi0.89b\demo\simple
```

Then run the sample database application that comes with the release. Use this command (assuming you have put the mckoi jar file in the jre\lib\ext directory):

```
java  SimpleApplicationDemo
```

If all is well, you will see some sample output like this, assuring you that the database libraries have been properly installed. If you do not see output like this, you will need to debug the problem based on the output you do see.

Output from Running SimpleApplicationDemo

```
Rows in 'Person' table: 12

Average age of people:  30.0833333333

All people that live in Africa:
  Grayham Downer
  Judith Brown
  Timothy French

All people that listen to either Beatles or Oasis:
  Grayham Downer listens to Beatles
  Ivan Wilson listens to Beatles
   ...
```

After you have the database example running, proceed to the next section to see how your Java application code establishes a connection with a database prior to sending across various SQL commands. We will finish up this section by saying a few words about the evolution of the JDBC.

JDBC was originally an acronym for "Java Data Base Connectivity," and is now held by Sun marketing not to be an acronym at all. JDBC was developed independently of the JDK, and first bundled with it in JDK 1.1. The package name is `java.sql`. Your database code may also use the `java.math` package that supports arbitrary-precision arithmetic. JDBC development continued to add more advanced features, creating JDBC version 2.0. Part of the JDBC 2.0 library was bundled with Java 2 (the release that is also known as JDK 1.2), and part of it was not. Table 27-3 summarizes the situation.

Table 27–3 JDBC Versions

JDBC Version	Bundled With	Package Name	Contents
JDBC 1.0 (previously called 1.2)	JDK 1.1	java.sql	Basic java client to database connectivity.
JDBC 2.0 core API	JDK 1.2 and later	java.sql	Added features such as scrollable results sets, batch updates, new datatypes for SQL-3, and programmatic updates using the result set.
JDBC 2.0 optional API	J2EE 1.2 and later	javax.sql	Can be downloaded from *java.sun.com/products/jdbc/*. Contains database server-side functionality. Prepares the ground for the use of database-aware Java beans.
JDBC 2.1 optional API	not bundled	javax.sql	Incremental improvement and additions over the 2.0 API.
JDBC 3.0 core API	JDK 1.4 and later	java.sql	Adds support for connection pooling, statement pooling, migration path to the Connector Architecture.

The Mckoi database manager implements the JDBC 2.0 core API.

Connecting to the Database

A database works in the classic client/server way. There is one database and many clients talk to it. (Larger enterprises may have multiple databases, but these can be considered independent for the purpose of this chapter). The clients are typically remote systems communicating over TCP/IP networks. They may talk directly to the database (called a "2-tier" system) or to a business logic server that talks to the database (known as a "3-tier" system).

How does a client or business logic program initiate a dialog with a database manager? JDBC uses a piece of software called a *database driver*. The database driver is specific to each vendor, and it is a library level example of the Adaptor design pattern. It knows how to connect to its database, send requests over TCP/IP, and how to listen for replies from the database. Just as an operating system device driver hides the peculiarities of an I/O device from the kernel and presents a standard interface for system calls, each JDBC driver hides the vagaries of its particular database and presents a standard interface to Java programs that use JDBC.

Putting it another way, the purpose of a JDBC database driver is to know the low-level protocol for talking with its database at one end, and with JDBC classes and methods at the other end. It acts like a human language interpreter, moving information from one end and putting it in a standard form that is comprehensible to the other end (see Figure 27-1). You typically get a JDBC database driver from the database vendor. There are several different kinds of database drivers, depending on whether it is written in Java or native code, or whether it talks directly to the database or through another data access protocol such as Microsoft's ODBC. None of that matters much to the applications programmer. As long as you have a working JDBC driver, you don't care how it works. Essentially, all commercial and non-commercial databases now have excellent support for access from Java programs. There are good third-party libraries that can be used to access the Microsoft database products.

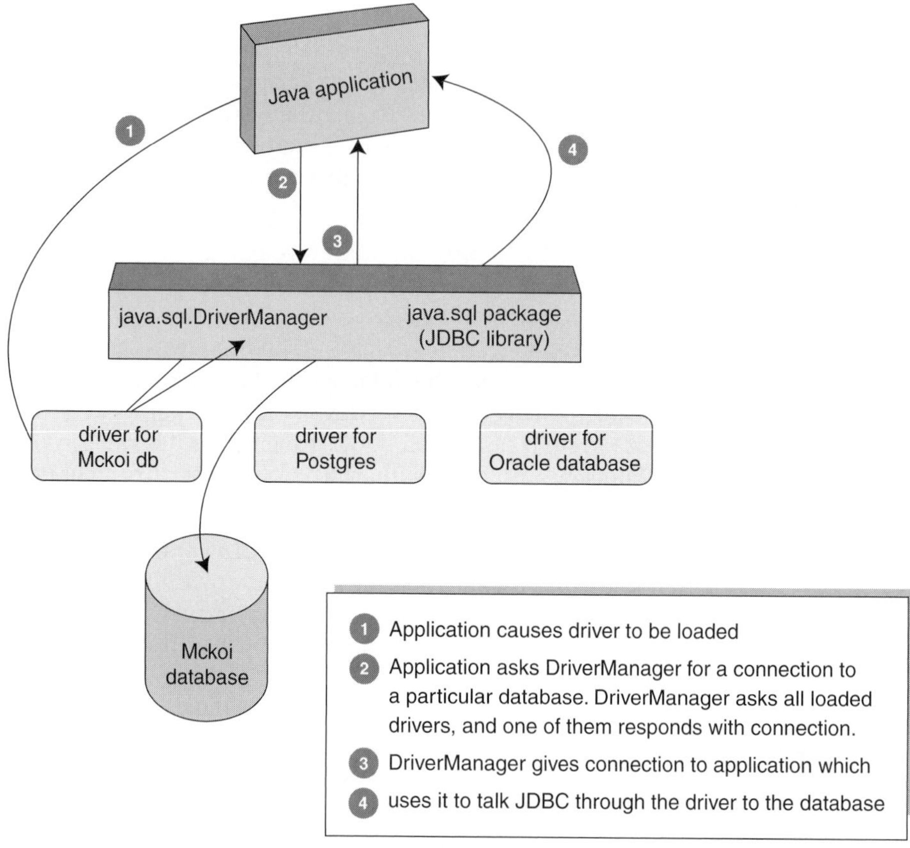

Figure 27–1 How JDBC establishes a connection between your code and a database.

First, you do a class.forName on the JDBC driver name. That causes its class to be loaded into the JVM that's executing your program.

```
Class.forName("com.mckoi.JDBCDriver");
```

You don't need to create an instance of the driver class. Simply getting it loaded is enough. Here's how it works. Each JDBC driver has a static initializer that is run when the class is loaded, and in that code the driver registers itself with the JDBC. You can also load a JDBC driver into the DriverManager by adding an entry to the `sql.drivers` property of the JVM. For example

```
java -Dsql.drivers=com.mckoi.JDBCDriver  ...
```

If you do this, you don't need the above call to Class.forName. Whichever approach you take, JDBC now knows about this driver, and can make calls to it. The JDBC driver does 90% of the workthat is done in JDBC. Since Mckoi is an open source product, you can inspect the code to confirm how this works for yourself.

Next, your Java application program asks for a *connection* to the database, using a string that looks like a URL as an argument. The JDBC library has a class called `java.sql.Connection` that knows how to use that string to guide it in its search for the right database.

Interface vs. Class That Implements the Interface

Some of the key JDBC things, like Connection, Statement, and ResultSet are actually interfaces, not classes. Here and throughout, we don't make an unnecessary distinction between an interface and a class that implements that interface. When we say "you get a Connection," you actually get an instance of some class that implements the Connection interface. You can store references to it in variables of type Connection, and you can use it to call all the methods defined in the Connection interface.

If you're ever curious about what class is behind some interface, you can easily find out its name. For any non-null reference x,

```
x.getClass().getName()
```

returns the fully qualified name of the class of the object referenced by x. If you are even more curious, you can then use reflection to dump out the names of its fields and methods.

As Patricia Shanahan (an expert programmer who sometimes answers questions on Usenet's Java groups) put it: "Never depend on this information in your programming. A method whose contract requires it to return a Connection may return instances of different classes in different implementations. It may even return instances of different classes in the same implementation under subtly different circumstances. The fact that it returns a Connection is part of its contract. The actual class of the returned object is implementation. Part of the art of object-oriented programming is firmly ignoring implementation details of one class when working on another class. Focus instead on the contracts between the classes, and the implementation details of the class you are working on."

The exact format of the pseudo-URL string will vary with each database, but it typically starts with "jdbc:" to indicate the protocol you will be using, just as "http:" indicates to a web server that you will be using the hypertext transport protocol. The string will then go on to give some indication of the database host name, the port number, and a database-specific subprotocol to use. The Mckoi database uses a pseudo-URL like this:

```
String url = "jdbc:mckoi:local://ExampleDB.conf?create=true";
```

That URL names a file called ExampleDB.conf on the local host in the current working directory that holds configuration information on the database. The parameter in the URL says that we expect to be creating a database in our program. Sun seems to want database implementors to cope with database creation commands based on SQL, not attributes passed in the URL. There aren't any JDBC drivers that actually support that today. Sun's preferred approach adds complexity because it would require a database to be able to parse SQL commands before it exists. The 'create=true' attribute to create a database is vendor-specific, but it's also how Cloudscape (see Table 27-1) works for embedded databases. The exact form of the pseudo-URL will vary from vendor to vendor. You need to read the documentation that comes with the database. Then your code will call a static method of the overall JDBC driver manager to get you a connection based on that string, and strings representing a username and password.

```
connection = java.sql.DriverManager.getConnection(url, user, passwd);
```

Behind the scenes, the DriverManager calls every JDBC driver that has registered, and asks it if that is a URL it can use to guide it to its database. If we have prepared the ground correctly, the URL will be recognized by at least one of the drivers. The first driver to connect to its database with this URL, username, and password, will be used as the channel of communication. The application program gets back a "Connection" object. (Strictly speaking, it gets an object that implements the Connection interface.) The session has been established, and the connection is now used for communication between your program and the database. Why doesn't the application simply talk directly to the driver? It could do that, but then you don't have a single standard library anymore—you have a collection of 50 different protocols and conventions for talking to 50 different databases. The point of the JDBC is to avoid that.

Connecting to a database is an expensive (time-consuming) operation. You would never design a servlet system that opened a new connection for every `doPost()` request. Most databases have a way to share connections among several different processes. This arrangement is known as "connection pooling." JDBC 2.0 introduced a new and preferred approach to getting a connection. Instead of using a Driver directly, you use a DataSource object which you configure and register with a naming service (e.g., LDAP, YP, NIS+) that uses the Java Naming and Directory Interface (JNDI). That is intended for enterprise-level software and takes a lot more setting up, so we'll stick to simple drivers in this chapter.

In summary, your application program knows which database it wants to talk to, and hence which database driver it needs to load. The JDBC driver manager knows how to establish the JDBC end of a database connection, and the driver knows how to establish the database end. They do it. The driver manager gives you back a connection into which you can pour standard SQL queries and get results.

Executing SQL Statements

Now we are at the point where we can start issuing SQL commands to our database and getting back results. We do this through a Statement object that we get from the connection object described in the previous section. Table 27-4 shows several methods in Connection.

Table 27–4 Some Methods of `java.sql.Connection`

Method	Purpose
`Statement createStatement()`	Returns a statement object that is used to send SQL to the database.
`PreparedStatement prepareStatement(String sql)`	Returns an object that can be used for sending parameterized SQL statements.
`CallableStatement prepareCall(String sql)`	Returns an object that can be used for calling stored procedures.
`DataBaseMetaData getMetaData()`	Gets an object that supplies database configuration information.
`boolean isClosed()`	Reports whether the database is currently open or not.
`void setReadonly(boolean yn)`	Restores/removes read-only mode, allowing certain database optimizations.
`void commit()`	Makes all changes permanent since the previous commit/rollback.
`void rollback()`	Undoes and discards all changes done since the previous commit/rollback.
`void setAutoCommit(boolean yn)`	Restores/removes auto-commit mode, which does an automatic commit after each statement.
`void close()`	Closes the connection and releases the JDBC resources for it.

You will invoke these methods on the `java.sql.Connection` object that you get back from the JDBC driver manager, as shown in an upcoming. You use a connection to create a Statement object. The statement object has methods that let you send SQL to the database. Thankfully, statements are blissfully simple. You send SQL queries as strings. In other words, the JDBC designers did not try to force-fit object-oriented programming onto SQL, perhaps by creating a Select class. Here's how you send a select query to the database:

```
Statement myStmt = connection.createStatement();
ResultSet myResult;
myResult= myStmt.executeQuery( "SELECT * FROM Person;" );
```

The executeQuery() method takes a string as an argument. The string contains the SQL statement that you want to execute. In the code fragment above, the SQL asks for all data to be returned from the Person table. There is an object that holds your result set. Here, we've called it myResult and it belongs to the ResultSet class. We'll talk more about ResultSet in a minute. Once you have a Statement object, you call one of its methods, shown in Table 27-5, to send SQL to the database. Statement has more methods than these, but these are the ones you'll use most.

Standard SQL has an optional ";" at the end of each SQL statement. You can leave it off. It is omitted in all the tutorials at Javasoft.

Table 27–5 `java.sql.statement` Methods to Execute SQL

SQL Statement	JDBC Statement to Use	Type of Its Return Value	Comment
SELECT	`executeQuery(String sql)`	`ResultSet`	The return value will hold the data extracted from the database.
INSERT, UPDATE, DELETE, CREATE, DROP	`executeUpdate(String sql)`	`int`	The return value will give the count of the number of rows changed (for insert, update, or delete statements), or zero otherwise.
stored procedure with multiple results	`execute(String sql)`	`boolean`	The return value is true if the first result is a ResultSet, false otherwise. You get the actual results by calling another method of the statement class.

The different SQL statements have different return values. Some of them have no return value, some of them return the number of rows they affected, and the select statement returns all the data it pulled out of the database. To cope with these different possible results, you need to call a different method depending on what kind of SQL statement you are executing. The most interesting case is the select statement that gets back an entire result set of data. The next section describes how this data is conveyed to your Java program.

Almost every JDBC interaction with a database can throw an exception, and you need to handle it appropriately in your code. JDBC defines four exceptions at present: `SQLException` (the most common), `SQLWarning`, `BatchUpdateException`, and `DataTruncation`. It is very important to write each handler so it outputs meaningful error messages for every exception it gets. If you don't pay attention to this, you will find it much harder to debug database problems and error situations.

Threads and Database Programming

Older databases sometimes have support for asynchronous SQL operations, meaning that you can start another SQL statement before you get the results back from the past one. Java doesn't need to use this kind of SQL because you can get the same effect by issuing the statements in separate Java threads. Your JDBC programs will be more portable if you avoid doing this in SQL.

When you write multithreaded Java code that uses JDBC, you must synchronize all your accesses to all shared data as usual. Shared data means any data that is accessed in more than one thread and also written by at least one of the threads. As always, it is the programmer's responsibility to do this. If you do not properly synchronize data access, the data can be updated or read inconsistently (with a value partly from one thread and partly from another). That leaves your code with hard-to-debug data races and data corruption problems.

You look for these potential bugs in your code by examining all the data that each thread accesses. If there are any variables that may be accessed by two threads at once, you need to synchronize the access. Chapter 11 on threads has an example of this issue, and how to do the synchronization.

Mckoi database has a visual query tool!

The Mckoi database is excellent software and provides some wonderful learning opportunities. The source code includes a visual SQL query tool, as shown in Figure 27-2. This is a Swing application that allows you to type in SQL queries in the upper window, press the "run" button, and see the results interactively.

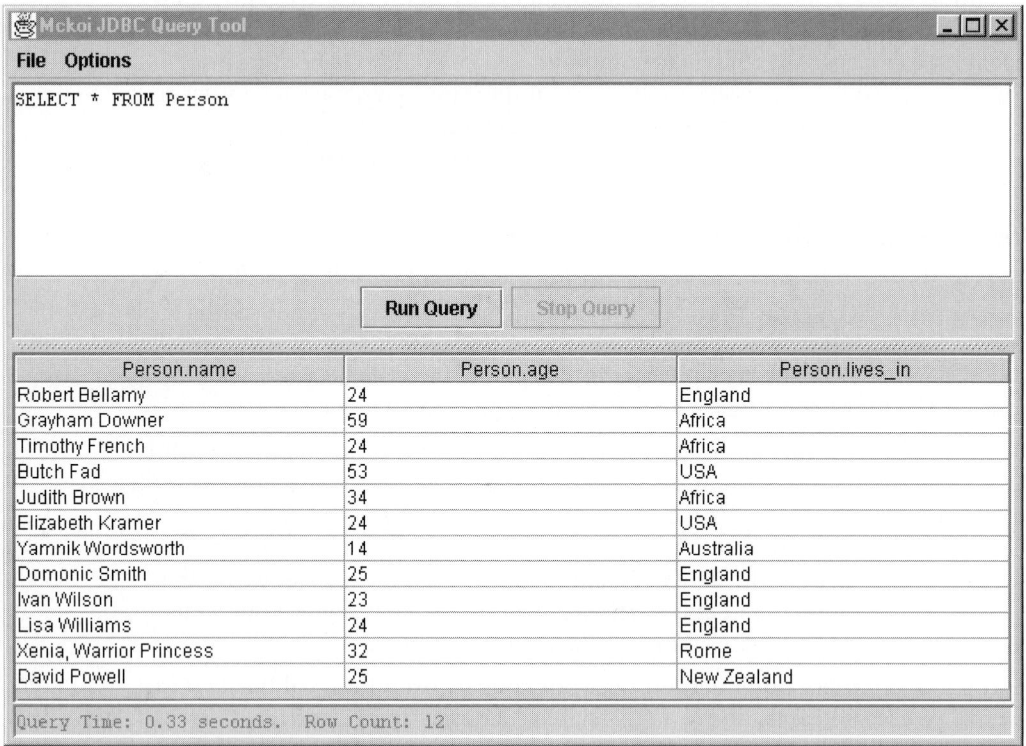

Figure 27–2 Mckoi GUI.

The Mckoi program was invoked with these commands:

```
cd \mckoi\demo\simple
java com.mckoi.tools.JDBCQueryTool -url "jdbc:mckoi:local:/ExampleDB.conf"
-u user -p "pass1212"
```

There are two commands there, shown on three lines to fit on this page.

Result Sets

As we saw in the previous chapter, the SELECT statement extracts data from a database. Here's an example which should be prefaced with the warning that columns are numbered starting with 1, not zero. That is an SQL convention that really had to be respected by Java. If we run this Java code fragment,

```
ResultSet result;
result = statement.executeQuery( " SELECT Person.name, Person.age "
                                + "FROM Person "
                                + "WHERE Person.age = 24 " );
while (result.next()) {
    String p = result.getString(1);
    int a = result.getInt(2);
        System.out.println( p + " is " + a + " years");
}
```

we'll get output like this:

```
Robert Bellamy is 24 years
Timothy French is 24 years
Elizabeth Kramer is 24 years
```

Relating that output to the code fragment shows how the ResultSet object can hold multiple values. I like to think of ResultSet as being similar to a 2D array. Instead of incrementing the most significant index variable, you call the result method next(). Each time you call next(), you are moved on to the next record in the result set. You need to call next() before you can see the first result record, and it returns false when there are no more result records, so it is convenient for controlling a while loop. That does make it different from an Iterator, however, so be alert to that difference. As a reminder, the Iterator next() method returns the next *object*, not a true/false value. A true/false value can be returned for a result set next() because there is another set of methods for actually getting the data. Read on to find out what!

You get individual values from a column within a record by calling one of the many methods whose signature looks like this:

```
SomeType  getSomeType( colNumberOrName );
```

The argument can be the name of the attribute, or the column number (which starts at 1, remember). Thus, the class ResultSet has methods `getBlob()`, `getBigDecimal()`, `getDate()`, `getBytes()`, `getInt()`, `getLong()`, `getString()`, `getObject()`, and so on, for all the Java types that represent SQL types and for a column name and column number argument. The getObject() is interesting. If the database supports it, you can put a Java object into the database! You can then retrieve it later, and invoke methods on it. So your database may be able to store and catalog serialized Java objects as well as data.

Column numbers should be used for columns that are not explicitly named in the query, such as when you do a "select '*'". Column names can be unreliable in this case, but otherwise they document the intent of your program better. Another advantage of using column names vs. column index for the ResultSet 'get' methods is that your code doesn't break when your query changes to include more columns. Access by name might run into limitations of JDBC drivers, though. Some drivers allow access to the result set columns only in the order of the index. If you use by name and try to access columns out of order, you will get an exception. You can see all of the get-methods if you review the javadoc HTML pages for `java.sql.ResultSet`.

Pitfall: Reusing Statements

Notice that a result set is assigned by the return value of a method of `Statement`. Normally, we would expect to be able to invoke a second execute() method on the same statement, assign the return value to a different result set, and proceed on our merry way. There is, however, a hidden pitfall to this!

Only one result set at a time can be open for a given statement. When you reuse a statement object, it closes whatever the previous result set was for that statement object. That means if you are going through a result set and executing more statements based on what you find, you must use an additional statement object. Otherwise, the second statement makes you lose the results of the first statement, which you are still processing. Here's some invalid code that shows what can go wrong:

```
ResultSet result1, result2
result1 = myStmt.executeQuery( someSQLString );
while (result1.next()) {
    ...
    result2 = myStmt.executeQuery( someSQLString2 ); // NO!  blows
                                                     //away result1
}
```

The problem is that the while loop uses result1, but result1 is destroyed when a second query is issued from the same myStmt object. Reusing the `myStmt` object will close the `result1` result set. Instead, do this:

```
...
Statement myOtherStmt = connection.createStatement();
while (result1.next()) {
    ...
    result2 = myOtherStmt.executeQuery( someSQLString ); // OK.
}
```

Of course, if you never have two statements active simultaneously, you only need one statement and result set object which you can reuse for all your queries.

Good programming practice says that you should close Statement objects explicitly when they are no longer needed, with a statement like this:

```
myStmt.close();
```

Closing a statement when you are finished with it is important because it frees up resources (like locks and caches) on both the server and the client.

Cursor Support

A default ResultSet object is not updatable and has a cursor that moves forward only. With this type of Result Set you can only go through the result records once, and only from the first row to the last row in order. That's not very convenient, so JDBC 2.0 brought in some new methods that let you specify (when you create a statement) that you want something better than the default. In this code example,

```
Statement stmt = conn.createStatement(
                    ResultSet.TYPE_SCROLL_INSENSITIVE,
                    ResultSet.CONCUR_UPDATABLE  );
```

all result sets created by that statement will:

- be scrollable. You can move backwards and forwards among the records of the result set. A cursor indicates the current position in the result set.
- not sense updates by others that occur after your result set was constructed. That is, despite possible updates to the database from elsewhere, your result set will not change. This may or may not be what you want.
- be updatable. If a result set is updatable, it means you can call a method to change its value, and then another method to put that same change back in the database too. This is very handy when the query results are being reviewed by a person online. They can type a new value for some field, and your program can move that to the result set and get it to update the database without formulating a whole new SQL query.

If a database cannot support the result set configuration you have requested, it will carry on processing and return a result set that it can complete. It will also add a warning to your connection object. So it is a good idea to check for warnings before and after creating a customized result set. The method getWarnings() of the Connection class will do this check. If you try to do something that is not supported on your result set, it will raise an SQLException. See the fields of the ResultSet class for other options.

Batching SQL Statements and Transactions

Performance has always been one of the top concerns of database vendors, and they often go to some lengths to find ways to speed up queries. One of the bottlenecks is the time taken to package up a query, ship it over TCP/IP, and get it into the database where the SQL interpreter can start working on it. In other words, the network latency has a cost.

To reduce the overhead of network latency, many vendors support a way to batch several SQL statements together and send them to the database as a group. You can batch together any statements that have an int return type, which basically means "any SQL statements except for select." You can see why. You are sending over a group of SQL statements to be executed together, but there is no mechanism defined for getting back the result set for each select. It is not that hard to invent such a mechanism (e.g., executing a batch returns an array of ResultSet), but this has not been done.

To bundle a group of SQL statements in a batch, you create a Statement object as usual:

```
Statement myStmt = conn.createStatement();
```

Then, instead of issuing an execute call for the statement, you instead do a series of addBatch(), like this:

```
myStmt.addBatch( myNonSelectSQL0 );
myStmt.addBatch( myNonSelectSQL1 );
myStmt.addBatch( myNonSelectSQL2 );
```

Finally, when you are ready to send the whole batch to the database, invoke the executeBatch() method:

```
int [] res = myStmt.executeBatch();
```

Batching SQL statements is so easy, there's no reason to avoid it. That will cause all the statements to be sent to the database, and executed as a batch one after the other. The results come back in the form of an array of int, where the ith element holds the row count result of the ith statement in the batch (or zero if it did not return a row count).

Support for batches of statements came in with JDBC 2.0, but is not supported in the beta version of the Mckoi database used here. However, it is an easy feature to add, and will probably be in the Mckoi final release.

Transactions

In the previous chapter we referred to "database integrity" and explained how a fairly common situation required either all of a group of statements to be executed or else none of them. The way you do this is to group the statements together in a "transaction." You execute the transaction in a temporary working area internal to the database. Then, based on other information from your environment, you either "commit" or "rollback" the transaction. Committing the transaction means you let all the data from the working area be copied to the database so your statements have taken effect. A rollback of the transaction means you delete the working area without copying it to the main database so none of your statements affect the database.

Transaction commitment is done through the Connection object. When a JDBC driver starts up, the Connection is in auto-commit mode. That means the Connection automatically commits changes after executing each individual statement. You can turn that off and control when commits or rollbacks are done by invoking this method on your Connection object:

```
boolean savedCommitValue = conn.getAutoCommit();  // save the current value
conn.setAutoCommit(false);      // turn off stmt-by-stmt commits
```

Then execute as many SQL statements as makes sense for your transaction; these will frequently be grouped in a batch. Look to see if they all completed successfully, and commit the transaction. You can also restore the old setting of auto-commit:

```
int [] res = myStmt.executeBatch();
conn.commit();     // commit the changes
conn.setAutoCommit(savedCommitValue);  // restore previous value.
```

If, however, an SQLException was raised, part of the recovery from that might be to issue a rollback:

```
conn.rollback();  // drop the partially completed changes.
```

The statements within a transaction are all the statements that you issued on a given connection since the previous commit() or rollback(). Another way of looking at this is to note that Connection and transaction are almost synonymous—you can only have one open transaction per connection. So if you want to update a database concurrently and transactionally, the most practical way can be to use one connection per transaction per thread.

Prepared Statements and Stored Procedures

Another way to boost performance is to precompile the SQL statement using what is termed a "prepared statement." That technique and the related one of "stored procedures" are described in this section.

A SQL statement is precompiled and stored in a PreparedStatement object. This object can then be used to efficiently execute this statement multiple times, often changing some of the values at runtime. You get a PreparedStatement with a method of your Connection object. It's easiest to see with a code example:

```
PreparedStatement pstmt = conn.prepareStatement(
    "UPDATE EMPLOYEES SET SALARY = ? WHERE ID = ?");

pstmt.setBigDecimal(1, 150000.00);
pstmt.setInt(2, linden4303);
pstmt.executeUpdate();

pstmt.setBigDecimal(1, 85000.00);
pstmt.setInt(2, jenkins2705);
pstmt.executeUpdate();
```

That code will set employee linden4303's salary to $150,000, and employee jenkins2705's salary to $85,000. The question marks in the SQL query represent data values that will be filled in before the statement is executed. It works like arguments to a procedure, with one difference: any of the question mark fields that you don't change will retain whatever value you have previously set them to, so you only need to set fields that change.

PreparedStatement has its own versions of the methods `executeQuery()`, `executeUpdate()`, and `execute()`. In particular, PreparedStatement objects do not take an SQL string as a parameter because they already contain the precompiled SQL statement you previously created.

Let's move on to take a look at stored procedures. As we saw in the previous chapter, these are a group of SQL statements bundled together as one unit that can be called from your program. That's where the "procedure" part of the name comes from. The "stored" part of the name is because the procedure can be precompiled by the SQL interpreter and actually stored in the database. A stored procedure is used when you have a group of SQL statements that, taken together, carry out some task like adding a new account and initializing it. Up until now, stored procedures could not be moved outside the database, and could not be linked to software components or external libraries. These disadvantages disappear when you write stored procedures in Java.

You have two choices for creating stored procedures. You can create them using SQL commands to install and manage stored procedures, and submit these commands using `executeUpdate()` in the normal way. Or, you can write the stored procedure following the SQLJ conventions. SQLJ is an industry standard covering how to embed SQL statements into Java methods and how to use Java methods for stored procedures. There is more information on SQLJ at *www.sqlj.org*.

Using SQLJ means writing a stand-alone Java program to contain your stored procedure. This is exciting and interesting because it means that even your stored procedures are now portable between different databases. Write a public static void method in a Java class. That method will have the usual code to get a Connection, create a Statement, and execute it. You compile it and put it in a jar file. Then you use the SQLJ library to install the jar file in the database management system. There is a special SQL syntax (which varies between databases) that lets you invoke your stored procedure. We won't cover the specialized technique here, except to say that there are full examples in the "Further Reading" section at the end of the chapter.

Complete Example

This section shows the complete program to create, update, and select from a database using JDBC. A longer version of this code comes with the Mckoi database and can be found in directory `c:\mckoi\demo\simple`. The code has been split into two programs there for convenience, one to create the tables, and one to query them.

```
/**
 * Demonstrates how to use JDBC.
 */

import java.sql.*;

public class Example {

  public static void main(String[] args) {

    // Register the Mckoi JDBC Driver
    try {
      Class.forName("com.mckoi.JDBCDriver");
    }
    catch (Exception e) {
      System.out.println("Can't load JDBC Driver. " +
                         "Make sure classpath is correct");
      return;
    }

    // This URL specifies we are creating a local database.  The
    // config file for the database is found at './ExampleDB.conf'
    // The 'create=true' argument means we want to create the database.
    // If the database already exists, it can not be created.
    // So delete .\data\*  when you want to run this again.
    String url = "jdbc:mckoi:local://ExampleDB.conf?create=true";

    //  Use a real username/password in a real application
    String username = "user";
    String password = "pass1212";

    // Make a connection with the database.
    Connection connection;
    try {
      connection = DriverManager.getConnection(url, username, password);
    }
    catch (SQLException e) {
      System.out.println("Connect problem: " + e.getMessage());
      return;
    }

    // --- Set up the database ---
    try {
```

```
      // Create a Statement object to execute the queries on,
      Statement statement = connection.createStatement();
      ResultSet result;

      System.out.println("-- Creating Tables --");

      // Create a Person table,
      statement.executeUpdate(
  "    CREATE TABLE Person ( " +
  "       name       VARCHAR(100) PRIMARY KEY, " +
  "       age        INTEGER, " +
  "       lives_in   VARCHAR(100) ) " );

      System.out.println("-- Inserting Data --");

      statement.executeUpdate(
  "    INSERT INTO Person ( name, age, lives_in ) VALUES "
  + "       ( 'Robert Bellamy', 24, 'England' ), "
  + "       ( 'Grayham Downer', null, 'Africa' ), "
  + "       ( 'Timothy French', 24, 'Africa' ), "
  + "       ( 'Butch Fad', 53, 'USA' ), "
  + "       ( 'Judith Brown', 34, 'Africa' ) ");

      System.out.println("-- SQL queries --");
      // get average age of the people
      result = statement.executeQuery("SELECT AVG(age) FROM Person");
      if (result.next()) {
         System.out.println("Av. age:  " + result.getDouble(1));
      }
      System.out.println();
      // List the names of all the people that live in Africa
      result = statement.executeQuery(
        "SELECT name FROM Person WHERE lives_in = 'Africa' ");

      System.out.println("All people that live in Africa:");
      while (result.next()) {
         System.out.println("  " + result.getString(1));
      }

      // Close the statement and the connection.
      statement.close();
      connection.close();

    }
    catch (SQLException e) {
      System.out.println(
      "An SQLException occurred: " + e.getMessage());
    }
    catch (Exception e) {
      e.printStackTrace(System.err);
    }
  }
}
```

Make sure the three Mckoi jar files are in your classpath, then you can compile and run this code with these commands:

```
javac Example.java
java Example
```

The output will look like this:

```
-- Creating Tables --
-- Inserting Data --
-- SQL queries --
Av. age:  27.0

All people that live in Africa:
  Grayham Downer
  Timothy French
  Judith Brown
```

Database and Result Set Metadata

"Meta-*anything*" is a higher or second-order version of the *anything*. Metadata is data about data. The classic example of metadata is file and directory information on your disk drive. You don't directly put it there, but you need it to keep track of your real data, and it is maintained by the system on your behalf. Databases have a large amount of metadata describing their particular capabilities and configuration.

The database metadata is going to be different for each database, and JDBC lets you get hold of it through the `java.sql.DatabaseMetaData` interface. You get an instance of the Metadata class by invoking a method of Connection. There you will find 100 or so fields and methods that you can use to find out specific details on the database. For example, it can tell you if the database supports transactions, and if so, to what level.

You use the database metadata when you know your code is going to run against several different databases. By looking at the metadata, your code can discover the individual features of a database, and perhaps take advantage of performance-related options. Often, but not always, there is a slower more standard way to achieve an effect, and you may prefer to write your database application code that uses that, instead of querying the database about its advanced features. Using database metadata is an advanced technique, beyond the scope of this book. The Javadoc documentation is extensive if you want to pursue this topic further.

Result sets also have metadata. An object of type `java.sql.ResultSetMetaData` can get information about the columns in a ResultSet object. Here is an example. The following code fragment creates a ResultSet and gets the corresponding ResultSetMetaData object from it. The code then uses that object to find out two pieces of information about the result set.. It calls two methods, one to find out how many columns the result has, and one to learn whether the first column in the result set can be used in a WHERE clause (i.e., it is a "searchable" column).

```
ResultSet result = statement.executeQuery(
    "SELECT c1, c2 FROM myTable; "

ResultSetMetaData rsmd = result.getMetaData();
int numberCols = rsmd.getColumnCount();
boolean b = rsmd.isSearchable(1);
```

Further Reading

There are some excellent book-length treatments of relational databases and JDBC in particular. One book I like is the *JDBC API Tutorial and Reference* (Addison Wesley, Reading: MA, 1999), by Graham Hamilton and Rick Cattell, and then by Maydene Fisher, and then by Seth White and Mark Hapner, and finally by Maydene and Seth again. If you buy this book, be sure to get the most up-to-date edition!

In addition, Sun has an online tutorial on JDBC at *java.sun.com/docs/books/tutorial/jdbc/index.html*. This contains some of the same material in the JDBC API Tutorial book.

Exercises

1. Run the javadoc tool to create the javadoc files for the packages of the Mckoi database, and browse the API. The database comes with the Java source code that implements it. The file is called src.zip. Unzip it, cd to the src directory that it creates, work out what the package names are (they mirror the directory names), and run javadoc on them. Look at some of the source code with an editor, and browse the javadoc-generated API documentation for the same files. How useful is javadoc to you? Why? How far does the code follow the Sun recommended code conventions at *java.sun.com/docs/codeconv/html/CodeConvTOC.doc.html*?
2. Write a JDBC program to display the name and age of everyone in the Person table who is older than 39. This question builds on a similar one in the previous chapter that asked you to write the SQL statement. Now the exercise asks that you put it into a JDBC program and actually run it.
3. Write a JDBC program to display the name of everyone in the Person table who lives in a NATO country and doesn't listen to the Beatles. Be careful to exclude people who listen to other bands as well as the Beatles. You will need a subquery for this.This question builds on a similar one in the previous chapter that asked you to write the SQL statement. Now the exercise asks that you put it into a JDBC program and actually run it.
4. Modify your program from the previous question to submit an invalid SQL query. How do the database and your program respond?
5. Write the JDBC code to create and populate a table for the CD inventory of an online store. Each CD is either domestic or imported. These details are stored for all CDs: artist, title, price, quantity in stock. Imported CDs also have these fields: country of origin, genre, non-discount status, language, and lead time for reorder. Write some instance data describing your five favorite CDs (include a couple of imported CDs, too), and populate your database.
6. Update your code from the previous exercise question to allow it to work interactively with the user. The user should be able to type in the title of a CD, and the database should return all the data it holds on that CD.

Light Relief—Hear Java Speak! See Java on a PDA!

This is a brief light relief section because I inserted it at the very last minute as the book went to press. Now that the book is finished, I had the time to go web surfing again and discovered two amazing products.

The first one is another free download from IBM's alphaworks. They call it the "Self Voicing Kit," and it lets your Java applications speak! You should buzz over to *www.alphaworks.ibm.com/tech/svk* right now and download the 11 MB speech kit for Windows. Install it by unzipping the download and then running

```
java install
```

Then run an example application like this:

```
cd c:/jdk1.4b3/demo/jfc/SwingSet2
java -jar SwingSet2
```

That will start up a Swing demo, and it will be accompanied by a voice that comments on what you are doing and identifies components on the screen. This is intended as an evaluation, so the library times out after 45 minutes. But it is an amazing proof of concept. It works and it works well. The download includes everything you need to make Java talk.

The Self Voicing Kit can make a Java application automatically speak to the end user. It is quick to add a speaking interface, too. It uses the "accessibility" hooks that allow disabled users to operate their PC (large fonts, etc., and now spoken descriptions of what's on the screen). Wonderful!

The second amazing Java thing that I stumbled across today is a Java OS for the Compaq iPAC Pocket PC. Leading edge PDAs now have the spec of a PC from a few years ago (200MHz CPU with 64 MB memory) and are powerful enough to run J2SE. You can buy the $20 Jeode JVM for the Compaq from Insignia Solutions and run Java Micro Edition. Or you can get the $100 Java OS from SavaJe Technologies and run full Java 2 Standard Edition 1.3.1 on your iPAQ or Psion netBook! You can develop Java programs on your desktop and deploy them onto the PDA with ease—as long as the application plus libraries fit in 60 MB and on a 240 by 320 pixel screen. Version 1.0 supports the Compaq iPAQ 32 MB and 64 MB color models such as the iPAQ H3600. The next release of iPAQ will come bundled with the Jeode JVM and Bluetooth (wireless connectivity standard) support. You can download a 30-day Java evaluation from *www.savaje.com* and then buy the license online to remove the time restriction. Wow! Full Java on a PDA! I don't know about you, but this gadget is an immediate "must have" for me.

The SavaJe software includes several applications that run in the limited PDA memory. There is a browser, mp3 player, email client, a personal information manager, games, an editor, the MS-Office compatible ThinkFree suite, and so on. Add on an ethernet adapter, and you can run this PDA as a Java-based web server! Throw in a folding keyboard from ThinkOutside, and now you're cooking with gas.

You can buy these products from Handandgo at their website, *www.handandgo.com*. Looking at their html files, it is clear they make extensive use of Java servlets to run the site! It's amazing what you can find when you have time to web surf. Now I'm getting a Java-capable iPAQ; I will probably never again have free time to surf.

Chapter 28

XML and Java

This chapter is in three parts. The first part describes XML, what it's for, and how you use it. It's straightforward and can be described in a couple of sections in the chapter. The largest part of this chapter describes Java support for XML, covering how you access and update XML documents. The XML world defines two different algorithms for accessing XML documents ("everything at once" versus "piece by piece"), and Java supports them both. We put together a Java program that uses each of these algorithms. The third part of the chapter explains how to download and configure the Java library for XML so you can trying running the code for yourself.

You'll probably be relieved to hear that the basics of XML can be learned in a few minutes, though it takes a while longer to master the "alphabet soup" of all the accompanying tools and standards. XML is a set of rules, guidelines, and conventions for describing structured data in a plain text editable file. The abbreviation XML stands for "eXtensible Mark-up Language." It's related to the HTML used to write web pages, and has a similar appearance of text with mark-up tags sprinkled through it. HTML mark-up tags are things like `<br>` (break to a new line), `<table>` (start a table), and `<li>` (make an entry in a list). In HTML the set of mark-up tags are fixed in advance, and the only purpose for most of them is to guide the way something looks on the screen. With XML, you define your own tags and attributes (and thus it is "extensible") and you give them meaning, and that meaning goes way beyond minor points like the font size to use when printing something out.

Don't make the mistake of thinking that XML is merely "HTML on steroids." Although we approach it from HTML to make it easy to explain, XML does much more than HTML does. XML offers the following advantages:

- it is an archival representation of data. Because its format is in plain text and carried around with the data, it can never be lost. That contrasts with binary representations of a file which all too easily become outmoded (e.g., do you have any old word processor files that you no longer have a way to read?). If this was all it did, it would be enough to justify its existence.
- it provides a way to web-publish files that can be directly processed by computer, rather than merely human-readable text and pictures.
- it is plain text, so it can be read by people without special tools.
- it can easily be transformed into HTML, or PDF, or data structures internal to a program, or any other format yet to be dreamed up, so it is "future-proof."
- it's portable, open, and a standard, which makes it a great fit with Java.

We will see these benefits as we go through this chapter. XML holds the promise of taking web-based systems to the next level by supporting data interchange everywhere. The web made everyone into a publisher of human-readable HTML files. XML lets everyone become a publisher or consumer of computer-readable data files.

Keep that concept in mind as we go through this example. We'll start with HTML because it's a good way to get into XML. Let's say you have an online business selling CDs of popular music. You'll probably have a catalog of your inventory online, so that customers know what's in stock. *Amazon.com* works exactly like this. One possibility for storing your inventory is to put it in an HTML table. Each row will hold information on a particular CD title, and each column will be the details you keep about a CD—the title, artist, price, number in stock, and so on. The HTML for some of your online inventory might look like this:

```
<table>
<tr> <th>title</th>   <th>artist</th>   <th>price</th>  <th>stock</th>  </tr>

<tr> <td>The Tubes</td>   <td>The Tubes</td>   <td>22</td>  <td>3</td>  </tr>

<tr> <td>Some Girls</td>   <td>Rolling Stones</td>   <td>25</td>  <td>5</td>  </tr>

<tr> <td>Tubthumper</td>   <td>Chumbawamba</td>   <td>17</td>  <td>6</td>  </tr>
</table>
```

We are using tags like `<tr>` to define table rows. When you display it in a web page, it looks like Figure 28-1.

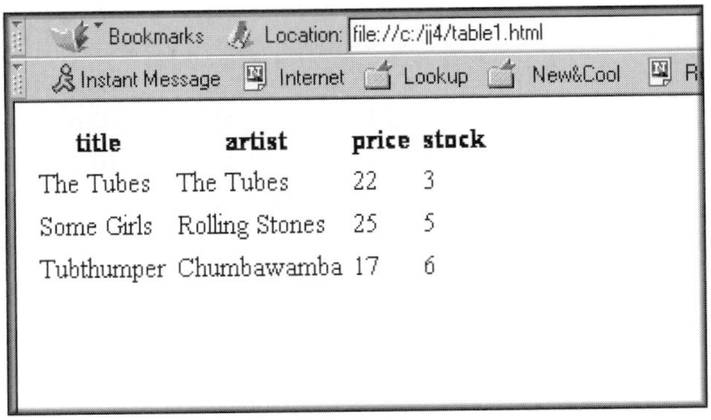

Figure 28–1 HTML table displayed in a browser.

The HTML table is a reasonable format for displaying data, but it's no help for all the other things you might want to do with your data, like search it, update it, or share it with others. Say we want to find all CDs by some particular artist. We can look for that string in the HTML file, but HTML doesn't have any way to restrict the search to the "artist" column. When we find the string, we can't easily tell if it's in the title column or the artist column or somewhere else again. HTML tables aren't very useful for holding data with a variable number of elements. Say imported CDs have additional fields relating to country, genre, non-discount status, and so on. With HTML, we have to add those fields to all CDs, or put imported CDs in a special table of their own, or find some other hack.

This is where XML comes in. The basic idea is that you represent your data in character form, and each field (or "element," as it is properly called) has tags that say what it is. It looks that straightforward! Just as with HTML, XML tags consist of an opening angle bracket followed by a string and a closing angle bracket. The XML version of your online CD catalog might look like this:

```
<cd> <title>The Tubes</title>    <artist>The Tubes</artist>
    <price>22</price>          <qty>3</qty>  </cd>

<cd> <title>Some Girls</title>   <artist>Rolling Stones</artist>
    <price>25</price>  <qty>5</qty>  </cd>

<cd> <title>Tubthumper</title>   <artist>Chumbawamba</artist>
    <price>17</price>  <qty>6</qty>  </cd>
```

It looks trivial, but the simple act of storing everything as character data and wrapping it with a pair of labels saying what it is opens up some powerful possibilities that we will get into shortly. XML is intended for some entirely different uses than displaying in a browser. In fact, most browsers ignore tags that they don't recognize, so if you browse an XML file you'll just get the embedded text without tags (unless the browser recognizes XML, as recent versions of Microsoft's Internet Explorer do).

Should we also wrap HTML around the XML so it can be displayed in a browser? You could do that, but it is not the usual approach. XML is usually consumed by data-processing programs, not by a browser. The purpose of XML is to make it easy for enterprise programs to pass around data together with their structure. It's much more common to keep the data as records in a database, extract and convert it into XML on demand, pass the XML around, then have a servlet or JSP program read the XML and transform it into HTML on the fly as it sends the data to a browser. The Java XSLT library does exactly that. Let us go on to make a few perhaps obvious remarks about the rules of XML.

Summary of the XML/HTML Key Differences

- HTML was created to *display data* and focus on *how the data looks*
- XML was created to *describe data* and focus on *what the data is*
- HTML is used to make text presentable and readable by people
- XML is a format to store and exchange data. It can be read by computers and people
- XML is a portable way to describe data for a program
- Java is a portable way to process data in a program

Some Rules of XML

XML follows the same kind of hierarchical data structuring rules that apply throughout most programming languages, and therefore XML can represent the same kind of data that we are used to dealing with in our programs. As we'll see later in the chapter, you can always build a tree data structure out of a well-formed XML file and you can always write out a tree into an XML file. When you want to send XML data to someone, the XML file form is handy. When you want to process the data, the in-memory tree-form is handy. The purpose of the Java XML API is to provide classes that make it easy to go from one form to the other, and to grab data on the way.

Notice that all XML tags come in matched pairs of a begin tag and an end tag that surround the data they are describing, like this:

```
<someTagName> some data appears here   </someTagName>
```

The whole thing—start tag, data, and end tag—is called an *element*.

You can nest elements inside elements, and the end tag for a nested element must come before the end tag of the thing that contains it. Here is an example of some XML that is not valid:

```
<cd>   <title>White Christmas  </cd>  </title>
```

It's not valid because the title field (or "element" to use the proper term) is nested inside the cd element, but there is no end tag for it before we reach the cd end tag. This proper nesting requirement makes it really easy to check if a file has properly nested XML. You can just push start tags onto a stack as they come in. When you reach an end tag, it should match the tag on the top of the stack. If it does, pop the opening tag from the stack. If the tag doesn't match, the file has badly-nested XML.

Just as some HTML tags can have several extra arguments or "attributes," so can XML tags. The HTML `<img>` tag is an example of an HTML tag with several attributes. The `<img>` tag has attributes that specify the name of an image file, the kind of alignment on the page, and even the width and height in pixels of the image. It might look like this:

```
<img  src="cover.jpg"  height="150"   width="100"  align="right">
```

In HTML, we can leave off the quotes around attribute values unless the values contain spaces. In XML, attribute values are always placed in quotation marks, and you must not put commas in between attributes. We could equally describe our CD inventory using attributes like this:

```
<cd  title="The Tubes"  artist="The Tubes"  price="22"  qty="3"> </cd>
```

As frequently happens in programming, a software designer can express an idea in several different ways. Some experts recommend avoiding the use of attributes in XML where possible for technical reasons having to do with expressiveness.

Comments have the same appearance as in HTML, and can be put in a file using this tag (everything between the two pairs of dashes is a comment):

```
<!-- comments  -->
```

XML tags are case-sensitive. XML is generally much stricter about what constitutes a good document than is HTML. This strictness makes it easier for a program to read in an XML file and understand its structure. It doesn't have to check for 50 different ways of doing something. An XML document that keeps all the rules about always having a matching closing tag, all tags being properly nested, and so on is called a *"well-formed "* document. There is a complete list of all the rules in the XML FAQ at *www.ucc.ie/xml/*.

The Document Type Definition (DTD)

There is another level of data validation in addition to a document being "well-formed." You also want to be able to check that the document contains only elements that you expect, all the elements that you expect, and that they only appear where expected. For example, we know this is not a valid CD inventory entry:

```
<cd>  <price>22</price>   <qty>3</qty>  </cd>
```

It's not valid because it doesn't have a title or artist field. Although we have 3 in stock, we can't say what it is 3 of.

XML files therefore usually have a Document Type Definition or "DTD" that specifies how the elements can appear. The DTD expresses which tags can appear, in what order, and how they can be nested. The DTD can be part of the same file, or stored separately in another place. A well-formed document that also has a DTD and that conforms to its DTD is called *valid*.

The DTD is itself written using something close to XML tags, and there is a proposal underway to align the DTD language more closely to XML. You don't need to be able to read or write a DTD to understand this chapter, but we'll go over the basics anyway. There is a way to specify that some fields are optional and thus might not be present. In other words, it's the usual type of "a *foo* is any number of *bars* followed by at least one *frotz*" grammar that we see throughout programming, with its own set of rules for how you express it. Here's a DTD that specifies our CD inventory XML file.

```
<!ELEMENT inventory (cd)* >
   <!ELEMENT cd (title, artist, price, qty)>
        <!ELEMENT title (#PCDATA)>
        <!ELEMENT artist (#PCDATA)>
        <!ELEMENT price (#PCDATA)>
        <!ELEMENT qty (#PCDATA)>
```

White space is not significant in an XML file, so we can indent elements to suggest to the human reader how they are nested. The first line says that the outermost tag, the top-level of our document, will be named "inventory," and this is followed by zero or more "cd" elements (that's what the asterisk indicates). Each cd element has four parts: title, artist, price, and qty, in that order. Definitions of those follow in the DTD. "#PCDATA" means that the element contains only "parsed character data," and not tags or other XML information.

When you get down to the bottom level, every element is either "CDATA"—character data that is not examined by the parser—or "PCDATA"—parsed character data meaning the string of an element. The nesting rule automatically forces a certain simplicity on every XML document which takes on the structure known in computer science circles as a tree.

XML documents begin with a tag that says which version of XML they contain, like this:

```
<?xml version="1.0"?>
```

This line is known as the "declaration" and it may also contain additional information, in the form of more attributes, about the character set and so on. By convention, the next tag gives the name of the root element of the document. It also has the DTD nested within it, or it gives the filename if the DTD is in another file. Here's what the tag looks like when it says "the DTD is in a file called "invfile.dtd":

```
<!DOCTYPE inventory  SYSTEM "inv-file.dtd" >
```

The version and DTD information is called the "prolog," which comes at the start of an XML document. The marked-up data part of the XML file is called the "document instance." It's an instance of the data described by the DTD.

Figure 28-2 shows the different sections of an XML document and the names given to them. This example shows how the DTD looks when it is part of the XML file, rather than a separate file.

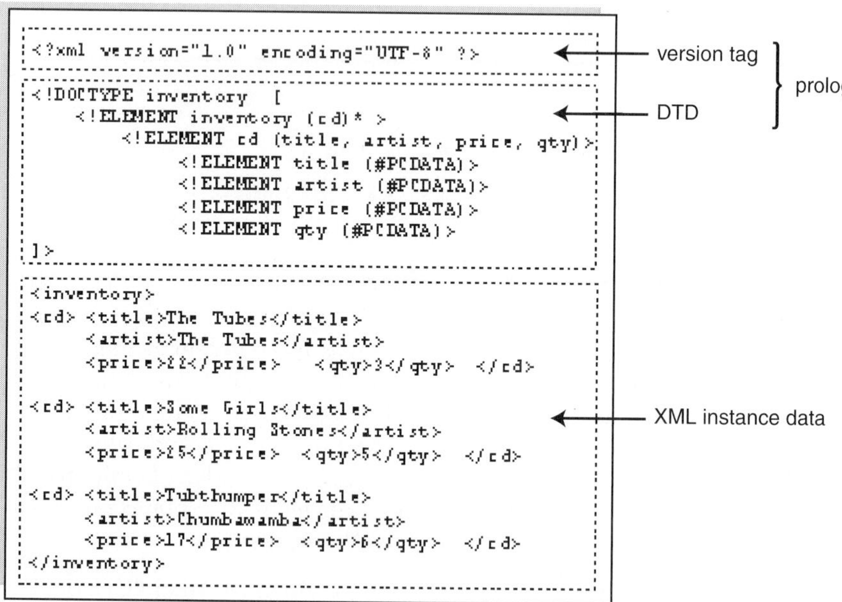

Figure 28–2 The parts of an XML file.

An important recent feature of XML is "namespaces." A "namespace" is a computer science term for a place where a bunch of names (identifiers) can exist without interfering with any other bunches of names that you might have laying around. For instance, an individual Java method forms a namespace. You can give variables in a method any names you like, and they won't collide with the names you have in any other method. A java package forms a namespace. When you refer to something by its full name, including the package name and class name, you unambiguously say what it is, and it cannot get mixed up with any other name that has identical parts. If we refer to "List" in our Java code, it may not be clear what we mean. If we write java.util.List or java.awt.List, we are saying which List we mean unambiguously by stating the namespace (the package) it belongs to. The reference cannot be confused with any other.

XML supports namespaces, so the markup tags that you define won't collide with any similarly-named tags from someone else. When you give the name of a tag at the start of an element, you can also supply an attribute for that tag, saying which namespace it comes from. The attribute name is "xmlns" meaning "XML NameSpace," and it looks like this:

```
<artist xmlns="http://www.example.com/inventory" >
Rolling Stones
</artist>
```

This says that the artist element, and any elements contained within it, are the ones that belong to the namespace defined at *www.example.com/inventory*. You define a namespace within a DTD by adding a "xmlns=something" attribute to the element's tag. By mentioning a namespace in the XML as in the example above, the CD inventory "artist" element will not be confused with any other element that uses the name "artist." Namespaces are useful when you are building up big DTDs describing data from several domains. However, note that the Java XML parsers do not support namespaces in the current release.

Here's a longer example of a DTD giving the XML format of Shakespearean plays! This shows the power of XML—you can use it to describe just about any structured data. This example is taken from the documentation accompanying Sun's JAXP library. It was written by Jon Bosak, the chief architect of XML. You'll notice a few more DTD conventions. A "?" means that element is optional. A "+" means there must be at least one of those things, and possibly more. You can group elements together inside parentheses.

DTD for Shakespeare's Plays

```
<!-- DTD for Shakespeare    J. Bosak    1994.03.01, 1997.01.02 -->
<!-- Revised for case sensitivity 1997.09.10 -->
<!-- Revised for XML 1.0 conformity 1998.01.27 (thanks to Eve Maler) -->

<!-- <!ENTITY amp "&#38;#38;"> -->
<!ELEMENT PLAY     (TITLE, FM, PERSONAE, SCNDESCR, PLAYSUBT, INDUCT?,
                                            PROLOGUE?, ACT+, EPILOGUE?)>
<!ELEMENT TITLE    (#PCDATA)>
<!ELEMENT FM       (P+)>
<!ELEMENT P        (#PCDATA)>
<!ELEMENT PERSONAE (TITLE, (PERSONA | PGROUP)+)>
<!ELEMENT PGROUP   (PERSONA+, GRPDESCR)>
<!ELEMENT PERSONA  (#PCDATA)>
<!ELEMENT GRPDESCR (#PCDATA)>
<!ELEMENT SCNDESCR (#PCDATA)>
<!ELEMENT PLAYSUBT (#PCDATA)>
<!ELEMENT INDUCT   (TITLE, SUBTITLE*, (SCENE+|(SPEECH|STAGEDIR|SUBHEAD)+))>
<!ELEMENT ACT      (TITLE, SUBTITLE*, PROLOGUE?, SCENE+, EPILOGUE?)>
<!ELEMENT SCENE    (TITLE, SUBTITLE*, (SPEECH | STAGEDIR | SUBHEAD)+)>
<!ELEMENT PROLOGUE (TITLE, SUBTITLE*, (STAGEDIR | SPEECH)+)>
<!ELEMENT EPILOGUE (TITLE, SUBTITLE*, (STAGEDIR | SPEECH)+)>
<!ELEMENT SPEECH   (SPEAKER+, (LINE | STAGEDIR | SUBHEAD)+)>
<!ELEMENT SPEAKER  (#PCDATA)>
<!ELEMENT LINE     (#PCDATA | STAGEDIR)*>
<!ELEMENT STAGEDIR (#PCDATA)>
<!ELEMENT SUBTITLE (#PCDATA)>
<!ELEMENT SUBHEAD  (#PCDATA)>
```

The DTD says that a Shakespearean play consists of the title, followed by the FM ("Front Matter"—a publishing term), personae, a scene description, a play subtext, a possible induction, a possible prologue, at least one (and maybe many) act, then finally, an optional epilogue. I asked Jon Bosak why he didn't use white space to better format this DTD. He explained that it's hard to do for non-trivial DTDs, although people are doing it more now with schemas (data descriptions) that are truly based on XML.

One programmer recently wrote a DTD describing the format of strip cartoons and published it on the *slashdot.com* website. It's a very flexible data description language! You don't need to be able to read and write DTDs as part of your work, but it doesn't hurt. There are automated tools called DTD editors that let you specify data relationships in a user-friendly way and automatically generate the corresponding DTD. There are a few additional DTD entries and conventions, but this summary provides a strong enough foundation of XML to present the Java features in the rest of the chapter.

What Is XML Used For?

There seems to be agreement from all sides that XML has a bright future. Microsoft chief executive Steve Ballmer said that he thinks use of XML will be a critically important trend in the industry. Why is this? What motivated XML's design? XML was developed in the mid 1990s under the leadership of Sun Microsystems employee Jon Bosak. Jon was looking for ways to use the Internet for more than just information delivery and presentation. He wanted to create a framework that would allow information to be self-describing. That way applications could guarantee that they could access just about any data. That in turn would clear the path to intelligent data-sharing between different organizations. And *that* in turn would allow more and much better applications to be written and increase the demand for servers to run them on. Well, that last part isn't a goal, but it's certainly a great side-effect for anyone in the computer hardware industry.

Information access might not sound like a problem in these days of web publishing, but it used to be a significant barrier. The web is still not a good medium for arbitrary binary data or data that is not text, pictures, or audio. A few years ago, every hardware manufacturer had a different implementation of floating-point hardware, and the formats were incompatible between different computers. If you had a tape of floating-point data from an application run on a DEC minicomputer, you had to go through unreasonable effort to process it on another manufacturer's mainframe. IBM promoted its EBCDIC (Extended Binary Coded Decimal Interchange Code) convention over the ASCII (American Standard Code for Information Interchange) codeset standardized in the rest of the Western world. People who wanted to see their printouts in Japanese resorted to a variety of non-standard approaches. By storing everything in character strings, XML avoids problems of incompatible byte order (big-endian/little-endian) that continue to plague people sharing data in binary formats. By stipulating Unicode or UTF encoding for the strings, XML opens up access to all the locales in the world, just as Java does.

XML makes your data independent of any vendor or implementation or application software. In the 1960s, IBM launched a transaction processing environment called CICS. CICS was an acronym for "Customer Information Control System." When a site used CICS, after a while it usually became completely dependent on it, and had to buy large and continuing amounts of hardware and support from IBM in order to keep functioning. People used to joke that it was the customer that was being controlled, not the information. But it was no joke if you were in that position. Modern software applications cause the same kind of single-vendor lock-in today. XML goes a long way to freeing your data from this hidden burden. But note this key point: just because something is published in XML does not make it openly available. The DTD and semantic meaning of the tags must also be published before anyone can make sense of non-trivial documents.

So XML makes it possible for otherwise incompatible computer systems to share data in a way that all can read and write. XML markup can also be read by people because it is just ordinary text. So what new things can be done with XML? XML opens up the prospect of data comparisons and data sharing at every level on the web. If you want to buy a digital camera online today, you might spend a few hours visiting several retailer websites and jotting down your comparison shopping notes. With XML, you take a copy of the merchants' product datasheets and run an automated comparison sorted in order of the product characteristics that matter most to you. Even more important, if you're a business that needs to buy 1,000 digital cameras for resale, XML lets you put this business-to-business transaction up for bid in an automated way.

Two things have to happen for automated XML bids and comparisons to occur. First, suppliers have to use a common DTD for describing their wares online. Second, someone has to write the comparison software, probably as a browser plug-in. Neither of these is outlandish. Various industry groups have already started to cooperate on common data descriptions. The best known are RosettaNet for electronics, and Acord for insurance. The development community is also working on XML-based protocols to let software components and applications communicate using standard Internet HTTP. The leading contender here is SOAP—Simple Object Access Protocol—from IBM, HP, Microsoft, and others.

As one white paper pointed out, the applications that will drive the acceptance of XML are those that cannot be accomplished within the limitations of HTML. These applications can be classified in four broad categories:

1. Applications that require the Web client to work with two or more different databases (e.g., comparison shopping).
2. Applications that want to move a significant proportion of the processing load from the Web server to the Web client.
3. Applications that require the Web client to present different views of the same data to different users.
4. Applications in which intelligent Web agents attempt to tailor information discovery to the needs of individual users.

The alternative to XML for these applications is proprietary code embedded as "script elements" in HTML documents and delivered in conjunction with proprietary browser plug-ins or Java applets. XML gives content providers a data format that does not tie them to particular script languages, authoring tools, and delivery engines. XML supports a standardized, vendor-independent, level playing field upon which different authoring and delivery tools may freely compete.

XML Versions and Glossary

Table 28-1 contains the latest version numbers relating to XML. This chapter describes the most up-to-date version of everything available at the time of this writing (Winter 2001).

Table 28–1 XML-Related Version Numbers

API	Version Number	Description
JAXP	ver 1.1	Java API for XML processing. Includes an XSLT framework based on TrAX (Transformation API for XML) plus updates to the parsing API to support DOM Level 2 and SAX version 2.0. The remainder of this chapter has more information on JAXP.
XSLT	ver 1	XSLT is a conversion language standardized by W3C that can be used to put XML data in some other form such as HTML, PDF, or a different XML format. For example, you can use XSLT to convert an XML document in a format used by one company to the format used by another company. See *www.zvon.org* for a tutorial on "eXtensible Stylesheet Language Transformations" (XSLT).
SAXP	ver 2.0	Simple API for XML Parsing. This is covered in the rest of this chapter.
DOM	level 2	Document Object Model, which is another API for XML parsing. This is covered in the rest of this chapter.
JAXM	ver 0.92	Java Architecture for XML Messaging. A new specification that describes a Java library for XML-based messaging protocols. Objects and arguments (messages) will be turned into XML and sent to other processes and processors as streams of characters.
JAXB	early access	Java Architecture for XML Binding. A convenient new Java library for XML parsing under development by Sun and released in draft form as this text went to print.

Table 28-2 contains a glossary of terms that you can review and refer back to as necessary.

As should be clear from the alphabet soup of different libraries and versions, XML is an emerging technology, and Java support for XML is evolving rapidly—on Internet time in fact.

Table 28–2 XML-Related Glossary

Name	Example	Description
start tag	<artist>	Marks the beginning of an element.
end tag	</artist>	Marks the end of an element.
element	<price>17</price>	A unit of XML data, complete with its start and end tags.
DTD	see chapter text	Document Type Definition, specifying which tags are valid, and what are the acceptable ways of nesting them in the document.
entity	<	An entity is essentially a shorthand way of referring to something. Here, the four characters "<" form an entity representing a left chevron, which has special meaning if it appears literally. An entity is a distinct individual item that is included in an XML document by referencing its name. This item might be as small as an individual character, or a text string, or a complete other XML file, or it may be a reference to something defined earlier in this XML file. All entities have to be declared in the DTD before they can be used.
attribute	<foo someName="someValue" ...	The **someName="someValue"** string pair holds additional information or detail about an element.
JAXP	see chapter text	The Java API for XML processing. A package of classes that support a Java interface to XML. The package name is javax.xml, introduced in JDK 1.4
JAXB	n/a	The Java Architecture for XML Binding— a follow-up library to JAXP, which handles all the details of XML parsing and formatting. It can be more efficient than using a SAX (Simple API for XML) parser or an implementation of the DOM (Document Object Model) API. An early draft was released in July 2001.
XML	see chapter text	eXtensible Mark-up Language.
XSLT	see chapter text	eXtensible Stylesheet Language Transformations, a standard for transforming XML into text or other XML documents. An XSLT implementationis in JDK 1.4.
URI	ftp://ftp.best.com	Uniform Resource Identifier. The generic term for all types of names and addresses that refer to objects on the World Wide Web. A URL is one kind of URI.
URL	http://www.afu.com	Uniform Resource Locator. The address of a web site or web page. The first part of the address specifies the protocol to use (e.g., ftp, http). The second part of the address gives the IP address or domain name where the resource is located.

JAXP Library Contents

This is a good point to review the packages that make up the Java XML library, their purpose, and their classes. The different package names reflect the different origins of the code. The Java interfaces came from Sun Microsystems, the DOM implementation came from the W3C, and the SAX parser implementation came from yet a third organization.

> package: **`javax.xml.parsers`**
>
> purpose: is the Java interface to the XML standard for parsing
>
> contains these classes/interfaces: DocumentBuilderFactory, Document-Builder, SAXParserFactory, SAXParser. These get instances of a Parser and undertake a parse on an XML file.

> package: **`javax.xml.transform`**
>
> purpose: is the Java interface to the XML standard for tree transformation
>
> contains: classes to convert an XML tree into an HTML file or XML with a different DTD. Tree transformation is beyond the scope of this text, but you can read more about it by searching for "transform" at *java.sun.com*.

> package: **`org.w3c.dom`**
>
> purpose: has the classes that make up a DOM tree in memory
>
> contains these classes/interfaces: `Node` plus its subtypes: `Document`, `DocumentType`, `Element`, `Entity`, `Attr`, `Text`, etc.

> package: **`org.xml.sax`**
>
> purpose: has the classes that can be used to navigate the data returned in a SAX parse
>
> contains: two packages `org.xml.sax.ext` (extensions) and `org.xml.sax.helpers` plus these classes/interfaces: `Attributes`, `ContentHandler`, `EntityResolver`, `DTDHandler`, `XMLReader`. The helpers package contains the `DefaultHandler` class which is typically extended by one of your classes to handle a SAX parse, as explained below.

All the above packages are kept in a file called jaxp.jar. The JAXP distribution also includes two other jar files: crimson.jar and xalan.jar. Crimson.jar holds the DOM and SAX parser implementations. Xalan.jar contains the implementation of the xml transformation interface. Make sure that the right jar files are in your path for the features you are using.

Because of the seemingly unrelated package names, XML parsing may appear a little unorganized. Just remember it this way: You always need the java.xml.parsers package. And you need the package with "dom" in its name to do a DOM parse, or "sax" in its name to do a SAX parse. The SAX packages also have the error-handling classes for both kinds of parse.

Reading XML with DOM Parsers

XML documents are just text files, so you could read and write them using ordinary file I/O. But you'd miss the benefits of XML if you did that. Valid XML documents have a lot of structure to them, and we want to read them in a way that lets us check their validity, and also preserve the information about what fields they have and how they are laid out.

What we need is a program that reads a flat XML file and generates a tree data structure in memory containing all the information from the file. Ideally, this program should be general enough to build that structure for all possible valid XML files. Processing an XML file is called "parsing" it. Parsing is the computer science term (borrowed from compiler terminology) for reading something that has a fixed grammar, and checking that it corresponds to its grammar. The program is known as an "XML parser." The parser provides a service to application programs. Application programs hand the parser a stream of XML from a document file or URL, the parser does its work and then hands back a tree of Java objects that represents or "models" the document.

An XML parser that works this way is said to be a "Document Object Model" or "DOM" parser. The key aspect is that once the DOM parser starts, it carries on until the end and then hands back a complete tree representing the XML file. The DOM parser is very general and doesn't know anything about your customized XML tags. So how does it give you a tree that represents your XML? Well, the DOM API has some interfaces that allow any kind of data to be held in a tree. The parser has some classes that implement those interfaces, and it instantiates objects of those classes.

It's all kept pretty flexible, and allows different parsers to be plugged in and out without affecting your application code. Similarly, you get information out of the tree by calling routines specified in the DOM API. The Node interface is the primary datatype for the Document Object Model. It represents a single node in the document tree, and provides methods for navigating to child Node. Most of the other interfaces, like Document, Element, Entity, and Attr, extend Node. In the next section we will review the code for a simple program that uses a DOM parser. DOM parsers can be and are written in any language, but we are only concerned with Java implementations here.

A Program That Uses a DOM Parser

This section walks through a code example that instantiates and uses a DOM parser. If you want to try compiling this as you read the section, you'll need to download and install JDK 1.4 first.

The DOM parser is just a utility that takes incoming XML data and creates a data structure for your application program (servlet, or whatever) to do the real work. See Figure 28-3 for the diagram form of this situation.

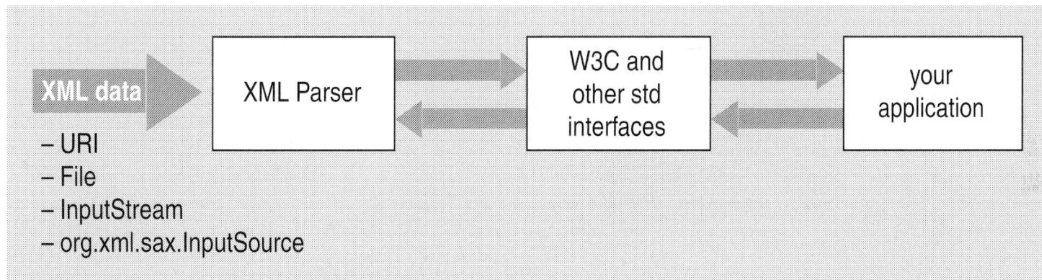

Figure 28–3 The flow of data from XML to your code.

The code we show in this section is the code that is "your application" in Figure 28-3. The JAXP library has code for the other two boxes. The interface is a little more involved than simply having our class call the parser methods. This unexpected slight complication happens because the Java library implementors wanted to make absolutely sure that the installations never got locked into one particular XML parser. It's always possible to swap the parser that comes with the library for another. To retain that flexibility, we instantiate the parser object in a funny way (the Factory design pattern), which we will explain later.

The program is going to read an XML file, get it parsed, and get back the output which is a tree of Java objects that mirror and represent the XML text file. Then the program will walk the tree, printing out what it finds. We hope it will be identical with what was read. In a real application, the code would do a lot more than merely echo the data; it would process it in some fashion, extracting, comparing, summarizing. However, adding a heavyweight application would complicate the example without any benefit. So our application simply echoes what it gets. The program we are presenting here is a simplified version of an example program called DOMEcho.java that comes with the JAXP library. The general skeleton of the code is this:

```
// import statements

public class DOMEcho {

    main(String[] args) {
      // get a Parser from the Factory
      // Parse the file, and get back a Document

      // do our application code
      // walk the Document, printing out nodes
      echo( myDoc );
    }

    echo( Node n ) {
      // print the data in this node

         for each child of this node,
             echo(child);
    }

}
```

The first part of the program, the import statements, looks like this:

```
import javax.xml.parsers.*;
import org.xml.sax.*;
import org.xml.sax.helpers.*;
import org.w3c.dom.*;
import java.io.*;
```

That shows the JAXP and I/O packages our program will use. The next part of the program is the fancy footwork that we warned you about to obtain an instance of a parser—without mentioning the actual class name of the concrete parser we are going to use. This is known as the Factory design pattern, and the description is coming up soon. For now, take it for granted that steps 1 and 2 give us a DOM parser instance.

```
public class DOMEcho {
    public static void main(String[] args) throws Exception {

      // Step 1: create a DocumentBuilderFactory
        DocumentBuilderFactory dbf =
            DocumentBuilderFactory.newInstance();
      // We can set various configuration choices on dbf now
      // (to ignore comments, do validation, etc)

     // Step 2: create a DocumentBuilder
        DocumentBuilder db = null;
        try {
            db = dbf.newDocumentBuilder();
        } catch (ParserConfigurationException pce) {
            System.err.println(pce);
            System.exit(1);
        }
        // Step 3: parse the input file
        Document doc = null;
        try {
            doc = db.parse(new File(args[0]));
        } catch (SAXException se) {
            System.err.println(se.getMessage());
            System.exit(1);
        } catch (IOException ioe) {
            System.err.println(ioe);
            System.exit(1);
        }

       // Step 4: echo the document
        echo( doc );

       }
```

That shows the key pieces of the main program. We will look at the code that echoes the document shortly, as it is an example of the data structure that the DOM parse hands back to your application. When you check the Javadoc html files for the JAXP library, you will see that the parse gives you back an object that fulfills the Document interface. Document in turn is a child of the more general Node interface.

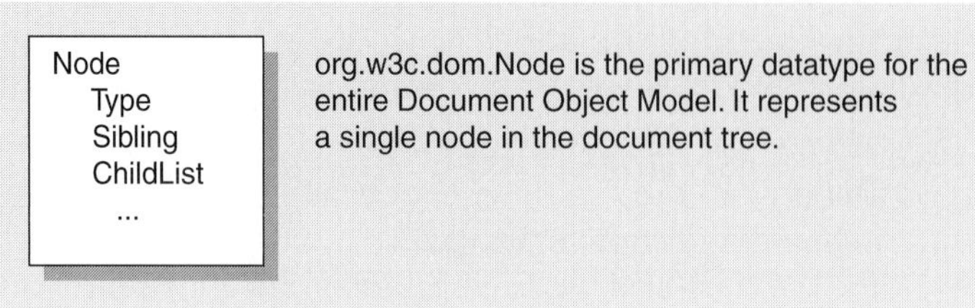

Figure 28–4 A Node represents an element, a comment, a CDATA section, an entity, and so on.

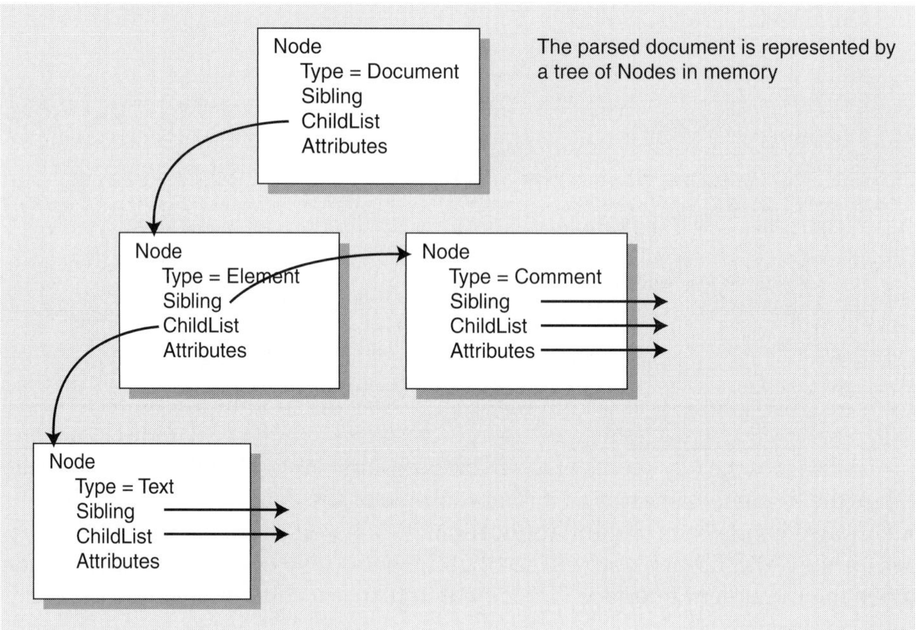

Figure 28–5 A DOM parse builds up a tree of Nodes.

Your tree is a tree of Nodes. Each element, entity, PCData, Attribute, etc., in your XML file will have a corresponding Node that represents it in the data structure handed back by the DOM parse. Node is an interface promising a dozen or so common operations: get siblings, get children, get type, get name, and so on.

Each Node has a list of child Nodes that are the elements contained within it. There is also a field that points to a collection of attributes, if the node has attributes. When you examine the class `org.w3c.dom.Node` using Javadoc, you will see that it has10 or 20 fields and methods allowing you to get and set data associated with the Node, as shown in Table 28-3.

Table 28–3 Methods of `org.w3c.dom.Node`

Method	Purpose
`getChildNodes()`	Returns a NodeList that contains all children of this node.
`hasChildNodes()`	Returns a boolean signifying if the node has children or not.
`getNextSibling()`	Returns the node immediately following this node, i.e., its next sibling.
`getNodeType()`	Returns an int code representing the type of the node, e.g., attribute, cdata section, comment, document, element, entity, etc.
`getNodeName()`	Returns a String representing the name of the node. For an element, this is its tag name.
`getNodeValue()`	Returns a String that means different things depending on what type of Node this is. An Element that just has PCData will have a child Node of type "text" and the node value that is the element's PCData.
`getParentNode()`	Returns the parent of this node.

You invoke these Node methods on the document value returned from the parse, as shown in the following example. Here is the remainder of the code. It does a depth-first traversal of a DOM tree and prints out what it finds. Once again, real application programs will do much more than just echo the data. We have omitted any processing of the XML data for simplicity here. All we do is echo the XML to prove that we have a tree that accurately reflects it.

```
  /**
    * Recursive routine to print out DOM tree nodes
    */
   private void echo(Node n) {
       int type = n.getNodeType();
       switch (type) {
       case Node.DOCUMENT_NODE:
           out.print("DOC:");
           break;
       case Node.DOCUMENT_TYPE_NODE:
           out.print("DOC_TYPE:");
           break;
       case Node.ELEMENT_NODE:
           out.print("ELEM:");
           break;
       case Node.TEXT_NODE:
           out.print("TEXT:");
           break;
       default:
           out.print("OTHER NODE: " + type);
           break;
       }

       out.print(" nodeName=\"" + n.getNodeName() + "\"");

       String val = n.getNodeValue();
       if (val != null) {
           if ( !(val.trim().equals(""))) {
               out.print(" nodeValue \""
                  + n.getNodeValue() + "\"");
           }
       }
       out.println();

// Print children if any
       for (Node child = n.getFirstChild(); child != null;
                child = child.getNextSibling()) {
           echo(child);
         }
   }
}
```

Note that the code above switches on the NodeType int field to deal with different types of Node. A better, more object-oriented way to do this is to use the instanceof operator:

```
private void echo(Node n) {
    if (n instanceof Document)
        out.print("DOC:");
    else if (n instanceof DocumentType)
        out.print("DOC_TYPE:");
    else if (n instanceof Element)
        out.print("ELEM:");
```

The Node interface is further specialized by child interfaces that extend it. The interfaces that extend the Node interface are Attr, CDATASection, CharacterData, Comment, Document, DocumentFragment, DocumentType, Element, Entity, EntityReference, Notation, ProcessingInstruction, and Text. These subinterfaces can do all the things that a Node can do, and have additional operations peculiar to their type that allow the getting and setting of data specific to that subtype.

As an example, the `org.w3c.dom.CharacterData` subinterface of `Node` adds a few methods to allow the inserting, deleting, and replacing of Strings. Table 28-4 lists the key methods of CharacterData. You should review Node and all its child interfaces using Javadoc when you start to use XML parsers.

Table 28–4 Methods of `org.w3c.dom.CharacterDat`

Method	Purpose
`getData()`	Returns the CharacterData of this Node.
`appendData(String s)`	Appends this string onto the end of the existing character data.
`insertData(int offset, String s)`	Inserts this string at the specified offset in the character data.
`replaceData(int offset, int count, String s)`	Replaces 'count' characters starting at the specified offset with the string s.
`setData(String s)`	Replaces the entire CharacterData of this node with this string.

You will invoke these methods on any Node to modify its character data.

The `Document` subinterface of `Node` is particularly useful, having a number of methods that allow you to retrieve information about the document as a whole, e.g.,get all the elements with a specified tagname. Some of the most important methods of `Document` are outlined in Table 28-5.

Table 28–5 Methods of `org.w3c.dom.Document`

Method	Purpose
`getElementsByTagName( String t)`	Returns a NodeList of all the Elements with a given tag name in the order in which they are encountered in a preorder traversal of the Document tree.
`createElement(String e)`	Creates an Element of the type specified.
`getDoctype()`	Returns the DTD for this document. The type of the return value is DocumentType.

You will invoke these methods on the document value returned from the parse.

Once you have parsed an XML file, it is really easy to query it, extract from it, update it, and so on. The XML is for storing data, moving data around, sharing data with applications that haven't yet been thought of, and sharing data with others outside your own organization (e.g., an industry group or an auction site). The purpose of the parser is to rapidly convert a flat XML file into the equivalent tree data structure that your code can easily access and process.

Reading an XML File—SAX Parsers

DOM level 1 was recommended as a standard by the World Wide Web consortium, W3C, in October 1998. In the years since then, a weakness in the DOM approach has become evident. It works fine for small and medium-sized amounts of data, up to, say, hundreds of megabytes. But DOM parsing doesn't work well for very large amounts of data, in the range of many gigabytes, which cannot necessarily fit in memory at once. In addition, it can waste a lot of time to process an entire document when you know that all you need is one small element a little way into the file.

To resolve these problems, a second algorithm for XML parsing was invented. It became known as the "Simple API for XML" or "SAX," and it's distinguishing characteristic is that it passes back XML elements to the calling program as it finds them. In other words, a SAX parser starts reading an XML stream, and whenever it notices a tag that starts an element, it tells the calling program. It does the same thing for closing tags too. The way a SAX parser communicates with the invoking program is via callbacks, just like event handlers for GUI programs.

The application program registers itself with the SAX parser, saying in effect "when you see one of these tags start, call this routine of mine." It is up to the application program what it does with the information. It may need to build a data structure, or add up values, or process all elements with one particular value, or whatever. For example, to search for all CDs by The Jam, you would look for all the artist elements where the PCDATA is "The Jam."

SAX parsing is very efficient with machine resources, but it also has a couple of drawbacks. The programmer has to write more code to interface to a SAX parser than to a DOM parser. Also, the programmer has to manually keep track of where he is in the parse in case the application needs this information (and that's a pretty big disadvantage). Finally, you can't "back up" to an earlier part of the document, or rearrange it, anymore than you can back up a serial data stream. You get the data as it flies by, and that's it.

The error handling for JAXP SAX and DOM applications are identical in that they share the same exceptions. The specifications require that validation errors are ignored by default. If you want to throw an exception in the event of a validation error, then you need to write a brief class that implements the `org.xml.sax.ErrorHandler` interface, and register it with your parser by calling the `setErrorHandler()` method of either `javax.xml.parsers.DocumentBuilder` or `org.xml.sax.XMLReader`. Error handling is the reason why DOM programs import classes from the `org.xml.sax` and `org.xml.sax.helpers` packages.

JAXP includes both SAX and DOM parsers. So which should you use in a given program? You will want to choose the parser with an eye on the following characteristics:

- SAX parsers are generally faster and use less resources, so they are a good choice for servlets and other transaction oriented requirements
- SAX parsers require more programming effort to set them up and interact with them
- SAX parsers are well suited to XML that contains structured data (e.g., serialized objects)
- DOM parsers are simpler to use
- DOM parsers require more memory and processor work
- DOM parsers are well suited to XML that contains actual documents (e.g., Office or Excel documents in XML form)

If it's still not clear, use a DOM parser, as it needs less coding on your part.

A Program That Uses a SAX Parser

This section walks through a code example of a SAX parser. Because we have already covered much of the background, it will seem shorter than the DOM example. Don't be fooled. The general skeleton of the code is this:

```
// import statements

public class MySAXEcho extends DefaultSAXHandler {

    main(String[] args) {
      // get a Parser
      // register my callbacks, and parse the file
    }

    // my routines that get called back
    public void startDocument() { ...}
    public void startElement( ...
    public void characters ( ...
    public void endElement(
  ...
}
```

The first part of the program, the import statements, looks like this:

```
import java.io.*;
import org.xml.sax.*;
import org.xml.sax.helpers.DefaultHandler;
import javax.xml.parsers.SAXParserFactory;
import javax.xml.parsers.ParserConfigurationException;
import javax.xml.parsers.SAXParser;
```

That shows the JAXP and I/O packages our program will use. The next part of the program is the fancy footwork to obtain an instance of a parser without mentioning the actual class name of the concrete parser we are going to use. As a reminder, it will be explained before the end of the chapter. For now, take it for granted that we end up with a SAX parser instance.

The next part of the program is critical. It shows how we register our routines for the callbacks. Rather than register each individual routine, the way we do with basic event handling in Swing, we make our class extend the class `org.xml.sax.helpers.DefaultHandler`. That class has 20 or so methods and is the default base class for SAX2 event handlers. When we extend that class, we can provide new implementations for any of the methods. Where we provide a new implementation, our version will be called when the corresponding SAX event occurs.

For those familiar with Swing, this is exactly the way the various Adapter classes, e.g., MouseAdapter, work.

```
public class MySAXEcho extends org.xml.sax.helpers.DefaultHandler {

    public static void main(String argv[]) {
        // Get a SAX Factory
        SAXParserFactory factory = SAXParserFactory.newInstance();

        // Use an instance of ourselves as the SAX event handler
        DefaultHandler me = new MySAXEcho();

        try {
            SAXParser sp  = factory.newSAXParser();

            // Parse the input
            sp.parse( new File(argv[0]), me);

        } catch (Throwable t) {
            t.printStackTrace();
        }
    }

    static private PrintStream  o = System.out;
```

The two lines in bold show where we create an instance of our class and then pass it as an argument to the parse routine, along with the XML file. At that point, our routines will start to be invoked by the SAX parser. The routines we have provided in this case are shown here:

```
    //============================================================
    // SAX DocumentHandler methods
    //============================================================

    public void startDocument()
    throws SAXException
    {
        o.println("In startDocument");
    }

    public void startElement(String namespaceURI,
                             String sName, // simple name (localName)
                             String qName, // qualified name
                             Attributes attrs)
    throws SAXException
    {
        o.print( "got elem <"+sName);
        if (attrs != null) {
            for (int i = 0; i < attrs.getLength(); i++) {
                o.println(attrs.getLocalName(i)+"=\""+attrs.getValue(i)+"\"");
            }
        }
        o.println("");
    }

    public void characters (char buf[], int offset, int len)
            throws SAXException {
        String s = new String(buf, offset, len);
        o.print(s);
    }

    public void endElement(String namespaceURI,
                           String sName, // simple name
                           String qName  // qualified name
                          )
    throws SAXException
    {
        o.println("</"+sName+"");
    }

}
```

And that's our complete SAX parser. In this case, we have provided the routines to get callbacks for the start of the document and each element, for the character data inside each element, and for the end of each element. A review of the DefaultHandler class will show all the possibilities. The code is on the CD that comes with this book. You should compile and test run the program.

A sample data file of a CD, complete with DTD, looks like this:

```
<?xml version="1.0"?>
<!DOCTYPE inventory [
<!ELEMENT inventory (cd)* >
   <!ELEMENT cd (title, artist, price, qty)>
      <!ELEMENT title (#PCDATA)>
      <!ELEMENT artist (#PCDATA)>
      <!ELEMENT price (#PCDATA)>
      <!ELEMENT qty (#PCDATA)>
]>

<inventory>
  <cd> <title>Some Girls</title>   <artist>Rolling Stones</artist>
     <price>25</price>  <qty>5</qty>  </cd>
</inventory>
```

This data file can be found on the CD. Compile and execute in the usual way:

```
javac SAXEcho.java
java SAXEcho  cd.xml
```

You will see output from the echo part of the code like this:

```
In startDocument
Some Girls</>
got elt <
>
Rolling Stones</>
got elt <
>
25</>
```

One of the exercises at the end of the chapter is to update the program to provide more readable output about the elements it finds.

The Factory Design Pattern

You can safely skip this section on first reading, as it simply describes how and why you use a design pattern with the JAXP library.

If you implement an XML parser in the most straightforward way, code that uses the parser will need implementation-specific knowledge of the parser (such as its classname). That's very undesirable. The whole XML initiative is intended to free your data from single platform lock-ins, so having your code tied to a particular parser undermines the objective. The Java API for XML Processing (JAXP) takes special steps to insulate the API from the specifics of any individual parser.

This makes the parser "pluggable," meaning you can replace the parsers that come with the library with any other compliant SAX or DOM parser. This is achieved by making sure that you never get a reference to the implementation class directly; you only ever work using an object of the interface type in the JAXP library. It's known as the "Factory" design pattern.

Factories have a simple function: churn out objects. Obviously, a factory is not needed to make an object. A simple call to a constructor will do it for you. However, the use of factories allows the library-writer to define an interface for creating an object, but let the Factory decide which exact class to instantiate. The Factory method allows your application classes use a general interface or abstract class, rather than a specific implementation. The interface or abstract class defines the methods that do the work. The implementation fulfills that interface, and is used by the application, but never directly seen by the application.

Figure 28-6 shows an abstract class called "Worker." Worker has exactly two methods: a() and b(). An interface can equally be used, but let's stick with an abstract class for the example. You also have some concrete classes that extend the abstract class (WorkByJane, WorkByPete, etc.). These are the different implementations that are available to you. They might differ in anything: one is fast but uses a lot of memory, another is slow but uses encryption to secure the data, a third might be able to reach remote resources.

The idea behind the factory pattern is that you don't want your application code to know about these implementation classes. You don't want it to be able to invoke the extra methods in the implementation, for example. You want a way to declare and use an instance of one of the implementation classes but have it be typed as the abstract worker class. You further want to do that with your application code seeing as little as possible of the implementation and ideally none. Figure 28-7 shows the Factory pattern that achieves this:

The factory has a method (usually static, though it doesn't have to be) that will return something that is the type of our abstract class, Worker. Here we have called this routine getWorker. It will actually send back a subtype of Worker, but as you know, if Dog is a subtype of Mammal, wherever a parameter or assignment calls for a Mammal you can give it a Dog. This is not true the other way

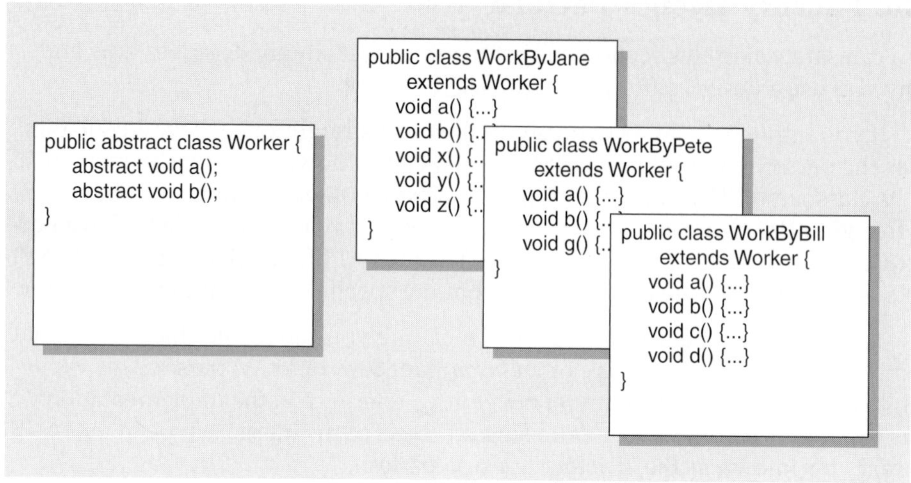

Figure 28–6 "Worker" abstract class.

```
public class MyFactory {

    static Worker getWorker( params... ) {
        //based on params,
        //choose Pete, Bill, or Jane
        ...
        return new WorkByPete();
    }
...
}
```

Figure 28–7 The Factory pattern.

around, of course, as you cannot supply a general class when a more specific one is called for. The Factory method getWorker will look at the parameters it was sent and decide which kind of Worker implementation is the best one to use: a fast one, a secure one, a small memory one, or whatever. Then it will instantiate one of these subclasses, and return it. Notice that *the return type is that of our abstract class, not one of the concrete subtypes.*

Our code that calls into the Factory will resemble Figure 28-8.

```
...
void myApplication() {
    ...
    Worker w;
    w = MyFactory.getWorker();
    w.a();
}
```

Figure 28–8 Getting an object from a Factory.

It gets back a Worker, and the only thing that can be done with a worker is to call a() or b(). There is no opportunity to call any of Pete or Jane's extra methods, shown in Figure 28-7.

You cannot instantiate a Worker object, because it's an abstract class. But by using the Factory pattern, you now hold a concrete object that is of type Worker. Describing how this works with XML parsers will bring some clarity to the Factory pattern.

When using an interface, you don't want to access the underlying implementation classes. If you break this rule, you might as well not be using an interface at all; you have locked yourself into one implementation. In the case of a DOM parser, you want to do everything through the interface, and not directly use the actual DOM parser that implements the interface. The interface is:

```
package org.w3c.dom;
public interface Document ... { ...
```

And the concrete class that implements the DOM parser currently looks something like this:

```
public class PetesPrettyGoodParser implements org.w3c.dom.Document { ...
```

But we don't want our code to be tied to any one implementation. That means you *don't* want your code to say:

```
class MyXMLApp { ...
    Document myDoc = new PetesPrettyGoodParser();     // Avoid this!
         ... = myDoc.petesSpecialMethod();       // Avoid this!
```

If you did that, you are building knowledge of Pete's Parser into your code and you can accidentally start calling additional methods of Pete's, which violates the intended API. Instead, we want a way to instantiate and access something that is a "PetesPrettyGoodParser," but without actually naming it. We want to create it and use it totally using interface methods. This is where the Factory Design Pattern comes in. The library code will have a ParserFactory class. The ParserFactory will have a static field or method that will give you a reference to the thing you are trying to keep out of your code. This field or method will typically be called something like "getInstance" or "newInstance." (If the library writer gave it a name of `newInstance`, don't confuse it with the method of the same name that has a similar purpose in class `java.lang.Class`.) The Factory method will look like this:

```
package javax.xml.parsers;
class DocumentBuilderFactory { ...
      static DocumentBuilderFactory newInstance() {

               ...
```

Design Pattern Summary

In summary, a classic "Factory" design pattern looks like this:

1. You have an interface or abstract class, Worker.
2. You have some implementations of that, WorkerBill, WorkerJane, WorkerFred.
3. You have a Factory that has a method, often static, often called "getSomething" or newSomething." It returns something of type "Worker." That method chooses which of the implementors to use. It does a new WorkerBill (say) and returns it as the supertype.

The application code now has a concrete class, but typed as the abstract superclass or interface. It cannot use more methods than are in the interface. Voila.

Factory Pattern Confusion in Java XML

The folks at Javasoft designed this with a double example of the factory pattern. First, you get a Factory, from that you get a ParserFactory, then you get a parser, then you parse. Even worse, they made the code more confusing by using the same class (DocumentBuilderFactory) for both Factories! The code looks like this:

```
// Step 1: instantiate a DocumentBuilderFactory
      DocumentBuilderFactory dbf =
          DocumentBuilderFactory.newInstance();
// Step 2:   Use the factory pattern again to get db
      DocumentBuilder db = dbf.newDocumentBuilder();
// Step 3: now actually use db as a parser
      Document doc = db.parse( "cd.xml" );
```

They wrote code to get a Factory using the Factory pattern! The algorithm used is "first get a factory instance, then use that to get a parser instance," but it would work just as well and be a lot clearer if DocumentBuilderFactory had a static factory method to return a DocumentBuilder directly.

I asked around in Javasoft to see why this was done, and the answer was it was a holdover from the early days of the API. The intent was to keep all the methods that configure the parser in one factory. Then once a parser had been configured and set up to be instantiated, you could use the builder class to get hold of the parser that had been configured and also use the convenience methods in there. For example, say you had just one factory and you started parsing and building a document. Then what would it mean if you changed one of the configurations in the middle? Does it affect the current parser or does it instantiate a new parser and take effect from then on? To avoid all this, once a parser has been configured, you can't change the configuration unless you get a new instance of the parser.

A much better way to solve the problem is to do what SAX 2.0 does if you try to reconfigure the parser during a parse, which is to throw an exception. This has the advantage of eliminating an extra class in the API and makes it easier to use. It's water under the bridge at this point, and we have to live with the unnecessary complexity. Moral: Keep your code obvious, and it will be easier to maintain.

Other Java XML Notes

The Document building code is not guaranteed to be well-behaved in threads. You may very well have many XML files to parse, and you may want to use a thread for each. An implementation of the DocumentBuilderFactory class is not guaranteed to be thread-safe. To avoid problems, the application can get a new instance of the DocumentBuilderFactory per thread, and they can be configured differently in terms of how much validation they do, whether they ignore comments and so on.

Here's how we use the Factory instance to get back a Parser which has the type of the abstract class `javax.xml.parsers.DocumentBuilder`:

```
... myDb = myDbf.newDocumentBuilder();
```

Now that we have a DocumentBuilder (which is actually a Pete'sPrettyGood-Parser, or equivalent), we can use it in a type-safe, future-proof way to parse an XML file and build the corresponding document, like this:

```
org.w3c.dom.Document doc = myDb.parse( new File("myData.xml"));
```

We did not simply move the dependency from your code into the runtime library. The JAXP runtime library has put the hooks in place to make it possible to switch parser implementations. The full details are the in the Specification document which you will download. However, to summarize, the runtime looks for a property file that contains the class name of any different parser you want to use. If the property is not found, it uses the default. So it all works as desired. Everything is hands-off. You're manipulating the tree by remote control, which admittedly makes this harder to follow.

Download and Install the Java XML Software (JAXP)

The JAXP package is a java extension that is downloaded separately from JDK 1.3. However, JDK 1.4 beta includes support for W3C DOM 1.0 API and the SAX parser 1.0 API. If time permits, JDK 1.4 FCS may instead have support for the W3C DOM 2.0 API and SAX parser 2.0 API. Sun intends to release JDK 1.4 some time in the first quarter of 2002. If the version 2.0 software is ready by the beta release of JDK 1.4, it will probably be in the final release of JDK 1.4. If you are using JDK 1.4 or later, you do not need to do this download step, as the software is already part of the release.

To get started with, go to the XML part of Sun's Java website at *java.sun.com/xml*

Click on the "downloads" link. If the website has been redesigned and this link has moved, simply search the website for the XML download. You should download two things:

- The Java API for XML Processing (JAXP) 1.1 **Reference Implementation.** There is a "click through" license agreement on this, and then you can download the 1.6MB file called jaxp-1_1.zip. This zip file contains three jar files that comprise the implementation, and a couple of hundred HTML files that provide the documentation in Javadoc form. No source code is currently available at the time of this writing.
- The Java API for XML Processing **Specification**.
  This is a PDF file about 1 MB in size. It's a 130-page document that provides an overview of the Java interface to XML. It also contains configuration information and some programming examples that will help you further explore the Java/XML relationship.

Create a top level directory on your disk called, say, "xml" and move the downloaded file "jaxp-1_1.zip" into that disk directory. Unpack the file in your xml directory. You could instead unpack the file under your JDK directory, and move the javadoc html into the same directory with all the Javadoc for the JDK, but that makes it hard to see what is new with JAXP. To unpack, you can use WinZip or the Java "jar" utility with these commands:

```
cd c:\xml
jar -xf jaxp-1_1.zip
```

That will create a directory tree in your "xml" directory containing the JAXP software and documentation. You should also move the specification PDF file into the xml directory. If you don't already have it on your system, you'll need to download the Acrobat PDF reader (it's free) from *www.adobe.com*. It's available as a stand-alone application and as a browser plug-in. Either is fine.

Now take a look at the jar files in your xml directory. There will be three of these, as outlined in Table 28-6.

Table 28–6 Jar Files in the jaxp-1_1.zip Download

Name of File	Contents
jaxp.jar	This file contains the JAXP-specific APIs.
crimson.jar	This file contains the interfaces and classes that make up the SAX and DOM APIs, as well as the reference implementation for the parser. To use a different parser, substitute it for this file. For example, you could put xerces.jar in place to use the parser from *apache.org*.
xalan.jar	This file contains the implementation classes for the XSLT transform package, used when you want to convert XML into HTML or an XML file with a different DTD. Using this is not difficult, but it is beyond the scope of this chapter.

Make these libraries visible to your java compiler and runtime. There are at least three ways to do that on a Windows system:

- Add the full pathname of each library to the $CLASSPATH variable in the autoexec.bat or other start-up file.
- Move the files to the `jre\lib\ext` subdirectory of your Java installation. Jar files in here are automatically regarded as part of the standard runtime library.
- Use the "-classpath" option to the compiler and JVM, and give the pathname to each of these three jar files. This is best done by writing a command batch file.

Note: these commands are for Windows. Make the obvious adjustments for Unix, Linux, Mac, etc. Be careful to get this right. You may already have a CLASSPATH variable, in which case you want to add to it, not replace it. If you used a batch file, execute it to make sure the variables are set. You can see what environment variables are set by typing "set" at the command line.

Running the Example Code

The next step is to try running one of the example XML programs that accompany the release. Go to your XML directory with this command:

```
cd c:\xml\jaxp-1.1\examples\DOMEcho
```

Then compile and run the sample DOMEcho application that comes with the release. This is a longer, fuller version of the DOMEcho presented here.

```
javac DOMEcho.java
java  DOMEcho  build.xml
```

You will see that the program prints out the nodes that it has read in. Note that if you don't provide a DTD for the sample data, you will have a non-validating parse by definition. The "build.xml" is an XML file that comes with the release. It is actually a file that is used to configure a part of the Tomcat servlet container that we saw in an earlier chapter. The output in part looks like this:

```
ELEM: nodeName="project"
      ATTR: nodeName="name" nodeValue="DOMEcho"
      ATTR: nodeName="default" nodeValue="main"
      ATTR: nodeName="basedir" nodeValue="."
    TEXT: nodeName="#text" nodeValue=[WS]
    COMM: nodeName="#comment" nodeValue=" The distribution top directory "
    TEXT: nodeName="#text" nodeValue=[WS]
    ELEM: nodeName="property"
        ATTR: nodeName="name" nodeValue="top"
        ATTR: nodeName="value" nodeValue="../.."
    TEXT: nodeName="#text" nodeValue=[WS]
    COMM: nodeName="#comment" nodeValue=" Common classpath "
    TEXT: nodeName="#text" nodeValue=[WS]
    ELEM: nodeName="path"
```

As Sun's JAXP specification points out, XML and Java form a marriage made in heaven. XML provides a cross platform way to describe data, and Java provides a cross-platform way to process data.

Further Reading

There is a centralized portal for people developing with XML languages at *www.xml.org*. The website was formed in 1999 by OASIS, the non-profit Organization for the Advancement of Structured Information Systems, to provide public access to XML information and XML Schemas. You can find everything there from tutorials to case studies.

The website *www.w3schools.com/dtd/default.asp* has a good DTD Tutorial under the title "Welcome to DTD School." It also has links to many other tutorials of interest to XML developers.

If you're interested in getting more information on XML and the Java XML API, be aware there are a few items we haven't covered. First, there is an additional XML mark-up tag, known as a "processing instruction." This is a piece of XML inherited from SGML, but not really a good fit. (SGML is the mother of all mark-up languages, too large and too complicated to ever get much use in the real world. XML and HTML are simplifications of SGML.) A processing instruction is used to link style sheets (regular HTML CSS style sheets) into documents. Second, the topics of both elements and attributes are deeper than we have room for here. We have not covered the third library in JAXP: the transformation library in javax.xml.transform.

There is an independently-developed open source library called JDOM. This is a Java API that does the same job as W3C's DOM. It was created as a more object-oriented and easier to use alternative to DOM, and there is a good possibility it will be adopted into JAXP (or even replace it). It has been adopted as Java Specification Request number 102, if you want to check on its progress. Please see the JDOM website at *www.jdom.org* for the most up-to-date information.

IBM offers a series of free tutorials on their website. There are tutorials covering parsers, DOM, SAX, and the transformation library. Go to *www.ibm.com/developerworks* and click or search on XML. You have to register at the site, but it is free and quick.

Exercises

1. Describe the Factory design pattern and state its use.
2. Write a DTD that describes a CD inventory file. Each CD is either domestic or imported. These details are stored for all CDs: artist, title, price, quantity in stock. Imported CDs also have these fields: "country of origin," genre, non-discount status, language, and lead time for reorder. Write some XML instance data describing your five favorite CDs (include a couple of imported CDs, too).
3. Validate your XML file from the previous question by running it against the DOMEcho program that comes with the Java XML library. In the output you get, explain what the text nodes with a value of "[WS]" are. Hint: Try varying the number of spaces and blank lines in your instance data, and seeing how that changes the output.
4. Rewrite the DTD describing Shakespearean plays making better use of names, comments, and indenting.
5. It is possible to implement a DOM parser using a SAX parser, and vice versa, although not particularly efficiently. Write a couple of paragraphs of explanation suggesting how both of these cases might be done.
6. Write a servlet that reads an XML file of a CD inventory and sends HTML to the browser, putting the data into a table.
7. Improve the output of the SAXEcho program to make it more presentable and understandable.
8. Write an application that uses a DOM parser to get CD information and outputs the total number of all kinds of CDs that you have in stock, and the total number by each artist. Remember that some artists may have several titles in print at once.

Some Light Relief—"View Source" on Kevin's Life

The 5K Contest first ran in the year 2000. It's a new annual challenge for web developers and HTML gurus to create the most interesting web page in less than 5120 bytes. That's right, all HTML, scripts, image, style sheets, and any other associated files must collectively total less than 5 kilobytes in size and be entirely self-contained (no server-side processing).

The 5k competition was originally conceived in the fall of 1999 after an argument about the acceptable file size of a template for a project at work. The creator says, "It took a long time to actually get it organized because, back in those days, we all worked hard at our soul-destroying dot.com jobs and didn't have time for fun personal projects."

The 5K size limit is pretty much the only rule, and some of the entries are a bit too Zen for a meat-and-potatoes guy like me, but everyone seems to be having a good time. There is the usual crop of games written in Javascript. You've got your Space Invaders, your Maze solvers, your Game of Life. It's the International Obfuscated C Code Competition (see my text "Expert C Programming"), updated for the new medium and the new millennium. 3D Tetris, post modernism, poetry, art, angst—it's all there, with clever use of javascript, style sheets, and DHTML. You can even enter an applet if you want.

One nice entry in 2001 is the Timepiece (shown in Figure 28-9). This is an animated clock showing seconds, minutes, hours, date, day-of-week, month, phase of moon, and year. You can choose the time zone.

Timepiece is incredibly busy to look at, but somehow the complexity adds to its appeal. All umpteen axes grind past each other as seconds tick away, a fusion of traffic, tectonics, and time. (Sorry, that Zen poetry style is catching. In less than 5K of Javascript code.) You can see all the 5K winners at *www.the5k.org/.*

One of the unexpected winners this year was, amazingly and appropriately, an XML entry. Think about it: XML is a "storing" thing, not a "doing" thing! So how can it compete with flashy graphic entries like the 3D Tetris or the Virtual Reality Dolphin? It competed with imagination. People are always looking for something fresh, something original, something that hasn't been done to death before.

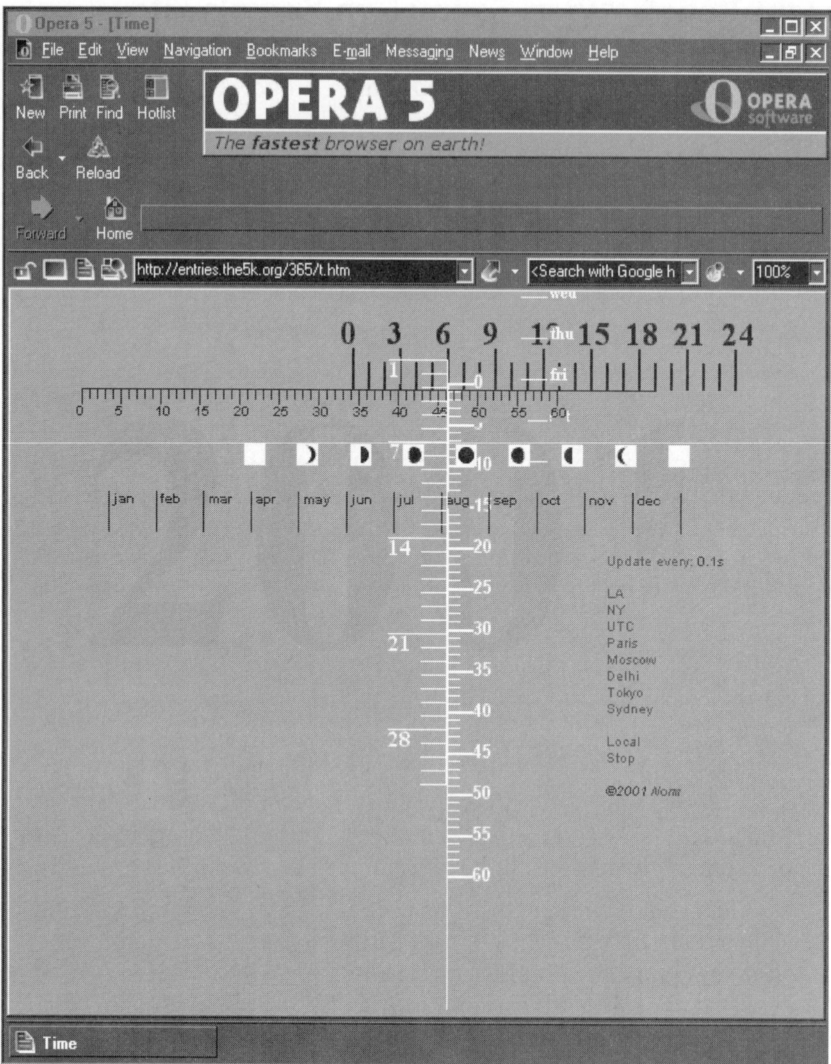

Figure 28–9 The Timepiece in under 5K bytes.

Winner Kevin Conboy described his entry as "a subtle comment on the pervasive nature of the Internet." He tried to imagine doing a "view source" on his life to see what an actual day would look like. Here is an extract from Kevin's essay entry—an XML diary. Kevin starts by getting up, washing, and dressing.

```
<!DOCTYPE KCML PUBLIC "-//KVC//DTD KCML 1.0 EXPERIMENTAL//EN"
"http://www.alternate.org/TR/REC-html40/loose.dtd"><br>
<day length='24' start='730' end='1046' name='kevinconboy'>
<wake>

<home temp='70' ac='true' tv='true' computer='false'>
<shower length='12' soap='ivory' shave='true'> </shower>
<style shirt='bananaRepublic' shorts='#000000'
shoes='bananaRepublic('sandals');'
  hat='false' boxers='true'> </style>
<kiss wife='true' son='true'></kiss>
<elevator down='true' up='false' occupied='true' conversation='no'>
</elevator>
</home>
```

Kevin lunches at a Mexican restaurant with three friends, and spends the afternoon working on graphics production for a client.

```
<lunch type='external' length='1' transport='walk' location='wahoos'>
<meal type='mexican'
companions='('vijayPatel','jeffVoreis','triciaChaya')'
src='chickenQuesadillas' beverage='mountainDew' refill='true'></meal>
</lunch>

<afternoon>
<task type='graphicsProduction' client='pearlIzumi'></task>
```

Finally, he drives home, has an evening meal, bathes his son, and soothes him to bed before watching a little TV and turning in himself.

```
<son activity='bath' cry='false'>
<bath length='15' clean='true' curSanity='('prevSanity+20');'> </bath>
<toSleep length='15' cry='true' blanket='false' pacifier='true'
bottle='false' curSanity='('prevSanity+30');'> </toSleep>
</son>

<television>
<program src='HBO' type='dennisMiller' entertain='true'>
</television>

</wake>
</day>
```

That very human sentiment of soothing his family strikes a chord. You (the reader) and I are both now near the end of the day, at the last sentence in the body of this book, and maybe we both feel the same way too: curSanity++; good night, dear programmer, sleep tight, and don't let the Tera byte.

Appendix A

Graphics Programming

- Colors
- Fonts and Font Metrics
- The Graphics Context
- Drawing Text, Lines, and Shapes
- Loading and Drawing Images
- Sounds
- Some Light Relief—Satan: Oscillate My Metallic Sonatas

This appendix covers the features of window programming associated with graphics rather than window GUIs. In this section we will cover color, fonts, and how to draw shapes on a Canvas or JPanel. We will then look at Images and some Image Processing. We'll finish up with an explanation and some sample programs showing Java's support for elementary audio output. More comprehensive support for sound is in the Java Media Framework, which is beyond the scope of this text.

The graphics features covered here are present in every version of Java from JDK 1.0 on. However, Java 2, JDK 1.2, introduced a richer, more sophisticated graphics model, known as Graphics 2D (two dimensional). It allows much finer control over the width of lines, coordinate transformations, filling shapes with colors and textures, and moving, rotating, or scaling text and graphics. The java.awt.Graphics object is augmented by a new subclass, java.awt.Graphics2D, which becomes the fundamental class for rendering shapes, text, and images.

Java is much more widely used for server programming than for client-side Graphics programs. Accordingly, we present the basic Java 1 Graphics features here, and refer interested readers to *java.sun.com/docs/books/tutorial/2d/index.html*, which is an online tutorial covering Graphics 2D.

Table A-1 lists the methods that cause the screen to be displayed.

Table A–1 Common Graphics Methods

Method	Description
`void repaint()`	You may call this to request that the window be refreshed. Typically, you would call it if you have changed the appearance of something and you want to see it on the screen. It calls update().
`void update(Graphics g)`	This routine exists to let you participate in painting the window. It defaults to clearing the area, then painting it, but you can conceivably override it to do something additional. Most of your programs, however, will not override this and will not call this.
`void paint(Graphics g)`	Will be called by the window system when the component needs to be redisplayed. You will not call this. You will override this if you dynamically change the appearance of the screen, and want to see it appear.

Colors

Naturally, Java allows you to put colors on the screen and there is a class called Color in the java.awt package. The basic color model used by Java is a common one in the computer industry. Colors are made up of a red, a green, and a blue component, each of which is described by a byte value saying how vivid that color is, ranging from 0 (darkest shade) to 255 (lightest shade). This is known as the RGB model. The actual color used in rendering will be the best match in the colors that are actually possible for a given output device. Images (like JPEG files) also have an "alpha" component that describes how transparent or opaque a pixel[1] is.

Again, this is stored in a byte, so it takes 32 bits just to store a single pixel on the screen. This is why some graphics programs can swamp your system. For large images, megabytes of data need to be moved around. The "alpha" comes in later with images; it isn't part of the Color class.

You need to experiment with this a little to get a feel for it. Figure A-1 shows an applet that allows you to set the R, G, and B values and see the resulting color mix.

To get these results, type in the following 30-line program (or copy it off the CD).

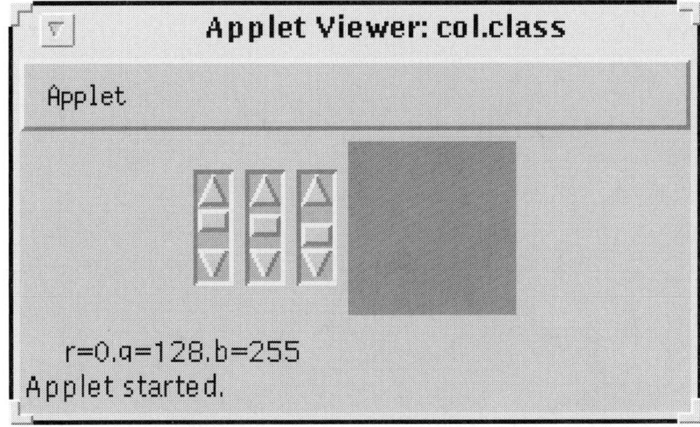

Figure A–1 The RGB can be set as shown here.

1. A pixel is a "Picture Element." It is a dot on a computer screen. When people say screens are 1024 by 768 (or whatever), they are referring to the number of pixels it can display. A pixel is like a grain of sand. By itself it is almost unnoticeable; nothing happens until you have thousands of them.

```
// <applet code=col.class   height=100 width=300>  </applet>
//
//  An applet to show how colors are made up of three values,
//  0-255 representing each of red, green, and blue.
//  Uses the JDK 1.1 event model

import java.awt.*;
import java.awt.event.*;
import java.applet.*;
public class col extends Applet {

    Scrollbar s1 = new Scrollbar(Scrollbar.VERTICAL,0,50,0,305);
    Scrollbar s2 = new Scrollbar(Scrollbar.VERTICAL,0,50,0,305);
     int x=50;
    Scrollbar s3 = new Scrollbar(Scrollbar.VERTICAL,0,x,0,255+x);
    Canvas c = new Canvas();

    int r,g,b;
    public void init () {
       s1.setUnitIncrement(10); s1.setBlockIncrement(25);
       s2.setUnitIncrement(10); s2.setBlockIncrement(25);
       s3.setUnitIncrement(10); s3.setBlockIncrement(25);
       add(s1); add(s2); add(s3); add(c);
       ScrAdj sa = new ScrAdj();
       s1.addAdjustmentListener(sa);
       s2.addAdjustmentListener(sa);
       s3.addAdjustmentListener(sa);
       c.setSize(75,75);
    }

    public void paint(Graphics gr) {
       c.setBackground(new Color(r,g,b) );
       gr.drawString("r="+r+ ",g="+g+ ",b="+b, 20,100);
    }


    class ScrAdj implements AdjustmentListener {
      public void adjustmentValueChanged(AdjustmentEvent ae) {
        System.out.println("ae="+ae);
        Scrollbar s = (Scrollbar) ae.getAdjustable();
             if (s==s1) r=ae.getValue();
        else if (s==s2) g=ae.getValue();
        else            b=ae.getValue();
        repaint();
      }
   }

}
```

We've already seen how you can use a Color object to set the color of a component. Here's an example of how that might be done in practice:

```
Frame f = new Frame("my frame");
f.setForeground( Color.white );

f.setBackground( new Color(255,175,175) ); //pink
```

The class Color has the following methods and constants, among others:

```
public final class Color {

     public final static Color white = new Color(255, 255, 255);
     public final static Color gray = new Color(128, 128, 128);
     public final static Color black = new Color(0, 0, 0);
     public final static Color red = new Color(255, 0, 0);
     public final static Color pink = new Color(255, 175, 175);
     public final static Color orange = new Color(255, 200, 0);
     public final static Color yellow = new Color(255, 255, 0);
     public final static Color green = new Color(0, 255, 0);
     public final static Color magenta= new Color(255, 0, 255);
     public final static Color cyan = new Color(0, 255, 255);
     public final static Color blue = new Color(0, 0, 255);

     public Color(int r, int g, int b);
     public Color(int rgb);
     public Color(float r, float g, float b);

     public int getRed();
     public int getGreen();
     public int getBlue();
     public int getRGB();

     public Color brighter();
     public Color darker();

     public static int HSBtoRGB(float hue, float saturation, float
brightness);
     public static float[] RGBtoHSB(int r, int g, int b, float[] hsbvals);
     public static Color getHSBColor(float h, float s, float b);
}
```

There's an alternative color model, known as HSB, meaning *Hue, Saturation,* and *Brightness.* Java doesn't use this, but it allows easy translations using the methods just described.

So When Will I Use the `paint()`, `repaint()`, or `update()` Methods? If you just use the static display typical of a GUI, you might never need to override any of the three above methods. You can often just setVisible (true) Components as needed. Let's explain when you use paint().

Normally, the window system keeps track of what you have put on the screen. If you obscure it with other windows and then bring it to the front, the window system is responsible for restoring the state.

If, however, you wish to *change* what you have put on the screen (say you have displayed a GIF that you now want to replace with something else), this would be accomplished by overriding paint(). Code in init() can get something on the screen to begin with. Code in paint() can change the screen and get something different up there. You call repaint() to signal to the window system that it needs to update the screen. The window system will then call your paint() method to put the new image on the screen. It's done this way because paint takes an argument (a Graphics context) that you use but don't normally create yourself. Repaint() doesn't need any arguments.

Repaint() calls update() which calls clear() and then paint(). You might override update() if you are doing some advanced graphics work and you know that you only need a small portion of the screen to be changed (e.g., in an animation). Update gives you the opportunity to achieve this by providing a point where you can insert your own code between repaint() and paint(). In addition, the following will repaint just the stated size rectangle at the given coordinates:

```
repaint(x,y,w,h);
```

Paint may be called by the runtime independent of update whenever it thinks the screen needs refreshing.

In summary, you don't call paint() yourself. You may override it, but the understanding is always that it will be called for you at the times the window system thinks it needs to update the screen. If you want to force the window system to think that, then call "repaint()."

Repaint() simply lodges a request to update the screen and returns immediately. Its effect is asynchronous, and if there are several paint requests outstanding it is possible that only the last `paint()` will be done.

Fonts and Font Metrics

Fonts and information about font size are encapsulated into two classes: Font and FontMetrics. Just as with Colors, whatever font is current will be used in all text drawing operations in the AWT. However, it will not be used in operations like System.out.println. Think about it: those are Stream operations that merely push data in and out of files, and not to the screen. Only the window system cares about the physical appearance of that data.

Notice in the following example that the "foo" text will appear in the current font.

```
    paint(Graphics g) {
     g.drawString("foo",10,10);
}
```

You're given a default font to start you off, then you can change any of the characteristics, or construct a new font and set it as the font to use.

Try modifying the "mobile button" program q.java, so that the button has a background color of red, a foreground color of white, and is labeled in italic courier size 18 point. The source is on the CD. Setting colors on buttons was buggy in JDK 1.0.2.

You can construct a new font with this:

```
Font loud = new Font  ("TimesRoman", Font.BOLD, 18);
```

You can make that the current font for any Component (any Button, Label, MenuItem, Canvas) or Graphics object with this:

```
this.setFont(loud);
```

The constructor for a Font is simply this:

```
public Font( String name, int style, int size);
```

You can set the font (Courier, Helvetica, etc.), the style (plain, bold, italic, or combinations of the three), and the size (8 point, 10 point, 12 point, etc.) any way you like.

Different computer systems will have fonts that are similar but have different names. The reason font names vary is that owners of the font can charge for using its name. For example, the closest thing available to the Windows Windings font on Unix is called Zapf Dingbats (really). It's a screwy font, so everyone gives it a screwy name. Java copes with this by mapping your font request to the closest

font, size, and style that is on the underlying system. These five font names can be taken for granted:

- Times Roman
- Courier
- Helvetica
- Symbol (The font will be different on different systems.)
- Dialog

Fonts are very straightforward. The FontMetrics class allows you to compute the exact position of Strings, namely, how wide and high they are in terms of pixels. This will allow you to lay out strings exactly centered or to mix Strings of different styles and get the spacing right. You might do this if you were writing a word processor in Java, but it's a bit fussy for everyday use. Figure A-2 shows how the terms relate to typeface measurements.

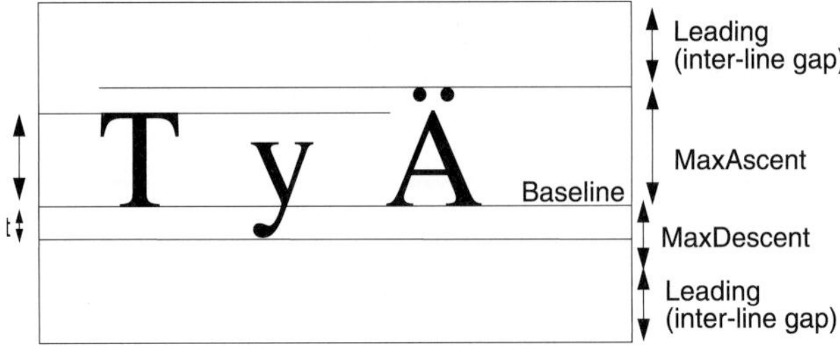

FontMetrics

getLeading() is the standard line spacing for the font. This is the amount of space between the max descent of one line and the maximum ascent of the next line.

getAscent() is the distance from the baseline to the top of most characters in the font.

getMaxAscent() is the distance from the baseline to the highest pixel painted of any character in the font. This may be the same as the ascent.

Figure A–2 FontMetrics terms as they relate to typeface measurements.

FontMetrics has these methods, which return values in units of a pixel (a dot on the screen).

```
public abstract class FontMetrics {
    public Font getFont() {

    public int getLeading(); // print term for line spacing
    public int getAscent();
    public int getDescent();
    public int getHeight() // leading + ascent + descent

    public int getMaxAscent() {
    public int getMaxDescent() {

    // For backward compatibility only.
    public int getMaxDecent() // some programmers can't spell...

    public int charWidth(char ch);
    public int stringWidth(String str);
}
```

The font metrics give you the real measurements of the font that is actually in use on your system, not the theoretical measurements of the font you asked for. The two may well be different.

The Graphics Context

A Graphics object is what you ultimately draw lines, shapes, and text on. It is also called a "graphics context" in some window systems because it bundles together information about a drawable area, plus font, color, clipping region, and other situational factors. If you look at the code in $JAVAHOME/src/java/awt/Graphics.java, you will see that it is an abstract class:

```
public abstract class Graphics { ...
```

It cannot therefore be instantiated directly, and you will never see code like the following:

```
Graphics gr = new Graphics(); // NO!
```

The most common way to obtain a Graphics object is as the argument to a paint() routine in a Canvas or Panel. (You'll actually get some concrete subclass of graphics, the details of which you never need worry about). You can explicitly ask for the Graphics object belonging to any Component or any Image with the call:

```
myComponent mc ...

Graphics mg = mc.getGraphics();
```

When you call getGraphics() it is usually for an Image, Panel, or Canvas. It's unlikely you'll want to get the Graphics object for anything else, such as [illegible]
There is too much peer behavior associated with it for you to be able to [illegible]
sensibly. When you have a Graphics object, you can draw on it and later [illegible]
the screen. You can clip it (shrink the drawing area). You can modify the [illegible]
and fonts. A common reason for explicitly getting the Graphics context [illegible]
Image is to do double-buffering. Another reason is to draw over an Image you have read in. All these techniques are explained in this chapter. If you do explicitly call this:

```
Graphics g = myPanel.getGraphics();
```

make sure you also call this when you are done with it:

```
g.dispose();
```

Graphics objects take up operating system resources (more than just memory), and a window system may have a limited number of them. When you clean them up explicitly without waiting for garbage collection to kick in, your system will tick along more smoothly.

Drawing Text, Lines, and Shapes

These are the methods of Graphics that draw text, lines, and shapes. Most of these come in two varieties: a drawXXX and a fillXXX. The first puts an empty outline on the screen, the second puts the outline and fills the interior with a solid color. In both cases the foreground color is used. A graphics object has the method `setColor(Color c)` to change the foreground color, but it doesn't have any direct way to change the background color. The underlying panel (or whatever) must do that, as shown in the following cases.

```
public void drawString(String str, int x, int y);
```

Here, the string is placed at location x,y on this component. For example:

```
public void paint(Graphics g) {
     g.drawString("The dentist whined incessantly", 10, 15);
}
```

A common pitfall with this method and the next two methods is drawing with y coordinate zero. That makes the characters disappear as they will be almost completely off the top of the canvas.

```
public void drawChars(char data[], int offset, int length, int x, int y)
public void drawBytes(byte data[], int offset, int length, int x, int y)
```

These two methods place characters or bytes from the array data[offset] to data[offset+length-1] on the component starting at location (x,y).

```
public void drawLine(int x1, int y1, int x2, int y2);
```

A line one pixel wide is drawn from (x1,y1) to (x2,y2). Drawing lines thicker than one pixel requires the use of Java 2D. The workaround is to use the fillPolygon described later. Like all of these methods, the rendering is done in whatever you have set the color to. The default foreground color is black.

```
public void drawRect(int x, int y, int width, int height);
public void fillRect(int x, int y, int width, int height);
```

A rectangle of the stated width and height is drawn with its top left corner at (x,y). There is also a `void clearRect(x,y,w,h)` that gets rid of a rectangle.

```
public void draw3DRect(int x, int y, int width, int height, boolean raised);

public void fill3DRect(int x, int y, int width, int height, boolean raised);
```

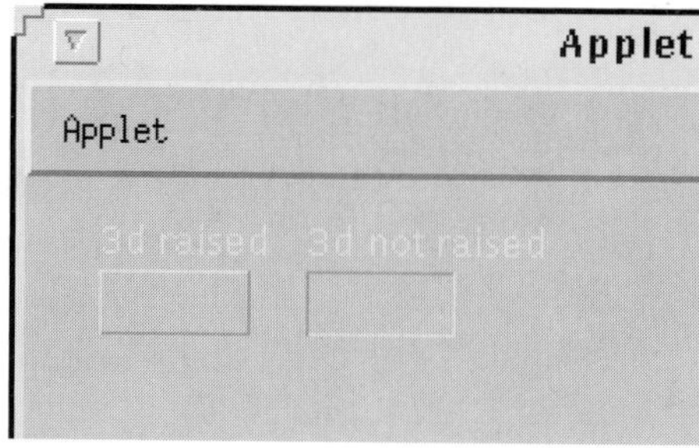

Figure A–3
3D raised and unraised.

A rectangle of the stated width and height is drawn with its top left corner at (x,y). The rectangle is artfully shaded on two sides to make it appear to be standing out (raised=true) or to be impressed (raised=false). A raised rectangle is shaded with brighter color, and a non-raised one with a darker color. Figure A-3 shows some 3D rectangles.

Here is the code that generated the screen capture:

```
// <applet code=graf.class height=300 width=500> </applet>
import java.awt.*;
import java.applet.*;
public class graf  extends Applet {

    public void paint(Graphics g) {
        g.setColor(Color.cyan);
        g.drawString("3d raised", 25,25);
        g.draw3DRect(25,30,50,20,true);
        g.drawString("3d not raised", 95,25);
        g.draw3DRect(95,30,50,20,false);
    }
}
```

Here are two more ways to draw a rectangle:

```
public void drawRoundRect(int x, int y, int width, int height, int
  arcWidth, int arcHeight);
public void fillRoundRect(int x, int y, int width, int height, int
  arcWidth, int arcHeight);
```

These are like drawRect and fillRect, only these rectangles have rounded corners.

You control the diameter of the rounded corners by setting the width and height of the curved portion in pixels. If you use values that are comparable to the

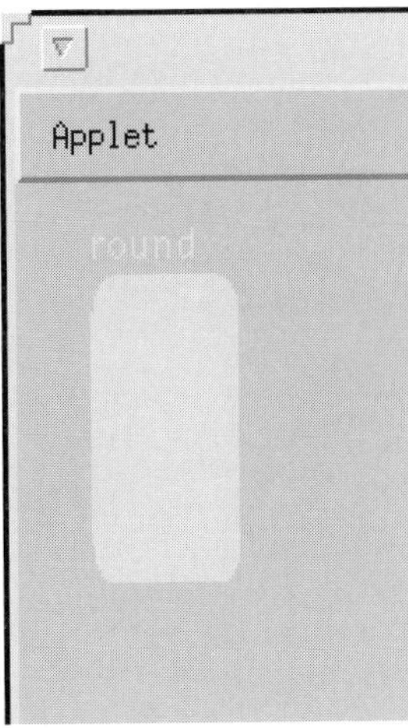

Figure A–4
A rounded rectangle.

width and height of the rectangle, you end up with an oval not a rectangle, as shown in Figure A-4. Rule of thumb: Use arc width and height that are 15-25% of the rectangle width and height.

Here is the code that generated the diagram:

```
// <applet code=graf.class   height=300 width=500> </applet>
import java.awt.*;
import java.applet.*;
public class graf  extends Applet {

    public void paint(Graphics g) {
        g.setColor(Color.cyan);
        g.drawString("round", 25,25);
        g.fillRoundRect(25,30, 50,100,15,25);
    }
}
```

```
public void drawOval(int x, int y, int width, int height);
public void fillOval(int x, int y, int width, int height);
```

These two methods draw ovals. The arguments are easy to understand if you compare the methods to drawRect(). The oval that is drawn is one that fits exactly in the rectangle of that width and height. The imaginary rectangle's top left corner is at the (x,y) location (see Figure A-5).

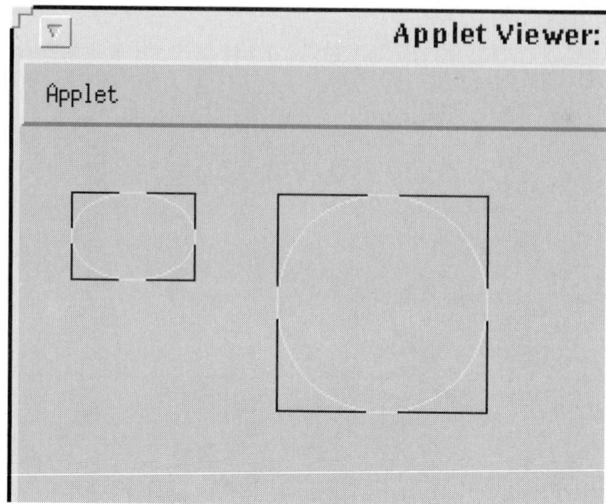

Figure A–5 Two ovals and their bounding rectangles.

Here is the code that generated the diagram:

```
// <applet code=graf.class height=300 width=500> </applet>
import java.awt.*;
import java.applet.*;
public class graf  extends Applet {

    public void paint(Graphics g) {
        g.drawRect(25,30, 60,40);
        g.drawRect(125,30, 100,100);

        g.setColor(Color.cyan);
        g.drawOval(25,30, 60,40);
        g.drawOval(125,30, 100,100);
    }
}
```

As can be seen, an oval with the width=height is a circle.

```
public void drawArc(int x, int y, int width, int height,
               int startAngle, int arcAngle);
public void fillArc(int x, int y, int width, int height,
               int startAngle, int arcAngle);
```

Again, the starting point for understanding these two methods is the rectangle located at (x,y). Then imagine dividing the rectangle into four quadrants. The x axis from the origin of the quadrants represents 0 degrees. The starting point for the arc is the offset from this line: 90 is straight up (along the y axis), 270 is straight down.

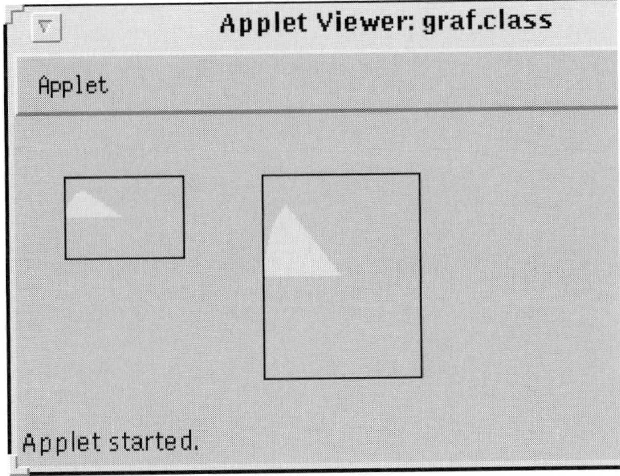

Figure A–6 An arc has the same concept of a bounding box as an oval.

Finally, the arcAngle is how many degrees to sweep from that starting point. See Figure A-6. Note that it is *not* the end angle as many people assume. A negative arcAngle sweeps clockwise, and a positive one counter clockwise. You never need use a negative angle because an arc sweeping 40 degrees forward from 90 degrees is the same as an arc sweeping 40 degrees back from 50 degrees.

Here is the code that generated the diagram:

```
import java.awt.*;
import java.applet.*;
public class graf  extends Applet {

    public void paint(Graphics g) {
        g.drawRect(25,30, 60,40);
        g.drawRect(125,30, 80,100);
        g.setColor(Color.cyan);
        g.fillArc(25,30, 60,40, 135,45);
        g.fillArc(125,30, 80,100, 135,45);
    }
}
```

```
public void drawPolygon(int xPoints[], int yPoints[], int nPoints);
public void fillPolygon(int xPoints[], int yPoints[], int nPoints);
```

Polygons are shapes with an arbitrary number of straight sides. To draw or fill one using these methods, you provide an array of x coordinates and an array of corresponding y coordinates along with the total number of points.

If you want the polygon to be drawn closed, you have to duplicate the starting point at the end of the arrays. Figure A-7 is an example of polygons.

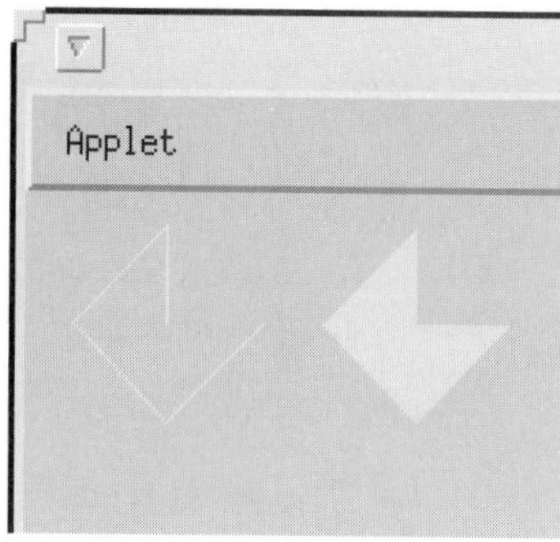

Figure A–7
A filled polygon connects its end points automatically as it fills.

Here is the code that generated the diagram:

```
// <applet   code=graf.class height=300 width=500> </applet>
import java.awt.*;
import java.applet.*;
public class graf  extends Applet {

     public void paint(Graphics g) {
          g.setColor(Color.cyan);
          int x_vals[] = {75,45,15,45,45 };
          int y_vals[] = {40,70,40,10,40 };

          g.drawPolygon(x_vals, y_vals, x_vals.length);

          for (int i=0;i<5;i++) x_vals[i]+=80;
          g.fillPolygon(x_vals, y_vals, x_vals.length);
     }
}
```

```
public void drawPolygon(Polygon p);
public void fillPolygon(Polygon p);
```

These two overloaded methods draw or fill a Polygon object. A Polygon object is constructed from the same arrays of (x,y) pairs as used previously:

```
Polygon(int xPoints[], int yPoints[], int nPoints);
```

You pass in the number of points if you only want the first N elements of the array to form the polygon. However, you can also add new points to a polygon by simply calling this method with an (x,y) pair:

```
pol.addPoint(10,20);
```

A Polygon also knows what its bounding box is.

That concludes most of the important routines for drawing text, lines, and shapes. The next section covers the topic of loading images into memory and rendering (drawing) them onto a graphics context.

Loading and Drawing Images

An Image, as the name suggests, holds a picture in memory. Originally, a picture will have been scanned in and stored in a file in GIF, JPEG, raster, PostScript, or other format. Java can currently only process the GIF and JPEG format.

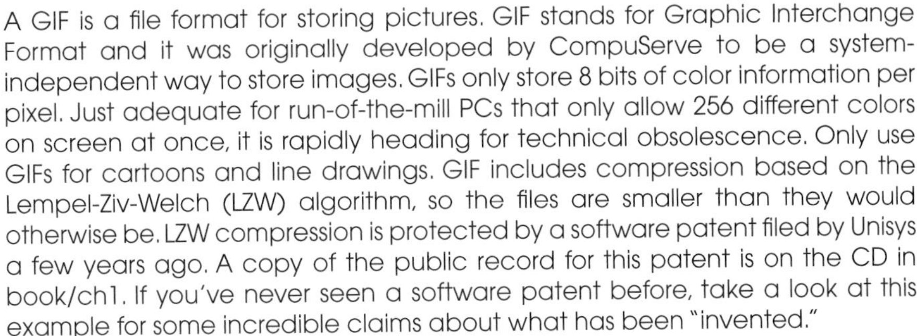

Image File Formats

A GIF is a file format for storing pictures. GIF stands for Graphic Interchange Format and it was originally developed by CompuServe to be a system-independent way to store images. GIFs only store 8 bits of color information per pixel. Just adequate for run-of-the-mill PCs that only allow 256 different colors on screen at once, it is rapidly heading for technical obsolescence. Only use GIFs for cartoons and line drawings. GIF includes compression based on the Lempel-Ziv-Welch (LZW) algorithm, so the files are smaller than they would otherwise be. LZW compression is protected by a software patent filed by Unisys a few years ago. A copy of the public record for this patent is on the CD in book/ch1. If you've never seen a software patent before, take a look at this example for some incredible claims about what has been "invented."

A JPEG is a newer and superior file format for compressing images. It's an acronym for Joint Photographic Experts Group (the committee that wrote the standard). An image in JPEG format can take much less storage space than the same picture in GIF format. However, the JPEG format also allows you to trade off image quality against storage needs—more requires more. When you save an image in JPEG format, you can specify a percentage for the image quality. JPEG stores full color information: 24 bits per pixel.

Before you can draw an Image onto a Graphics object, you must have an Image to draw. The most common way of getting one is to load it from a file. Another way of getting an Image is to call createImage() for a particular Component. We'll start by dealing with an image in GIF or JPEG format in a file. An image can be displayed in either an applet or an application. The two alternatives vary slightly.

Loading an Image File in an Application

Here is some code to display a file in an application. We create a Frame, read in the image file from our URL, instantiate a canvas, and off we go.

The only novelty about this is the way we get the image. We use the toolkit which is available in the AWT. It provides a getImage() method for applications. Note that you can get an Image from an URL (i.e., anywhere) as well as from a local file specified by a pathname as shown here.

```
import java.awt.*;
import java.net.*;
public class display {

    static public void main(String a[]) {
        Image i = Toolkit.getDefaultToolkit().getImage("dickens.jpg");
        Frame f = new Frame("my frame");

        myCanvas mc = new myCanvas(i);
        f.resize(350,200);
        f.add(mc);
        f.show();
    }
}

class myCanvas extends Canvas {
    Image saved_i;
    public myCanvas(Image i) {
       this.resize(300,200);
       saved_i = i;
    }

    public void paint(Graphics g){
       g.drawImage(saved_i, 10, 10, this);
    }
}
```

There are plenty of pitfalls to avoid when you type in this code. If you get one of these wrong, your image will not appear and you will not get any kind of helpful error message either. Here are some potential problems:

- You must give the frame a size in order to see it!
- If you provide a file name which doesn't exist or can't be accessed, it will fail silently. The same if you use the URL alternative for getImage.
- If you don't give the canvas a size, it won't show up.

  If you get all this correct, Figure A-8 will appear.

Figure A–8 See Dickens lay down—on the Internet sometimes they *do* know you're a dog.

Loading an Image File in an Applet

To load an image file in an Applet, we simply reference its URL. File access is usually restricted in an Applet, so there is no getImage that takes a pathname as an argument. Recall, however, that an URL can point to a resource anywhere on the Internet, so if the file is local to your system it can find it (if your security manager allows your applet to read local files). The Applet method is:

```
public Image getImage(URL url);
```

It allows you to specify a complete absolute URL to the image file. Some examples would be these:

```
URL u1 = new URL("http://sparcs/images/ball.jpg");     //remote
URL u2 = new URL("file:///home/linden/puppy.jpg"); // local
```

The other alternative lets you specify an URL and an image filename that is relative to where the URL points.

```
public Image getImage(URL url, String name);
```

This is more common in an applet because the image files are usually stored in the same directory as the HTML document or the class files. For these cases you can use the following code:

```
getDocumentBase() // the URL of the document containing the applet
getCodeBase() // the URL of the applet class file
```

So an example would be this:

```
Image i;
  ...
i=getImage( getDocumentBase(), "puppy.jpg");
```

Note there is a pitfall here! A very common mistake is to try to call getImage() to initialize the image as you declare it, like this:

```
Image i1 = getImage(getDocumentBase(), "spot.jpg");
```

That compiles without a problem, but (if the Image is declared outside any method, as normal) it fails at runtime like this:

```
java.lang.NullPointerException
     at java.applet.Applet.getDocumentBase(Applet.java:59)
     at jpg.<init>(jpg.java:7)
     at sun.applet.AppletPanel.runLoader(AppletPanel.java:386)
```

The reason is that before the init() method of an Applet is called there isn't enough structure in place for calls to other methods of Applet to succeed. You can't do much with an Applet until its init() method has been called, which is the right place to put this getImage() call.

If you can't remember which methods belong to Applet, just use the following rule of thumb: In an applet, don't call any methods to initialize data fields in their declaration. Instead, declare them, then initialize them separately in the init() method.

A related pitfall concerns the createImage() method. Many people want to create an Image in the constructor of, for example, a Canvas.

```
     public class MyCanvas extends Canvas{
          Image myImage;
          Graphics myGraphics;

          public MyCanvas(){
               myImage=this.createImage(100,50); //  this returns Null.
               myGraphics=myImage.getGraphics(); // so this throws
NullPtrExcptn.
          }
```

The createImage() method does not work until *after* the Canvas has been added to a Container. So in general you can't create the Image in the constructor. One workaround is to also add the Canvas to its Container in the constructor. This is because a peer for the Canvas component must have been created before we can get its image. But we are still in the class constructor, so unless we force peer cre-

ation by doing an add(), createImage here will always fail and return a null pointer. These limitations are defects in the design of this Java library.

The code using getImage () brings the image into memory, and holds it in the Image object. The next step is to render it on the screen.

How Do You Get a Java Applet to Load an HTML Page Into the Browser? The method `this.getAppletContext().showDocument(URL)` will make the browser load the page from the specified URL. There is also a version that takes a String argument:

```
public abstract void showDocument(URL url, String target)
```

The string says where to show it:

- `_self` Bring the URL up in the current frame.
- `_parent` Bring it up in the parent frame.
- `_top` Show it in the top-most frame.
- `_blank` Show it in a new unnamed frame.

Similarly, the following will put the message on the browser status line:

```
this.getAppletContext().showStatus("Get out in the fresh air more.");
```

Drawing an Image Onto a Graphics Object

The Graphics object has four variations of the drawImage() method:

- ```
  public boolean drawImage(Image img, int x, int y,
  ImageObserver observer);
  ```

  This draws the specified image at the specified coordinates (x, y). The image is cut off as necessary if it is larger than the area it is being drawn onto.

- ```
  public boolean drawImage(Image img, int x, int y,
  int width, int height,
  ImageObserver observer);
  ```

  This scales the image as needed to fit within the width and height specified as it draws it. Depending on the values you supply, that might change the proportions of the picture, stretching or shrinking it in one direction.

- ```
  public boolean drawImage(Image img, int x, int y,
  Color bgcolor,
  ImageObserver observer);
  ```
  ```

- `public boolean drawImage(Image img, int x, int y,`
  `int width, int height,`
  `Color bgcolor,`
  `ImageObserver observer);.`

These last two methods are just variations on the first, with the addition of providing a solid background color behind the image being drawn.

An Applet is an example of an ImageObserver, so wherever one is required, we can just provide the "this" of an Applet. The entire code to load and display a file in an Applet is thus just this:

```
// <applet code=jpg.class height=250  width=300> </applet>
import java.awt.*;
import java.applet.*;

public class jpg extends Applet {

    Image i;

    public void init() {
        i=getImage( getDocumentBase(), "puppy.jpg");
    }

    public void paint(Graphics g) {
        boolean b = g.drawImage(i,25,25, this);
    }
}
```

Running this code results in Figure A-9 appearing on the screen.

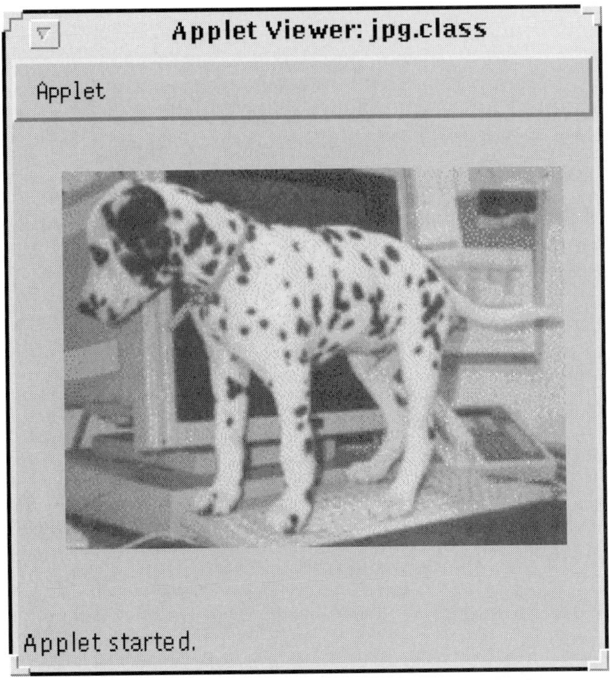

Figure A–9 See young Dickens do the "Type-5 Keyboard Macarena."

The ImageObserver Argument

Let's get back to the ImageObserver argument used in drawImage. When you call getImage() to bring an image file into memory, the method returns at once, and in the background at some point a separate thread starts reading the file off disk somewhere on the Internet. That incoming image data is said to be an observable event. And you can specify who or what is going to observe it.

As a matter of fact, Component implements the ImageObserver interface. Every button, frame, canvas, panel, label, etc., is an ImageObserver and able to register its interest in observing incoming images. An applet being a subclass of Panel is also therefore an ImageObserver. We normally just put "this" down as the argument and the right thing happens by default. As the image comes in gradually, more and more of it is painted onto the screen.

Why have an ImageObserver? Why not just use Observer/Observable? Through an oversight or by design, Observable is a class, not an interface. Any class wishing to be observable must use up its one chance to inherit. In the case of Image, it was better to provide the specialized interface ImageObserver.

Why bother with an Observer at all, though? The reason it's done this way, instead of the obvious implementation of making getImage() stall until the bytes are loaded, is twofold:

1. The human factors of waiting for an image file to load are truly horrible. In other words, few things make users angrier than being forced to sit idle while some hideous GIF loads scanline by scanline.
2. Everyone would end up writing every getImage() as a separate thread. This way, your applet is decoupled from the slow net for free.

Better yet, as pieces of the image are gradually loaded into memory, there will be a number of times when there is enough information to call ImageObserver.imageUpdate(). It may be called when the image file header has been read, when we have decoded enough to know the height of the image, when we know the width, and when the entire transfer has been completed.

The Component class contains an imageUpdate() method. When it is called, it schedules a repaint, allowing a little more of the image to be drawn without interfering at all with your thread of control. There are a couple of properties shown in Table A-2 that affect this.

Table A–2 System Properties

Property	Effect
`awt.image.incrementaldraw`	True: (default) Draw parts of an image as it arrives. False: Don't draw until all the image is loaded.
`awt.image.redrawrate`	The default value is 100. It is the minimum period in milliseconds between calls to repaint for images. This property only applies if the first one is true.

JDK 1.0 doesn't support setting an individual property. You change a property by instantiating a new property table based on the system one, then appending your modifications.

The following code updates the entire system properties table. If you just want to add one or two properties, you can't do it directly, but you can do it indirectly. You create a new properties table, supplying the system properties table to the constructor. You add properties one by one to your new table. When you search, if a property isn't found in your new table, the program will proceed to look in the system properties table. Clumsy, but it works.

```
import java.io.*;
import java.util.*;

public class read {

  public static void main(String args[]) {
    try {

      // get the standard system properties into a property table
      Properties MyProps = new Properties(System.getProperties());

      // add my new properties to that table
      MyProps.put( "awt.image.incrementaldraw", "true" );
      MyProps.put( "awt.image.redrawrate", "50" );

      // set that table as the system property table.
      System.setProperties(MyProps);

      // list all properties
      System.getProperties().list(System.out);

     } catch (Exception e) {e.printStackTrace();}

   }
}
```

When you change a property, the change only lasts for as long as your program runs. If you want to permanently change a property you need to write the property file out to disk (with your change) and read it back in at the start of each program.

You can save a property table to a file with this:

```
// save a property table to a file
FileOutputStream fos = new FileOutputStream("banana.txt");
MyProps.save(fos, "my own properties");
fos.close();
```

You can read a property table back from a file with this:

```
// read in a property table from a file
FileInputStream fis = new FileInputStream("banana.txt");
MyProps.load(fis);
fis.close();
```

Image Update

If you want to retain really tight control over an incoming image you can overload imageUpdate() in your applet that will override the regular version in the Component parent class. Whenever there is more information available, your imageUpdate() will be called repeatedly until you return a value of false to indicate that you've got enough information. The following code example will clarify how this works:

```
import java.applet.*;
import java.awt.*;

public class iu extends Applet {
   Image   i;
       int times=0, flags=0,wd=0,ht=0;

    public void init() {
       i = getImage(getDocumentBase(), "spots.jpeg" );
       wd = i.getWidth(this);  System.err.println("INIT:wd="+wd);
       ht = i.getHeight(this);  System.err.println("INIT:ht="+ht);
    }

    public boolean imageUpdate(Image i, int flags,
                              int x, int y, int w, int h) {
                if (times++<5)
                    System.err.println("my IMAGEUPDATE: flags="
                                  +flags+ " w="+w+ " h="+h);
                return true;
    }

    public void paint (Graphics g) {
       g.drawImage(i,50,50, this);

    }

}
```

This clearly shows how imageUpdate is a callback routine. Experiment with this example (invoke with the usual HTML file), including removing the limitation of five prints in the middle of imageUpdate (done so that the information doesn't scroll off the screen the first time you try it).

The Media Tracker

The ImageObserver interface is good for really low-level control of loading media files. But for some purposes it's a bit too low-level. If you just want to wait till a file is loaded completely, and you don't care to hear about the 57 intermediate stages of loading it, then the MediaTracker class is for you.

MediaTracker is actually built using ImageObserver, and it allows you to track the status of a number of media objects. Media objects could include audio clips, though currently only images are supported.

To use MediaTracker, simply create an instance and then call `addImage()` for each image to be tracked. Each image can be assigned a unique ID for indentification purposes. The IDs control the priority order in which the images are fetched, as well as identifying unique subsets of the images that can be waited on independently. You then `waitForID(n)`, which will suspend the thread until the image is completely loaded. The methods `isErrorAny()` and `isErrorID(i)` let you know if everything went OK for all the images or for a particular ID group.

Here is an example of the MediaTracker in use:

```
public void init() {
     MediaTracker t = new MediaTracker (this);
     Image i = getImage (getDocumentBase "spots.gif");
     t.addImage (i,1);
     try    {t.waitForID(1);}
     catch  (InterruptedException ie) {return;}
     //Image is now in memory, ready to draw
}
```

Image Processing

By putting together the basic classes that have already been described, and sprinkling a couple of new ones in, some pretty sophisticated image processing can be achieved. This section will describe the standard techniques for getting smoother animation by overriding update and double buffering. Start with this brief applet. The following code and JPEG image files are on the CD.

```
//<applet  code=pin.class   width=600 height=350>  </applet>
import java.awt.*;
import java.awt.event.*;
import java.awt.image.*;

public class pin extends java.applet.Applet {
    Image spirit, rolls;
    int new_x=550;
    int new_y=100;

    public void init () {
        spirit = getImage(getDocumentBase(), "spirit.jpg");
        rolls = getImage(getDocumentBase(), "rolls.jpg");
        addMouseMotionListener( new MouseMotionListener () {
         public void mouseDragged(MouseEvent e){
             System.out.println("what a drag");
             new_x=e.getX();
             new_y=e.getY();
             repaint();
         }
         public void mouseMoved(MouseEvent e){}
    } );
    }


    public void paint (Graphics g) {
        g.setColor(Color.gray);
        g.fillRect(0,0,getSize().width, getSize().height );
        g.drawImage (rolls,5, 5, this);
        g.drawImage (spirit, new_x-25, new_y-25, this);
    }


}
```

The code implements a simple "pin-the-tail-on-the-donkey" game. In other words, you can use the mouse to drag the image of the Spirit of Ecstasy over to its place on the Rolls-Royce radiator. Incidentally, the Spirit of Ecstasy was modeled on a real person: Eleanor Thornton. She was the paramour of early motoring pioneer, the second Lord Montagu. He artfully suggested to his pals on the Rolls-Royce board in 1911 that their cars would be enhanced by a graceful radiator mascot, and he "just happened to know a good one." Sadly, Eleanor Thornton perished in a tragic torpedo mishap in 1915 (Lord Montagu was on the same boat wearing an inflatable cork waistcoat and he made it back to England in time to read his obituary in *The Times*). Thornton's spirit lives on, immortalized on the bonnet of every Rolls-Royce motor car for the last ninety years. But I digress. The applet screen looks like that in Figure A-10.

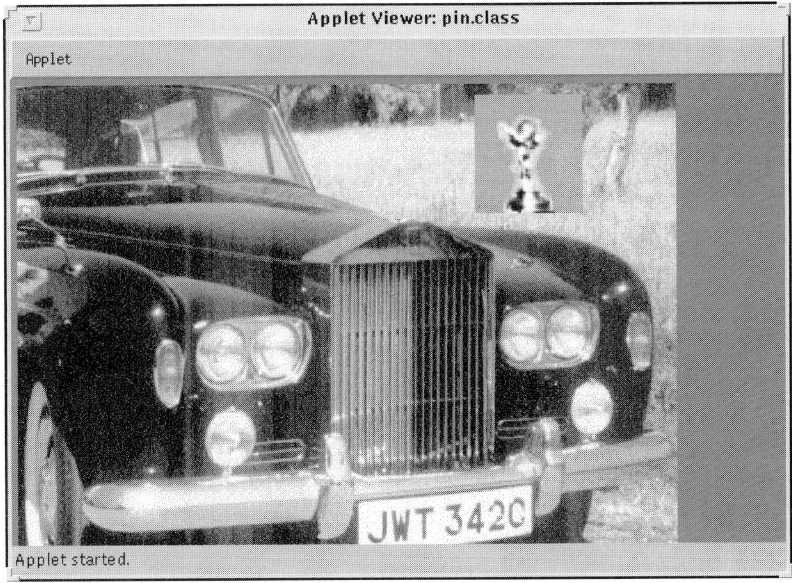

Figure A–10 A moment of silence for Eleanor Thornton.

When you run the code you will notice that the applet flickers annoyingly as you drag the mouse. The flickering problem is a well-known artifact of imaging programs in all languages. To fix this, there are some Java-specific things to try and some algorithmic things to try. The first and easiest improvement is to look at the default implementation of one of the utility routines, update().

As we drag the mouse, each event causes the new_x and new_y coordinates to be noted, then a request to repaint() is made. Repaint will call Component.update, which looks like the following code:

```
public void update(Graphics g) {
    g.setColor(getBackground());
    g.fillRect(0, 0, width, height);
    g.setColor(getForeground());
    paint(g);
}
```

It sets the color to the background color, then fills the whole Graphics context with it (in other words erases whatever image is currently there). It then sets the foreground color, and calls paint.

However, we are already painting the whole background in our paint routine. So, repaint calls update which paints the whole panel, then calls paint, which again paints the whole panel. (Voila: A flicker or flash will occur because an unnecessary clear/paint is done.) We could remove the fillRect() in paint, for it was put there precisely to demonstrate this flicker as a teaching example (and it represents some more general background painting that you may do). A better solution is to override update(), and provide your own version that doesn't clear the applet panel.

```
public void update(Graphics g) {
    paint(g);
}
```

You can (and should) do this whenever your paint routine updates the entire component. If your paint didn't update the entire component, then you couldn't override update in this manner. You'd get pieces of the old image left in place as you dragged it to a new location. Overriding update with a more sensible version reduces flashing considerably, but doesn't eliminate it. For that we'll use a technique called double buffering or offscreen imaging (they mean the same thing).

Double Buffering

Double buffering, or *offscreen imaging* (a more accurate description), is the process of doing all your (slow) drawing to a graphics area in memory. When the entire image is complete, it zaps it up onto the screen in one (fast) operation. The overall time is slightly longer because of the overhead, but the overall effect is stunning because the new graphics context appears instantly.

The following code makes the image rendering double buffered:

```
//<applet  code=pin2.class   width=600 height=350>  </applet>
// same as pin, but uses double buffered output.
// PvdL.
import java.awt.*;
import java.awt.event.*;
import java.awt.image.*;

public class pin2 extends java.applet.Applet {
    Image spirit, rolls;
    Image myOffScreenImage;
    Graphics myOffScreenGraphics;
    int new_x=550;
    int new_y=100;

    public void init () {
        spirit = getImage(getDocumentBase(), "spirit.jpg");
        rolls = getImage(getDocumentBase(), "rolls.jpg");
        myOffScreenImage= createImage(
                    getSize().width, getSize().height );
        myOffScreenGraphics = myOffScreenImage.getGraphics();
        addMouseMotionListener( new MouseMotionListener () {
           public void mouseDragged(MouseEvent e){
               System.out.println("what a drag");
               new_x=e.getX();
               new_y=e.getY();
               repaint();
           }
           public void mouseMoved(MouseEvent e){}
       } );
    }

    public void paint (Graphics g) {
        g.setColor(Color.gray);
        g.fillRect(0,0,getSize().width, getSize().height );
        g.drawImage (rolls,5, 5, this);
        g.drawImage (spirit, new_x-25, new_y-25, this);
    }

    public void update(Graphics g) {
          paint(myOffScreenGraphics);     // draws on the db
          // draws the double buffer onto applet
          g.drawImage(myOffScreenImage,0,0, this);
     }

}
```

We don't change paint() at all. Paint will still do its rendering thing onto whatever Graphics context you give it. Here's where the magic comes in. We have added two off-screen objects:

```
Image myOffScreenImage;
Graphics myOffScreenGraphics;
```

In init() these two are initialized. We create an Image the same size of the applet. Then we get a graphics context for it. Now the clever part. We modify update so *first* it paints the offscreen image myOffScreenGraphics. It simply uses the regular call to paint, with myOffScreenGraphics as the argument. That painting won't appear on the screen, as it would if the AWT had called paint with the Graphics object for the applet. Instead, it goes to myOffScreenGraphics object. (Sorry to belabor the point, but it is important to understand this thoroughly.)

Finally, instead of update() calling only paint(), as it did in the previous version, we now do a very quick g.drawImage() to get the just-painted myOffScreen-Image onto the Applet's graphics context! Drawing a single preconstructed image onto the screen is a lot faster than building up a screenful of images one at a time. And that is double buffering.

Clipping Rectangles

The final possible optimization is to use a clipping rectangle to only draw where the image has changed. Clipping is a standard graphics technique to optimize the amount of (slow) drawing that takes place. When you clip, you are telling the paint routine "I know that the only changes in this image are inside this rectangle, so you need only paint inside the rectangle. Everything else remains unchanged."

The clipRect method of Graphics follows:

```
public void clipRect(int x, int y, int width, int height);
```

This cuts down the size of the area that is painted to just the *intersection* of what it was and the new rectangle specified by the arguments. This is an optimization used in animations and other graphics programming to speed up output and make it smoother. Many people have complained about the way the clipping rectangle can only be reduced in size. So JDK 1.1 added this method to set the current clip to the specified rectangle:

```
setClip(int x, int y, int width, int height)
```

Rendering doesn't take place outside this area.

Depending on how much can be clipped and how long it takes to calculate the overall image, clipping can save a lot of time and effort. Clipping works best on big images where only a little changes at a time. It's tailor-made for animations.

Taking Images Apart: java.awt.image

Java features some pretty substantial support for pulling Images apart to get at individual pixels. It also has a class that takes bytes from memory and assembles them into an Image. One problem with mastering this area of Java is that there is a lot of classes, generality, and infrastructure. As with the stream I/O classes, the profusion of abstractions creates a learning barrier for programmers.

We'll look at two concrete classes in java.awt.image that allow you to have absolute control over your screen images, namely:

- PixelGrabber: implements the abstract class ImageConsumer.
- MemoryImageSource: implements the abstract class ImageProducer.

As the names suggest, ImageConsumer takes an Image away from you (giving you something else you'd rather have, like an array of pixels), while ImageProducer takes something and gives you back the Image that it created from it.

Here's how PixelGrabber works:

1. You construct a new instance of the class supplying the image (or ImageProducer) and lots of sizes and an int array as arguments:

   ```
   PixelGrabber pg = new PixelGrabber ( .... );
   ```

2. You call grabPixels() which fills the int array with the pixels from the image:

   ```
   pg.grabPixels();
   ```

3. You check the status to see if all bits were grabbed without problems:

   ```
   if (pg.status() & ImageObserver.ALLBITS) != 0)
         // we grabbed all the bits OK
   ```

The two constructors of PixelGrabber are:

```
public PixelGrabber(Image img, int x, int y, int w, int h,  int[] pix, int
off, int scansize);

public PixelGrabber(ImageProducer ip, int x, int y, int w, int h, int[]
pix, int off, int scansize);
```

As you can see, the second constructor has an ImageProducer as its first parameter, but the other arguments (defined here) are the same.

- `img` is the image from which to retrieve pixels
- x is the x coordinate of the upper-left corner of the rectangle of pixels to retrieve from the image, relative to the default (unscaled) size of the image

- `y` is the y coordinate of the upper-left corner of the rectangle of pixels to retrieve from the image
- `w` is the width of the rectangle of pixels to retrieve
- `h` is the height of the rectangle of pixels to retrieve
- `pix` is the array of integers which are to be used to hold the RGB pixels retrieved from the image
- `off` is the offset into the array of where to store the first pixel
- `scansize` is the distance from one row of pixels to the next in the array

Here's how MemoryImageSource works. It is essentially the complement of PixelGrabber. It reads an int array of pixels and gives you back the corresponding image. First, you construct a new instance of the class MemoryImageSource supplying arguments of the int array, and lots of sizes (height, width, scanline size, etc.). That will get you a MemoryImageSource object, which implements ImageProducer, and hence can be fed into the Component.createImage() method to obtain a real renderable Image.

There are six constructors for MemoryImageSource. The simplest one is:

```
public MemoryImageSource(int w, int h, int pix[],
                                    int off, int scan)
```

This instantiates a w-by-h MemoryImageSource starting from the pix[off] element in the array of pixels, and with scan pixels in each line. The other five constructors allow various combinations of with and without HashTables and ColorModels.

Transparent Backgrounds

We are going to use these two classes on our image of the Spirit of Ecstasy. We are going to grab the pixels and turn all the pink ones transparent by setting the alpha byte to zero. If the alpha value of a pixel is 0, it is totally invisible. If the alpha value is 255, it is totally solid color. Values in between allow for varying degrees of translucence or opacity. Since the background is mostly pink, this will turn it transparent and allow Eleanor Thornton to be seamlessly reunited with her pedestal.

How Do I Turn the Background of My Image Transparent? In general, there is no way to say, "Filter this image and give it a transparent background." You need a way to identify what is a background pixel and what is a foreground pixel. Here we are using color to identify the background. If the foreground is a regular shape you could use (x,y) position. For more on this, read on.

I touched up these images in Adobe Photoshop beforehand to give them a uniform pink background and sharper edges. If your company won't spring for Adobe Photoshop so you can play around with stuff like this, use the freeware "Gimp" image software that can do many of the same things. It's on the CD.

To minimize the learning curve here, let's highlight the new code by making this class extend the class pin2 above. Notice what we are doing here. We already have a class pin2 that does most of what we want. Instead of copying all that code into a new file and starting hacking from scratch, we just create a new class that *extends* pin2. Then, in our new class, we place new versions of the methods that we want to replace in pin2. Our new methods will override the corresponding methods in pin2. We have reused pin2 by extending it and adding the changed functionality. The compiler has done most of the work for us. We only have to test the features that have changed. (Isn't object-oriented programming wonderful?)

```
//<applet  code=transp.class   width=600 height=350>  </applet>
// double buffered
// transparent image
// Peter van der Linden, Sept 1996, Silicon Valley, Calif.
import java.awt.*;
import java.awt.image.*;

public class transp extends pin2 {

     public void init () {
          spirit = getImage(getDocumentBase(), "spirit.jpg");
          rolls = getImage(getDocumentBase(), "rolls.jpg");
          myOffScreenImage= createImage(size().width, size().height );
          myOffScreenGraphics = myOffScreenImage.getGraphics();

          spirit = getRidOfPink(spirit);   // filter the image

     }


     int  width=475, height=265;

     public Image getRidOfPink(Image im) {
          try {
     // grab the pixels from the image
               int[] pgPixels = new int [width*height];
               PixelGrabber pg = new PixelGrabber (im, 0, 0,
                    width, height, pgPixels, 0, width);

     if (pg.grabPixels() && ((pg.status() & ImageObserver.ALLBITS) != 0))
{
          // Now change some of the bits
               for (int y=0;y<height;y++) {
                    for (int x=0;x<width;x++) {
                         int i = y*width+x;
                         int a = (pgPixels[i] & 0xff000000)>>24;
                         int r = (pgPixels[i] & 0x00ff0000)>>16;
                         int g = (pgPixels[i] & 0x0000ff00)>>8;
                         int b = pgPixels[i] & 0x000000ff;
                         // turn the pink-ish pixels transparent.
                         if (r>200 && g>100&&g<200&&b>100&&b<200) {
                              a=0;
                              pgPixels[i] =  a  | (r<<16) | (g<<8) | b;
                         }
               }
          }
          im = createImage (new MemoryImageSource (width, height,
pgPixels, 0, width));
          }
      } catch (InterruptedException e) { e.printStackTrace (); }
      return im;
     }
}
```

We have overridden init() to add the filtering statement:

```
spirit = getRidOfPink(spirit);    // filter the image
```

And we have added the routine getRidOfPink(). That routine looks fearsome at first, but it quickly breaks down into four simple stages:

1. Grab the pixels.
2. Look at each individual pixel. You may be wondering why the pixel array isn't two dimensional, just as an image is. The reason is to keep it closer to the model the hardware uses. Frame buffer (graphics adapter) and CPU memory is one dimensional.
3. If the RGB values are within the range of "generally pink," then make the pixel transparent by setting its alpha value to 0.
4. Reassemble the pixel array into an image with MemoryImageSource.

It's as simple as that. When you run this, you see a picture like that in Figure A-11.

Comparing this image with Figure A-10, you'll see that the ugly pink background has disappeared.

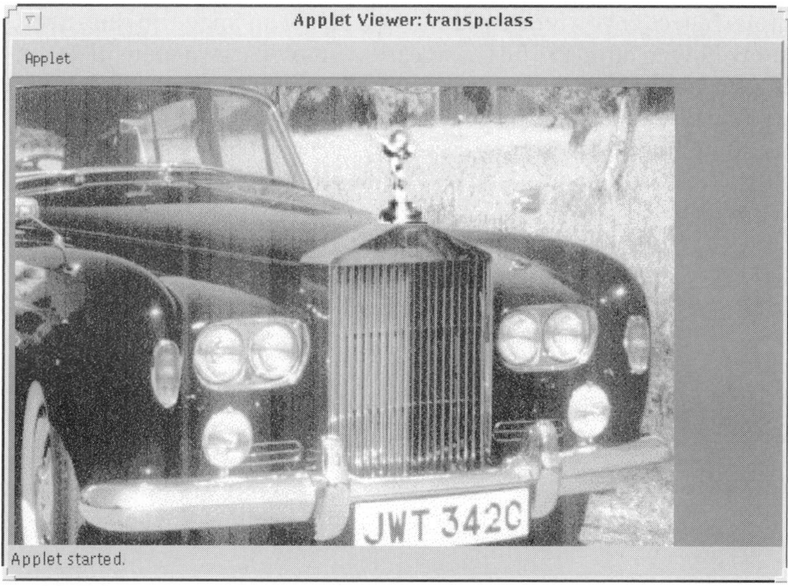

Figure A–11 Eleanor transparently on her pedestal.

Note that it is a very expensive operation to grab pixels and look at them. To help your program performance you should do this as sparingly as possible, and look at as few pixels as you can. Don't grab pixels from the whole image if you don't need to. On a SPARCstation 5 desktop computer, this applet took about five seconds to initialize. On an Intel Pentium 66Mhz system, it took about twice as long.

How Do I Save to a File an Image I Have Created on the Screen? The beauty of pixel grabbing is that it turns a picture into an array of ints. You can do anything you like with that array of ints including process it, send it down a socket, or write it out to a file. If you write it out to a file, you have saved your image to disk. It will not be in a recognized standard format like GIF or JPEG, and you will not get the benefit of compression, but it does let you save an image to a file.

The final point is that the java.awt.image package has a couple of other specialized classes for filtering RGB values and for chaining ImageProducers together so you can do multiple filtering.

Exercise: Try filtering an image by adapting the code above. Turn the black Rolls-Royce into a pink one.

Animation

Animation is the last major Image Processing topic we are going to cover, and it is thankfully simple. In fact, if you already know how to get an image on the screen, you already know how to animate. Just as in cartoon movies, Java animation consists of showing several images (known as "frames") in quick succession. The human eye has a quality called *persistence* that means a series of slightly different frames fools us into thinking we see movement. When we change the entire image, it is called "frame animation." When we just change a small area of the image, that area is called a "sprite" and we do "sprite animation."

So all we do for animation is bring all our frames in memory and display them one after the other. If we need to we will also use double buffering and clipping to make things appear smoother. There is a cheesy example of animation that comes with the JDK in directory $JAVAHOME/demo/Animator. If you go to that directory, you can run the following to see some jumping beans.

```
appletviewer  example4.html
```

The CD that comes with this book has a Java program to save images to disk in JPEG format in the goodies directory.

You can also review the Animator.java source code. As an example, let's make Dickens the Dalmatian wag his tail in Figure A-12.

Before we show the code, let's look at the Java idiom for starting a thread in an applet. You don't need a user thread in an applet if all you do is respond to GUI events. You *do* need one if you are animating, though.

Figure A–12 See Dickens wag his tail.

```
public class foo extends java.applet.Applet {

     public void init() { ... }

     public void start() { ... }

     public void stop() { ... }

     public void paint (Graphics g) { ... }

}
```

Figure A–13 Framework of a normal applet.

A regular applet has the framework shown in Figure A-13.

To give yourself a thread, the idiom is that you do these five things:

- Make your applet class implement Runnable.
- Add the run() method of the thread. Inside here will be the statements to do all the work that your thread must do.
- Declare a Thread object: `Thread t;`.
- Inside start(), instantiate the thread with this applet:

  ```
  t = new Thread(this);
  ```

- The thread running:

  ```
  t.start();
  ```

- Inside stop(), stop the thread running by this:

  ```
  t.stop();
  t=null;  // so it can be garbage collected.
  ```

```
public class foo extends java.applet.Applet
implements Runnable{

   Thread t;

   public void run()  { ...}

   public void init() { ... }

   public void start() {
      t = new Thread(this);
      t.start();    }

   public void stop() {
      t.stop();
      t=null;        }

   public void paint (Graphics g) { ... }

}
```

Figure A–14 Threaded applet.

So that the applet framework with a thread looks like Figure A-14.

Here is the code to animate the tail. It closely follows the preceding framework. Again, by making this extend the "transp" class of the previous example, we can present the minimum new code. It's not too surprising that we can use the framework of the "pin-the-silver-lady-on-the-Rolls" code as the basis of the "animate the dog's tail" program. They both involve putting images on the screen and moving them about. All animation programs will have the same general form.

```
//<applet  code=wag.class   width=280 height=200>  </applet>
// double buffered, transparent image, animation
import java.awt.*;
import java.awt.image.*;
import java.awt.event.*;

public class wag extends transp implements Runnable {
    Image dal, appendage, tail1, tail2;
    Font f;

    public void init () {
        tail1 = getImage(getDocumentBase(), "tail.jpg");
        tail2 = getImage(getDocumentBase(), "tail2.jpg");
        dal = getImage(getDocumentBase(), "dickens.jpg");
        dal = getRidOfPink(dal);
        tail1 = getRidOfPink(tail1);
        tail2 = getRidOfPink(tail2);
        appendage=tail2;

        addMouseMotionListener( new MouseMotionListener () {
           public void mouseDragged(MouseEvent e){
               System.out.println("what a drag");
               new_x=e.getX();
               new_y=e.getY();
               repaint();
           }
           public void mouseMoved(MouseEvent e){}
        } );

        f = new Font("Helvetica", Font.BOLD, 18);

        myOffScreenImage = createImage(getSize().width, getSize().height
);
        myOffScreenGraphics = myOffScreenImage.getGraphics();

    }

    public void paint (Graphics g) {
        g.setColor(Color.lightGray);
        g.fillRect(0,0,getSize().width, getSize().height );
        g.setColor(Color.yellow);
        g.setFont(f);
        g.drawString("Dickens is a happy dog",10,20);
        g.drawImage (appendage, 10, 50, this);
        appendage= (appendage==tail2?tail1:tail2); // swap frames
        g.drawImage (dal, 35, 65, this);
    }

       public void run() {
       while (true) {
            try{Thread.sleep( 100 ); }
            catch(InterruptedException ie){}
            repaint();
```

```
            }
        }

        Thread t;

        public void start() {
            t = new Thread(this);
            t.start();
        }
        public void stop() {
            t.stop();
            t = null;
        }
}
```

The init() method brings in an extra image, tail2.jpg, which looks similar to tail, but is slightly displaced. All the images are filtered to give them a transparent background.

The two tails look like those shown in Figures A-15 and A-16.

Figure A–15
Dickens tail can look like this.

FigureA–16
. . or this.

I created Figure A-15 from Figure A-14 by rotating it ten degrees in Adobe Photoshop (image rotation is one of the features that xv doesn't offer). If you don't have Photoshop, it doesn't matter—you now know enough Java to whip up a special purpose program to do any image processing you want!

In the paint method, I added some text at the top just for fun. The only other change is we now draw an "appendage" instead of a tail. The appendage just holds a reference to either tail1 or tail2. Immediately after we have drawn the appendage, this line:

```
appendage= (appendage==tail2?tail1:tail2); // swap frames
```

swaps it over to point to the other one. In this way, when paint is called, it alternates between Figure A-15 and Figure A-16. Another way to accomplish this is to change what appendage refers to in the run() routine. It doesn't have to alternate between two images; you may have dozens in your animation.

The run routine just spins in an infinite loop, sleeping for a tenth of a second, then issuing a repaint request. About twenty-four frames per second is all you need to fool the eye into seeing continuous motion. Here we're running at ten frames per second.

The start() instantiates and kicks the thread off. The stop() is equally important. It's very poor programming to leave a thread running after the user leaves a page, so you should kill the thread in the stop routine. And that is image animation. Finally, putting the whole thing together so you can see all the code in one place, here is the program written without inheritance:

```
//<applet  code=fullwag.class   width=280 height=200>  </applet>
// double buffered
// transparent image
// animated tail
// Peter van der Linden

import java.awt.*;
import java.awt.image.*;
import java.awt.event.*;
import java.applet.*;

public class fullwag extends Applet implements Runnable {
    Image dal, appendage, tail1, tail2;
    Image myOffScreenImage;
    Font f;
    Graphics myOffScreenGraphics;

    public void update(Graphics g) {
        paint(myOffScreenGraphics);    // draws on double buffer
          // draws the db onto applet
                g.drawImage(myOffScreenImage,0,0, this);
}
    int  width=475, height=265;

    public Image getRidOfPink(Image im) {
        try {
     // grab the pixels from the image
            int[] pgPixels = new int [width*height];
            PixelGrabber pg = new PixelGrabber (im, 0, 0,
                      width, height, pgPixels, 0, width);

    if (pg.grabPixels() &&
            ((pg.status() & ImageObserver.ALLBITS) != 0)) {
     // Now change some of the bits
        for (int y=0;y<height;y++) {
           for (int x=0;x<width;x++) {
                   int i = y*width+x;
                   int a = (pgPixels[i] & 0xff000000)>>24;
                   int r = (pgPixels[i] & 0x00ff0000)>>16;
                   int g = (pgPixels[i] & 0x0000ff00)>>8;
                   int b = pgPixels[i] & 0x000000ff;
                   // turn the pink-ish pixels transparent.
                   if (r>200 && g>100&&g<200&&b>100&&b<200) {
                      a=0;
                      pgPixels[i] =  a  | (r<<16) | (g<<8) | b;
                   }
           }
        }
        im = createImage (new MemoryImageSource (width, height,
                                                    pgPixels, 0,
width));
        }
      } catch (InterruptedException e) { e.printStackTrace (); }
```

```
        return im;
    }

    public void init () {
        tail1 = getImage(getDocumentBase(), "tail.jpg");
        tail2 = getImage(getDocumentBase(), "tail2.jpg");
        dal = getImage(getDocumentBase(), "dickens.jpg");
        dal = getRidOfPink(dal);
        tail1 = getRidOfPink(tail1);
        tail2 = getRidOfPink(tail2);
        appendage=tail2;
        f = new Font("Helvetica", Font.BOLD, 18);
                myOffScreenImage = createImage(getSize().width,

getSize().height );
        myOffScreenGraphics = myOffScreenImage.getGraphics();
    }

    public void paint (Graphics g) {
        g.setColor(Color.lightGray);
        g.fillRect(0,0,getSize().width, getSize().height );
        g.setColor(Color.yellow);
        g.setFont(f);
        g.drawString("Dickens is a happy dog",10,20);
        g.drawImage (appendage, 10, 50, this);
        appendage= (appendage==tail2?tail1:tail2); // swap frames
        g.drawImage (dal, 35, 65, this);
    }

      public void run() {
      while (true) {
           try{Thread.sleep( 100 ); }
           catch(InterruptedException ie){}
           repaint();
          }
      }
      Thread t;
      public void start() {
          t = new Thread(this);
          t.start();
      }
              public void stop() {
          t.stop();
          t = null;
      }
```

Table A–3 Some Image Processing Utilities

Windows	Use Star Office for GIMP. GIMP is on the CD.
Solaris	Use Star Office.
Macintosh	Macintosh image processing software can be downloaded from: ftp://rever.nmsu.edu/pub/macfaq/JPEGView or ftp://rever.nmsu.edu/pub/macfaq/GIF_Converter.sit.bin.

Now Try These Exercises

1. Add to the filtering to turn Dickens into a black lab by turning all his white fur black.
2. Change the animation so the "tail wags the dog."

Sounds

Applets have some simple methods to play sound files. The 1.1 release can only deal with sounds in the .au format. The Java library that supports sound files was greatly improved for JDK 1.2. It now enables playback of sound files in WAV, AIFF, AU, MIDI, and RMF format with much higher sound quality. The API has not changed and the methods are the same, but there is a big increase in the types of different sound files they can handle. Also in JDK 1.2, applications can now access sound files by calling the new static method "newAudioClip()" from class java.applet.Applet.

You can browse the site *cuiwww.unige.ch/OSG/AudioFormats* which describes the implementation of all the popular sound file formats including .wav (Windows), .au (Sun and NeXT), and .aif (Macintosh and SGI).

There are four kinds of information making up a Digital Audio stream. The man (manual) page explains that digital audio data represents a quantized approximation of an analog audio signal waveform. In the simplest case, these quantized numbers represent the amplitude of the input waveform at particular sampling intervals. I hate it when man pages (the UNIX online documentation) read like dictionary entries instead of making a reasonable attempt at explaining something.

Sample Rate. This says how many times per second we sample (take a reading from) our noise source. Java 1.1 supports only 8000Hz, while Java 1.2 supports many more.

Encoding. The encoding says how the audio data is represented. Java uses μ-law encoding (pronounced mew-law) which is the standard CCITT G.711 for voice data used by telephone companies in the United States, Canada, and Japan.

There is an alternative A-law encoding (also part of G.711) which is the standard encoding for telephony elsewhere in the world. A-law and μ-law audio data are sampled at a rate of 8000 samples per second with 12-bit precision, with the data compressed to 8-bit samples. The resulting audio data quality is equivalent to that of standard analog telephone service, meaning, in technical terms, pretty crappy.

Precision. Precision indicates the number of bits used to store each audio sample. For instance, μ-law and A-law data are stored with 8-bit precision: 16-bit precision is common elsewhere and now available in Java.

Channels. This says whether the audio is mono or multichannel. Since it is basically telephone audio, Java 1.1 is mono (single channel). Java 1.2 has stereo.

For a standard audio CD the audio is sampled at 44.1KHz, which means that for every second of music (or silence, or the conductor coughing) the CD has to take 44,100 16-bit samples for each of the two stereo channels.

To summarize, JDK 1.1 supports sounds encoded as mono (1 channel), 8-bit (as opposed to 16), and μ-law (not A-law or CD quality). The whole is stored in .au files (not .wav or .aif).

One minute of monaural audio recorded in μ-law format at 8KHz requires about 0.5MB of storage, while the standard Compact Disc audio format (stereo 16-bit linear PCM data sampled at 44.1KHz) requires approximately 10MB per minute.

Table A–4 Some Sound Utilities

Windows	One sound utility that works is SOund eXchange or SoX, available at *www.spies.com/Sox*. There are many others that work and also a few that don't. Use it with sox file.wav -r 8012 -U -b file.au.
Solaris	One Solaris Unix sound utility that works is /usr/demo/SOUND/bin/soundtool. Another is audiotool. All modern desktop SPARCs (with the exception of the SS4) come with the audio hardware and software needed to record input from line-in or headphone jack. I recorded my message on the CD in the goodies directory using the little microphone that came with my SS5. It plugs into a port on the back. You can also use audiorecord to record the incoming audio data in any format supported by the audio device. For example, use the following to record fifteen seconds of CD quality sound to file foo.au: /bin/audiorecord -p line -c 2 -s 44.1k -e linear -t 15 foo.au Use the following to record 15 seconds of 8 Khz ulaw data (default) to file foo.au: /bin/audiorecord -p line -t 15 foo.au You can use audiotool to edit the resulting file if needed.
Macintosh	One Mac sound utility that works is ConvertMachine at http://www.kagi.com/rod/default.html.

Here is a minimal applet to play a sound effect:

```
import java.applet.*;
public class noise extends Applet {
    public void init() {
        play( getCodeBase(), "danger.au");
    }
}
```

The file "danger.au" is on the CD. It makes a noise like a drumstick rattling on the side of a tin cup. The program would be invoked from the usual HTML file:

```
<applet code=noise.class  width = 150 height =100> </applet>
```

The applet directory $JAVAHOME/src/java/applet contains several other useful methods:

```
public AudioClip getAudioClip(URL url)
```

Once you have retrieved an AudioClip from an URL, you can play it once, play it in a loop continuously, or cease playing it with the methods `play()`, `loop()`, or `stop()`.

If you play it continuously, make sure that you stop playing it in the stop() method, called when the applet's Panel is no longer on the screen. Otherwise, the noise will continue longer than you probably want.

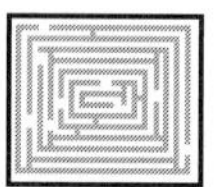

Write an applet that plays a sound file and evaluates it for hidden Satanic messages. There is an easy way to do this and a hard way. The easy way is to play the sound file, and then conclude:

```
println("That contained 0 Satanic messages \n");
```

The hard way would actually involve some analysis of the sound waveforms, but it would probably produce exactly the same result.

In the first edition of this book I threw down the challenge to readers inviting them to submit code to play a sound file backwards. It would be a non-trivial task to figure out the .au format and do that, but alert programmer Manfred Thole from Germany realized that the task would be considerably simplified by using one of the vendor-specific classes that turns a FileInputStream into an AudioStream. This was a clever piece of programming to get the job done more simply. The code follows.

```
import java.io.*;
import sun.audio.*;


/**
*
 * This application plays audio files backwards!
 * Only applicable for "8-bit u-law 8kHz mono" encoded audio files.
 * Usage: BackwardAudio audio-file-to-play-backwards
 */



public class BackwardAudio {

  static void swap(byte [] b) {
    int l = b.length;
    int i;
    byte tmp;

    for (i = 0; i < l/2; i++) {
      tmp = b[i];
      b[i] = b[l-i-1];
      b[l-i-1] = tmp;
    }
  }


  public static void main(String[] args) {

    AudioPlayer ap = AudioPlayer.player;
    AudioStream as = null;
    byte [] ad = null;

    if ( args.length != 1 ) {
      System.err.println("Usage: BackwardAudio audio-file-to-play-
backwards");
      return;
    }
    try {
      as = new AudioStream(new FileInputStream(args[0]));
      // Some files give strange results...
      // Maybe they have an incorrect file header.
      if ( as.getLength() < 1 ) {
        System.err.println("Length: "+as.getLength()+"!");
        return;
      }
      ad = new byte[as.getLength()];
      as.read(ad, 0, as.getLength()-1);
      swap(ad);
      //ap.start(new ByteArrayInputStream(ad));
      ap.start(new AudioDataStream(new AudioData(ad)));
      // We have to wait for the ap daemon thread to play the sound!
```

```
      Thread.sleep(as.getLength()/8+100);
    }
    catch (FileNotFoundException fne) {
      System.err.println(fne);

    }
    catch (IOException ioe) {
      System.err.println(ioe);
    }
    catch (InterruptedException ie) {
      System.err.println(ie);
    }
  }
}
```

As well as the java.*.* hierarchy of packages, Java vendors can supply vendor-specific packages under <vendor>.* Sun has a large number of sun.* packages that it does not tell you about explicitly. Good programmers will find them because good programmers tend to investigate on their own.

The classes are in the $JAVAHOME/jre/lib/rt.jar. Copy this file somewhere safe, and unzip it. By the way, this is the file that the JDK README warns you not to unzip. I think they are trying to use reverse psychology.

You'll see all the standard java.*.* classes in there, and several dozen interesting looking Sun ones, too, including these:

```
Extracting: sun/misc/Ref.class
Extracting: sun/misc/MessageUtils.class
Extracting: sun/misc/CEStreamExhausted.class
Extracting: sun/misc/UUEncoder.class
Extracting: sun/misc/CharacterEncoder.class
Extracting: sun/misc/HexDumpEncoder.class
Extracting: sun/misc/UUDecoder.class
Extracting: sun/misc/BASE64Encoder.class
Extracting: sun/misc/UCDecoder.class
Extracting: sun/misc/CacheEnumerator.class
Extracting: sun/misc/Timeable.class
Extracting: sun/misc/TimerThread.class
Extracting: sun/misc/UCEncoder.class
Extracting: sun/misc/CRC16.class
Extracting: sun/misc/ConditionLock.class
Extracting: sun/misc/BASE64Decoder.class
Extracting: sun/misc/CacheEntry.class
Extracting: sun/misc/CEFormatException.class
Extracting: sun/misc/Timer.class
Extracting: sun/misc/TimerTickThread.class
Extracting: sun/misc/Lock.class
Extracting: sun/misc/CharacterDecoder.class
Extracting: sun/misc/Cache.class
  Creating: sun/audio/
Extracting: sun/audio/AudioStream.class
Extracting: sun/audio/InvalidAudioFormatException.class
Extracting: sun/audio/AudioStreamSequence.class
Extracting: sun/audio/ContinuousAudioDataStream.class
Extracting: sun/audio/AudioDevice.class
Extracting: sun/audio/AudioPlayer.class
Extracting: sun/audio/AudioData.class
Extracting: sun/audio/AudioTranslatorStream.class
Extracting: sun/audio/NativeAudioStream.class
Extracting: sun/audio/AudioDataStream.class
```

That gives you the package name. Of course, remember that you can use javap to look at any of these methods!

```
      % javap sun.audio.AudioStream
Compiled from AudioStream.java
public class sun.audio.AudioStream extends java.io.FilterInputStream {
    sun.audio.NativeAudioStream audioIn;
    public sun.audio.AudioStream(java.io.InputStream);
    public int read(byte [],int,int);
    public sun.audio.AudioData getData();
    public int getLength();
}
```

Fuller documentation on these Sun classes has been put together by some Swedish programmers and is available at: *www.cdt.luth.se/java/doc/sun*.

Be sure you are clear that the classes in the vendor-specific hierarchy are intended solely for a vendor's use to implement the public APIs in the JDK. So Sun might change these classes around without notice. Use these at your own risk; they may change, and they make programs nonportable. The real way to play sounds now is with the Java Media Framework. But that didn't exist when this program was written.

Some Light Relief—Satan: Oscillate My Metallic Sonatas

Some people claim that "backwards masking" conceals satanic messages in popular music. They believe that if you play the music backwards (like reading the phrase above backwards) a hidden message will be revealed.

You can easily play a piece of music backwards by recording it onto a cassette tape. Then take the cassette apart by unscrewing the little screws, and swap the reels left to right (don't flip them upside down). You will have to thread the tape a little differently onto one spool.

You've done it correctly if the feed and take-up spools revolve in opposite directions to each other when you hit "play." Rewind once to remove this anomaly, and away you go with your backwards masking. This experiment is so much fun, you should drop whatever you're doing (you're probably reading a book) and go and try this *right now.*

For advanced students: overdub a tape to produce a gimmicked version on which you have added some suitable wording ("Sacrifice homework. Cthulu is our thesis advisor. Wear leather and stay out late on Fridays. Stack dirty dishes in the sink, and cut in line at supermarkets"). Leave the tape out for a suitable colleague to "discover" your backwards masked work.

Finally, I urge you to try running the Backward audio class on the file yenrab.au on the CD:

```
java  BackwardAudio  yenrab.au
```

If that sound file isn't evidence of demonic possession, I don't know what is.

Appendix B

Obsolete Components of the Abstract Window Toolkit

This appendix describes the components of the Abstract Window Toolkit (AWT) that have been replaced by the Swing components. The AWT components are described here because there are two circumstances when you may run into them: when you maintain old code, and when you are asked to write code that must run in the obsolete JDK 1.0 environment.

The Java AWT interface offers the functions that are common to all window systems. The AWT code then uses the underlying native (or "peer") window system to actually render the screen images and manipulate GUI objects. The AWT thus consists of a series of abstract interfaces along with Java code to map them into the actual native code on each system. This is why it is an *abstract* window toolkit; it is not tailored for a specific computer but offers the same API on all.

How the Java Abstract Window Toolkit Works

The AWT currently requires the native window system to be running on the platform because it uses the native window system to support windows within Java. Figure B-1 shows how the AWT interacts with the native window system.

Mnemonic: Peer objects let your Java runtime "peer" at the underlying window implementation. They are only of interest to people porting the Java Development Kit. To a Java applications programmer, all window system code is written in Java.

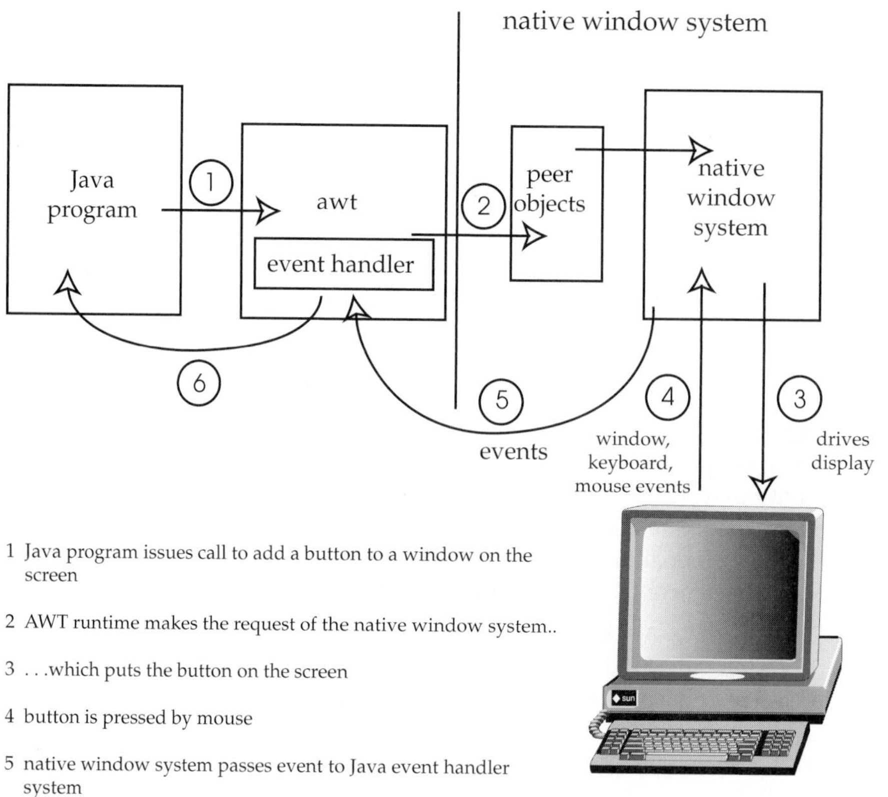
native window system
Java program
1
awt
event handler
2
peer objects
native window system
6
5
4
3
events
window, keyboard, mouse events
drives display
1 Java program issues call to add a button to a window on the screen
2 AWT runtime makes the request of the native window system..
3 . . .which puts the button on the screen
4 button is pressed by mouse
5 native window system passes event to Java event handler system
6 and from there into Java app's code

Figure B–1 How the Java abstract window toolkit works.

Controls, Containers, Events

In this appendix, I use the PC term *control* to mean the group of all the GUI things that users can press, scroll, choose between, type into, draw on, etc. In the Unix world, a control is called a *widget*. Neither control nor widget is a Java term, and in reality there is no control class. It's so useful, however, to be able to say "control" instead of "GUI thing that the user interacts with" or "Components plus menus" that we use the term here wherever convenient. Because each control is a subclass of `Component`, each control (button, etc.) also inherits all the methods and data fields of `Component`.

The important top-level classes that make up the AWT are shown in Figure B-2.

The basic idea is that you:

- Declare controls. You can subclass them to add to the behavior, but this is often not necessary.
- Add the controls to a container. Again, subclassing is possible but frequently not necessary.
- Implement an interface to get the event handler that responds to control activity.

We will look at all the dozen or so individual controls in depth.

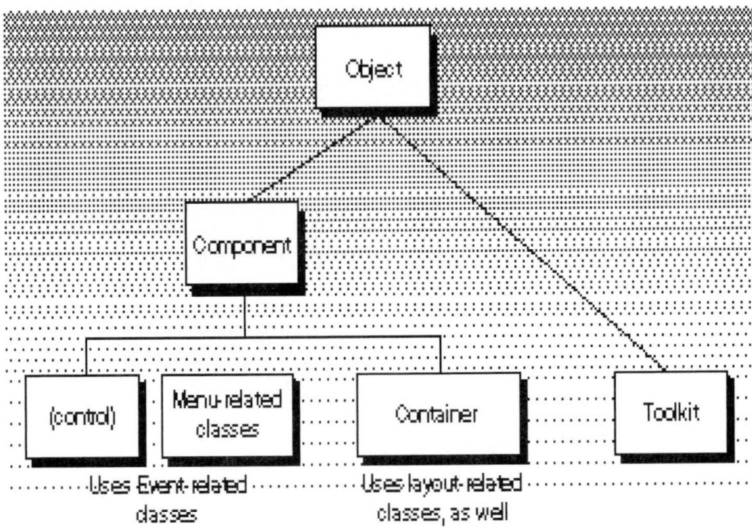

Figure B–2 The most important of the AWT classes.

Overview of Controls

The controls are: `Button`, `Canvas`, `Checkbox`, `Choice`, `Label`, `List`, `Scrollbar`, `TextField`, `TextArea`, and the variations on `Menu`. Each control has methods appropriate to what it does. The `Scrollbar` control has methods to set the width, orientation, and height of scrollbars, for instance. We'll examine each individual control in depth later in the appendix. One obvious control that is missing is a control into which you can write HTML and have it automatically formatted. More controls were added with the Java Foundation Classes, adopted from Netscape's Internet Foundation Classes. These were announced for the JDK 1.2 release.

At this point we now have enough background knowledge of the various GUI elements to present an in-depth treatment of how they talk to your code. Read on for the fascinating details!

Summary of AWT Event Handling: JDK1.0 vs JDK 1.1

Event-handling changed completely in JDK 1.1 mostly in order to better accommodate JavaBeans. In the JDK 1.0.2, the event-handling callbacks were based on inheritance. Your event-handling code had to be subclassed from `Component` so it would override the `Component`'s `handleEvent()` or `action()` method. You may see this code when you maintain older Java programs.

In the JDK 1.1, the callbacks are based on delegation: there is an interface for listening to each kind of event (mouse event, button event, scrollbar event, etc.). When an event occurs, the window system calls a method of a class that implements the specific listener interface. You create a class of your own that implements the appropriate interface, and register it with the window system. When that event occurs, the method that you have delegated (appointed) will be called back by the window system.

Never use a mixture of the two event models in the same program. That is not supported and will lead to bugs that can only be solved by a rewrite.

All About AWT Controls (Components)

We now start looking at individual controls in detail and to describe the kinds of event they can generate. Almost the whole of window programming is learning about the different objects that you can put on the screen (windows, scrollbars, buttons, etc.) and how to drive them. This section explains how to register for and process the events (input) that you get back from controls. A control isn't a free-standing thing; it is always added to a `Container` such as an `Applet`, `Frame`, `Panel`, or `Window`, with a method call like `MyContainer.add( myComponent )`. The controls that we will cover here are buttons, text fields, scrollbars, mouse events, and so on. The class hierarchy is quite flat. The controls shown in Figure B-3 are all subclasses of the general class `Component` that we have already seen.

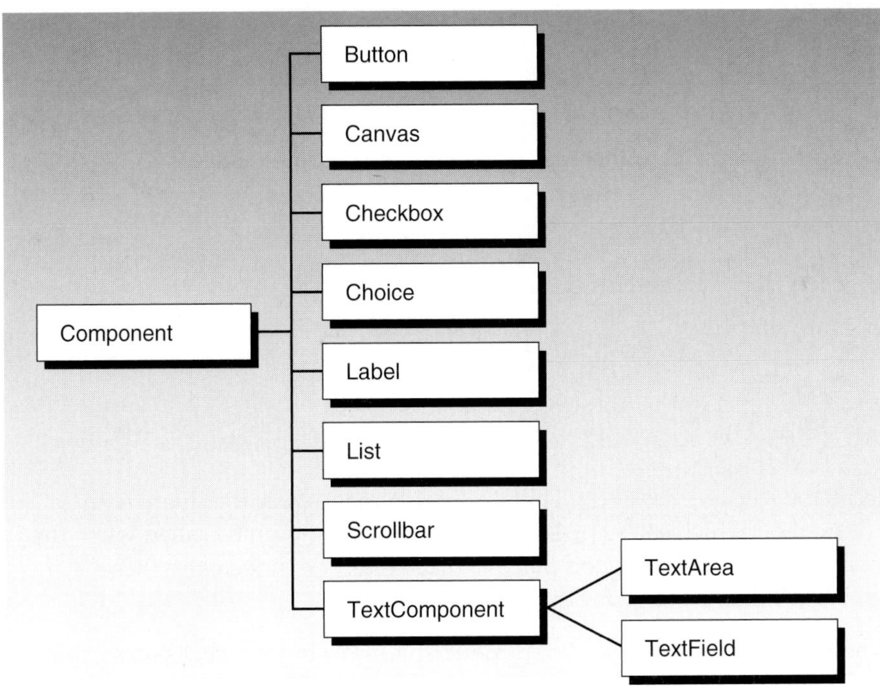

Figure B–3 The controls (visible AWT objects) of Java.

These classes are the controls or building blocks from which you will create your GUI. What you do with all these components is:

1. Add them to a container (usually `Frame` or `Applet`), then display the container with the `show()` method.

2. Register your event handler, using the `addXxxListener()` method of the control. This will tell the window system which routine of yours should be called when the user presses buttons, makes selections, etc., to process the event.

Fortunately, both of these activities are quite straightforward, and we'll cover them here in source code, words, and pictures. The `add` method can be applied to a `Frame` in an application, like this:

```
Frame f = new Frame();
                    ...
f.add( something );
```

Or, it can be applied to the `Applet`'s panel in an applet, like so:

```
public static void init () {
     this.add( something );
```

Or, more simply:

```
public static void init () {
     add( something );
```

Recall the `Applet` life cycle. That discussion made clear that there is an `init()` method which each `Applet` should override. It will be called when the Applet is loaded, and it is a good place to place the code that creates these GUI objects. We will use `init()` for that purpose.

Whenever a user operates a `Component` (presses a button, clicks on a choice), an event is generated. The `XxxEvent` argument is a class that can be seen in the `awt/event` directory. It contains much information about the coordinates of the event, the time it occurred, and the kind of event that it was. If the event was a keypress, it has the value of the key. If the event was a selection from a list, it has the string chosen.

Having explained the general theory of controls and control events, let's take a look at how they appear on the screen and the typical code to handle them.

`Button`

What it is: This is a GUI button. You can program the action that takes place when the button is pressed

What it looks like on screen:

The code to create it:

```
Button b = new Button("peach");
     add(b);
```

The code to retrieve user input from it:

```
     MyBHClass myButtonHandler = new MyBHClass();

     public void init() {
          add(apple);
          apple.addActionListener(myButtonHandler);
     }
}

class MyBHClass implements java.awt.event.ActionListener {
     int i=1;

     public void actionPerformed(ActionEvent e) {
          // this gets called when button pressed...
               String s = e.paramString(); // gets the button label
     }
}
```

An event-handler this small would typically be written using an inner class, and we will use inner classes for the rest of the examples.

In an applet, you will typically override the `init()` method and, inside it, call the `add()` method to add these objects to your Applet's panel. In an application, there is no predetermined convention, and you can set the objects where you like. (*Note:* in future examples in this section, we won't bother repeating the context that this is part of the `init()` method in an applet).

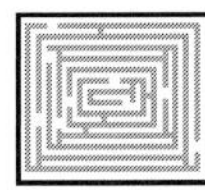

Program an "Alice in Wonderland" applet: a panel with two buttons, one of which makes the panel grow larger, the other smaller. The `Component` method

```
setSize(int, int)
```

will resize a `Panel` or other `Container`. (Easy—about 20 lines of code.)

Canvas

What it is: A Canvas is a screen area that you can use for drawing graphics or receiving user input. A Canvas usually is subclassed to add the behavior you need, especially when you use it to display a GIF or JPEG image. A Canvas contains almost no methods. All its functionality is either inherited from Component (setting font, color, size) or from functionality you add when you extend the class.

To draw on a canvas, you supply your own version of the paint(Graphics g) method. To do that, you need to extend the class and override the paint() method for this Canvas. A more descriptive name for the paint() method would be do_this_to_draw_me(). That gives you a Graphics context (the argument to paint()), which is used in all drawing operations. The many methods of Graphics let you render (the fancy graphics word for "draw") lines, shapes, text, etc., on the screen.

What it looks like on screen:

The screen capture is not very exciting, merely showing a rectangular area that has been highlighted with a different color to make it visible (see code below). Canvases are relatively inert until you extend them and use them to display images or do other graphics programming.

The code to create it: This code gives the Canvas a red color, so you can distinguish it from the Panel (as long as your *Applet* panel isn't red to begin with, of course). The code then gives the Canvas a size of 80 pixels wide by 40 pixels high and adds it to the Applet.

```
Canvas n = new Canvas();

n.setBackground(Color.red);
n.setSize(80,40);
add(n);
```

Note that you cannot draw on objects of class Canvas. You must extend Canvas and override the paint() method and do your drawing in that routine. The paint() method needs to contain all the statements to draw everything that you

want to see in the canvas at that time. Here is how you would extend Canvas to provide a surface that you can draw on:

```
// <applet code=can.class width=250 height=100>  </applet>
import java.awt.*;
import java.applet.*;
public class can extends Applet {
     myCanvas c = new myCanvas();

     public void init() {
          c.setSize(200,50);
          add(c);
     }
}

class myCanvas extends Canvas{
     public void paint(Graphics g) {
          g.drawString("don't go in the basement", 10,25);
          g.drawLine(10,35, 165,35);
     }
}
```

You can compile and execute this by typing

```
javac can.java appletviewer can.java
```

A window like this is displayed on the screen:

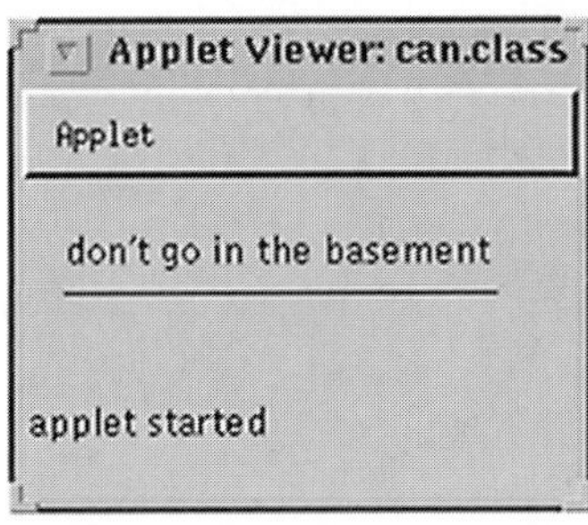

A `Canvas` is similar to a `Panel`, in that you can draw on it, render images, and accept events. A `Canvas` is not a container, however, so you cannot add other components to it. Here is how you would accept mouse events on a Canvas.

```
//  <applet code=can.class width=250 height=100> </applet>
import java.awt.*;
import java.awt.event.*;
import java.applet.*;
public class can extends Applet {
     Canvas c = new Canvas();

     public void init() {
          c.setSize(200,50);
          c.setEnabled(true);
          c.setBackground(Color.blue);
          c.addMouseListener ( new MouseListener() {
               public void mouseEntered(java.awt.event.MouseEvent e)
                    {System.out.println(e.toString() );}
               public void mouseClicked(java.awt.event.MouseEvent e) {}
               public void mousePressed(java.awt.event.MouseEvent e) {}
               public void mouseReleased(java.awt.event.MouseEvent e) {}
               public void mouseExited(java.awt.event.MouseEvent e) {}
               });
          add(c);
     }
}
```

The preceding code handles the event fired when the mouse enters the blue canvas. If you run it, you'll see something like this.

```
% appletviewer can.java
java.awt.event.MouseEvent[MOUSE_ENTERED,(131,49),mods=0,clickCount
  =0]  on canvas0
```

Adapter Classes

Here is an example showing how the `MouseAdapter` class is used when all we are interested in is the mouse entering the `Canvas`.

```
//  <applet code=can.class width=250 height=100>  </applet> import java.awt.*;
import java.awt.event.*;
import java.applet.*;
public class can extends Applet {
     Canvas c = new Canvas();

     public void init() {
          c.setSize(200,50);
          c.setEnabled(true);
          c.setBackground(Color.blue);
          c.addMouseListener ( new MouseAdapter() {
               public void mouseEntered(java.awt.event.MouseEvent e)
                    {System.out.println(e.toString() );}
               });
          add(c);
     }
}
```

Here is an example of how a game program might capture individual key presses in an applet as they are made. Note that the output is to `System.out`, which isn't displayed in a browser unless you bring up the right window. This example is best run in the applet viewer.

```
// <applet code=game.class height=200 width=300> </applet>
import java.awt.*;
import java.awt.event.*;
import java.applet.*;
public class game  extends Applet {

     public void init() {
          requestFocus(); // a component must have the focus to get
                              //key events
          addKeyListener(
               new KeyAdapter() {
               public void keyPressed(java.awt.event.KeyEvent e)
                    { System.out.println("got "+e.getKeyChar()); }
               } // end anon class
          ); // end method call
     }
}
```

The `requestFocus()` call is a `Component` method to ask that keyboard input be directed to this control. Having to explicitly ask for the focus is a change from JDK 1.0.2. The `Component` must be visible on the screen for the `requestFocus()` to succeed. A `FocusGained` event will then be delivered if there's a listener for it.

Let's continue with our description of the individual controls.

Checkbox

What it is: A checkbox screen object that represents a boolean choice: "pressed" or "not pressed" or "on" or "off." Usually some text explains the choice. For example, "Press for fries" would have a Checkbox "button" allowing yes or no.

What it looks like on screen:

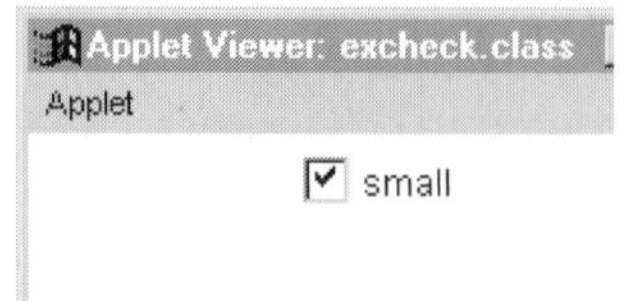

The code to create it:

```
Checkbox cb  = new Checkbox("small");
add(cb);
```

The code to retrieve user input from it: Checkbox generates `ItemEvent`. The code to register an `ItemListener` looks like this:

```
//  <applet code=excheck.class width=250 height=100>  </applet> import
java.awt.*;
import java.awt.event.*;
import java.applet.*;
public class excheck extends Applet {
     Checkbox c1 = new Checkbox("small");

     public void init() {
          c1.addItemListener ( new ItemListener() {
               public void itemStateChanged(java.awt.event.ItemEvent ie)
               { System.out.println(ie.paramString() );}
     });
          add(c1);
     }
}
```

In this example, as in most of them, we simply print out a String representation of the event that has occurred. Running the applet and clicking the checkbox will cause this output in the system console:

```
appletviewer excheck.java
ITEM_STATE_CHANGED,item=small,stateChange=SELECTED
ITEM_STATE_CHANGED,item=small,stateChange=DESELECTED
```

Handlers in real programs will do more useful actions: assign values, create objects, etc., as necessary. The ItemEvent contains fields and methods that specify which object generated the event and whether it was selected or deselected.

CheckboxGroup

What it is: There is a way to group a series of checkboxes to create a `CheckboxGroup` of *radio buttons*. The term "radio buttons" arises from the old manual station selection buttons in car radios. When you pressed in one of the buttons, all the others would pop out and be deselected. `CheckboxGroups` work the same way.

What it looks like on screen:

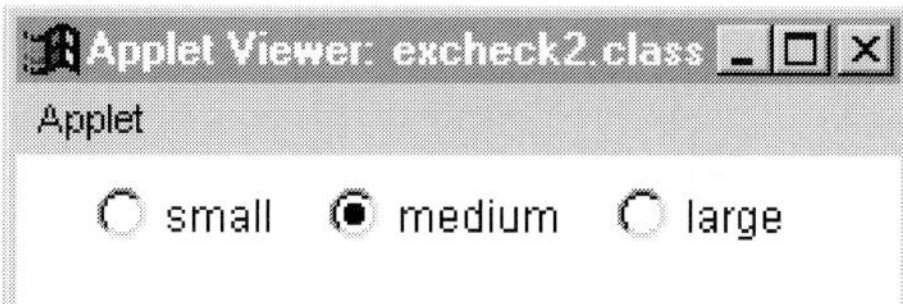

On Windows 95, mutually-exclusive checkboxes are round, while multiple-selection checkboxes are square. This is one of those "look and feel" differences that vary between window systems.

The code to create it: You first instantiate a `CheckboxGroup` object, then use that in each `Checkbox` constructor, along with a parameter saying whether it is selected or not. This ensures that only one of those Checkbox buttons will be allowed to be on at a time.

```
//  <applet code=excheck2.class width=250 height=100>  </applet>
import java.awt.*;
import java.awt.event.*;
import java.applet.*;
public class excheck2 extends Applet {
     CheckboxGroup cbg = new CheckboxGroup();

     Checkbox c1 = new Checkbox("small", false,  cbg);
     Checkbox c2 = new Checkbox("medium", false, cbg);
     Checkbox c3 = new Checkbox("large",  true,  cbg);

     ItemListener ie = new ItemListener () {
          public void itemStateChanged(java.awt.event.ItemEvent ie)
               { System.out.println(ie.toString());}
          };
     public void init() {
          c1.addItemListener ( ie );
          c2.addItemListener ( ie );
          c3.addItemListener ( ie );
          add(c1);
          add(c2);
          add(c3);
     }
}
```

Note here that we are using the same, one instance of an inner class as the handler for events from all three of these Checkboxes. It is common to have one handler for several related objects, and let the handler decode which of them actually caused the event. We couldn't do this if we had created an anonymous class, because we would not have kept a reference to use in the later `addItemListener()` calls.

`Choice`

What it is: This is a pop-up list, akin to a pull-down menu, which allows a selection from several text strings. When you hold down the mouse button on the choice, a list of all the other choices appears and you can move the mouse over the one you want.

What it looks like on screen:

Choices are very similar to the `List` control. Lists look a little more like text; Choices look a little more like buttons and menus. When you click the mouse on a `Choice`, it pops up the full range of choices, looking like this:

The code to create it:

```
<applet code=exchoice.class width=250 height=100>  </applet> import
java.awt.*;
import java.awt.event.*;
import java.applet.*;
public class exchoice extends Applet {
     Choice c = new Choice();

     public void init() {
          add(c);
          c.addItem("lemon");
          c.addItem("orange");
          c.addItem("lime");
     ItemListener il = new ItemListener () {
          public void itemStateChanged(java.awt.event.ItemEvent ie)
               { System.out.println(ie.getItem()); }
          };

        c.addItemListener ( il );
     }
}
```

Note that it is perfectly feasible to build the items in a Choice list dynamically. If you wanted to, you could build at runtime a `Choice` representing every file in a directory. A control called `FileDialog` does this for you, however.

Label

What it is: This is a very simple component. It is just a string of text that appears on screen. The text can be left, right, or center aligned according to an argument to the constructor. The default is left aligned.

What it looks like on screen:

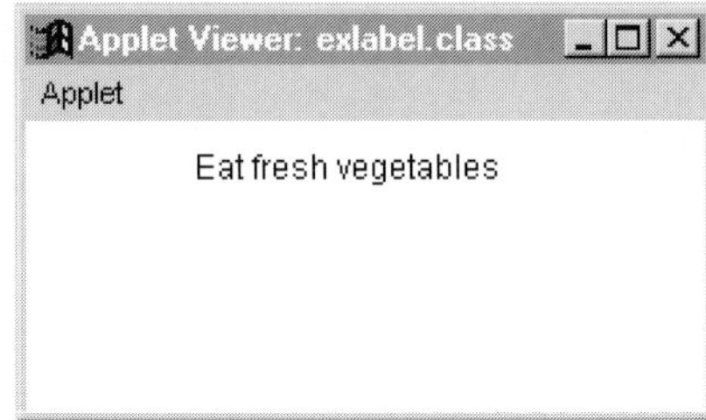

The code to create it:

```
//  <applet code=exlabel.class width=250 height=100>  </applet>
import java.awt.*;
import java.awt.event.*;
import java.applet.*;
public class exlabel extends Applet {
     String s = "Eat fresh vegetables";
     Label l = new Label(s);

     public void init() {
          add(l);
     }
}
```

Labels do not generate any events in and of themselves. However, it is possible to change the text of a label (perhaps in response to an event from a different component).

Labels are typically used as a cheap, fast way to get some text on the screen and to label other controls with descriptions or instructions. People often want to know how to get a multiline label (or a multiline button). There is no direct way. You will have to program the functionality in for yourself, by extending the class `Canvas` or `Component` to do what you want.

List

What it is: Lists are very similar to Choices, in that you can select from several text alternatives. With a Choice, only the top selection is visible until you click the mouse on it to bring them all up. With a List, many or all of the selections are visible on the screen with no mousing needed.

A List also allows the user to select one or several entries (single or multiple selection is configurable). A Choice only allows one entry at a time to be chosen.

What it looks like on screen:

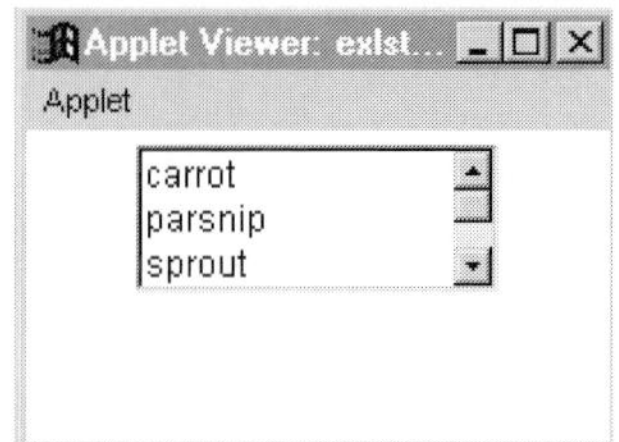

The code to create it: This creates a scrolling list with three items visible initially and does not allow multiple selections at the same time (multiple selections is false).

```
//<applet code=exlist.class width=200 height=100> </applet> import
java.awt.*;
import java.awt.event.*;
import java.applet.*;

public class exlist extends Applet {
     List l = new List(3,false);

     public void init() {
          add(l);
          l.addItem("carrot");
          l.addItem("parsnip");
          l.addItem("sprout");
          l.addItem("cabbage");
          l.addItem("turnip");
          ItemListener il = new ItemListener () {
               public void itemStateChanged(java.awt.event.ItemEvent ie)
          { System.out.println(ie.getItem() ); }
               };
          l.addItemListener ( il );
     }
}
```

The code to retrieve user input from it: The `ItemListener` is called when the selection is made by clicking on the list entry. Unlike a Choice, which returns the text string representing the selection, a `List` selection event returns an integer in the range 0 to N, representing the selection of the zeroth to Nth item.

The `List` class (not the `ItemEvent` class) has methods to turn that list index into a String and to get an array containing the indexes of all currently selected elements.

```
public String getItem(int index);
public synchronized int[] getSelectedIndexes();
```

`Scrollbar`

What it is: A scrollbar is a box that can be dragged between two end points. Dragging the box, or clicking on an end point, will generate events that say how far along the range the box is.

You don't have to use `Scrollbar` much, as scrollbars are given to you automatically on several controls (`TextArea`, `Choice`, and `ScrollPane`). When you do use one, it is typically related by your code to some other control. When the user moves the scrollbar, your program reads the incoming event and makes a related change in the other control. Often, that involves changing the visual appearance, but it doesn't have to. A scrollbar could be used to input numeric values between two end points.

What it looks like on screen:

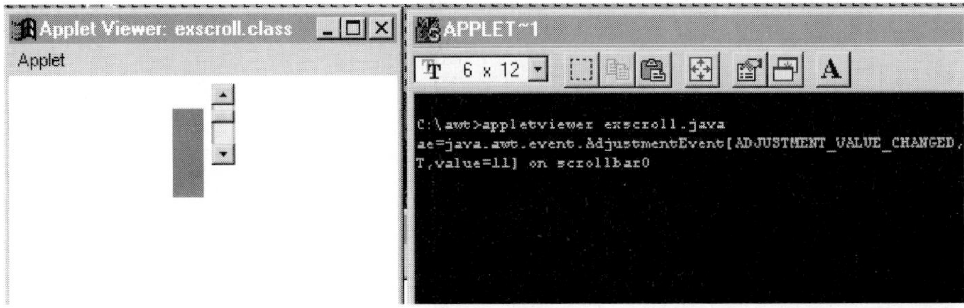

The code to create it:

```
public void init() {
     Scrollbar s = new Scrollbar(Scrollbar.VERTICAL,20,10,5,35);
     add(s);
```

The arguments are:

- whether the bar should go up `Scrollbar.VERTICAL` or along `Scrollbar.HORIZONTAL`
- the initial setting for the bar (here, 20), which should be a value between the high and low ends of the scale
- the length of the slider box (here, 10)
- the value at the low end of the scale (here, 5)
- the value at the high end of the scale (here, 35)

The code to retrieve user input from it: Scrollbars have various methods for getting and setting the values, but the method you'll use most is `public int getValue()`. There is a method of this name in both the `Scrollbar` class and the `AdjustmentEvent` class. When you call it, it returns the current value of the `Scrollbar` or (when you invoke it on the `AdjustmentEvent` object), the value that it had when this event was generated.

Here is an example of using `Scrollbar` to input a numeric value. It draws a simple bar graph by resizing a canvas according to the scroll value.

```
// <applet code=A.class height=200 width=300> </applet>

import java.awt.*;
import java.awt.event.*;
import java.applet.*;
public class A  extends Applet {

     public void init() {
          resize(250,200);

          final Canvas n      = new Canvas();
          n.setBackground(Color.red);
          n.setSize(20,20);
          add(n);

          Scrollbar s  = new Scrollbar(Scrollbar.VERTICAL,10,20,1,75);
          add(s);
          s.addAdjustmentListener(
               new AdjustmentListener() {
                    public void adjustmentValueChanged(AdjustmentEvent ae)
{
                         System.out.println("ae="+ae);
                         n.setSize( 20, ae.getValue() *5 );
                         repaint();
                    }
               }
          );
     }
}
```

Now that JDK 1.1 has introduced the `ScrollPane` container type, scrollbars don't need to be programmed explicitly nearly so much.

TextField

What it is: A `TextField` is a field into which the user can type a single line of characters. The number of characters displayed is configurable. A TextField can also be given an initial value of characters. Changing the field is called editing it, and editing can be enabled or disabled.

The `TextField` component sets its background color differently, depending on whether the `TextField` is editable, or not. If the `Textfield` can be edited, the background is set to `backgroundColor.brighter();` if it is not editable, the whole text field is set to the same color as the background color.

What it looks like on screen:

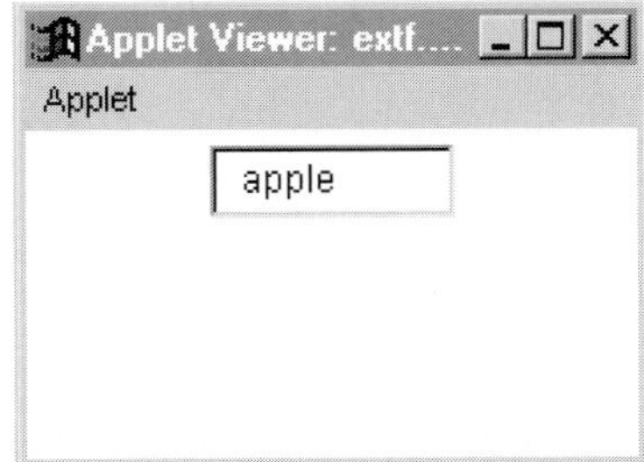

The code to create it: This code creates a `TextField` with eight characters showing, and initialized to with the characters "apple". You can type different characters in there and more than eight, but only eight will show at a time.

```
TextField tf = new TextField("apple",8);
add(tf);
```

The code to retrieve user input from it: A `TextField` causes an event when a Return is entered in the field. At that point, the `ActionEvent` method `getActionCommand()` will retrieve the text.

```
//<applet code=extf.class height=100 width=200> </applet>
import java.applet.*;
import java.awt.*;
import java.awt.event.*;

public class extf extends Applet {
     TextField tf = new TextField("apple",8);
     public void init() {
          add(tf);
          tf.addActionListener(
               new ActionListener()
               {
                    public void actionPerformed(ActionEvent e) {
                         System.out.println("field is"
                              +e.getActionCommand());
                    }
               } // end anon class
          ); // end method call
     }
}
```

Remember that any component can register to receive any kind of event. A useful thing you might want to do is register a `KeyListener` for the text field. You could use this to filter incoming keystrokes, perhaps validating them. The code below will make the text field beep if you type any non-numeric input.

```
//<applet code=extf2.class height=100 width=200> </applet>
import java.applet.*;
import java.awt.*;
import java.awt.event.*;

public class extf2 extends Applet {

     TextField tf = new TextField("numbers only",14);

     public void init() {
          add(tf);

          tf.addKeyListener( new KeyAdapter() {
                    public void keyPressed(KeyEvent e) {
                         char k = e.getKeyChar();
                         if (k<'0' || k>'9'){
                              tf.getToolkit().beep();
                              e.setKeyChar('0');
                         }
                    }
               } // end anon class
          ); // end method call
          tf.addActionListener(  new ActionListener() {
                    public void actionPerformed(ActionEvent e) {
                         System.out.println("got "+e.getActionCommand());
                    }
               } // end anon class
          ); // end method call
     }
}
```

A `KeyListener` is registered with the text field. As keystrokes come in, it examines them and converts any non-numerics to the character "0", effectively forcing the field to be numeric. An `ActionListener` is registered with the text field too. The `ActionListener` retrieves the entire numeric string when the user presses Return.

Note: A bug in the Windows 95 version of JDK 1.1.1 prevents the `setKeyChar()` method from changing the character to zero.

A better approach would be to allow the character to be typed, and then use the `getText()` and `setText()` methods of the `TextComponent` parent class to remove the non-numeric characters.

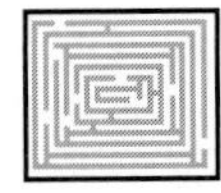

Finally, note the `setFont()` method, which will use a different font in the component. A typical call looks like this:

```
myTextArea.setFont(
new Font("FONTNAME", FONTSTYLE, FONTSIZE) );
```

Where `FONTNAME` is the name of the font (e.g., Dialog, TimesRoman) as a String. `FONTSTYLE` is `Font.PLAIN`, `Font.ITALIC`, `Font.BOLD` or any additive combination (e.g., `Font.ITALIC+Font.BOLD`). `FONTSIZE` is an int representing the size of the font, (e.g., 12 means 12 point).

TextArea

What it is: A TextField that is several lines long. It can be set to allow editing or read-only modes.

What it looks like on screen:

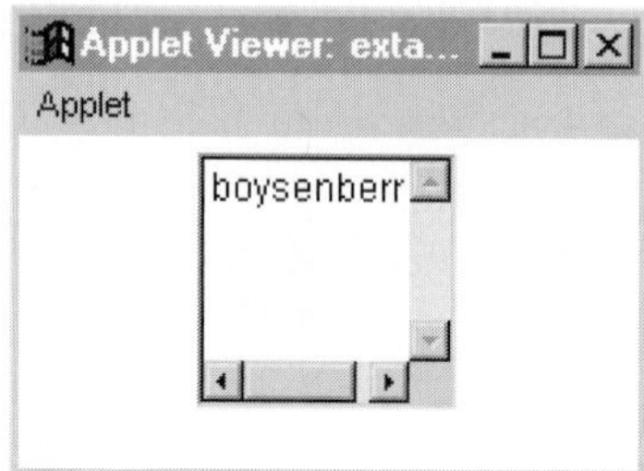

The code to create it:

```
TextArea t = new TextArea("boysenberry", 4, 9);
add(t);
```

This creates a text area of four lines, each showing nine characters. The first line shows the first nine characters of the string "boysenberry." You can place text on the next line in the initializer by embedding a '\n' character in the string.

TextAreas automatically come with scrollbars, so you can type an unbounded amount of text.

```
//<applet code=exta.class height=100 width=200> </applet>
import java.applet.*;
import java.awt.*;
import java.awt.event.*;

public class exta extends Applet {

     TextArea ta = new TextArea("boysenberry", 4, 9);

     public void init() {
          add(ta);

          ta.addTextListener(  new TextListener()
               {
                    public void textValueChanged(java.awt.event.TextEvent
e)
                         { System.out.println("got "+ta.getText()); }
                    } // end anon class
               ); // end method call
     }
}
```

Like all of these controls, `TextAreas` use the underlying native window system control and are subject to the same limitations of the underlying window system. Under Microsoft Windows, TextAreas can only hold 32K of characters, less a few K for overhead. A big benefit of moving to peerless, pure Java components is to lose platform-specific limitations.

Unlike a `TextField`, a TextArea might have embedded newlines, so a newline can't be used to cause the event that says, "I am ready to give up my value." The same solution is used as with a multiple-selection list. Use another control, say, a button or checkbox, to signal that the text is ready to be picked up. Alternatively, as in this example, you simply can pull in the text for the whole area as each new character comes in.

Menus: Design

In an eccentric design choice, menus are not Components—they are an on-screen thing that isn't a subclass of `Component`. This inconsistency was originally perpetrated to reflect the same design limitation in Microsoft Windows, namely, menus in Win32 are not first-class controls.

The terminology of menus is shown in Figure B-4.

The Menu-related classes match the terminology shown in Figure B-4. We have a `MenuBar` class on which menus can be placed. Each menu can have zero or more `MenuItems`. Because menus aren't Components, we have two additional classes: `MenuComponent` and `MenuContainer`.

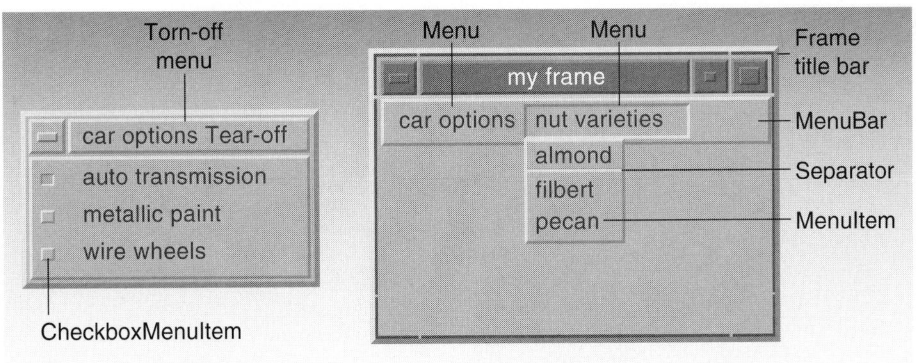

Figure B–4 The terminology of menus.

`Menu`: *Class*

What it is: A Frame can hold a `MenuBar`, which can have several pull-down menus. The `MenuBar` has its top edge on the top edge of the `Frame`, so if you add anything to (0,0) on the `Frame`, the `MenuBar` will obscure it. The `MenuBar` holds the names of each `Menu` that has been added to it. Each pull-down menu has selectable `MenuItems` on it, each identified by a String. You can populate a menu with menu items and also with other menus. The second case is a multilevel menu.

What it looks like on screen:

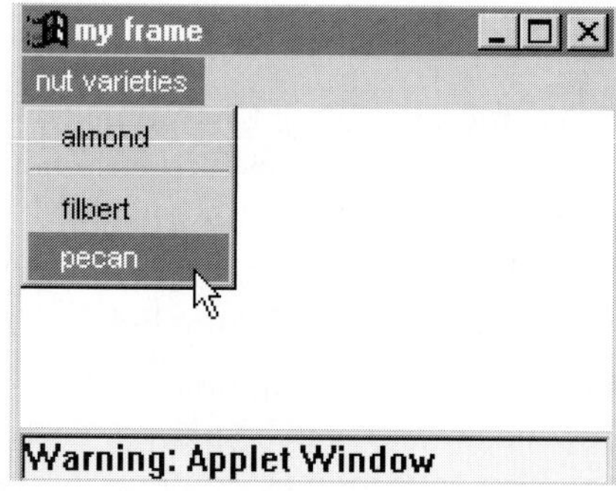

The code to create it:

```
//<applet code=exmenu.class height=100 width=200> </applet>
import java.applet.*;
import java.awt.*;
import java.awt.event.*;

public class exmenu extends Applet {

     Frame f = new Frame("my frame");
     MenuBar mb = new MenuBar();
     Menu nuts = new Menu("nut varieties", /*tearoff=*/ true);

     public void init() {
          nuts.add(new MenuItem("almond"));
          nuts.add(new MenuItem("-") );    // a separator in the menu
          nuts.add(new MenuItem("filbert"));
          nuts.add(new MenuItem("pecan"));

          mb.add(nuts);
          f.setSize(500,100);
          f.setMenuBar(mb);
          f.show();
```

The code to retrieve user input from it `MenuItems` can be handled by registering an `Event` with the `Menu`, like this:

```
nuts.addActionListener(
     new ActionListener()
     {
          public void actionPerformed(ActionEvent e) {
               System.out.println("field is "+e.getActionCommand());
          }
     } // end anon class
); // end method call
```

A *tear-off* menu is one that remains visible even after you take your finger off the mouse button and click elsewhere. Not all window systems support tear-off menus, and the boolean is simply ignored in that case. Under CDE (the Unix window system), a tear-off menu is indicated by a dotted line across the top of the menu.

CheckboxMenuItem

An alternative kind of `MenuItem` is a `CheckboxMenuItem`. This variety of `MenuItem` allows on/off selection/deselection, possibly several at once. It looks like the `Checkbox` control that we saw earlier.

What it looks like on screen:

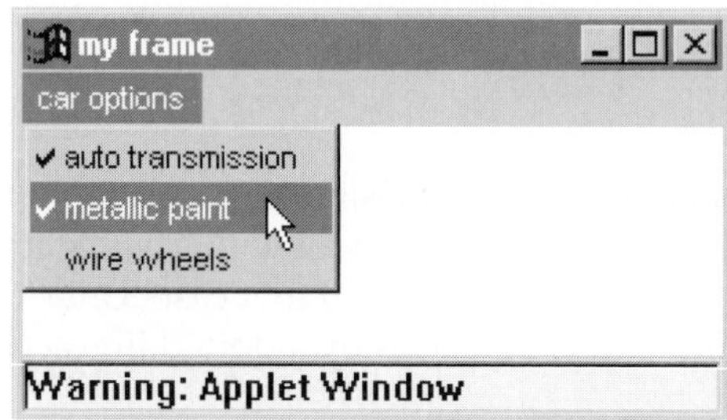

As the name suggests, this is a menu item that can be checked off or selected (like a checkbox). You receive ItemEvents from this kind of control, to say whether it is currently selected or not. Other than that, it works like a `MenuItem`, because it is a subclass of `MenuItem`.

With all these `Menu` gadgets, there are more methods than are shown here. A menu item can be disabled so it can't be selected, then later it can be enabled again.

There are menu item shortcuts, which are single-character keyboard accelerators that cause a menu event when you type them, just as if you had selected a menu item. A menu item shortcut can be set and changed with methods in the `MenuItem` class.

```
MenuItem myItem = new MenuItem("Open...");
myMenu.add(myItem);
myItem.setShortcut(new MenuShortcut((int)'O', false);
```

Note that under Windows, the standard controls parse their text names for special characters that indicate a letter in the control's text should be underlined (indicating a shortcut). For OS/2, the special character is ~; for Win32, it is &. Java does not support this feature.

The code to create it:

```
//<applet code=exmenu2.class height=100 width=200> </applet> import java.applet.*;
import java.awt.*;
import java.awt.event.*;

public class exmenu2 extends Applet {

      Frame f = new Frame("my frame");
      MenuBar mb = new MenuBar();
      Menu car = new Menu("car options", /*tearoff=*/ true);

      public void init() {
            CheckboxMenuItem cbm1 = new CheckboxMenuItem(
                                          "auto transmission");
            CheckboxMenuItem cbm2 = new CheckboxMenuItem(
                                          "metallic paint");
            CheckboxMenuItem cbm3 = new CheckboxMenuItem(
                                          "wire wheels");

            options action = new options();
            cbm1.addItemListener(action);
            cbm2.addItemListener(action);
            cbm3.addItemListener(action);

            car.add(cbm1); car.add(cbm2); car.add(cbm3);

            mb.add(car);
            f.setSize(500,100);
            f.setMenuBar(mb);
            f.show();
      }
}

class options implements ItemListener {
      public void itemStateChanged(ItemEvent e) {
            System.out.println("field is "+e.toString());
      }
}
```

Pop-up Menus

As well as pull-down menus, most modern systems have pop-up menus, which are menus that are not attached to a menu bar on a Frame. Pop-up menus are usually triggered by clicking or holding down a mouse button over a Container. One of the mouse event methods is `PopupTrigger()`, allowing you to check on this eventuality and if so display the pop-up menu at the (x,y) coordinates of the mouse. On Unix, the right mouse button is the trigger for a pop-up.

Pop-up menus, introduced in JDK 1.1, made menus much more useful in applets. Until then, people had tended not to use menus in applets, because the top-level container is a `Panel` (not a `Frame`) and so can't have a `MenuBar` added to it. You can create Frames in applets, but they are independent windows, floating free on the desktop.

What it looks like on screen:

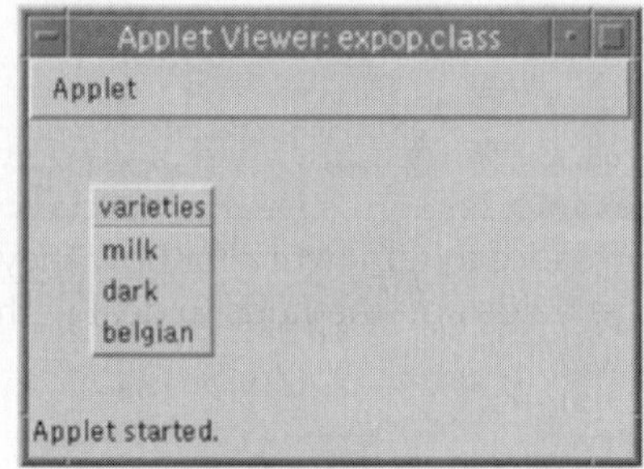

The code to create it:

```
//<applet code=expop.class height=100 width=200> </applet>
import java.applet.*;
import java.awt.*;
import java.awt.event.*;

public class expop extends Applet {

     PopupMenu choc = new PopupMenu("varieties");

     public void init() {
          choc.add(new MenuItem("milk"));
          choc.add(new MenuItem("dark"));
          choc.add(new MenuItem("belgian"));

          add(choc);

          final Applet app = this;
          addMouseListener( new MouseAdapter() {
               public void mousePressed(MouseEvent e) {
                    if (e.isPopupTrigger())
                         choc.show(app,30,30);
          } } );
          choc.addActionListener(
               new ActionListener()
               {
                    public void actionPerformed(ActionEvent e) {
                         System.out.println("field is
"+e.getActionCommand());
                    }
               }
          // end anon class
); // end method call
     }
}
```

All About Containers

The previous section describes all the controls of JDK 1.1, now let's take a look at the Containers that hold them. To refresh our memories, the class hierarchy for containers is as shown in Figure B-5.

On the following pages, we will outline each of these containers, suggest typical uses, and show code examples. `Container` is the class that groups together a number of controls and provides a framework for how they will be positioned on the screen. `Container` has fields and methods to deal with:

- The layout manager used to automatically position controls
- Forcing the layout to be done
- Refreshing the appearance on screen
- Adding a `ContainerListener` for `ContainerEvents`
- Adding, removing, and getting a list of any of the controls
- Size (current, preferred, minimum, and maximum)
- Requesting the window focus
- A `paint()` routine that will render it on the screen

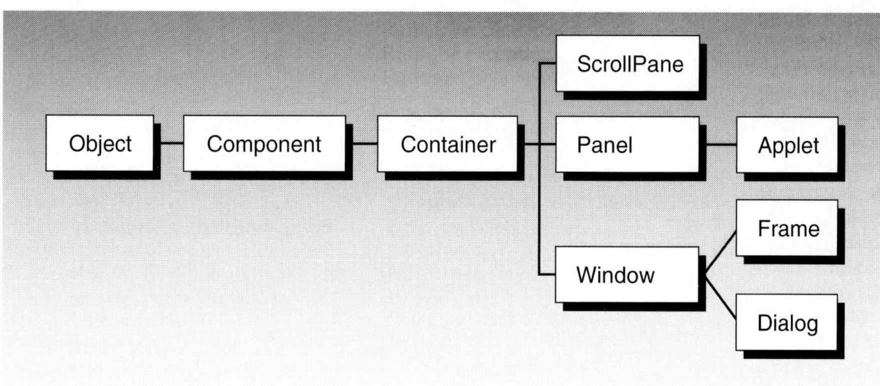

Figure B–5 Class hierarchy of containers.

Container has methods to get and set many of these attributes. Since a Container is a subclass of Component. It also has all the Component fields. You can and should review the Container methods by running

```
javap java.awt.Container
```

On the following pages we will review the different kinds (subclasses) of Container in the AWT. Containers are for holding, positioning, and displaying all the controls you add to them. When you have finished adding or changing the components in a Container, you typically call these three methods on the Container:

```
myContainer.invalidate();  // tell AWT it needs laying out
myContainer.validate();    // ask AWT to lay it out
myContainer.show();        // make it visible
```

These methods aren't needed if you are just adding to an applet, but you will need to use them in your more complicated programs.

ScrollPane

What it is: `ScrollPane` is a `Container` that implements automatic horizontal and/or vertical scrolling for a single child component. You will create a `ScrollPane`, call `setSize()` on it to give it a size, then add some other control to it. The control you add will often be a canvas with an image, though it can be any single component (such as a panel full of buttons).

You can ask for scrollbars never, as needed, or always. Note the inconsistent use of capitals; we have a `Scrollbar` but a `ScrollPane`.

What it looks like on screen:

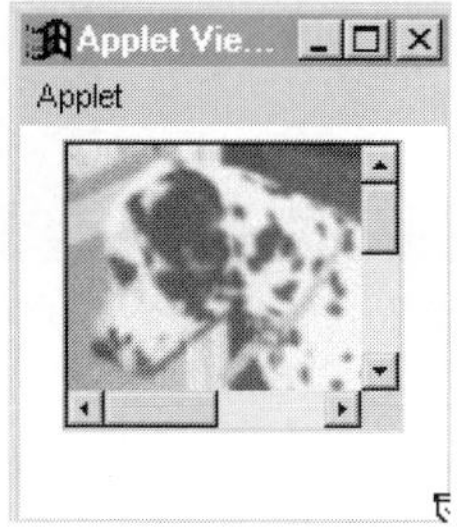

The code to create it:

```
//<applet code=exsp.class width=150 height=130 > </applet>
import java.awt.*;
import java.applet.*;
import java.awt.event.*;
public class exsp extends Applet  {
     public void init() {
          Image i = getImage(getDocumentBase(),"puppy.jpg");
          myCanvas mc = new myCanvas(i);

          ScrollPane sp = new ScrollPane();
          sp.setSize(120,100);
          sp.add(mc);
          sp.add(mc);

          add(sp);
     }
}

class myCanvas extends Canvas {
     Image si;
     public myCanvas(Image i) { this.setSize(200,200); si=i;}
     public void paint(Graphics g) { g.drawImage(si,0,0,this);}
}
```

`Window`

What it is: This `Container` is a totally blank window. It doesn't even have a border. You can display messages by putting Labels on it. Typically you don't use `Window` directly but use its more useful subclasses (`Frame` and `Dialog`).

Windows can be modal, meaning they prevent all other windows from responding until they are dealt with (usually with a checkbox). `Window` has a few methods to do with bringing it to the front or back, packing (resizing to preferred size,) or showing (making it visible).

What it looks like on screen:

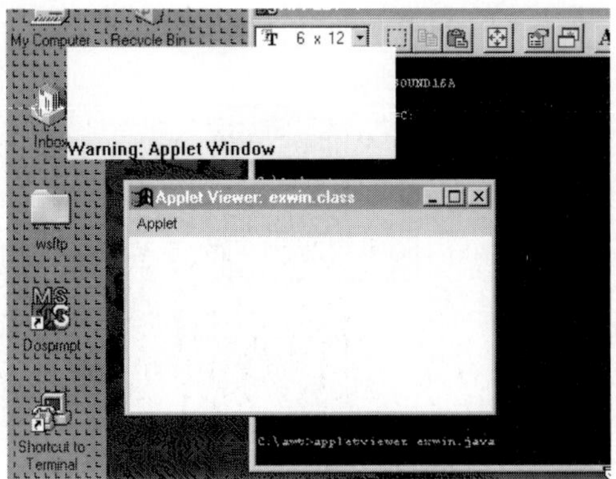

The code to create it:

```
//<applet code=exwin.class width=275 height=125 > </applet> import java.awt.*;
import java.applet.*;
import java.awt.event.*;
public class discern extends Applet {

      public void init() {

      Component c = this.getParent();
      while (Connell && !(c instanceof Frame)) c=c.getParent();

      Window w = new Window( (Frame)c);
      w.setBounds(50,50,250,100);
      w.show();
      }
}
```

The public constructor of `Window` needs to know the `Frame` that it belongs to, so we walk up the parent tree until we find it. This repeated `getParent()` code is a Java idiom you will see in AWT code from time to time.

For security purposes, the browser will typically make sure any `Window` or subclass of `Window` popped up from an untrusted applet will contain a line of text warning that it is an "untrusted window" or an "applet window." This message ensures the user of an applet will never be in any doubt about the origin of the window. Without this clear label, it would be too easy to pop up a window that looked like it came from the operating system and ask for confidential information to send back to the applet server. It is not possible for an applet to prevent this security label from being shown.

Frame

What it is: A `Frame` is a window that also has a title bar, a menu bar, a border (known as the inset), and that can be closed to an icon. In JDK 1.0.2, the cursor could be set for a `Frame` (only). In JDK 1.1, this restriction was lifted, and the cursor can now be set for each individual `Component`.

The origin of a `Frame` is its top left corner. You can draw on a `Frame` just as you can on a `Canvas`. When you create a `Frame`, it is not physically displayed inside the applet or other Container but is a separate free-floating window on the monitor.

What it looks like on screen:

The code to create it:

```
import java.awt.*;
public class exfr {
     static Frame f = new Frame("cherry");

     public static void main(String[] a) {
          f.setBounds(100,50,300,100);
          f.show();
     }
}
```

Note that this is an application, but frames can equally be displayed from an applet, as in the code below.

```
//<applet code=exfr2.class width=275 height=125 > </applet>
import java.awt.*;
import java.applet.*;
import java.awt.event.*;
public class exfr2 extends Applet {

     public void init() {
          Frame f = new Frame("Frame of an Applet");
          f.setBounds(100,50,300,100);
          f.show();
     }
}
```

What it looks like on screen:

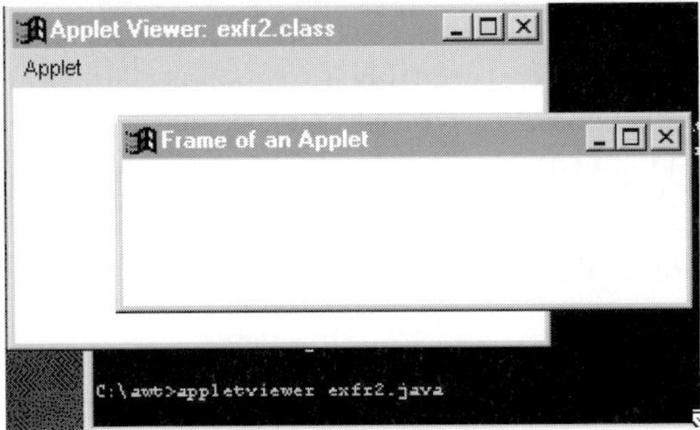

Here is how you associate a file containing an icon with a Frame, so that when you close the Frame, it collapses to the icon.

```
// load the image from a file Toolkit
t = MyFrame.getToolkit();
Image FrameIcon = t.getImage(filename);
if (FrameIcon != null) {
     // change the icon
     MyFrame.setIconImage(FrameIcon);
}
```

The file name should point to a GIF or JPEG file that is the icon you want to use. Typically, this image will be thumbnail-sized, 32 x 32 pixels or so.

You will usually want to put in the three or four lines of code that deal with a top level window (Frame, etc) being quit or destroyed (when the user has finished with it—this is usually a standard choice on the frame menu bar).

The code looks like:

```
class wl extends WindowAdapter {
     Window w;
     public wl(Window w) {
          this.w=w;
     }
     public void windowClosed(WindowEvent e) {
          w.setVisible(false);
          w=null;
     }
}
```

You could also exit the application. That would be appropriate when the user quits from the top-level window. For a lower-level window, the right thing to do may be to hide the window and release the resource for garbage collection by removing any pointers to it.

Panel

What it is: A `Panel` is a generic container that is always in some other container. It does not float loose on the desktop, as `Window` and `Frame` do. A panel is used when you want to group several controls inside your GUI. For example, you might have several buttons that go together, as shown in the next screen capture. Adding them all to a Panel allows them to be treated as one unit, all displayed together, and laid out on the screen under the same set of rules.

The code to create it:

```
//<applet code=expan.class width=275 height=125 > </applet>
import java.awt.*;
import java.applet.*;
import java.awt.event.*;

public class expan extends Applet  {

     public void init() {

          final Panel p = new Panel();
          add(p);
          invalidate();
          validate();

          final Button b1 = new Button("beep");
          b1.addActionListener( new ActionListener() {
               public void actionPerformed(ActionEvent e) {
               b1.getToolkit().beep(); } } // end anon class
          ); // end method call

          Button b2 = new Button("change color");
          b2.addActionListener( new ActionListener() {
               public void actionPerformed(ActionEvent e) {
               Color c = p.getBackground()==Color.red? Color.white:
                    Color.red;
               p.setBackground( c );
               b1.setEnabled(false);  } } // end anon class
          ); // end method call
          p.add(b1);  p.add(b2);
     }
}
```

This code displays two buttons, one of which beeps, and the other of which changes the panel color. Once the panel color has been changed, the beeping button is disabled. Note how that changes its appearance on the screen.

What it looks like on screen:

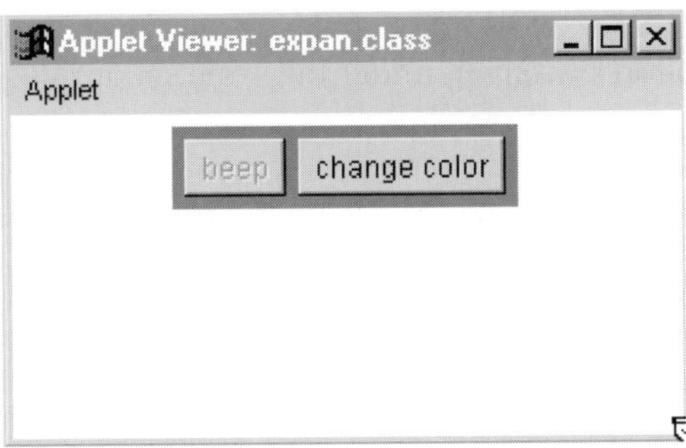

`Applet`

Applet is a subclass of Panel. The major thing this says is that applets come ready-made with some GUI stuff in place. Figure B-6 is another example screen capture of an applet.

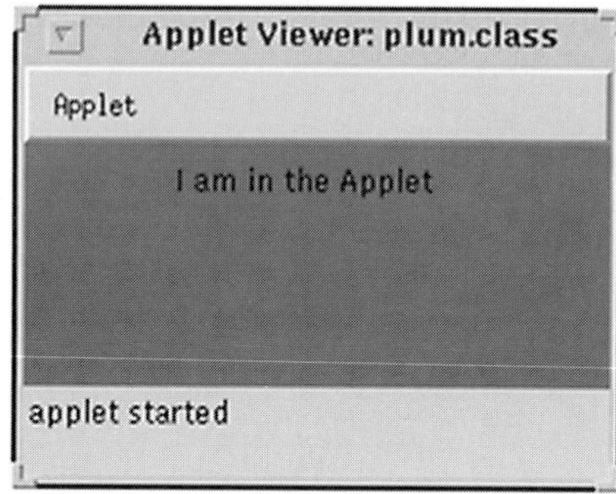

Figure B–6 Just another applet.

Here is the code that created that applet:

```
import java.awt.*;
import java.applet.*;

public class plum extends Applet {

    public void init() {
       setBackground(Color.green);
       resize(250,100);
    }

    public void paint(Graphics g) {
       g.drawString("I am in the Applet", 35,15);
    }

}
```

One advantage of an applet over an application for a GUI program is that you can start adding components and displaying them without needing to create an underlying backdrop, as one already exists.

Here are some popular methods of Applet:

```
public URL getDocumentBase() //the URL of the page
                               containing the applet
public URL getCodeBase() //the URL of the applet code

public String getParameter(String name)
public void resize(int width, int height)

public void showStatus(String msg)
public Image getImage(URL url) //bring in an image
public Image getImage(URL url, String name)

public AudioClip getAudioClip(URL url) //bring in a sound file
public void play(URL url)
```

Applet has other methods too. The source can be seen in $JAVAHOME/src/java/applet/Applet.java

Dialog

What it is: A `Dialog` is a top-level, free-floating window like `Frame`. `Dialog` lacks the menu bar and iconification of `Frame`. A `Dialog` is the way you show a line of text to the user, often relating to the most recent action, such as, "Really overwrite the file? Y/N."

According to a boolean mode parameter in the constructor, a `Dialog` can be modal or modeless. Modal Dialogs disable all other AWT windows until the modal Dialog is no longer on the screen.

What it looks like on screen:

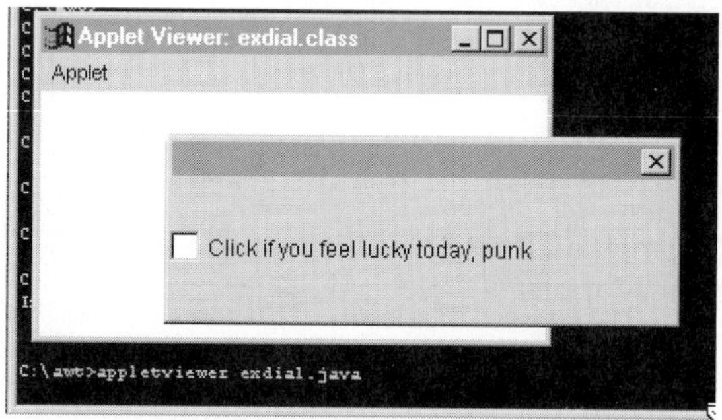

The code to create it:

```
//<applet code=exdial.class width=275 height=125 > </applet> import java.awt.*;
import java.applet.*;
import java.awt.event.*;

public class exdial extends Applet  {

     public void init() {

          Component c = this.getParent();
          while (c!=null && !(c instanceof Frame)) c=c.getParent();

          final Dialog d = new Dialog((Frame)c);
          Checkbox c1 = new Checkbox("Click if you feel lucky today, punk");
          c1.addItemListener ( new ItemListener() {
               public void itemStateChanged(java.awt.event.ItemEvent ie)
                    { d.setVisible(false); }
               });
          d.add(c1);
          d.setBounds(50,50, 280,100);
          d.show();
     }
}
```

FileDialog

What it is: `FileDialog` is a `Container`, but you are not supposed to add anything to it. It is a `Container` by virtue of being a subclass of `Window`. `FileDialog` brings up the native "file selection" control, allowing you to choose a file in the file system. A list of files in the current directory is displayed, optionally filtered by some criteria such as "only include files that end in `.gif`."

A `FileDialog` can be either a Load dialog, allowing you to select a file for input, or a Save dialog, allowing you to specify a file for output.

What it looks like on screen:

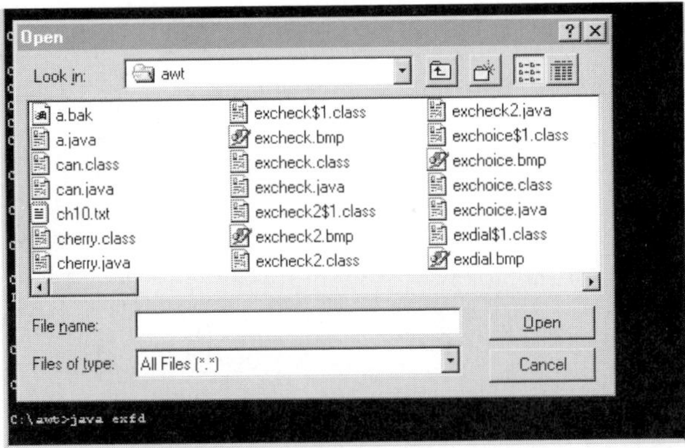

The code to create it:

```
import java.awt.*;
import java.awt.event.*;
import java.io.*;
public class exfd {

     public static void main(String args[]) {

          Frame f = new Frame("myFrame");
          final FileDialog fd = new FileDialog(f,"get a GIF file");

          fd.show();
          fd.setFilenameFilter(new myFilter());

          System.out.println("Filter is " + fd.getFilenameFilter() );

          String s = fd.getFile();
          System.out.println("You chose file "+ s );
     }
}
class myFilter implements FilenameFilter { // broken on Windows

     public boolean accept(File dir, String name) {
          return( name.endsWith(".gif") );
     }
}
```

The `FileDialog` control is only of use in applications and trusted applets because you cannot usually see the client file system in an untrusted applet running in a browser.

A bug in JDK 1.0 and 1.1 (all versions) meant the `accept()` method was never called at all on Windows.

Don't forget that most operating systems have case sensitive file names, so `foo.gif` is different from `foo.GIF`.

To summarize:

1. Use the javax.swing components in preference to the java.awt components.
2. The AWT components are shown in this appendix because you might find them in old code or even have to write new code for very old browsers.
3. Don't mix old and new events styles. Don't mix AWT and Swing components.

Appendix C

Powers of 2 and ISO 8859

Refer to Table C-1 for Powers of 2

With *n* bits in integer two's complement format, you can count:

unsigned from 0 to (one less than 2^n)

signed from -2^{n-1} to (one less than 2^{n-1})

Refer to Table C-2 for ISO 8859

Characters 0x0 to 0x1F are the C0 (control) characters, defined in ISO/IEC 6429:1992

Characters 0x20 to 0x7E are the G0 graphics characters of the 7-bit code set defined in ISO/IEC 646-1991(E)—essentially the 7-bit ASCII characters.

Characters 0x80 to 0x9F are the C1 (control) characters, defined in ISO/IEC 6429:1992

The unshaded characters comprise the Latin-1 code set defined in ISO/IEC 8859-1:1987 though the symbols "Φ" and "Φ" (0xDE and 0xFE) are approximations to the capital and small Icelandic letter "thorn." The actual letters are too weird to be in character sets anywhere outside a 12-mile radius of Reykjavík.

Table C–1 Powers-of-Two from 2^1 to 2^{64}

2^{1}	2	2^{17}	131,072	2^{33}	8,589,934,592	2^{49}	562,949,953,421,312
2^{2}	4	2^{18}	262,144	2^{34}	17,179,869,184	2^{50}	1,125,899,906,842,624
2^{3}	8	2^{19} **megabyte**	524,288	2^{35}	34,359,738,368	2^{51}	2,251,799,813,685,248
2^{4}	16	2^{20}	1,048,576	2^{36}	68,719,476,736	2^{52}	4,503,599,627,370,496
2^{5}	32	2^{21}	2,097,152	2^{37}	137,438,953,472	2^{53}	9,007,199,254,740,992
2^{6}	64	2^{22}	4,194,304	2^{38}	274,877,906,944	2^{54}	18,014,398,509,481,984
2^{7}	128	2^{23}	8,388,608	2^{39} **terabyte**	549,755,813,888	2^{55}	36,028,797,018,963,968
2^{8}	256	2^{24}	16,777,216	2^{40}	1,099,511,627,776	2^{56}	72,057,594,037,927,936
2^{9} **kilobyte**	512	2^{25}	33,554,432	2^{41}	2,199,023,255,552	2^{57}	144,115,188,075,855,872
2^{10}	1,024	2^{26}	67,108,864	2^{42}	4,398,046,511,104	2^{58}	288,230,376,151,711,744
2^{11}	2,048	2^{27}	134,217,728	2^{43}	8,796,093,022,208	2^{59}	576,460,752,303,423,488
2^{12}	4,096	2^{28}	268,435,456	2^{44}	17,592,186,044,416	2^{60}	1,152,921,504,606,846,976
2^{13}	8,192	2^{29} **gigabyte**	536,870,912	2^{45}	35,184,372,088,832	2^{61}	2,305,843,009,213,693,952
2^{14}	16,384	2^{30}	1,073,741,824	2^{46}	70,368,744,177,664	2^{62}	4,611,686,018,427,387,904
2^{15}	32,768	2^{31}	2,147,483,648	2^{47}	140,737,488,355,328	2^{63} **bubbabyte**	9,223,372,036,854,775,808
2^{16}	65,536	2^{32}	4,294,967,296	2^{48}	281,474,976,710,656	2^{64}	18,446,744,073,709,551,616

Table C-2 ISO 8859 8-Bit Latin-1 Character Set and Control Characters

Least significant 4 bits of the byte

Most Significant 4 Bits of the Byte

	0	1	2	3	4	5	6	7	8	9	A	B	C	D	E	F
0	nul	soh	stx	etx	eot	enq	ack	bel	bs	ht	lf\n	vt	ff	cr\r	so	si
1	dle	dc1	dc2	dc3	dc4	nak	syn	etb	can	em	sub	esc	is_4	is_3	is_2	is_1
2	space	!	"	#	$	%	&	'	(	)	*	+	,	-	.	/
3	0	1	2	3	4	5	6	7	8	9	:	;	<	=	>	?
4	@	A	B	C	D	E	F	G	H	I	J	K	L	M	N	O
5	P	Q	R	S	T	U	V	W	X	Y	Z	[	\	]	^	_
6	'	a	b	c	d	e	f	g	h	i	j	k	l	m	n	o
7	p	q	r	s	t	u	v	w	x	y	z	{	|	}	~	del
8	n/a	n/a	bph	nbh	n/a	nel	ssa	esa	hts	htj	vts	pld	plu	ri	ss2	ss3
9	dcs	pu1	pu2	sts	cch	mw	spa	epa	sos	n/a	sci	csi	st	osc	pm	apc
A	nbsp	¡	¢	£	¤	¥	¦	§	¨	©	a	«	¬	shy	®	¯
B	°	±	2	3	´	µ	¶	•	¸	1	o	»	$^1/_4$	$^1/_2$	$^3/_4$	¿
C	À	Á	Â	Ã	Ä	Å	Æ	Ç	È	É	Ê	Ë	Ì	Í	Î	Ï
D	D	Ñ	Ò	Ó	Ô	Õ	Ö	¥	Ø	Ù	Ú	Û	Ü	Y	F	b
E	à	á	â	ã	ä	å	æ	ç	è	é	ê	ë	ì	í	î	ï
F	∂	ñ	ò	ó	ô	õ	ö	Π	ø	ù	ú	û	ü	y	F	ÿ

Index

A

B

C

D

E

H

I

J

K

O

P

1095

U

V

W

X

Z